VATICAN II
Assessment
and Perspectives

VATICAN II

Assessment
and Perspectives

Twenty-five Years After
(1962–1987)

VOLUME TWO

Edited by RENÉ LATOURELLE

WITHDRAWN

PAULIST PRESS/ NEW YORK/ MAHWAH

The publication of this project has been helped immensely by generous gifts from trustees of the Gregorian University Foundation and other friends. Specific contributions were made by Mr. John Brogan, Mr. and Mrs. Cyril Nigg, and Mr. and Mrs. John T. Ryan, Jr. To them and all others whose assistance made possible this publication—in French, German, and Italian as well as English—warmest thanks from the writer and editor.

Copyright © 1989
René Latourelle, S.J.

Library of Congress Cataloging-in-Publication Data

Vatican II: Assessment and perspectives: twenty-five years after
    (1962–1987)/edited by René Latourelle.
        p.   cm.
      1. Vatican Council (2nd: 1962–1965).   2. Catholic
    Church—Doctrines—History—20th century.   3.Catholic
    Church—History—20th century.   I. Latourelle, René.
    BX830 1962.V322   1988   262'.52   87-35972
    ISBN 0-8091-0412-1 (v. 1)
    ISBN 0-8091-0413-X (v. 2)

Published by Paulist Press
997 Macarthur Blvd.
Mahwah, NJ 07430

Printed and bound in the
United States of America

A Note on the English Translation

Except where the author of a given article is making his own translation (in which case the English translation is based on this), or in quotations found in already published English translations of works cited by the various authors, the translation of the Holy Scriptures used is *The Holy Bible,* Revised Standard Version, Catholic Edition (London: Catholic Truth Society, 1966). However, in some cases, the Jerusalem Bible and the New American Bible have been consulted.

Except where the author of a given article is making his own translation (in which case the English translation is based on this), the translation of the Council documents used is that found in A. Flannery (gen. ed.), *Vatican Council II: The Conciliar and Post Conciliar Documents* (Collegeville, MN: Liturgical Press, revised edition 1984). However, on some occasions, the translation found in W.M. Abbott (gen. ed.), *The Documents of Vatican II* (New York: Guild Press, 1966), has been consulted.

Except where the author of a given article is making his own translation (in which case the English translation is based on this), the translation of the 1983 Code of Canon Law used is that produced by the Canon Law Society of America (Washington, DC, 1983). However, on some occasions, the translation produced by the Canon Law Society of Great Britain and Ireland (London, 1983) has also been consulted.

Works quoted in the text of articles: If an already published English translation could be found, this has been used—as will be seen from the relative notes. However, if no English translation could be found, the present translators translated such quotations

from the original-language version of the works in question—
again, as will be seen from the relative notes.

Works quoted in notes: All such quotations have been left in
the original language, and have not been translated into English.

Apart from the various people whose names appear at the end
of the different articles as translators or cotranslators, the following have assisted with library research and/or advice: Philip Gil-
lespie and Rev. Father Robert Hagan, S.J.

Leslie Wearne

Acknowledgments

The English edition of the present work has been made possible thanks to the generosity and large-scale contributions of a group of benefactors in the United States and Canada. We wish to express our deep gratitude to all these persons.

We should also like to address our sincere thanks to Miss Leslie Wearne, who is responsible for coordinating the English translation, and also to the whole team of translators.

René Latourelle, S.J.
Editor

Abbreviations

1. Abbreviations of the books of the Bible are those used in A. Flannery (gen. ed.), *Vatican Council II: The Conciliar and Post Conciliar Documents*.

2. *Abbreviations of Council Documents:*

AA   *Apostolicam actuositatem*, Decree on the Apostolate of the Laity

AG   *Ad gentes*, Decree on the Missionary Activity of the Church

CD   *Christus Dominus*, Decree on the Pastoral Office of Bishops in the Church

DH   *Dignitatis humanae*, Declaration on Religious Freedom

DV   *Dei Verbum*, Dogmatic Constitution on Divine Revelation

GE   *Gravissimum educationis*, Declaration on Christian Education

GS   *Gaudium et spes*, Pastoral Constitution on the Church in the Modern World

IM   *Inter mirifica*, Decree on the Means of Social Communication

LG   *Lumen gentium*, Dogmatic Constitution on the Church

NA   *Nostra aetate*, Declaration on the Relation of the Church to Nonchristian Religions

OE   *Orientalium Ecclesiarum*, Decree on the Catholic Eastern Churches

OT   *Optatam totius*, Decree on the Training of Priests

PC   *Perfectae caritatis*, Decree on the Up-to-Date Renewal of Religious Life

PO   *Presbyterorum ordinis*, Decree on the Ministry and Life of Priests

SC   *Sacrosanctam concilium*, Constitution on the Sacred Liturgy

UR   *Unitatis redintegratio*, Decree on Ecumenism

3. *Other abbreviations:*

AAS   *Acta Apostolicae Sedis* (Rome, 1909–   )

AS   *Acta Synodalia S. Concilii Oecumenici Vaticani II*, 26 vols. (Vatican City, 1970–1980)

ASS   *Acta Sanctae Sedis* (Rome, 1865–1908)

CIC   *Codex Juris Canonici* (The Code of Canon Law)

DS   H. Denzinger and A. Schönmetzter, *Enchiridion Symbolorum, Definitionum et Declarationum de rebus fidei et morum* (Freiburg im Breisgau, 1965)

Mansi J.D. Mansi, *Sacrorum Conciliorum nova et amplissima collectio* (Florence, 1759)

PG   *Patrologia Graeca*, ed. J.P. Migne (Paris, 1857–1866)

PL   *Patrologia Latina*, ed. J.P. Migne (Paris, 1844–1855)

Apart from this, the authors of certain articles use a system of abbreviations generally accepted in their specific fields of study when citing specialized publications dealing with their own disciplines.

Contents

PART IV

LITURGY
AND
SACRAMENTS

CHAPTER 22

The Principal Manifestation of the Church (SC 41)

Pedro Romano Rocha, S.J.

Summary

The author takes as his starting point the conciliar texts that emphasize the relationship between liturgical celebration and the nature of the Church, and on this basis seeks to pinpoint the image of the Church contained in the *General Instruction to the Roman Missal* and in the *Order of the Mass*. Among the various expressions regarding the subject, he highlights that of "people of God that is hierarchically ordered" and stresses the importance the new missal gives to the "people who gather together" for the celebration of the Mass.

The Constitution *Sacrosanctum concilium* sets forth the main aspects of the liturgy, showing the Church as the subject of the liturgical actions and as intimately linked to everything involved in divine worship. Although the aim of the document was not that of providing a definition of the Church (a task that would be left to *Lumen gentium*), at several points, it does either directly or indirectly offer elements pointing to a specific conception of the Church.[1] Thus, for instance, we have number 2, which speaks of the "real nature of the true Church"; number 26, in which the Church is called "the holy people, united and arranged under their bishops"; and number 41, according to which the celebration of the liturgy around the same

3

altar and presided over by the bishop, contains "the principal manifestation of the Church."

Reflection on the liturgy, therefore, automatically leads to reflection on the Church, inasmuch as the two are closely linked. Moreover, from its beginnings, the liturgical movement was of course accompanied by ecclesiological concern and developed most easily where Christians were interested in an in-depth study on the mystery of the Church. In this persepctive, it is also easier to understand *Sacrosanctum concilium* when, as early as its introduction, it says that it is seeking to fulfill the objectives set by the Council, at the heart of which today's Church was involved—in other words, the task of always increasing the growth of the Christian life among the faithful, improving the adaptation of the institutions of the Church to the needs of our times, and making the Church a more living sign in our world (SC 1).

There is thus a relationship between the liturgy and the nature of the Church, and this brings us to the question of whether we can arrive at an ecclesiology on the basis of our liturgical celebrations,[2] and, if so, what image of the Church can be seen in our celebrations?

On the other hand, *Sacrosanctum concilium* states that "Although the sacred liturgy is principally the worship of the divine majesty it likewise contains much instruction for the faithful" (SC 33). It goes on to state that "The rites should be distinguished by a noble simplicity. They should be short, [and] . . . within the people's powers of comprehension, and normally should not require much explanation" (SC 34). This means that the actual celebration and the texts used should be a catechesis.[3] And this leads us to another question: What teaching is given by our liturgical actions? Twenty-five years after the Council, it is now reasonable to consider whether, thanks to the new way of living the liturgy that has resulted from the conciliar texts,[4] we can recognize certain features of the conciliar teaching on the Church.

Without wishing to oversimplify, we can say that in its celebrations, the preconciliar liturgy presented a view of the Church that was more or less static, set in its features and words, and hieratic. On the one hand, we had a group of members of the Church—the clergy—who performed the sacred functions, and on the other, the people who were simply "present," "as strangers or silent spectators" (SC 48), and very often as passive ones, too. This partly corresponded to the image people had of the Church: on the one hand, the hierarchy, who govern, celebrate, sanctify, teach, and so on; and on the other hand, the people, who listen, receive the divine grace, obey, follow instructions, and so on.

Now, although the Council did not deny the role of the hierarchy or the powers it had received from Christ, it recalled that in the first place, the Church is the people called by God with a view to its salvation; a holy people, gathered together and organized under the authority of the bishops; a priestly community; a body with members that are of course different from one another but that even so are organically united in the Holy Spirit by the same faith, the same sacraments, and the same government; the universal sacrament of salvation, which is offered to all people.

Does liturgical celebration usually manifest this community dimension and this missionary vocation? The liturgy had to be made less clerical, more ecclesial, and more open to participation, and in such participation it is easier for Christians to realize that they are the Church that Christ associates with himself in the exercise of his priesthood in order to offer worship to the Father and sanctify men (SC 7). This is the objective of the conciliar Constitution on the Liturgy.

The Thinking of the Constitution on the Liturgy

Study of *Sacrosanctum concilium* reveals a close relationship between liturgical celebration and the Church in its nature, members, and image. If we make a survey of the articles concerned with this subject, we find the following statements:

> . . . it is through the liturgy, especially, that the faithful are enabled to express in their lives and manifest to others the mystery of Christ and the real nature of the true Church (SC 2).
> The liturgy daily builds up those who are in the Church, making of them a holy temple of the Lord . . . [and] increases their power . . . to show forth the Church, a sign lifted up among the nations, to those who are outside . . . [ibid.].
> . . . all the faithful should be led to that full, conscious, and active participation in liturgical celebrations which is de-

manded by the very nature of the liturgy, and to which the
Christian people, "a chosen race, a royal priesthood, a holy
nation, a redeemed people" (1 Pet. 2:9, 4–5), have a right and
an obligation by reason of their baptism (SC 14).

Liturgical services are not private functions but are celebrations of the Church which is . . . "the holy people united and
arranged under their bishops" (St. Cyprian, "On the Unity of
the Catholic Church," 7) (SC 26).

. . . liturgical services pertain to the whole Body of the
Church. They manifest it, and have effects upon it (*ibid.*).

. . . all . . . must be convinced that the principal manifestation of the Church consists in the full, active participation
of all God's holy people in the same liturgical celebrations,
especially in the same Eucharist (SC 41).

. . . lesser groupings of the faithful. Among these, parishes,
set up locally under a pastor who takes the place of the bishop,
are the most important, for in some way they represent the
visible Church constituted throughout the world (SC 42)

Apart from these articles, which can be described as fundamental with regard to the relationship between liturgy and Church,
we must add another series that take participation as their special
starting point in indicating how this ecclesial action is to be put
into practice. These texts are grouped under the title "Norms
Drawn from the Hierarchic and Communal Nature of the Liturgy" (Nos. 26 to 32). Apart from number 26, which I have
already noted, and in view of the immediate and wide-ranging
implications for the *Order of Mass,* I would recall numbers 30 and
31, to which I shall return in due course. Here, it is enough to
highlight number 28:

. . . each person, minister, or layman who has an office to
perform, should carry out all and only those parts which pertain to his office by the nature of the right and the norms of
the liturgy.

The Witness of the Books

Following *Sacrosanctum concilium* and the various documents
connected with it, a revision of the liturgical books was under-
taken, with a view to a general renewal of the liturgy as called for

by the Council.[5] Liturgical texts have always been a reflection of the life and thinking of the Church—and, we might say, of the cultural environment in the different eras in which they have been composed and used. They are witnesses that always speak of the life of the Church of their times, even after they have passed out of living use. Bearing this in mind, what image of our Church will our books give? We can at least state that they entail and manifest a view of the Church that corresponds to the thought of the Council, and that this view was not so visible in the previous books. For example, we have only to take a look at the introductions to the new rites of the sacraments in order to see the references to the documents of the Council.

The aim of this short study is that of discovering how far the conception of the Church underlying *Sacrosanctum concilium* and confirmed in *Lumen gentium* is effectively expressed in the books now in use. Given the breadth of the subject, I shall confine myself to the area of the Church as the "holy people, united and arranged," acting in the liturgical service; and with regard to celebrations themselves, I shall concentrate on the Mass, because it is the summit of the liturgy and the most frequent liturgical action in the normal life of the Christian people.

I shall study the celebration as it is found in the Roman Missal (second typical edition, 1975) in two documents of different types: the *General Instruction of the Roman Missal* (= GI) and the *Order of Mass* (= OM). The former presents and explains the celebration of the Mass, whereas the latter directs this celebration in practical terms, with the succession of actions and texts common to every Mass. The reflection found in the *General Instruction* constitutes the link between the principles laid down in the Constitution *Sacrosanctum concilium* and the present *Order of Mass*.

The Meaning of the *General Instruction* of the *Roman Missal*

Is there a relationship between this document and the celebration of the Mass? The answer is provided by Paul VI, who states that the *General Instruction* gives the new regulations for the celebration of the eucharistic sacrifice, as regards not only the performance of the rites, but also the specific functions of each of the participants.[6] It was produced with a view to this celebration, in order to guide and help the community—both ministers and faithful—in its action, bearing in mind the spirit and instructions of *Sacrosanctum concilium.* It is a type of catechesis that takes as its basis the doctrine on the Mass and then develops this in decidedly pastoral terms. It has its place between the conciliar documents[7] and the present Roman Missal—or, narrowing the frame of reference, between the Constitution *Sacrosanctum concilium* and the missal.[8]

With regard to the subject of the present study—the image of the Church, the people of God—the role of this people in the celebration of the Eucharist is presented or described at several points in the *General Instruction,* and these references can be divided into three groups: the first is the general introduction, of a more doctrinal nature, found in the Introduction, Chapter I (Nos. 1–6), and Chapter III (Nos. 58–73); the second gives the description of the celebration in a more catechetical and pastoral perspective, and is found in Chapter II (Nos. 7–57); and the third is found in the part that we can describe as of a ritual orientation, that is, Chapter IV (and especially Nos. 74–141). The *Order of Mass* found in the actual body of the missal corresponds on the whole to this last chapter, and the same expressions are often used. A number of references of interest are also found in Chapter V, in the section dealing with the place in which the celebration takes place, and I shall also bear these references in mind.

The Action of Christ and the People
of God Hierarchically Assembled

Since it is not possible to examine this rich document in all its breadth, I shall confine myself to stressing this first statement at the very beginning of the first chapter, as a sort of preliminary introduction. And it is well worth stressing, inasmuch as it expresses the spirit of the document: "The celebration of Mass is the action of Christ and the people of God hierarchically assembled . . . [and] is the center of the whole Christian life" (GI 1). The Eucharist is presented not so much as an action of the celebrant, to which the people associate themselves, but rather as the action of the whole people of God, assembled in a "here-and-now" and constituted in the totality and diversity of its members as they exercise their different functions. Inasmuch as the priest–minister holds the place of Christ, his presence and action are indispensable if the priestly people is to be able to exercise its priesthood, although this presence and action do not constitute the whole action of the ecclesial community or take its place.

We would recall that the formulation sketched out in *Sacrosanctum concilium* was developed in greater depth in the Constitution on the Church, for example, in numbers 10 and 11:

> Taking part in the eucharistic sacrifice, the source and summit of the Christian life, they [the faithful] offer the divine victim to God and themselves along with it. And so it is that, both in the offering and in Holy Communion, each in his own way, though not of course indiscriminately, has his own part to play in the liturgical action (*LG* 11).

And the Decree on the Ministry and Life of Priests would also take up and further develop this relationship between the ministry of priests and the priestly action of the community (*PO* 2, 5, 6).

It is true that the efficacy and dignity of the eucharistic celebration, which is the action of Christ and the Church, are not dependent on the actual presence of the faithful. However, it is also true that their presence and participation show more clearly the ecclesial nature of the liturgical action, as the *General Instruction* points out in a timely reminder (No. 4).

Toward the end, the basic idea of number 1 will be brought up again in connection with the place in which the celebration takes place. It is stated that even the arrangement of the places of the different members of the assembly should show that the community is hierarchically structured in the differences in functions and ministries. However, it is immediately added that this hierarchical arrangement must also clearly express the unity of the whole people of God (No. 257).

Meaning and Importance of the *Order of Mass*

In conformity with the *General Instruction,* the present *Order of Mass* starts from the principle that the presence and participation of the assembled community is not accidental or secondary, but that on the contrary it is required by the celebration and is part of the latter. *Sacrosanctum concilium* lays clear stress on the attention to be paid to the different forms of participation: "To promote active participation, the people should be encouraged to take part by means of acclamations, responses, psalms, antiphons, hymns, as well as by actions, gestures and bodily attitudes . . ." (SC 30). The following article is even more explicit: "When the liturgical books are being revised, the people's parts must be carefully indicated by the rubrics" (SC 31).

And this is what has been done: with its numerous references to the actions of the people, the new *Order of Mass* bears witness to the fact. These rubrical indications are more than disciplinary regulations and will be seen as the result of a theologically richer conception of the celebrations. With this in view, and in response to the previously cited instructions in *Sacrosanctum concilium*, the *General Instruction* includes three articles (Nos. 14, 15, and 16) in which these elements are provided with a doctrinal framework and basis.[9]

We can therefore understand that the *Order of Mass* devoted a great deal of attention to the people, and referred to them very often. Anybody who pays attention to the *Order of Mass* will find this presence of the people expanded at every point and its many actions described in detail. The word *populus* (the people) appears over thirty times, and the term *fideles* (the faithful) is also sometimes used, alternating with *populus*. This *populus* or these *fideles* respond, acclaim, pray, sing, and offer, according to the different moments and the orientation of their interventions.

In the same line, we should note that on several occasions, these actions are carried out by the people together with the priest, as is indicated by the term *omnes* (all) or the expression *una cum* (one with). In other words, at certain points in the celebration, the action of the presiding priest is not distinguished from that of the other members of the gathering. Thus, the priest *et* (and) the faithful make the sign of the cross at the beginning of the celebration; *omnes simul* (all in the same way) confess their sins; *omnes una* (all as one) pray in silence; *omnes*, seated, listen to the word of God, and at the end exclaim, "Thanks be to God"; the priest *una cum populo* (one with the people) concludes the preface by singing, "Holy, holy, holy . . ."; *una cum populo* he says the Lord's Prayer, and shows his sentiments of humility before taking communion. In an appendix, we give a summary of the *Order of Mass* with the interventions of the people.

This very detailed explanation of the actions of the faithful is all the more significant in that in the previous missal, the people were practically ignored, both in the description of the rite and in the *Order of Mass* itself. The dialogues, responses, and acclamations belonged to the *minister* or *ministri* (the assistant or assistants)—in other words, to the acolytes, and sometimes to the deacon or subdeacon, and possibly to the choir.

In this connection, it should be noted that one of the last editions, *iuxta typicam,* of the "Tridentine" Missal (1964) inexplicably retained the style of previous editions, despite the fact that the Instruction *De musica sacra et sacra liturgia* (3 September 1958) had already dealt with the active and conscious participation of the members of the faithful in the celebration of the Mass clearly and at length, giving a detailed listing of the moments when they are to participate through dialogue, acclamations, or singing.[10] Moreover, the new rite for Holy Week had already broken ground in this direction.[11]

The Celebration of the Mass According to the *General Instruction* and the *Order of Mass*

Before discussing the actual course of the celebration as described in Chapter II of the *General Instruction,* it seems necessary to look at Chapter III, which is devoted to "Offices and Ministries in the Mass," and to draw attention to its opening article (No. 58), and especially to its second section, which is concerned with the "Office and Function of the People of God" (Nos. 62–64).

Number 58 basically summarizes the content of numbers 14, 26, and 28 of *Sacrosanctum concilium,* highlighting the fact that "in the assembly which gathers for the Mass," each person, "whether minister or layman," has the right and duty to participate in the celebration according to his functions, doing all and only that which belongs to him. This article concludes by stating that in this way, the actual unfolding of the celebration enables the Church to be seen as it is, made up of different members and ministries.

The second section, entitled "Office and Function of the People of God," deserves special mention inasmuch as it contains something that is in a sense new. Whereas the previous ritual of the Mass was concerned almost exclusively with the priest and assistants, here the people also come to the forefront as an object of the concern of the *Order of Mass*. The *General Instruction* repeats certain expressions that are among the most beautiful in *Sacrosanctum concilium* in order to describe the action of the Christian community in the liturgy:

> . . . the faithful form a holy people, a chosen race, a royal priesthood: they give thanks to the Father and offer the victim not only through the hands of the priest but also with him, and they learn to offer themselves (*GI* 62).

The immediate inspiration for this text is found in *Sacrosanctum concilium* 48, in the part devoted to the eucharistic mystery, as a note tells us. However, it also draws inspiration for certain fundamental articles in the first chapter of the Constitution—and specifically numbers 14, 26, and 41—which highlight the role of the community as the agent of liturgical actions. When Christians act in this way, in virtue of their baptism, they express the nature of the Church.

The Introductory Rites

Having described the function of the people of God in general terms, the *General Instruction* gives practical details of the exercise of this function.

In the description of the structure of the Mass, the introductory rites play an important role inasmuch as they help to create the community. It begins by stating that the people of God is "gathered together [*in unum convocatur*]" "to celebrate the memorial of the Lord or eucharistic sacrifice." It states that in this local congregation (*coadunatione locale*[12]) of the Church—"in the assembly itself, which is gathered in his name"—Christ is really present (*GI* 7).

The *General Instruction* then goes on to describe the "Introductory Rites," and says that the purpose of these rites is to "make the assembled people a unified community."

The description of the rites then follows. The starting point is the fact of the assembled community (or *populo congregato*), while the priest enters with the ministers and the entrance song begins.[13] Among the other purposes of this song is that of "deepening the unity of the people." Having mentioned the greeting addressed to the community by the priest, its significance is explained as "expressing the presence of the Lord to the assembled community." Further, "this greeting and the people's response manifest the mystery of the Church that is gathered together" (*GI* 28). It would be difficult to express more clearly the importance of these "preliminary" actions and their relationship to the mystery of the Church.

"The Assembled People"

Without trying to overstrain the texts, we cannot help but be struck by the insistent use of the term *congregare* (to gather together) and related terms in the *General Instruction*. In the second chapter alone, which is devoted to the main elements of the celebration itself, the term recurs more than ten times. And the expression *populo congregato* (assembled people), which is so strongly emphasized by the *General Instruction* and the *Order of Mass,* is clearly emblematic of the role of the community in the celebration.

As has already been observed, in both the instructions on the ritual (known by the first words of the title, *Ritus servandus*) and in the *Order of Mass* itself, the previous missal more or less ignored the presence and action of the community in order to concentrate almost exclusively on the person of the priest. On the contrary, our missal describes the celebration, both in the *General Instruction* and in the *Order of Mass,* beginning with an explicit reference to the person of the priest. However, when our missal describes the celebration, both in the *General Instruction* and in the *Order of Mass,* it begins with an explicit reference to the assembled people of God. Let us compare the two texts.

Previous missal	*Present missal*
Ritus servandus in celebratione Missae	[The celebration in the *General Instruction*]
I. De praeparatione sacerdotis . . .	Introitus

Sacerdos celebraturus Missam,
praevia confessione . . .

> *Populo congregato,* dum ingreditur sacerdos cum ministris, cantus ad introitum incipitur (*GI* 25)

[And, a little further on:]
II. De ingressu sacerdotis
Sacerdos omnibus paramentis indutus, accipit manu sinistra calicem . . .

[In the opening of the *Order of Mass*:]
Sacerdos paratus, cum ingreditur ad altare, . . . signat se signo crucis . . .

> [Opening of the *Order of Mass*:]
> Ritus initiales: *Populo congregato,* sacerdos cum ministris ad altare accedit, dum cantus ad introitum paragitur [OM 1]
> [A little further on:]
> Cantu ad introitum absoluto, *sacerdos et fideles,* stantes, signant se, dum sacerdos dicit: In nomine Patris . . . [OM 2]

This comparison is confined to the entrance rite alone, but it could easily be extended to many other elements. However, even a simple glance at it as it stands reveals that the attention of the author of the *Ritus servandus* was concentrated on the celebrating priest, whereas in the *General Instruction* and the new *Order of Mass* the accent has been moved and is now placed primarily on the community.

The accent on the "assembled people" is no accident. That expression indicates the importance of the presence and action of the people in the liturgy, and especially in that of the Mass, the normal celebration of which presupposes the gathering together of the people. This is why the missal calls such a celebration ("Mass with a Congregation") the "common form" (*forma typica*).[14]

This people is not assembled simply through its own initiative, but is there because God has called and gathered it together: ". . . this people is thus the people of God . . . called together by the Lord" (*GI,* Introduction 5). It is gathered together in the name of the Father and of the Son and of the Holy Spirit, as the priest and faithful proclaim at the beginning of the celebration.[15] And at the heart of the eucharistic action, the Church recalls that the Father never ceases to gather his people together (Eucharistic Prayer III).

We would recall in passing that the *Order of Mass* of John Burckard, which dates from the end of the fifteenth century and which provided a good deal of the basis for the *Ritus servandus* of the "Tridentine" Missal (to such an extent that certain authors less correctly identify the two documents with one another), bore in mind the presence of the people and their actions. It often speaks of the *"interessentes" missae* (the faithful who are present and who participate in the Mass) and of what they must do in the course of the celebration.[16] From this point of view, the *Ritus servandus* represents a backward step in comparison with the *Order* of Burckard.

As far as the expression "assembled people" is concerned, we should also add similar expressions used by the *General Instruction*, such as the following: "the people of God . . . *gathered together into one*" (No. 7); "the faithful who *gather into one*" (No. 19); "the faithful . . . *gathered together*" (*ibid.*); "the *assembled* people" (No. 24); and "the people of God . . . *called together*" (No. 259).

Reflection on these references to the "people called and assembled" and to the "faithful who gather together" inevitably puts us in mind of the writings of the early Church. It will suffice to mention the *Didachè* and the first *Apology* of St. Justin. Both these texts deal with the Sunday celebration, and the first element highlighted is the gathering together of the people.

Didachè:
κατὰ κυριακὴν δὲ κυρίου συναχθέντες, κλάσατε ἄρτον καὶ εὐχαριστήσατε.
(On the Lord's own day, assemble in common to break bread and offer thanks.)[17]

St. Justin Martyr:
καὶ τῇ τοῦ ἡλίου λεγομένῃ ἡμέρᾳ, πάντων κατὰ πόλεις ἢ ἀγροὺς μενόντων ἐπὶ τὸ αὐτὸ συνέλευσις γίνεται.
(On the day which is called Sun-day, all, whether they live in the town or in the country, gather in the same place.)[18]

These texts in turn lead us to the first letter to the Corinthians, in which Paul speaks of the Eucharist as celebrated in the
assemblies of the *ecclesia* or community. The link between the
terms of the *General Instruction* and those given by the Vulgate is
clear: "For, in the first place, when you *assemble as a church*
[*convenientibus* vobis *in ecclesiam*] . . . when you *meet together as
one* [*convenientibus* ergo vobis *in unum*] . . ." (1 Cor. 11:18, 20);
"So then, . . . when you *come together* [*convenitis*] to eat, . . .
lest you *come together* [*conveniatis*] to eat, . . . lest you *come together* [*conveniatis*] to be condemned" (1 Cor. 11:33–34).

We would also note in connection with the texts cited that
the expression *in unum convenire* is the one chosen by *Sacrosanctum concilium* when it speaks of the Sunday celebration: "For
on this day Christ's faithful are bound to come together [*in unum
convenire*]" (SC 106).

The Liturgy of the Word

Before discussing the rites themselves, we should note the extent to which the *General Instruction* takes up the terms used in
Sacrosanctum concilium, highlighting and emphasizing the Church
as the special place for the reading and hearing of the word of God:
"When the Sacred Scriptures are read in the Church, God himself
speaks to his people, and it is Christ, present in his word, who
proclaims the Gospel" (*GI* 9).

In the description of this liturgy, we are always aware of the
presence of the community as it listens, responds, acclaims. After emphasizing that God speaks to his people, the document
adds that the people in turn make this word their own through
their chants, and express their adherence to it through the profession of faith (No. 33). There is one moment of particular importance in which the ecclesial character of the common priesthood
of the faithful is expressed, and this is the general intercessions,
or prayer of the faithful, in which the Church can be seen as the
community concerned over the good of mankind and interceding
on its behalf (No. 45).

In this connection, we would recall the richness and vigor
with which the Introduction to the second edition of the
Lectionary stresses the relationship between the celebration of
the word in the Mass and the Church as the people of God

gathered together in assembly. On the one hand, they state that the Church is built up and grows by listening to the word. On the other hand, they stress the role of the community in the announcement and proclamation of this word, and above all they highlight the activity of the Spirit, who constantly leads the Church to increased awareness of itself as people of God in which the action begun in ancient times is fully accomplished: "Whenever, therefore, the Church, *gathered* by the Holy Spirit *for liturgical celebration,* announces and proclaims the word of God, it has the experience of being a new people. . . ." How different this is from a purely ritual, anonymous, and incomprehensible reading!

At the end of the description of the Liturgy of the Word, having explained the profession of faith, the *General Instruction,* almost as an afterthought, very decidedly assigns the concept of agent of the eucharistic celebration to the people: "*In the profession of faith . . . the people* have the opportunity to respond and give assent . . . before *they begin to celebrate* the eucharist" (No. 43).

The Eucharistic Liturgy

With regard to the preparation of the gifts, both the *General Instruction* and the *Order of Mass* are anxious to highlight the part played by the assembly, especially in their explanations of the meaning of the offering of the gifts intended for the liturgical action and for the needs of the community, particularly those who are in distress (*GI* 49). The *Order of Mass* explains this intervention of the people with expressions that were not usual in the rubrical context: "It is desirable that the *participation of the faithful* be expressed by members of the congregation bringing up the bread and wine *for the celebration of the eucharist* or other gifts *for the needs of the Church and the poor.*"

When the *General Instruction* came to speak of the eucharistic prayer, which is the center and summit of the whole celebration, it was bound to stress the action of the community. Although this prayer of course belongs to the priest, he is aware of not being alone, for with him he has the assembly of which he is the president: ". . . the priest invites the people to lift their hearts to God . . . [and] unites them with himself in the prayer he addresses in their name to the Father through Jesus Christ" (*GI*

54). And it then gives the meaning of this prayer in very explicit terms: "The meaning of the prayer is that the *whole congregation joins Christ* in acknowledging the works of God and *in offering the sacrifice*" (cf. *ibid.*: ". . . he unites them with himself in the prayer . . . that the whole congregation joins Christ . . .").

The following article gives more details on the action of the people during this great prayer: ". . . *in the name of the entire holy people,*"[19] the priest glorifies God the Father, and then the congregation unites itself with the heavenly praises in the *Sanctus*. The text explains that this acclamation "*forms part* of the eucharistic prayer, and *all the people join with the priest* in singing or reciting it." The *Order of Mass* uses a similar expression: "At the end of the preface, *together with the people,* [*the priest*] *concludes it.* . . ." A little later, speaking of the offering that the Church "*here and now assembled*" offers to the Father in the Holy Spirit, the *General Instruction* describes the role of the community here at the summit of the celebration: "The Church's intention is that the faithful not only offer the spotless victim but also learn to offer themselves" (No. 55f.). Lastly, in the final doxology, the *Instruction* recalls the value of the acclamation of the people, in which the whole eucharistic action "is confirmed and concluded" (No. 55h).

Celebration and Church

The fourth chapter of the *General Instruction* is devoted to the different forms of celebration. It begins by echoing the statement of *Sacrosanctum concilium* 41 in which the local Church, the role of the bishop, and the presence of the people are emphasized:

> Among the various ways of celebrating the eucharist in the local Church, first place should be given to Mass at which the bishop presides with the college of presbyters and the ministers, and with the people taking full and active part. This is the principal sign of the Church (*GI* 74)

We should note the importance given to the celebration as the outstanding manifestation of the Church.

Taking this ideal context as a basis, the document moves on to the more normal case of Mass celebrated with some other type of community, speaking first of the parish community. In this case, its supremely ecclesial character is also stressed: it "has special meaning in representing the universal Church gathered at a given time and place" (GI 75).

We shall not follow the full development of this description, which is marked by its rubrical tone. However, we would observe that even in this secondary context, the aspect of assembled community is consistently highlighted, and the typical expression already noted before reappears here: "The priest and the ministers, . . . *when the people have assembled . . .*" (No. 82). Then we have references to the action of the people at important points in the celebration. For example, at the end of the collect, "all . . . make the acclamation"; at the general intercessions, "the people take part"; in the preparation of the gifts, "it is fitting that the participation of the faithful be expressed."

The Place of the Celebration

In order to complete the principles formulated with regard to the celebration and its rite, it would seem helpful to recall what the *General Instruction* has to say in its fifth chapter on the place in which the celebration takes place. Here again we find the key ideas that have accompanied us until now.

It is stated from the outset that in order to celebrate the Eucharist, the people of God "is normally assembled in a church" (GI 253). After emphasizing the duty to embellish the place of celebration and make it worthy, the document notes the respect that should be accorded to this place because of the relationship between the church as place of worship and the Church as community: "The faithful should see the cathedral church and their own church as signs of the spiritual Church which their Christian vocation commissions them to build and extend" (No. 255). Behind these expressions, we can discern a very rich doctrinal line that the liturgy then develops in the rite for the dedication of a church, and that we find in the introductory notes to the new rite of dedication.[20]

Having given the general principles, the *General Instruction* moves on to discuss their practical application, describing how to arrange the general layout, the sanctuary, the altar, the celebrant's chair, the lectern, and so on. Under all the norms, we can constantly feel the principle of the "assembled community," the people of God that is gathered together and has an organic and hierarchical structure. "The general plan of the building should suggest in some way this image of community," and while the elements must express the diversity of offices, "they should at the same time form a complete and organic whole which clearly expresses the *unity of the people of God*" (GI 257).

The altar deserves special treatment. It is defined as the "table of the Lord," and "the people of God *is called together* to share in this table" (No. 259). Its position should show that it is truly the center toward which the attention of the *whole gathering of the faithful* is spontaneously drawn (No. 262).

Manifestation of the Church?

We have seen that the liturgical books of the Mass are concerned to make the celebration more alive, and in this way to make it a manifestation of the Church. Even so, we may wonder whether our liturgy of the Mass does in fact normally fulfill this objective.

It must be recognized that many communities have renewed the style of their celebrations, which are no longer simply the concern of the clergy, but are an action in which the assembly takes part according to the various ministries. In these celebrations, we find a sort of echo of the different activities and aspirations of the local community: welcome, proclamation of the gospel, shared prayer, fraternal assistance and mutual support, pastoral concern. It might be said that a community with liturgical commitment tends to have apostolic commitment, in line with the thought expressed in *Sacrosanctum concilium* 10:

> The liturgy . . . moves the faithful . . . to become "of one heart in love"; it prays that they hold fast in their lives to what they have grasped by their faith. The renewal in the Eucharist of the covenant between the Lord and man draws the faithful and sets them aflame with Christ's insistent love.

However, we also know that people have often been satisfied simply to change the texts, the rites and the language, without taking into account the requirements of a truly coherent liturgy.

Further liturgical catechesis is still needed[21] so that the books can be used with awareness, and the words and actions of the rite can be the expression of the faith and life of each Christian and of the community as a whole. Only then will we be able to say that the celebration is an expression of the Church as priestly people, as community of faith and charity.

Translated from the French by Leslie Wearne.

Appendix

Ordo Missae (Roman Missal, second typical edition, 1975)

(Opening)

1. *Populo congregato* . . . sacerdos cum ministris ad altare acce-dit. . . .
2. . . . sacerdos *et fideles*, stantes, signant se. . . . *Populus* respondet: Amen.
   Deinde sacerdos, manus extendens, *populum* salutat. . . . Populus respondet: . . . .
3. Sacerdos . . . potest brevissimis verbis introducere *fideles*. . . . Sacerdos *fideles* invitat ad paenitentiam. . . . Postea *omnes simul* faciunt confessionem. . . . *Populus* respondet: Amen.
6. Et *omnes una* cum sacerdote . . . orant . . .[22]; sacerdos . . . dicit orationem, qua finita, *populus* acclamat: Amen.
7. Quam [lectionem] *omnes sedentes auscultant*. . . . *Omnes* accla-mant: Deo gratias.
8. Psalmista . . . psalmum dicit, *populo* responsum proferente.
9. *Omnes* acclamant: Deo gratias.
12. [At the gospel], *populus* respondet: Et cum. . . . *Populus* acclamat: Gloria tibi Domine. . . .
13. . . . *omnibus* acclamantibus: Laus tibi Christe!
15. [At the Creed] . . . *omnes* se inclinant.
16. Deinde fit oratio universalis seu *oratio fidelium*.[23]
18. Expedit ut *fideles* participationem suam oblatione manifestent. . . .
19. . . . in fine *populus* acclamare potest: Benedictus Deus in saecula.
23. . . . diaconus incensat sacerdotem et *populum*.
25. Stans . . . versus ad *populum* . . . dicit: Orate. . . . *Populus* re-spondet: Suscipiat. . . .
26. Qua finita, *populus* acclamat: Amen.
27. [Eucharistic Prayer:] *Populus* respondet. . . . In fine autem prae-fationis . . . *una cum populo,* ipsam praefationem concludit, cantans. . . .

91. Hostiam consecratam ostendit *populo.* . . .
92. . . . calicem ostendit *populo.* . . .
93. . . . et *populus* prosequitur, acclamans: Mortem tuam. . . .
100. *Populus* acclamat: Amen.
125. [Communion] . . . *una cum populo* pergit: Pater noster. . . .
126. *Populus* orationem concludit, acclamans: Quia tuum est. . . .
127. *Populus* respondet: Amen.
128. Sacerdos *ad populum* conversus. . . . *Populus* respondet: Et cum. . . .
129. Et *omnes* . . . pacem et caritatem sibi invicem significant.
133. . . . *ad populum* versus . . . et *una cum populo* semel subdit: Domine non sum dignus. . . .
135. . . accedit *ad communicandos,* et hostiam . . . *unicuique* eorum ostendit. . . . *Communicandus* respondet: Amen. Et communicatur.
140. Et *omnes una cum* sacerdote per aliquod temporis spatium in silentio orant. . . . *Populus* in fine acclamat: Amen.
141. [Conclusion] Sequuntur . . . breves annuntiationes *ad populum.*
142. Sacerdos versus *ad populum.* . . . *Populus* respondet: Et cum. . . . Sacerdos benedicit *populum.* . . . *Populus* respondet: Amen.
143. Diaconus . . . *ad populum* versus. . . . *Populus* respondet: Deo gratias.

Notes

1. The ecclesiology underlying *Sacrosanctum concilium* already gives a glimpse of the great principles that will then be developed in *Lumen gentium:* even so, had *Sancrosanctum concilium* been drafted and discussed later, it would certainly have been enriched by the reflection of the Fathers and by the doctrine set forth in texts such as *Lumen gentium, Presbyterorum ordinis,* and *Gaudium et spes.* These documents were to enrich the introductions (or *praenotanda*) to the new liturgical books, which, taking the principles of *Sacrosanctum concilium* as their starting point, benefited from the later texts.

2. In this connection, cf.: A. Decourtray, "Esquisses de l'Eglise d'après la constitution *de sacra liturgia,*" *La Maison-Dieu,* 78 (1964), 40–63, which appeared immediately after the promulgation of the Constitution; I. Oñatibia, "La eclesiologia en la Sacrosanctum Concilium," *Notitiae,* 19 (1983), 648–660, a study forming part of the series of works published by the review of the Sacred Congregation for the Sacraments and Divine Worship on the twentieth anniversary of *Sacrosanctam concilium;* D. Sartore, "Chiesa e Liturgia," in D. Sartore and A. Triacca (eds.), *Nuovo Dizionario di Liturgia* (Rome, 1984), 248–259.

3. Here we can apply the statement of the Instruction *Eucharisticum mysterium* of 25 May 1967: "Catechesis of the Mass should take the rites and prayers as its starting point. . . . Suitable catechesis . . . should take as its starting point the mysteries of the liturgical year and the rites and prayers which are part of the celebration. It should clarify their meaning . . ." (No. 15).

4. P.R. Rocha, "No 20° aniversário da constituição litúrgica," *Brotéria,* 118 (1984), 508–522.

5. The terms used by *Sacrosanctum concilium* are clear: for example, *instauratio* (Nos. 21, 33), *recognoscere* (Nos. 25, 31, 50), *restituere* (No. 50).

6. Paul VI, Apostolic Constitution *Missale Romanum* (3 April 1969), promulgating the new missal.

7. Apart from the very frequent citations of *Sacrosanctum concilium* (more than fifty), the document also cites *Lumen gentium, Presbyterorum ordinis, Christus Dominus, Unitatis redintegratio,* and *Dei Verbum.*

8. Between *Sacrosanctum concilium* and the *General Instruction,* the Instruction *Eucharisticum mysterium* helped to enrich and define the doctrine of active participation in the Mass. Taking as its starting point the relationship between "ministerial priesthood" and "common priesthood" (No. 11), the document states: "It should be made clear that all who gather for the Eucharist constitute that holy people which, together with the ministers, plays its part in the sacred action" (No. 12). It should be observed that the *General Instruction* cites *Eucharisticum mysterium* very often (some twenty-five times).

9. In numbers 14–16, the *General Instruction* gives the reasons for the importance attributed to these elements (dialogue, acclamations, responses) by appealing to the community character of the Mass, and states that they are the means of greater communion between priest and people, and clearly express the action of the whole community.

10. The change would begin in 1965, when the Council for the Proper Implementation of the Constitution on the Sacred Liturgy and the Sacred Congregation of Rites published a new edition of the *Order of Mass* in accordance with the modifications laid down in the instruction *Inter oecumenici* (26 September 1964). This *Order of Mass* was as a whole still that of the Tridentine Missal, although it did already take the presence of the people into account and assumed their active participation. This presence is indicated in the rubrics: "Ministri vel circumstantes respondent . . . faciunt confessionem"; the antiphons, the *Kyrie* and the *Gloria* are sung or recited "a schola vel a populo"; the "oratio communis seu fidelium" is also envisaged; and the *Sanctus-Benedictus* is sung by the celebrant "una cum ministris, clero et populo." Although the description of the rite, the *Ritus servandus,* still retained a good deal of the earlier style, it also took into account the presence of the people and their interventions, in accordance with the modifications introduced in the *Order of Mass*. This was an intermediate stage while the new missal was still being awaited.

11. As early as 1956, the new order for Holy Week mentioned the people and their interventions in its rubrics. And in the semiofficial commentary published by Edizioni Liturgiche, the importance of this "new departure" is repeatedly recalled. The rubric stated, "Cui omnes respondent . . . ," and a note emphasized the *omnes:* "Notetur spiritus pastoralis huius rubricae." And then a little later: "*Omnes:* nota pastoralis; ante dicebatur: 'Chorus respondet.' " A. Bugnini and C. Braga, *Ordo Hebdomadae Sancate instauratus* (Rome, 1956), 50, 53.

12. We would note the preference for the adjective "local" to indicate the assembled church. Later on the local church would be spoken of in connection with the Mass as presided over by the bishop (No. 74) and it would be said that the eucharistic community represents the universal Church. The *ecclesia* is present wherever the people are gathered together in the liturgical assembly. See also, for example, *Lumen gentium* 26.

13. Echoing this expression, the *Order of Mass* would open the celebration in almost identical terms: "After the people have assembled, the priest and the ministers go to the altar while the entrance song is being sung" (No. 1).

14. See GI 82: "*Common form*. Introductory rites. The priest and the ministers put on their vestments and, *when the people have assembled. . . .*" The "common form" is that of "*Mass with a congregation*" (No. 77), the "normal" Mass, which is described first among the various forms of celebration.

15. Drawing inspiration from St. Cyprian (*De oratione dominicale* 23), *Lumen gentium* would also say that the Church is seen to be "a people *brought into unity* with the unity of the Father, the Son and the Holy Spirit" (No. 4).

16. There is an edition of the *Ordo Missae* of Burckard printed in 1498 (L. Hain, *Repertorium Bibliographicum*, No. 4102). J. Wickham Legg, in his work *Tracts on the Mass* (London, 1904), reproduces the edition printed in Rome in 1502, and this is what I am using here. Burckard's *Ordo Missae* is conceived in the perspective of the Mass as celebrated "sine cantu et sine ministris," in other words, what would be called "low Mass," without deacon or subdeacon. Even so, the author frequently speaks of "*interessentes*" *missae*, or the faithful who are present and participate in the Mass. At the outset, he gives details of the positions they must observe: kneeling, standing, sitting (Legg, *Tracts on the Mass*, 134–135). He then states that the *minister* and the *in-*

teressentes respond to the verses of the psalm *Iudica me*, say the *Confiteor* and the *Misereatur* (*ibid.*, 135–136), alternate the *Kyrie* (*ibid.*, 139), respond to the *Orate, fratres* (*ibid.*, 152), and so on. Basically, this ritual printed in 1502 contains what almost amounts to a description of the "Dialogue Mass" that was to create some problems at the beginning of the present century. Burckard goes further when it comes to defining the attitude of the people in the "low Mass." For example, even if the *interessentes* do not understand the celebrant and have no knowledge of Latin, they must not recite other prayers or *officia* (?), but must make an effort to pay attention and to unite themselves with what the celebrant is saying and doing: together with the priest, the faithful must offer, implore, pray, and so on (*ibid.*, 135). Burckard also envisages the possibility of gifts brought by the people ("si sint qui volentes offerre"—*ibid.*, 149); similarly, he envisages the gesture of peace toward the *interessentibus* (*ibid.*, 162) and the communion of the faithful after that of the priest (*ibid.*, 165). He warns the celebrant to speak the texts in a sufficiently comprehensible tone of voice so that he can be heard by those present, and, with a certain dry humor, says that the priest should not linger overlong over the *Memento*, "ne circumstantibus sit molestus" (*ibid.*, 154).

17. *Didachè*, 14, 1; English translation from J. Quasten and J.C. Plumpe (eds.), *Ancient Christian Writers*, 6 (New York, 1978), 23. We would note the Latin version of this text chosen by J. Quasten, *Monumenta eucharistica et liturgica vetustissima*, Florilegium Patristicum 7 (Bonn, 1935), 12: "Die autem dominica *congregati*, frangite panem et gratias agite."

18. St. Justin Martyr, *Apologia I*, 67, 3, in G. Rauschen (ed.), *S. Justini Apologiae duae*, Florilegium Patristicum 2, revised edition (Bonn, 1911), 108–109; English translation from L. Deiss (ed.), *Early Sources of the Liturgy* (London, 1967), 25. We would note the Latin version chosen by Rauschen: "Et die qui dicitur solis omnium qui in urbibus et in agris habitant *in unum* fit *conventus.*"

19. The expression recalls that of the Roman Canon: ". . . nos servi tui sed et plebs tua sancta. . . ."

20. In this connection, see S. Marsili, "Dal tempio locale al tempio spirituale," in *Il Tempio. Atti della XVIII Settimana liturgica nazionale a Monreale, 28 agosto—1 settembre 1967* (n.c., 1968), 51–63. On the basis of the new rite for dedication, see J.S. Peixoto, "A Igreja templo vivo de Deus. A liturgia do Comum da Dedicação. A eucologia do Comum da Dedicação," *Humanística e Teologia*, 5 (1984), 219–233, 319–335, with an up-to-date bibliography.

21. Rocha, "No 20° aniversário da constituição litúrgica," 512–517.

22. GI 88 describes the dynamics of the invitation to prayer and the actual prayer of the people more clearly: "*Sacerdos populum ad orantum invitat* . . . dicens Oremus. Et *omnes una cum sacerdote ad breve tempus silentes orant.* . . .

23. GI 99 is more explicit: "Deinde, *populo pro sua parte participante,* fit oratio universalis seu oratio fidelium. . . ."

CHAPTER 23

The Divine Office:
Monastic Choir, Prayer Book,
or Liturgy of the People of God?
An Evaluation of the New Liturgy
of the Hours in its Historical Context

Robert Taft, S.J.

Summary

One aspect of Vatican II that inspired liturgical renewal has not
met with success: the attempt to make the Divine Office true
parish "liturgy" once again. The roots of the failure lie (1) in the
history of the hours in the medieval West, a history of monas-
ticization and privatization; and (2) in the ignorance of other,
more pastoral models of the hours seen in the early history of the
Divine Office and in several eastern traditions. But the flexibility
of the new *Liturgy of the Hours* makes them adaptable to more
popular forms of common worship if only we had the interest,
initiative, and imagination to do so.

In the overwhelming chorus of approving voices that hailed
the liturgical reforms of Vatican II, a discordant note has been
heard.[1] It concerns the new Liturgy of the Hours. In spite of
conciliar and postconciliar efforts, there has been little substantive progress in restoring the Divine Office as an integral part of
parish worship in the Roman Rite. To understand some of the

reasons for this failure in the generally positive liturgical work of
the past decades, let us look at what contemporary historiogra-
phy of the Divine Office tells us about its origins and meaning in
the life of the Church.[2] Before deciding what to do about the
office, one must know what it was meant to be.

The Liturgy of the Hours:
Origins and Meaning in the Life of the Church

Since the appearance in 1945 of Dom Gregory Dix's classic *The
Shape of the Liturgy*, it has been customary to fit the office under the
heading of "sanctification of time," as a "liturgy of time" distinct
from the "eschatalogical" Eucharist. Furthermore, Dix sees the
office as the result of a fourth-century revolution in the spirit of
worship. In the pre-Nicene period, when secular life was pagan,
he argues, liturgy and daily life were distinct and even opposed.
When the monastic movement swept the fourth-century world, it
brought in its train a new emphasis on personal edification in
Christian worship. Hippolytus' *Apostolic Tradition* presents a re-
gime of prayer "recognizably semi-monastic in character," which
"represents the purely *personal* aspect of devotion, and stands quite
apart . . . from the corporate worship of the *ecclesia*. . . . The
corporate worship of the pre-Nicene christians . . . was over-
whelmingly a 'world-renouncing' cultus, which deliberately and
rigidly rejected the whole idea of sanctifying and expressing towards God the life of human society in general. . . ."[3]
Such is the scenario drawn by Dix, all of which, he says, was
to change in the fourth century when the pre-Nicene system of
private prayer, developed by the monks into a large part of their
public worship, leads to the introduction of services of praise into
the public worship of the secular churches. The older worship
stressed the corporate action of the Church. The new offices,
though done in common, are intended chiefly to express and
evoke the devotion of the individual worshiper, and are "a direct
result of the monastic–ascetic movement."[4]
Let us examine this historical model proposed by Dix to see,
first, whether another interpretation might not accord better
with the facts, and, second, what such a revisionist view might
mean in the light of recent liturgical reforms.

The Emergence of a Fixed Cycle of Daily Prayer
in the Third Century

From the New Testament and *Didachè* 8:2–3, we know that the early Christians prayed daily, alone or in common, at certain times of the day or night. But it is only from the beginning of the third century that evidence for a system of specifically Christian daily prayer at set times begins to accumulate. We see this in Clement of Alexandria, Origen, Tertullian, Cyprian, and Hippolytus.

1. *The Cursus.* The evidence is diverse enough to exclude any facile attempt to harmonize it all into one prayer system without doing violence to the facts. Among the Egyptians, we hear of morning–noon–evening–night prayer, but nothing about the forms or content of this daily prayer.[5] The Egyptian sources are concerned less with *times* and *kinds* of prayer than with *unceasing* prayer. The exhortation to *incessant* prayer, repeated four times in the New Testament (1 Thess. 5:16–18; Eph. 6:18; Col. 4:2; Lk. 18:1 and 21:36), will remain fundamental to the Egyptian tradition and, through it, will become the basis for monastic prayer. Christians were to pray unceasingly, and the times mentioned, all of them normal chronological points of reference in ancient culture, were simply the Egyptian way of saying that Christians must pray "morning, noon, and night"—in other words, always.

With the North Africans and the *Apostolic Tradition*, we are closer to the full series of hours that will eventually coalesce into the fourth-century cursus: prayer on rising, at the third, sixth, ninth hours, in the evening, and during the night.[6]

2. *Content of the Prayer.* In the third century, these hours of prayer also begin to assume some form and commonality. Tertullian tells us that Christian daily prayers were said alone or in the company of others, that hymns and biblical psalms were used, and both he and the *Apostolic Tradition* indicate that sometimes the psalms were executed responsorially.[7] But apart from the sacramental rites, the only Christian service that had evolved a clear ritual shape in this period is the *agape*, an occasional fraternal meal held in the evening.[8] The service began with the lighting of the lamps, a practical necessity to provide light for the service. But even among non-Christians, the lighting of the evening lamp had a deeper meaning. Pagans were accustomed to

greet the light with the exclamation, "*Chaire phôs agathon* [Hail, good light]!" or "*Chaire phôs philon* [Hail, friendly light]!"[9] And Clement of Alexandria, *Protrepticus* 11, 114:1, recommends that we greet the true God with "Hail, light!" So even before the development of evening prayer into a formal liturgical office, Christian domestic piety had inherited and christianized the pagan custom of greeting the evening lamp. The spirit of this Christian *lucernarium* can be seen in the following *agape* prayer from the Ethiopic version of the *Apostolic Tradition*:

> 26. When the bishop is present, and evening has come, a deacon brings in a lamp; and standing in the midst of all the faithful who are present (the bishop) shall give thanks. . . . And he shall pray thus, saying: "We give you thanks, Lord, through your Son Jesus Christ our Lord, through whom you have shone upon us and revealed to us the inextinguishable light. So when we have completed the length of the day and have come to the beginning of the night, and have satisfied ourselves with the light of day which you created for our satisfying; and since now through your grace we do not lack the light of evening, we praise and glorify you through your Son Jesus Christ our Lord. . . ."[10]

3. *Meaning.* Here we see the beginnings of what will become the common interpretation of the incipient Christian cursus of daily prayer—its "theology"—especially in cathedral usage. Evening and morning, at the setting and rising of the sun, remind us of Jesus' passover from death to life, and of his second coming. *1 Clem.* 24:1–3 at the end of the first century is our earliest witness to this symbolism:

> Let us consider, beloved, how the Lord continually manifests to us the resurrection to come, whose first fruits he made Christ by raising him from the dead. We see, beloved, that the resurrection was accomplished according to the time. Day and night make visible to us a resurrection. Night goes to sleep, the day rises; the day departs, the night follows.

In third-century sources, such imagery is applied directly to morning and evening prayer, as we read in Cyprian, *On the Lord's Prayer* 34–36:

Likewise at sunset and the passing of the day it is necessary to pray. For since Christ is the true sun and the true day, when we pray and ask, as the sun and the day of the world recede, that the light may come upon us again, we pray for the coming of Christ, which provides us with the grace of eternal light. . . .

The practice of orientation in prayer witnessed to by Clement, Origen, and Tertullian[11] was also related to this symbolism of Christ as sun of justice and light of the world, as well as to the eschatological expectation of the second coming of the Lord, "for as the lightning comes from the East and shines as far as the West, so will be the coming of the Son of man" (Mt. 24:27).

Clement, *Pedagogue* 2:9, is also our first witness to the eschatological character of Christian prayer at night, a fundamental trait of all Christian vigils:

We must therefore sleep so as to be easily awakened. For it is said: "Let your loins be girt, and your lamps burning, and be like those who are waiting for their master to come home from the marriage feast . . ." (Lk. 12:35–37). . . . Therefore at night we ought to rise often and bless God. For blessed are they who watch for him, and so make themselves like the angels, whom we call "watchers."

So by the third century, Christian daily prayer has acquired not only a certain consistency and form, but also a rationale. The rising sun and the light of the evening lamp at vesperal prayer symbolize Christ, the light of the world. The day hours recall the passion of the Markan account; the third hour is also a memorial of the descent of the Holy Spirit at Pentecost. Night prayer is eschatological, like the watch for the coming of the bridegroom, and the unceasing praise of angels.

Was this "liturgical" or "private" prayer? The question is anachronistic. Christians prayed. Whether they did so alone or in company, depended not on the nature of the prayer, but on who happened to be around when the hour for prayer arrived. The point was to pray. In times of persecution, or during the workday, that usually meant alone. When they could come together, they did so, because the very nature of church means to congregate. But alone or together, the prayer was the same.

The Cathedral Office in the Fourth Century

After the Peace of Constantine in 313, Christian worship, formerly the furtive affair of a persecuted minority, becomes an integral part of the daily public life of the Roman Empire. The Liturgy of the Hours was part of this explosion of liturgical development. In this period, three types of office evolve: (1) cathedral, (2) Egyptian–monastic, and (3) urban–monastic. These are not three successive stages in the development of one office, but three distinct types of office that evolved in three separate areas of church life. The first two evolved simultaneously from the midfourth century. The third, a synthesis of the first two, is already visible in the last quarter of the same century.

The office of the secular churches is called "cathedral" rather than "parochial," because for centuries it was the bishop's church that was the center of all liturgical life. This office comprised popular services characterized by symbol and ceremony (light, incense, processions, etc.), by chant (responsories, antiphons, hymns), by diversity of ministries (bishop, presbyter, deacon, reader, psalmist, etc.), and by psalmody that was limited and select, rather than current and complete. That is, the psalms were not read continuously according to their numerical order in the Bible. Rather, certain psalms or sections of psalms were chosen for their suitability to the hour or service. Furthermore, the cathedral services were offices of praise and intercession, not a Liturgy of the Word. Contrary to popular misconception, there were no scripture lessons in the early cathedral office except in Egypt and Cappadocia.[12]

We first hear of this office at the beginning of the fourth century, from Eusebius of Caesarea in Palestine (ca. 263–339). In his *Commentary on Ps. 64:9*, he tells us "that throughout the whole world in the churches of God at the morning rising of the sun and at the evening hours, hymns, praises, and truly divine delights are offered to God." From that time on, we have fourth-century evidence for such popular services in Egypt, Cappadocia, Cyprus, Antioch and its environs, Constantinople, and Palestine.[13] What is more remarkable, the sources agree on the basic framework of these offices: morning praise and evensong opened with a fixed psalm—Psalm 62/63 or 50/51 in the morning and Psalm 140/141 in the evening—and concluded with intercessions for the needs of the people. To this basic skeleton, other elements were added according to the time, place, and character of the service, all within the same fourth century. At morning prayer, for example, we see the *Gloria in excelsis* and the psalms of lauds; in the evening, a hymn to accompany the lamplighting, and an offering of incense with Psalm 140. Occasionally, we hear of a reading and a homily.

We do not have space to unroll all the evidence here. Let's just glance at our earliest examples, from Cappadocia, where we see a cathedral office still quite close to its domestic roots. Gregory of Nyssa (d. 394), in his *Life of St. Macrina*, describes the death of his sister in 379. The day before, Gregory wished to remain with the failing Macrina, "But," he tells us, "the chant of the singers called to the thanksgiving for the light, and she sent me off to the church."[14] In the *Apostolic Tradition* of Hippolytus (ca. 215), we saw that this lamplighting was in conjunction with the *agape*, and included a prayer of thanksgiving for the light. By the last quarter of the fourth century in Cappadocia, this ritual and its name have been incorporated into cathedral vespers. We see this new development as early as 374 in Gregory Nazianus's eulogy for his father.[15]

On the Holy Spirit 29 (73), by another of Macrina's brothers, St. Basil, provides us with the precious information that this "thanksgiving for the light" was the evening hymn *Phôs hilaron*, which is still the lamplighting hymn of Byzantine vespers according to the tradition of St. Sabas. It is one of the earliest extant Christian hymns, a song of praise to Christ, the true light shining in the darkness of the world. Basil says the hymn was ancient even in his time, so old that he did not even know who wrote it:

> It seemed fitting to our fathers not to receive the gift of the evening light in silence, but to give thanks immediately upon its appearance. We cannot say who was the father of the words of the thanksgiving for the light. But the people utter the ancient formula, and those that say, "We praise you Father, Son and Holy Spirit of God" were never thought impious by anyone.

Basil also seems to have known the "angel of peace" litany, a traditional formula of dismissal at the end of the evening office. In *Letter 11*, he writes:

After passing, by God's grace, the whole day in the company of
our children, and having celebrated for the Lord a truly complete feast . . . we sent them on to your lordship in good
health, after praying God the lover of humankind to give them
an angel of peace as an aid and traveling companion. . . .[16]

We find the same thing in Syria. Around 380, the *Apostolic
Constitutions* (II, 59) refers to Psalms 62 and 140 as the opening
psalms for the two daily services, and even gives the text of the
lengthy intercessions, concluding with the "angel of peace" bid-
dings, a final blessing, and dismissal (VIII, 34–39).[17] Half a century later, Theodoret (ca. 393–466), bishop of Cyrus, a small
town east of Antioch, testifies to the ceremonial embellishment of
this basic framework in his *Questions on Exodus* 28 (*post* 453),
when he speaks of "the incense and the light of the lamps that we
offer to God, as well as the service of the mysteries of the holy
table."[18] In other words, in addition to the Eucharist, Christian
worship included offices with a light ritual and the use of incense.

As for developments in morning prayer, the lauds psalms are
already referred to at the end of the century by Chrysostom in
Antioch and Cassian in Bethlehem,[19] and in other sources of the
period, we hear of such elements as the *Gloria in excelsis* and an
Old-Testament canticle.[20] Although the western evidence is later, the same basic structure and developments can be seen there
too. Gregory of Tours (ca. 540–595), for example, describes
morning prayer as comprising the *Miserere* (Ps. 50/51), the
Benedicite canticle of Daniel 3: 57–88, the lauds psalms, and
concluding intercessions.[21]

What could be simpler than these popular devotions? The
whole local community is there, bishop, clergy, people. Skilled
cantors intone the various verses, while popular participation is
assured through a limited repertory of fixed refrains and hymns.
The service opens with a fixed invitatory psalm, chosen to set
the tone. Two or three other select hymns, psalms, or biblical
canticles follow. Then the deacon proclaims the litanies for the
people's intentions. The brief service ends with a collect and
final blessing of the bishop, then off to work or home to supper
and bed.

Chrysostom in Antioch around 390 gives the motivation for
the two daily cathedral synaxes in his *Baptismal Catechesis* VIII,
17–18:

Be very diligent in coming here early in the morning to bring prayers and praises to the God of all, and to give thanks for the benefits already received, and to entreat him to deign to be a close ally for protection in the future. . . . But let each one go to his affairs with fear and trembling, and so pass the time of day as one obliged to return here in the evening to give the master an account of the entire day and to ask pardon for failures. For it is impossible . . . to avoid being liable for all sorts of faults. . . . And that is why every evening we must ask the master's pardon for all these faults. . . .

Then we must pass the time of night in sobriety and thus be ready to present ourselves again at the morning praise. . . .[22]

In his *Commentary on Psalm 140*, Chrysostom repeats the same teaching,[23] and similar explanations are given by Basil, Cassian, and others.[24] So the theory is as uncomplicated as the structure. In the morning, we gather to consecrate the day to God by opening it with his praises, thanking him for past graces and imploring him continued protection during the coming day. At night, we return to thank him for the day's graces, ask pardon for its failings, and seek protection from the terrors of night—very real fears in the days before electricity and a more sophisticated understanding of the nature of dreams and sleep. To put it in contemporary terms, cathedral morning prayer was a sort of morning offering in common, and vespers a common examination of conscience and act of contrition.

The Egyptian Monastic Office

While the formation of the cathedral hours was underway, a parallel series of offices was evolving in monastic communities. John Cassian, who lived in Scetis, the present Wadi an-Natrun, sixty-five kilometers northwest of Cairo, from about 380 until 399, has left us a detailed description of the usage of Lower Egypt.[25] There were only two offices, one at cockcrow, in the wee hours of the morning, and one in the evening. Both offices comprised twelve psalms, with private prayer, prostration, and a collect after each. The prayer concluded with the *Gloria Patri* and two lessons from Sacred Scripture.

The other Egyptian monastic office for which we have evidence is that of the cenobitic foundations initiated by Pachomius

(d. 346) around 320 at Tabennesi in the Nile valley of the
"Thebaid" north of Thebes.[26] At the synaxis, the seated monks
continued their traditional handiwork of weaving rushes into
baskets and mats while the appointed individuals went in turn to
the ambo to recite a biblical passage (not necessarily a psalm).
After each passage, the reader gave a signal and all rose, made
the sign of the cross on the forehead, and recited the Our Father
with arms extended in the form of a cross. At a second signal,
they blessed themselves again and prostrated themselves on the
ground, bemoaning their sins. Then they rose, blessed themselves again, and prayed in silence. After a final signal, they sat
down once more to recommence the whole cycle.

What we see in these Egyptian sources is a pure monastic
office. As in the cathedral system, there were only two hours, at
the beginning and end of the day. But that is where the similarity
ends, for the monastic office was not a liturgical ceremony so
much as a meditation on Sacred Scripture done in common.

Here, too, it would be anachronistic to ask if this was "private"
or "liturgical" prayer. For the early monks, there was but one
prayer, always personal, sometimes done in common with others,
sometimes alone in the secret of one's heart. In monastic literature
during the foundational epoch, the only difference between solitary prayer and common prayer was whether there was more than
one person present. The very vocabulary of prayer in the earliest
monastic documents betrays the same mentality.[27] The term
"synaxis" is used indifferently for common assemblies as well as for
the prayer of solitaries. And the Pachomian sources use the same
nomenclature (*meletan, apostêthizein*) to refer to meditation on
Sacred Scripture alone or at the common synaxis.[28] The point was
not with whom one prayed, nor where, nor in what form, nor at
what fixed times nor in how many common synaxes, but that one's
very life be totally prayer. The Pachomians did the offices together, the anchorites of Scetis assembled only on weekends, but
in their minds this in no way changed the nature of their prayer.

The Urban Monastic Office

But the Egyptian desert was not the only fourth-century monastic cradle. Ephiphanius of Salamis, in his treatise *On the Faith*
23:2 written around 374–377, informs us that "some monks re-
side in the cities, others settle in monasteries and withdraw a

great distance." By the end of the century, in addition to the pure cathedral and monastic offices, mixed offices were developed by monks living near urban centers in Palestine, Mesopotamia, Syria, and Cappadocia. These monks were in contact with the life of the secular churches and adopted cathedral usages into their offices without, however, abandoning the continuous monastic psalmody inherited, seemingly, from Lower Egypt.[29]

So by the end of the fourth century, urban monks outside Egypt had carried the evolution of the Liturgy of the Hours three steps further:

1. They effected a synthesis of monastic and cathedral usages by adopting elements of cathedral morning and evening prayer, while retaining the continuous monastic psalmody at the beginning and end of the monastic day.
2. They filled out the daily horarium by creating the formal liturgical hours of terce, sext, and none at the other traditional times of Christian private prayer.
3. They introduced a new office, compline, as bedtime prayer, thus duplicating vespers. For in both the Egyptian and cathedral systems, it is at vespers that we review and conclude the day.

This is the sort of hybrid office described for the monasteries of Palestine, Mesopotamia, and Gaul by Cassian; for Antioch by Chrysostom; for Caesarea by Basil; and for Italy by the Rule of the Master and by Benedict.[30] Although the basic ingredients remain the same, the recipe varied from place to place. In general, eastern offices outside Egypt and Ethiopia preserved better the integrity of the old cathedral hours.[31] But in Rome, where the great basilicas were served by monastic communities, the monastic character predominated.[32] An abridged form of this largely monastic Roman office was the daily prayer of the Papal Curia under Innocent III in 1213–1216, was in turn adapted and spread across thirteenth-century Europe by the Friars Minor, and was ultimately codified in the reform of the office that issued after the Council of Trent.[33]

Some Conclusions from Tradition: Toward a Theology of the Liturgy of the Hours

This history has carried us a long way from Gregory Dix. He said the office was a direct result of the monastic movement. But we have seen it to be in direct continuity with a tradition of daily prayer that existed before anyone ever heard of monasticism. He criticized the cathedral offices for being more an expression of individual piety than a corporate action of the Church. But the fourth-century *Apostolic Constitutions* II, 59, is quite explicit on just this point:

> When you teach, bishop, command and exhort the people to frequent the church regularly, morning and evening every day, and not to forsake it at all, but to assemble continually, and not diminish the Church by absenting themselves and making the Body of Christ lack a member. For it is not only said for the benefit of the priests, but let each of the laity hear what was said by the Lord as spoken to himself: "He who is not with me is against me, and he who does not gather with me scatters" (Mt. 12:30). Do not scatter yourselves by not gathering together, you who are members of Christ . . . but assemble each day morning and evening, singing psalms and praying in the Lord's houses, in the morning saying Ps. 62, and in the evening Ps. 140. But especially on the Sabbath and the Lord's Day of the resurrection of the Lord, meet even more diligently, sending up praise to God. . . .[34]

The conclusion alone, which refers indiscriminately to the daily office and Sunday Eucharist, shows there is no basis for distinguishing between the Mass as a "corporate action of the Church" and fourth-century "offices of devotion."

As for the accusation that the spirit of these services, directed at edification, was a novelty, there is no difference whatever between this and the spirit of Christian assemblies in the New Testament itself, where the purpose of the synaxis was precisely to build up the People of God into one Body of Christ.

And how can one seriously set Eucharist and hours in opposition, one as "eschatological," the other a "sanctification of time," when the early writers explicitly relate the symbolism of morning, evening, and night prayer to the Second Coming of Christ and to the resurrection of the body at the Last Judgment? In these early sources, it is clear that the hours take their meaning not from daily life as opposed to an other-worldly eschatological expectation, nor from the natural cycle of morning and evening, nor from personal devotion and edification as distinct from the worship of the community. Rather, they take their meaning from that which alone gives meaning to all of Christian worship and life: the paschal mystery of salvation in Christ Jesus. All liturgy is a celebration of Christian life, and the same is true of the Liturgy of the Hours. It is no more, no less than a common celebration of what we have become in Christ.

Morning praise and evensong, with baptism and eucharist, were the principle ways in which the early Church exercised this *leitourgia*. There is no special mystical significance about morning and evening as times of prayer. They are the beginning and end of the day, and so it was perfectly natural to select them as the "symbolic moments" in which to express what must be the quality of the whole day. The symbolism was not arbitrary, but drawn from the New Testament itself, where darkness is sin and evil, light is grace and salvation, and Jesus is the light of the world. So in the early Church, baptism was called *phôtismos*, "illumination," and those about to be baptized were *phôtizomenoi, illuminandi*, those about to be enlightened. And Christians prayed facing East, seeing in the rising sun a symbol of the Risen Lord, light of the world.

Because the natural phenomenon that characterizes the beginning and end of the day is the waxing and waning of daylight, what could be more normal than to flesh out morning and evening prayer with texts and rites that reveal the morning and evening as sacraments of this mystery of salvation in Christ? So when we begin the day with prayer, the rising sun calls to mind that true Sun of Justice in whose rising we received the light of salvation. Basil, Chrysostom, Cassian, and the *Apostolic Constitutions* VII, 38–39, all make it clear that morning praise serves to consecrate the day to the works of God, to thank him for benefits received, especially the benefit of redemption in the rising of his Son, to rekindle our desire for him as a remedy against sin during the beginning day, and to ask his continued help.[35]

In the evening, after the day's work is done, we turn once more to God in prayer. The passing of day reminds us of the darkness of Christ's passion and death, and of the passing nature of all earthly creation. But the gift of light reminds us again of Christ, the light of the world. As in morning prayer, the service of evensong ends with intercessions for the needs of all humankind. Then, in the collect and final blessing, we thank God for the graces of the day, above all for the grace of the Risen Christ, ask pardon for the sins of the day, and request protection during the coming night.[36]

The request for protection during the darkness of the night has eschatological overtones: the bridegroom will come at night and we must be found waiting, lamps in hand (Mt. 25:1–13). This is a standard theme of night prayer; so is the cosmic theme of those at vigil joining their voices to those of the angels and all creation in praise of God, as in the *Benedicite* of Daniel, while the world sleeps.[37]

So the earliest tradition of noneucharistic public prayer had nothing to do with theories of "sanctification of time," with *kairos* and *chronos*, with a liturgy of "time" or "history" as distinct from the "eschatological" Eucharist. Rather, the morning office dedicates the new day to God, and the evening office at the close of day leads us to reflect on the hours just passed, with thanksgiving for the good they have brought and sorrow for the evil we have done.

Note the limpid simplicity of the early Church's liturgical theology reflected in the basic structure and spirit of morning praise and evensong. Like prayer in both the Old and New Testament, they are a glorification of God that wells up from the joyful proclamation of his saving deeds: "The almighty has done great things for me! Holy is his name!" (Lk. 1:49). This is the core of biblical and liturgical prayer: remembrance, praise, and thanksgiving—which can then flow into petition for the continuance of God's saving care in our present time of need. In the early liturgical tradition, what we recall and celebrate is one unique event, the paschal mystery in its totality, the mystery of Christ and of our salvation in him. This is the meaning of baptism; it is the meaning of Eucharist; it is the meaning of the Divine Office as well.

Hence, the Liturgy of the Hours, like all Christian liturgy, is a proclamation of the salvation received in Christ, a song of praise and thanksgiving for that gift, and a cry of hope in its final fulfillment. It is not monastic or clerical prayer, but simply the prayer of the People of God. That is why *Apostolic Constitutions* II, 59, already cited,[38] exhorts the congregation to be present regularly at the offices of morning prayer and evensong, and states explicitly that this exhortation is directed not just at the clergy, but at the laity as well. One often hears that certain categories and groups in the Church are "deputed" to pray the office in the Church's name. Now one can pray for everyone, including the Church. But no one can pray *in place of* anyone else, like some living prayer wheel that spins on vicariously while the world goes on about its business. Some can be called to assume freely the obligations of a life totally dedicated to prayer in common, but not in the sense that they are "official pray-ers" for others who thereby can consider themselves freed from the evangelical command to pray always. The burden of common prayer is incumbent on all. No early monk or nun at prayer had any idea of "performing an act in the name of the Church."[39] This purely Latin notion is largely the result of urban monasticism in the West from the fifth–sixth centuries, when monastic communities served major city sanctuaries such as the great Roman basilicas, and were responsible for the public cult.

So the "liturgical mystique" of modern monasticism owes more to the neogothic religious revival of nineteenth-century romanticism than to the Fathers of the Church. For the early monks, life was one continual prayer,[40] with no compartmentalization into "liturgical" prayer and other kinds of prayer and work. They prayed while they worked and worked while they prayed. Wherever they were, refectory, oratory, workshop, cell, the differences were only accidental.

Attendance at the office did not exhaust a monk's obligation to pray any more than going to the cathedral hours absolved the laity from living out the paschal mystery during the rest of the day. Christian liturgy is a symbol of life, Christ's self-sacrificing life and our life in him, and unless the mystery celebrated becomes a mystery lived, it is done in vain. When Christians stand vigil before God, they are doing no more than expressing in symbolic form what must be the basic stance of every moment of their lives. This is the meaning of all liturgy, including the cathedral and monastic hours. The only difference between the laity and the monks is that the monks turned the symbol into life. The early anchorites *lived* liturgy rather than celebrating it: their whole life was one continuous vigil before the living God.

From Liturgy to Prayer Book:
The Office Becomes a Breviary in the West

Only later does the office become an exclusively clerical obligation, and only *much* later, in the general western trend toward privatization of an already clericalized liturgy, does the once common prayer of the People of God become a prayer book for the clergy's private use.

Today, of course, there is a reaction against this clerical obligation—but not necessarily the right one. The western obligation to "recite the breviary" is taken to be a relatively recent product of a legalism ill-suited to the modern mentality. The truth of the matter is somewhat more nuanced. For it is not at all untraditional that the hours be considered obligatory. The *novelty* is to think that only the *clergy* is obliged. In the early Church, it was just as much an obligation of the priest's mother-in-law as of the priest himself. What is untraditional, therefore, is not the *obligation* of the office, but its *clericalization*. As with so much else in the history of the Church, what was once the property of the entire People of God has degenerated into a clerical residue of what it was originally meant to be. One must not, of course, blame the lower clergy for this. They were the chief victims of developments beyond their control. When the office grew into an insupportable burden and continued to be celebrated in Latin, the laity simply dropped out, and the clergy could no longer celebrate it in public and get anything else done in the course of the day.

The Reformed Office: A Critique

With the advent of the liturgical movement and the resulting Vatican II *Constitution on the Sacred Liturgy* came hope in the Liturgy of the Hours becoming *liturgy* once again. Has this hope been fulfilled?

The Vatican II reform did manage to solve the problems of language and length, but many believe that the unwillingness to make a more radical break with not just the forms, but with the mentality of this past, has marred the recent reform of the Roman Office. In the post-Vatican II discussions on the Office, more than one informed voice was raised urging the case for a popular "cathedral" office suitable for public celebration in the parishes. But when one reads Annibale Bugnini's recent account of the deliberations of the commission for the reform of the office,[41] three things are clear:

1. The overriding concern of the commission was to produce a prayer book for clergy and religious.

2. It was simply presumed that this prayer would be done, for the most part, in private. Celebration "with the people," as they call it, was envisioned and even desired, but the whole tenor and vocabulary of the discussions show that this was the exception and not the point of departure for understanding the hours.

3. The historical basis underlying much of the discussion was gravely deficient, based as it was almost exclusively on postmedieval Latin tradition.

These same defects of clericalism, privatization, and ignorance of early and eastern tradition can be seen also in the discussions of eucharistic concelebration, and indeed are endemic to much of the western liturgical enterprise. In the postconciliar commission's debates on the office, one sees this problem surface, for instance, in criticisms that the office was too "monastic."[42] What was meant was that it has elements designed for common use—as if historically this were a characteristic of monastic rather than secular usage! Similarly, objections against the introduction of general intercessions at the end of lauds and vespers shows a total unawareness of the huge place such petitions held in early cathedral usage.[43]

Under these conditions, it is not surprising that the new Roman *Liturgy of the Hours* bears a monastic stamp. Such an office, more a contemplative prayer than a popular devotional service, may be eminently suitable for the private prayer of clergy and religious. But this skirts the real issue, which is whether the Liturgy of the Hours should be a prayer book for the clergy, or something more.

But I do not wish to play Cassandra. Flexibility is one of the hallmarks of post-Vatican II Roman Catholic worship. Furthermore, the desire for a truly public celebration of the new *Liturgy of the Hours*, and what is more important, its underlying theology, find pride of place in the excellent *General Instruction on the Liturgy of the Hours* of 2 February 1971.[44] All one needs is a little imagination. Taking a page from the new U.S. *Lutheran Book of Worship* or Episcopal *Book of Common Prayer*, some communities have found that a *lucernarium* can easily be used to open "official" vespers, and this is certainly in accord with the spirit of the *General Instruction*. Furthermore, that same document provides for such a variety of hymnody and types of psalmody that the real problem is not so much the limitations of the office itself, as the incompetence of those unable to celebrate it properly and the indifference of those who fail to celebrate it at all.

What the future will bring is not for the historian to predict. But in the days before television, Vatican II, and the rise of urban street crime, the devout also attended Benediction, novena devotions, forty hours, etc. As Carl Dehne has shown in his fine article on Catholic private devotions, these services filled a real need and were the true successors to the cathedral office in the West.[45] Perhaps it is time for western Catholics to ask themselves once again whether a tradition of daily worship that for all practical purposes is limited to the Eucharist is really offering a balanced diet. Is a restoration of parish hours a viable possibility? That is for the pastoral liturgist to decide. All the historian can do do is remove obstacles to understanding produced by a misreading of the past.

Notes

1. W.G. Storey, "The Liturgy of the Hours. Principles and Practice," *Worship*, 46 (1972), 194–203; *id.* "The Hours for the People," *Liturgy*, 18/5 (1973), 3–7; *id.* "Parish Worship. The Liturgy of the Hours," *Worship*, 49 (1975), 2–12; *id.* "The Liturgy of the Hours: Cathedral vs. Monastery," *Worship*, 50 (1976), 50–70; W.J. Grisbrooke, "The Divine Office and Public Worship," *Studia liturgica*, 8 (1971–1972), 155–159; C. Dehne, "Roman Catholic Popular Devotions," in J. Gallen (ed.), *Christians at Prayer*, Liturgical Studies (Notre Dame/London, 1977), 83–99. The reform of the office and critiques of it are reviewed in Th. A. Schnitker, *Publica oratio. Laudes matutinae und Vesper als Gemeindegottesdienste in diesem Jahrhundert. Eine liturgiehistorische und liturgietheologische Untersuchung* (Münster dissertation, 1977), 34–87, esp. 78–84.

2. For a complete treatment, see R. Taft, *The Liturgy of the Hours in East and West. The Origins of the Divine Office and its Meaning for Today* (Collegeville, MN, 1985).

3. *The Shape of the Liturgy* (Westminster, 1945), 324.

4. *Ibid.*, 326, 328.

5. Clement, *Stromata*, VII, 7, 40:3, 39:3–4; *Pedagogue*, 2:9–10; Origen, *On Prayer*, 12:2.

6. *Apostolic Tradition*, 35, 41; Tertullian, *On Prayer*, 25–27; *To his Wife*, II, 4:2; *On Fasting*, 9–10; Cyprian, *On the Lord's Prayer*, 34–36.

7. Tertullian, *On Prayer*, 27; *Apostolic Tradition*, 25.

8. Tertullian, *Apology*, 39:18; *Apostolic Tradition*, 25.

9. See F.J. Dölger, "Lumen Christi," *Antike und Christentum*, 5 (1936), 1–43.

10. G.J. Cuming (trans.), *Hippolytus. A Text for Students*, Grove Liturgical Studies 8 (Bramcote, 1976), 23.

11. Clement, *Stromata*, VII, 7, 43:6–7; Origen, *On Prayer*, 32; Tertullian, *Apology*, 16; *Ad nationes*, 1:13.

12. See Taft, *The Liturgy of the Hours*, Chap. 3.

13. See *ibid.*, Chaps. 3 and 5 for complete information on the early cathedral office in these areas.

14. "Grégoire de Nysse," in P. Maraval (ed.), *Vie de s. Macrine*, SC 178 (Paris, 1971), Chap. 22, 212.

15. *Oratio*, *18*, 28–29, PG, 35, 1017–1021.

16. S. Basile, *Lettres*, vol. 1, Y. Courtonne (ed.), (Paris, 1957), 41.

17. F.X. Funk (ed.), *Didascalia et Constitutiones apostolorum* (Paderborn, 1905), I, 171, 540–548; cf. VIII, 6–9, *ibid.*, 478–488.

18. PG, 80, 284.

19. Chrysostom, *In 1 Tim hom. 14*, 3–4; Cassian, *Inst.* III, 3–6. On the interpretation of these texts, see R. Taft, "*Quaestiones disputatae* in the History of the Liturgy of the Hours: The Origins of Nocturns, Matins, Prime," *Worship*, 58 (1984), 130–158.

20. E.g., Chrysostom, *In Matt hom. 68* (69), 3: *Apostolic Constitution*, VII, 47, F.X. Funk (ed.), I, 454–456; Basil, *Letter 2*, 2 Y. Courtonne (ed.), I, 6; PS.-Athanasius, *De virginitate*, 20 (ca. 370), E. von der Goltz (ed.), *De virginitate*, TU 29, Heft 2a (Leipzig, 1905), 55–56.

21. *Vitae patrum*, 6:7, MGH, *Serm.* I, 685 (= PL 71, 1034).

22. A. Wenger (ed.), "Jean Chrysostome," *Huit catéchèses baptismales inédites*, SC 50 (Paris, 1957), 256–257.

23. PG, 55, 426–430.

24. Basil, *Longer Rules*, 37:2–5; Cassian, *Conferences*, 21:6; *Apostolic Constitution*, VIII, 34, 37–38, F.X. Funk (ed.), I, 540–542, 544–548.

25. *Inst.*, II, 5–11; III, 2; cf. Taft, *The Liturgy of the Hours*, Chap. 4.

26. See Taft, *loc. cit.* for the relevant documents.

27. *Loc. cit.* and A. Veilleux, *La liturgie dans le cénobitisme pachômien au quatrième siècle*, Studia Anselmiana 57 (Rome, 1968), 293ff.

28. Veilleux, *La liturgie*, 308.

29. See Taft, *The Liturgy of the Hours*, Chap. 5.

30. Relevant sources cited in *ibid.*, Chaps. 5 and 7.

31. See *ibid.*, Part II.

32. *Ibid.*, Chap. 7, and G. Ferrari, *Early Roman Monasteries*, Studi di antichità cristiana 23 (Vatican City, 1957), xix, 365–375.

33. Taft, *The Liturgy of the Hours*, Chap. 19, and esp. S.J.P. Van

Dijk and J. Hazelden Walker, *The Origins of the Modern Roman Liturgy. The Liturgy of the Papal Court and the Franciscan Order in the Thirteenth Century* (London/Westminster, MD, 1960).

34. Funk, I, 171–173.

35. Notes 23–24 above.

36. *Loc. cit.*

37. Clement, *Pedagogue*, 2:9; *Apostolic Tradition*, 41, Chrysostom, *In 1 Tim hom. 14*, 4. For later vigils, see Taft, *The Liturgy of the Hours*, Chap. 9.

38. Above at note 34.

39. A. de Vogüé, *La Règle du s. Benoît*, VII: *Commentaire doctrinal et spirituel*, SC hors série (Paris, 1977), 193ff.

40. E.g., Tertullian, *On Prayer*, 25; Cyprian, *On the Lord's Prayer*, 35; *The Canons of Hippolytus*, 21, PO 31, 387–389; *Apostolic Constitution*, II, 59, VIII, 34, F.X. Funk (ed.), I, 171–173, 540–542; Chrysostom, *Baptismal Catechesis*, VIII, 17–18, A. Wenger, (ed.), 256–257; *Expos. in Ps. 140*, 3; Cassian, *Inst.*, II, 3:1, III, 3:8–11.

41. *La riforma liturgica (1948–1975)*, Bibliotheca Ephemerides liturgicae, Subsidia 30 (Rome, 1983), 482–557, *passim*, esp. 482–483, 503.

42. *Ibid.*, 503.

43. *Ibid.*, 543, note 2.

44. Text in R. Kaczynski (ed.), *Enchiridion documentorum instaurationis liturgicae* (Rome, 1976), doc. 141, 734–782; International Commission on English in the Liturgy (ed.), *Documents on the Liturgy 1963–1979. Conciliar, Papal and Curial Texts* (Collegeville, MN, 1982), doc. 426, 1091–1132.

45. Cited above, note 1.

CHAPTER 24

The Teaching of Vatican II on Baptism

A Stimulus for Theology

Karl J. Becker, S.J.

Summary

By their content, the documents of the magisterium have a normative value; they are also stimuli for reflection inasmuch as their statements leave certain questions open. This is particularly true for the teaching of the Second Vatican Council on baptism. The various declarations scattered through several of the documents insist not only on new aspects, restoring forgotten truths; but they also provide an orientation for theological research on questions that are not yet resolved, and that are not so simple, such as those of the relationships between baptism and faith, between baptism and the Church, and between baptism and confirmation.

———————

The last Council did not promulgate a document on baptism.

The first chapter of the Fourth Lateran Council presented a profession of faith for the Middle Ages. In the third part, devoted to the Church, we find a well-thought-out pronouncement on baptism, expressed in terms of the situation of the time. This pronouncement speaks principally of the rite and the effect, but also of the recipient and the minister. The Council of Florence developed a general sacramental teaching in its Decree for the

Armenians, in which it dealt with each of the seven sacraments. It is well known that the closely followed basis for this Decree was a treatise by Thomas Aquinas, which, for each sacrament, kept to the points mentioned by Lateran IV concerning baptism. However, even as concerns baptism, the Council of Florence repeatedly made its own alterations in the text of St. Thomas.[1] The most detailed declaration is that given by the Council of Trent in its seventh session, where fourteen canons are devoted to baptism. The intention of the Fathers of the Council was to reply to their contemporary opponents, but not to present an exhaustive, self-contained account.

There is no such individual document in Vatican II in which we can find the teaching of this Council on baptism as has been the case for these previous Councils. We have to assemble this teaching from numerous texts dealing with other matters, but which also speak of this subject.

This work of assembly is our *first task*. The texts come principally from *Lumen gentium, Sacrosanctum concilium,* and *Ad gentes,* but we must also take into account every individual remark from the other conciliar documents, such as *Orientalium ecclesiarum, Unitatis redintegratio, Apostolicam actuositatem,* and *Presbyterorum ordinis.* It is not an easy matter to smooth out the tensions that become evident as we go about our task. They could hardly be absent from documents that have passed through several thousand hands. These were based more on Encyclicals than on specific texts from earlier Councils and they have the intention of describing, teaching, admonishing, and encouraging. In these documents, it is not always clear whether precedence is given to words that are spiritual and moving or else to a content that is thought and formulated in a precise manner, or whether the intention is to present biblical teaching or else to express tradition in biblical words. However, all these observations should not obscure the basic intention: the Council intended presenting a *unified* teaching, in the diversity of the documents, of the style—and of the sometimes frankly peculiar Latin.

Alongside this first task, which is necessary as a preparatory step, we have a *second task,* which corresponds to the real purpose of this article. A clearly formulated, unambiguous declaration on the part of the magisterium often gives rise to further questions. Open questions should not obscure clear teaching.

Fidelity to the teaching must not, however, deprive the theologian of the joy to be found in discussing the unresolved question. There are more than enough such problems connected with the teaching of the last Council as concerns baptism. This can readily be understood, for it was the clearly stated intention of Vatican II not to pronounce upon any dogmatic controversy, but rather to speak to its contemporaries about faith in a suitable form, giving fuller value than had previously been the case to the riches of Scripture and Tradition.

Both tasks will be dealt with here *together*, in such a way that individual points of the Council's teaching on baptism will be presented and considered as regards their content and their openness to unresolved questions.

We cannot engage on a study of the sources here, partly because the proportions of a brief article are insufficient for this purpose, and partly—and above all—because a Council has the intention of producing a text that has a clear content as it stands and not one that requires a study of the sources in order to be comprehensible. We shall, however, give a brief survey of the teaching on baptism as found in the preconciliar manuals. It is against precisely this background that the novelties and new concerns of the conciliar doctrine on baptism become entirely accessible, both as regards their clear content and also in their unresolved questions.

The Manuals Before the Council

The principal points of the teaching on baptism that were already prefigured in the brief mention in the Fourth Lateran Council—which did, however, indicate a direction—and that were then developed in the small treatise of St. Thomas *On the Articles of Faith and the Sacraments of the Church,* the basis for the later Decree for the Armenians, represented the basic structure of the teaching on baptism in the nineteenth and twentieth centuries, slightly extended under the influence of Trent. The points presented by the manuals are the following: its institution, its matter and form, its minister, its recipient, its necessity, and its effect.

As regards the institution, the manuals speak of its institution by Jesus Christ (not simply by God!).

As regards matter, we find *ablutio* (washing) with water. This could be performed by *immersio* (plunging), *infusio* (pouring), or *aspersio* (sprinkling). The form is the expressed invocation of the Trinity in three Persons, which express the action and the person of the minister. Baptism in the name of Christ is often evoked and rejected.

The authors of the manuals consider the ordinary minister to be a bishop or a priest. A deacon is an extraordinary minister, and, in case of need, anyone can baptize.

The recipient of baptism is an adult with an intention as the condition for at least valid reception, and with a disposition, in connection with which faith and repentance are often mentioned, for fruitful reception. A child before the age of reason can also be a recipient. For the baptism to be administered *licitly*, it must be the child of Catholic parents, even though it is not yet capable of making an act of faith by itself.

Baptism is necessary for salvation. However, in certain circumstances, baptism with water can be replaced by baptism of desire or baptism of blood.

The effect of baptism is the forgiveness of sins and guilt, and the infusion of grace.

Naturally, there are differences here. Perrone takes his lead as regards the order and presentation of the material mostly from the canons of the Council of Trent, whereas Billot takes his more from the *Quaestiones* of St. Thomas, which it is his intention to explain. Many authors do not speak of the character at all, since they have already dealt with it when speaking of the sacraments in general; others mention it, and even connect it with the teaching on the universal (*sic!*) priesthood. Not all the authors are content with merely listing one negative effect (forgiveness of sins) and one positive one (infusion of grace); some speak of incorporation into the Church, and d'Alès, going far beyond Thomas, collects all the effects of baptism from Scripture and the Fathers. However, all these and other differences cannot destroy the general impression: the account given by the manuals continually turns around the same subjects.

The Council repudiates none of these statements. Indeed, from time to time, it mentions one or another of them, for example, that everyone can baptize (*LG* 17). However, its particular interest is directed toward quite different aspects of baptism.

Let us try to deal with these one by one.

The Rite

Only a few references deal with the rite of baptism.

The numbers of *Sacrosanctum concilium* deal with the ceremonies, that is to say, that part of the administration of the sacraments that is briefly designated by St. Thomas as "what appertains to a certain solemnity of the sacrament,"[2] and which is later called "the ceremonial part." A few numbers of this document present the norms according to which a liturgical rite must be celebrated if it is to be considered a sacramental rite. The first norm, which is the revealed truth of the sacrament of baptism, can be found in number 69, where the text requires that the new "rite for supplying what was omitted in the baptism of an infant" must reflect the fact that the infant baptized in conditions of emergency has already been received into the Church, or when the same number requires that the new rite for the conversion to the Catholic faith of those who have already been baptized provide for their reception "into the communion of the Church," which implies that this cannot have taken place in baptism outside the Church. The second norm, that of human nature in its form as modeled by a particular culture, can be seen in number 65, where it is allowed that features of initiation ceremonies of various peoples may be received into the liturgy, if they can be reconciled with Christianity. *Sacrosanctum concilium* 66 and 67 recall both these norms when they require that the reform of the baptismal rites takes the catechumenate into account, and that in infant baptism, the situation of small children and that of their parents and godparents be taken into account.

However, in these norms, we are not dealing with a peculiarity that concerns baptism alone. This is why we shall not accord them more dettailed consideration. The case of *Lumen gentium* 7b is different. It states concerning baptism:

In this sacred rite fellowship in Christ's death and resurrection is symbolized and is brought about: "For we were buried with him by means of baptism into death"; and if "we have been united with him in the likeness of his death, we shall be so in the likeness of his resurrection also" (Rom. 6:4–5).

Here, in the first sentence, we find the rite of baptism described as a representation and realization of union with the death and resurrection of Christ. We are therefore dealing here with the part that St. Thomas calls "what is necessary for the sacrament,"[3] and that is otherwise known as "the essential part"—not "the substance of the sacrament"—that is to say, the part that symbolizes and effects grace. In the second sentence, a quotation from Scripture is given as an explanation.

Already this _second_ sentence presents a small problem. Was it really the intention of the Council to decide a scientific debate among exegetes? Some exegetes considered that Paul had derived his teaching on dying and rising with Christ from the _immersio_ and _emersio_ (or immersion and emergence); others do not hold this opinion. It would be quite contrary to the intentions of the Council to consider the text cited as a decision, for the Council wished to avoid taking up controversies between schools and deciding them. Here we have a quotation from Scripture that is to be understood in the sense of a centuries-old patristic and theological exegetical tradition, which is certainly a meaningful and valuable way of interpreting texts, even if it is not the form of historical exegesis based on sound principles, as is customary today.

What is really surprising is the _first_ sentence of this text. _Repraesentatur_ ("is represented" or "symbolized") was accepted by an overwhelming majority of bishops, of whom by far the most came from the Latin-rite church, with the consequence that in their dioceses, the rite of pouring was used without exception for baptism. Hence, we cannot speak of a visual representation of dying with Christ and rising again with him in baptism in their rite. Since, however, the sacraments have their effect by their signification, how can we speak of _efficitur_ ("is effected" or "brought about") with regard to dying and rising again with Christ?

In searching for a reply, we must first consider the _linguistic_ situation of the Council, where only very few Fathers thought in Latin, whereas the vast majority thought exclusively in their mother tongue, which they then expressed in Latin words. We must ask, in these circumstances, what concepts, ideas, and maybe feelings may have been aroused by _repreaesentare_ as opposed to _significare_? It will doubtless prove extremely difficult to establish the answer. Hence, this reference should not be overinterpreted, whether for or against.

However, the text then obliges us to make a _theological_ reflec-

tion. Under the influence of the *Summa theologica,* an opinion of
St. Thomas has been much diffused, and has also found its way
into the rituals of baptism,[4] to the effect that the action of
baptism is the bodily washing, which might be performed
whether by immersion or else by sprinking or pouring.[5] All these
various actions are linked to Scripture: washing in 1 Corinthians
6:11 and Hebrews 10:22; immersion in Romans 6:4–5; sprinkling
in Hebrews 10:22; and pouring in Ezekiel 36:25. Each of these
four expressions indicates an aspect of the effect of baptism that
the other three do not mention explicitly; thus none of them
fully expresses the effect of baptism. Leaving aside the origin of
the washing, which is considered to be necessary, Thomas and
the theology and liturgical baptismal practice of the Church that
follow him appear to consider that alongside the washing, the
rite of baptism must always have only *one* of the three more
detailed prescriptions of the rite, but that none of the three is
necessary, nor are all three together. This means that the opinion is held (whether consciously or unconsciously) that the sign
of baptism that effects the grace does not represent the whole
effect symbolically, but only part of it.[6] However, this means
that, at least as concerns baptism, we must be very cautious in
speaking of the sign producing the effect. Furthermore, we must
ask whether the awareness of the Church, the emphasis (not the
truth) of baptismal doctrine can shift, and even whether such
shifts may have produced at least some change in the "essential
part" of the rite of baptism from the thirteenth century onwards.
Lastly, we must ask whether it is possible that such changes can
be made today, and, if so, to what extent.

However, we must also gain a clearer conception of the symbolical character of baptism. Faith alone concerning baptism
contains the entire fullness of the effect of baptism. The visible
action of baptism must be interpreted by taking this faith as our
starting point. The action makes one or more aspects of the
effect of baptism visible by representation. For the others, the
visible action is merely an occasion that recalls them. In this
sense, we could say that the action of pouring[7] symbolizes the
washing away of sins and the infusion of graces, but secondarily
also represents union with the death and resurrection of Christ,
and effects what it signifies both symbolically and representa-
tively. This could give a meaningful interpretation of the conciliar text or, maybe better, the text could give rise to a necessary

consideration concerning the rite of baptism, and also a reflection on baptismal instruction without which it is not possible to understand the fullness of what the symbolical action is intended to impart and evoke.

New Birth From Faith and Baptism

The Teaching of Vatican II

As concerns the relationship of faith and baptism, the manuals have little to say. If they mention it at all, it is in the form of a brief observation regarding the disposition necessary for baptism. Here faith is mentioned (also repentance, sometimes with reference to Trent or else to other documents). Vatican II certainly refers to this mention when it states in *Sacrosanctum concilium* 59 that faith is a condition for the sacraments—and thus also for baptism. It does, however, go further than this when, in *Sacrosanctum concilium* 10, it says that the goal of apostolic work is that "all those who have been made the sons of God through faith and baptism" should be united in the Church for the praise of God. *Ad gentes* 21b is also unequivocal: lay people are born again in the Church through faith and baptism. This juxtaposition of faith and baptism cannot be sufficiently explained by the distinction of disposition (faith) and cause (baptism).

This precision is not a matter of chance, but, rather, the conscious emphasis of a biblical teaching. Let us leave aside for the moment the consideration that bishops who were acquainted only with the practice of infant baptism are here taking the position of rebirth from faith. The answer is in part well known, but in part can be found in the following reflections. It is more important to observe that the Council juxtaposes a biblical teaching that had been much neglected in theology concerning rebirth from the word or preaching, in other words, faith, with a theologically precisely studied teaching on rebirth from baptism, whereby it indicates a fact and a relationship that it does not itself explain.

Lumen gentium 9a gives two biblical points of reference that in the sacred Scriptures themselves cannot be reconciled:

For those who believe in Christ, who are *reborn*, not from a corruptible seed, but from an incorruptible one through the word of the living God (cf. 1 Pet. 1:23), not from flesh, but from water and the Holy Spirit (cf. Jn. 3:5–6), are finally established as "a chosen race."

In this connection, we must also take into account *Unitatis redintegratio* 22a, which takes up Colossians 2:12 into its baptismal teaching. According to the words of the apostle, we are buried with Christ in *baptism*. In him, we are also raised again through *faith* in the action of God, who raised him from the dead. A clear indication is also found in *Ad gentes* 6c, which states that Christ sent the disciples into the whole world so that men, having been reborn by the word of God (cf. 1 Pet. 1:23), might through baptism be joined to the Church.

At this point, there can be no further doubt as to the teaching of the Council, according to which, on the basis of 1 Peter 1:23, a new birth is granted by the word of God.

This doctrine of rebirth from baptism and faith or the word was achieved through taking into account certain passages from the Bible along with a teaching marked by a long development of faith. This doctrine is now taken further by the Council in two developments that, although each has biblical bases, when taken together go beyond the confines of Scripture.

The first development is the list of the persons taking an active part in this rebirth. Through the ministry of the *bishops, Christ* preaches the word of God to all, he administers the sacraments to the faithful, and incorporates new members into his body through the rebirth granted from above (*LG* 21a). The *Holy Spirit* arouses the obedience of faith through the seed of the word, begets those who believe in Christ to new life in baptism, and gathers them into one people (*AG* 15a). With reference to 1 Corinthians 4:15 and 1 Peter 1:23, the Council also teaches that *priests* have spiritually begotten the believers through baptism and teaching (*LG* 28e).

The second development shows a separation in time and in content between rebirth from baptism and rebirth from faith. In the Decree on the Church's Missionary Activity, it is stated that the newly converted person begins his path "already sharing through faith in the mystery of the death and resurrection," whereby he passes from the old to the new man (*AG* 13b). However, it then states that in the sacraments of initiation, the neophytes are freed from the power of darkness, "having died, been buried, and risen with Christ" (AG 14b). Thus, according to the Council, it appears there are two ways of being connected with Christ's death and resurrection, and these two ways do not coincide within time; one way is through faith, and the other through baptism. If we go on to read *Ad gentes* 15a, we shall see that the Holy Spirit prompts faith through the seed of the word and then grants new life in baptism, and we might try to show a link with *Lumen gentium* 64, where two stages are mentioned: a conception from the Holy Spirit and a birth from God.

The following text from the Constitution on the Church, which explains the Church in terms of Mary, belongs not just to these two stages but, furthermore, actually to both of these developments: "The Church . . . by receiving the word of God in faith becomes herself a mother. By preaching and baptism she brings forth sons, who are conceived of the Holy Spirit and born of God, to a new and immortal life" (*LG* 64). This text belongs to the first development because it again mentions one of the factors of this rebirth, this time the Church; it belongs to the second development because it speaks of a separation—which is not necessarily to be seen in terms of time—between the effects of faith and baptism, and expresses this in terms of conception and birth. However, this text becomes fully comprehensible only by a reference to the teaching of the Fathers, which is developed in it.

Patristic Witness

Let us start by eliminating a preliminary difficulty with this text, namely, how a rebirth from faith and baptism can be expressed in terms of conception and birth. When dealing with a form of analogy whereby the use of natural categories to indicate supernatural realities is always partially inappropriate, we must not let ourselves be inhibited by such difficulties. We must, however, bear them in mind.

Let us also eliminate a second difficulty. It is true that the verb *generare* in classical theology often means only "to beget," not "to bear," and thus could not be used at all for Mother Church. However, in Augustine, it means simply "to bring forth," and thus it can be used for a mother and for Mother Church who brings forth her children in baptism "from the selfsame sacraments, as from the seed of her husband."[8]

The real difficulty lies in the pair of concepts "conceived from the Holy Spirit" and "born from God." It is true that each of these is borrowed from the teachings of the Fathers, but the combination of them as found in the Council does not occur in the Fathers.

The origin of the approach that sees in Mary a type of the Church is well known. Ambrose writes: "Truly wedded, yet a virgin [i.e., Mary]; for she is a type of the Church, which is immaculate yet married. As a virgin it conceives us from the Spirit, and bears us as a virgin without pangs."[9]

Here Ambrose reads a conception from the Spirit and a painfree birth from the comparison of Mary with the Church for the Christian. There is no mention of a birth *from* God or a birth from preaching and baptism.

Augustine takes us a step further. Although he does not give the typology of Mary as the Church, he distinguishes at the beginning of Christian life a "being convinced" and a "being born," although it is true that he does not complete these with the phrases "from the Holy Spirit" and "from God." Augustine sees the conception as taking place in the beginnings of belief, and the birth in baptism: "Certain beginnings of faith therefore occur, which are similar to conceptions, but it is also necessary to be born in order to attain eternal life."[10] Here he obviously has the catechumen in mind, who has been conceived as an adult in and through the beginnings of his faith, and who will be born in and through baptism.

In his Commentary on Luke, St. Bede the Venerable's thought depends at this point on Ambrose, whom he sometimes follows word for word, and he combines Ambrose's ideas with those of Augustine. In this, he writes the following about Christ, whom he sees in the Christian: "He is conceived daily through faith in the virginal womb, that is, in the soul of believers, and he is born through baptism."[11] Thus, two ideas are merged in Bede. One is taken from Ambrose, and sees the beginning of Christian life in terms of the beginning of Christ's life, in a conception from the Holy Spirit and a pain-free birth. The other comes from Augustine and sees the beginning of Christian life in terms of its course in the life of an adult catechumen in the Church, in a conception from faith, or, better, the beginnings of his faith, and a birth to life from baptism. Bede has both of these ideas and brings them into contact with each other by his expression "the virginal womb"; "womb" is

also found in Augustine, both the word and the idea of Mother
Church, and "virginal" is added by Bede from Ambrose, who saw a
prototype of the "virgin Church" in the "virgin Mary." However,
from the combination of the two, Bede produces something quite
different, "the soul of believers."

Thus, Lumen gentium 64 in a text that is not easy to understand, combines the ideas of three Fathers of the Church: Ambrose, Augustine, and Bede. This gives us considerable help in
understanding the relationship of Mary with the Church. However, in order to explain rebirth from faith and from baptism,
Lumen gentium 64 employs two further ideas, namely, conception
from the Holy Spirit, which is taken from christology or mario-
logy, and birth from God, which is taken from baptismal doctrine. The union of these two ideas cannot be found in patristic
teaching, nor in the typology of Mary for the Church. It must be
explained from ideas to be found elsewhere in theology.

Traces of this Teaching in the History of Theology

This beginning of life from faith and baptism can also be found
in later theology. Hugh of St. Victor writes: "And again, effective grace is not enough to sanctify man, if he will not receive
that sanctification which is to be found in God's sacraments."[12]
Here a power is attributed to effective grace, which, although it
is insufficient without the sacraments, does not, however, for
this reason lose its saving power.

Richard of St. Victor distinguishes three manners in which
one can be "a member of Christ": by predestination, by preparation, and by incorporation. For the second manner, that of preparation, Richard is thinking of repentance, but also of the faith
that precedes or can precede a sacrament, in the present instance
the sacraments of baptism or penance.[13] This line of thought
follows a rather different path from that of Hugh, but it is certain
that Richard considers faith to have a power of uniting men with
Christ, albeit not completely.

Thomas Aquinas never expressly makes the relationship between faith and baptism the subject of a specific article, but he
speaks of it so often that we find a more complete picture than in
the writings of Hugh and Richard of St. Victor. We shall select
just a few passages, which will show us the richness and breadth

of his thought.[14] The order of the following presentation is not found in Thomas in this form.

In a first step, Thomas juxtaposes faith and sacraments in the meaning they have for the working out of Christ's Passion in us. He writes: "The power of Christ's Passion is conjoined to us through faith and the sacraments." However, this comes about in different ways. The union through faith is brought about "through an act of the soul," that through the sacraments "through use of external things."[15]

How are these two manners of creating a link with the power of Christ's Passion to be found in baptism? As a second step, Thomas gives a reply to this that surprises us as it ascribes both to faith and also to the sacraments an influence on sacramental grace. Thomas takes as his point of departure the distinction between *sacramentum et res* and *res tantum*, and then names two things that belong *ad ultimam rem sacramenti*: "rebirth, which belongs to the fact that through baptism man begins a new life of justice; and illumination, which belongs specifically to faith, through which man receives spiritual life."[16] Here again, as before, we find the concepts of both faith and baptism, both directed to a new life. However, what is difficult about this answer of Thomas is that this "illumination," which belongs to faith, is considered as the *res sacramenti*, or at least as one of its features. Now we must ask if the faith is beside or in baptism, and if it is in it, is not "the act of the soul" effective *in* the "use of external things," thereby participating in producing the final effect? Can this be reconciled with the theory of *opus operatum*?

In a third step, the situation is somewhat clarified, because Thomas distinguishes two illuminations.

Thomas explains that in baptism we are born again to spiritual life through union with Christ the head. From him, "the spiritual sense" flows out into the members, and "the knowledge of the truth," from which derives also "the spiritual movement" that is set in motion by "the instinct of grace." Once again we have an illumination and an infusion of grace. This is the same as in the previous text. But Thomas gives two supplementary explanations. Prior to baptism, already believing adults are "mentally" incorporated into Christ, and through baptism they are also incorporated into him "bodily, that is, through the visible sacrament." However, the intention to receive the sacrament also belongs to this first form of incorporation. Finally, Thomas distinguishes the following two points: the teacher illumines the neophytes externally, through his ministry and through the catechism, but God illumines them interiorly.[17]

Thus, Thomas recognizes two illuminations and incorporations into Christ. He ascribes the first to the teacher, or in other words to faith; in the case of an adult, this takes place prior to baptism. The other takes place in baptism itself; it is a work wrought by God.

However, this is not all that Thomas has to say concerning the relationship of baptism and faith. There is also a fourth step, ascribing to faith an influence on the effect of the sacrament: "Baptism is the sacrament of faith, since it involves a profession of the Christian faith"[18]; "Baptism is called 'the sacrament of faith,' which is the beginning of spiritual life"[19]; "The faith of the Church and of the person baptized contributes to the efficacy of baptism; for this reason those who are baptized make a profession of faith, and baptism is called 'the sacrament of faith.' "[20] Here Thomas is certainly not speaking of the *habitus fidei* (habit of faith), but, rather, of the act of confessing faith at the moment of baptism. It is *this act* that is decisive for the power of baptism. However, this is too much for a simple disposition.

Further Development of these References

We can make use of these references in order to develop a consideration of the teaching of Vatican II.

In the Bible, we find two kinds of rebirth or, maybe better, two ways of considering it, and, corresponding to these, two ways of leading to them: a rebirth from acceptance of the preaching, from faith, and a rebirth from reception of the sacrament of baptism. Through knowledge and personal acceptance of this, the first gives a new life-style, which represents a community of life with Christ in thought, feeling, and behavior. It is certain that the individual is carried and supported along this path by helping grace. The second gives a new being and a new life-force, which is imparted by an operation of Christ in the Holy Spirit, both of whom make use of the human minister.

These two kinds of rebirth, or ways of considering it, do not necessarily coincide, as is evident if we think of the genuine faith of one who is not or maybe not yet baptized, or else of another who is baptized but who is not yet capable of believing at all.

However, both kinds are interrelated. This relationship can exist in the first place in a context of *time*. The sacrament of baptism as the act of the recipient is a profession of faith, that is, an act that confesses faith externally. Thereby, rebirth through faith—or at least an expression of life of the individual reborn through faith—occurs at the moment of rebirth, through the new life-force. As such, this is only an identity within the context of time.

This relationship is also a correspondence according to *content*. Rebirth through faith is a penetration into the individual truths of revelation, whether realities, promises, or commandments, which are grasped or accepted individually and which require a new life-force, which is given through the sacrament of baptism. Rebirth through baptism as an action of the minister gives a new life-force and grace, faith, hope, and love as *habitūs*, which, however, require knowledge of faith in order to come to fulfillment. Thus, both kinds of rebirth have a mutual need of each other in order to bring to fulfillment all they contain. Only together do they comprise entire rebirth.

The considerations we have made up to this point have not yet provided an explanation for justification by faith as taught by the Bible and the contribution of faith for the efficacy of baptism, as taught by Thomas. We must go one step further.

The relationship of the two types of rebirth must also constitute an influence of faith on the content of the sacrament of baptism.

A preliminary consideration concerns the expression "sacrament of faith" for baptism. We are now accustomed to call *all* the sacraments "sacraments of faith." This is right and proper, yet it is especially appropriate for baptism, not just because for several centuries it was the first and only sacrament to bear this name, nor only because in the first centuries, the sacrament was administered with the threefold question and answer concerning the profession of faith instead of today's baptismal formula, for this name remained restricted to baptism for quite a time after the West had introduced the baptismal formula everywhere. Thus, a special relationship to faith must have been perceived in baptism that was not present in the other sacraments. We must try to specify the nature of this relationship.

It is here that the real reflection begins: the basic action of faith takes place or is performed in baptism. This basic action is

the following: the individual can be informed about the Christian revelation purely as regards the content, and may be seized
by enthusiasm, or take an interest, consider assent, or be inclined toward it—or however we may describe all the steps there
can be in a human life on the way to Christ. Finally, the person
decides to believe in Christ. To believe in Christ means letting
one's personal identity depend on him as its assurance. When a
person takes a decision such as this, he must accept it in its
totality, and thus also in his thoughts and desires (it is here that
the aspect of "considering to be true" has its indispensable place
in personal belief). However, such a decision, which accepts
Christ as a person, must also take seriously and carry out his
wishes and the demands he makes of the person. Now the first
matter he demands is baptism for the forgiveness of sins: baptism
that takes the person into Christ, whereby only then is his life
fully dependent on Christ, or incorporated into him.

Thus, the fundamental opinion of faith has only been made
completely once the believer carries out the action that incorporates his life into Christ, not only into the Christ of the past, but
also into the Christ of the present.[21] Here we perceive the special
character of baptism as the sacrament of faith. Here, too, we
perceive the special meaning of faith for baptism, which is more
than just a disposition. The adult must wish to bring to fulfillment his act of faith in baptism as the action of the recipient and
let it be brought to fulfillment through baptism as the action of
Christ in the minister. The rebirth given from faith can find its
fulfillment only in baptism.

None of this affects the doctrine of *opus operatum.* However,
faith is lifted well above the level of a simple disposition, and an
internal connection between faith and baptism becomes visible.
It seems to me that one could take this reflection on the teaching
of Vatican II further along this line.

Yet first we must consider the Church.

Baptism and Access to the Church

In contrast to the previous subject, here the preconciliar manuals give certain statements on this topic. It is sometimes generally
affirmed that baptism incorporates the neophyte into the Church,
or into the mystical body of Christ. This observation can be di-

vided into various levels. Through a valid baptism, the person becomes a member of the body of Christ, but through fruitful baptism the person becomes a living member. We may also find the affirmation to the effect that although, if someone is excommunicated he or she is no longer a member of the Church, but can still be subject to its jurisdiction. Frequently, we find the baptismal character contemplated simply as incorporated into the Church or into the body of Christ, and sometimes the obligation is deduced from this to hold firmly to the Catholic faith and to take one's place within the Church.

There is no entirely clear and unified teaching to be found in the manuals.

The Teaching of Vatican II

Both the texts of previous Councils with which these manuals are acquainted are also present in the awareness of Vatican II. Florence declared in its Decree for the Armenians, concerning baptism: ". . . through it . . . we are made part of the Church" (DS 1314). And in its Decree on Penance, the Council of Trent observed that the Church has no jurisdiction over anyone "who has not previously entered it through the doorway of baptism" (DS 1671).

Vatican II itself has three series of statements on this subject.

The first follows faithfully these two texts with which we are already familiar. Since it speaks of Catholics, it has no great problems in speaking of the relationship between baptism and Church, or else the body of Christ and the people of God, without losing itself in finer details or more precise distinctions.

Men enter the *Church* through baptism as through a door (*LG* 14a). Believers are incorporated into the Church through baptism (*LG* 11a).

Following 1 Corinthians 12:13, the Council states that we are baptized into a *body* (*LG* 7b). Christ incorporates new members into his body through rebirth from above (*LG* 21a). The laity are inserted into the mystical body of Christ through baptism (*AA* 3a).

All people must be incorporated through baptism into Christ, and into the *Church*, which is his *body* (*AG* 7a). Through baptism, people must be added to the Church, which is the body of the incarnate word (cf. *AG* 6c).

In baptism, the Christian faithful are made the *people* of God (cf. *LG* 31a). Through baptism, priests lead people into the people of God (*PO* 5a). The Holy Spirit begets the faithful through baptism into new life, and gathers them together in the people of God (*AG* 15a).

All these statements follow the line of the traditional teaching of the Church, but they do not take into account finer distinctions or gradations.

Alongside these statements, we find a second series, which is also restricted to Catholics, but which lists other elements of Church membership apart from baptism.

According to *Lumen gentium* 14b and *Orientalium ecclesiarum* 2, the Catholic church is composed of persons who, under the prompting of the Holy Spirit, are united by the threefold bond of faith, the sacraments, and the leadership and communion of the Church. Thus, it would appear that for Catholics, baptism is not sufficient for reception into the Church. If this is the case for adults, we must ask what the position is for children.

In the third series of statements, which are made in an ecumenical context, the necessity for an explanation of this question is thrown into even sharper relief.

The problem already appears in the first Constitution of the Council, in a text dealing as such with a practical question of liturgical reform. On the one hand, "The Order for Supplying Omitted Elements for a Baptized Infant" is to express the fact that the child "has already been received into the Church" (*SC* 69a). On the other hand, "a new rite is to be drawn up for converts who have already been validly baptized. It should indicate that they are now admitted to communion with the Church" (*SC* 69b). Now we must ask what the distinction is between the Church and the communion of the Church. Is a child baptized in the Catholic Church not yet in the communion of the Church, or, if it is, through what means? If baptism effects reception into the Church, what is added by the conversion to effect in addition communion with the Church?

Lumen gentium 15 says concerning baptized non-Catholics only that the Church feels itself to be joined (*conjunctam*) to them for several reasons. It is not stated whether their baptism has incorporated them into the Church, or maybe only incompletely so.

The Decree on Ecumenism takes as its basis the idea of different degrees of *communio:* "For men who believe in Christ and who have been properly baptized are put in some, though imperfect, communion with the Catholic Church" (*UR* 3a). Here the use of the term *communio* is not the same as in *Sacrosanctum concilium* 69, since there it is only by conversion that the individual is admitted to *communio* with the Church; nor is it the same as in *Lumen gentium* 14 and 15, since there it was one of the three bonds that hold the Catholic Church together. Here in *Unitatis Redintegratio,* we find different degrees of *communio.* This concept had not been previously mentioned, but neither had it been rejected; as a genus, it is not merely equivalent with recognition of the ecclesiastical hierarchy, but is seen in a different manner as being together in things that derive from Christ.

Further on, we find the same Decree stating that the divisions in Christianity prevent the fullness of catholicity being achieved in its sons "who, joined to her by baptism, are yet separated from full communion with her" (*UR* 4h).

Here again, the Council avoids speaking of an incomplete incorporation into the Church through baptism, and, once again, we have here the idea of different degrees of *communio* as a basis. I intentionally leave the Latin word here, since an English translation expressing only the idea of community (a possible translation as such) would not distinguish sufficiently clearly between the concepts of *communio* (communion) and *communitas* (community).

This cautious reserve is seen as its clearest in *Unitatis redintegratio* 22. This section gives the doctrine of incorporation into Christ through baptism, but avoids speaking of incorporation into the Church. The second paragraph begins: "Baptism, therefore, constitutes the sacramental bond of unity existing among all who through it are reborn." The paragraph then goes on to state that baptism is only a beginning and needs to be completed in three directions, by a complete profession of faith, by complete incorporation into the institution of salvation, and by being fully ordered into the eucharistic community. In point of fact, we find here once again the three bonds spoken of in *Lumen gentium* 14 and *Orientalium ecclesiarum* 2, albeit in a different context; however, the question remains whether this "complete incorporation" into the institution of salvation presumes a non-complete incorporation through baptism.

The Council never states that there are members of the

Church who, although they are baptized, do not hold the Catholic faith, nor that there are baptized non-Catholics who are incorporated into the Church, albeit incompletely. It is here that we see the tension between the third series of statements and the first, which, although it was speaking in the context of Catholics, did appear to state in a general form that through baptism an individual is incorporated and ordered into the Church, the body of Christ and the people of God.

The Difficulties of the Question

Thus, the question is the following: What is the meaning of baptism for entry into the Church?

Before seeking to answer this question, we must make sure we understand exactly what we are asking. This will involve above all examining the two concepts "Church" and "baptism." Not everything we shall say here concerning the concept of the Church can or should be reduced to a single answer, but, rather, it should provide a background against which we may attempt to answer a more precisely specified question.

First of all, not always is the same concept linked with the word "Church." It may mean "the Catholic Church"; it may mean "the Church of Christ," a concept that does not specify more closely the relationship with the Catholic Church; and it can also simply avoid both of these qualifications and mean just "the community of Christian believers." Here I am not concerned with the truth of these various ideas, but I only wish to point out that which concept may be the premise of a certain line of research, in the course of which, consequently, not only can the question shift, but also, during the considerations, a concept may change, either slightly or more profoundly. At present, what matters is that we must be clear at the outset about what is actually meant by "Church."

Next, in our question, we must see what the relationship is between the concept "Church" and the three well-known expressions the Bible uses for it: the people of God, the body of Christ, and the temple of the Holy Spirit.

The Council calls the Church the *people of God:* "the Church or people of God" (*LG* 13b); "the people of the New Covenant, which is the Church" (*UR* 22); "it is true that the Church is the new people of God" (*NA* 4f).

The following statement—that the Church is the body of Christ—does, however, occur more frequently: "in his body which is the Church" (*LG* 14a; also *LG* 48b, 49, 52; *AA* 2, 7a; cf. "the mystical body of Christ" in *OE* 2 and *AA* 2; "the body of the Word incarnate" in *AG* 6c). *Apostolicam actuositatem* 18a, when describing the Church, speaks of the *people of God* and the *body of Christ* together.

However, in relation to the Church, *all three biblical expressions* are employed *together*: priests share in Christ's ministry, "through which the Church here on earth is being ceaselessly built up into the people of God, Christ's body and the temple of the Spirit" (*PO* 1; cf. also *LG* 17 and *AG* 7b).

However, this teaching of the Council leaves several questions open.

What is the difference between these three concepts as used in the natural domain and as used in the area of the Old Testament or even in the New Testament? A single example will suffice to explain this: Is it right to see a common feature of the natural and supernatural meanings of the word "people" in the fact that a person is born into a people and is thus subject to its laws whether he wills it or not? Certain theologians take this for granted in the natural domain and then at once apply it to the baptized person who has become a member of the people of God by his character and thus, whether he wills it or not, is subject to its laws.

There is a further question we must answer: Do these three images (now understood in the supernatural domain) refer to the same aspect of the Church or not?

Let us begin with examples from other subjects. Christ is God and Christ is man. However, his divine nature is not his human nature. Christ the man is the son of Mary and the servant of God, yet his being a son is not the same as his being a servant.

Let us apply this same principle to the Church. The Church is the people of God, the temple of the Holy Spirit, and the body of Christ. Could it be that its being the people of God is not equivalent to its being the body of Christ, nor to its being the temple of the Spirit? We cannot simply reject this possibility out of hand on the grounds that it is meaningless, for, to start with, in each of the three images, a different Person of the Holy Trinity is mentioned. Their role cannot be called "appropriation," since this could not apply to Christ as concerns his human nature, and since this hardly fits the Holy Spirit either, because he dwells within the temple as one who is sent, and this mission is not an appropriation. And would it not also be better to understand "God" in the Pauline sense as the Person of the Father? This would mean that each of the three images reflects something different in the Church, because each refers to a different divine Person in a manner particular to that respective Person. What is more, the images of people, body, and temple are different in themselves, a community of persons, a part of a person, and an inanimate object. Furthermore, we must bear in mind that "temple" can be used both of the individual and of the ecclesial community, whereas "people" and "body" cannot be used of the individual believer. Does this not also suggest a variety of characteristic features of the Church itself that are being severally indicated here?

We have not posed all these questions rhetorically, in order simply to steer the answer in a particular direction. However, these questions must be carefully considered, whatever the final answer may prove to be.

In this meditation on the Church, the concept of the member begins to appear. In Latin, the word *membrum* immediately evokes another: *corpus* (body). Yet Richard of St. Victor sees no difficulty in explaining it as "member (or element) of the building."[22] This gives us quite a different slant on understanding the supernatural reality of the member of the Church, which may be seen as a member of a body, and thus as something alive, as a member or element of a building or a chain, and thus as something inanimate, but also as a member of a community, and thus as a person. This will have considerable consequences if we come to speak of Church membership. If we take as our starting point the idea of belonging to the Church, we may easily incorporate all these different aspects into the single concept.

The Council avoids all these difficulties. In *Lumen gentium* 14, it refers back to the "society of the Church" into which we are incorporated under certain conditions. In *Orientalium ecclesiarum*, it states that the Catholic Church is composed of believers who are joined by certain bonds, and in *Unitatis Redintegratio*, the Council bases all its teaching on the idea of communion. Here we cannot avoid recalling Augustine, according to whom all Cornelius' prayers and alms could avail him nothing, "unless he were incorporated into the Church by the *bond* of Christian *society* and peace."

However, following this, he comes to know Christ through Peter, "and once baptized by him he is joined to the Christian people and the fellowship of *communion*."[23] For the moment, let us bear in mind only that Augustine takes as his starting point none of the three images that Vatican II took from the Bible, but other ideas, from which, later in the same polemic against the Donatists, he is led to discuss the significance of Catholic and Donatist baptism for entry into the Church.

This will suffice to indicate the context within which our question must be placed.

For baptism, I should undertake a similar discussion of the concept. In order to avoid repetition, I shall link it along with certain references to its relation to entry into the Church.

Toward an Answer: The Concept and Influence of Baptism

Regarding our subject, in the manuals, baptism seems generally to be the sacrament that impresses the initial character, for we find constant repetitions of the statement that baptism makes a person a member of the Church because it confers a character. In order better to evaluate this demonstration, it will be helpful to examine a Brief of Benedict XIV, which is quoted as the source for Canon 87 of the 1917 Code, and according to which one becomes a person in the Church through baptism.

Benedict XIV depends on Suarez, who in turn depends on Augustine. However, in this tradition, certain shifts in the thought process occur.

In his work *De Baptismo contra Donatistas*, Augustine deals with a pastoral problem. Someone is in danger of death, can find no Catholic to administer baptism to him, yet desires to become a Catholic. Thus, in order to receive baptism, which is necessary for salvation, he goes to a non-Catholic and is baptized by him. If he then dies, Augustine considers he has died a Catholic. If he escapes death and is then joined to the Catholic Church, Augustine not only admits what he has done, but goes so far as to praise him since he did not wish to leave this life without baptism and, at the same time, in his heart he had never been separated from the Catholic Church.[24]

Suarez refers to this passage in his *Defensio fidei Catholicae*. He states that one becomes a member of the Catholic Church through a properly administered baptism, since one receives the true righteousness and faith of Christ through baptism, along with the character of Christ. He uses as his demonstration for this statement the previously mentioned passage from Augustine, and then goes on to say that the same holds true for a child below the age of reason, even if it is baptized by a heretical minister at the request of heretical parents.[25] Suarez agrees with Augustine that "faith" is necessary; however, he understands this, at least for the child below the age of reason, as infused faith, or as *habitus* (habit), whereas Augustine meant an act of faith that was intended as an act of Christian faith. Furthermore, Suarez explicitly mentions the baptismal character, which is not mentioned by Augustine, and which, at least at a first reading of the text, is not to be found even as a concept.

Benedict XIV, in his Letter *Singulari* of 9 February 1749, discusses the same case of an infant baptism, and quotes this passage from Suarez with approval, but, although he follows Suarez in speaking of the *habitus fidei* (habit of faith), he links membership of the Catholic Church with the validity of the baptism. This becomes even clearer when he counters the claim that such a child, baptized by a heretic, is outside the Catholic Church by replying that it did, after all, receive the character if the proper form and matter were employed for the baptism.[26] Thus, here membership of the Catholic Church is now linked only to the character. In Augustine, it was the will expressed in an act of faith to be and to remain Catholic that justified this membership or that was at least irreplaceable for it; in Suarez, who refers back to him, it was the infused faith, (supernatural) righteousness, and the character; whereas in Benedict XIV, who refers back to Suarez and who mentions the *habitus fidei*, it is now only the character.

Heinrich Kleibern, who composed the first volume of the *Theologia Wirceburgensis* only a few years after the Brief *Singulari*, holds the contrasting opinion that the character is not the union itself with the Catholic Church, but only the sign of this union, whether present or past.[27] If we go back from the eighteenth to the twelfth century, we can even find an opinion that does not so much as mention the character (indeed, this concept had not yet made its appearance). Hugh of St. Victor is of the opinion that the Church is the body of Christ, which receives its life from the one Spirit and which is united and sanctified by the one faith:

> For if someone has not the Spirit of Christ, he is not a member of Christ. . . . Through faith we are made members, and through love we are given life. . . . Moreover, in sacrament we are united by baptism and we are given life by the body and blood of Christ. Through baptism we are made members of the body, whereas by the body of Christ we are made sharers of life-giving.[28]

Thus, it would appear that we cannot find an answer to the problem of whether baptism signfies entry into the Church if we consider baptism simply as the rite that confers the first character. We shall be able to give an answer only if we understand the full meaning of baptism, as it was certainly perceived by Augustine and as it was also still perceived by the Middle Ages.

A Response: The Full Concept of Baptism in Its Significance

As the administration of the sacrament, baptism is the sign and cause of a character, of grace, and of the three infused theological virtues.

As the reception of the sacrament, baptism is the sign of faith, whether we say "the sacrament of faith" with Augustine or employ along with Thomas the additional expression "profession of faith."

These two features do not simply occur alongside one another within a rite, but belong essentially to its internal unity. In the foregoing discussion on "Baptism and Faith," I attempted to demonstrate this.

However, baptism is also (both in the action of the minister and in that of the recipient) a service of the Catholic Church. Augustine would call it a "sign of faith." A relationship with the Catholic Church can already be seen in its feature as profession of faith. The believer wishes to receive his faith from the hand of the Catholic Church and he declares that he wishes to live in it. As such, this cannot be called a Church service. However, both acts, that of the minister and that of the recipient, are also (and thus not only) a prayer to God to grant the effect of baptism, and a prayer of the Church in the minister and for the Church in the recipient, the believer who is entering the Church, to grant new life and configuration with Christ. Such a prayer constitutes recognition of God's majesty and our dependence on him, and is thus a Church service.

A baptism such as the one we have just described can be in the fullest sense a sign and cause of grace, a sacrament of faith, and a sign of faith—in the Augustinian sense. It is the baptism of a Catholic, and *this* baptism incorporates the neophyte into the Catholic Church. If someone does not receive *this* baptism, he is not a member of it. This in no way changes the principle that wherever sacraments, above all baptism, truths of faith, and order of the Catholic Church have been preserved after divisions, or have maybe been reacquired, these very features create common ground with the Catholic Church, a *communio* through which these Christians are in relationship with the Church—are ordered toward it, or inserted into it, or however else Vatican II may have expressed this. For, to adopt Augustine's words, part of the Catholic Church has been preserved in the separated communities.

As concerns baptism, the administration can have had its effect only in a diminished form, and the reception can likewise not express the full Catholic profession of faith. It lies beyond the limits of our task to investigate where the boundary posts stand as to whether such baptisms are admissible for membership in the Catholic Church or not. One point is certain: *only* a baptism that is intended as a confession of this Catholic Church and that is administered within it effects incorporation into the Catholic Church.

A further difficulty derives from the principle that there is no salvation outside the Church. This would imply that all non-Catholics would be deprived of salvation. A response to this difficulty must be based on *Lumen gentium* 14a, which is also quoted in *Ad gentes* 7a, and which is well known in connection with this subject. However, a discussion of this point would take us beyond the limits of our present subject.

Incorporation into Christ

It is difficult to understand why baptism as dying and rising again with Christ—leaving aside occasional observations—is ab-

sent from the manuals as a separate theological subject. Might
the reason come from the *Catechismus ad parochos,* which recommends baptism as a mystery for contemplation and imitation[29]
without ever speaking of an effect of baptism as its basis? Whatever the case may be, the Council gave renewed prominence to
this teaching from Scripture and Tradition and accorded it special emphasis.

The Teaching of Vatican II

For a proper understanding of this subject, we must return to
the question of rebirth and mention one of its consequences that
was already mentioned in the Bible and that was taken up again
by the Council: through baptism, we have become children of
God (*LG* 11a and b; cf. *SC* 6 and *AG* 14b). A first reason for this
truth is our sharing in the divine nature (*LG* 40a; cf. *UR* 22a).
Several aspects of this participation have been precisely thought
through by theology. However, a second, more profound reason
is given alongside this one: ". . . united in Christ . . . , we are
truly called and indeed are children of God" (*LG* 48d). Our
dignity derives from our rebirth in Christ (cf. *LG* 32b).

Here we gain a first glimpse of a question that will become
clearer from the relationship that baptism creates with Christ, as
the Council teaches.

Alongside the doctrine of *rebirth* in Christ (*LG* 32b; *AG* 7b),
the Council recalls in the first place that through baptism we are
incorporated into Christ (*LG* 31a; *UR* 3a; *AG* 7a and 15e; cf. also
the quotation from Gal. 3:27 in *UR* 2b), we are bound to him
(*LG* 15), and are conformed to him (*LG* 7b).

This relationship with Christ is more precisely indicated as a
relationship with the paschal mystery of Christ. This mystery is
described in part by the death, burial, and resurrection of Christ,
into which the individual is assumed by baptism (*SC* 6; cf. *AG*
14b, where it is true that the expression "paschal mystery" is
lacking alongside the mention of these three events). The biblical background is unmistakable, yet we must bear in mind that
just a little earlier, without baptism being apparently in view, the
paschal mystery is seen with the words of the Roman Canon in
the passion, resurrection, and ascension (*SC* 5). In three other
passages referring to baptism, the burial is missing: through configuration with the death of Christ, we are bound to the paschal

mystery (GS 22d); through baptism, we are taken up into the death and resurrection of Christ (LG 7b) and incorporated into the crucified and glorified Christ (UR 22a). In these latter two references, the expression "paschal mystery" is also lacking.

In *Lumen gentium* 7e, it might be the case that being taken into the mysteries of the life of Christ and into configuration with him, in his death and resurrection, refers to the whole of the Christian's life, and not just to baptism. Furthermore, a relationship with the paschal mystery is offered to all men (GS 22e).

Hence, the teaching we find cannot be easily organized into a unity.

Reflection

There can be no doubt that the gift received in baptism *originates* from Christ. However, this is not what is being discussed in this passage. The Council teaches that this gift *is* a relationship with Christ, and here we see a question that is thrown into sharper relief by the mention of the paschal mystery.

Let us start by excluding three questions that could well be posed but that do not refer to the precise problem with which we are concerned. There is a *linguistic* problem: the translation of this Latin word (which, if I am not mistaken, is a translation from an expression originating from a modern language) evokes quite different words, concepts, and ideas in romance languages than from those it evokes in others. Next, there is a *biblical* problem: the Bible presents no fully unified doctrine concerning our being taken into the death, burial, and resurrection of Christ, but rather a basic tendency that is expressed in various forms that cannot always be easily harmonized with one another.

Lastly, there is a *theological* problem: we find the paschal mystery described as participation in the death, burial and resurrection, in the passion, resurrection and ascension, in the crucifixion and glorification, in the death, and in the death and resurrection. Here, too, we see that a basic idea was presented to the Council that was not to be given rigorously precise formulation.

Let us limit ourselves to the basic nub of the question: sharing in the death and resurrection of Christ.

Is this expression just an impressive rhetorical figure for the effect of the death and resurrection of Christ in baptism? This is obviously not so, for however justified this conviction regarding such an effect, Scripture, Tradition, and magisterium see in baptism something effected that is conceptually different.[30] We must ask what this is, and the reply must be grace: it takes away sins, and gives the new life and the new righteousness. It is the basis for divine filiation. However, this grace is described as sharing in the divine nature. But how can a sharing in the divine nature be the basis for sharing in the death and resurrection of Christ, both of which are events from the life of Christ as a man? Only a man can die and thus only a man can rise again. Divine nature, even by participation, can surely not be capable of these things.

Sharing in Christ's soul is not mentioned in the sources of revelation and would appear unthinkable. The same holds true for sharing in the (physical) body of Christ. The only possibility would appear to be that sharing (not communication of the divine nature, which we are not discussing here) in the divine nature first existed in Christ the Man and was fashioned by his human actions, above all by what he wrought in his death and resurrection. The baptized person shares in this grace of Christ as fashioned by his human life—the expression "grace" as such deserves an explanation and justification—and, since this grace has been fashioned above all by what Christ wrought in his death and resurrection, also by these two events: the baptized person has this power of grace from Christ and receives it as the basis for his life.

In the conception of the Council, this relationship begins already in the catechumenate through faith (AG 13b). This is simply a development of the doctrine of rebirth from faith and baptism, which we have already discussed. The Council also teaches that God offers *all* men the opportunity of entering into a relationship with the mystery of Christ's death and resurrection (GS 22e). This simply represents a continuation of the idea that every grace is not only given by Christ, but also conformed and fashioned by Christ. However, this takes us beyond the limits of the problem of baptism.

Baptism and the Spirit

When speaking of baptism, the manuals never mention the sending or gift of the Holy Spirit as an effect of baptism. However, this silence should not be interpreted too hastily, as we can see from their teaching on confirmation, which in certain cases also deals with baptism. Thus, Diekamp-Jüssen states when discussing the effect of confirmation: "Baptism also confers the Holy Spirit (Jn. 3:5; Tit. 3:5)."[31] This statement can also be found in other authors, but with a twofold background of the Spirit as the giver and the Spirit as the gift. The first of these can clearly be seen in B. Neunhäuser, who states that baptism gives "remission of sins and—fundamentally—the gift of the Holy Spirit," since in it are combined the action of the neophyte and the mercy of God, "who gives Christian salvation through his Spirit."[32] The expression "through his Holy Spirit" could mean the Spirit as a gift, but does seem rather to signify, at least for my linguistic understanding, the originator of grace, the Spirit as agent.

Let us first of all follow this line of the Council, the Spirit as the originator of grace.

The classical teaching concerning the minister of baptism is well known. The bishop (*LG* 21b), the priest (*LG* 28d and *PO* 5a), the deacon (*LG* 29a) baptizes; everyone can baptize (*LG* 17). Indeed, the Council goes yet further, following Augustine: Christ baptizes in the human ministers (*SC* 7a and *LG* 21a); even more, in baptism, the Holy Spirit begets the neophyte to new life (*AG* 15a; cf. *AG* 7b and *LG* 11b). Of course, it is true that this is a tenet of general sacramental doctrine, for the statement that Christ baptizes (*SC* 7a) is given only as an example for a doctrine that holds good for all sacraments. The Council states explicitly and repeats, furthermore, that sacraments are conferred by the Holy Spirit (*LG* 12b and 50c; *AA* 3d).

Thus, this point, which was not mentioned at all, or too little, in the manuals, is certain: *through the Holy Spirit,* Christ confers baptism in the human minister. This relationship of the Spirit with baptism is the clear teaching of the Church and requires further fundamental theological consideration: whether and how the risen Christ, who is thus man, could send the Spirit who, after all, is God; how the action of Christ and that of the Spirit are combined; how we are to understand the presence of the Spirit as an agent in baptism; or how we are to understand the action of the Spirit in the sacraments and in other actions of the Church, both in its common and diverse aspects.

However, these are all questions that refer to all the sacraments and that are therefore not confined to baptismal doctrine. We shall not discuss them here, as they will not provide the answer to another question, namely, whether the Spirit is given as a Person in baptism; whether we say "in some way" or not changes nothing of the substance of the question.

Let us attempt to clarify this question at least by means of a few introductory steps.

Baptism and Confirmation

Introduction to the Problem

If we wish to find out whether the Spirit comes as a gift, we must ask three questions in our context. First, does confirmation confer the Holy Spirit? Next, do baptism and confirmation both confer the Holy Spirit? And lastly, if so, what is the difference in reception of the Spirit in these two sacraments?

We find a surprising situation in these manuals. The first question does not receive a clear response, since the Holy Spirit is seen not at all, or hardly so, as a gift. The second question receives no reply in the treatises on baptism, although we can sometimes find a statement in the account given of confirmation that is in the order of a positive reply and that partially touches the third question. L. Billot considers that every sacrament gives the Holy Spirit because every sacrament confers created grace along with the uncreated, indwelling Trinity. This indwelling is, however, especially appropriated to the Holy Spirit: it is only a matter of working out the special aims of each sacrament, in other words, the special aids encapsulated in each sacramental grace.[33] Thus, Billot considers that the Holy Spirit is conferred in every sacrament. M. Premm states that the Holy Spirit is already given in some way in baptism "insofar as in every infusion of sanctifying grace, the Father, the Son and the Holy Spirit also enter the soul and take up their dwelling-place therein."[34] I shall not try to show whether Premm's view can be fully reconciled with that of Billot; in any case, he too derives the gift of the Spirit in baptism from the doctrine of indwelling.

The doctrine of indwelling is naturally well known to all theologians and goes without saying, yet its consequences for baptism and confirmation, which become evident in these examples, seem rarely to have been drawn. In any case, it remains debatable whether this view does justice to the special relationship of the Holy Spirit to confirmation as found in Scripture and Tradition.

The Council

Concerning confirmation, the Council teaches what had always been known and was accepted by the magisterium and theologians, namely, that in confirmation a special power of the Holy Spirit is conferred (*LG* 11a and *AG* 11a). We also find the classical doctrine to the effect that the Holy Spirit indwells the believer as in a temple (e.g., *LG* 4 and 9b). However, in these passages, it never states whether this indwelling has its origin in baptism or in confirmation.

The original draft of *Lumen gentium* 10a would have given a sufficient basis for seeing the communication of the Spirit not in baptism but in confirmation.[35] The promulgated text no longer permits this interpretation, but leaves the whole question open: "The baptized, by regeneration and the anointing of the Holy Spirit, are consecrated to be a spiritual house. . . ."

This is also the case in other passages in *Lumen gentium*. In number 15, we find, alongside baptism, through which non-Catholics are also joined to Christ, the action of the Holy Spirit in them. Now since many of them do not have confirmation, one is bound to think of a gift of the Spirit conferred in baptism. However, the statements go no further than the Spirit as the giver of grace and maybe also as the originator of "actual grace." Number 31 speaks expressly of baptism, but says nothing concerning the Holy Spirit; yet this silence must not be interpreted as a negative reply to our question, especially since number 34b states concerning the laity that they are "dedicated to Christ and anointed by the Holy Spirit." However, this fits—just like the similar parallel in 48d—the juxtaposition we found before in the quotation from number 10a.

Lumen gentium clearly teaches that Christ's faithful are equipped with the Holy Spirit and it sees in them a personal presence of the Spirit; however, the Council does not state whether this is to be ascribed to baptism or to confirmation or else whether to baptism as a first step and confirmation as a second.

The Decree on the Church's Missionary Activity appears at first glance to represent a progress, or even a development of doctrine. According to *Ad gentes* 11a, the faithful must manifest the new man they have put on through baptism and the power of the Holy Spirit by which they have been strengthened

through confirmation. Here, too, one could view this strengthening through the Spirit as the increase of an initial filling with
the Spirit, already operated in baptism. Yet the Council maintains silence on this point. *Ad gentes* 14b repeats *Sacrosanctum
concilium* 6 word for word and, without mentioning baptism,
confirmation, or the Eucharist by name, it specifies their nature
as dying with Christ, being buried and rising again with him,
through reception of the Spirit of sonship and through the
"memorial" or "commemoration" of the death and resurrection
of Christ. Here the "they receive the spirit," written in lower-
case in the Constitution on the Liturgy, becomes "they receive
the Spirit," with a capital letter in the Decree on Missionary
Activity. Yet this change, however much it may give prominence to the Spirit as a Person, decides nothing for our question as to which sacrament confers him, since the three sacraments are not mentioned by name. Nor does *Ad gentes* 15e go
beyond the parallels of a contact with Christ and a filling with
the Spirit, with which we are already acquainted from *Lumen
gentium* 34b and 48d.

Thus, Vatican II offers no support for the claim that baptism
confers the Holy Spirit. Equally, nowhere does it state unequivo-
cally that confirmation confers the Spirit as a Person.

Considerations

This puts us in a new situation. So far, we had subjects that
the Council was proposing for the Church's renewed attention,
such as rebirth from faith and baptism, or the Spirit as the minister of baptism. These are statements that give theology a sure
point of departure for its speculative work. Apart from these, we
were faced with a fresh path, involving the members of the
Church, and Christians as inserted into the Church, and this
meant that we had to examine anew and in greater breadth a
subject that is already familiar but that had formerly been dealt
with rather simplistically. Here, however, we have a question
that was purposely left open.

The Council makes no decision regarding the question of
whether baptism or confirmation confers the Spirit, but it does
help us to see and to express more clearly certain points periph-
eral to this question.

In the first place, we have already seen the theme of the

temple of the Holy Spirit. This doctrine, which rests on a solid basis in Scripture and Tradition, is not simply equivalent to the theological doctrine of uncreated grace. The discussion on this subject is well known, especially as regards the question of whether the indwelling of the Spirit is a *proprium* or an appropriation. Reference to Scripture and Tradition must first of all show us what part of this discussion is dogma and what part is theological opinion—however tenable this may be—and whether in this doctrine really only *one* truth is proposed or whether several are mixed together, so that a satisfactory account of the subject is quite impossible.

Another question that presents itself for our consideration is whether in the past we saw the Holy Spirit clearly enough as a Person in the gift of confirmation. It would appear that the authors always spoke only of grace and power, given by the Spirit for a specific purpose, but they did not take sufficiently into account the doctrine of Scripture and the Fathers to the effect that the Holy Spirit comes as a Person.

This, however, leads us to another question: that of whether we can consider the Spirit as the effect of the sacrament of confirmation. This is obviously not possible. It may be objected that although he himself can certainly not be the effect, his presence could well be. Yet this cannot be so easily equated with created grace. Maybe we must give renewed and stronger attention to the biblical and also to augustinian doctrine on confirmation, to the effect that the minister must pray to God to give himself, in other words, that *one* feature of the action of administration of confirmation, namely, the prayer to God to come, must receive greater and renewed attention?

These considerations, the development of which would take us way beyond the limits of this article, will certainly provide a good basis for a clear statement of the question and a better presentation of the relationship both of baptism and also of confirmation with the Holy Spirit as gift.

Baptism and the Priesthood of Believers

This title covers four individual subjects that cause few problems when treated separately, but that present a number of questions when seen in their relationship to each other.

The Royal Priesthood

Our first text in *Sacrosanctum concilium* 14a quotes the biblical passage 1 Peter 2:9 as a proof for the statement of the Council to the effect that the Christian people have, because of their baptism, the right and duty to participate in the liturgy. The same quotation is employed in *Lumen gentium* 9a to describe the goal of rebirth from faith and baptism. Similarly, in *Ad gentes* 15a, it accompanies the statement that the Holy Spirit begets Christ's faithful in baptism to new life and unites them as a people. Here, however, this global statement is the preparation for an admonition addressed to missionaries to build up living Christian communities that are a sign of God's presence in the world. In *Apostolicam actuositatem* 3a, we once again find the expression "royal priesthood" as part of a statement by the Council that, however, is intended to recall 1 Peter 2:4–10 and to explain that the lay apostolate has its basis in baptism and confirmation. In all these cases, *sacerdotium* means priesthood in the sense of a group or body; *regale* remains, as in the Bible, not at all clear. It is nonetheless certain that this global expression always refers to a task of man derived from baptism, which places him before God.

The expression is found a fifth time in *Presbyterorum ordinis* 2a, but not in a context related to baptism, and then a sixth time in *Lumen gentium* 10b, which we shall deal with now.

The Common Priesthood

Lumen gentium intentionally situates this concept of the common priesthood between that of the holy priesthood[36] and that of the royal priesthood.

The first section of this number is thought out and expressed in biblical terms. The baptized are consecrated into a holy priesthood through rebirth and anointing with the Holy Spirit. This is how we must translate *sacerdotium sanctum* here, with reference to the biblical text that is recognizable in the background. The Council twice describes this consecration in biblical words: presenting spiritual sacrifices to God, and witnessing before men to what God and Christ have done.

The second section presents a covert shift in terminology, going from priesthood as a category to priesthood as a capacity and task possessed by the individual members of this category. It calls this "the common priesthood." This expression has its origins in Luther, in whose writings it signifies the alleged priestly quality of all believers and effectively denies any other particular priesthood of Orders. In Vatican II, it represents the same affirmation as in Luther, but in place of the denial, we now find the tacit recognition of an ordained priesthood and the essential difference of the latter from the priesthood of all believers.

At the end of the second section, this common priesthood is now called "the royal priesthood," with priesthood being understood as a capacity and task and not as a category, and it is described in terms of certain activities. The faithful "participate in the offering of the Eucharist. They exercise that priesthood, too, by the reception of the sacraments, prayer and thanksgiving, the witness of a holy life, abnegation and active charity." In the first line, we again recognize the spiritual sacrifices of the Bible, although here they are understood as applying to the offering of the Eucharist, without, however, excluding other uses of this fundamental biblical concept. Those who understand the reception of the sacraments as "the worship of the Christian religion" will understand their role here as consisting primarily of prayer and thanksgiving. In connection with the witness of a holy life, we can recognize a biblical feature: that of announcing the wonderful deeds of God (which was called in witness by the council itself in the previous section). The other examples, to which we must return in due course, are at first glance not immediately easily coordinated. Be that as it may, in *Lumen gentium* 10a, we find a list of the activities of the common and the royal priesthood in the fundamental biblical descriptions of the holy priesthood.

We are certainly justified in concluding that for the Council, the biblical doctrine of the priesthood that in its scriptural context is called holy or royal is clarified and expressed by means of examples taken from Tradition. The concept is enriched in this way and further developed from priesthood as a category to priesthood as a capacity or task, and is then called the common or royal priesthood in the new sense.

Sharing in the Three Offices of Christ

The development of the concept goes further.

On the basis of their baptism, the faithful are a royal priesthood (in the biblical sense) and possess the common or royal priesthood (in the sense of the magisterium). On the basis of their baptism, the members of Christ's faithful share in the priestly, prophetic, and kingly office of Christ (LG 31a; cf. AA 2 and 10a; AG 15b). We must ask the meaning of these new words and how they stand in relation to the foregoing terminology from Lumen gentium 10.

The priestly office is intended to carry out a spiritual service in God's honor and for the salvation of men (LG 34b). The prophetic office makes believers witnesses to the faith in their daily life (LG 35a). The kingly office renders them capable of conquering the kingdom of sin in royal liberty, self-denial, and a holy life, and of establishing the kingdom of Christ in themselves and in others (LG 36a).

We have already encountered one of these adjectives: "kingly" or "royal." However, it was then employed as a more specific qualification for the priesthood, in both senses, and not as a function associated with the priesthood in either sense. "Priesthood" appeared previously to mean the whole of the capacities and tasks imparted to the Christian in baptism, whereas here "priestly" appears only to be one feature alongside two others. "Prophetic" had already appeared in Lumen gentium 12, but there it was at first difficult to classify and was not one of a series of three.

Now "priesthood" is clearly seen as a broad concept of priesthood that contains within itself all three "offices"—including the priestly office in the narrower sense, for the spiritual service found in Lumen gentium 34, which is a feature of the priestly office, can be found again in the offering of the Eucharist, the reception of the sacraments, and in prayer and thanksgiving in Lumen gentium 10. The prophetic office with the task of bearing witness is found almost word for word amongst the examples of the activities of the common priesthood, and likewise the kingly office is found almost word for word there in the "abnegation and active charity" of Lumen gentium 10, and fits both the spiritual service and the prophetic office of bearing witness. (Here the question is thrown up as to whether these three offices can really be so clearly distinguished one from another.[37] However, this is not our subject here.)

Hence, although the Council does not state this in so many words, it nonetheless teaches by its content that the common priesthood is composed of the three offices, namely the priestly (in the stricter sense) task, the prophetic task, or that of witness, and the kingly task, or that of a life following Christ. According to *Lumen gentium* 10, this common priesthood is based on rebirth and anointing with the Spirit, and, according to *Lumen gentium* 31, it is based on baptism. Does this mean that confirmation is not part of the foundation of the common priesthood? When we take into consideration the fact that *Sacrosanctum concilium* 41a and *Ad gentes* 15a also give baptism and nothing else as the foundation for the royal priesthood in the biblical sense, the question only becomes more pointed.

The Apostolate

Of course, here it is not a question of the apostolate of the successors of the apostles, but rather, that of the apostolate of all the faithful. We are given this charge by the Lord himself through baptism and confirmation (*LG* 33b). This same statement is found in *Apostolicam actuositatem* 3a, but here the two sacraments are more precisely defined: inserted through baptism into the mystical body of Christ, and strengthened through confirmation with the power of the Holy Spirit, we receive the right and duty of the apostolate.

Already in *Lumen gentium* 33b, the description of the apostolate is strongly reminiscent of what is elsewhere called the prophetic office. The equivalence is still clearer in *Apostolicam actuositatem* 6.

However, if this is the case, how can it be said that the apostolate is based on two sacraments, namely baptism *and* confirmation? Here I detect a certain tension, which is not a contradiction, both in *Lumen gentium* and in the Council as a whole. If it is true that in the Constitution on the Church, the Council wished to avoid a clear pronouncement when describing the common priesthood in *Lumen gentium* 10 as to whether confirmation is involved here, if what is called the prophetic office in *Lumen gentium* 12 and above all in 31 and 35 is included in this common priesthood, and if this prophetic office is the apostolate of the faithful and this apostolate is founded upon baptism and confirmation, then an observation and a question must be expressed.

The unavoidable observation is that this common priesthood is founded in baptism and confirmation. This observation does not provide a solution to the relationship of baptism, confirmation, and the Spirit, which we have already discussed, but *Lumen gentium* 33 does provide an answer to the question left open in *Lumen gentium* 10.

The question comes from the motivation of the apostolate. If the apostolate concerns only the prophetic office, but the prophetic office consists of bearing witness in life and word, then confirmation must be the sole foundation for the apostolate of the faithful, as it gives power and the charge of witness. How then are we to understand the Council when it sees baptism *and* confirmation as the foundation of the apostolate? The answer must be found in *Apostolicam actuositatem*. In number 3a, following the mention of baptism as insertion into the mystical body of Christ and of confirmation as strengthening with the power of the Holy Spirit, we find the biblical parallels to this from 1 Peter 2:4–10 concerning the offering of spiritual sacrifices and then concerning witness for Christ throughout the world. Number 4a then adds that the fruitfulness of this apostolate depends on a living relationship with Christ. Hence, the Council does not only wish to state that it is true that the charge of the apostolate is given by confirmation, but that confirmation necessarily presumes baptism and that baptism is given for the apostolate as the precondition for confirmation. The Council wishes to say more than this. Sanctification of self—in other words, a living relationship with Christ—is the interior power that makes witness for Christ convincing. Without this, it produces an empty activism; without it, the soul is lacking in witness for Christ.

Recapitulation

In these four subjects, old teaching is given in words that are in part new. Only through baptism and confirmation is Christian life fully founded. Baptism gives conquest over sin with the duty to renew this constantly in our own lives; in configuration to Christ, it gives us a new life with the duty of living in conformity with this: we may call this "the kingly office," if we like. However, the Christian must not simply live like Christ, but also spread his message through word and example: we may call this "the prophetic office," if we like; this has nothing to do with ecclesial futurology, and we may also refer to it as "apostolate." All these tasks in a Christian life must be borne by our will to acknowledge and honor God, above all by sharing in the sacrifice of the Mass and reception of the sacraments: we may call this "the priestly office," if we like. This all sounds very simple, yet the true depths of Christian life can be expressed only in simple words. However, the teaching of the Council has the value of setting before us the essential internal relationship of baptism and confirmation. A Christian life that limits itself to itself and does not wish to convince others to join it is only incomplete, or, to put it another way, public activity for Christ originating from a person who is not holy or who does not at least strive for holiness, will be only frenetic and ineffective. If the conciliar texts have managed to present this teaching more incisively, they have achieved their goal.

The Rights and Duties of the Baptized

When speaking of the effect of baptism, the customary manuals concentrated almost exclusively on being, but spoke very little of duties. There were certain exceptions. In a *Corollarium*, Tanquerey sees baptism as an obligation to a new life in Christ.[38] In an appendix on the "value for life" of baptism, Premm sees it as the basis for an obligation to service of God, to whom one now belongs entirely.[39] Otherwise we find nothing. This silence concerning duties may be connected with the *Catechismus ad Parochos*, which was certainly acquainted with an obligation deriving from baptism, but which saw its basis in the baptismal vows.[40] It might be that this led to a failure to give express consideration to the consequences of the effect of the sacraments for Christian duties.

It is here that Vatican II brought new emphases.

The fundamental statement is to be found in *Lumen gentium* 40a. Through baptism, the disciples of Christ share in the divine nature and thus are truly sanctified. This means they must preserve and fulfill the holiness they have received by their life.

Here the Council takes as its starting point one of the attributes of the divine nature—holiness—in which we share through baptism, as its basis for the possibility and duty of a holy life. It is necessary to follow this point, to understand this grace as sharing in the grace of Christ, and then to see in it the basis for the possibility and duty of a life following Christ. This means living out the commandment of love just as Christ lived it out and taught it, and thus not just the commandment to love one's neighbor, which was already found in the Old Testament ("Love your neighbor as yourself"), but above all making the commandment of brotherly love the foundation of life from baptism ("Love one another as I have loved you"). It is no coincidence that shortly before the passage we have cited, the Council gives this very commandment for the Christian.

This, however, also throws fresh light on rebirth from faith and baptism. Both of these together constitute the foundation for the rights and duties of the Christian, faith in a consciously accepted duty, and baptism through the urge produced by the grace to correspond to this sense of duty.

Here we are on the seam joining dogmatic and moral theology, which must be more clearly defined precisely in the doctrine on baptism.

Alongside this general statement of the rights and duties of the baptized, the Council gives special prominence to two areas in which they are situated.

The first area is that of the liturgy. On the basis of baptism, the baptized person has the right and duty of active participation (SC 14a). One of the two foundations for this feature of baptism is given by the Council in Lumen gentium 11a: through their character, the baptized are appointed to Christian religious worship.

This statement must be completed in two directions. One of these lies in the distinction of classical theology to the effect that the character appoints the subject to external worship and the grace to interior worship. These two forms of worship are not identical, but they belong very closely together. External and interior worship must combine in the liturgy, working together like body and soul. However, the interior worship that is accomplished in daily life must also be consciously seen and performed in its dual relationship with the liturgy, its source and its goal.

The other direction lies in the particular form of worship that we call liturgy today. In Sacrosanctum concilium 48, the Council recommends that the faithful learn to offer the immaculate victim of the Mass not only through the hands of the priest, but also together with him, as they also offer themselves. Lumen gentium 10b goes still further. It derives this offering from the royal priesthood and then (see para a.) from rebirth in baptism, after which it adds reception of the sacraments. Here we find theological themes that have never been heard of before in baptismal doctrine, such as the obligation and right to participate in the Mass. The very necessity of participating in the Mass finds its basis in baptism, from which we find a commandment communicated in revelation itself. The Church has merely specified the frequency. We also find the reception of the sacraments. By taking up the old expression "sacraments of faith," the Council indicates con- fession of faith as a feature of reception. It also, however, gives equal emphasis to the other feature: that they are worship, here in the special form of a prayer to God to grant the help he has promised of the grace imparted through signs. This prayer is at the same time a recognition of man's dependence on God and of God's readiness to help. Only when taken together do this profes- sion of faith and worship give the proper setting for reception of the sacraments.

This is the first area in which the Council indicates the rights and duties of the baptized. The second area concerns witness for Christ.

In the foregoing section, when commenting on *Lumen gentium* 33b and *Apostolicam actuositatem* 3a, we showed how this duty and right have their basis in baptism and confirmation. Here we must consider the complex problems of *Lumen gentium* 11a. Ac- cording to this text, we are obliged by baptism to profess our faith before men, and by confirmation to spread and to defend the faith as witnesses of Christ. How are these two statements related to each other, for, given the different character of the sacra- ments, it can surely not be true that the same thing is intended twice over?

The goal of the baptismal obligation might be to express exter- nally and also fully humanly one's assent to Christ, which must at first perforce be primarily an interior assent. It is not necessary that this take place before men, for a worthy attitude, for exam- ple in personal prayer, where one is seen by no one else, is also such a fully human assent. However, in many cases, this will take place before others because human life is always a living together with others. But the consequence of this external profession is that others recognize what I confess and affirm. In contrast, the goal of the obligation related to confirmation is to win others for this faith and at least to defend it so that others do not lose it. Of course, these two obligations belong together, since the interior, strong, and therefore expressed, conviction of faith (which derives from baptism) must constitute the soul of the concern to convince others (which comes from confirmation).

Ad gentes 36a extends the scope of this consideration, which up to this point was limited to baptism and confirmation. As members of Christ, incorporated into him through baptism, confirmation, and the Eucharist, all believers have the duty to contribute toward the increase of his body. While in *Lumen gentium* 11 the difficulty was to distinguish confirmation from baptism, here we have the task of understanding why the Eucharist has been added to justify a duty that would appear to have its basis in confirmation. However, this brings us to our next section.

Sacraments of Initiation

Before the theological subject itself, we must deal with a semantic point that may well have an influence on our theological considerations.

The Concept of Initiation

A first concept of *initiatio* is that of the non-Christian rites of initiation that still exist in certain cultures (*SC* 65). However, apart from this, the word is always used in a Christian context, where a second concept is that of introduction into the priestly manner of thinking and living (*OC* 11c), and a third is that of introduction into (theological) studies (*OT* 14b). A fourth concept is that of entry into Christian life and knowledge of faith (*AG* 14a and b). It is within this framework that the concept of the sacraments of Christian initiation is employed. Let us leave aside the fact that here the concept of initiation is a genus admitting two different species, the non-Christian (cf. *SC* 65) and the Christian one. Apart from this, there is a certain vacillation as to whether the expression *initiationis christianae sacramenta* means the sacraments *belonging to the introduction* into Christian life and thought, or the sacraments *constituting initiation* into Christian life. The context in *Ad gentes* favors the former, whereas other passages such as *Sacrosanctum concilium* 71a and *Presbyterorum ordinis* 2c tend more toward the latter. We must remember that the terminology of the Council was fluctuating slightly since the very matter under discussion was not entirely clear. Thus, *initiatio* remains both introduction and initation.

This linguistic observation now brings us face to face with the problem we have already dealt with when speaking of rebirth from faith and baptism. What was mentioned there concerning introduction into faith and initiation in the sacrament of baptism must now be extended to other sacraments. We must ask to which others.

The Sacraments of Initiation

Presbyterorum ordinis 2c states that ordination to the priest-hood presupposes the sacraments of initiation. The minimum demanded by the plural form must be baptism and confirmation. In *Sacrosanctum concilium* 71a, the same must be understood for the sacraments of initation. It is true that it cannot be excluded that the Eucharist may also be intended. However, in *Ad gentes* 14b, we are obliged to think of *three* sacraments of initiation:

> Then, having been delivered from the powers of darkness through the sacraments of Christian initiation, and having died, been buried, and risen with Christ, they receive the Spirit of adoption of children and celebrate with the whole people of God the memorial of the Lord's death and resurrection.

If anyone should have the reasonable doubt, after the above comparison between *Sacrosanctum concilium* 6 and this passage from *Ad gentes* 14, whether "the Spirit of adoption of children" is truly a reference to confirmation, there is a clear text in *Ad gentes* 36a, even though the words "sacraments of initiation" do not appear in it: ". . . incorporated into him and made like him by baptism, confirmation and the Eucharist, all the faithful . . ."

Presbyterorum ordinis 5b points in the same direction.

The Meaning of Initiation

This statement on the part of the Council can be justified by the liturgical unity of initiation in the early centuries of the Church. This was a *liturgical* unity because all three sacraments were cele-brated in a unified rite, which was composite but continuous. The Council refers back to a unity of initiation without fully restoring this unity *liturgically*. Hence, this statement can intend only a unity of *content* for initiation, which still obtains even when the liturgical unity is interrupted, sometimes by a space of several years. This question of the unity of content acquires added importance from the fact that the sequence is sometimes inverted (baptism–Eucharist–confirmation), or else a further sacrament (penance) intrudes into the series—indeed, it is stated (not by the Council) that this intrusion is necessary in certain cases.

Here we must ask what *initiatio* understood as "initiation" actually means, when as a liturgical unity it often no longer exists and is no longer sought after for each individual case.

The internal connection between baptism and confirmation derives from the fact that they are the Good Friday, Easter, and Pentecost of the Christian life. In the life of Christ, these three events are the accomplishment of his work of salvation and the inception of its distribution to men. In his death, he prays to his Father to forgive men's faults, and he expresses his readiness to accept on their behalf the friendship the Father offers them. By raising him from the dead, the Father recognizes this readiness, forgives, and concludes a pact of friendship with mankind in his Son Jesus Christ. However, it is the Holy Spirit who must take on the task of distributing the gifts of salvation and reception into the friendship of God with Christ, as well as rendering it possible for men, who can live like Christ, to progress in maturity by winning others for Christ. This is why the risen Christ must first receive the Spirit (whom he always possessed for himself) for others, so that he may pass him on to them. Baptism means being taken into the death and resurrection of Christ, and confirmation means being taken into this reception of the Spirit of Christ, just as occurred for the apostles at Pentecost. The unity of baptism and confirmation must be seen from the life of Christ. There is no other convincing access.

However, this new life is the life of God and the life of Christ, and it is thus beyond the capacity of man to bring it to realization corresponding to the power within it, even if it is entrusted to man's activity and can and must be used by him. This is why man himself must enter into relationship with Christ himself, God and man, so that *he*, in and with man, may take on the full realization of this life of grace. In the sacrifice of the Mass, the Christian comes into contact with Christ's death and with the risen Christ in communion. However, since this is the glorified

Lord, filled with the Spirit, who meets him here, he must also do this in the Spirit of the Lord, and thus as one who is confirmed.

It is precisely the Mass that shows us afresh the importance of the unity of introduction and initiation. For baptism, we have already discussed this topic when speaking of rebirth; it is significant in the same sense for confirmation. In the Mass, it is thrown into relief by the fact that the liturgy of the word and the eucharistic liturgy "form but one single act of worship" (SC 56).

Moreover, these considerations require us to distinguish two facets of the Mass. It is certainly a sacrament of initiation, but, unlike baptism and confirmation, it is not only this. It is also the apex and the nucleus of the whole of Christian life (LG 11a and the statements that follow from it for the activity of the Church in SC 10a, AG 9b, PO 5b and 6e).

Baptism and Religious Life

In two passages, the Council speaks of the link between baptism and life according to the three evangelical counsels. The Constitution on the Church sees in a life based on the vows a way of obtaining richer fruits of baptismal grace, since the person is freed from the hindrances standing in the way of the love and service of God and is more profoundly consecrated to obedience of God (LG 44a). The Decree on the Renewal of Religious Life sees in this life of the evangelical counsels a special consecration to God, rooted in baptismal consecration, to which it gives fuller expression (PC 5a).

Let us try taking up the opening given us by the Council, but only in order to gain a better understanding of baptism, and not in order to offer a complete theology of the religious life.

The three vows of poverty, celibacy, and obedience are on the one hand a renunciation of property, marriage, and running one's own life, in other words, of the three major goods of human life: of things subject to one's own disposal, of another person who completes and fulfills one, and of oneself. On the other hand, they signify freedom from property, marriage, and the kind of life one runs oneself. Both of these, renunciation and freedom, are taken on for a lifetime.

A decision for life of this nature can only be understood from the viewpoint of Christ.

In his own life, Christ renounced possessions, marriage, and a self-chosen life-style: he had come to do the Father's will. This attitude is seen at its clearest in Gethsemane, in his readiness to denounce a decision based on his own assessment, which was and could only be good, in order willingly to take on what the Father willed. It was on the cross that this attitude reached its climax, choosing the more difficult alternative before him inasmuch as it was the Father's will, not for itself as such. This attitude and the resultant decision to accept death overcame sin and the consequences of sin in all men.

In his resurrection, Christ gains an immediate encounter with God such as he did not possess on this earth as a man; he is no longer reliant on things and men in order to find God and himself, and as a man, as opposed to being God, he has no freedom any more; for in God, all that is created is better known and possessed than was ever possible on earth, and he who possesses in God the fulfillment of his expectations can no longer be free with respect to him. With its own consequences, the resurrection also contributes in its own way to overcoming sin and the consequences of sin.

The life of the three vows is a special sharing in the death and resurrection of Christ. Renunciation of property, marriage, and a personal life-style is a renunciation of the highest values that enable a person to mature and grow, and this renunciation is for a lifetime. This is hard, and a cross that can only be taken up for Christ's sake and in order to follow him especially, and only if and because God calls one to do it. However, a life of the three vows also means being free of property, marriage, and a personal life-style, and this is something beautiful, because it derives from God and configuration with Christ. But here the correct sequence must be respected. Only by going through the cross can one share in the resurrection. This was true for Christ, and it is also true for the life of the three vows. Hence, such a life, owing to the greater renunciation and greater freedom, is a more complete liberation from the hindrances that in sins or the consequences of sin stand in the way of God's service, and it is also a greater stimulus and opportunity for love.

From this vantage point, in the context of the other ideas of the Council, we can return to a more profound view of baptism. We have already seen that the Council particularly emphasizes baptism as a death and resurrection with Christ. We have also already seen how very much the Council emphasizes duty. We can now start our considerations at this point.

Configuration with the death of Christ, which is brought about in baptism and which incorporates us into his life of grace, is a power and a task with three characteristic features: first, to do the Father's will, then to learn to renounce valuable goods for God's sake, and lastly, as a result of these two attitudes, to overcome the might of sin and disorder that lives in us. This will of the Father—and the reununciation that is its consequence—as can be seen in Christ, can be learned from his teaching in an exemplary manner. This is the impressed character of every baptismal grace; but it can go yet further into the life of Christ, which renounces possessions, marriage, and a personal life-style totally and for ever. This is a particular vocation from God, which does, however, presuppose the fundamental character of baptism.

Configuration with the resurrection of Christ, which is brought about in baptism and similarly incorporates us into his life of grace, is the capacity to have an encounter with God, as a result of which, precisely because God fills us entirely, we are given a more profound approach to created things, to other people, and to ourselves than is possible purely naturally for man, who comes to God from created things. A beginning of this is given in baptismal grace, which is a sharing in the life of the Trinity and the three virtues that are especially directed toward God. A more profound way of living out this aspect of baptismal grace comes from God's call to live in freedom from property, marriage, and a personal life-style.

Thus, from the vantage point of the religious life, we can obtain a more precise view of baptism, but also of confirmation; for if baptism finds its completion in confirmation and only the two sacraments taken together can provide a perfect foundation for the Christian, whereas confirmation is the foundation for witness for Christ as a possibility and as a task, then the religious life must also be founded on confirmation as the completion of baptism, and it must be a witness for Christ. Conversely, it is also true that confirmation presupposes baptism, and thus witness presupposes sanctification. Maybe the very weakness of the religious life today can make it clear that confirmation can have no effect if previously one has not taken baptism seriously.

Concluding Considerations

The individual points proposed for our attention by the Council in various contexts combine to form a framework into which the principal points from the manuals, which were already well known, can easily be integrated. This framework is that of the encounter of various persons who have dealings with each other, whereby they meet at a specific moment determined by an action called a sacrament.

The risen Christ acts in the action of the Spirit, who is sent by him, through a human minister. This man must have the conscious desire to act in the service of these two divine Persons (whatever degree of consciousness must be involved). In this way, his action becomes an act of worship for the glory of God and the salvation of man: this man acknowledges that he stands in the service of God and that he is passing on God's help in his name.

The person receiving this sacrament must come before this divine action in faith, and this faith is expressed in the external action of his coming and receiving. This faith accepts the truth of this sacrament of baptism, but also the whole Catholic faith, a faith that already has a path behind it, along which this person has acknowledged God and his Son Jesus Christ, and which reaches its climax in the reception of baptism. What the adult must build up in himself prior to baptism must take place in a child after baptism. The parents or their representatives and the godparents as representatives of the Church, who can also be representatives of the parents, must promise to do their part so as to make it possible for the child to learn this path to faith.

However, the action of the recipient is also an act of worship, a prayer to God to obtain the promised gift, and an acknowledgment that his own Christian life cannot be led without God's help, and that God is prepared to grant this help.

The actions of both these persons, the minister and the recipient, must express what has been stated before; here the minister's action must above all indicate the gift of Christ himself. This indication receives its symbolic power at the occasion of a natural action only from revelation, yet it can never fully express the gift. Hence, it is all the more necessary to have knowledge of the truth of faith of this sacrament of baptism and to receive it with faith in the sense of the Catholic Church.

In this encounter (but not *through* it); the believer is made to
share in the life of the Holy Trinity; the believer becomes a child
of God and enters into an interior relationship with him. This
sharing has the same form it had in the man Jesus Christ; it is
above all characterized by the death and resurrection of Christ.
In this encounter, not only is the person taken into Jesus Christ,
but is also received into the Catholic Church through the gift of
the Trinitarian life configured to Christ and through a profession
of faith in the sense of the Catholic Church that he or she
recognizes. If someone does not possess, fully or at all, these two
means of incorporation into the Catholic Church through baptism, he or she is not at all or not fully a member of the Catholic
Church. Someone who is not a member at all may have more or
less in common with the Church according to how much,
through common faith or maybe even without it, he or she
possesses structures that Christ has entrusted to the Catholic
Church as their guardian.

This faith together with the gift becomes a foundation for
rights and duties in Catholic life. To do God's will, to renounce
good things for God's sake, to overcome sins and the consequences of sin—all these become the Christian's life task, as
prefigured in grace and expressed in words in faith. It becomes
possible and a life task to share in a new encounter with God,
which leads to a new encounter with oneself and with other
people and nonhuman creatures. This whole life task finds its
climax in sharing in the eucharistic sacrifice and Communion,
but is also accomplished in reception of the sacraments and in an
active Christian life. All this is the priestly office—or an act of
worship. This worship cannot be performed without the manifestation of Christ in a person, without conquering oneself and
denying oneself, in other words without the kingly office. Both
of these together must produce a witness for Christ before others,
the prophetic office or the apostolate of the faithful.

In this latter office, we already find mention of the necessary
complement of baptism. Christ the risen mediator was fully
equipped for his task only once he had received the Spirit,
through whom he was to act and who was to bear witness to him.
The Christian is fully incorporated into Christ only once he or
she has received this Spirit in Person, so as to bear witness to
Christ.

However, this Christian life, based in baptism and confirmation, must be lived together with Christ, who even today still bears within himself the offering of his death, and who, risen from the dead, lives eternally in immediate proximity to God. The Eucharist is the completion of the foundation of the Christian person as an agent, and is the point of departure and the center of his or her life for Christ and God.

This is an outline of the baptismal doctrine, the development of which the Council entrusts to theologians as their task.

Translated from the German by Ronald Sway.

Notes

1. J. de Guibert, "Le décret du Concile de Florence pour les Arméniens. Sa valeur dogmatique," *BullLittEccl*, 10 (1919), 81–85, 150–162, 195–215; as concerns the doctrine of baptism, cf. 197–199.

2. Thomas Aquinas, *Summa theologica*, III, 66, a. 10 c.

3. Cf. *ibid.*

4. Here I do not discuss the difference between rituals before and after the Second Vatican Council.

5. Thomas Aquinas, *Summa theologica*, III, 66, a. 7 c.

6. Cf. here the cautious indication given by A. d'Alès, *De Baptismo et Confirmatione* (Paris, 1927), 95: "Symbolismus Baptismi, ad captum hominum accomodatus, aliquando priores partes tribuit exclusioni peccatorum, cui homo, intellecta egesta sua, operam dat convertendo se ad Deum, qui est auctor vitae."

7. I prefer not to discuss here the difference between *effusio* (as in Thomas) and *infusio* (as in today's *Rite of Baptism*).

8. The quotation: Augustine, *De Baptismo contra Donatistas* I, 10, 14, in *PL*, 43, 117; concerning the meaning of the word *generare*, cf. the whole text of I, 10, 13–14, in *ibid.*, 116–118.

9. Ambrose, *Expositio Evangelii secundum Lucam* II, 7, in *PL*, 15, 1555B.

10. The quotation: Augustine, *De diversis quaestionibus ad Simplicianum*, I, 2, 2, in *PL*, 40, 112. Cf. for the whole distinction discussed above between conception and birth, this whole number (*PL*, 40, 111–112), and Augustine, *Expositio ad Galatos* 38, in *CSEL*, 84, 106f, or *PL*, 35, 2131f. These two passages of Augustine demand much more detailed study in order to present the multiplicity of their thought concerning our subject more precisely and more considerately than is possible here.

11. Bede, *In Lucae Evangelium Expositio* I, 2, in *PL*, 92, 330D.

12. Hugh of St. Victor, *De sacramentis Christianae fidei* I, 9, 8, in *PL*, 176, 328B.

13. Richard of St. Victor, *De potestate ligandi et solvendi* 20, in *PL*, 196, 1172B–1173A.

14. Cf. the detailed account given by J. Gaillard, "Les sacrements de la foi," *Revue Thomiste*, 67 (1959), 5–31, 270–309. Cf. also L. Villette, *Foi et sacrament*, vol. 2, "De Saint Thomas à Karl Barth" (Paris, 1964), 19–55.

15. Thomas Aquinas, *Summa theologiae*, III, 62, a. 6 c.

16. *Ibid.*

17. *Ibid.*, III, 69, a. 5 c, and *ad* 1 and *ad* 2.

18. *Ibid.*, III, 71, a. 1 c.

19. *Ibid.*, III, 73, a. 3 *ad* 3.

20. *Ibid.*, III, 39, a. 5 c.

21. Cf. in this connection, the general statement by Thomas Aquinas, *ibid.*, III, 84, a. 5 *ad* 2: "Faith itself also requires that, through the power of Christ's passion which works in the sacraments of the Church, we seek to be justified from sin."

22. Cf. Richard of St. Victor, *De potestate ligandi et solvendi* 20, in *PL*, 196, 1172C.

23. Augustine, *De Baptismo contra Donatistas* I, 8, 10, in *PL*, 43, 115.

24. *Ibid.*, I, 2, 3, in *PL*, 43, 110.

25. Franciscus Suarez, *Defensio Fidei Catholicae* I, 24, 2, in *Opera Omnia*, 24 (Paris, 1859), 117.

26. Benedict XIV, Brief *Singulari* (9 February 1749), 12–13, in *Codicis Juris Canonici Fontes*, 2 (Rome, 1928), 197.

27. Heinrich Kleiber, *Theologia Wirceburgensis*, 2 (Paris, 1852[2]), 94 (*Resp. ad Inst.* 2).

28. Hugh of St. Victor, *De sacramentis christianae fidei* II, 2, 2, in *PL*, 176, 416B. Cf. for a more detailed account H. Weisweiler, *Die Wirksamkeit der Sakramente nach Hugo von St. Victor* (Freiburg im Breisgau, 1932), 96–125. Cf. also A.M. Landgraf, "Sünde und Gliedschaft am geheimnisvollen Leib," in *Dogmengeschichte der Frühscholastik*, 4/2 (Regensburg, 1956), 48–49; for the questions of faith, esp. 62–64, 76–81.

29. *Cathechismus ex decreto Concilii Tridentini ad Parochos* II, Chap. II, "De Baptismi Sacramento," no. 1 (Rome, 1871), 144.

30. I do not refer here to *Lumen gentium* 7b, which speaks of all the sacraments, because this text requires a very detailed study, which would, however, take us into the field of general sacramental doctrine.

31. Diekamp-Jussen, *Katholische Dogmatik*, 3 (Münster, 1962[13]), 107.

32. B. Neunheuser, "Taufe" 4, Systematisch 3, *LThK*, 9 (1964), 1318.

33. L. Billot, *De Ecclesiae sacramentis*, 1 (Rome, 1931[7]), 291.

34. M. Premm, *Katholische Glaubenskunde*, 3/1 (Vienna, 1957[2]), 168.

35. Cf. the path taken by the various drafts of the text in G. Alberigo and F. Magistretti, *Constitutionis Dogmaticae "Lumen Gentium" Synopsis Historica* (Bologna, 1975), 47 (lines 14–16, 45).

36. "Holy priesthood" is also found in *PO* 2a. This expression is no doubt adopted from 1 Pt. 2:5.

37. It is also clear from *LG* 12 that the Council was not at pains to employ carefully considered and precise terminology. This passage mentions that the people of God "also" share in the prophetic office. This statement is surprising since the three offices have not yet been mentioned at all, and the "also" appears to refer back to the common priesthood of *LG* 10. There, it is true, the witness of life was one of the examples of priestly activity; now it makes a fresh appearance under the name of the prophetic office.

38. A. Tanquerey, *Synopsis Theologiae Dogmaticae*, 3 (Paris, 1930[22]), 343.

39. Premm, *Katholische Glaubenskunde*, 3/1, 139.

40. *Catechismus ad Parochos*, "De baptismi sacramento" 2 (p. 145), 77 (p. 178).

CHAPTER 25

Penance and Reconciliation in Vatican II

Pierre Adnès, S.J.

Summary

Anyone who looked to Vatican II for a doctrine on penance, however undeveloped and unexpanded, would certainly be disappointed. Even so, the Council makes a relatively large number of passing references to penance or penitence, both as a sacrament and as a Christian virtue. It will certainly be informative to make a methodical listing of these fleeting references in order to carry out an evaluation that can lead to increased understanding of a not unimportant aspect of the Council, and that can also encourage theology to carry out further and deeper reflection on the subject.

Vatican II refers quite frequently to Christian penance or penitence, although such references are mostly incidental. The word *paenitentia*—together with the related words *paenitens*, *paenitentialis*, and *paeniteo*—are found at least thirty times in the conciliar documents, and seven of these refer directly to the sacrament of penance.

If we are to take the texts in chronological order, we should begin with the Constitution on the Sacred Liturgy, *Sacrosanctum concilium*, and from the very first chapter of this document, the preaching of repentance is presented as a fundamental aspect of the evangelizing mission of the Church and its activity. The Church proclaims salvation to nonbelievers so that they "may be converted from their ways, doing penance," and "must ever preach faith and penance to believers" (SC 9). In religious language, the word "penance" has many meanings: repentance and conversion, expiation or reparation for sins committed, mortification of bad tendencies, and so on. None of these meanings is excluded here, since none of the scripture references referred to in a note is particularly illuminating, apart from Acts 2:38, which speaks of *metanoia*. When believers are involved, repentance–conversion will naturally be expressed in and through the reception of a special sacrament, for which the Church must "dispose" them, as it does for the other sacraments.

Penance as a sacrament is explicitly referred to in Chapter III, which deals with sacraments other than the Eucharist. The definition that opens this chapter deserves our attention, because it is also applied to penance as a sacrament, throwing light on its theological underpinnings: "The purpose of the sacraments is to sanctify men, to build up the Body of Christ, and, finally, to give worship to God. Because they are signs they also instruct" (SC 59). The first draft presented for discussion at the Fourth General Congregation on 22 October 1962 mentioned only two purposes for the sacraments: the sanctification of men and the worship offered to God.[1] The Council Fathers expressed the wish to see "the social and ecclesial aspect in each of the sacraments expressed in simple and effective terms," and it was therefore proposed that the text should state that "the sacraments are ordered to the offering of the desired worship to God by means of the sanctification of the members of the Body of Christ."[2] The final version of the Constitution complies with these wishes by adding a third purpose to the two already mentioned: that of the building up of the body of Christ, which briefly but in formal terms stresses the ecclesial and communitarian dimension of the sacraments in general—a dimension that is of great importance for a full understanding of penance as a sacrament.

We should also note the statement that all the sacraments "draw their power" from the "paschal mystery of the Passion, death and resurrection of Christ" (SC 61). And penance is obviously not an exception. Theology must therefore try to clarify the relationship of this sacrament with the paschal mystery inasmuch as it expresses one aspect of this mystery, and also show how it is an act of worship offered to God just as the other sacraments are. It must certainly be admitted that twenty-five years after the Council, even the first steps toward the fulfillment of this task have hardly been taken.

In order to justify a revision of the sacramental rites (which is the subject of this chapter), the Constitution then says that with the passage of time "there have crept into the rites of the sacraments and sacramentals certain features which have rendered their nature and purpose far from clear to the people of today" (SC 62). The following paragraphs note specific points on which the individual sacraments need revision. The remark on the sacrament of penance is strikingly terse: "The rite and formulae of Penance are to be revised so that they more clearly express both the nature and effect of the sacrament" (SC 72). This was clearly a way of pointing out (but without suggesting any specific modification) the inadequate nature of the ritual laid down for the sacrament of penance, the form of which then in use went back to the Roman Ritual of 1614.

This article (No. 72) is interesting because it is the only text referring to the sacrament of penance that seems to have caused some stir on the floor of the Council during discussions (at the Thirteenth and Fourteenth General Congregations, on 6 and 7 November 1962). The proposed schema mentioned only the effect of the sacrament, stating simply: "The rite and formulae of Penance are to be revised so that they more clearly express the *effect* of the sacrament."[3] The extreme brevity of this statement caused some perplexity: How could the Fathers vote either for or against a statement that was written in such generic terms? They would have preferred more explicit indications as to the type of reform envisaged, and said that it would be helpful at least to insert the fact that it should be done "insofar as is necessary."[4] Certain Fathers obviously feared changes of which they would not be told and that would be beyond their control.

In actual fact, the article on penance had been divested of the statement that the commission entrusted with drafting Chapter III had originally been given as an appendix. This statement had proposed the reestablishment of the ancient practice of the imposition of hands, which had been used as a sign of reconciliation with the Church in the first centuries, and which the post-tridentine ritual had modified, reducing it to a simple raising of the hand in the direction of the penitent; it had also proposed

the revision of the words concerning excommunication that precede the sacramental formula of absolution and are almost always
superfluous.[5] These indications were certainly meager, but even
so the orientation was valid, and the two proposals would be at
least partially implemented in the new *Rite of Penance*, which no
longer insists on the formula of absolution from censures before
absolution from sins, and which also envisages the imposition of
hands on the penitent's head, which can replace the holding up
of the right hand during the absolution (Nos. 19 and 46). The
latter is obviously the only sacramental gesture possible in cases
where there is a grille between the penitent and the confessor—
and the faithful who so wish are free to make use of this arrangement (cf. Canon 964, §2).

Strangely enough, four bishops called for a shortening and
simplification of the sacramental rite for pastoral reasons, saying
that in the case of numerous penitents, it could be reduced to the
single formula that expresses the essence of the sacrament and
that the posttridentine ritual reserved for cases where there was a
danger of death.[6] However, the liturgical reform in the new *Rite
of Penance* would certainly not take the form of any shortening or
simplification, although it did retain the prescription of the old
ritual on the imminent danger of death (No. 21). As regards
jurisdiction, two Fathers asked that bishops could confess "anywhere in the world"—a privilege granted to cardinals in the 1917
Code—and a third wanted priests to be granted a similar faculty
at least in their own country.[7] The 1983 Code would fulfill these
wishes (Canon 967, §§1 and 2).

Only two bishops stressed the ecclesial nature of sin, and
hence that of penance, which should be expressed in the sacramental rite, inasmuch as sin is not simply a turning away from
God, but also a break with the community of the faithful,[8] and
the restoration or increase of grace through the sacrament benefits each individual and also the whole mystical body.[9]

The question of collective absolution was raised by two other
bishops, one of whom asked, but "tentatively and interroga-
tively," for some broadening of the cases in which such absolution is permitted for the good of souls,[10] and the other that the
future ritual should expressly define the cases in which it was
authorized, in order to make sure that in such a serious matter,
people did not act according to their own personal criteria.[11]
This question would come to the forefront in the years following

the Council and would lead to the publication of the *Pastoral Norms for Imparting Communal Sacramental Absolution* of the Sacred Congregation for the Doctrine of the Faith (16 June 1972). However, it did not apparently attract much attention at the time of the Council, and had not yet become a contemporary concern.

The article was eventually voted on, but with the addition of the word "nature" before "effect."[12] Although this change may seem minor and relatively insignificant, it is worth taking a look at the explanation given by the spokesperson of the commission entrusted with the revision of the text when it was presented for the last time (at the Forty-Eighth General Congregation, on 15 October 1963), in which was stated that this addition had been made in order to respond to the request of a number of Fathers who wanted "the renewed rite of the sacrament of penance to express its nature—especially social and ecclesial—more clearly."[13]

As far as the drafting of the rite itself was concerned, which would have to be submitted for the approval of the Pope in the last instance, the Fathers of the Council were content to leave this up to the Holy See. Ten years would pass between the approval of the Constitution *Sacrosanctum concilium* (on 4 December 1963) and the promulgation of the new *Rite of Penance* by the Sacred Congregation for Divine Worship (on 2 December 1973), and at least seven of these years would be needed for the two successive work groups to reach a satisfactory implementation of this very brief article (No. 72).[14] The drafting process of this rite was probably more difficult than that of any of the others.

Penance is again referred to by the Constitution *Sacrosanctum concilium* in connection with the seasons of the liturgical year: ". . . in the various seasons of the year and in keeping with her traditional discipline, the Church completes the formation of the faithful by means of pious practices for soul and body, by instruction, prayer, and works of penance and mercy" (SC 105). The outstanding season for penance is of course Lent, to which two long articles are then devoted.

The first recalls the character of Lent, which is twofold, being both baptismal and penitential, and then its purpose, which is that of preparing for the celebration of the paschal mystery through the hearing of the word of God and through more intense prayer. The Council hopes that this twofold character will be more clearly expressed both in the liturgy and in catechesis.

> . . . catechesis, as well as pointing out the social conse-
> quences of sin, must impress on the minds of the faithful the
> distinctive character of penance as a detestation of sin because
> it is an offense against God. The role of the Church in peniten-
> tial practices is not to be passed over, and the need to pray for
> sinners should be emphasized (SC 109).

This is certainly the first time that any document of the magisterium has stressed both the theological and social dimensions
of sin, although the social consequences of sin are not described
in any detail. It is to be supposed that such consequences are
above all of an ecclesial order, since the sin of one member of the
Church has direct repercussions for the whole body of the
Church and not only for human society in general. Nor is the
"role of the Church in penitential practices" described in any
greater detail, although we can suppose that reference is being
made here to the already mentioned mission of the Church to
preach conversion and to foster a disposition to the sacrament
that it is one of its functions to dispense.

The following article, which deals specifically with penance in
the lenten season, states that such penance "should be not only
internal and individual but also external and social" (SC 110).
Lenten penance will thus be expressed outwardly through practical actions, taking on a communitarian and ecclesial aspect.
During Lent, the whole Church must be seen in a state of
penance.

We move from pastoral to dogmatic theology with the Constitution *Lumen gentium,* the document containing one of the most
important texts of Vatican II on the sacrament of penance, in
which it is attributed a twofold effect: God's pardon and reconciliation with the Church (LG 11). This teaching represents a fairly
amazing departure if we realize that until then no document of
the magisterium had ever mentioned such a thing.[15] Even so, the
idea itself was not new but completely traditional, and it will
maybe be helpful to recall its long history in order to gain a better
understanding of the statement of the Council.

In early Christianity, penitential discipline used the word "reconciliation" to indicate the final and culminating act of the process of canonical penance. The *Gelasian Sacramentary* calls this rite the "sacrament of reconciliation."[16] Through it, the penitent receives the "peace of the Church."[17] This term expresses the ecclesial dimension of the pardon that ended the state of visible separation from the community that had been imposed on the penitent. Reconciliation with God and reconciliation with the Church were closely bound together for early Christians, with the latter constituting the sign and guarantee of the former.

Even after the disappearance of public penance and the establishment in the early Middle Ages of what is called "private" penance, there was still the conviction that reconciliation with the Church was among the effects of this sacrament—as is witnessed to by many scholastic theologians, who took such reconciliation as one of the reasons for the need of priestly absolution before communion in the case of mortal sin.[18] Even so, when the Council of Trent dealt with penance, it defined it as a sacrament "instituted by Christ our Lord to reconcile the faithful with God himself as often as they fall into sin after baptism" (14th Session, Canon 1, DS 1701; cf. DS 1674), without so much as mentioning any reconciliation with the Church, although certain sixteenth- and seventeenth-century theologians did still remember this dimension.[19]

The fact that an item of truth has been forgotten does not mean that it is being denied. In the present century, in a thesis for the Gregorian University under the direction of Maurice de la Taille, Bartolomeu Xiberta performed the admirable task of once again drawing the attention of theologians to the concept of reconciliation with the Church, which he held to be "the proper and immediate fruit of sacramental absolution."[20] The Fathers of the Church would have seen such reconciliation as the intermediate effect between the outward sensible sign and the specific grace of the sacrament, which our theology refers to as *res-et-sacramentum*. Although the underlying concept of Xiberta's thesis was at first given a reserved or negative reception, in due course it came to exercise considerable influence on the contemporary theology of sacramental penance.[21]

However, the declaration of Vatican II on reconciliation with the Church has its own history. It is found in a paragraph that has the aim of showing how the common priesthood of all the faithful is exercised in the sacraments. The original draft did not mention all the sacraments.[22] Many Fathers were puzzled by the omission of penance, the anointing of the sick, and orders, and some of them presented interventions in the name of large groups of bishops.[23]

A first effort at including penance was made in a proposal by Cardinal Suenens dealing with the rearrangement of the chapters of the Constitution. This is found among the Acts of the Thirty-Seventh General Congregation (30 September 1963), but was not distributed to the Fathers until the Forty-Fourth General Congregation (9 October 1963). As regards penance, it states: "The faithful, in approaching the sacrament of penance, implore reconciliation with the priestly community and pardon from the mercy of the Lord, whilst the community itself toils incessantly for their conversion."[24] As is suggested by the order in which the effects of the sacrament are listed, this text seems to take reconciliation with the Church, which precedes God's pardon, as the immediate and intermediate effect of penance. This was in fact the essential point of Xiberta's thesis. However, since this opinion was not unanimously shared by theologians, any appearance of approving it would have been controversial, and the Council did not wish to take sides in disputed questions.

Another text was therefore produced by the theological commission and submitted to the Fathers at the Eightieth General Congregation (15 September 1964). In this text, the order in which the effects are listed has been reversed, and their simultaneity is affirmed: "They who fittingly approach the sacrament of penance obtain pardon from the mercy of God and at the same time are reconciled with the Church, which toils unceasingly for their conversion with love, prayers and example."[25] The commission responsible for this amended formulation explained: "With regard to the sacrament of penance, the commission wished to stress the communitarian aspect, although not in such a way that diversity of opinion is brought to an end."[26] It is important to note this statement, because as it now stands, the text could be taken as supporting the opinion of Xiberta's opponents, who do not of course deny reconciliation with the Church, but see it merely as a consequence of reconciliation with God or as a parallel effect. However, those responsible for drafting the text specifically state that they did not wish to resolve the debate and define the relationship between the pardon obtained from God's mercy and reconciliation with the Church. They were satisfied with a simple juxtaposition.

Lastly, during the 113th General Congregation (on 30 October 1964), a final revision appeared. This time the aim was not to modify the text, but simply to fill it out with two additions, the intention of which was that of showing why the sacrament of penance was a twofold effect of pardon granted by God and recon-ciliation with the Church. The reason springs from the actual nature of sin, which has a twofold theological and ecclesial dimen-sion, inasmuch as it is an "offense" against God and a "wound" to the Church.[27] These additions were accepted without difficulty,[28] so that the definitive text could thus be produced:

> Those who approach the sacrament of Penance obtain pardon from God's mercy for the offense committed against him, and are, at the same time, reconciled with the Church which they have wounded by their sins and which by charity, by example and by prayer labors for their conversion (*LG* 11).

The final statement indicates that the Church acts not only through the administration of the sacramental rite, but also through the use of other means (prayer, example, charity) that aim at bringing about the conversion of sinners, whose penance forms the sacrament. In this perspective, there is no member of the community who does not have a role to play in helping his or her neighbor.

The very term "reconciliation" suggests that there is a situation or disunion or a type of rupture, if not of actual enmity, between the sinful Christian and the Church. The doctrine later formu-lated by the Council on membership of the Church can throw light on this question. Among the elements that constitute *full* incorporation into this *society* of the Church, the Council lists not only overall acceptance of its structure and all the means of salva-tion instituted in it, but also the interior possession of the "Spirit of Christ" (*LG* 14). This expression most probably means the possession of the divine life of grace and the theological virtue of charity, as directly opposed to serious or mortal sin. This in turn means that sinners who have lost this life are no longer fully incorporated into the Church, although they still belong to it.[29]

They remain in the bosom of the Church "in body" but not "in heart," as the Council explains, citing Saint Augustine (*De baptismo contra Donatistas* V, 28, 39). Serious sin, therefore, alters the sinner's relationship to the Church, although it does not completely cancel his membership. Through sin, the sinner has inwardly withdrawn from living union with the Church, and from this point of view he or she has set up an invisible but real internal condition of separation between himself or herself and the Church. Now this separation from the Church as spiritual community is bound to entail a corresponding loss of full communion with the Church in its visible and institutional aspect as an established and organized society, precisely because of the intrinsic unity between the invisible and visible aspects in the Church, which is referred to by the Council in a previous paragraph (*LG* 8). And it is this loss of communion that explains the need for external and sacramental reconciliation.[30]

Viewed within the context of the doctrine of the sacramentality of the Church—one of the most outstanding elements of the teaching of the Constitution *Lumen gentium*—the question of reconciliation with the Church takes on a very special significance. If the Church, which is the body of Christ, is "in the nature of sacrament, a sign and instrument, that is, of communion with God" (*LG* 1), "the universal sacrament of salvation" (*LG* 48), it is difficult to see how it is possible to stop at juxtaposing the reentry of the penitent sinner into grace with God and reconciliation with the Church without developing the two elements. It would surely be logical to deduce that this reconciliation with the Church plays a primordial role in the reentry of the penitent sinner into grace with God, of which such reconciliation would be the sign, the means, the guarantee, the requirement and the disposing cause (in other words, the *res-et-sacramentum*). However, the Council preferred not to draw this conclusion in express terms, and we must therefore be careful not to make it say what it did not in fact say. Even so, there is nothing to prevent us from going beyond the actual letter of the text if we have good reason to do so.

Sinners obviously harm themselves above all, but we still have to understand better why their sin means that they harm the Church, inflicting a "wound" on it (*LG* 11). In order to stay within the conceptual framework of the Constitution *Lumen gentium,* we can answer this question by referring to the already mentioned idea of the sacramentality of the Church. It can be said that the sinful Christian wounds the Church in its effective existence as sign and instrument of salvation.

The sinner wounds it in its existence as sign by making this sign less meaningful because when he or she no longer has the Spirit of Christ, or grace, he or she is no longer the living sign of this divine grace to which, as a member of the Church, he or she has the mission of bearing witness in the world. The witness of the Church is dimmed through sin.

By wilfully remaining in his or her condition of sinfulness, the sinful Christian also wounds the Church in its existence as instrument of salvation by setting himself or herself against the grace that flows from the Church and that the Church has the task of effectively communicating. He or she becomes an obstacle to this dynamic process of sanctification, to some extent nullifying it in his or her own person, and thus preventing it from spreading outwards, and limiting its action in the world so far as this depends on him or her.

When we come to consider things from the viewpoint of the *res* or final effect to which the sacramentality of the Church is ordered—which consists of the salvation of men and women through sanctification—it will be seen that the sinful Christian is like a dead branch still attached to the trunk of the Church but no longer drawing nourishment from the sap. Indeed, it is the tree that will find its life-force weakened. Now the life-force of the people of God is indivisible from its real and effective holiness, and the presence of the sinful Christian within the bosom of the people of God reduces the holiness of the Church, lowering its level.

The term "reconciliation" recurs later in the Constitution *Lumen gentium* in connection with priests and their sacred function: "And on behalf of the faithful who are moved to sorrow or are stricken with sickness they exercise in an eminent degree a ministry of reconciliation and comfort" (*LG* 28). In this text, "reconciliation" means the sacrament itself and not simply its effect. The word became popular in the wake of Vatican II, and today it is normal to speak of the "sacrament of reconciliation." This is due not only to the Council, but more probably to the new *Rite of Penance,* which couples the term "penance," which is found in the actual title of the rite, with that of "reconciliation," which is found in the titles of various chapters. The name of a sacrament is of some importance, and overemphasis on "reconciliation," understood as the action of God who pardons and of the Church that mediates this pardon by means of its own pardon, entails a risk of forgetting that the aim of the sacrament is that of sacramentalizing the actions of the penitent and his or her conversion, and that fundamentally it is therefore "penance," without which there could be no "reconciliation."

However, the real problem is that at first glance this name is ill-suited to the sacrament when venial sins are concerned, and especially when the sacrament is repeated frequently. The more natural word to use here should be "purification," inasmuch as the Christian who sins venially is not separated from the intimate life of the Church and does not lose full communion with it, unlike the case of the person who sins mortally. Even so, it is still valid to speak of reconciliation, although in a decidedly analogical way. We can say that insofar as the Christian consciously resists the divine principle of the life of the Church, which is love, and hampers the free and full unfolding of this love without himself or herself, he or she is in a way opposing the Church, and allowing a gap to be created between himself or herself and the fullness of ecclesial life—a gap that is secret, although not without a certain repercussion on his or her visible membership of the Church because of the intrinsic unity between the invisible and visible aspects in the Church. This life will no longer shine forth in him or her—or at least not to the extent it should. The Church can certainly grant its pardon, its peace, and a certain form of reconciliation with itself to a Christian in such a condition, who has moved away from it through his or her own fault. And, if we consider that reconciliation with the Church is the *res-et-sacramentum* or intermediate effect of the sacrament of penance, we are entitled to say that by means of such reconciliation, the person will acquire—not of course a new and radical participation in the Spirit of the Church, who is the Spirit of Christ, the Holy Spirit, and whom he or she has not lost through venial sin—but a deeper participation in this Spirit, an increase in habitual grace, an awakening of active charity, the fervor of which is remissive of venial sin, and as a consequence God's pardon. Even though the sacramental process of penance applies only very analogically in the case of venial sin, there is still the immediate significance of this process, or its ecclesial dimension.[31]

The Church with which sinners are reconciled, and which helps bring about their conversion by its example, prayer, and charity, is presented in another equally well-known text as itself doing penance (*LG* 8). There is a clear paradox here. On the one hand, the Church is involved in the penance of the sinner only inasmuch as it carries out a mission of conversion and a ministry of reconciliation, while on the other, it is itself the subject of penance. In this text, which incidentally precedes that on the ecclesial dimension of the conversion and reconciliation of the sinner, the Constitution *Lumen gentium* discusses the holiness of the Church. Although it is a true holiness, it must not be seen as identical with that of Christ, who,

> . . . "holy, innocent and undefiled" (Heb. 7:26), knew nothing of sin (2 Cor. 5:21) but came only to expiate the sins of the people (Heb 2:17). The Church, however, clasping sinners to her bosom, at once holy and always in need of purification, follows constantly the path of penance and renewal (*LG* 8).

The first draft of this text spoke of the Church as a "congregation of the righteous." In the course of the Thirty-Seventh General Congregation (20 October 1963), the Conference of German-language Bishops and the Conference of Scandinavian Bishops proposed that this expression, although traditional, should be replaced with "at once holy and sinful."[32] However, this suggestion was accepted only after the word "sinful" had been changed to "always in need of purification," in order to avoid saying that the Church is sinful.

However, is this Church that does penance the same Church as the one that reconciles sinners? We are not concerned here with the classic problem of how the Church can be both holy and full of sinners, but rather with explaining how a Church that does penance because it is in constant need of purification and renewal can at the same time reconcile sinners with itself and work toward their conversion with its example, prayer, and charity. Is it because sin and holiness do not have equal power in the

Church, so that the holiness of the Church will finally prevail, and thus enjoys a sort of precedence over its state of sin? Although it is sinful, and despite its state of sin, the Church would therefore be able to come to the assistance of sinners through its holiness. On the other hand, would it not be more logical to admit that the concept of the Church is not a univocal one? When we refer to the Church, we can mean the community of Christians as a whole, members and heads. It is the people of the New Testament, on pilgrimage through history, which has its roots in the people of the Old Testament, and which is as sinful as the latter was because it is made up of men. There is nobody in the Church, apart from the Most Blessed Virgin Mary, who does not "strive to conquer sin and increase in holiness" (LG 65). However, not all people are sinners to the same extent. The concept of sin is analogical, and not all are on the same level. There are those who have lost the life of grace, and those whose venial faults mean that they resist the influence of this life or neglect it, although this does not mean that they are no longer righteous in the theological sense of the term. Even outstanding saints are not exempt from certain imperfections. However, this view of the Church, which we can call "sociologico-religious" and which sees the Church merely as the congregation of the faithful, only provides us with an incomplete and maybe very inaccurate idea of the Church. Emphasis on the Church as the people of God should not make us lose sight of the true essence of the Church.

If we no longer consider the Church from the empirical point of view as a collectivity, but from an ontological point of view as mystery and sacrament and in its constitutive relationship with Christ and the Spirit, it is properly and by definition "the society set up by Christ and vivified by his Spirit, with the precise aim of fighting and conquering sin."[33] Even so, it does not present itself to the faithful as an abstract and disincarnated entity that would exist even apart from its members. However, although it does indeed encompass the latter, it is much more than their sum: it is the kingdom of God and of his grace as already present among us. Insofar as its members commit serious sin and lose the Spirit of Christ, they are separated from it and are no longer in full communion with it, and if they sin venially, they still tend to put a certain distance between themselves and it. Sin has an absolutely antiecclesial character. It is a break with the Church, or at least a movement away from it. Hence, any sinfulness there may be in us does not belong to the Church taken in its deep and most authentic being. It is the mission of the Church to fight against sin, not only in the world, but in its own members, and to be the sacrament of reconciliation with God for them.

It is interesting to see that the Constitution *Lumen gentium* moves from the mystery of the Church (Chapter I) to the people of God (Chapter II). As mystery, the Church is already "the seed and the beginning" of the kingdom of God on earth (*LG* 5). It is the mystical body of Christ, who constitutes it for himself through the communication of his Spirit to his brethren, "who are called together from every nation" (*LG* 7). It is this Church, "our mother," who "exhorts her children to purification and renewal so that the sign of Christ may shine more brightly over the face of the Church" (*LG* 15). Here the Church is no longer presented as herself doing penance, but as exhorting her children to do so.

The difficulty is that we are dealing with texts coming from different theological backgrounds, and because they are only brief statements or passing references, the Constitution *Lumen gentium* did not take the trouble to show how they were to be harmonized. At all events, we must be careful not to be selective and unilateral in our reading and interpretation.

If we now consider the other documents of the Council, we shall see that the Decree on the Ministry and Life of Priests, *Presbyterorum ordinis,* is the one containing proportionally the most references to penance as a sacrament. Speaking of priests as ministers of the sacraments, the Decree states: "By Baptism priests introduce men into the People of God; by the sacrament of Penance they reconcile sinners with God and the Church" (*PO* 5). This is clearly an echo of *Lumen gentium,* which introduced the original formulation of a twofold reconciliation with God and with the Church. However, in *Lumen gentium,* it is the faithful, in virtue of their common priesthood, who beseech God's pardon and are reconciled with the Church, whereas in *Presbyterorum ordinis,* it is the priests who exercise their ministerial priesthood in reconciling sinners.

They are told that they should be very willing and approachable in the exercise of this ministry:

. . . they are united with the intention and the charity of Christ when they administer the sacraments. They do this in a special way when they show themselves to be always available to administer the sacrament of Penance whenever it is reasonably requested by the faithful (*PO* 13).

Their duty is not limited simply to administering it, but also includes training the faithful to receive it:

In the spirit of Christ the Pastor, they instruct them to submit their sins to the Church with a contrite heart in the sacrament of Penance, so that they may be daily more and more converted to the Lord (*PO* 5).

They themselves will be the first to receive the sacrament of penance:

The ministers of sacramental grace are intimately united to Christ the Savior and Pastor through the fruitful reception of Penance. If it is prepared for by a daily examination of conscience, it is a powerful incentive to the essential conversion of heart to the love of the Father of mercies (*PO* 18).

This is the only text in which the Council speaks of frequent confession, and the element that commends it is its spiritual usefulness.

The Decree *Christus Dominus* on the Pastoral Office of Bishops in the Church in turn stresses the usefulness of confession in general and says that parish priests should be available for it:

Parish priests must bear constantly in mind how much the sacrament of penance contributes to the development of the Christian life and should therefore be readily available for the hearing of the confessions of the faithful (*CD* 30).

According to the Decree on the Catholic Eastern Churches, *Orientalium Ecclesiarum*, penance, together with the Eucharist and the anointing of the sick, is a sacrament that Catholics may request from ministers of the separated Eastern Churches "as often as necessity or true spiritual benefit recommends such action, and access to a Catholic priest is physically or morally impossible," and that it can also be given to separated Eastern Christians "if they are rightly disposed and make such request of their own accord" (*OE* 27).

In the Decree on the Up-to-Date Renewal of Religious Life, *Perfectae caritatis,* the Council addresses religious superiors and says that they should allow those subject to them "due liberty with regard to the sacrament of penance and the direction of conscience" (*PC* 14). It is to be assumed that this freedom refers to the choice of confessor and the frequency of confession. And this would apply in a similar way to all members of the faithful.

Apart from the above, in various documents, the Council makes penance, considered now as a virtue, one of the supernatural means attributed with an apostolic and missionary effectiveness. Thus, through their works of penance or mortification, the righteous can contribute to the spiritual welfare of their neighbor. Such works are of benefit not only to themselves, but also to others, and especially if they are offered to God with a specific intention. The idea appears more than once, and in this regard, a number of texts are worth citing, in view of the fact that they are little known and represent a certain aspect of spirituality adopted by the Council.

In the Decree on the Ministry and Life of Priests, *Presbyterorum ordinis,* the Council states: ". . . the ecclesial community exercises a truly motherly function in leading souls to Christ by its charity, its prayer, its example and its penitential works" (*PO* 6). In its chapter devoted to the different types of apostolate, the Decree on the Apostolate of the Laity, *Apostolicam actuositatem,* states:

> All should remember that by public worship and by prayer, by penance and the willing acceptance of the toil and hardships of life by which they resemble the suffering Christ (cf. 2 Cor. 4:10; Col. 1:24), they can reach all men and contribute to the salvation of the entire world (*AA* 16).

For its part, the Decree on the Missionary Activity of the Church, *Ad gentes,* teaches us that the whole people of God must cooperate in the missionary apostolate: "From this renewed spirit prayers and works of penance will be spontaneously offered to God that by his grace he might make fruitful the work of missionaries" (*AG* 36). The apostolate of penance and prayer will be the special concern of those who suffer: "It is the task of the bishop to raise up among his people, especially among those who are sick or afflicted, souls who with a generous heart will offer prayers and works of penance to God . . ." (AG 38). However, institutes of contemplative life also have a similar duty: "Institutes of the contemplative life, by their prayers, penances and trials, are of the greatest importance in the conversion of souls" (AG 40). And the Decree on the Up-to-date Renewal of Religious Life, *Perfectae caritatis*, says that in the "constant prayer and willing penance" of their members, who "give themselves over to God alone," these same institutes have "a hidden apostolic fruitfulness" (PC 7). Further, according to the Decree on the Pastoral Office of Bishops in the Church, *Christus Dominus*, all religious have the duty of working for the building and growth of the whole mystical body and for the good of local churches, and they will "promote these objectives primarily by means of prayer, works of penance, and by the example of their own lives. The sacred Synod earnestly exhorts them to develop an ever-increasing esteem and zeal for these practices" (CD 33). Lastly, with a view to fostering vocations to the priesthood, in the Decree on the Training of Priests, *Optatum totius*, "The Council, first of all, recommends the traditional aids towards this general cooperation, such as: unceasing prayer [and] Christian penance . . . " (OT 2).

There is nothing particularly new in all this, and the Council itself speaks of "traditional means." Even so, it is certainly worth noting the fact that it emphasizes these means of prayer and penance particularly in function of the concepts of apostolate and mission.

In conclusion, if we try to pinpoint the most striking keynote of the texts considered, it would most probably appear to be the concern of the Council to highlight the social aspect of sin and the sacrament of penance.

This concern then reappears in various postconciliar documents of the papal magisterium. In the Apostolic Constitution *Indulgentiarum doctrina* (1 January 1967) on the Revision of Indulgences, Paul VI explains that "a supernatural solidarity reigns among men, with the consequence that the sin of one person harms other people, just as one person's holiness helps others."[34] In the Apostolic Constitution (18 February 1966) on the Penitential Discipline of the Church, *Paenitemini*, which aims at the introduction of new legislation on fasting and abstinence, the Church is seen as a penitent community, whose penance means not only participation in Christ's work of expiation, but also continual conversion and renewal—"a renewal which must be implemented not only interiorly and individually but also externally and socially"—and also the practice of mortification, which shows people "the right way to use earthly goods."[35] The Apostolic Exhortation (8 December 1973) on Reconciliation within the Church, *Paterna cum benevolentia,* offers a complementary point of view: the Church, "established by Christ as a permanent sign of the reconciliation accomplished by him in accordance with the will of the Father," is a community of "reconciled people" and also by its nature a "reconciling" community.[36]

These themes are taken up by John Paul II in his postsynodal Apostolic Exhortation (2 December 1984) on Reconciliation and Penance in the Mission of the Church Today, *Reconciliatio et paenitentia,* which speaks of the inevitable social repercussions of any sin, even the most personal and secret, for the community of the Church and the whole human family, in virtue of a solidarity that is not only mysterious and imperceptible, but also real and concrete, and is a sort of communion of saints in reverse, so that "one can speak of a communion of sin, whereby a soul that lowers itself through sin drags down with itself the Church and, in some way, the whole world."[37] In order to act as reconciler and thus to fulfill its mission, the Church "must begin by being a reconciled Church," and "is called upon to give an example of reconciliation particularly within herself."[38] The passage is of course concerned with the tensions and divisions that wound the Church from within. However, it also shows the close link between the mission of the Church and its duty of internal purification as people of God.

However, it is to be regretted that the actual idea of the reconciliation of the sinful Christian with the Church has in fact received so little explicit echo either in theology or in official postconciliar documents. This concept was almost totally absent from the 1938 Synod on Penance and from the Apostolic Exhortation that followed it. We should consider whether what we have here is maybe a truth that is once more on its way to being forgotten.

Translated from the French by Leslie Wearne.

Notes

1. AS, I/I, 283.

2. Intervention of the Auxiliary Bishop of Lyons, M. Maziers, AS, I/II, 174–175.

3. AS, I/I, 285. In the schema, what eventually became number 72 was numbered 56.

4. AS, I/II, 164 (Cardinal M. Browne); 180 (M.A. de Carvalho, Bishop of Angra in the Azores); 343 (W. Godfrey, Archbishop of Westminster); 348 (V. Brizgys, Coadjutor Bishop of Kaunas in Lithuania); 380 (A. Sépinski, Minister General O.F.M.).

5. AS, II/II, 558–559.

6. AS, I/II, 168, 178, 320, 346.

7. AS, I/II, 170, 358, 364.

8. AS, I/II, 174 (M. Maziers, Auxiliary Bishop of Lyons).

9. AS, I/II, 188 (A. Barbero, Bishop of Vigevano in Italy).

10. AS, I/II, 178 (T. Botero Salazar, Archbishop of Medellin).

11. AS, I/II, 362 (A. Fares, Archbishop of Catanzaro in Italy).

12. This was asked by two abbots general of monastic congregations: AS, I/II, 377 (J. Prou, O.S.B., Solesmes); 380 (G. Sortais, O.C.R.).

13. Archbishop Paul Hinan of Atlanta, AS, II/II, 567: "Plures Patres petierunt ut recognitio ritus Sacramenti Poenitentiae eius naturam praesertim socialem et ecclesialem clarius exprimat. Commissio censuit hanc emendationem recipiendam esse per insertionem verborum 'naturem et' ante verbum 'effectum.' " Who are these *plures Patres*? They cannot be the two abbots general of the previous note, since they do not mention this aspect of the sacrament of penance. They are thus at least the two bishops of notes 8 and 9.

14. A. Bugnini, *La Riforma liturgica* (Rome, 1983), 646–664.

15. K. Rahner, "Reconciliantur cum Ecclesia," in *Populus Dei. Studi in onore del Card. A. Ottoviani*, 2 (Rome, 1969), 1087.

16. Ed. L.C. Mohlbert (Rome, 1960), No. 363.

17. St. Cyprian, *Epist.* 57, 4, 2 (ed. Bayard, p. 157); St. Augustine, *De baptismo contra Donatistas*, III, 18, 23, in *PL*, 23, 150.

18. St. Bonaventure, *In IV Sent.*, d. 16, dub. 12 (Quaracchi, 1889, p. 401); d. 17, p. 3, a. 3, q. 2 (p. 460); St. Albert the Great, *De Eucharistia*, p. 2, q. 1, in Aschendorff (ed.), *Opera omnia*, 26 (Münster, 1958), 65; St. Thomas Aquinas, *In IV Sent.*, d. 17, q. 3, a. 3, q. 5, ad 3; *Suppl.*, q. 8, a. 2, ad 3; *Super Iam Epist. ad. Cor.*, XI, lect. 7, in R. Cai (ed.) (Turin, 1953), n. 690, p. 364; Richard of Mediavalle, *In IV Sent.*, d. 9, a. 2, q. 2 (Brescia, 1591), 111; Duns Scotus, *Opus Oxoniense*, IV, d. 9, q. unica, in *Opera omnia*, 17 (Paris, 1894), 119; Gabriel Biel,

Canonis Missae Expositio, lect. VIII, ed. Oberman-Courtenay, 1 (Weisbaden, 1963), 34.

19. F. Suarez, *De Sacramento Eucharistiae*, q. 80, disp. 6, sect. 3, n. 7, in *Opera omnia*, 21 (Paris, 1861), 468; J. de Lugo, *De Sacramento Eucharistiae*, disp. 14, sect. 4, n. 66, in *Disputationes*, 4 (Paris, 1868), 86.

20. *Clavis Ecclesiae. De ordine absolutionis sacramentalis ad reconciliationem cum Ecclesia* (Rome, 1922), 11.

21. For bibliography, see P. Adnès, "Pénitence," *Dictionnaire de Spiritualité*, 12, 994–995.

22. AS, II/I, 258–259.

23. Thus, Cardinal de Barros Camara, Archbishop of Rio de Janeiro, and ninety-one Brazilian bishops (*AS*, II/III, 55), and Bishop Joseph Schröffer of Eichstadt in Germany and sixty-nine German-language Fathers (*AS*, II/III, 17).

24. AS, II/I, 326; cf. II/III, 408.

25. AS, III/I, 184–185.

26. AS, III/I, 197.

27. AS, III/VI, 96.

28. AS, III/VI, 103–105.

29. This interpretation is supported by the statement made by the commission to justify the addition of the possession of the Spirit of Christ to the original schema: "Quia peccatores Ecclesiae non plene incorporantur, etsi ad Ecclesiam pertinent, Commissio statuit adiungere secundum Rom. 8, 9: 'Spiritum Christi habentes' " (*AS*, III/I, 203).

30. F. Coccopalmiero, "Sacramento della penitenza e comunione con la Chiesa," *Communio*, 40 (July–August 1978), 54–64; *id.*, "Quid significent verba 'Spiritum Christi habentes.' *Lumen Gentium* 14, 2," *Periodica*, 68 (1979), 253–276.

31. K. Rahner, "Vom Sinne der häufigen Andachtsbeichte," in *Schriften zur Theologie*, 3 (Einsiedeln, 1959³), 211–225; English translation, "The Meaning of Frequent Confession," in *Theological Investigations*, 3 (London, 1974), 177–190.

32. AS, II/I, 294.

33. Monsignor Philips, *L'Eglise et son mystère au II° concile du Vatican*, 1 (Paris, 1968), 125.

34. II, 1, in *AAS*, 59 (1967), 9; English translation in Flannery (gen. ed.), *Vatican Council II*, 65.

35. Intro., in *AAS*, 58 (1966), 177–178; English translation in Flannery (gen. ed.), *Vatican II: More Postconciliar Documents*, 1.

36. AAS, 67 (1975); English translation, *L'Osservatore Romano* (English edition) (26 December 1974), 1–2.

37. II, I, 16, in *AAS*, 77 (1985), 214–215; English translation by the Vatican Polyglot Press (London, 1984), 51.

38. I, II, 9, in *AAS*, 77 (1985), 202–203; English translation, 31.

CHAPTER 26

Sacrifice

François Bourassa, S.J.

Summary

This article discusses, without attempting to be exhaustive, the theology of sacrifice. Within such limitation, it examines the teaching of the Council relative to sacrifice, including reference to the debates that took place just prior to it and analysis of the conclusions reached in the conciliar documents; analyzes sacrifice systematically and in depth as structure of the religious relationship for the purpose of responding to the fundamental problem of how to reconcile the need for sacrifice with the transcendency of divine love; and demonstrates how "true sacrifice" is reached, through a series of propositions that contain the fundamental teaching of the Church. The article concludes with a brief review of the subject discussed, which is intended also to be helpful in individual reflection on the theme and to encourage participation with one's own life in the one sacrifice of Christ "in Spirit and in Truth."

Introduction

At the beginning of Vatican Council II, a great number of questions on the agenda regarding the theology of sacrifice were being studied and discussed. These questions involved the *Eucharist* as sacrifice, the sacrifice of *the cross*, and, ultimately, the fundamental question as to the meaning and very *nature of sacrifice* as structure of the religious relationship.

The Council responded to these questions by emphasizing that the sacrifice that Christ offered up by dying on the cross for the salvation of the world is always present in his Church in the eucharistic sacrifice: "Christ loved the Church and gave himself up for her—a fragrant offering and sacrifice—that he might sanctify her" (Eph. 5:2, 25, 26).

Nevertheless, certain questions regarding the nature of sacrifice that were raised prior to the Council remained unresolved. Within the limitations of this article, we shall examine the Council teaching on sacrifice, discuss the problems still unresolved, and, proceeding from the clear teaching of the Council and the conclusions flowing from the debates, attempt to provide a new focus on the basic questions.

The Teaching of the Council

The doctrine of Vatican II on sacrifice has its natural context, so to speak, in the Constitutions *Sacrosanctum concilium,* on the liturgy, and *Lumen gentium,* on the mystery of the Church.[1] These make manifest that the Church was born, exists, and lives in the sacrifice of Christ Redeemer.[2]

This teaching of the Council on sacrifice may be articulated around three basic truths.

The first is concerned with the sacrifice of the cross. Christ actualized the eternal design of the Father by bringing all persons into friendship with the living God. He performed this work by his whole life, culminating it with *death on the cross.* This offering to the Father is the sacrifice of his consecrated life from its beginning to its unique concluding act.

The second regards the Eucharist. To complete his divine work, Christ instituted the *Eucharist* and entrusted it to his Church so that he might be present to all persons in his unique sacrifice "until he comes."

The third involves the essence of sacrifice. God's design is realized in the Church and in the Eucharist in such a way that through each of them he has given all members of the Christian community and each member individually the power to offer themselves to God in union with Christ.[3] This teaching necessarily implies an idea and a theology of *sacrifice* that explains the *nature* of this religious relationship as willed and established by God in Christ.

The Sacrifice of the Cross

In speaking of the sacrifice of the cross, the documents of the Council repeat the traditional teaching of the Church in the numerous declarations that have been made on the eucharistic sacrifice.

"As often as the sacrifice of the cross by which 'Christ our Pasch is sacrificed' (1 Cor. 5:7) is celebrated on the altar, the work of our redemption is carried out" (LG 3; SC 2).

Priests, as ministers of the sacred mysteries, "act in a special way in the person of Christ, who gave himself as a victim to sanctify men . . . *as they celebrate the mystery of the Lord's death*" (PO 13).

The decree on ecumenism recalls that God's design was accomplished in the sacrifice of Christ, who "before offering himself up as a spotless victim upon the altar of the cross, prayed to his Father for those who believe, saying 'that all may be one, as you, Father, one in me and I in you; I pray that they may be one in us' " (UR 2).

This doctrine reveals to us the internal unity in God, who manifests himself in the sacrificial death of Christ. This sacrifice is not an accessory property of his human condition, but an exigency of his divine nature, of the life and unity of God in love:

> The glory that you have given me I have given to them, that they may be one even as we are one . . . so that the world may know . . . that you have loved them even as you have loved me . . . that the love with which you have loved me may be in them, and I in them (Jn. 17:22–26).

Recalling the unique role of Mary, who embodies the love of the whole Church for Christ, the Council declares that "Mary . . . committing herself wholeheartedly and impeded by no sin to God's saving will, devoted herself totally, as a handmaid of the Lord, to the person and work of her Son . . . presented him to the Lord in the temple. . . ." And having preserved this consecration through all her life, "she faithfully persevered in her union with her Son unto the cross, where she stood, in keeping with the divine plan (Jn. 19:25), enduring with her only begotten Son the intensity of his suffering, associating herself in his sacrifice with a mother's heart, and lovingly consenting to the immolation of the victim, which was born of her . . . " (LG 56–58).

The Eucharistic Sacrifice

Vatican II concerned itself with the eucharistic sacrifice chiefly in the Constitution on the Sacred Liturgy and the Decree on the Ministry and Life of Priests. It also dealt with this subject in an incidental way in various other documents.[4]

To have a more precise idea of the question the Council faced, it is convenient to recall that the fundamental problems regarding sacrifice were chiefly raised after the Reformation in the seventeenth century, and that they revolved around the relationship between the sacrifice of the cross and the Eucharist. The discussion began among reform theologians, but it quickly engendered various efforts of posttridentine theology in the Catholic Church regarding the sacrificial character of the eucharistic celebration.

In this way, ideas advanced prior to the Council, and which were being debated in the period just before it, received wide consensus on the following three main points.

1. *The Unicity of Christ's Sacrifice.* There is one single sacrifice of Christ, which is of infinite value, and which culminates in his offering of himself and his immolation on the cross once and for all. In this one oblation, we have all been sanctified.[5]
2. *The Specifically "Sacramental" Character of the Eucharistic Sacrifice as Representation of the One Sacrifice of Christ on the Cross.* The Eucharist does not add another sacrifice; it is one and the same sacrifice offered on the cross and made present[6] on the altar in the celebration of the eucharistic supper.
3. *The Participation of Christians in this Sacrifice.* Christians participate actively in the eucharistic sacrifice, the source and summit of the Christian life, by offering the divine Victim to God and themselves along with it (LG 11).

Regarding the unicity of the sacrifice of Christ, the following comments are pertinent.

In the *Eucharist*, Christ actualizes the *sacrifice of the cross*, while for its part, the *Church* finds in this admirable mystery its plenitude, offering itself as a sacrifice in and through the *one sacrifice of Jesus Christ.*[7] (Here the theology of the mystical body is directly implied, and this in turn involves ecclesiology and christology.) The Church lives solely by this grace of the Redemption won by Christ through his sacrifice. Reciprocally, Christ desired from all eternity to obtain the fulfillment of his mission "in his body which is the Church."

His offering of himself on the cross is his personal "realization" and his "sanctification" in the "perfecting of his work," which is the work of the Father.[8]

In his death, Christ reached the fullness of his love for the Father and for the Church: "Christ loved the Church and *gave (paredôken)* himself up for her that he might sanctify her . . . with the Word" (Eph. 5:25–26): "for their sake I consecrate myself that they also may be consecrated in truth" (Jn. 17:19).

The Eucharist, therefore, will be the *one sacrifice* of Christ on the cross if his body and blood, made present under the appearances of bread and wine,[9] constitute the *one victim.*

As to the Eucharist–Christ relationship, the Council expressed the relationship between the Eucharist and the cross in the one sacrifice of Christ in this way: the Mass is a *sacramental sacrifice*[10]—in the sense of the dogmatic definition of the sacraments of the New Law (DS 1600–1612)—which, under the symbols of ritual celebration, "represent" and "make present" the one sacrifice of Christ in order to perpetuate it in the Church. The Church in turn offers it to Christians so that they may be intimately associated with the mystery of Christ's love in his death and resurrection.

The strictly sacrificial action is accomplished *in the consecration* of the bread and wine into the body and blood of the Lord; his body offered up for the life of the world, his blood shed for all for the remission of sin. This is accomplished when the priest, in virtue of the power given to the apostles by Christ, reproduces, "makes present," through the same gestures and words, the same action of Christ. For this reason, the eucharistic celebration has the same efficacy as the sacrifice of the cross.[11]

The Eucharist, which perpetuates the sacrifice of Christ, requires that there be in it the *same victim* as that of the cross, the *same priest* (DS 1739–1741, 1743), exactly as he himself desired to celebrate it in the last supper.

This is a sacrifice that is made present in virtue of Christ's word now pronounced by the priest, whom he has made a participant in his priestly function.[12]

As to *the participation of Christians in this sacrifice*, the following comments may be made.

Christians, who are members of Christ's body, participate in this sacrifice, which is the "source and summit of the Christian life," and they themselves are the ones who offer the divine victim and themselves with the victim (*LG* 11), through the ministry of the priest (*PO* 2), giving testimony of Christ's sacrifice to the whole world (*AG* 15).

The priest places their lives on the altar, making them "spiritual victims" in Christ and asking God "to fashion us for himself 'as an eternal gift' " (*SC* 12).

From this sacrifice, he receives grace and strength (*SC* 48) to collaborate with God's design by actualizing his work in the world and by expressing with every word and action the true nature of the Church (*SC* 2). This Mass unites him to all Christians in one single body (*LG* 50; *SC* 2) and makes him grow day by day through Christ in the holiness of God (*SC* 48).

Other statements emphasize still more the unicity of the sacrifice. In the Eucharist, a twofold act of consecration is performed: the Church offers up and it offers itself up through the ministry of the priest acting in the name of Christ. The eucharistic sacrifice entails *communion* as an integral component, but this is not a constituent element of the sacrificial act.[13]

The Nature of the Sacrifice

In places in the conciliar documents where the Eucharist is discussed, there is indirect mention of the elements that constitute the nature of sacrifice as an essential form in religion.

When studying these elements, it becomes clear that the significance and the very nature of sacrifice as a fundamental form of the religious relationship has received its real meaning from the sacrifice of Christ. The Council affirms this radically genuine meaning in upholding the unicity of Christ's sacrifice: "it is the unique sacrifice of the New Testament," which replaces all the sacrifices of the old law. Accordingly, there is no need for any other; Christ has performed this one once and for all on the cross in offering himself to the Father as a spotless victim.[14]

For this reason, our study of the conciliar documents must begin with the sacrifice of Christ before delving further into the questions raised.

In order to effect our salvation, Christ *"offered himself on the cross"*[15] as a sacrifice pleasing to the Father. He is the only mediator (Heb. 9:15) between God and men,[16] the High Priest who offers himself up personally in the passion.[17] He is at the same time priest and victim, the "divine victim."[18]

The cause of this indescribable and unique act was love. Such an abasement can be explained in no other way: infinite love for the Father and love for humanity, a sacrifice undergone in obedience,[19] unutterable pain in order to redeem us and to unite us as one single people. The consequence of this marvelous work is that *"the whole redeemed city,* that is, the whole assembly and community of the saints, should be offered as a universal sacrifice to God through the High Priest who offered himself in the passion for us that we might be the body of so great a head."[20]

And so that we might participate in his sacrifice in its eternal fruits, "he instituted the eucharistic sacrifice of his Body and Blood to *perpetuate the sacrifice of the cross* throughout the ages until he should come again."[21]

Thus, the Council reveals to us the true meaning and very nature of sacrifice as the form of the religious relationship. Because of this illumination, we are able to discover its essential properties, which will now be examined.

Sacrifice is in the first place an offering to God (LG 11), an offering of something belonging to man that puts him in contact and in friendly dialogue with his creator in a loving relationship that brings man to offer himself, to make of himself a living sacrifice (PO 2). This relational form is developed chiefly in an environment of worship (LG 50), which for the Christian is in the Eucharist (SC 2), where it acquires a sacramental dimension.

Sacrifice also possesses a spiritual aspect (SC 12) in virtue of which the faithful unite themselves to the sacrifice offered by the priest (PO 2), an offering that unites all the baptized among themselves (LG 50), builds the community, and strengthens each of its members (SC 48).

True sacrifice is that which is performed "in Spirit and in

Truth," only thus is it a sublime medium of union with the Father and with one's neighbor. In working our redemption, it invites us to bring the sacrifice of Christ to all men, and it showers abundant graces on the whole community so that it may live in charity and be inflamed with apostolic zeal (*AD* 15).

Other Points Regarding Sacrifice
Commented Upon by the Council

Taken as a whole, the conciliar documents gave enormous importance to the *work of the Holy Spirit* in the Church as the supreme gift of Christ's love. On this most important point, the liturgical reform desired by the Council reconstructed the epiclesis of the Holy Spirit, especially with regard to the eucharistic sacrifice.

The Council also insists on the liturgy "as the means through which 'the work of our redemption is accomplished'[22] especially in the divine *sacrifice of the Eucharist*" (SC 2).

On the widely disputed question regarding *oblation and immolation* in sacrifice, the documents as a whole, following a long tradition, practically identify immolation and oblation by declaring that there is immolation and oblation at the same time both in the Eucharist and on the cross.

Nevertheless, a certain distinction between the two may be perceived. In the sacrificial ritual of the Old Testament, while many rites may signify oblation, only ritual death is properly immolation. This is, however, ultimately included as a form of oblation. Thus, in dying on the Cross, Christ freely immolated himself to the Father.

Immolation may also be understood in the metaphorical or mystical sense of offering up; the giving up of one's own life to God in the faithful accomplishment of duty is in itself an immolation.

To dissipate certain ambiguous interpretations regarding the eucharistic sacrifice, we can also mention the distinction Pius XII made between ritual and sacramental immolation. The latter is an act of the priest alone, who acts in the place of Christ, who offers himself as priest in the sacrifice of himself. At the same time, the priest makes this offering in the name of the whole Church. Thus, Christ realizes his own immolation–oblation on the altar and through this places himself in the hands of the

Church, making it possible for it to enter into communion with the plenitude of his one sacrifice.[23]

Taken as a whole, these elements provide a first truth, namely, that of *the unicity of Christ's sacrifice* celebrated in the Eucharist, by which "we have been sanctified through the offering of the body of Christ once for all" (Heb. 10:10).

Sacrifice as Structure of the Religious Relationship

In the period before the Council, *the idea of sacrifice as the structure of the religious relationship* was questioned even among Christians. This was a tendency that developed chiefly as a consequence of ignoring the sacrificial aspect of the Redemption and of the Eucharist in expounding the Christian mystery.

The reason for this attitude is not necessarily irreligious; to the contrary, it is a religious sentiment that accounts for this silence, the idea of God and of a religious relationship appearing incompatible with the idea of honoring God and entering into a relationship with him through sacrifice.

Theological questioning was not long in coming, and it arose, to begin with, relative to sacrifice as a religious practice, chiefly in light of Christ's sacrifice. What is the purpose of celebrating a sacrifice? What is the nature of sacrifice as a religious relationship? What aspect of God does Christ's sacrifice reveal to us?

Objections of Concern to Theology

The objections that the theology of the Redemption is called upon to deal with in holding to the idea of sacrifice as essential are being raised currently for particular reasons that are in opposition to the idea of sacrifice as structure of the religious relationship. It is accordingly necessary for theology to correct certain erroneous concepts regarding sacrifice, which are the source of this opposition.

These objectives may be grouped in the three following categories:

1. *The Mythical Character of Sacrifice.* Sacrifice according to this theory is an archaic idea linked to a mythicizing mentality that is foreign to modern culture.
2. *Incompatibility of Sacrifice with God's Mercy.* This difficulty

arises when expiatory sacrifice is considered as placating God's anger. Can the God of life be pleased with death? Can God find satisfaction in the death of an innocent person?

3. *The Problem Related to the Transcendency and Purity of Charity.* The same question is raised in metaphysics and in transcendental ethics. God is *transcendent* and *agape* by his very being. No action of a creature can reach him, either to obtain his grace or to offend him. Sin cannot affect him; it is an evil that man inflicts on himself. *Agape is gratuitous love,* generous, *anterior* to any action of creatures. This question seems to ignore the fact that the relationship with God is before all else communion and *friendship,* [24] a relationship of love without limit and without measure. If one thinks that the difficulty is overcome by explaining the sacrifice as a simple intercessory prayer, one simply puts the problem aside without resolving it.

The Fundamental Explanation of Sacrifice

Regarding the first difficulty, it is necessary to recall the fundamental meaning of sacrifice. This involves *a forgotten truth.* All these objections rely in one way or another on a first truth that is the basis for the theology of sacrifice, that "true sacrifice" is founded on the transcendency of God and of his Agape; and if this be set aside, no conclusion can be drawn concerning incompatibility between sacrifice and "worship in Spirit and in truth."[25]

The theology of sacrifice is as old as revelation and systematic treatment of it is found in the most classic Christian theology. However, what is essential in this theology is the interpretation that revelation (Old Testament and New Testament) has furnished it with under God's own inspiration.

The Latin term *sacrificio* is, in accord with the biblical idea of sanctification, an interpretation and a theological synthesis of the ritual thus designated. In Hebrew, a distinction is made between the rite (*asham*) and the offering "for sin" (*hattah*), whereas the Greek of the Septuagint and the New Testament includes both rites under a common name, generally the term *thysia: prespherein thysian hyper amartiôn* (cf. Heb. 10:12). Therefore, the Latin translation continued a semantic evolution already developed in the internal logic of the inspired text.

As regards the meaning of the sacrificial rites, the Old Testament contains the interpretations of the levitical liturgy and of prophetic theology in a kind of dialectic (thesis, antithesis, synthesis).

On the one side, the prophets and psalmists denounce as worthless the rites adopted from the pagans, while on the other, the priestly tradition retains and codifies them religiously as having been instituted by Moses under the inspiration of God: Israel has been consecrated by Moses under the inspiration of God: Israel has been consecrated as a kingdom of priests dedicated to the worship of the living God (cf. Ex. 19:5–6).

The theology of the prophets, psalmists, and sages of Israel developed the basic truths about the religious relationship, the "true sacrifice": "Behold, to obey is better than sacrifice" (1 Sam. 15:22); "for I desire steadfast love and not sacrifice, the *knowledge of God* rather than burnt offerings" (Hos. 6:6). For God sacrifice is *contriteness of heart* (Ps. 51:19); "When he said . . . 'You have neither desired nor taken pleasure in sacrifices and offerings and burnt offerings' . . . he added, 'Lo, I have come to do your will' " (Heb. 10:5–10).

The theology of deutero-Isaiah furnishes a sublime expression in the figure of the servant of Yahweh, who although innocent fulfills God's plan by facing suffering and death and "offering his life" in expiation of the sins of the people. This teaching expresses the greatness of God's love and omnipotence, as well as the dignity of man, created in the image of God and recreated by him in a most praiseworthy manner.

Another essential element in the theology of the prophets is the concept of the rites, taken as a whole, being *an institution established by God himself* for the sake of his people in accordance with a process of *offering* and *acceptance*.

- *The sacrificial act* is God's work, since it has value in his sight only if it is *performed by his representative* (the priest) chosen, called, and consecrated by him.
- This action is not of a more or less mysterious nature, but is rather a *meeting between persons*: a person freely offers the sacrifice, which is accepted by God. Only in this way does the sacrifice have value.
- The effect of these rites is the *sanctification* not only of the victim offered but also of everything related to the worship (cf. Lev. 20:26).

The New Testament illuminates this theology of the prophets. In the eucharistic rite, Christians commemorate the death of Christ as the one sacrifice. The apostolic writings themselves announce that Christ is the fulfillment of the law and that his death and resurrection are the *true and only sacrifice*.

The words and acts of Jesus are the perfect fulfillment of the Father's will. For St. John, the life of Jesus was "to work the works of the Father," and it was lived in a liturgical atmosphere for the purpose of announcing the true worship that is to be rendered to the Father (cf. Jn. 17:17–19).

In the other New Testament writings, particularly in the letters of St. Paul and especially in the letter to the Hebrews, the theology of the sacrifice of Christ appears in thematic presentations (see Eph. 5:25; 1 Pet. 3:18; cf. *PO* 21).

The *teaching of the Church*, faithful to the teaching received from the apostles, is that: (1) spiritual sacrifice (*thysia pneumatika*) (see 1 Pet. 2:5) involves man's interior transformation, (2) transcendency and primacy of the divine action is in virtue of charity, (3) the transcendency of the divine action is revealed in the unity of the sacrifice of Christ in which we are all sanctified.

Discussion

Myth and Reality. In considering the *mythical* character of sacrifice, it has been proposed that *demythification* be the rule of interpretation.

The "true sacrifice" is looked for, worship "in Spirit and in truth," which is the heart of revelation and of Christian theology. God has intervened in the history of men and has made an eternal covenant with them, to which he remains faithful and which has had its culmination in the incarnation of his Son.

In mythical language, there remains an elevated human thought, an expression of religious and moral ideas, just as there is in the highest philosophical thought.

Expiatory Sacrifice. A distinction must be made between what involves the sacrifice as such and what specifically involves expiation (the expiatory character of sacrifice).

Expiation as such is not based on the nature of sacrifice as essential form of the religious relationship. Nevertheless, *the sinful condition of man* makes the sacrifice assume this particularity.

A brief explanation of the meaning of the terms is useful here.

Biblically, the term *expiation* signifies a process of reparation that *avoids punishment* (DS 1543, 1690, 1692). Expiation is an alternative to punishment, "*aut satisfactio aut poena*" (St. Anselm). Expiation is purification from sin to the extent that sin is involved as a factor affecting the personal relationship of man with God, and it implies an action of God repairing the damage.

It seems that originally rites of expiation were distinct from sacrifices. Expiation was gradually incorporated into sacrifice as a prelude to the offering: "First be reconciled to your brother, and then come and offer your gift" (Mt. 5:24). When expiation has been incorporated into the sacrifice, the sacrifice does not merely imply the idea of expiation, but becomes expiation.

Expiation "in Spirit and in Truth." In considering expiation in its spiritual and moral reality, its basic meaning and its various modalities may be distinguished.

In its fundamental meaning, expiation is essentially purification from sin and sanctification of the creature, because sin is an antireligious attitude of man that denies or interrupts his relationship with God. It is a rupture of the covenant, an offense against God.

Purification is the restoration of man to the communion of life and love with God. The first and gratuitous initiative is God's. It is he who first expiates sins, because since he loves he pardons. Man for his part freely accepts God's gift, which implies, given the very nature of love, that man abandons his wrong ways and acknowledges that he is a sinner in the sight of God. For conversion of heart (*metanoia*), man must die to sin to rise again with Christ to love. The life of God in man demands that he breathe the pure love of God. God's justice consists of satisfying the conditions for love (1 Jn. 4:18).

Perfect communion with God demands of man love and total fidelity. This is impossible for man, and even more impossible for the sinful man. It is in this that the abundant riches of the love of a God who saves and who pardons are manifested (1 Jn. 4:10).

This is the meaning of the doctrine of merit and of satisfaction that, being in harmony with the divine love, is far from contradicting the transcendency and charity of God, but rather finds in them the grounds of its existence. Love is the only thing that is pleasing to God and that can satisfy the exigencies of pure love, as well as the requirements for life and friendship with him. Love converts man, purifies him, and truly expiates his sin.

Satisfaction is man's personal share in the expiation process. It is important not to confuse satisfaction with a penal substitute.

According to this theory (erroneously attributed to St. Anselm), "the justice of the law" cannot be satisfied except by punishment for sin. And the wages of sin is death, eternal condemnation. In the expiatory sacrifice, the victim suffers the punishment in place of the guilty person (substitution). It is in this manner that the sinner is freed from punishment.

God removes the punishment, not the sin. Man is justified in such a way that God no longer imputes his sin to him, his justice having been satisfied by the death of Christ.

According to the doctrine of the Church, the justice and holiness of God are based on his fidelity and love. Thus, the satisfaction is infinitely greater than the "justice of the law." The punishments called "temporal" are nothing but the fruit of love, its purification for the sake of a more perfect communion with love. As to the expiatory sacrifice, in the ritual sacrifice, which is an expression of the interior sacrifice, the victim must be unblemished. Its immolation is the offering of a life to God in testimony of love. So it is with the sacrifice of Christ. He is the spotless victim (Heb. 9:14), like us in all things except sin. Christ, delivered up to suffering and death, suffers the abandonment of the Father on the cross, not his reprobation. He dies for love, placing his life in the Father's hands so that he may receive it back in the Spirit (Jn. 10:17–18).

Christ dies for us, in our place, but above all in solidarity with our human condition, in order to communicate to us what he alone possesses. Therefore, his sacrifice is the salvation of the world, not as pure substitution but by way of solidarity. In the consummation of his work, Christ gives the fullness of the Spirit. The mystery of communion in Christ implies, therefore, the remission of sins through interior conversion in love.

Death as a Sacrifice to God. The idea that the death of a living being can be a religious act intended to honor God and obtain his favor is, beyond doubt, the chief difficulty concerning sacrifice. The inspired authors reveal to us the salvific value of the death of Christ. The theological interpretation that the inspired authors have given is the norm of interpretation. In the Bible, death is considered the ultimate enigma. It is the enemy of God, destined to be overcome. God has created man for immortality.

Man, through sin, has made himself the slave of death. Presented with man's repeated rejection, the Son of God becomes
man to give us the bread of heaven. Ultimate rejection of him
will be the second death. Christ met not only with a lack of
acceptance by man, but also with hostility and hatred, but he
was faithful in his love and from the cross confirmed his pardon
while placing his life in the Father's hands.

The death of Christ is the supreme gift of his life for the love of
God, an offering of himself as a sacrifice pleasing to God (Eph.
5:2, 25; Jn. 17:17, 19).

*The Necessity and Transcendency of Divine Justice and Mercy
(Mt. 26:54 and passim).* On the part of God, it is the necessary
faithfulness of divine love, which having been proclaimed in the
Eucharist, involves God's honor. This concerns a necessity of
love that love alone can comprehend (cf. Jn. 14:12).

On the part of man, it is needed for salvation. It was needed to
overcome man's resistance and to make him reach up to the
extreme limits of love. In light of the boundless proliferation and
diffusion of sin, nothing can free man from the power of death
except the power of boundless love.

On the part of Christ, liberty in limitless love was necessary. It
was necessary that Jesus be infinitely certain and conscious of the
message he had received. Jesus died conscious of the fact that he
was offering himself as an expiatory sacrifice, because that is
what the gift of his own life was for the one who obtained
remission of sins once and for all.

Jesus is priest and also victim of love for the Father and for
men. Because of his great love for man he delivered himself up to
death to save him.

Absolute Necessity. It was necessary that he be God, the God
who gives life. It was necessary that he give himself for pure love,
so that it might be the supreme gift. It was necessary that he
make a gift of himself, so that it might be a gift of love (Jn. 3:16;
1 Jn. 4:910).

Excess of Charity. Out of the superabundance of love God has
for us, he chose this course, that of taking our sin upon himself.

"So That the Sinful Body Might Be Destroyed" (Rom. 6:6). If the
sacrificial immolation cannot be comprehended as a chastise-
ment, it may be understood as a punishment, which would
equally demand a sacrifice.

This explanation has also been questioned. If sacrifice has honoring God as its objective, is it possible to render homage to God by the destruction of what he has made and gives to man as a pledge of his love? An answer has already been given to this question, because in primitive religious ideas this rite was considered a symbolic act by means of which man signifies that he was giving himself up in acknowledgment of the sovereign dominion of God. Man abandons himself totally to God.

We are at this point directed to a figurative and symbolic interpretation. In 1 Corinthians 15, St. Paul gives us a twofold interpretation of death. In one sense, death is the wages of sin, but in Christ, it becomes the destruction of sin and death.

In being immolated and placed on the altar, the victim has been transferred to the dominion of God, transformed by the sacred fire that is the sign and instrument of the divine action, while the smoke of the holocaust rises up toward God.

In this world, because of the sin and his mortal state, man is deprived of the glory of God. Death freely accepted and endured for love of God frees man from his condition of life in this world, so that he may find welcome and refreshment in the life of God (cf. Rom. 6:1–14).

The Shedding of Blood

Directly connected with the immolation of the victim of the sacrifice on the altar is the rite of the shedding of blood.

The letter to the Hebrews associates *the death* of Christ to the oblation of his sacrifice and *the shedding of his blood for the remission of sins.*

> Christ entered once for all into the Holy Place, taking not the blood of goats and of calves but his own blood, thus securing an eternal redemption . . . how much more shall the blood of Christ, who through the Eternal Spirit offered himself up without blemish to God, purify your conscience from dead works to serve the living God. Therefore he is the mediator of a new covenant so that those who are called may receive promised eternal inheritance, since a death has occurred which redeems them from the transgressions . . . everything is *purified with blood,* for *without shedding of blood there is no remission* (Heb. 9:6–26).

The shedding of blood is linked to *death*. From a profane point of view, it is a synonym for death. In any event, the shedding of blood is not different from the immolation of the victim.

In biblical language, blood is tied to life and is considered a sacred substance par excellence and at the same time God's property.

Blood in sacrificial rites, whether poured onto the ground or sprinkled on the altar, is not a gift of man to God but an act of recognition toward the author of life: "I have given it for you upon the altar to make atonement for your souls . . ." (Lev. 17:11).

The altar that sanctifies the gifts is itself sanctified by the blood.

The sprinkling of the blood is a means of covenant; on the one side, it is spilled on the altar, the sanctuary, and the cover of the Ark of the covenant, the throne of God; and on the other, on the people, thus establishing community of life between them and God: "Behold the blood of the covenant which the LORD has made with you" (Ex. 24:8).

The rite of the sprinkling of the blood may be celebrated as an *offering* of man to God. Thus, *to shed one's own blood* is equivalent *to giving one's own life*; to give one's own life to God is "to place it in his hands."

The blood of Christ is, according to Hebrews 9 and 10, at the same time the blood of the covenant and of the expiation. It is chiefly in the shedding of his own blood, "offering himself to God through the Holy Spirit" that he "sanctifies himself" and us, freeing us from every stain of sin (cf. Rev. 1:5; 5:9). Through this blood *shed for us*, we enter into communion with his sacrifice.

The Passion: Sacrifice Through Suffering

Suffering. "The Son of Man must suffer many things. . . . He had to suffer all these things" (Mk. 8:31).

The suffering of the passion and death of Christ is a single mystery as regards its salvific value. However, it gives rise to some questions relative to its religious value and the meaning the latter has in sacrifice.

St. Thomas says that Christ "offered himself up for us in his passion, and because he bore it voluntarily, it was extremely pleasing to God since it was done out of love. Hence it follows that the passion of Christ was a true sacrifice. . . ."[26]

Vatican Council II has reminded us of the importance of this truth (*LG* 7, 11, 34, 58, 61, and others), which has also been fully set forth in the Encyclical *Salvifici Doloris:* "The Church, which is born of the mystery of the Redemption on the cross of Christ, is obligated to try to meet man particularly along the way of suffering" (*SD* 3).

By way of synthesizing, we may say that the nature of sacrifice involves three elements: (1) the reality of the evil that is suffered (personally or united in solidarity with others), (2) that there is no suffering where there is no awareness of the evil suffered, and (3) that our nature tends to reject any kind of evil suffered.

In analyzing the phenomenon of suffering coldly, a question inevitably arises as to how man's suffering can be a sacrifice pleasing to God.

In attempting to answer this, it is necessary to ask relative to the suffering of Christ what its cause and purpose were.

The Source of the Suffering. Christ assumed human nature entirely, entering fully into the world of suffering (*SD* 18).

There is a threefold source of suffering: man's limited nature; his lack of God's glory in his historical situation, which is due to sin; and actual sin, real and existing.

The source of all Christ's suffering is love in all its "divine profundity" (*SD* 18), because of the fact that the man Jesus Christ who suffers is the only begotten Son in person (*SD* 17).

The Passion. Jesus Christ was obedient unto death in faithfulness to the love that unites him to the Father. The degree of suffering that he voluntarily underwent—*multa pati*—is an indication of the intensity and profundity of his love. His suffering becomes the embodiment in the weakness of mortal man of a love that was given for all without limit.

Suffering as a Sacrifice to God. How can the suffering of the beloved Son be a sacrifice to God?

The Sacrifice to God in Suffering. The single perfect thing pleasing to the Father is love, and that alone is able to restore communion of life with Him. And in any event, to suffer for the sake of the good is the most sublime kind of love in a world lacking the glory of God.

The Profundity and Intensity of the Suffering of Christ. Only the "incomparable profundity and intensity of the suffering which the Man who is the only begotten Son had to undergo can make us fully appreciate the depth of his sacrifice" (SD 18).

We come face to face here with the divine and human mystery involved in this same subject, the suffering of one who is God and Man (cf. SD 18).

The sublimity of this mystery can only be glimpsed by considering the evil that afflicted Christ, namely, sin; the consciousness he had of this evil and of its consequences; and the intensity and profundity of love, which is the source of all suffering.

Sacrifice in the Spirit. ". . . who through the eternal Spirit offered himself without blemish to God . . ." (Heb. 9:14). In his love for his Father, Jesus also loves his own and consecrates himself "for them" (Jn. 17:19).

For Us

Christ died for our sins and arose from the dead for our justification.

Vatican II and numerous contemporary documents have recorded the fundamental truths that clarify our *knowledge of this mystery.*

The sacrifice of Christ is unique, and this implies that he accomplished it personally to make us sharers in the divine life; that the salvation of man consists of communion with this sacrifice, which is specifically accomplished for the Church in the Eucharist; that the Eucharist is the only sacrifice of Christ that the Church as his Mystical Body offers; and that a profound unity exists between the personal sacrifice of Christ and that of Christians.

At the same time, the documents have clarified two essential elements of the sacrifice and its salvific function, namely, the resurrection of Christ and the primordial role of the Spirit in the sacrifice of Christ.

The Resurrection of Christ in virtue of the Spirit is, in a first sense, the acceptance of the sacrifice on the Father's part.

Lastly, this teaching answers the question as to how the sacrifice of Christ effects the salvation of men.

In participating in the sacrifice of Christ, man lives Christ's very life, and in remaining in his love, man is nourished by his merits and enjoys the fruits of the expiation worked by his perfect sacrifice.

It is first of all in virtue of the Spirit of Christ that is given in this same sacrifice and effectuated always in the Church that man enters into the mystery of the divine unity.

Substitution of Penalty. The concept of penal substitution involves, first, transfer of the sins to the victim who substitutes for the sinner, and, second, the expiation of the guilty person through the death of the victim.

Expiation thus eliminates punishment for this reason: it involves a fundamental action of God, who reestablishes his covenant through the rite of blood, and a corresponding action of man, who rejects and makes amends for his fault and again offers his life to God.

In biblical language, punishment for sin is attributed to the wrath of God. Scripture ordinarily uses allegorical and metaphorical language that cannot be well understood if what is behind it in the intention of the narration or of the expression is not taken into consideration. "The wrath of God" is, in the Bible, an anger that is holy, the passionate expression of a great love. Love is passion for the good. Wrath is the form love takes when faced with an evil that is opposed to the good loved. The wrath of God explains and manifests the holiness of a God who is love, and the feeling of repulsion that the soul experiences in the presence of sin is accordingly the best guarantee of our salvation.

When the term is explained, it becomes clear that it is love that motivates Yahweh to institute the expiation toward him that redounds ultimately to the benefit of man himself.

Transcendency and Solidarity. The religious relationship is not simply a metaphysical relationship, but rather a total moral union and community of life between persons. In ritual celebrations, this religious unity is found established in a visible way.

Because of the divine transcendancy and out of its very nature, the love that is God is love that by its very essence gives itself, love that generates love, and it thus possesses the reciprocity that is characteristic of friendship.

Jesus Christ, in offering himself voluntarily to the Father on behalf of his brothers, unites them in friendship with God.

From the social side of this religious concept, God accepts the sacrifice of Jesus Christ on behalf of his brothers; Christ has joined himself to them in an eternal covenant in order to give them "the life that is in him." In this way, he brings solidarity to its highest living expression.

Christians now live the very life of Christ, motivated by love for God and their brothers, and manifesting the moral and mystical virtue of charity. To live in charity has always been thought of by the Church as a mark of excellence and holiness in Christians in the sight of God.[27]

We can conclude this second part by saying that Christ died "for our sins," that is, *because* of our sins that had separated us from God. He died for *us*, shed his blood and sanctified himself equally for us so as to give us his life and the fullness of his love, "so that we might live in him." In his suffering, he bore the whole weight of the sin that afflicts our humanity, *multa pati* (*SD* 17–19), an abyss of pain that cannot be explained except by the infinite measure of his love (*SD* 16, 18, 20). He alone has lived in the infinite dimension of love.[28] A love that only God can live in the Spirit. Of its profound fullness, we have all received. In his death, "he gave us the Spirit" in fullness also, *paredoken to Pneuma.*

The True Sacrifice

The Bible and Church Tradition recognize as the true and only sacrifice the sacrifice "in Spirit and in Truth."

The sacrifice as a special expression of religious feeling appears in a very complex form that is the fruit of a long historical evolution that goes from the law and the prophets up to its summit in the prayer and offering of Christ "in Spirit and in Truth." This is sacrifice considered in its sacramental concept, in its historical reality, and in its theological depth.

Excellent studies on the nature of religious sacrifice are available today (it is not our intention, however, to go into that in this article), and the more progress they make, the wider becomes the theological horizon they reveal. For this reason, the remarks that follow are being made solely as theological rumination having the ontological aspect of sacrifice as its subject as well, since these two points of view (the theological and the ontological) influence one another reciprocally.

The Interpretive Principle

It is necessary to bear in mind that the great figures in theology, such as St. Thomas and St. Augustine, consider "true sacrifice" to be the interior and spiritual sacrifice of the creature, the visible and ritual sacrifice being the visible expression of interior sacrifice. This same insistence is present in the documents of Vatican II. It is a position in contrast with that of a few modern theologians who consider only the visible and ritual sacrifice as true sacrifice or sacrifice in the proper sense.

We must not forget that in biblical revelation, sacrifice was from the beginning the *ritual* action that man used to express his religious sentiments and to establish in some way his relationship with divinity. This cultural form of natural religions was adopted by Israel and transformed by the prophets, under the divine inspiration and in function of Yahwism, to celebrate its intimacy with Yahweh, God the Creator, "Living God," God of the covenant. Thus, the covenant of Sinai was established with the blood of victims in order to be constantly renewed in the liturgical institution of *expiation.*

However, at the same time, the preaching of the prophets and the theology of the inspired Palestinians and sages never ceased to furnish reminders that the "truth" set forth and celebrated in the liturgical ceremonies is "knowledge of God," obedience, and mercy. The sacrifice of expiation is that of a contrite heart, conversion of heart (Ez. 36:26–27; cf. Jn. 31:31–34), which is announced explicitly in the New Testament revelation that speaks of the worship of the "true worshipers in Spirit and in Truth."

The apostles and prophets of the New Testament announced the works of salvation in Christ and, faithful to the instruction of their master, adopted the religious language that crystallized the spiritual hope of Israel and of the nations: Christ actualizes the loving design of the Father with obedience even until death. It was an obedience that culminated in the sacrifice of his life, "his body given up and his blood shed" in the Spirit of Love, a sacrifice ratified by the Father in his resurrection by the Spirit. This is the one sacrifice pleasing to the Father, which restores all men to true communion with the living God.

One may think about sacrifice in its primitive and original sense, for example, ritual sacrifices, death of a hero, death of a martyr, etc., without understanding the profound nature of sacrifice.

It is only in considering the *reality* of ritual sacrifices that we can understand that they only expressed the hope of the reality of the love of Christ.

With this change of perspective in mind, we ought to say with

St. Augustine that true sacrifice is first of all the mystery through which the creature is united with his creator to form a single society (*koinonia*) with him,[29] "so that you may have fellowship with us; and our fellowship is with the Father and with his Son, Jesus Christ" (1 Jn. 1:3).

This theology of sacrifice "in Truth," set forth in Scripture and taught by the Church, was magisterially explicated by St. Augustine: the salvation of humanity is in the redeemed city built on the one true sacrifice of Christ that has become that of Christians in the Eucharist.

To comprehend this rich teaching more deeply, let us separate it into a series of propositions.

A fundamental *principle* that is derived from the biblical data defines *ritual* sacrifice or "mystery" as a sign and symbol of the *real*—"true"—sacrifice, which consists of:

1. The offering of man to God, dedicating his entire life to him. God accepts it, thereby establishing a bond of friendship and communion of life. This action constitutes for man the essential structure of the religious relationship, including all his feelings toward God. These include "knowledge" of God, "to know the one true God," "to proclaim his 'glory,' " which is at the same time adoration and thanksgiving"; gratitude for the gifts received from him, which has its consummation in Jesus Christ: "being thankful for the gift of God"; petition, which neither desires nor seeks anything but communion and his "will," his design of love regarding men; and atonement for sin, since as sin is ingratitude toward God and a rupture of the bond of friendship, man's sacrifice in offering himself necessarily implies reparation for the offense and restoration of friendship.

2. The sacrifice is hence also this unique "mystery" by means of which man passes from his condition of profane existence— "life in this world"—to the condition of "life with God"; he passes from "death to life"; from egoism—living for oneself —to life with God in Christ.

The Purpose of Sacrifice Is Holiness
(The Holiness of a Person in Union with God)

In the sacrificial ritual, the gifts offered are consecrated by the sacrifice; man himself is *sanctified* by his sacrifice.

"I *sanctify* myself for them so that they also may be *sanctified* in truth" (Jn. 17:19). "Christ loved the Church and *gave himself up for her*—a fragrant offering and sacrifice to God—that he might sanctify her . . . so that she might not have any spot or wrinkle or any such thing, but that she might be holy and without blemish" (Eph. 5:2, 25–27).

What is *holy* and *sacred* (in the etymological sense) is what is separated from the profane domain and set apart, which is to say, dedicated to God.

Only God is holy, and no creature can be holy except to the extent of its *union with he who is Holy*. In this relationship, everything is sanctified—the articles and utensils of worship, persons, priests, and the whole people inasmuch as they are God's property.

From this point of view, in light of the divine transcendency, the religious relationship of man with God cannot be other than sacrifice as access to the one who is holy.

Sacrifice as Knowledge and Love

Spiritual creatures could not enter into communion with God except *by way of knowledge of and love for God, faith, and charity*. "God is Spirit and must be worshiped in Spirit and in Truth," "eternal life is to *know* the one true God . . . if you want to have life, love God with all your heart . . . ," etc.

This proposition contains two most important truths that are mutually implied in the definition of sacrifice "in Truth."

The first truth defines the very essence of religion, namely, to know the destiny of man created in the image and likeness of God so that he may be transformed into that same image by the Spirit of the Lord in knowing the truth and charity that God is.

The second truth explains the sacrificial meaning of the work of Christ in reuniting all men in the communion of his love.

Sacrifice Is the Ontological and Absolutely Necessary Condition for the Holiness of All Creatures

"God alone is the holy one and sanctifier" (*PO* 5). His Spirit is the *Holy* Spirit, in whom he sanctifies all things. A creature cannot exist in plenitude except by reaching that state, and this it cannot do by itself. *To reach the state of being holy* through the omnipotent action of God is the purpose of sacrifice.

This ontological movement is the true *Pasch*: "*he passed* from death to life" in virtue of charity, a movement that can be performed only through the one "way," Christ. Thus, sacrifice is the communion of all humanity with God and in God, realized through the ministry of priests.[30]

Sacrifice is by its nature separate from sin because of its being the *essential* form of the religious relationship, prior to and beyond the situation created by sin. However, because of our sinful condition, it becomes a sacrifice of expiation that restores our relationship with God.

The Beginning and End of this Movement

The first beginning, as also the end, of this movement is not the creature but God himself. God is the author of sacrifice. It is commonly thought that sacrifice is a work of man, and this is true insofar as sacrifice explains the hope and attitude of man and involves his personal action in which he commits his own life. However, this defines only one part of the reality. This perspective must be completed by establishing that its beginning and origin are God himself.

It is "a work of God" (Jn. 4:34) that is given to men so that they may bring its fulfillment

in Christ . . . the mystery of salvation has been revealed as mystery of *God the Father who offers the sacrifice* for the redemption of mankind. . . . The redeeming sacrifice is . . . for . . . the Father who decreed that salvation be brought to humanity in this way. . . . *The action of the Father who offers his Son in sacrifice is the submission of love*. . . .[31]

St. Thomas says that the passion of Christ was the true sacrifice, infinitely pleasing to the Father "because of the charity" which was its motivation.[32] And God the Father is himself the "author" of this because he "inspired in him the desire to suffer for us, inflaming him with charity."[33]

The charity of the three divine persons is the basis of the Redemption; it indeed influenced the human will of Jesus Christ and penetrated his adorable heart, inspiring it with this same charity. . . .[34]

Properly speaking, the divine quality of sacrifice appears most clearly in *ritual* sacrifice, the sacrament of *real* sacrifice.

As regards *sacramental* sacrifice (the New Testament sets forth clearly the institution of the Eucharist by Christ), it is to God that *institution* of the sacrifice is attributed. He himself instituted the *priesthood* through which the priest consecrates in his name the gifts of men. God is likewise the author of the gifts that man offers. This explains the "eucharistic" character of the sacrifice. It is he also who *sanctifies* the gifts at the moment when he *accepts* them, which is represented ritually in the coming down on the altar of the *sacred* fire. Finally, it is God who again gives to men, in the communion at the altar, the gifts sanctified by the sacrifice.

As concerns *real* sacrifice, God is the author of all gifts: "He has loved first of all." God is first in every instant, in existence, life, love, freedom. . . . *He gives himself* first. It is again God who, through the pouring out of his love into our hearts, solicits and inspires the gift of man, and grants to him through the gift of the Spirit *the possibility of giving his very self* to God. Such is the meaning of this doctrine of the faith that teaches the absolute need of the grace of God for the work of salvation from the beginning of faith and ever afterwards; the meritorious value of the action of man justified in the Spirit of God, which is "the work of God" in him; and the function of the *priesthood* in the sacrifice, which is "to work the works of God." The priest is the man elected, consecrated by God, and clothed in his Spirit to promote the coming together of all men in the Church, in the unity of God, and the communion of the body of Christ and of his word (*PO* 2 and 6). From this point of view, every Christian possesses the priestly role through anointing of the Spirit (*AA* 2, 3, 10).

Ontologically, it is indispensable that God bring this action to its conclusion. Ultimately, it is he who is the *author* of merit, that is to say, the author of the action of man in accepting the gift of God and giving himself to God. The same is true regarding "recompense"; "in thus crowning his own gifts," God is "the author and perfecter of faith."

Sacrifice Is Essentially a Paschal "Mystery"

Sacrifice is "mysterious" in that it is a process of death and resurrection. It is *Pasch* in that it is a "passage from death to life."

For the creature, the ontological and absolutely necessary condition for sacrifice is that it be an *exodus*, a going out of oneself, a going to the beyond. For a created being to reach intimacy with the living God necessarily involves passing beyond the confines of its fragile nature. Man created in the image of God cannot reach fulfillment except by transcending himself in his spiritual activity, through which he enjoys the possibility of reaching the presence of God. *Charity* is a *passage* and a liberation from the narrowness of selfishness to an opening into "the infinite spaces of love." If God were not he who requires every creature to reach toward the infinite, then he would not be God. If his love did not require man to leave everything in order to possess him and to seek always to find him, then he would not be God either.

Therefore, the creature must overcome the limitations of his created nature because the finality of his striving demands it. This is the positive meaning of Christian self-denial and abnegation: "if any man would come after me, let him deny himself and take up his cross daily and *follow me*," which means passing from this world to the Father (Lk. 9:23).

The Ecclesial Dimension of Sacrifice

Multi unum corpus in Chrsito, hoc est sacrificium christianorum, quod etiam *sacramento altaris* fidelibus noto frequentat Ecclesia, ubi ei demonstratur quod in ea re quam offert et ipsa offeratur.[35]

Thus, the Church defines its existence on earth for the sacrifice of humanity in Christ.

Christ is always present in his Church. . . . He is present *in the Sacrifice of the Mass*, not only in the person of his *minister*, "the same now offering through the ministry of priests . . . ," but especially *in the eucharistic species* (SC 7; PO 2).
. . . all . . . should come together to praise God in the midst of his *Church*, to take part in the Sacrifice and to eat the Lord's Supper (SC 10).

The Historical Dimension

Man exists in time, this is his place, but it is God who, through his Spirit, directs time to its fulfillment in him, when all things will be fulfilled in the plenitude of God. *Craens tempora, generas aeterna.* Thus he unites in himself, in his day, all times. *The one sacrifice, and all history beginning with Abel the just.*[36] "By faith Abel offered to God a more acceptable sacrifice. . . . By faith Abraham offered up Isaac, who was his only son. . . . By faith Moses left Egypt. . . . By faith they crossed the Red Sea . . . (Heb. 11).

Cosmic Liturgy

"All creation is, through man, the promise of a transcendental unity under a single head, Christ. It is a creation turned toward him that groans with the pains of birth, awaiting the revelation of the Son of the Most High. God did not cease to work after the creation but through the *sacrifice* continues to keep it directed toward him, so as to bring it back to his divine rest on the holy day."

Sacrifice, an initiative made actual by God and begun by Christ is his death on the cross, has for its end the gathering of all things in him, in his Church, "so that the oblation of the nations may be pleasing and sanctified by the Holy Spirit" (Rom. 15:16) and that all things "may find fulfillment in the fullness of God" (*PO* 2, *AA* 2, 5, 7; *Dominicae cenae,* 9).

The Eschatological Dimension

For this reason, sacrifice is necessarily *eschatological.* "We proclaim the death of the Lord until he comes." This character is an essential and necessary aspect of sacrifice, it is consummation, the new creation, the new heaven, and new earth. It is not, therefore, something arbitrary, imposed from outside, but a necessary finality of creation from its beginning.

All things must reach their fulfillment in God, whose kingdom will have no end. It is impossible to conceive of a beyond outside of God: "I am the first and the last" (Rev. 1:17).

The Christological and Priestly Dimension

Christ is the one mediator between God and man, chosen and established by God as eternal *priest* to realize the "work of God," sacrifice "in Spirit and in Truth."

This essential element of the true sacrifice involves and reveals the Trinitary structure of the sacrifice. Let us now see the christological dimension.

Christ is (1) Son of God in person, who offers himself to his *Father* in this capacity in virtue of the Holy Spirit, and he is the object of the Father's gratification in the fullness of the Spirit. (2) He is the Son of God *incarnate, in a body of sin,* and in this condition he made himself obedient unto death on the cross, having been offered up once and for all in his death and glorified in his resurrection. (3) Clothed as man with the plenitude of the spirit received from the Father in his dignity as only son, he realizes his sacrifice for the sanctification of all men *through the Spirit* dwelling in him. These three elements are what give Christ his unique function as mediator and eternal priest, and they involve the Trinitarian dimension of his true sacrifice.

This *real* sacrifice, or this mystery, of the reuniting of all things and of humanity around God could have been put forward by God in a purely spiritual manner by showing man his design of love, but man rejected God's first offer. Nevertheless God's faithfulness remains forever.

To "save those who were lost," his own Son made himself *flesh* "descended from David" (Rom. 1:3), and "it is not with angels that he is concerned but with the descendants of Abraham" (Heb. 2:16). In the sacrifice of this Son, man returns to God. "No one has ascended into heaven but he who descended from heaven, the Son of man" (Jn. 3:13). Thus, the mystery was accomplished through a movement of going–returning: a descent from God in the flesh, but with the intent of returning "there where he formerly was" in virtue of the Spirit. This is revealed as the structure of the eucharistic sacrifice: "you will see the Son of man going up to where he was."

The state of "body of sin" that Christ assumed to accomplish his sacrifice involves three elements:

1. That he is of our human race. "For he who sanctifies and those who are sanctified have all one origin. That is why he is not ashamed to call them brethren" (Heb. 2:11).
2. In his incarnation, he assumed a humanity subject to suffering and death (Heb. 2:4), "a man of suffering," "like his brethren in every respect" (Heb. 2:17): "he *suffered, died,* and was buried."
3. In coming to a *world of sin,* hostile to the design of God, he faced the hostility of men and hatred of all kinds to make love

for love triumph. This particular economy of the incarnation was not absolutely necessary, but rather a superabundance of love on the part of God. "Many waters cannot quench love" (Cant. 8:7).

The Trinitarian Dimension

"True worshipers will worship the Father in Spirit and in Truth" (Jn. 4:23). In the New Testament and Christian liturgical texts, sacrifice is essentially a Trinitarian mystery. The one sacrifice offered by man, which effects his entry into communion of life with God and reconciles him to God by expiating his sin, is the sacrifice offered by *Christ,* only son of God, in the fullness of the Spirit, offering himself to the *Father* and offering himself through the Holy Spirit (Heb. 9:14; Rom. 15:16). This Trinitarian structure is the very nature of sanctification.

"God is Spirit," God is life, "the living God"; and the life that he gives us is life in him. *Life in God,* life eternal, is Love.

The love that God reveals to us, and that he *pours into our hearts through the gift of the Spirit,* so that we may live in him, is the "*Love* (without measure) with which *the Father loved the Son* before the creation of the world" in the fullness of the Spirit: "the Father loves the Son and has given all things into his hand . . ." (Jn. 3:35); "The glory which you have given me I have given to them . . . your love for me before the foundation of the world . . . (I have given) that they may become perfectly one . . . even as you, Father, are in me and I in you, that they also may be in us . . . (Jn. 17:21–26).

It is then *in the sacrifice of Christ,* in his death and resurrection—the culmination of love—that God has revealed himself to us in all the splendor of his charity, to give us life in him in the fullness of the Spirit.

In this life in him, in which he *gives us his sacrifice,* is his Spirit in which he has offered himself. "When he said, 'it is finished,' he bowed his head and gave up his Spirit" (Jn. 19:30; cf. 7:39). And when he appeared in the midst of the apostles in the evening of the resurrection, "he breathed on them and said to them, 'Receive the Holy Spirit' " (Jn. 20:22). "Being therefore exalted at the right hand of God, and having received from the Father the promise of the Holy Spirit" (Acts 2:33; Tit. 3:6). It is equally *his own sacrifice,* "his body delivered up and his blood shed," which he gives to the Church to offer it life in the *commandment of love* (Jn. 15:4, 9–13).

The sacrifice of Christ reveals to us "the truth of Love" (*SD* 18) that is God, so that we may have life in Him: "By this we know love, that he laid down his life for us; and we ought to lay down our lives for the brethren" (1 Jn. 3:16). The sacrifice of Christ is essentially the very structure of the charity that gives life, the charity that is the Trinity.

Love is *the gift of oneself* in its very nature and in its transcendency, "It is without limit that God *gives* the Spirit—the vivifying Holy Spirit: the Father loves the Son and has given everything to him. . . ."

The Father, from whom comes "every perfect gift" (Jas. 1:17). "He is the living God," he who possesses life itself and gives it without measure. To be a Father is to generate, to *give life*. For God, to give the life that is in him is to give himself fully in order to generate his Only Begotten, who is not another god but one God with Him, in the fullness of his Love and "the communion of the Spirit," vivifying him and finding in him everything pleasing to himself: "Everything you have is mine; the Father and I are one; you Father in me, and I in you."

The Son, consubstantial with the Father and the object of his approval, "Son of his Love," "also possesses life in Him *as only Son of the Father*," which is to say: living by the Father, possessing the life that is in the Father. Thus, Love engenders Love.

Finally, the Son makes us know the Father because he lives all the love that is the very substance of the Father, accepting it always as the perfect gift of his love. In the same way, the Father always accepts the Holy Spirit, the gift of love of his Son, finding the gift of the love of his Only Begotten pleasing, a love without limits in his image, "as the Father loves me."

It is in *the Holy Spirit* of the Father and of the Son that everything is sanctified. Christ sanctifies himself by offering himself to the Father to be pleasing to him in the one same Spirit. "The eternal Spirit" is thus the sacred fire of the one sacrifice "in Spirit and in Truth," because he is the divine fire of love.

Conclusion

The Council doctrine reiterates and decrees the traditional teaching of the Church regarding sacrifice, a subject on which several aspects were perhaps left vague in the course of prior debates. Certain new expressions and declarations help in the main to clarify questions that are old but that recur constantly, and they thus incorporate the most recent statements of the magisterium. Even more important, however, is their role in corroborating through synthesis various other points related to the subject under consideration.

This brings us back to the original question, namely, how to reconcile sacrifice with the transcendency of charity.

True sacrifice is *the gift of oneself* to God, the culmination of love. And love is, by its very nature and transcendency, the *gift of self* without reserve. This deals not simply with a condition extrinsic to or accessory to the life that God gives us in his Son, but to his own life. "Life is in his Son" means that it is eternally the "gift of God"; it is life that is always an effusion of his love; it is a fountain that springs up to eternal life.

The Father is the "living God," he "from whom comes every perfect gift," the source of all Life and all Love. It is he who eternally loves his Son and has entrusted eternal life to him. With him in the communion of the Holy Spirit he is one God; in him he finds gratification in the reciprocal gift of his love.

Thus is the first element of sacrifice revealed. It is before all else "a work of God," "a gift of God." "In this is the Charity of God toward us made manifest in that he has sent (given) his only Son—he in whom all his love resides—so that we may live through him." For this gift that he has given to us in his only Son, "God's love has been poured into our hearts through the Holy Spirit who has been given to us" (Rom. 5:5).

To be "in Truth," this life must be *received* directly from God and accepted consciously and freely.

For man, living the life of God personally must be first of all knowing the true God who is Love as he has made himself known in his Son Jesus Christ, "knowing the gift of God," and letting himself be drawn to it, acknowledging constantly that Life is he who is infinitely greater and is that which he cannot possess by himself, but that *receiving* it always as a pure gift of the merciful love of God is the way to possess it. It is like something constantly new, because one may expect it as "the bread of Life," "our daily bread."

Such is the first form of Love in us: *Voluptas non voluntas*, the attraction of Love, received by acknowledging what is "given by the Father" (Jn. 6:44, 66). It is the highest gift of the Spirit who makes Christ dwell in our hearts through faith, so as to give us, together with all the saints, the ineffable splendor of the Love of God in Christ (Eph. 3:14–19; Rom. 8:39).

Antecedent to the creation of the world, the very life of the Son of God in the Father is living the fullness of Life and of Love; he receives it and possesses it eternally of the Father as the "perfect gift" of his Love.

Love also seeks love. This is its nature. The acknowledgment of the gift of God arouses in the heart of man a sentiment of reciprocal love that makes him wish to give himself in turn, in the purest joy, the exaltation of the Spirit. This requires and gives Love: joy not only in being loved, but also in loving everlastingly without limit. That this is the nature of love, only love can comprehend; love (like knowing, like being, like the good) is a primordial reality, transcendent, unfathomable, which has been revealed to us in experiencing charity.

Before all else, and in the same measure, it is the gift of the Father to the Son, who makes him live in his love: "For this reason the Father loves me, because I lay down my life. . . . I lay it down of my own accord. . . . This charge I have received from my Father" (Jn. 10:17–18).

> The divine dimension of the redemption . . . is realized . . . in the fact of making love the creative force through which man again possesses access to the fullness of life and holiness which comes from God. . . . It is love which not only creates the good but also makes it possible to share in the very life of God—Father, Son, and Holy Spirit. In fact, he who loves wishes to give himself. The cross of Christ on Calvary rises up out of that *admirable commercium,* of that admirable communication of God himself with man, so that man, in giving himself to God, and with himself all the visible world, may share in the divine life, and that as adoptive son he may share in the truth and in the life which are in God and come from God.[37]

In the Eucharist is the mystery of the sacrifice that Christ made of himself to the Father on the altar of the cross (and which is continually renewed by his command): a sacrifice that the Father accepted, reciprocating his Son's offering of the total gift of himself, which he made in being "obedient unto death," *with*

his own paternal offering, that is, with the gift of new and immortal life in the resurrection, because the Father is the first source
and the giver of life from the beginning. That new life, which
involves the corporal life of Christ crucified, has become the
efficacious sign of the new gift granted to humanity, the gift of
the Holy Spirit, through whom the divine life which the Father
possesses in himself and gives to his Son is communicated to all
men who are united with Christ.[38]

With respect to the transcendency of charity, the purity of the
gift offered to God in true sacrifice is ensured by two elements,
namely, (1) the fact of acceptance on the part of the one offering, in the fundamental sense of acknowledgment, which makes
of his gift a *Eucharist,* a gift to God in response to his gifts; this is
manifested in the eucharistic prayer both in the ritual of acceptance and in the communion of the gifts sanctified by God; and
(2) the fact that the desire to give oneself is always enlightened
by the awareness of one's impotence with respect to primordial
love ("of he who loved first"), and as regards perfect reciprocity
for the gift that alone can establish true communion of love.
Here enter in the function of the *priest* chosen by God and of the
spotless victim. Here also the meaning of the one sacrifice is
clear. Only one whose love could equal the love of God could
offer to God the gift of a love capable of giving him eternal joy
through the offering of himself in a love beyond measure that
only the very spirit of God could inspire. "Jesus Christ, Son of
the living God, has become our reconciliation with the Father.
He indeed, and only he, has given satisfaction to the eternal love
of the Father."[39]

Thus, God's love for us is so complete that to reach true
communion of life and love with us, he went so far as "to give his
only Son," first of all to love us in him with all the love with
which he loves his son—the first grace that Christ asks for "his
own" in his sacrifice. The Father did this to give us the gift that
he has himself given to his Son, which is *to love like him* and *in
him:* "Love one another as I have loved you . . . as the Father
loves me, remain in my love." This is impossible for man but
"possible for God." The love of God in Christ goes as far as *to give
us the fullness of the Spirit* of his Son, in which he has given us the
capacity to love like him and in him.

Such is the definition of the meaning of love in terms of
redemption. Such is the mystery of redemption as it is defined by

love. *The only Son is the one who takes this love of the Father and gives it to the Father,* by bringing it to the world. The only Son is the one who gives himself through this love for the salvation of the world, so that every human being, his brother and his sister, may have eternal life.[40]

In his sacrifice, Christ, united to the will of the Father, reached the culmination of love in virtue of the Spirit, and in the intensity of his love for his own, he makes them in this same sacrifice the supreme gift of his love and communicates to them these three things that subsequently are one: (1) the infinite riches of this his sacrifice embodied in the fullness of his love, "take and eat *my body offered up* and *my blood shed,* whoever eats me will possess life; (2) his commandment, the same one he *received* from the Father and through which he remains forever in his love; and (3) his Spirit, "he gave the Spirit," in blood and in water, "the Spirit which gives life."

> *The gift of the Holy Spirit* is the first outward sign of the generosity of his love. . . . This consoling Spirit, the divine person who is the mutual love of the Father and the Son is sent by both of them . . . he fills souls with divine charity . . . this outpouring of divine love has its origin also in the heart of our Savior. . . . This charity is a gift both of the heart of Jesus and of his Spirit; and this Spirit is himself the Spirit of the Father and the Son . . . this divine charity which wells up from the heart of the Word incarnate is poured into the soul of every believer through the power of the Holy Spirit.[41]
>
> We are led to recognize in the Holy Spirit (the one) who brings about in human hearts reconciliation with Christ and with God . . . the Holy Spirit who is the spirit of love and unity fulfills in actuality the purpose of Christ's redemptive sacrifice, the bringing together of the children of God.[42]

The one sacrifice, the sacrifice "in Spirit and in Truth," is that alone that has been given to man that he may live in fellowship of life and of love with Christ in the eternal offering that he makes of himself in the Holy Spirit, an offering pleasing and acceptable to God in the one and the same Spirit of Holiness. The only Son of God alone, he who *is life,* lives in all its fullness the life of God in the infinite consciousness of receiving it and *welcoming* it eternally as the gift of the Father's love, and hence in an eternal *Eucharist,* which is alone the cause of the Father's joy in the gift of his love before the creation of the world. It is he, and only he, who has fully reciprocated the eternal love of the Father (*RH* 9, 1, c).

In this exchange of love and mutual giving, then, sacrifice is the "consummation in unity" of the Father and the Son in fellowship of the Spirit, which in the sacrament has become the sacrifice of the Church:

> For their sake I consecrate myself that they also may be consecrated in truth (that is, in Me). Your word is Truth . . . that they also may be in us, as you Father are in me and I in you. . . . That the love with which you have loved me may be in them, and I too in them . . . that they may become perfectly one . . . in the Spirit" (Jn. 17: 17–26; cf. Eph. 4:3; 2 Cor. 13:13).

Translated from the French by Edward Hughes, Rogelio Alcántara,
and Michael Mitchell.

Notes

1. LG 11, 28, 50.
2. John Paul II, Bull, *Aperite portas Domini,* §3 (*AAS,* 75 [1983], 89); *Redemptor hominis,* 7; General Audience for the Year of the Redemption (*Documentation catholique,* 80 [1983], 134); etc.
3. AG 15; LG 11; SC 12.
4. LG 3, 10, 11, 34, 58; PO 2, 5, 13; UR 2; AA 3; and cf. Paul VI, *Mysterium fidei,* 2–5, 27–38; Paul VI, *Credo of the People of God* for the Year of Faith (1968), 24 and 26; John Paul II, Letter *Dominicae cenae* 1980, §2–5, 8, 9.
5. LG 28; SC 5, 7, 47; Paul VI, *Mysterium fidei,* 27, 32, 34; John Paul II, *Dominicae cenae,* §8, 9.
6. According to the traditional vocabulary of theology and of the documents of the magisterium, the sacrifice of the cross is *represented* (*repraesentatur*). Translations of recent documents already render this term by *make present.* The Latin text of two recent documents makes the point clear in the same way:
Paul VI, *Credo of the People of God* (1968), 24: "Nos credimus Missam quae a sacerdote in persona Christi, vi potestatis per sacramentum Ordinis receptae, celebratur, quaeque ab eo Christi et membrorum eius mystici corporis nomine offertur, revera esse Calvariae

Sacrificium, quod nostris in altaribus *sacramentaliter praesens efficitur.*" 26: "Una atque individua Christi Domini in coelis gloriosi existentia non multiplicatur, sed Sacramento *praesens efficitur* variis in terrarum orbis locis ubi Eucharisticum Sacrificium peragitur. . . ."

John Paul II, *Dominicae cenae,* 9: "In primis est Eucharistia sacrificium; redemptionis videlicet eodemque tempore sacrificium Novi Foederis, sicut credimus ac manifeste profitentur etiam Ecclesiae Orientis; plura quidem abhinc saecula Ecclesia Graeca docuit: '. . . hodiernum sacrificium sic profecto est ut illud quod olim unigenitum incarnatum Verbum obtulit, ab eo nunc hodie ut tunc offertur, cum *idem sit unicum sacrificium.'* Quodcirca, cum *praesens redditur unicum hoc salutis nostrae sacrificium,* homo et mundus Deo restituuntur per paschalem Redemptionis novitatem." Cf. General Audience, 1, 8 June 1983 (*Documentation catholique,* 80 [1983], 673, §2; 674, §2).

7. LG 10, 11; SC 48; PO 2; Paul VI, *Mysterium fidei,* 31, 32; John Paul II, *Dominicae cenae,* 2, 8, 9; SD 24.

8. Christ is said to be "made perfect" by God through his sacrifice (Heb. 2:10; 5:9; 7:28), just as the Father "sanctifies" him by investing him with his dignity as Son of God (Jn. 10:36; cf. Heb. 5:5, 9–10; Rom. 1:4), just as he *sanctifies* himself by his sacrifice (Jn. 17:19). In the LXX, these terms *teleioô* (Lev. 8; Ex. 29) (to fulfill or make perfect), and *agiazoô* (Lev. 21:6–8; Ex. 28–30), have the same meaning, namely the consecration of priests and levites. *Teleioô* signifies more exactly the rite of consecration, which consists in "*filling* or *heaping up*" the hands of those chosen with the gifts offered to God, to fit them for their function of divine *service* (abd), carrying out *the work* or *the works* of God (ergon). Hebrews 10:14 seems to point to the equivalence of these two terms: Christ "by a single offering has *perfected* (filled) for all time those who are *sanctified.*" There may be an allusion to this consecration of Christ in John 3:35; 13:3: "The Father has *given all things into his hand*" or "*his hands,*" to "carry out *his work,*" just as it is the Father who has *given* him his *work* or his *works* to carry out on the sabbath (Jn. 4:34; 5:17, 20, 36; 9:4; 10:37: 17:4; 14:10, 12; 19:30, 31).

9. Pius XII, *Mediator dei* (AAS, 39 [1947], 548ff.); cf. Paul VI, *Mysterium fidei,* 46; Paul VI, *Credo of the People of God,* 24–25 (AAS, 60 [1968], 442).

10. PO 2, 5; Paul VI, *Credo of the People of God* (1968), 24 (see note 6); John Paul II, *Dominicae cenae* 3, 4; 8, 9.

11. Pius XII, *Mediator Dei* (AAS, 39 [1947], 535, 562); Allocutions: in AAS, 46 (1954), 667; 48 (1956), 715–16; John Paul II, *Dominicae cenae,* 8, 9.

12. Numerous documents of the magisterium regarding this point have recalled "the authentic Catholic doctrine" (*Documentation catholique* [1983], 337). See among others LG 10, 17, 26, 29; PO 2 and 5;

Pius XII, *Mediator Dei* (*AAS*, 39 [1947], 535, 562); Allocutions: in *AAS*, 46 [1954], 667; 48 [1956], 715–716; Paul VI, *Mysterium fidei*, 34–35; Paul VI, *Credo of the People of God* [1968], 24 (see note 4); Synod of Bishops, 1971, 4 (*Documentation catholique*, 69 [1972], 5–6); John Paul II, Letter *Nuevo incipiente nostro*, 1979, 2–5; (*Documentation catholique*, 76 [1980], 301–302, 304–306); Address to the Dutch Bishops, 22 January 1980, 3 (*Documentation catholique*, 80 [1983], 337); Sacred Congregation for the Doctrine of the Faith, *Mysterium ëcclesiae* (1973), 6 (*Documentation catholique*, 70 [1973], 668–670); Letter on the Minister of the Eucharist, 1983 (*Documentation catholique*, 80 [1983], 885–887); etc.

13. Pius XII, *Mediator Dei* (*AAS*, 39 [1947], 562ff.); Allocutions: in *AAS*, 46 [1954], 667, [1956], 716; cf. John Paul II, *Dominicae cenae* 8, 9.

14. *LG* 28; cf. Heb. 9:11–28.

15. *SC* 7.

16. *PO* 2.

17. *PO* 2, citing St. Augustine, *De civitate Dei*, 10, 16; *PL* 41, 284.

18. *LG* 11.

19. *SD* 18.

20. *PO* 2.

21. *SC* 47.

22. Roman Missal, Secret for Ninth Sunday after Pentecost.

23. Pius XII, *Mediator Dei* (*AAS*, 39 [1947], 535, 562); Allocutions: in *AAS*, 46 [1954], 666–667, [1956], 716; Paul VI, *Credo of the People of God* [1968], 24; John Paul II, *Dominicae cenae*, 8–9.

24. Cf. St. Thomas, *Suppl.* 12, 2, c; 14, 1, c; 4 c.

25. This question is again being discussed, so great is the interest, with reservations, that this kind of religious experience stimulates in the modern mentality, as, for example, in many studies performed in the various branches of the humanistic sciences, such as anthropology, ethnology, psychology, religious sociology, etc.

26. St. Thomas, *ST*, III, 48, 3.

27. DS 1545–1549; 1576; 1582; 1689–1693; 1712–1714.

28. John Paul II, *Redemptor hominis*, 9; *Dominicae cenae* II, 8–9.

29. St. Thomas, *ST*, III, 22, 2; II a II ae, 85, 2, 3, etc.

30. *PO* 2; cf. *LG* 10, 34, 58; *UR* 2.

31. John Paul II, Audience for the Jubilee of the Redemption (*Documentation catholique*, 80 [1983], 519ff.); St. Thomas, *ST*, III, 48, 3, c.

32. St. Thomas, *ST*, III, 48, 3, c, 1 m and 3 m.

33. St. Thomas, *ST*, III, 47, 3, c; cf. 3, 48, 5, c.

34. St. Thomas, *ST*, III, 48, 5; Pius XII, *Haurietis aquas*, *AAS*, (1956), 338.

35. St. Augustine, *De civitate Dei*, 1, 1.

36. *Ibid.*

37. John Paul II, *Dives in misericordia*, V, §7.

38. John Paul II, *Redemptor hominis*, §20.

39. John Paul II, *Redemptor hominis*, §9.

40. John Paul II, "Letter to Priests for Holy Thursday," (*Documentation catholique*, 80 [1983], 334).

41. Pius XII, *Haurietis aquas*, 48ff. (*AAS*, 48 [1956], 334ff.).

42. John Paul II, General Audience, Pentecost 1983 (*Documentation catholique*, 80 [1983], 615).

CHAPTER 27

"Lay Ministries" and Their Foundations in the Documents of Vatican II

Louis Ligier, S.J.

Summary

In its paragraphs on the laity, the Constitution *Lumen gentium* most unexpectedly stated that lay people could "supply" sacred functions (No. 35d*). Analysis of the text in question and its context makes it possible to clarify the type of function meant. The two Decrees on the Church's Missionary Activity and on the Apostolate of Lay People help us to fill out the meaning of this statement of *Lumen gentium*. These contributions are of importance in the context of the 1987 synod on the vocation and mission of lay people in the Church and the world.

Although it may be true that the Second Vatican Council consigned many of the problems concerning the laity to the Decree *Apostolicam actuositatem* and also to *Ad gentes*, the Dogmatic Constitution *Lumen gentium* does in fact contain the treat-

*The author refers to number 35c, in line with the Latin text. However, in keeping with the policy followed in the English version of the other articles in the present collection, this paragraph is referred to here as number 35d, in line with Father Flannery's translation of the Council documents. (It might be noted that the same paragraph appears as 35e in Father Abbott's translation.)— *Translator*

ment of the essential points of its theology and deal with the basis of many problems.

The main question of the definition of lay people was progressively clarified thanks to the successive drafts and their discussion.[1] It is eventually found at the beginning of the present Chapter IV of the Constitution, where it is stated that the laity are members of the people of God who are distinct from priests and religious, but who are incorporated into Christ through baptism and thus share in their own way in his priestly, prophetic, and kingly office, exercising the mission of the whole Christian people in the Church and the world. Their specific characteristic is that they are secular, and their vocation is that of seeking the kingdom of God in the administration of temporal things by directing them toward God.[2] Lastly, as sharers in the priesthood of Christ, and thus as worshipers, lay people have the role and task of "consecrating the world itself to God."[3]

With regard to their cooperation with the hierarchy, which is also of importance and on which we shall dwell here, although the question is undeniably dealt with in greater depth in the Decree *Apostolicam actuositatem*, it is considered, and indeed treated, in the Constitution itself, especially in numbers 33–36, which first indicate the general orientations of the priesthood of the laity and then develop its three dimensions as priestly, prophetic, and kingly. In this connection, before we consider number 35, the most important passage is number 33—as even its position indicates.

Number 33 first of all emphasizes the vocation of the laity to work for the advancement of the Church as so many living members, and for its permanent sanctification, devoting all their resources to this.

The same paragraph seeks to highlight the foundation of this vocation—in other words, the Christian initiation they have received, with the sacraments defining it (baptism, confirmation, and Eucharist). Thus sanctified and vivified, the laity can ensure the presence of the Church in the world, which, through them, becomes "the salt of the earth."[4] All Christians without exception are called to "this apostolate," which concerns them all equally: "Thus, every lay person, through those gifts given to him, is at once the witness and the living instrument of the mission of the Church itself, 'according to the measure of Christ's bestowal.' " These are the terms in which the first part of the paragraph speaks, and it then winds up by returning to the same concept: "All the laity, then, have the exalted duty of working for the ever greater spread of the divine plan of salvation to all men, of every epoch and all over the earth."

In between, however, having clearly attributed this common vocation, as founded on the sacraments of Christian initiation, to all Christians, the article inserts an important interpolation expressed in a separate paragraph. This interpolation concerns two forms of ministry that place the laity in relationship to the hierarchy.

In the case of the first, it confines itself to stating that the laity "can be called in different ways to more immediate cooperation in the apostolate of the hierarchy." Alongside their general vocation, which has already been described, they can therefore have a special vocation that is not shared by all of them and the effect of which is to make them cooperate more directly with the apostolate of the hierarchy. Without giving further details of the form such collaboration takes, the Council Fathers limit themselves at the outset to recalling how in the early Church "men and women . . . helped the apostle Paul in the Gospel, laboring much in the Lord."

The same paragraph then uses a well-turned *praeterea* to state that the laity have "the capacity of being *appointed* [or *assumed*] by the hierarchy to some ecclesiastical offices with a view to a spiritual end." As Father Constantino Koser, O.F.M., observed at the time in Baraúna's commentary, what was being referred to here was a type of apostolate different from the previous one, and well-established historically.[5] And this capacity would only be limited by the will of Christ, who, having instituted a specific sacrament, required the reception of the sacrament of Orders in order to perform certain functions in the Church, as is the case for consecration of the Eucharist, absolution of sins, and also "the exercise of a jurisdictional magisterium."[6]

The two faculties thus noted and distinguished by Koser both entail the requirement that in order to exercise this capacity and thus share in ecclesiastical functions, such lay people must be "appointed" or "assumed" for this by the hierarchy.

There is then a last case, which is also noted in Koser's commentary[7]—although in our opinion he did not give it its true importance and position. The Constitution itself mentions it in number 35d, where it recognizes that "when there are no sacred ministers or when these are impeded under persecution, some lay people supply sacred functions to the best of their ability." It is worth studying this passage carefully. It appears that this "supplementary" service is, of itself, exceptional for lay people, especially since, immediately after it is mentioned, the same number 35 returns once more to the approach familiar since number 33, or, in other words, the fact that "many of them [the laity] expend all their energies in apostolic work" of an ordinary nature (which is precisely what is referred to in number 33), and that "the whole laity must cooperate in spreading and in building up the kingdom of Christ."

This shows that a truly exceptional and particularly remarkable cooperation is intended. Whereas in number 33 lay people called to cooperate more directly with the apostolate of the hierarchy must be "appointed" by the hierarchy for their ecclesiastical functions, here in number 35d they perform such tasks "to the best of their ability" without apparently having to be appointed for this by the authorities. In any case, it is difficult to see how the authorities could in fact make such appointments in the specifically mentioned case of persecution! Be that as it may, the question is: Which ministerial functions are intended in number 35d?

In order to answer this question, we must bear in mind the general context of number 35d, as well as its overall style.

The context of our passage is clear, and concerns the "prophetic" function of Christ and the hierarchy—a prophetic function in which the laity also share in their own way. Thus, our text particularly highlights the mission of people united by marriage. The catechesis of their children is their "specific vocation," although the passage then goes further, and encompasses the work carried out at school: there is nothing forcing us to be satisfied to recognize only the catechetical ministry of parents, and this applies equally to that of professors entrusted with the catechetical care of school children. Lay people are also called to "diligently apply themselves to a more profound knowledge of revealed truth" and to "earnestly beg of God the gift of wisdom."

On the other hand, if we also take into account the style and vocabulary of number 35, we must note that when the Council says that some lay people provide a "supplementary" service, it intends this to be used for *sacred* functions, "when there are no *sacred* ministers or when these are impeded under persecution."

This means that these "functions" and "ministers" are both "sacred." We may, of course, be surprised to see that in the prophetic context, to which we have just referred, this theme of sacrality is contradicted. Taken in itself, this theme would have seemed more natural in the previous article (No. 34), which dealt with the specifically priestly role of Christ and his ministers. And maybe its present position is a simple oversight. Be that as it may, the Council clearly states here that lay people do have this capacity: they can in certain circumstances "stand in" for ministers of the Church in order to perform cultal and sacramental functions in their place.

Thus, apart from the two specific missions already noted in number 33, we must add that of number 35d. And there are, indeed, analogies between these missions. However, there is the difference between them that the first require not only a capacity or potential to be found in the lay person, but also a call and an appointment to be issued by the hierarchy, whereas, as we have already noted, the mission described in number 35d does not (at least apparently and explicitly) require the intervention of the hierarchy, since it concerns times of persecution and the absence of hierarchical ministers.

In the face of this fact—or, we should say, in the face of the possibility of such power being granted to lay people—we may be surprised not only over the existence of this statement and the recognition of its meaning, but above all over the fact that it has hardly been invoked or utilized since the Council. It might have been expected that on its basis theologians who were concerned with cases where for one reason or another the faithful are deprived of the celebrations essential to Christian worship, such as those of the Mass, the confession of sins, and the anointing of the sick, would have made use of this passage at least in reference to the case of emergencies.

It is also surprising that the statements of the magisterium, which is so careful to correct faulty interpretations of the conciliar texts, and so concerned to reserve the power to celebrate Mass to bishops and ordained priests,[8] should not have seen fit to clarify this passage, for example, whenever they condemned the path of "illegality"[9] or "alternative ministerial practices,"[10] especially since they had to take into account Paul VI's Motu proprio *Ministeria quaedam* of 15 August 1972, and state precisely which ministries he authorized to be created.[11]

However, without going as far afield as this, the first question is to see whether this passage from *Lumen gentium* 35d cannot be interpreted on the basis of the later Decrees of Vatican II, especially *Apostolicam actuositatem* and *Ad gentes*.

Consultation of the Decrees of Vatican II

If we were faced here with the task of an in-depth study of the Decree *Apostolican actuositatem* as a whole, we should have to take into account its whole history—which is, in fact, well summarized by its secretary, Bishop Achille Glorieux.[12] We should also have to consult the two articles drafted by the lay people Rosemary Goldie and Jan Grootaers, the first of which reveals the complex multiplicity of the problems encountered,[13] and the second is striking for its vigorous and forceful style.[14] However, our task is fortunately a simpler one: here we have simply to define the relationship of the laity to the hierarchy, and especially in the cases described in *Lumen gentium* 33 and 35.

If we are not mistaken, we need to consult Chapter V of the Decree, "The Order to Be Observed," particularly number 24. This chapter and particularly this article are of interest in that they arrange the various forms of lay apostolate according to their relation to ecclesiastical authority. Three types of lay initiative and movement are distinguished, both from the point of view of their nature and from that of their relation to the hierarchy.

1. The *first group* (lines 6–11 of the Latin text of No. 24) concerns those initiatives and movements that fall as such within the ordinary and specific mission of the laity[15] and are in no way dependent on the hierarchy. Note 2, which is retained in the definitive version, bears witness to this, giving the example of the Saint Vincent de Paul Conferences and the "pious associations" of lay people set up by Ozanam in the last century and highly praised by eighty Fathers at the First Vatican Council— although their canonical status was not established until 13 November 1920 with a document from the Sacred Congregation of the Council.[16] *Apostolicam actuositatem* states that this type of apostolic movement owes its origin to the free initiative of lay people, and that their activities are carried out under their own responsibility, although the hierarchy may possibly praise and commend them. Apart from this, the hierarchy is looked to for

its "approval" or "recognition" when these institutions claim the title of "Catholic" either for themselves or their activities. However, it is admitted that in such a context, this approval is to be seen as an isolated specific act; in other words, it does not set up any stable bond between the institution in question and the hierarchy. This first type of lay apostolate, therefore, does not envisage any official supervision or direction by the hierarchy.

However, immediately after this, the same article 24 broadens to embrace various forms of the apostolate that are explicitly recognized by the hierarchy: "Certain types of the lay apostolate are explicitly recognized by the hierarchy though in different ways" (lines 12–13). These forms of apostolate are then listed in the following lines (13–33), thus concluding the article. In this listing, we find two categories in which we shall recognize our other two groups.

2. The *second group* (lines 16–22) encompasses "apostolic associations and undertakings aiming immediately at a spiritual goal," and over these the hierarchy exercises a special responsibility because of its general apostolic mission, and it will choose and foster them in a special way. For all that, this does not mean that the authority of the Church intends changing their nature or the distinction between the two tasks. It will neither absorb them nor take them over, and it leaves them the activity, autonomy, and freedom of initiative necessary to the laity. We should also note that ecclesiastical authority does not entrust them with any specific "responsibility" or "function," whether similar or not to that of priests. It is simply anxious to make sure that their activity, over which the movements themselves retain freedom of choice and initiative, takes a form that is in accordance with the apostolic responsibility of the hierarchy itself.

This relationship to the hierarchy is based on the latter's role of organizing the apostolate according to the given circumstances, and is expressed in the term "mandate." This word had cropped up a number of times during the drafting process of *Lumen gentium,* but had fortunately been avoided until this point. The Constitution on the Church had preferred to place the accent on the dogmatic sacramental basis of the apostolate— that is, baptism, confirmation, and the Eucharist—and the term "mandate," with its connotations of ecclesiastical authority, only appears here in our Decree. The context is similar to the one in which this concept was originally formulated and developed between 1945 and 1960, when it was so hotly debated in connection with Catholic Action and its various groups (in Germany, Italy, and France). If the "mandate" is placed within this perspective, it is not seen as suppressing either the autonomy of the movement or its freedom of choice and initiative: its sole intention is that of ensuring harmony between the activities carried out by the laity and the apostolate for which the hierarchy has overall responsibility.

3. With the *third and last group* (lines 22–32), ecclesiastical authority finally gives the laity specific "functions" and "responsibilities" of their own that have their place within the framework of pastoral responsibilities: "Finally, the hierarchy entrusts the laity with certain charges more closely connected with the functions of pastors." Examples are given: ". . . in the teaching of Christian doctrine, for example, in certain liturgical actions, in the care of souls." We cannot help noting how the presentation of these forms of the apostolate has changed from that of previous passages: we are no longer dealing with lay associations or institutions, founded by the laity and for the laity, and with their own specific orientation and function; here we are dealing simply with lay people. We rightly think of individuals, since only individuals can carry out such personalized tasks that entail invitation, duty, subordination, and direction. These lay people are entrusted with "functions" or "charges" that are defined by comparing them to the *officia* of pastors—in other words, in keeping with the sense of the word *officium* in *Presbyterorum ordinis* 17 and 20, pastoral "functions," "charges," and "offices." (In our view, the word "duties" given by the French and English translations of *Apostolicam actuositatem* 24 is too weak and vague.)

Thus, when we come to this last group, the relationship of laity to hierarchy is of a totally new type, inasmuch as the hierarchy entrusts lay people with "functions" that fall within the range of charges or functions that it normally fulfills through its own ministers. These *munera* are "entrusted" (*commissa*) to lay people. The general concept of *mandatum* is therefore abandoned and is replaced by that of *missio*, which then receives a stronger sense since it is used with regard to lay people and in connection with a mission in which they are entirely subject to ecclesiastical authority: "In virtue of this mission the laity are fully subject to superior ecclesiastical control in regard to the exercise of these charges"!

Remarks. We can now make a few observations on the three concepts encountered in connection with the three groups of associations of lay people: *consensus, mandatum,* and *missio.*

The first remark is that each of these concepts is used in clearly distinct cases, and each, therefore, has a different value. The first, *consensus,* is used for the first group, and applies to lay associations, institutions, and movements, understood as a group and in accordance with the general and specific vocation of lay people. The second term, *mandatum,* does not apply to all lay institutions, but, as the text indicates, only to "certain" of them, which are discerned by ecclesiastical authority in order to ensure coordination between their action and its own; this applies notably to Catholic Action, as it was viewed particularly by Pius XI. The third term, *missio,* is not required either for all lay institutions or for Catholic Action, but solely for lay people who are chosen individually and to whom the hierarchy entrusts functions that fall within the range of pastoral ministries.

The second remark is that each of these terms expresses different types of involvement on the part of the hierarchy.

Consensus (consent, assent, approval) is a minor, isolated, or momentary involvement that ecclesiastical authority—as, indeed, any authority—is led to grant when there is agreement on common ground. It also presumes a lay initiative, to which ecclesiastical authority then gives its "approval." Thus, although any Catholic movement has some right to present itself as "Catholic," since it is in fact so, before making such claims, the consent of the hierarchy is desirable, because it is not the only Catholic movement that exists, and its activity could possibly compromise that of others. For this reason, the activity of any Catholic institution can be the subject of such *consensus* on the part of the hierarchy. *Mandatum,* on the other hand, as we have just seen, is no longer applied to all lay institutions. It indicates a stable bond and commitment. It compromises neither the freedom nor the autonomy of the movement, but, by coordinating its initiatives with those of Church authorities, it confirms their value and importance for the Church. The concept of *missio* is applied to individuals rather than to groups, because of the "tasks" or "charges" that the former receive and that give them a "similarity" to pastors; these "charges" imply dependence and submission in the exercise of the charge received.

Lastly, the meaning of these terms—and especially that of

missio and *mandatum,* since that of *consensus* is more obvious and secondary—is in fact clarified by the notes provided in the conciliar drafts, as well as in other passages of texts approved by the Council, and above all in the discussions that took place in the Council Hall.

Conciliar Clarifications

1. The concept of *mandatum* was discussed on two occasions: on 23 September 1965, in the course of General Congregation 134 (VC 20); and again, prior to the final vote, on 9 November 1965, in the course of General Congregation 156 (VC 24). However, this concept and that of *missio,* together with the "charge" possibly conferred on lay people by the hierarchy (cf. *Lumen gentium* 33 and 35d), had been the subject of notes presented during General Congregation 95, as early as 6 October 1964 (VC 13, p. 383).[17]

To start with, the following are the two explanations concerning *mandatum* and *missio:*

To distinguish between the concepts of *mandatum* and *missio canonica,* the following points are to be noted:

Mandatum by which is meant that act of ecclesiastical authority to which the Supreme Pontiff and many Bishops have had recourse in past years, through which any apostolate of the laity directed to a specific (often spiritual) end may be conjoined to that specifically hierarchical apostolate which is proper to the Bishop. Thus, the lay apostolate is granted hierarchical approval and, in some way, takes to itself a part of that very authority. This is done, however, in a way which safeguards the proper and distinct natures of the two apostolates.

Missio canonica in our context is the act of ecclesiastical authority by which certain offices [*munera*] are entrusted to members of the lay state which, of right, are linked more closely to the duties of the hierarchy. It does not deal with the delegation of the power of Orders or of jurisdiction but simply the utilization of a person in the lay state either due to an insufficient number of available clergy or else a greater facility in the field of the work in question. In such cases the lay person shares in a real sense in the apostolate of the hierarchy but, in that we are dealing here with activities not pertaining to the lay state, this activity is fully dependent upon the delega-tion of authority on the part of the hierarchy. Such activities are referred to as the "lay apostolate" not by reason of their object but rather by reason of their subject only—that is to say, due to the fact that a lay person exercises it.

In this, therefore, *mandatum* differs from *missio canonica:* whereas through *missio canonica* tasks proper to the clerical state are entrusted to lay people, who of themselves have no proper competence in such matters, by means of a *mandatum* the hierarchy unites to itself certain apostolic activities under-taken by the laity in their own right. A *mandatum* is given, therefore, so that a specific group of lay persons may act not simply in their own name—which they may always do—but in the name of the ecclesiastical authority.

The concept of *mandatum* was in fact discussed twice in con-nection with the Decree on the Apostolate of Lay People: on 23 September 1965, during General Congregation 134, and then, at the time of the final voting, on 9 November 1965, during Gen-eral Congregation 156.

a. The September discussion was in connection with two *Modi.* The first of these came from some Fathers who asked "that the word *mandatum* be avoided in that it is controversial" (VC 20, 354). The spokesman replied that it was precisely for this reason that the commission had added "in various ecclesiastical documents." Other Fathers had gone further and expressly called for deeper theological explanations as to *mandatum* and *missio:* "The terms *mandatum* and *missio* require fuller theological study" (*ibid.*). The response was: "But this would be to exceed the limits of this Decree, which is primarily practical, and would be to enter into controversial matters which was not the intention of the commission" (*ibid.*).

b. Before the final vote in November, two questions con-nected with the two September *Modi* were brought up. One Father again asked: "May the reference to *mandatum* be removed in that it is unclear in its formulation?" and the answer was: "Not possible; such an action would go against the text approved by the majority of the Fathers" (VC 24, 110). Lastly, a group of fifteen Fathers returned to the addition the commission had made of "in various ecclesiastical documents" before the words "referred to as *mandatum*," and asked that it be nuanced as follows: "in certain ecclesiastical documents it may be called *mandatum*" (*ibid.*). The spokesman objected that this would change the sense: "Not possible; the approved meaning would thereby be changed" (*ibid.*).

2. We find a number of clarifying interventions with regard to *missio*.

a. We would first of all recall that in September, the request for "deeper theological explanations" referred to *missio* as well as *mandatum*. And, as we saw, the commission refused to enter into this thorny question, since it had no intention itself of settling the controversy (cf. previous page).

b. However, on the same date, another *Modus* asked for a return to the previous text, which had read: ". . . mission, which is called 'canonical' " (cf. "the act . . . which is called a mandate"). The spokesman replied that these words had been omitted by the commission "lest it enter into controversial canonical matters" (VC 20, 354). As we shall see, this answer would not be sufficient.

c. As could have been foreseen, the request was repeated at the time of discussions on the Decree on the Church's Missionary Activity *Ad gentes* 17c, which we mentioned before. This text formally requested the "missio *canonica*" for catechists. As was to be expected, a *Modus* called for the elimination of the adjective *canonica*, since it had been eliminated in *Apostolicam actuositatem* 24: ". . . for this word was rejected from the Decree on the Apostolate of Lay People" (General Congregation 165, VC 25, 52)! Although the reason given was a valid one, the spokesman replied: "All things having been duly considered, the *Modus* is not accepted: because, although the established law does not yet recognize such thing as 'canonical mission,' the practice of such is widespread, and not only in mission territories" (*ibid.*).

A number of conclusions with regard to our two concepts can be drawn from this clarification provided in the Council Hall in answer to well-founded questions.

(i) The first conclusions concern the *missio*. It is first of all clear that the *missio* (*simpliciter*) of *Apostolicam actuositatem* 24 and the *missio canonica* of *Ad gentes* 17 are practically identical in actual fact. The only difference is that *Apostolicam actuositatem* explicitly refuses to enter into discussions of a canonical order.

The respective motivations of the two commissions are also of interest. That given for *Apostolicam actuositatem* 24 indicates that the Council was aware that the concept of "canonical mission" was no longer applied today to people in the current Code. The *Ad gentes* commission contradicts this by saying that practice is in advance of the law, and that in fact the term "canonical mission" is already in current use in connection with catechists in the missions and elsewhere.

(ii) A number of conclusions can also be drawn about the concept of mandate.

(a) Everybody recognizes that this is a much-debated subject. The objectors repeated this up to the last moment, and the commission did not deny it. It is also accepted that it is unclear, which is why a number of Fathers asked for the provision of deeper theological reasons as was the case for *missio*. This would seem to indicate that the information provided at General Congregation 95 in October 1964 (VC 13, p. 383) had not been judged sufficient or had been forgotten.

(b) Nevertheless, the concept of *mandatum* was upheld by the commission because, as it was careful to point out, it is in fact used in various Church documents. It also refused to tone down or nuance the formula by writing that this act of the hierarchy "may" be called a mandate "in certain Church documents."

(c) Further, from the historical point of view, the whole debate roused by this question of mandate prior to the Council will no doubt be recalled. We would, for example, cite the following: K. Rahner, "Laineapostolat," in *Schriften zur Theologie*, 2 (Einsiedeln, 1955), 339–373 (English translation, "Notes on the Lay Apostolate," in *Theological Investigations*, 2 [London, 1975], 319–353); C. Baumgartner, "Formes diverses de l'apostolat des laïcs," *Christus*, 4 (1957), 9–34; and the following commentaries on the conciliar Decree *Apostolicam actuositatem* in *Unam Sanctam* 75 (Paris, 1970): A. Glorieux, "Histoire du Décret 'Apostolicam actuositatem' sur l'apostolat des laïcs," 91–141; Y. Congar, "Apports, richesses et limites du Décret," 157–190; J. Grootaers, "Quatre ans après. Un texte qui est loin déjà," 215–239; F. Varillon, *Beauté du monde et souffrance des hommes* (Paris, 1980), 89–106.

For the present and the future, it would therefore seem to be wise, on the basis of the official documents that define and legitimize its meaning, to restrict the use of this concept of mandate to the problems and questions in regard to which it has been used especially by the Holy See, and to be careful not to use it outside these limits. It should thus be limited to expressing the relationship of the movements of Catholic Action with the hierarchy at the time when the use of the mandate was necessary.

Conclusions

However brief it may have been, this summary of the teaching of Vatican II on the apostolate of the laity in its relation to the hierarchy, and especially on the "supplying" of sacred functions by lay people, will, we hope, have revealed not only the main passages in which this doctrine is defined, but also, and above all, the main positive elements constituting it and marking its limits.

1. The main passages are found first of all in the Constitution *Lumen gentium*, and specifically in the two articles 33 and 35. In 33c, where the two faculties are noted, it is first pointed out that today, as at the time of Saint Paul, lay people can cooperate more directly with the apostolate of the hierarchy. Moreover, the Council does not hesitate to state that lay people also have the specific capacity of being appointed by the hierarchy to exercise certain ecclesiastical "offices" (*ad qua dam munera ecclesiastica*). The affirmation of this possibility makes it possible to understand another important text found in the Decree *Apostolicam actuositatem* 24, which we have already noted and analyzed.

The Constitution *Lumen gentium* also contributes a complementary element to the previous one, and one which could in fact move beyond it, although without completely explaining it. We are referring to the "supply" ministries of number 35d. The capacity attributed to lay people in this connection is so full that it would appear that it can be exercised without any proper intervention on the part of the hierarchy. Thus, in the case of persecution, or when "sacred ministers" are lacking, lay people can act as "replacements" (*pro facultate supplent*). This power of "supplying" that is thus attributed to lay people could have done with further clarification. We have pointed out how it can be viewed on the basis of the text and context of paragraph 35d.

2. However, we must also refer to the Decree *Apostolicam actuositatem* 24 (lines 23–27), since this text in turn—or at least

to some extent—allows us to define this doctrine further and to recognize its limits.

The limits are in fact more clearly defined, for, unlike *Lumen gentium* 35d, *Apostolicam actuositatem* 24, lines 23–27, only refers to the ministries that the hierarchy can entrust to lay people in virtue of the "mission" it entrusts to them. We would thus be remaining as such within the context of *Lumen gentium* 33c, which also postulates a hierarchical mission: ". . . being assumed by the hierarchy." However, the drafting of *Apostolicam actuositatem* 24 had led the commission to define the three types of ministry that the hierarchy can entrust to lay people. The text in question is as follows, as it was given in a note of 6 October 1964 in the course of General Congregation 95 (*VC* 13, 383):

Offices which the sacred hierarchy is accustomed to delegate fall into the following categories:

(a) *Liturgical action.* Several liturgical functions normally linked to the Minor Orders are frequently delegated to the lay sacristan or acolyte. In mission lands, or where persecution is greater, permission in these matters is more broadly given.

(b) *The preaching of the word of God.* Concerning the duty of a parish priest to gather to himself suitable persons for the catechizing of young children, see the Code of Canon Law, Canon 1333 §1. In mission territories the preaching of the word of God as such is entrusted to the catechists to a larger degree.

(c) *The care of souls.* Concerning the necessity in certain Catholic nations of committing the care of souls to certain selected lay persons, see Pius XII's Radio Message to the German Catholic congress (*AAS*, 40 [1948], 419–420). In mission lands lay catechists, strengthened by canonical mission, act as pastors of souls, exercising the whole gamut of pastoral duties save those requiring sacred orders.

How then does *Lumen gentium* 35d fit in with the context just described? Is it permissible to appeal to the latter—and hence to *Apostolicam actuositatem* 24, lines 23–27—in order to comment on it?

The answer would appear to be that it is. The conciliar note we have just quoted explicitly recognizes this with regard to "liturgical acts," since it makes a very precise exception for cases such as those of *Lumen gentium* 35d: ". . . in mission lands, or where persecution is greater, permission in these matters is more broadly given."

Nevertheless, however positive the answer provided by this note may be, the fact remains that instead of suggesting that our texts from *Lumen gentium* 33 and 35 are to be treated differently, it brings them closer together.

There is, therefore, no need to go, as Koser's commentary quoted above suggests,[18] and examine the files of the commission on *Lumen gentium* 33 in order to see if they provide some clarification of the final phrase: ". . . being appointed by the hierarchy to some ecclesiastical offices *with a view to a spiritual end.*"

There is no point either in reflecting on whether *Lumen gentium* 35d does or does not disregard the hierarchical *missio* under the pretext of circumstances of persecution or the lack of sacred ministers. It is more logical to conclude that if this mission is not explicitly mentioned, this is because of the obvious, implicitly understood, impossibility of the case in question. In any case, as is expressly stated in the note quoted before, the powers of the laity spoken of in *Lumen gentium* 35d are limited by the divine institution of Orders. As Koser's commentary also says,[19] it is of course possible to grant a favored treatment to the historical limits and to the limits of the ecclesiastical institution, but there are still the limits established by the institution of Orders by Christ. Within the context of the "liturgical acts" and the "care of souls" attributed to them by *Apostolicam actuositatem* 24, lines 23–27, lay people would still be incapable of performing those ministries that require sacred Orders, as is plainly stated in the note quoted.

Translated from the French by Leslie Wearne.

Notes

1. In connection with this point, we would refer to the commentary on *Lumen gentium* published by G. Baraùna (French edition: Y.M.-J. Congar, *Unam Sanctam* 51c), esp. the article of E. Schillebeeckx, "La définition typologique du laïc chrétien," vol. 3, 1013–1034.

2. *Ibid.*, 1060–1063.

3. M.-D. Chenu, "Les laïcs et la 'consecratio mundi,' " in *ibid.*, 1035–1054.

4. *LG* 33b.

5. C. Koser, "La coopération des laïcs avec la hiérarchie sur le plan de l'épiscopat," in Baraùna (ed.), *Unam Sanctam* 51c, 3, 1055–1078, citing the thesis of A. Doglio, *De capacitate laicorum ad potestatem Ecclesiasticam praesertim iudicialem* (Rome, 1962).

6. Koser, "La coopération des laïcs avec la hiérarchie," 1067.

7. *Ibid.*

8. *Epistula ad Ecclesiae catholicae Episcopos de quibusdam quaestionibus ad Eucharistiae ministrum spectantibus*, in *AAS*, 75 (1983), 1001–1009.

9. E. Schillebeeckx, *Le ministère dans l'Eglise* (Paris, 1981), 121–124.

10. *Ibid.*, 129–132.

11. *AAS*, 44 (1972), 529–534. We would add the Motu proprio on the diaconate, *Ad pascendum*, published the same day, in *AAS*, 44 (1972), 534–540.

12. "Histoire du Décret 'Apostolicam actuositatem' sur l'apostolat des laïcs," in Vatican II, *L'apostolat des laïcs, Unam Sanctam* 75 (Paris, 1970), 91–140.

13. "Le panorama de l'apostolat des laïcs," in *ibid.*, 141–156.

14. "Quatre ans après. Un texte qui est loin déjà," in *ibid.*, 215–238.

15. Thus, it is presented in the first paragraphs of *Lumen gentium* 30–33.

16. Sacred Congregation of the Council, *Resolutio Corrienten* (13 November 1920), in *AAS*, 13 (1921), 137–140.

17. The abbreviation *VC* refers to the second part of the volumes containing the documentation of Vatican II, in other words, the part containing the General Congregations (Vatican II, General Congregations).

18. Cf. Koser, "La coopération des laïcs avec la hiérarchie," 1068.

19. *Ibid.*, 1067.

CHAPTER 28

Vatican II and Marriage
The Sacred Foundations of the Order of Creation in Natural Marriage

Monsignor Bernard de Lanversin

Summary

Through the nuptial blessing of the bride, the liturgy of marriage has always been concerned to indicate its deep respect for the natural values of the order of creation, in the union of man and woman. The Second Vatican Council was also keen to integrate these natural values into the concept of marriage, as the human mind perceives them today in the penetration of the mysteries of creation. This "plan of God" with regard to man and woman is the sacred basis on which, in Jesus Christ, the sacrament of Christian marriage can be seen. In its definition of marriage, the conciliar Constitution *Gaudium et spes*, therefore, included the concepts of sexuality and human love, which belong to the order of creation. This would be the starting point for the whole teaching of Pope John Paul II on the "origins" and "basis" of marriage, and also for the evolution of the jurisprudence of the Roman Rota.

Father, you have made the union of man and wife so holy a mystery that it symbolizes the marriage of Christ and his Church.

Father, by your plan man and woman are united, and married life has been established as the one blessing that was not forfeited by original sin or washed away by the flood.

Look with love upon this woman, your daughter, now joined to her husband in marriage. She asks your blessing. . . .

In these liturgical terms of the traditional Nuptial Blessing of the Roman Missal, which are substantially repeated in the new Rite of Marriage,[1] we can see one of the perspectives of the reflection of the Second Vatican Council. Not only did the Fathers of the Council highlight the sacrament of the union of man and woman as symbolizing the union of Christ and the Church (which was energetically affirmed in a complementary way in the Dogmatic Constitution *Lumen gentium* on the Church and in the Pastoral Constitution *Gaudium et spes* on the Church in the Modern World), but they also restored the appreciation of the sacred institution of marriage, willed by God "from the beginning," and with its source in the mystery and sacred order of creation. In this way, it would seem that in its natural and original foundation, the reality of marriage has been detached from the institutional and juridical structure that modern societies had attributed to it by force of circumstances because of the very role of the family in national life. Although the proliferation of such legislation does, of course, enable us to see how fragile this precious "reality" is and how much it needs to be protected and guaranteed, for many of our contemporaries, it still obscures the deep reality of marriage—the union of man and woman in all its mystery—to the benefit of the institution, in the modern and juridical sense of this term.[2]

From the very start of the drafting process of *Gaudium et spes*, those responsible were aware of the perspective brought out by Pope Paul VI in his first Encyclical, *Ecclesiam suam*, in which he stressed

> . . . the need for the Church to have an understanding of the problems of the world in their own true dimension. It was necessary as *captatio benevolentiae*, and was essential for a true appreciation of the human and social problems upon which the light of the gospel must be shone. And more fundamentally still, it was necessary for a firm grasp of the work of God in creation: not only at the beginning of time, but also here and now in a world that is undergoing rapid change as it hastens into its future.[3]

As we know, the order of creation is taken up by the order of salvation. This is why marriage as constituted by God the Creator is already a sign of the promise of God's faithfulness, which is fully revealed in Jesus Christ. It is therefore through Christ, and beyond the whole order of creation, that the deepest essence of marriage is revealed—an essence that can be grasped only by faith. And this must be constantly borne in mind in the study we propose to carry out. We want to consider not so much the sacramental aspect of marriage (which will be the subject of another contribution to this collection), but rather how the Council sought to restore to "natural marriage," as rooted in the order of creation, its sacred character in the eyes of our contemporaries, while taking up in modern terms the eternal values that are lived out in the union of man and woman. With this end in view, we shall seek to highlight two elements that were a feature of the work of the Council Fathers and that have encouraged the reflection of the Church in the decades since the Council: the globality of human nature in its physical and psychological aspects, and the value and significance of marital love.

The Significance of the Human Body
in the Structure of the Personal Subject

When the text referred to as Schema XIII, later to become the Constitution *Gaudium et spes*, was presented to the Fathers in the third session of the Council, it already had a long history. Together with a number of other bishops, Cardinal Suenens declared that "the present theology of marriage is linked to out-of-date knowledge. Medical and psychological discoveries showing the specific character of human sexuality must be integrated into it."[4] The period immediately following the Second World War had seen a real explosion in the biomedical field, leading to deeper knowledge of the mechanisms involved in the major functions of the human body. Evidence of this can be found in the great number of allocutions of Pius XII concerned with biology and medicine, especially toward the end of his papacy—that is, after 1950. Most of these addresses were given to gatherings of specialists in the different disciplines concerned with the human body: military surgeons or physicians, biologists, anesthetists, urologists, gynecologists, and so on. In most cases, the Pope was called on to answer specific questions asked by practitioners and research experts who seemed bewildered by the speed and extent of their discoveries, and were aware of the ethical problems posed by their application to human beings. The field of sexuality was also caught up in this broad process of research and discovery on the vital functions of human nature. In this connection, we should in particular remember that it was Pius XII, in his famous allocution to midwives on 29 October 1951, who was the first to have the courage to return human sexuality to its existential context of marriage partners as was intended in the order of creation: "The same Creator . . . has also decreed that in this function [of procreation] the partners should experience pleasure and happiness of body and spirit. Husband and wife, therefore, by seeking and enjoying this pleasure do no wrong. They accept what the Creator has destined for them."[5] The novelty of this text does not lie in the importance given to love within marriage, since a great many Fathers of the Church and theologians had already spoken of marital love in sublime terms. "However, for them, it was essentially seen as a spiritual love, an affectivity moved by charity, desexualized so to speak, whereas Pius XII attributes to it a physical and sexual . . . as well as spiritual dimension."[6]

However, even at that time, people realized that the sphere of sexuality went well beyond the sphere of social and moral regulations applied to the area of anatomy or physiology, which were related more to man's genital functions. People came to realize that the ordering of human sexuality is also very deeply rooted in flesh and blood, and concerns a whole infinitely broader range of factors. About ten years after the close of the Council, specialists were able to consider a whole series of "stages," each with its importance in the development of the human being. Thus, we should consider:

1. To start with, there is a *chromosomic sex* springing from genetics, which can differentiate between different sexual chromosomes (XX for a woman, and XY for a man) within the formula of the basic cell structure of each individual. This will then influence all further types of differentiation.
2. There is then a *gonadic sex,* which distinguishes the woman as bearing genital organs of a female type (ovaries), whereas genital organs of a male type (testicles) appear in the man.

However, even at this stage, the experts discern an *enzymatic sex*, in other words, the existence of compound substances that have enabled the chromosomic elements of stage 1 to bring about the different gonadic processes that followed it in the development of the individual.

3. There is also *endocrinian sex*, which involves the hormonal secretions produced by the endocrine glands (stage 2) and released directly into the individual's bloodstream so that they reach the whole organism. Endocrinian sex is, therefore, essentially—but not exclusively—related to the gonads, and determines the exterior aspect of the individual (the following stage).

4. There is then sex related to the *secondary sexual characteristics*, in other words, the outer morphology of each individual: external genital organs, build, amount and distribution of hair, tone of voice, and so on. This is what is normally referred to as "civil status" or "legal" sex.

5. *Psychological sex* is made up of the various affective and intellectual characteristics proper to each sex.

6. *Functional sex* is based on the individual's ability to accomplish sexual intercourse in the strict sense of the term, whether or not this is followed by procreation.

7. *Social sex* refers to the person's life in society, inasuch as the role of each of the two sexes—quite apart from the person's "love life"—is generally different (for example, in family life and even in professional life).

8. Specialists even recognize what they call a *grammatical sex*, which develops in the course of the person's education, so that he or she learns to conform to the grammatical gender (masculine or feminine) with which he or she is notionally identified.

We know, of course, from clinical experience and pathological psychology that on the basis of one of the above-listed levels, we cannot be sure of being able to forecast the following level or levels (or, indeed, the reverse). However, sexologists do admit that in the normal development of the human being, it is gradually and through the lived experience of the "social and grammatical" sexes that we have built up our sexuality, learned our sexual role, and used the biological mechanisms that existed within us from the start (and biologists and psychologists are agreed on this point). Apart from this, these factors will take on new force with the onset of puberty, undoubtedly under the influence of factors springing from the endocrinian sex. We must also recognize that human beings have a large degree of "freedom" over the movement from one level to another.[7] Here we can see the broad gamut of fields in which recent results of controlled research affect the definition of sexuality while still recognizing that these concepts are interconnected and overlapping in what it has been agreed to refer to as human sexuality.

If we also consider the research sphere, it should be observed that despite the biologist's awareness that his competence does not extend to the fields of psychology and human medicine, he or she cannot sidestep the question of whether the sexual behavior of animals can throw some light on human behavior. It is true that it would at first appear that the major mechanisms studied in animals are also present in human beings (for example, endocrinologically speaking, our species is not fundamentally different from that of animal species, and the hypothalamic and rhinencephalic structures of our brain seem to play similar roles). These physiological mechanisms are, so to speak, the roots linking our species to the animal world. However, the research student is very much struck by the great importance in human beings of the higher mechanisms for the control of sexual activity. Thus, although sexual activation and its control by the higher centers can be exercised *in conjunction* with the individual's neuroendocrinian roots, it is striking to observe the possibility of a total implementation *in contradiction* with these neuroendocrinian roots. It is therefore clear that, although we can examine the data established for laboratory animals, any transportation to the human species is bound to be extremely risky because of the totally different importance of the control of the higher nervous centers in human beings. Even so, we must recognize that knowledge of mechanisms as established for a simpler model can throw light on the rules of much more complex behavior such as that found in human beings.

Lastly, it is significant to see that biologists recognize that man's

> . . . independence of physiological determinism is seen in *sexual control* and in *fidelity*, which can also be seen from experience. Since this margin of autonomy in the implementation of

some type of behavior sometimes goes against the bases that are common to other animal species, is it not here that we see the emergence on the human level of what is called *freedom*, with its limits and fragility but also with its incredible power?[8]

During the same period, we have been able to observe the more or less comparable development of research in the areas of sociopsychology, psychiatry, and depth psychology. Such research has made it possible to establish that the wisdom of human beings lies in assuming the most probable sex in which they are born (in other words, each sex can only be assumed psychologically in recognizing the other); in dominating a real situation by recognizing their individual determining qualities and obeying them, or at least voluntarily conforming with them; in recognizing the deepening of human love with time ("growing old together" does not appear antibiological, since there are other animal species that live as more or less faithful couples); in accepting educational parenthood, since human young have the good fortune to be born incomplete and therefore educable, in the sense of a stable affective relationship, which is an inestimable value; and lastly in admitting the true equality of dignity of the two sexes, in family life, work life, social life, and so on—all elements tending to narrow the gap between the psychological characteristics of each sex, which for a long time in the past were held to be purely biological.

Lastly, we would note that in the field of the "choice of partner" within the framework of the marriage union, psychological research has enabled us to arrive at the concept of "critical faculty," which entered into jurisprudence on 3 December 1957 with a sentence of Monsignor Felici. This sentence recognized that apart from the faculties of knowledge, which lie in the simple apprehension of what is "true," there is need of a *critical faculty*, which can be defined as follows: the power to judge and reason, in other words, the power to assemble judgments or a series of pieces of information, and to deduce a new judgment on their basis—a judgment capable of leading to action. Since then, and thanks to the collaboration of physicians, psychologists, and jurists, it has been possible to establish a certain number of definite facts with regard to human responsibility, and in the canonical sphere, jurisprudence has been able to define the psychological conditions required in order for a human being to be able to establish an interpersonal relationship of a matrimonial order.

If we consider the declarations made by some of the Fathers of the Council as early as the first discussions on the schema presented to them, we can see that they were very well aware of all these established facts concerning relations between man and woman in setting up a matrimonial relationship. Thus, we find the Auxiliary Bishop of Mayence, Monsignor Reuss, declaring: "Sexuality cannot and must not be viewed only from the biological point of view: it is different from any sort of non-human sexuality, and has repercussions on the whole human person."[9] Pope Paul VI's words at the opening of the second session of the Council apply more to the mystery of man and woman as united in marriage than to any other sphere:

> The world should understand that the Church looks on it with deep comprehension and real admiration, and sincerely wishes not to dominate it but to serve it, not to belittle it but to increase its dignity, not to condemn it but to sustain and save it.[10]

This is not the place to describe all the vicissitudes of the drafting process of the Constitution *Gaudium et spes*, since this has already been done with greater expertise by others who themselves took part in the debates.[11] The important point here is to realize that "never before had a Council spoken on the directly temporal aspects of Christian life in an extended and systematic manner. And the gestation was not easy. . . ." Whatever their particular sympathies, the majority of theologians

> . . . rebelled against anything that might seem an empirical analysis of the world. They declared in strong tones that a Council must proceed according to the surest theological method, in other words, starting from the principles of revelation, from which norms of faith and morals are drawn in the temporal order.

And this is why

> . . . for this document, which belonged to a new type, a new method had to be invented. If the reader wants to interpret

the Constitution correctly and pursue the dialogue it initiates with the world, he must grasp this new method, which was slowly worked out and remained imperfect up to the last stage of the Constitution.[12]

At the end of this process of development, the text of the Constitution could declare that "The intimate partnership of life and the love which constitutes the married state has been established by the creator and endowed by him with its own proper laws,"[13] and for all men and women, the institution of marriage enters into this partnership, as was willed and established in the order of creation. Following this, the thinking of those responsible for drafting the document is situated less in an overly juridical and contract-oriented view of the institution (although we would hasten to add that this aspect retains its full value) than in the perspective of a more personalistic ethics, especially with regard to the values of marital sexuality:

> . . . true love between husband and wife as manifested in the worthy customs of various times and peoples . . . [is] experienced in tenderness and action, and permeates their whole lives; besides, this love is actually developed and increased by the exercise of it. This is a far cry from mere erotic attraction, which is pursued in selfishness and soon fades away in wretchedness.[14]

Far from turning away from the biological and psychological sciences and depriving itself of their findings, the Council was not afraid to appeal here to all those who have devoted themselves to study and research in this field:

> Experts in other sciences, particularly biology, medicine, social science and psychology, can be of service to the welfare of marriage and the family and the peace of mind of people, if by pooling their findings they try to clarify thoroughly the different conditions favoring the proper regulation of births.[15]

However, it is important never to lose sight of the link between each of these various elements of contemporary science and what is fundamental and essentially personal for each individual, whether man or woman, as well as for their mutual relationship:

Man's sexuality and the faculty of reproduction wondrously surpass the endowments of lower forms of life; therefore the acts proper to married life are to be ordered according to authentic human dignity and must be honored with the greatest reverence.[16]

Hence the acts in marriage by which the intimate and chaste union of the spouses takes place are noble and honorable; the truly human performance of these acts fosters the self-giving they signify and enriches the spouses in joy and gratitude.[17]

In these texts, we can see the outcome of the thinking of the Council on this specific point of the integration of human physical and physiological values within the reality of marriage. It can be summarized as follows: recognition of the value of sexual acts within marriage, as dynamics of procreation, as expression of love, and as factors in personal growth:

For God himself is the author of marriage and has endowed it with various benefits and with various ends in view: all of these have a very important bearing on the continuation of the human race, on the personal development and eternal destiny of every member of the family. . . .[18]

In keeping with this line of thinking, the Council twice states that a healthy sex education should be ensured, both in this Constitution (49c) and in another document which we could consider here as a decree of practical application—the Declaration *Gravissimum educationis* on Christian Education—and in which it is stated that

. . . children and young people should be helped to develop harmoniously their physical, moral and intellectual qualities. They should be trained to acquire gradually a more perfect sense of responsibility in the proper development of their own lives by constant effort and in the pursuit of liberty. . . . As they grow older they should receive a positive and prudent education in matters relating to sex.[19]

Everybody is called to assist in this task of education and formation:

Teachers must remember that . . . above all they should work in close cooperation with the parents. In the entire educational program they should, together with the parents, make full allowance for the difference of sex and for the particular role which providence has appointed to each sex in the family and in society.[20]

Still along the same lines as the principles just set forth, the reflection of the Church then continued, expressed every time the need was felt in documents of the magisterium on these questions involving the foundations of human nature: the Encyclical *Humanae vitae* of Paul VI in 1968, the Declaration *Personae humanae* of the Sacred Congregation for the Doctrine of the Faith in 1975, the Apostolic Exhortation *Familiaris consortio* of John Paul II in 1981, following a Synod of Bishops that told him of their pastoral experience and their anxieties, and, most recently, the Instruction of the Sacred Congregation for the Doctrine of the Faith on Respect for Human Life in Its Origin and on the Dignity of Procreation, of 22 February 1987. These various documents all help to explain more clearly to our contemporaries how the connection between the "unitive aspect" and the "procreative aspect" of sexuality defines in an exclusive manner the truly marital implementation of human sexuality. Pope John Paul II has also emphasized this in his teaching on marriage, but he has also stressed the following point:

Contemporary biophysiology can provide us with a great deal of precise information on human sexuality. However, knowledge of the personal dignity of the human body and of sex also comes from other sources. And a very special source is the Word of God itself. . . . Turning to it should mean rediscovering the significance of the human body and its personal significance for communion.[21]

The Adoption of the Values of Human Love

In his intervention at the last session of the Council, Bishop De Roo of Victoria, Canada, had the following to say in the course of the final debate on marriage and the family:

Married people tell us that marital love is a very deep spiritual experience. It throws light into their very depths, showing them what they mean for one another, and highlighting their mutual communion in an irrevocable union. Through this love, and in a sort of synthesis, they grasp the unity of the mysterious plan of their lives, as well as the bonds linking them to God the Creator. In an almost tangible manner they are united in the love of God, and through their conjugal life they can glimpse the fact that God is the source of life and happiness. [22]

Bishop De Roo continued:

This Council will work towards the redemption of the whole of humanity by proclaiming the positive values of marital love. Never has the world had more need to recognize the divine plan in virtue of which man shares in the divine creative Love, and in this way to discover his dignity. [23]

We must also recognize that from the beginning of the drafting process of the text of the Constitution, and even before it was presented to the Fathers for discussion, those responsible for Schema XIII were keen to take into account the contribution of the human sciences such as psychology, which has very effectively shown that love is one of the deepest purposes of sexuality. And if there is one human sentiment today that is seen as enhancing and expressing freedom, this is certainly human love. Such enhancement of love is the result on the one hand of the refining of morals because of an increased awareness, under the influence of personalist philosophies, that people are made to love, and on the other hand of the gaining of freedom under every form. Love has often been taken as the symbol of an unqualified liberation, but there can be a deep ambiguity here, since love can be taken as covering a multitude of very different things. [24] Indeed, some of the Fathers of the Council were so convinced of the backwardness of Catholic thinking on this point that they attributed excessive importance to these values; and since (at least at the beginning) they saw no need to explain precisely what they meant by "marital love," the ambiguity was complete. Only gradually, as they came to understand the need to explain what they meant and to avoid ambiguities, did the Council try to link marital love to a voluntary commitment, rendered sublime by charity. This was the gist of what Cardinal Brown had to say when he asked for the provision of a definition of the "love of friendship," which helps the spouses not only in the upbringing of their children but also in their own happiness. Moreover, he added that human and Christian virtue, as well as the stability of marriage, require that their love, which is almost always the prime mover for the couple, should be a love that is "authentic and sincere, and controls the senses."[25] This then meant in the thinking of the drafters of the text that the characteristics of unity and indissolubility of marriage were not only conditions of the matrimonial contract, but requirements of true marital love.

Those responsible for drafting the conciliar text were certainly faced with considerable problems: on the one hand, they wanted to keep a greater place for love in the matrimonial union, and therefore made an effort to absorb and integrate the modern values of personalist philosophy, and on the other hand, they did not want to face this task without, as we have seen, guaranteeing the true values of human sexuality. Thus, in the course of the drafting process, the passages concerned with love within marriage were gradually broadened and nuanced, and it seemed necessary to note its specific character on the psychological and sexual level. Sexuality was then no longer seen as having the sole purpose of procreation, but also as helping fulfill the need to share together and to find a true mutual blossoming in marital love as expressed sexually.

It was also a question of showing how marital love was taken up by charity without losing its own true nature. On the psychological level itself, charity and marital love have very different orientations: the charity of a human being is never other than a reflection of the divine *Agape*, and it has no need to find a value to which to attach itself since it creates the value itself (on this basis, it would be related to the love of mercy and to the exercise of forgiveness); marital love, on the other hand, like friendship (of which it is a variant) can only live in mutuality.[26] In the drafting of the text of the Constitution, it was therefore necessary to avoid the interpretation that would have implied the absorption of the concept of marital love by the virtue of charity. As would be shown in the final text, marital love can thus be supremely human inasmuch as it starts from a person taken in all of his or her aspects (spirit, body, mind, will, heart) and is

oriented toward another person, who is also taken in all of his or
her dimensions and orientations: "A love like that, bringing
together the human and the divine, leads the partners to a free
and mutual gift of self, experienced in tenderness and action, and
permeates their whole lives."[27]

Some Fathers also saw a risk in the unqualified acceptance of
certain teachings of modern psychology, and protested against a
possible confusion between marital love and passion with all its
affective consequences. In this perspective, the bishops of Asia
played a moderating role in the discussion by observing that the
schema "demonstrated a completely western tone and does not
take into account the manner in which marriage is seen in the
various cultures of Asia. . . ." The spokesman for these bishops
continued: "You marry because you love one another, whereas
we love one another because we are united in marriage." In this
perspective, the main stress must be laid

> . . . not on the contract, the act through which the couple
> bind themselves to one another, but on the permanent asso-
> ciation for the whole life of the husband with his wife, which
> is of a sacred character. It is not necessary to lay the stress on
> the reasons of love, because . . . love is often born after
> marriage.[28]

In the definition given in the final text, the Council in fact
emphasized the aspect of the "partnership of the spouses in marriage," and took into account the voluntary aspect of marital love
and the help that God's grace brings to it by purifying it:

> Many of our contemporaries, too, have a high regard for true
> love between husband and wife as manifested in the worthy
> customs of various times and peoples. Married love is an emi-
> nently human love because it is an affection between two
> persons rooted in the will and it embraces the good of the
> whole person; it can enrich the sentiments of the spirit and
> their physical expression with a unique dignity and ennoble
> them as the special elements and signs of the friendship proper
> to marriage.[29]

Lastly, it should be observed that from the very beginning of the
Constitution, marriage is described as a community or partner-

ship. The term "community" occurs three times in the very first paragraph of this section, once in the more specific form of "community of love":

> The well-being of the individual person and of both human and Christian society is closely bound up with the healthy state of that *community produced by marriage and family*. Hence Christians and all men who hold *this community* in high esteem sincerely rejoice in the various ways by which men today find help in fostering this *community of love*. . . .[30]

Community first of all involves a psychological union between persons linked by a sympathy and a similarity of ideals. It changes the "I" and "you" into a "we," which can dispense with strictly hierarchized structures, but which transcends the individuals and tends to prevent them from regaining their autonomy. Thus, when the Council sees marriage as a community, it gives much more attention to personalist concerns, although in no way diminishing stability. "It seems here that we have moved from the juridical level, on which contract and institution enclosed marriage, to the psychological and moral level."[31]

However, although we have been concerned to integrate these psychological and moral values into our approach to the institution of marriage, we must not lose sight of the fact that precisely in the interests of those concerned, the Church has to provide a definition in the precise terms of canon law of this complex reality that involves the different areas of the voluntary commitment of persons, their state of life, and the sacramental order.

As we know, the efficient cause of marriage—that which establishes two baptized people in the married state of life—is the consent they express outwardly in specific circumstances laid down by the law and liturgy of the Church, in other words, according to the canonical form of marriage. It is a free act of the will through which two people give themselves radically to one another.

The nature of this consent cannot be viewed philosophically and theologically as behavior that is in the strict sense creative of the married state as such, but it should be seen as consent *in obedience* to the call expressed by God, who, through natural law and the law of the gospel, has instituted marriage and established it with its own rules that are absolutely independent of human decision and judgment. This is why in its deepest and most totalizing dimensions, the state of married life is established and has its source on the personal level because of the "consent." And in the Church, this consent has a juridical dimension inasmuch as it obeys the regulations of canon law. Through a special law, canon law should in fact express the requirements of charity that are encompassed in the very vocation of the baptized in the Church.

The question then arises of the extent to which charity or "marital love" can be translated into law concerning the constitution of the married state within the Church through the consent of the spouses. It cannot extend to the point of translating marital charity into the required consent, since this would in fact destroy the institution of marriage as such by introducing subjectivism into it. Experiences belonging only to the realm of human subjectivity cannot be introduced into the juridical realm, for they would place man in an autonomous position with regard to the objective values of natural law and the law of the gospel. If an institution is as such based on the subjective behavior of those who adhere to it, this amounts to denying the institution and reducing it to a simple factor that is wholly dependent on the subjectivity of those who claim to belong to it. This is what Pope Paul VI was referring to in the warning he gave in his address to the Tribunal of the Rota on 9 February 1976 with regard to proponents of certain trends who "regard married love as an element of such great importance even in law that they subordinate to it the very validity of the nuptial bond, thus opening the way to practically unrestricted divorce."[32] Thus, in the new Code of Canon Law, which is "the Code of the Council and, in this sense, . . . the 'final conciliar document,' which doubtlessly will constitute its strength and its value, its unity and its dissemination,"[33] Canon 1055, which doctrinally speaking repeats the terms of the Constitution *Gaudium et spes* 48a, does not include the concept of marital love in the definition of marriage:

> The matrimonial covenant, by which a man and a woman establish between themselves a *partnership of the whole of life,* is by its nature ordered toward the good of the spouses and the procreation and education of offspring; this covenant between baptized persons has been raised by Christ the Lord to the dignity of a sacrament.[34]

But if this marital love, as gift and function, grace and vocation, expresses the characteristics of a state of married life in the Church, this fact must be recognized in a certain way by canon law, inasmuch as the law must express the objective structure of marriage in the Church, both in the natural order and in the supernatural order.[35] This is why marital love can be expressed on the one hand in law through its requirements, and by nature it is endowed with two fundamental requirements—unity and fidelity (which are expressed as follows in Canon 1056: "The essential properties of marriage are unity and indissolubility, which in Christian marriage obtain a special firmness in virtue of the sacrament"), while on the other hand, marital love is expressed juridically in its effects and in a specific way through the sexual act, which is fulfilled "if the parties have performed between themselves in a human manner the conjugal act which is per se suitable for the generation of children" (Canon 1061, §1); here the juridical structure is expressed by adapting the specific bond of the matrimonial covenant, as duty and right, to its bodily fulfillment in the union of the spouses.

Despite everything, the study of specific cases submitted to canonists has forced jurisprudence to examine "marital love or charity" as an at least predetermining component of matrimonial consent. In a very deep-reaching study carried out prior to the promulgation of the Code, Monsignor Grocholewski was led to consider two components of marital love: the one is more affective, and might be described with the term "complaisance" (as well as "concupiscence," which is derived from it in the philosophical and scholastic sense of the term, and which should not be viewed solely as a simple sexual desire); the other, which is deeper and can be viewed as the essential core of marital love, is the aspect of "benevolence," and consists of a permanent disposition and behavior through which one person brings about the good of the other. Referring to the teaching of the Council, Pope Paul VI dealt with this more explicitly in his Encyclical Humanae vitae 9. It is important to quote this passage because of the prominence it has since taken on in the jurisprudence that has made use of it:

This love is first of all *fully human*, that is to say, of the senses and of the spirit at the same time. It is not, then, a simple transport of instinct and sentiment, but also, and principally, *an act of the free will,* intended to endure and to grow by means of the joys and sorrows of daily life, in such a way that husband and wife become one only heart and one only soul, and to-gether attain their human perfection.

Then, this love is *total,* that is to say, it is a very special form of personal friendship, in which husband and wife gener-ously share everything. . . . Whoever truly loves his marriage partner loves not only for what he receives, but for the part-ner's self. . . .

Again, this love is *faithful* and *exclusive* until death. . . .

The example of so many married persons down through the centuries shows, not only that fidelity is according to the nature of marriage, but also that it is a source of profound and lasting happiness.[36]

This said, and to return to Monsignor Grocholewski's study, in that this "essential core" of marital love, this "benevolence," consists of a permanent disposition to act for the good of the other, it is the only element essential in order to speak of authen-tic love. Moreover, love is in general all the higher and all the closer to the love of God in proportion to the predominance and purity of this element of "benevolence." This aspect of love is dealt with both by Saint Paul, who compares marital love to that of Christ and the Church, and also by many documents of the magisterium of the Church in which spouses are exhorted to cultivate their love within marriage. This essential element of marital love *can* have a certain juridical value to the extent that it is under the influence of the free will (as Pope Paul VI noted). However, if the nature of marriage is seen as "a partnership of the whole of life," it *must* be recognized that there is a certain juridi-cal value in this element that contributes to the formation of a "partnership of life," and is for this reason linked to marriage in a proportion analogical to the "ordering to children," to unity, and to indissolubility.[37]

Even so, it should be noted that the jurisprudence of the Roman Rota is still very prudent with regard to these ideas, and does not forget that the conciliar Constitution *Gaudium et spes* was expressly declared to be "pastoral" and was therefore promul-gated not in order to establish some new doctrine on the institu-tions it discusses, but primarily so that people could use an al-ready established and defined doctrine in order to draw elements useful for a full understanding of these institutions themselves. And the "partnership of life" should in fact be seen as the natural *consequence* of the act of will through which the matrimonial union is constituted. Similarly, the "love of benevolence" as described previously would be seen more as one of the *predetermining* elements of the specific act of will through which the spouses "through an irrevocable covenant mutually give and accept each other" (Canon 1057), just as afterwards this "permanent disposition" sustains the partnership of the whole of life, which is set up through the voluntary and free consent of the spouses.

At this point, we should like to leave aside the specifically canonical question in order to show how, in our opinion, by taking on the deeply human values resulting from the development of modern science, the Council, and especially the Constitution *Gaudium et spes* (which, as we should bear in mind, should never be separated from the Constitution *Lumen gentium* on the Church), can provide a response to certain trends—indeed, let us bluntly call them "deviations"—in the social order that have arisen since then in the field with which we are concerned:

> It is in fact precisely within a crisis of the human element that the juridical problems raised by unmarried couples seem to take root. Especially in the so-called "economically developed" world the individual feels oppressed by two types of society which mortify his dignity, his proper freedom and his autonomy: the consumer society, in which technology and bureaucracy paralyze his private initiative and in which the stronger exploit the weaker; and the society of dialectical and practical materialism, in which everything is ordered from above and the individual is lost in the anonymous mass. Along the axis that passes from one pole of these two societies to the other he does not find enough space to develop his personality and let it blossom. An alienation from the institution—any institution—is then set up within him. He reserves to himself the sole area of social life in which he can be his own master: the family. He sets up a *de facto* ménage, on the margins of the institution.[38]

Unfortunately, "in such situations individuals find the way is open to highhandedness, illusions, violence, and injustice of every type, especially against the weakest."[39] When the Pastoral

Constitution *Gaudium et spes* detaches the "mystery of marriage
between man and woman" from overinstitutionalization and
from overdependence on elements of positive law, it addresses
such people "who have been traumatized by our civilization," in
order to help them understand the deep and positive values to
which they aspire. The language of marital love in the first place
expresses the reciprocal love of the spouses,

> . . . since each couple here has its own manner of speaking.
> Even so, however personal this language of love may be and
> must become within a couple, it does have certain significance
> of which no couple could claim to be either the source or
> master. It is taken up and becomes part of an order that goes
> well beyond their own power. The love of the spouses—"their
> love" in the most intimate and private sense of the term—is
> both "themselves" but also "more than themselves." Humanity
> is directly involved in them, not simply because only love, as
> communion and sharing, can define humanity in its essence,
> but also and no less truly because the love of the spouses is and
> must remain the entrance-way, the only source, the only con-
> dition worthy of a human being, when it comes to introducing
> him into the mystery of existence. It therefore has the supreme
> beauty of a communion that must be total and that is made in
> order to become creative in its own way.[40]

For the spouses, this marital love is

> . . . the personal gift of self which is proper and exclusive to
> them, and which brings them both to the communion of their
> beings with a view to a reciprocal personal development and
> improvement, in order to work with God in generating and
> educating new lives.[41]

This study needs completing with an analysis of the teachings
of Pope John Paul II on marriage. In these teachings, which are
in direct line with the principles set forth by the Council even in
its "pastoral" perspectives, we can see how the Pope builds an
authentic anthropology on the mystery of the union of man and
woman as this was conceived by God "from the very beginning"
in the sacred order of creation, before it was "consecrated" by
Jesus Christ in order to become a sacrament of the new law.

While the Council was able to tell the modern world what the spouses are as united in marriage, it is just as important to proclaim where they come from and also to show the fulfillment toward which they are oriented, and this would seem to be the fruit of the teaching of Pope John Paul II in the course of the first two years of his papacy, together with the reminders he constantly addresses to married people during his apostolic journeys.

In conclusion, we should like to express one regret, and this is that the conciliar Constitution *Gaudium et spes* did not place marital love more explicitly within the perspective of its absolute model, which is the love in God of the three persons of the Holy Trinity.

As the Constitution *Lumen gentium* tells us, the Church is nothing other than the Holy Trinity exteriorizing itself in the world and in history, so that the Church flows from the Trinity like water from a spring. The mystery of the family is exactly the same. In the book of Genesis, God says, "Let us make man in our image, after our likeness," and he made them man and woman. This means that within the couple there is something of God, I would even say the heart of God, the core of divinity that is manifested in the man and woman who love one another, inasmuch as on its own level the family possesses the same characteristics as the Holy Trinity. [42]

We must, however, distinguish between the image of God in the natural order, the order of creation, which has been the more particular object of the present study, and in the supernatural order, which will be the subject of other contributions, especially in the study of the sacramental nature of marriage.

Thus, between nonbaptized people the marital and family union only has a very loose and almost external relationship with the Trinity. Such a relationship is established through God's creative action which is common to the three divine Persons, who act *ad extra* not as distinct from one another but as consubstantial, in other words as endowed with a single nature. It is therefore not surprising if a unique operation that proceeds from the whole Trinity leaves a trinitarian stamp on created things—a stamp that is found at the different levels of creation, at least as a trace or image, but that shines forth in incomparable fashion in the community formed by the couple and the family, because this community reflects the most trinitarian quality of the Holy Trinity—in other words, the life of love which unites the divine Persons.[43]

It is true that, as we have glimpsed them in the drafting process of the Constitution *Gaudium et spes,* the approach of the drafters and the thought of the Fathers of the Council paid close attention to the experience of contemporary men and women, which made it very difficult to formulate propositions springing from lines of thought that were different if not actually in opposition. To make up for this, however, the thought process and theological expression used in the drafting of the Constitution *Lumen gentium* took as their starting point the central mystery of our faith—that of the Holy Trinity. The two Constitutions are therefore mutually complementary, and, as we have said, they should not be separated in Christian reflection. Nobody who studies this matter can ignore the complementary nature of the bonds uniting these two texts, especially in the interests of those to whom they are addressed: the men and women of our times. Through these two great documents, the thought of the Council

. . . wanted to make sure that even an atheist reading the text would find nothing contrary to the truth but would also perceive the anguished distress of the Church over the oppression of her children and the mutilation that people suffer without God, and would clearly feel that the Church loves him too with a true and unchanging love.[44]

Translated from the French by Leslie Wearne.

Notes

1. *The Rites of the Catholic Church as revised by the Second Vatican Council,* English translation prepared by the International Commission on English in the Liturgy (New York, 1983), Rite of Marriage 33, p. 564.

2. J.-M. Aubert, "L'Eglise et la Société" (Chapter II, "Famille et Mariage"), in J.-M. Aubert and R. Metz (eds.), *Le Droit et les Institutions de l'Eglise Catholique Latine de la fin du XIIIᵉ siècle à 1978,* Histoire du Droit et des Institutions de l'Eglise d'Occident 18 (Paris, 1980), 500.

3. Bishop McGrath of Santiago de Varaguas, Panama, in Y. Congar and M. Peuchmaurd (eds.), *Vatican II: L'Eglise dans le monde de ce temps*, 3 vols., Unam Sanctam 65a, b, c (Paris, 1967), 2, 28–29.

4. P. Delhaye, "Dignité du mariage et de la Famille," in *ibid.*, 2, 401.

5. *AAS*, 43 (1951), 835–854; English translation in J. Neuner and J. Dupuis (eds.), *The Christian Faith* (Bangalore, 1978), 612.

6. Aubert, "L'Eglise et la Société," 501.

7. H. Pequignot, "Sexe et degré de liberté," *Le concours Medical* (4 January 1975, special issue on "La Sexualité"), 5–8.

8. J.P. Signoret and J.C. Thiery, "Bases neuro-physiologiques et endocriniennes de l'activité sexuelle," *Le concours Medical* (4 January 1975), 79ff.

9. Delhaye, "Dignité du mariage et de la Famille," 404.

10. R. Tucci, "Introduction historique et doctrinale," in Congar and Peuchmaurd (eds.), *Vatican II: L'Eglise dans le monde de ce temps*, 2, 54.

11. G.M. Garrone (ed.), *Vatican II: Constitution Pastorale "Gaudium et Spes,"* 2 vols. (Paris, 1967).

12. McGrath, in Congar and Peuchmaurd (eds.), *Vatican II: L'Eglise dans le monde de ce temps*, 2, 18–19.

13. GS 48a.

14. GS 49a.

15. GS 52d.

16. GS 51c.

17. GS 49b.

18. GS 48a.

19. GE 1.

20. GE 8.

21. John Paul II, Allocution of 20 April 1980, 3.

22. 128th General Congregation (21 September 1965), in G. Caprile (ed.), *Concilio Vaticano II*, 5 vols. (Rome, 1965–1969), 5, 137.

23. *Ibid.*

24. Aubert, "L'Eglise et la Société," 492.

25. Caprile (ed.), *Concilio Vatican II*, 139.

26. Delhaye, "Dignité du mariage et de la Famille," 432.

27. GS 49a.

28. Intervention of Bishop Djajasepoetra of Djakarta, 20 November 1964, in Caprile (ed.), *Concilio Vaticano II*, 5, 493.

29. GS 49a.

30. GS 47a.

31. Delhaye, "Dignité du mariage et de la Famille," 124.

32. *AAS*, 68 (1976), 204–207; English translation in *L'Osservatore Romano*, English edition (26 February 1976), 3.

33. John Paul II, Address to Bishops and Priests in Canon Law Course at the Pontifical Gregorian University, 21 November 1983; English translation in *L'Osservatore Romano*, English edition (30 January 1984), 4.

34. Canon 1055.

35. C. Caffara, "Caritas conjugalis et consensus matrimonialis," *Periodica*, 65/4 (1976), 613–618.

36. Encyclical *Humanae vitae* (25 July 1968), 9, in *AAS*, 60 (1968), 481–503; English translation by St. Paul Publications (Homebush, N.S.W., 1981), 10.

37. Z. Grocholewski, "De communione vitae in novo schemate DE MATRIMONIO, et de momento juridico amoris conjugalis," *Periodica*, 65/4 (1976), 479.

38. Monsignor Eid, Intervention at the 11th Colloquium of the Council of Europe on European Law, *Communicationes*, 13/2 (1981), 459.

39. *Ibid.*, 455.

40. G. Martelet, "Signification de l'Encyclique *Humanae Vitae*," in *Paul VI et la Modernité*, Collection Ecole Française de Rome 72 (Rome, 1976), 403.

41. *Humanae vitae* 8.

42. Cardinal Daneels, Archbishop of Malines-Bruxelles, Pastoral Letter "L'Eglise à la Maison," *Bulletin officiel de l'Archidiocèse de Malines Bruxelles*, 6 (June–July 1986), 86.

43. P. Adnès, "Matrimonio e mistero Trinitario," in P. Adnès and S. Garofalo (eds.), *Amore et stabilità nel matrimonio* (Rome, 1976), 22.

44. Caprile (ed.), *Concilio Vaticano II*, 4, 494–495, notes 16–17; presentation in the Council Hall of the text of the Constitution by Archbishop Garrone of Toulouse.

CHAPTER 29

The Canonical Significance of Marital Communion

Monsignor Antoni Stankiewicz

Summary

The article consists of three sections: Marital communion in preconciliar canonical tradition. Marital communion in the Pastoral Constitution *Gaudium et spes*. Marital communion and the partnership of the whole life.

———
———

Now, after more than twenty-five years, if we read what the Pastoral Constitution *Gaudium et spes* has to say on marriage,[1] and especially on marital communion, we shall be in a position to evaluate its innovating significance. Since the promulgation of the conciliar documents, canonical doctrine has been constantly rediscovering in *Gaudium et spes* a personalistic breadth to the concept of marriage, defined as "the intimate partnership of life and marital love."[2] As seen in *Gaudium et spes,* the fullness of marital communion, which is the source of family communion or the "domestic church,"[3] embraces the persons of husband and wife on the basis of the covenant of love that is mutual self-giving and acceptance in a community of life and marital love.

Marital communion arises on the basis of the harmonized wills of husband and wife, and of their love for one another, and encompasses both the spiritual and bodily dimensions of the persons, through which they express themselves and enter into the interpersonal marital relationship.

The unitary and full view of the grafting of these two dimensions of the personality in a total communion of two persons may
be lacking if emphasis is placed on one of them at the expense of
the other by recognizing the essential contribution of one and
seeing the other as merely complementary or secondary in the
formation of marital communion. However, full understanding
of marital communion and its essential and secondary elements
also depends on the historical view of matrimony as a natural
institution, and on the way in which we discern its elements of
communion. A short historical overview can illustrate better the
integration of the spiritual and bodily significance of marital
communion and bring out the unitary and personal view of this
as found in *Gaudium et spes.*

Marital Communion in Preconciliar
Canonical Tradition

Marital communion was highlighted in the well-known text of
Tertullian, who said that "there is no division in either spirit or
flesh" between husband and wife.[4] In later canonical tradition,
this concept came to be described with terms taken from Roman
law, such as *individua vitae consuetudo* (indissoluble community of
life)[5] or *consortium omnis vitae* (partnership of the whole life).[6]

The expression *individua vitae consuetudo,* which became established in doctrine and canonical legislation[7] in theological schools
prior to Gratian, referred to the two communal elements, that is,
individualiter commanendi et carnaliter commiscendi (indissoluble cohabitation and carnal union).[8] Thus, cohabitation and carnal
union came to be seen as characteristic of marital communion,
and entered into the object of consent, as Gratian in fact stated:
". . . consensus ergo cohabitandi et individuam vitae consuetudi-
nem retinendi eos coniuges facit" (thus, the consent to live together and maintain an indissoluble community of life makes
them into a married couple).[9]

Later on, however, there was a tendency to view marital communion as the *societas coniugalis* (marital society), so that marriage was constituted solely by *consensus coniugalis societatis* (consent to the marital society) and not by consent to exclusive
cohabitation and exclusive carnal union.[10] Marriage, therefore,
belonged to the genus of *relatio* (relation) and to the species of

coniunctio maxima (supreme union) of the spouses, that is, to the union *animorum et corporum* (of souls and bodies), which Saint Thomas described as that of *maxima amicitia* (supreme amity) and as constituting a *totius domesticae conversationis consortium* (community of total domestic intimacy).[11]

Although some people stated that marriage *non est essentialiter ipsa coniunctio carnalis* (is not essentially the carnal union itself) but an *associatio* (partnership or association),[12] another school of thought was beginning to give the priority to the bodily element in marital communion, which thus began a union *corporum et animorum* (of bodies and souls).[13]

Matrimonial consent, therefore, did not have any direct effect in the formation of the marital society, but *in mutuam corporum potestatem* (in the mutual right to dispose of the other's body),[14] and marital communion was narrowed down to bodily union, especially if we bear in mind that in the matrimonial contract, in the words of Duns Scotus, *est mutua datio corporum ad copulam carnalem* (there is a mutual gift of bodies with a view to carnal intercourse).[15]

It should be noted that emphasis on the bodily element in marital communion was not able to eliminate the significance of the spiritual element, so that in later canonical and moral thinking, we find alternations in the definition of the essential elements of marital communion, and especially in that of the object of consent.

On the one hand, therefore, the organic, biological, and reproductive view of communion continued, inasmuch as the essential object of consent was only the *mutua traditio corporis* (mutual gift of the body) and marriage became solely what Francis of Vitoria, for example, described as *quodam instrumentum ordinatum ad procreandos liberos* (a means as it were ordered to the procreation of free beings).[16]

On the other hand, without denying the essential place of bodily union, which comes from the mutual gift of the body for procreative ends, equal stress was laid on the spiritual element, understood as expression of the marital society. Thus, Peter of Ledesma wrote that in matrimony *consensus in societatem coniugalem divinitus institutum* (consent to the marital society instituted by God) was needed, apart from *in mutuam traditionem corporum* (to the mutual gift of bodies).[17]

Some people inserted the marital society into the expression of

Ulpian, so that it became *individua vitae societas* (indissoluble society of life),[18] although in practice it only meant *mutua habitatio* (cohabitation).[19]

In preconciliar canonical tradition, the concept of marital communion in the doctrine of Ponce de Leon deserves very close attention. This theologian saw the essence of marriage in the spiritual union of husband and wife, and considered that the *mutua coniunctio animorum* (mutual union of souls) must refer to the *naturalem* or *individuam vitae societatem cum diversitate sexus* (natural or indissoluble society of life between persons of different sexes).[20]

This spiritual approach to marital communion did not exclude bodily union, as based on the *potestas in corpus* (right over the body), or on the *obligatio ad carnalem copulam per consensum scilicet contrahentis explicitum vel implicitum* (duty to carnal intercourse through the consent, whether explicit or implicit, of the contractant),[21] but its true basis was the *vinculum mutuae societatis* (bond of mutual society).[22] Thus, the criterion of distinction between the matrimonial contract and other contracts lay in the obligation to the *individua vitae societas cum diversitate sexus* (indissoluble society of life between persons of different sexes) and not in the *obligatio ad carnalem copulam* (duty of carnal intercourse).[23] As a *vinculum mutuae societatis* (bond of mutual society), marital communion was, therefore, also the bond of mutual love, since marriage itself *ex essentia sua est vinculum mutuum amoris* (in its essence is the mutual bond of love).[24]

Against the background of this view, the prevalently corporalistic approach of the 1917 Code stands out. In this Code, marital communion was attributed only one essential element, which was the formal object of the consent of marriage *in fieri*: the *ius in corpus, perpetuum et exclusivum, in ordine ad actus per se aptos ad prolis generationem* (perpetual and exclusive right over the body, as ordered to acts suited of themselves to the generation of children).[25] Even the *societas permanens* (permanent society), which was the object of minimal knowledge, was described as having the exclusive aim of procreation.[26]

However, it cannot be said that the 1917 Code was unaware of the *communitas vitae* (community of life), the union of spirits, as based on the *mutuum adiutorium* (mutual aid) of husband and wife, which included *communio tori mensae et habitationis* (sharing of bed, board, and hearth). However, communion of life, which was described as *vitae consortium* (Canon 1130), *vitae consuetudo* (Canons 1131 and 1132), *vita communis* (Canons 1131 and 1132), and *vitae coniugalis communio* (Canon 1128), was viewed simply as a secondary element of marriage that could have canonical significance only within the perspective of separation of the spouses.

This was also the normally accepted teaching, as authoritatively expressed by Cardinal Gasparri, the craftsman of the Code, according to whom the *individua vitae consuetudo* (indissoluble community of life) meant primarily the *ius mutuum in corpus cum relativa obligatione* (right over the body of the other, and corresponding obligation) and only in second place, the *communio tori mensae et habitationis in unione animorum per mutuum amorem et in aliquali unione bonorum* (sharing of bed, board, and hearth, in the union of souls through mutual love and in a certain union of goods).[27] Apart from the *ius in corpus* (right to [the use of] the body), the *individua vitae consuetudo* also included the *ius-obligatio ad hanc vitae communionem* (right and duty to live this communion of life),[28] although this latter right was only secondary and was therefore part of the *integritatem potius quam ad essentiam matrimonii* (secondary part more than of the essence of marriage), so that the denial of the *ius ad vitae communionem* (right to communion of life) could not mean the nullity of the marriage.[29]

On the other hand, Cardinal Gasparri himself observed that at the time there were people who held the opinion (which he did not share) that the substance of marriage would not exist if consent to the sharing of bed, board, and hearth was not present in the celebration of the marriage.[30]

We can therefore conclude that in the period prior to the Second Vatican Council, the right to communion of life had canonical significance only in a secondary and not an essential manner. And the Encyclical *Casti connubii* of Pius XI did not broaden the canonical view of marriage, although this pontiff did understand it in the broader sense as *totius vitae communio, consuetudo, societas* (communion, community, society, of the whole of life), the primary reason or cause of which was the *mutua coniugum interior conformatio* (interior conforming of the spouses to one another) and the *assiduum sese invicem perficiendi studium* (persevering endeavor to bring each other to the state of perfection).[31] The community of life and actions of husband and wife, their integration, their reciprocal love, were subordinated to the primary aim of marriage, which was closely linked to the *ius in corpus* (right to the body).[32]

Marital Communion in the Pastoral Constitution *Gaudium et spes*

Community of Life and Marital Love

In ecclesial reflection on marriage in the period prior to the Council, people focused on its religious and social aspect, which was closely linked to the procreative aim,[33] while the personalistic aspect, and especially marital love, were seen as subordinate to procreation and the function instrumental in this.[34]

The conciliar debate revealed the inadequacy of the unilateral procreative approach to marriage, which *non est merum instrumentum procreationis* (is not merely a means of procreation), but also a *totius vitae consuetudo et communio* (community and communion of the whole life).[35]

The Council stresses the person and the communion of persons of different sexes that takes place in marriage, without detracting from its institutional character for procreative ends; it is thus defined in a personalistic and dynamic perspective as the *intima unio* (intimate union) of persons, as *communitas amoris* (community of love), and more precisely in the now classic expression *intima communitas vitae et amoris coniugalis* (intimate partnership of life and marital love).[36]

This partnership of life and marital love has its source in the marital covenant—that is, in the irrevocable personal consent with which the man and woman give themselves to one another and receive one another—and is oriented toward the good of persons—that is, the spouses, their offspring, and society.[37]

The bodily union of husband and wife had previously been interpreted in a biological and procreative key, but *Gaudium et spes* related it more to marital love, with its human and interpersonal significance. As "an eminently human love," marital love "embraces the good of the whole person" and therefore enriches "the sentiments of the spirit and their physical expression with a unique dignity and ennobles them as the special elements and signs of the friendship proper to marriage."[38] As John Paul II later

explained in his Apostolic Exhortation *Familiaris consortio*, bodily union "is realized in a truly human way only if it is an integral
part of the love by which a man and a woman commit themselves
totally to one another until death."[39]

When the acts of bodily communion proper to married people
(*actus coniugales*) are thus bound up with marital love, they not
only have a procreative and unitive significance, but express the
whole significance of mutual self-giving and become the sign of
dialectio coniugalis (marital pleasure or joy).[40]

Although we shall not enter here into an analysis of the
strictly theological dimension of marital love,[41] it is helpful to
emphasize the derivation of bodily communion, with its *ius in
corpus* (right to the body) from the *intima communitas vitae et
amoris coniugalis* (intimate partnership of life and marital love) to
which it owes its full human significance and its interpersonal
dimension.[42]

The central role of marital love in the partnership of life and
love, not as closed in on itself, but as open to procreation and
to the advancement and perfecting of the spouses, means that
marriage becomes the *institutum amoris coniugalis* (institution of
marital love) or institutionalized marital love.[43] Indeed, marital
love is the identifying element of the communion of marital
life. Husband and wife give themselves to this communion in
the covenant of love or in the free choice with which they
"accept the intimate community of life and love willed by God
himself."[44]

The Canonical Interpretation of the Partnership
of Life and Marital Love

Postconciliar discussion has brought to light a question in the
field of doctrine and canonical jurisprudence with regard to the
juridical interpretation to be attributed to the elements contained in the conciliar definition of marriage—in other words,
partnership of life and marital love.

Although it is clear that marriage becomes very precarious
without love and that deep communion between the spouses is a
guarantee of the stability of the marriage, the line of thought
strongly linked to the formulation of Canon 1081, §2, of the
1917 Code held from the beginning that *Gaudium et spes* did not

raise marital love and partnership of life to the level of a "juridically relevant category" alongside the three traditional goods of marriage."[45]

The partnership of life and marital love was, therefore, placed on the level of cohabitation and mutual aid, and thus was not essential but secondary and complementary for marriage.

As a result, marital love was not held to have any direct juridical significance; it was viewed as the *res facti,* or the psychological and affective element, which, since it was not subject to the control of the will, could not be an essential element of the formal object of matrimonial consent.[46]

Another line of thought in the field of doctrine and jurisprudence attributed essential canonical significance to the element of love and to the partnership of life.

Although the definition of marriage given in *Gaudium et spes* is mainly theological and pastoral, it still has canonical implications, especially if we remember the close connection between theological formulations and the canonical norms that must express theological and pastoral content in legislative terms.

It was therefore correct that in the conciliar definition, the intimate partnership of life and marital love was seen as the "intimate and first *ratio* of marriage,"[47] although not as its purpose, since marital love, like marriage, is, according to *Gaudium et spes,* "by nature ordered to the procreation and education of children."[48]

In this way, marital love came to be identified with consent— that is, love understood as a constitutive element of marriage *in fieri* in such a way that there can be no valid consent without love.[49]

In another perspective, it was held that marital love enters only indirectly into consent, or into its formal object, although it is not identified with the *consensus qui solum facit matrimonium* (consent that alone makes marriage).[50] The element of love would, therefore, not be involved in consent, but in the object of consent, inasmuch as only the partnership of life and marital love is set up through this consent.[51]

However, the distinction did not appear so clear-cut as to eradicate all doubts, so that some people held that marital love is juridically significant to marriage both *in fieri* and *in facto esse.*[52]

Apart from the element of love, there was also the element of the object of consent. However, the question was left open as to whether such communion of life encompassed all the marital rights and obligations included in the *tria bona* (three goods of marriage) and thus become identified with marriage itself, or whether it was a separate element that had still to be identified.[53]

The problem was not solved in the course of the revision of the 1917 Code, since the *ius ad communionem vitae* (right to communion of life), or, in other words, *ad ea quae vitae communionem essentialiter constituunt* (to those things that essentially constitute the communion of life),[54] was not directly included in the new canonical norms concerning the *elementa essentialia matrimonii* (essential elements of marriage).[55]

Marital Communion and the Partnership of the Whole Life

The Partnership of the Whole Life

Marital communion—that is, the communion of the persons of the spouses—has been constantly present in the papal magisterium since the Second Vatican Council, and is referred to in the present Code with the substantially Roman expression *totius vitae consortium* (partnership of the whole life).[56]

Through the matrimonial covenant, the spouses set up between them "a partnership of the whole of life [*totius vitae consortium*] [which] is by its nature ordered toward the good of the spouses and the procreation and education of offspring" (Canon 1055, §1).

The word *consortium*, which had replaced other equivalent terms such as *coniunctio* or *communio*, means that the *consortium coniugale* is seen as oriented toward the *consortio familiaris*, of which it is the source, and as encompassing the global and total nature of the communion of the persons of the spouses in its interpersonal aspect—and hence as independent of marital cohabitation, or what is called *convictus coniugalis*.[57]

In purely juridical terms, the *consortium totius vitae* expresses the concept of marital communion that is referred to in conciliar terms as the intimate partnership of life and marital love, and it therefore indicates the canonical fact of the marital communion that husband and wife bring into existence with the covenant of love of mutual self-giving, accepting it in the structure that was set up by divine command and willed by God himself.[58]

This marital communion has a dynamic dimension, since it

. . . is established and develops between husband and wife: by virtue of the covenant of married life, the man and woman "are no longer two but one flesh" (Mt. 19:6; cf. Gen. 2:29) and they are called to grow continually in their communion through day-to-day fidelity to their marriage promises of total mutual self-giving.[59]

Even so, the essential canonical significance only involves the setting up of marital communion and not its growth, although the latter can be significant in a secondary or complementary sense, so that its absence could lead to the separation of the spouses.[60]

The Essential Structure of the Partnership of the Whole Life

Two essential and foundational elements can be clearly distinguished in the structure of the *consortium totius vitae*, as expressed in the *bonum coniugum* (good of the spouses) and *bonum prolis* (good of the offspring). These are the spiritual and bodily elements through which the spouses share "their entire life-project, what they have and what they are."[61]

1. *Communion of Marital Love.* Since communion of persons cannot be set up without love,[62] within the structure of the marital partnership in ontological terms we can discern the communion of marital love, which is distinguished by the *elementum amoris* (element of love). The communion of marital love defines in a canonically significant way the communion of life that is set up by the spouses, constituting its essential dimension. Marriage can therefore be called the *institutum amoris coniugalis* (institution of marital love) and not only the *institutum procreationis* (institution of procreation), and in this way we overcome the preconciliar dualism between institution and marital love (inasmuch as the latter had no direct canonical significance).

According to Pianazzi, three components of marital love can be distinguished: the physical component, made up of sexual attraction and "bound up with the search for pleasure"; the affective component, which encompasses the aspect of falling in love, and expresses "the need and satisfaction of tenderness, intimacy, closeness, support, protection and the search and instinctive fulfillment of one's own sex with the values proper to the other"; and the spiritual component, which is the will to mutual self-giving, "wanting the good of the other, and the wish to accomplish this good within a deep and stable union of two lives—the wish to build up this good at every moment of life."[63]

Although these components of marital love are expressed in a "unitary and harmonic" manner, the spiritual component is basically dependent on the will of the spouses and can therefore be seen as the canonically significant element of the formal object of consent—or, in other words, of the mutual covenant of love. This element does not represent the direct object of sexual attraction or of the feelings, which are nonstable components of marital love and do not depend directly on the will; rather, it depends directly on the act of the will, as part of the mutual commitment of the spouses made at the moment of the expression of consent.

The spiritual component integrates and ennobles the other components of marital love, which thus become "fully human love" and "not a simple transport of instinct and sentiment but also, and principally, an act of the free will, intended to endure and to grow by means of the joys and sorrows of daily life."[64]

This volitive element of marital love—its *voluntatis affectus*[65]—is the foundation of an interpersonal relationship specific to the *dilectio coniugalis*,[66] that is, the communion of marital love, which is also based on sexual values and sentiment, and to which the spouses bind themselves in the liturgical and ecclesial act of consent, promising each other *ut eam/eum diligas et honores omnibus diebus vitae suae* (to love and honor her/him all the days of his/her life).[67]

This love, which, as *Gaudium et spes* declares, is "indissolubly faithful" inasmuch as it is "endorsed by mutual fidelity and, above all, consecrated by Christ's sacrament" (No. 49), therefore produces the communion of marital love that becomes an essential component of the partnership of the whole life. The right and obligation to the communion of marital love enters into the formal object of matrimonial consent—in other words, the covenant of marital love—as an essential element of matrimony. The absence of the right and obligation to the communion of marital love therefore means that matrimonial consent is invalid, as we find in Canon 1101, §2.

The intention of not making a total commitment to the right

and obligation to the communion of marital love, as a means of freeing oneself from the matrimonial bond and thus regaining complete freedom and starting a new life, has until now been considered by canon law within the framework of the rejection of the *bonum sacramenti,* that is, the absence of acceptance of the indissolubility of marriage.[68] However, the object of such an intention in fact refers directly to a lack of commitment to the obligation of the communion of marital love, inasmuch as this love "abides faithfully in mind and body in prosperity and adversity and hence excludes both adultery and divorce."[69]

Consequently, a marriage is also made invalid by the incapacity, for some reason of a psychological nature, to take on the obligation to set up the communion of marital love.[70]

It can also have indirect canonical relevance in the case of deception (*deceptio dolosa*), concerning some quality of the other party that of its very nature can seriously disturb the partnership of married life.[71] Thus, deception perpetrated in order to extort the consent of the other party—that is, to obtain the covenant of marital love—psychologically speaking produces a total lack of commitment to the obligation to maintain the communion of marital love. So long as the error caused by the deception remains, the establishment of the communion of marital love is merely apparent, because the covenant of marital love is invalid and the spouses cannot validly accept the intimate partnership of life and love willed by God.

2. *Sexual or Bodily Communion.* As we have already indicated, in canonical tradition, sexual or bodily communion of life[72] and the relative right and obligation to this have always been considered an essential component of marriage and of the formal object of consent.

Inasmuch as the bodily or sexual dimension of the partnership of the whole life is based on the marital right to bodily consummation with the acts proper to marital life,[73] it has essential canonical relevance both with regard to the capacity of the subjects to perform the conjugal act in its unitive and procreative significance, and also with regard to the exclusivity of the right and obligation to such acts, which express the mutual self-giving of the spouses, and thus constitute and bring about sexual communion.[74]

Although sexuality and marital love are not identical,[75] there is a partial overlapping between them within the framework of the partnership of the whole life, inasmuch as the exercise of the sexual function "is realized in a truly human way only if it is an integral part of the love by which a man and a woman commit themselves totally to one another until death."[76] In this way, the conjugal act is not simply a biophysiological fact, but takes on the value of an act of the persons, and of their mutual and total self-giving, assuming a personal, interpersonal, and transpersonal character, since it brings about intimacy and openness to new human life.[77]

Moreover, the conjugal act as performed in a truly human manner so that the spouses become "one single flesh" takes on canonical significance with regard to the consummation of the marriage[78] and makes the marital communion absolutely indissoluble.[79]

Translated from the Italian by Leslie Wearne.

Notes

1. GS 47–52.
2. *Ibid.*, 48.
3. LG 11.
4. Tertullian, *Ad uxorem*, II, VIII, 7, in *Corpus* Christianorum, 1, 393.
5. *Inst.* 1, 9, 1.
6. *Dig.* 23, 2, 1 (Modestin, *I Reg.*).
7. Cf. *Dict.* a.c. 1, C. XXVII, q. 2; *dict.* q. 1, C. XXIX; c. 11, X, II, 23 (Alexander III).
8. Cf. A. Stankiewicz, "De origine definitionis matrimonii in Decreto Gratiani," *Periodica*, 71 (1982), 222–223.
9. C. 3, C. XXVII, q. 2.
10. Peter Lombard, *Sententiae*, IV, d. 28, c. 4, n. 2.
11. Saint Thomas Aquinas, *Summa contra Gentiles*, III, c. 123.
12. Saint Thomas Aquinas, *In IV Sententiarum*, d. 28, q. 1, a. 4, sol.
13. Saint Bonaventure, *In IV Sententiarum*, d. 27, a. 1, q. 1, concl. nn. 4–5.
14. *Ibid.*, d. 28, a. un., q. 6, concl.
15. J. Duns Scotus, *Quaestiones in lib. IV Sententiarum*, d. 30, q. 2, n. 5.
16. Francis of Vitoria, *Summa Sacramentorum Ecclesiae* (Venice, 1629), n. 246.
17. Peter of Ledesma, *Tractatus de magno matrimonii sacramento* (Venice, 1595), q. 48, a. 1, p. 292.

18. Cf. F.X. Schmalzgrueber, *Ius ecclesiasticum universum* (Rome, 1844), t. IV, p. 1, tit. 1, n. 223.

19. Cf. T. Sanchez, *De sancto matrimonii sacramento* (Venice, 1619), lib. II, disp. 1, n. 8. Some people say that the *pactum numquam cohabitandi irritat nuptias;* cf. R. Le Picard, *La communauté de la vie conjugale. Obligation des époux* (Paris, 1930), 3.

20. Basil Ponce de Leon, *De sacramento matrimonii tractatus* (Lyons, 1640), lib. I, c. 28, n. 15; lib. VII, c. 57, n. 1.

21. On the *duplus consensus,* that is *in naturalem in diverso sexu societatem* and *in liberorum procreationem* which *supponat primum, et illum consequatur; ibid.,* lib. I, c. 18, n. 18.

22. *Ibid.*

23. *Ibid.*

24. *Ibid.,* lib. II, c. 2, n. 4.

25. Canon 1081, §2.

26. Canon 1082, §1.

27. P. Gasparri, *Tractatus canonicum de matrimonio,* 1 (Vatican City, 1932), 15, n. 6.

28. *Ibid.,* 2, 188, n. 1103.

29. *Ibid.,* 2, 7–8, n. 776; 189, n. 1105. For rulings of the Rota, cf. C. Holboeck, *Tractatus de jurisprudentia S.R. Rotae* (Graz/Vienna/Cologne, 1957), 253f.

30. Gasparri, *Tractatus canonicus de matrimonio,* 1, 16, n. 8.

31. Pius XI, Encyclical Letter *Casti connubii,* in *AAS,* 22 (1930), 548; English translation in J. Neuner and J. Dupuis (eds.), *The Christian Faith* (Bangalore, 1978), 499.

32. Supreme Sacred Congregation of the Sacred Office, 1 April 1944, in *AAS,* 36 (1944), 103.

33. Leo XIII, Encyclical Letter *Arcanum,* in *ASS,* 12 (1894), 388.

34. Pius XII, Allocution of 29 October 1951, in *AAS,* 43 (1951), 835–854.

35. Cf. L.C. Bernal, "Genesis de la doctrina sobre el amore conyugal de la constitución *Gaudium et Spes,*" *Ephemerides Theologicae Lovanienses,* 51 (1957), 64.

36. GS 48.

37. *Ibid.*

38. *Ibid.,* 49.

39. John Paul II, Apostolic Exhortation *Familiaris consortio,* 11, in *AAS,* 74 (1982), 92; English translation in A. Flannery (gen. ed.), *Vatican II: More Postconciliar Documents,* 2 (New York, 1982), 822.

40. GS 49.

41. Cf. J. Beyer, "Amoris humani donum divinae caritatis sacramentum," *Periodica,* 58 (1969), 123–138.

42. Cf. A. Favale, "Fini del matrimonio nel magistero del Concilio

Vaticano II," in A.M. Triacca (ed.), *Realtà e valori del sacramento del matrimonio* (Rome, 1976), 203.

43. C.A. Molina Melia, "La 'communitas vitae et amoris' en el Concilio Vaticano II," in *El "consortium totius vitae"* (Salamanca, 1986), 48.

44. John Paul II, *Familiaris consortio* 11; English translation, 823.

45. P. Fedele, "'L' 'ordinatio ad problem' e i fini del matrimonio con particolare riferimento alla costituzione 'Gaudium et Spes' del Concilio Vaticano II," in V. Fagiolo (ed.), *L'Amore Coniugale* (Vatican City, 1971), 38.

46. U. Navarrete, "Consenso matrimoniale e amore coniugale con particolare riferimento alla Cost. 'Gaudium et Spes,' " in *ibid.*, 213. For rulings of the Rota, cf. *Rom. Rotae Decisiones seu Sententiae*, 63 (1980), 468–473 (c. Palazzini, 2 June 1971, Nos. 3–17).

47. V. Fagiolo, "Essenza e fini del matrimonio secondo la Cost. past. 'Gaudium et Spes' del Vaticano II," in Fagiolo (ed.), *L'Amore Coniugale*, 97.

48. GS 50.

49. A. Gutierrez, *Il matrimonio: essenza-fine-amore coniugale* (Naples, 1974), 63; P.A. Bonnet, *L'essenza del matrimonio canonico. Contributo allo studio dell'amore coniugale* (Padua, 1976), 132. For rulings of the Rota, cf. *Rom. Rotae Decisiones seu Sententiae*, 62 (1980), 979–986 (c. Fagiolo, 30 October 1970, nn. 3–9).

50. Paul VI, Allocution to the Roman Rota, 9 February 1976, in *AAS*, 68 (1976), 206.

51. O. Fumagalli Carulli, *Il matrimonio canonico dopo il concilio. Capacità e consenso* (Milan, 1978), 170.

52. L. Vela, "La 'communitas vitae et amoris,' " in *El consenimiento matrimonial, hoy. Trabajos de la XV semana de derecho canonico* (Salamanca, 1976), 102.

53. U. Navarrete, "De iure ad vitae communionem," *Periodica*, 66 (1977), 259.

54. *Communicationes*, 9 (1977), 374–375.

55. Cf. Canon 1101, §2.

56. Canon 1055, §1. Cf. A. Mostaza Rodriguez, "El 'consortium totius vitae' en el nuevo Código de Derecho Canónico," in *El "consortium totius vitae,"* 83ff. The *consortium omnis vitae* was an essential element of marriage for the Romans; cf. C. Castello, "Consortium omnis vitae," in F. Biffi (ed.), *La definizione essenziale giuridica del matrimonio* (Rome, 1980), 63.

57. Canons 1151, 1152, §§1–2.

58. GS 48; John Paul II, *Familiaris consortio* 11.

59. John Paul II, *Familiaris consortio* 19.

60. Cf. Canons 1152–1153.

61. John Paul II, *Familiaris consortio* 19.

62. *Ibid.*, 18.

63. H. Pianazzi, "L'amore coniugale. Sue componenti e sua colloca-zione nei confronti della carità e dell'amicizia," in Triacca (ed.), *Realtà e valori del sacramento del matrimonio*, 284–287.

64. Paul VI, Encyclical Letter *Humanae vitae* 9, in *AAS*, 60 (1968), 486; English translation, St. Paul Publications (Homebush, N.S.W., 1981), 10.

65. GS 49.

66. *Ibid.*

67. *Ordo celebrandi matrimonium* (1972), No. 25.

68. Cf. *Rom. Rotae Decisiones seu Sententiae*, 64 (1981), 383 (c. Palazzini, 28 June 1972, No. 11).

69. GS 49.

70. Canon 1095, 3°.

71. Canon 1098. Cf. U. Navarrete, "Canon 1098 de errore doloso estne iuris naturalis an iuris positivi ecclesiae," *Periodica,* 76 (1987), 177ff.

72. John Paul II, *Familiaris consortio* 32.

73. Cf. Canon 1061, §1.

74. Cf. Canons 1084, §1; 1101, §2.

75. Favale, "Fini del matrimonio nel magisterio del Concilio Vati-cano II," 199.

76. John Paul II, *Familiaris consortio* 11.

77. *Ibid.* Cf. D. Tettamanzi, *Il procreare umano* (Casale Monferrato, 1985), 16.

78. Canon 1061, §1.

79. Canon 1142.

CHAPTER 30

Vatican Council II and Matrimonial Law
The Perspective of Canon 1095

Raymond L. Burke

Summary

The Code is the last conciliar document and, as John Paul II says, it puts the Council into the whole of life. The question is to know if the definition of marriage that the Code presents responds to the vision of the Council. The study of the texts confirm this: marriage is a divine vocation, a consecration of life and situates a particular state within the Church. That is why Canon 1095, which considers the validity of consent, responds perfectly to the values called into question by matrimonial consent and makes one see the importance of the psychological and physical aspects that could invalidate this consent and renders inviable the union that it ought to establish.

Introduction

In the fall following the promulgation of the revised Code of Canon Law, a special course of introduction to the new Code was given by the Faculty of Canon Law at the Pontifical Gregorian University. Laypersons, members of institutes of the consecrated life, priests and bishops from around the world took part in the special course. During the time of their study, the participants were received in special audience by the Holy Father, Pope John Paul II. In his discourse to the audience, the Holy Father, the Legislator of the 1983 Code, referred to the revised Code of Canon Law as the "last Conciliar document."[1] He went on to call it the first document "to bring the whole Council into the whole of life."[2]

Certainly, from an historical point of view, the Code of Canon Law completed the program of Church renewal, announced by Pope John XXIII on 25 January 1959.[3] More profoundly, however, the Code gives expression to the Church's discipline coherent with the Church's doctrine presented in the conciliar documents proper. While it is regrettable that the conciliar teaching lacks an explicit and systematic reflection on the essential place of canon law in Church life, for example, in the Dogmatic Constitution on the Church,[4] nevertheless, the service of Church discipline to the whole of Church life is implicit throughout the documents of the Council, also by explicit reference to canonical norms that must follow from the Council's teaching.[5]

By examining the overall structure of the revised Code and studying the individual canons, the Code's fidelity to its doctrinal foundation in the teaching of the Second Vatican Council is readily evident. The organization of the seven books of the Code according to the presentation of the Church as the hierarchically ordered People of God, sharing in the redemptive prophetic, priestly, and kingly mission of Christ, is the first and most striking evidence of the Code's fidelity to the Council. Likewise, the individual canons of the Code, many of which repeat verbatim the text of the conciliar documents, have their roots in the teaching on the Church and its mission, authentically proclaimed and illustrated by the Fathers of the Second Vatican Council. One example is the description of the marriage covenant given in Canons 1055, §1; 1056; and 1057, §2. The text of the canons is a synthesis of the first paragraph of number 48 of the Pastoral Constitution on the Church in the Modern World. The fidelity of the Code to the teaching of the Council even is seen in the canons that seem the least doctrinal, namely, the procedural norms of the Church, as has been demonstrated in a recent presentation of Bishop Zenon Grocholewski, Secretary of the Apostolic Signatura.[6]

If it is true that the Code of Canon Law brings the integral teaching of the Council into every dimension of life, the Legislator of the Code had to give particular attention to the origin and secure receptacle of human life in marriage and the family born of the matrimonial consent of man and woman. There could have been no more sensitive and critical concern for the Legislator than the correct interpretation, in Church discipline, of the Council's teaching on marriage and the family, on the "domestic Church."[7]

The purpose of the present study is to see, therefore, whether the practical norms regarding marriage in the Code of Canon Law truly reflect in juridic categories the truth about marriage presented anew at the Second Vatican Council. To respond to the question proposed by the study, it is necessary, first of all, to examine the teaching on marriage at the Second Vatican Council. Then, a single canon, completely new in the revised Code, namely, Canon 1095, will be examined regarding its fidelity to conciliar teaching. In a lengthier study, the same examination could be made of the other canons directly touching on marriage and the family.[8] For the present study, Canon 1095 will stand as a test case. At the end of the study, the conclusion to the question posed at the beginning can be drawn, also with respect to the interpretative significance of the conciliar documents for the understanding of Canon 1095.

Conciliar Teaching on Marriage

The Second Vatican Council presents marriage, first of all, as a divine vocation, a call from God, by which husband and wife are "established in a true order of persons."[9] In the Dogmatic Constitution on the Church, the "state of life and order" of married persons is called their proper gift in the People of God.[10] Marriage is, therefore, one of the adult forms of the originary baptismal vocation by which God constitutes his Church.

Marriage is a divine vocation. Therefore, its origin is not in man, either as individual or as society, but rather in God, three in one, and in his plan for creation redeemed by the passion, death, and resurrection of the Son.[11]

Marriage is a vocation. It is the response to a specific call. It is not simply the natural result of a developing relationship be-

tween a man and a woman. Rather, it is the response to the
invitation from God to give adult expression to the Christian
vocation received at Baptism, increased and strengthened at Confirmation, and nourished at the Table of the Eucharist. It is the
response to God's call to give specific adult form to the life of
Christ within the individual. [12]

The Christian vocation of Baptism takes adult form in marriage by the life of mutual and exclusive, indissoluble, and
procreative love of husband and wife. The Council Fathers
remind priests of their duty to foster "the vocation of spouses"
by various pastoral means, especially the proclamation of the
gospel and the celebration of the sacred liturgy. In a particular
manner, the married find strength and comfort through the
ministry of the priest. By fidelity to their vocation in both "joys
and sacrifices," the married follow in the way of Christ, share in
his passion, death, and resurrection, attain with him their eternal salvation. [13]

The Decree on the Apostolate of Laypersons describes the
specific mission that flows from the vocation (consecration) of
married persons, as opposed to the mission of those in other
ecclesial states of life. The Decree states that the vocation of the
married is

> To manifest and demonstrate the indissolubility and holiness
> of the marriage bond by their life; to affirm actively their right
> and duty (imparted to parents and guardians) to educate off-
> spring in a Christian manner; to defend the dignity and legiti-
> mate autonomy of the family. [14]

This text succinctly indicates the specific characteristics of the
mission of those called to the married life. The mission of the
married is, first of all, to make present in the world the love of
God by their faithful (mutual and exclusive), permanent (indissoluble), and life-giving (procreative) love for one another. By
carrying out the mission for which they have been consecrated by
God's grace in the Sacrament of Marriage, husband and wife
safeguard and foster the proper dignity of the family as the house-
hold of faith.

What is stated in the Decree on the Apostolate of Laypersons
is presented more amply in Chapter One of Part II of the Pastoral
Constitution on the Church in the Modern World. Most espe-

cially in number 48 of the Pastoral Constitution, the nature of the vocation to marriage is elaborated.

Number 48 states, first of all, what the origin of the married life is. It teaches that marriage is born of God's call and the response of man and woman to God's call "by irrevocable personal consent."[15] The Council Fathers further teach: "Thus, out of the human act by which the spouses mutually hand over and accept one another is born an institution [marriage] stable by divine ordering, also before society."[16]

The same text describes the state of life (the mission) that results from the response of the couple in the act of marriage consent. It is a state of life that is at one and the same time ordered to the salvation of the spouses, and to the procreation and education of children. The conciliar text does not permit that one end or purpose of marriage have precedence over or exclude the other. Rather, it includes both as equally essential to the happiness (salvation) God intends for those whom he calls to the married life. Both purposes of marriage postulate the indissolubility and exclusive unity of the love of marriage: "This intimate union, namely the mutual giving of two persons, as well as the good of the children require the complete fidelity of the spouses and demand their unbreakable unity."[17]

In summary, marriage is presented in the conciliar documents as the call to form, by personal consent, the bond of love that is, by its nature, exclusive, indissoluble, and procreative, and which has as its mission the salvation of the married parties, and the generation and development of human life, of the human family.

Before looking at Canon 1095, one additional aspect of the conciliar teaching, which has serious implications for the vocation to marriage, must be studied. Canon 1095 treats directly the effect of the psychological development and state of a person on the response to the vocation of marriage by irrevocable personal consent. It must be asked, therefore: Did the Council speak about the meaning of psychological development for the act of marriage consent?

In the Decree on Christian Education, the Council Fathers note specifically the importance of the science of psychology in assisting the harmonious development of the young person. The conciliar text states that the child or the young person is to be assisted "in acquiring gradually, once obstacles have been overcome by a generous and steadfast mind and heart, the more perfect understanding of the responsibility for his own life, rightly perfected by constant effort and pursued in true freedom."[18] Further, the text mentions as a specific aspect of the necessary assistance to the child or young person "positive and prudent sexual education as age increases."[19] The Council Fathers here, that is, in the very first number of the Decree on Christian Education, refer to the primary and ultimate goal of all true education: the knowledge of one's vocation in life and the acceptance of the same vocation with fidelity and generosity. In the same context, they indicate the importance of the findings in the science of psychology for the offering of true education.

With respect to the vocation to Holy Orders, the Council mandates that the human maturity required for acceptance of his vocation be fostered in the seminary student. The chief signs of the attainment of the required maturity are "a certain stability of mind and heart" and "the ability of making considered decisions" and "of judging rightly events and persons."[20] It is clear that sound psychological development is seen as necessary to the acceptance of the vocation to the priesthood. The degree of personal development of the individual must be proportionate to the call and the response to the vocation, according to the conciliar teaching. So, too, speaking of the relationship of Christian teaching to human culture, the Council insists that pastoral care be informed not only by the principles of theology, but also by the discoveries of the secular sciences, principally psychology and sociology. In such a manner, the conciliar text states, "the faithful will be led to the purer and more mature life of faith."[21]

If the Church is to help individuals to respond effectively to their vocations, it will have to take account of the findings of psychology, which are relevant to vocational response. For the translation into juridic categories of the truth about Christian marriage, the conciliar document demands that proper account of the psychology of the Christian vocation be taken.

Canon 1095

Canon 1095 is one of the completely new canons in the revised Code of Canon Law. Although the 1917 Code had made mention of causes of nullity of marriage because of *amentia* in Book IV on processes (Canon 1982), it made no mention of the so-called psychological grounds of nullity in the substantive law on marriage in Book III. It is not that such grounds were unknown, for references to *amentia* as a grounds of nullity are found in the early sources of canon law.[22] Likewise, the Roman Rota had developed an accepted jurisprudence in causes introduced under the heading of *amentia,* or of lack of discretion of judgment, the gradually preferred category for such factispecies.[23] It should be noted that the term amentia, used in the strictly canonical sense of a psychological state rendering invalid the act of marriage consent, was subject to equivocation because of its classical psychiatric usage in the sense of psychosis.[24]

There was, however, a certain hesitancy to define by codification the nature of the grounds, a hesitancy that persisted to the time of the revision of the Code.[25] Due to the rapid developments in the science of psychology and in the medical art of psychiatry, there was a natural fear of defining realities about which much was yet unknown. At the same time, the lack of any definition in the law led to a great deal of confusion in canonical doctrine and practice.[26]

The Pontifical Commission for the Revision of the Code of Canon Law took on the task of formulating legislation that would "more distinctly and more clearly" express the incapacity of giving valid marriage consent because of psychological difficulties.[27] The canon that resulted from the Commission's work reads:

Can. 1095—They are incapable of contracting marriage:

1° who lack the sufficient use of reason;

2° who suffer a serious lack of discretion of judgment regarding the essential matrimonial rights and duties to be handed over and accepted mutually;

3° who, for causes of a psychic nature, cannot assume the essential obligations of marriage.[28]

In order to understand correctly the intent of the legislation in Canon 1095, three clarifications must be made.

First, the whole of Canon 1095 treats incapacity to give consent because of a defective psychological state or development. Numbers 1 and 2 of the canon do not mention "psychic causes," as does number 3. The categories, sufficient use of reason and discretion of judgment, however, are taken from classical meta-physical psychology.[29] They refer to the gradual personal develop-ment in the capacity to act through orders or by oneself in matters of ever greater seriousness. In using these categories, it is not necessary to make reference to "psychic causes." Use of rea-son and discretion of judgment include in their meanings the gradual psychological integration of the individual, by which he is capable of actions of ever greater seriousness. Saint Thomas Aquinas provides a classical discussion of the nature of use of reason or discretion of judgment in practical judgments:

> Man differs, however, from other irrational creatures in this: That he is the master of his acts. Whence alone those actions of which man is the master are properly called human. Man is, however, master of his acts through reason and will: Whence also free will is said to be the faculty *of the will and reason.* Those actions, therefore, are called properly human, which proceed from deliberated will.[30]

Use of reason and discretion of judgment, therefore, refer to the capacity for the practical judgment to marry. When the same capacity is lacking in a person at a certain age, it is owed to some psychological deficiency, some lack of development or loss of development achieved already.

The second clarification has to do with the distinction be-tween numbers 1 and 2 of Canon 1095. Lack of sufficient use of reason and serious lack of discretion of judgment do not represent two distinct kinds of incapacity for marriage consent. Rather, they indicate two degrees of the same incapacity to form suffi-cient marriage consent.

In classical texts of philosophical psychology, use of reason and discretion of judgment are used interchangeably.[31] In the discussion of the Pontifical Commission for the Revision of the Code of Canon Law, it is clear that lack of sufficient use of reason is understood to be the most severe form of the serious lack of discretion of judgment.[32] Monsignor Antoni Stankiewicz, Auditor of the Roman Rota, commenting on the 1975 draft of the revised Code, wrote: "The criterion of the *use of reason* is implicit in the criterion of 'discretion of judgment proportionate to marriage' as its minimum essential element."[33] Since the lack of sufficient use of reason already is contained in the notion of serious lack of discretion of judgment, it is not correct to treat number 1 separately from number 2. Number 1 would apply to persons who lacked altogether the psychological integration requisite for marriage consent, for example, a person in the qualified state of epileptic psychosis.[34]

The third clarification has to do with the distinction of numbers 1 and 2 from number 3. Although the defect in number 3, as the text states explicitly, like in numbers 1 and 2, is owed to a defective psychological state or development, the nullifying effect number 3 produces is distinct from that of numbers 1 and 2. Whereas numbers 1 and 2 describe insufficiency in the act itself of consent, number 3 describes inefficacy of the act of consent, given the sufficiency of the act itself. Monsignor Mario Pompedda, Auditor of the Roman Rota, differentiates well numbers 1 and 2 from number 3:

In reality, Canon 1095, establishing a triple incapacity of contracting marriage, in the first two cases (numbers 1 and 2) considers the *subject* as productive of an inadequate psychological act, and in the third case (number 3) still formally the subject but placed in relationship with the *object* to which he is unequal, because his attempt to consent falls on a matter removed from his capacities, which, that is, he is not capable of having at his disposal for psychological reasons.[35]

Number 3 refers, therefore, to a distinct kind of nullity, concerning which canonical jurisprudence yet remains in the state of formation.

Having clarified the meaning of Canon 1095 in its three numbers, the initial question now can be asked: Does Canon 1095 interpret faithfully the teaching on marriage of the Second Vatican Council? There can be no question that the canon takes seriously the teaching that marriage is a divine vocation to which man and woman respond by the act of consent. Not only is Canon 1095 new because of its treatment of psychological causes of nullity of marriage, but even more so because it constitutes a general norm for the vocational response to marriage. In fact, it might have been placed more fittingly in a category by itself, that is, distinct from the impediments and the defects of consent.[36] Not having a place proper to itself, it rightly occupies the first place among the defects of consent, for it specifies the fundamental human development required for marriage consent.

Canon 1095, therefore, respects rightly the vocational nature of marriage. Marriage is a call to which one must give a response proportionate to the inherent rights and duties of the vocation (the mission inherent in the vocation). Canon 1095 specifies the state of mind and heart or the degree of personal development postulated by the response to God's call in the married life. It must be the development that permits the proper acknowledgment and weighing of a decision as important as the decision to marry.

What is more, Canon 1095 presents the act of marriage consent under the aspect of psychological development. The categories of use of reason and discretion of judgment describe, above all, the stage of personal development or integration. The incapacity to assume the rights and obligations of marriage describes the situation of one whose personal development permits him to choose the rights and obligations of marriage, but, because of some psychic deficiency, does not permit him to live up to the rights and responsibilities chosen in the married state.

Regarding the criteria by which the psychological incapacity is to be measured, the canon rightly refers to "the essential rights and duties of marriage to be handed over and accepted mutually" (Canon 1095, 2°) and to "the essential obligations of marriage" (Canon 1095, 3°). The discretion of judgment for marriage describes the understanding of and attraction to the vocation of mutual and exclusive, indissoluble, and procreative love. In other words, the mission that flows from the vocation (consecration) of marriage is the criterion by which discretion of judgment is measured. In the same manner, the incapacity to assume the essential obligations of marriage refers to the mission of marriage, described in the Council teaching, as the criterion for the capacity "to assume." Within the Code itself, the reference is to Canons 1055, §1; 1056; and 1057, §2, which canons, as mentioned earlier, are a synthesis of the conciliar teaching, especially in number 48 of the Pastoral Constitution on the Church in the Modern World.

With respect to the conciliar teaching concerning the implications of the advances in the science of psychology for vocational discernment and response, Canon 1095 is an explicit recognition of the new understanding of the importance of psychological development on practical judgments like marriage consent.

Conclusion

As is clear from the foregoing analysis, Canon 1095 faithfully interprets, in the language of Church discipline, the Second Vatican Council's teaching on marriage. Both in its attention to the vocation and mission of marriage, the capacity to discern and accept, proportionate to the mission proper to the vocation, and in its attention to the understanding brought to the situation by psychology, it corresponds to the teaching of the Council Fathers.

A further point, however, is to be made. If Canon 1095 faithfully interprets the teaching of the Second Vatican Council, then the teaching of the Second Vatican Council is the ultimate key to understanding the intention of the Legislator in giving the Church the particular norm in question. In the case of Canon 1095, this last observation has special importance. In the whole matter of paying attention to the findings of psychology and psychiatry regarding vocation, there is needed the proper tool by which psychological categories can be related to theological categories and eventually juridic categories. The interpretative tool required is the Christian anthropology that underlies both the theological–juridical discourse on marriage and the psychological discourse on marriage.[37] If such an interpretative tool is not employed, psychological and theological categories cannot be weighed together. Rather, either the theological–juridical reality of marriage will be considered alone, irrespective of the psychological factors present, or the psychological facts will be considered alone apart from the theological reality on which they have influence. The truth of this has been illustrated strikingly in an article by Giuseppe Versaldi, in which he analyzes the impact of narcissism on matrimonial consent.[38]

Finally, the fidelity of the Code of Canon Law to the conciliar teaching not only verifies the truth of Pope John Paul's reference to the Code as the "last Conciliar document," but it also indicates the way for the canonist and for Christ's faithful, in general, to understand the true meaning of the norms of Church discipline. Such understanding ensures that truth and charity will be served in the application of canonical norms. In the case of Canon 1095, it will ensure that the theological and psychological aspects of marriage consent will be integrated in decisions regarding nullity of marriage.

Notes

1. "Ultimo documento conciliare," Pope John Paul II, "Il Diritto Canonico inserisce il Concilio nella nostra vita," *Communicationes*, 15 (1983), 128.

2. "Inserisce tutto il Concilio in tutta la vita." Pope John Paul II, "Il Diritto Canonico," 128.

3. John Paul II, "Solemnis Allocutio ad Eminentissimos Cardinales in Urbe praesentes habita, die XXV Ianuarii anno MCMLIX, in coenobio Monachorum Benedictinorum ad Sancti Pauli extra Moenia, post Missarum solemnia, quibus Beatissimus Pater in Patriarchali Basilica Ostiensi interfuerat," *Acta Apostolicae Sedis*, 51 (1959), 68–69.

4. Alfons M. Stickler, "Teologia e Diritto canonico nella storia," in Arcisodalizio della Curia Romana (ed.), *Teologia e Diritto Canonico* (Vatican City: Liberia Editrice Vaticana, 1987), 30–31.

5. Sacrosanctum Concilium Oecumenicum Vaticanum II, "Constitutio Dogmatica de Ecclesia (Die 21 m. novembris a. 1964)," *Acta Apostolicae Sedis*, 57 (1965), No. 45. 1, hereafter cited as *LG*; Sacrosanctum Concilium Oecumenicum Vaticanum II, "Decretum de pastorali Episcoporum munere in Ecclesia (Die 28 m. octobris a. 1965)," *Acta Apostolicae Sedis*, 58 (1966), No. 44. 1; Sacrosanctum Concilium Oecumenicum Vaticanum II, "Decretum de institutione sacerdotali (Die 28 m. octobris a. 1965)," *Acta Apostolicae Sedis*, 58 (1966), No. 16. 4, hereafter cited as *OT*; Sacrosanctum Concilium Oecumenicum Vaticanum II, "Decretum de Apostolatu Laicorum (Die 18 m. novembris a. 1965)," *Acta Apostolicae Sedis*, 58 (1966), No. 1. 2, hereafter cited as *AA*; Sacrosanctum Concilium Oecumenicum Vaticanum II, "Decretum de activitate missionali Ecclesiae (Die 7 m. decembris a. 1965)," *Acta Apostolicae Sedis*, 58 (1966), No. 19. 2.

6. Zenon Grocholewski, "Aspetti teologici dell'attività giudiziaria della Chiesa," in Arcisodalizio della Curia Romana (ed.), *Teologia e Diritto Canonico*, (Vatican City: Libreria Editrice Vaticana, 1987), 195–208.

7. *LG*, No. 11. 2.

8. See, for example, J.M. Serrano Ruiz, G. Putrino, J.M. Castaño, M.F. Pompedda, P.A. Bonnet, A. Vitale, Z. Grocholewski, and F. Salerno, *Matrimonio canonico fra tradizione e rinnovamento*, Il Codice del Vaticano II (Bologna: Edizione Dehoniane, 1985).

9. "In vero ordine personarum constituti," Sacrosanctum Concilium Oecumenicum Vaticanum II, "Constitutio Pastoralis de Ecclesia in mundo huius temporis (Die 7 m. decembris a. 1965)," *Acta Apostolicae Sedis*, 58 (1966), No. 52. 6, hereafter cited as GS. For a theological presentation of the same matter, see Hans Urs von Balthasar, *Christlicher Stand* (Einsiedeln: Johannes Verlag, 1977), Part II, Chapter II.

10. "Suo vitae statu et ordine," *LG*, No. 11. 2.

11. *LG*, No. 11. 2; *GS*, No. 52. 6.

12. *LG*, No. 11. 1.

13. *GS*, No. 52. 6.

14. "Indissolubilitatem et sanctitatem vinculi matrimonialis vita sua manifestare et probare; ius et officium prolem christiane educandi, genitoribus et tutoribus inditum, strenue affirmare; dignitatem et legitimam autonomiam familiae defendere," *AA*, No. 11. 3.

15. "Irrevocabili consensu personali," *GS*, No. 48. 1.

16. "Ita actu humano, quo coniuges sese mutuo tradunt atque accipiunt, institutum ordinatione divina firmum oritur, etiam coram societate," *GS*, No. 48. 1.

17. "Quae intima unio, utpote mutua duarum personarum donatio, sicut et bonum liberorum, plenam coniugum fidem exigunt atque indissolubilem eorum unitatem urgent," *GS*, No. 48. 1.

18. "Ad gradatim acquirendum perfectiorem sensum responsabilitatis in propria vita continuo nisu recte excolenda et in vera libertate prosequenda, obstaculis magno et constanti animo superatis," Sacrosanctum Concilium Oecumenicum Vaticanum II, "Declaratio de educatione christiana (Die 28 m. octobris a. 1965)," *Acta Apostolicae Sedis*, 58 (1966), No. 1. 2, hereafter cited as GE.

19. "Positiva et prudenti educatione sexuali progrediente aetate," *GE*, No. 1. 2.

20. "Quadam animi stabilitate," "facultate ferendi ponderatas decisiones," "recta de eventibus et hominibus iudicandi ratione," *OT*, No. 11. 1.

21. "Fideles ad puriorem et maturiorem fidei vitam ducantur," *GS*, No. 62. 2.

22. C. 26, C. XXXII, q. 7; c. 24. X. IV. 1.

23. See, for example, Alexander Dordett, *Eheschließung und Geisteskrankheit: Eine Darstellung nach der Rechtsprechung der S. Romana Rota* (Vienna: Herder, 1977).

24. Dordett, *Eheschließung und Geisteskrankheit,* 21–22.

25. *Communicationes,* 7 (1965), 43–47.

26. Raymond L. Burke, *Lack of Discretion of Judgment Because of Schizophrenia: Doctrine and Recent Rotal Jurisprudence,* Analecta Gregoriana, Vol. 238 (Rome: Editrice Pontificia Università Gregoriana, 1986), 71–85.

27. "Distinctius et clarius," *Communicationes*, 3 (1971), 77.

28. "**Can. 1095**—Sunt incapaces matrimonii contrahendi:
1° qui sufficienti rationis usu carent;
2° qui laborant gravi defectu discretionis iudicii circa iura et officia matrimonialia essentialia mutuo tradenda et acceptanda;
3° qui ob causas naturae psychicae obligationes matrimonii essentiales assumere non valent."

29. See, for example, Paulus Siwek, *Psychologia Metaphysica*, 7th ed. (Rome: Apud Aedes Universitatis Pontificiae Gregorianae, 1965), 458–461, 473.

30. "Differt autem homo ab aliis irrationalibus creaturis in hoc, quod est suorum actuum dominus. Unde illae solae actiones vocantur proprie humanae, quarum homo est dominus. Est autem homo dominus suorum actuum per rationem et voluntatem: unde et liberum arbitrium esse dicitur facultas *voluntatis et rationis*. Illae ergo actiones proprie humanae dicuntur, quae ex voluntate deliberata procedunt." *ST*, Ia–IIae, q. 1, a. 1.

31. *Supplem.*, IIIae, q. 43, a. 2.

32. *Communicationes*, 9 (1977), 370.

33. "Il criterio dell'*usus rationis* è insito nel criterio della 'discretio iudicii matrimonio proportionata' come il suo minimo elemento essenziale." Antoni Stankiewicz, "L'incapacità psichica nel matrimonio: Terminologia, Criteri," *Ephemerides Iuris Canonici*, 36 (1980), 256.

34. See, for example, Coram Egan, 2. IV. 1981, *Il Diritto Ecclesiastico*, 92 (1982), II, 100–101.

35. "In realtà, il can. 1095, stabilendo una triplice incapacità di contrarre matrimonio nelle prime due fattispecie (nn. 1° e 2°) riguarda direttamente il *soggetto* in quanto produttivo di un atto psicologico inadeguato, e nella terza (n. 3°) ancora formalmente il soggetto ma posto in relazione con l'*oggetto* cui egli è impari, in quanto il suo conato di consentire cade su materia sottratta alle sue forze, di cui egli, cioè, per cause psichiche non è in grado di disporre," Mario F. Pompedda, "Incapacità di natura psichica," in *Matrimonio canonico fra tradizione e rinnovamento*, Il Codice del Vaticano II (Bologna: Edizioni Dehoniane, 1985), 134.

36. *Communicationes*, 3 (1971), 77; 7 (1975), 38–39, 43–44, 46–47.

37. See L.M. Rulla, *Anthropology of the Christian Vocation*, Vol. 1, Interdisciplinary Bases (Rome: Gregorian University Press, 1986), esp. 31–68.

38. Giuseppe Versaldi, "Via et ratio introducendi integram notionem christianam sexualitatis humanae in categorias canonicas," *Periodica de re morali canonica liturgica*, 75 (1986), 437–441.

PART V

THE CHURCH
AND
THE CHURCHES

CHAPTER 31

Universal Church, Particular Church, and Local Church at the Second Vatican Council and in the New Code of Canon Law

Gianfranco Ghirlanda, S.J.

Summary

In an allocution on 9 December 1983, Pope John Paul II said that "the Code of Canon Law, which is the last conciliar document, will also be the first to integrate the whole of the Council into the whole of life," since "in a certain sense this new Code could be understood as a great effort to translate this same conciliar ecclesiology into *canonical* language" (Apostolic Constitution *Sacrae disciplinae leges*). The present contribution points out the continuity between the ecclesiological teaching of the Council and the new Code, and shows how on some points, the former finds its completion in the latter, after twenty-five years of discussion and reflection. The key to the approach is the concept of communion, and more specifically that of hierarchical communion, and in this context, we see the significance that the personal elements of the people of God and of those who preside over it have in the definition of the universal, particular, and local Church.

The Church as Communion

The concept of communion can be seen as having primary and fundamental importance in the ecclesiology of Vatican II, inasmuch as it also throws light on the other definitions of the Church found in the conciliar teaching.

In the first paragraph of the Constitution *Lumen gentium,* the Church is defined "in Christ [as] in the nature of a sacrament or sign and instrument of intimate union with God, and of unity among all men."[1]

The Church is the sacrament of the communion of mankind with God who is one and three, and of men with one another. This means that the Church signifies this communion and brings it about: anybody who enters into communion with God is also in communion with his brethren; and all those who are united to God are united to one another. God is the source of communion, with the Church as instrument of this, so that it is the present action of the Spirit in and through the Church that brings about communion of men with God and with one another. In this way, the Church is constituted in its fullness inasmuch as it is by its nature communion, in the image of the communion between the three divine Persons.

The Church is the "sacrament or sign and instrument of intimate union with God and of unity among all men," and presents itself as "a people brought into unity from the unity of the Father, the Son and the Holy Spirit,"[2] inasmuch as this unity is the work of all three divine Persons. The Father "determined to call together in the holy Church those who should believe in Christ. . . . Made manifest in the outpouring of the Spirit, it [the Church] will be brought to glorious completion at the end of time,"[3] so that "all the just . . . will be gathered together with the Father in the universal Church."[4] Men become sons of the Father in virtue of the redemption wrought by Christ, and by sharing in the one eucharistic bread, they enter into deep union with the others who believe in Christ and who together form a single body in him: the Church.[5] The Spirit, who vivifies, sanctifies, and guides the Church, "unifies it in communion and in the works of ministry, . . . bestows upon her varied hierarchic and charismatic gifts, and in this way directs her; and he adorns her with his fruits."[6]

The communion of the faithful (*communio fidelium*), which

has its basis in baptism under the promptings of the Holy Spirit,[7] has a direct relationship with the Eucharist. Indeed, participation in the Eucharist leads to communion with Christ[8] and with the Trinity.[9] And communion between all the members of the Church[10] and between all the churches (communio inter ecclesias)[11] flows from this communion, in virtue of which the faithful are made partakers in the divine nature.[12] It is here, therefore, that we find the essential basis that constitutes the communion of life, faith, sacraments, and charity[13] between the faithful and between the churches.

This communion—which we can describe as "spiritual" since it is brought about by the working of the Spirit and unites all the faithful spiritually[14]—together with the doctrine of the apostles, the breaking of bread, and prayer, is to be seen as the same union (congregatio) and unity of the Christian community, whose source and basis is the Holy Spirit.[15] The Christian community is constituted by the different hierarchical and charismatic gifts and by the different ministries bestowed by the Holy Spirit.[16] This diversity means that even in the unity of communion, different members of the Church have different juridical situations, and there is thus a plurality of juridical relationships between the different members.[17]

This is a point of fundamental importance for any understanding of the nature of the Church in the thought of Vatican II as this is then reflected in the 1983 Code.

The Theological Commission's Preliminary Explanatory Note (or PEN) to Chapter III of Lumen gentium explicitly states that "communion" "is not to be understood as some vague sort of goodwill, but as something organic which calls for a juridical structure as well as being enkindled by charity."[18] Ecclesial communion cannot be only spiritual and invisible, but must also be juridical and visible. As Lumen gentium 8a in fact states, Christ himself "established and ever sustains here on earth his holy Church, the community of faith, hope and charity, as a visible organization through which he communicates truth and grace to all men." In this way, and in line with the definition of the Church as sacrament given in the first paragraph of the same Constitution, the Council is seeking to state in this passage that the community as visible organism of faith, hope, and charity is the instrument by means of which salvation is communicated to all men. And this takes place because

. . . the society structured with hierarchical organs and the mystical body of Christ, the visible society and the spiritual community, the earthly Church and the Church endowed with heavenly riches, are not to be thought of as two realities. On the contrary, they form one complex reality which comes together from a human and a divine element.

This statement, which is of major importance for any understanding of the ecclesiology of Vatican II,[19] is founded christologically on the analogy between the mystery of the incarnate Word and the mystery of the Church, according to which

As the assumed nature, inseparably united to him, serves the divine Word as a living organ of salvation, so, in a somewhat similar way, does the social structure of the Church serve the Spirit of Christ who vivifies it, in the building up of the body.[20]

This communion between the faithful and between churches, which is vivified by charity and organically structured, and which fully expresses the mystery of the Church, "subsists in the Catholic Church, which is governed by the successor of Peter and by the bishops in communion with him."[21] As we shall see more clearly, it is therefore not enough to define the Church solely as a spiritual communion created by the Holy Spirit between the faithful and between churches, but more fully as "ecclesiastical communion" and "hierarchical communion."

We shall examine these two concepts in greater detail in due course, but for now it is worth concentrating a moment on the fundamental structure of the Church in order to reach a deeper understanding of its actual nature as communion in the Spirit and created by the Spirit—and therefore also a deeper understanding of the different positions the faithful have in this communion. The Church is thus the communion, both spiritual and institutional, of all the baptized, in other words of all those who, through baptism, have been made partakers in the priestly, prophetic, and kingly mission or function (*munus*) of Christ, and who are called to share in the mission that God has entrusted the Church with accomplishing in the world.[22] So the fact that there is a true equality between all the Christian faithful with regard to both dignity and action[23] is the source of shared obligations and rights, although each Christian must fulfill and exercise these within the Church in a different way, inasmuch as there is also a true inequality between the members of the faithful.[24] Each individual Christian shares in the threefold mission or function (*munus*) of Christ in an individual manner, and hence in accordance with his or her juridical position and the mission he or she is called to fulfill within the Church[25] in view of the different hierarchical and charismatic gifts and the different types of ministry given to each person by the one Spirit.[26]

The fundamental structure of the Church should be seen as both charismatic and institutional.[27] In baptism, each person receives the same gift of the profession of faith, which entails obligations and rights that are common to all,[28] and among which a primary and very fundamental place must be attributed to those of professing the faith in a complete manner,[29] leading a life of holiness,[30] and in this way preserving communion with the Church,[31] which is the community of faith and charity.[32] And, parallel with this, a very fundamental place must be attributed to the right to receive the true and complete faith of the Church,[33] and hence the proclamation of the word of God and the sacraments, as spiritual goods necessary for salvation.[34] Each person lives out the gift received in baptism, and in this way fulfills the obligations and exercises the rights proper to his or her specific juridical position as determined by the charisms received from the Spirit, and hence in accordance with the functions and ministries he or she must carry out within the Church. Hence, the whole Church is made up of various orders, according to the different charisms and ministries flowing from them.[35] It must therefore be borne clearly in mind that the varying juridical positions of the faithful within the Church are not purely and simply a legal matter, but something theological, since within the sphere of the institutional life of the Church, they are the expression of the personal vocation of each person, and thus of his or her interior relationship with God. There is no contradiction between the charismatic and institutional dimensions of the Church, but rather a relationship of necessary correlation, inasmuch as a charism necessarily gives birth to an institution, that is, a series of intersubjective relationships supported by specific mutual obligations and rights. Both charism and institution as understood in these terms have their source in the Spirit, and the intervention of the Church only comes after this. Once those who have the charism of validating the authenticity of all the other charisms within the Church—in other words those who have hierarchical authority[36]—officially approve a charism, they provide norms defining the obligations to be fulfilled and the rights to be exercised and respected so that such a charism can be used within the Church for the common good. This gives rise to a canonical institution, although, in order to be truly such, this institution cannot but be in line with the action of the Spirit, because the norms given are and must be in accordance with the norms flowing from the charism itself.

It is therefore clear that the fundamental structure of the Church cannot be reduced to the ramifications of the distinction between laity and clergy (although this distinction may be essential), inasmuch as both laity and sacred ministry are charisms in the Church, within the framework of a much greater variety of charisms.

The general charism of the lay life, with its specific character of secularity,[37] is expressed more individually in personal charisms, which either remain free (in other words, without any official recognition in the Church), or are canonically institutionalized for the performance of specific offices or ministries.[38] This general lay charism together with the individual charisms give rise to specific obligations and rights, and all those who share in the same gift of the Spirit, form an "order" or "rank" within the Church.[39]

In the same way, the general charism of the sacred ministry is made specific in many more individual charisms. In this way, we have the charism of the general order of sacred ministers and the charisms of the various specific orders (deacons, presbyters, bishops, archbishops, metropolitans, primates, cardinal patriarchs, and the Supreme Pontiff), which in turn give rise to their own obligations and rights.[40]

Lastly, the general charism of life consecrated by the profession of the evangelical counsels, and the specific charisms of the different forms of consecration give rise both to the obligations and the rights proper to the order of all "consecrated people" in the Church, and to the specific obligations and rights of the individual institutes.[41]

We must therefore conclude that the organic unity of ecclesial communion is brought about precisely by the action of the Spirit, which gives rise to the basic charismatic and institutional structure of the Church. In this light, it is easier to understand the concepts of *ecclesiastical communion* and *hierarchical communion,* which we also find in the conciliar texts.

According to the teaching of the Council, ecclesiastical communion (*communio ecclesiastica*), which obviously always has Christ as its source and center,[42] exists between the local churches and Rome and also between the local churches themselves,[43] and is as such expressed in eucharistic concelebration.[44] This ecclesiastical communion constitutes fully Catholic communion (*plenitudo communionis catholicae*).[45] Although the Orthodox churches and the Protestant communities[46] do not live in this communion,[47] they are to varying degrees in spiritual communion with the Catholic Church,[48] in proportion to their varying degrees of communion of life, faith, sacraments, and charity, and to the varying degrees to which they manifest the fundamental charismatic and institutional structure of the Church—in which its hierarchical structure should also be included. The concept of communion is closely related to that of the incorporation of the individual baptized person into the Church, and this incorporation takes place in varying degrees according to the degree of union with Christ through the bonds of profession of faith, sacraments, ecclesiastical governance, and communion.[49]

Hierarchical communion (*hierarchica communio*) constitutes ecclesiastical or catholic communion and, in general, the full realization of the Church as communion. Although hierarchical communion is as such defined in relation to bishops and presbyters, it does, as we shall see, have primary importance also in relation to the definition of the Church.

With regard to bishops, hierarchical communion, as based on the common gift of the Spirit communicated to them in episcopal consecration and as established by the legitimation of the consecration itself,[50] points to the spiritual and organic or structural bond between bishops and the head of the college and its other members.[51] With regard to presbyters, in a similar way to bishops, and in virtue of union in the one priesthood and through legitimate ordination,[52] hierarchical communion points to the spiritual and organic or structural bond between presbyters and the order of bishops.[53] Lastly, with regard to deacons, we must say that, although hierarchical communion is never expressly mentioned in connection with them, and it is merely stated that they are ordained for the ministry and serve the people of God in communion with the bishop and his priests,[54] it cannot be denied that the communion spoken of here cannot be anything but hierarchical—or, in other words, organic and structural.

Hierarchical communion and ecclesiastical communion are mutually involved inasmuch as the latter can only exist if the former exists. Local churches, and therefore the faithful of which they are composed, are in ecclesiastical communion with Rome and with one another when their bishops retain hierarchical communion with the Bishop of Rome, who is the head of the college and the perpetual and visible source and foundation of faith and communion,[55] and with all the other members of the college.[56] In a similar way, we can say that the community of the faithful presided over by the presbyter is in ecclesiastical communion when the latter is in hierarchical communion with his bishop and the order of bishops as a whole.[57]

Ecclesiastical communion and hierarchical communion are made up of the spiritual element of grace together with the institutional element that is organic and structural, and these two aspects of communion fully express the complex nature of the Church and are a reflection of its fundamental charismatic and institutional structure.

Universal, Particular, and Local Churches

Catholic ecclesiastical communion is found on three levels: universal, particular, and local.

Vatican II is not very clear as regards terminology in this connection. The universal Catholic Church is never as such defined, but we can undoubtedly say that it is the whole people of God who, under the guidance of the Roman Pontiff and the college of bishops, is spread throughout the world.[58] It is therefore the universal communion of all the baptized, or, in other words, of all those who are "fully incorporated into the Church," inasmuch as,

. . . possessing the Spirit of Christ, [they] accept all the means of salvation given to the Church together with her entire organization, and who—by the bonds constituted by the profession of faith, the sacraments, ecclesiastical government, and communion—are joined in the visible structure of the

Church of Christ, who rules her through the Supreme Pontiff and the bishops.[59]

It is, moreover, made up of all the baptized who have different hierarchical and charismatic gifts and different ministries bestowed on them by the Holy Spirit, and therefore find themselves in different juridical circumstances.[60]

It is difficult to provide a satisfactory definition of the Church, but on the basis of the previously cited texts, we can speak of the Catholic Church only if the following essential elements are present: (1) an organic distinction between the members of the faithful, although always in the unity of the Holy Spirit; (2) full acceptance of the authority of the visible Church and of all the means of salvation instituted within it, particularly the Eucharist; (3) union with Christ in the visible body of the Church through the bonds of profession of faith, sacraments, ecclesiastical government, and communion[61]; and (4) the authority of the Supreme Pontiff and the bishops.

These essential elements are always the same whether we consider the Church on the universal, particular or local level. Indeed, the fact of being universal, particular or local should be seen as an accidental element of the Church, even though it must be recognized that the Church does not exist in abstract terms but only in its specific existence, whether universal, particular, or local. The Church, as subject, is one, and it is always the same in its essential elements, although it does change in its accidental elements, which are expressed through the adjective. The adjectives "universal," "particular," and "local" are correctly attributed to the Church as subject if the above-mentioned essential elements are found in the community defined with the terms "universal Church," "particular church," or "local church."[62]

The Church can be considered in the perspective of many accidental and distinguishing elements, but here it will suffice to take into direct consideration only the personal element and that of government. Even so, we should bear in mind that the personal element is bound up with the spatial element, which in turn involves the cultural element.

As concerns persons, the universal Church points to the relation of a subject—which is defined as "Church" inasmuch as it unites within itself the essential elements just listed—to the universality of the baptized scattered over the face of the earth.[63] In

this sense, the universal Church and the Catholic Church are
the same. However, the expression "Catholic Church" defines
the Church not only as to totality of persons and universality of
extent, but above all as to the difference established between it
and the Orthodox churches and the Protestant communities.[64]
Even so, this distinguishing factor does not cancel the other
sense of universality that emerges from the relationship to persons and space, although we must clearly understand that it does
not seek to affirm this directly. Indeed, to take a ridiculous
hypothesis, the Catholic Church would exist in its universality
even if it was restricted within very limited spatial limits, inasmuch as all the essential elements of the one Church of Christ
"which in the Creed we profess to be one, holy, catholic and
apostolic"[65] would still subsist even in such a minute Church.
Even in this case, that minute Church would be the "universal
sacrament of salvation."[66] On the other hand, even if the non-
Catholic communities and churches were scattered throughout
the whole world, they would not represent the elements of universality and catholicity, inasmuch as the one Church of Christ
would not subsist within them.[67]

Under the personal aspect, "particular church" points to the
relationship of the one unique subject, the Church, to a part of
the totality of the baptized. *Christus Dominus* 11a gives the definition of a diocese and also that of a particular church:

> A diocese is a section of the people of God entrusted to a
> bishop to be guided by him with the assistance of his clergy so
> that, loyal to its pastor and formed by him into one commu-
> nity in the Holy Spirit through the Gospel and the Eucharist,
> it constitutes one particular church in which the one, holy,
> catholic and apostolic Church of Christ is truly present and
> active.[68]

As can be seen, this definition also directly encompasses the
element of government and indirectly that of space. It consists of
the communion of the baptized as governed by the bishop, a
communion that is normally found within a clearly defined territory, although no explicit reference is made to the territorial
element, inasmuch as personal dioceses can also exist. We shall
consider the element of government in greater detail. Lastly, it

should be stated that the Council nearly always identifies particular church with diocese.[69]

There is also another concept of particular church to be found in the Council documents, and this is the communion of a part of the people of God that, while accepting the primacy of the See of Peter, has its own discipline, liturgical customs, and theological and spiritual heritage.[70] This definition also includes the elements of persons, territory (although not necessarily), government, and culture. In this sense, the expression "particular church" generally refers to the patriarchates, which have patriarchs at their head,[71] or to churches that are similar to patriarchates, some as major archbishoprics, presided over by archbishops,[72] or dioceses or groups of dioceses that have their own cultural traditions.[73] The variety of all these particular churches that are encompassed in the one unity clearly expresses the catholicity of the one and undivided Church.[74]

The Council also uses the expression "local church" to refer to a patriarchate or diocese,[75] although it should be observed that it uses "particular church" when speaking of a part of the people of God under the aspect less of territory than of rite, and of theological and spiritual tradition and of government, whereas it uses the expression "local church" for the same grouping when it is more particularly considering territory as the distinguishing factor.

The definition of "particular church" found in the new Code is completely in keeping with the teaching of Vatican II.[76] This definition is applied to dioceses,[77] territorial prelatures and abbacies,[78] apostolic vicariates or prefectures,[79] and apostolic administrations.[80] The personal element can be seen in all these definitions; in other words, from the perspective of the people of God,[81] the relevant element is that of government, in other words, that of the person who presides over the particular church. As far as the territorial element is concerned, it is explicitly stated that the portion of the people of God in question is normally restricted to a specific territory, although it is also accepted that within the same territory particular churches can be set up that are distinguished on the basis of the rite of the faithful or some similar reason.[82]

Lastly, we must clearly state that a portion of the people of God is to be considered a church when it is formed in the image of the universal Church,[83] in other words, when it possesses all the elements essential to the actual nature of the Church and some distinguishing individual element, such as a particular portion of the people of God, or a particular rite, territory, or organs of government. This is why the one Catholic Church exists within and from the particular churches.[84]

Only once does the Council refer to the portion of the people of God under the care of a specific priest as a "local church."[85] Such a portion is more frequently referred to with the expression "local assembly of the faithful" (*congregatio localis fidelium*)[86] or simply as the "assembly of the faithful" (*congregatio fidelium*)[87] or "local community" (*communitas localis*).[88] Such a local community is the communion of the baptized as presided over by the priest, who "represents in a certain sense the bishop,"[89] especially in the celebration of the Eucharist, which is the center of the life of the Christian assembly.[90] Each local community "in some way represents the visible Church constituted throughout the world,"[91] inasmuch as priests "render the universal Church visible in their locality and contribute efficaciously towards building up the whole body of Christ."[92] This is why the local community can be referred to as the Church of God,[93] since in it, too, we find the elements essential to the nature of the Church and the distinguishing accidental elements of organs of government and territory. However, whereas in the case of the particular church, the territorial element is not particularly important as against the other elements, in the case of the local church, it carries greater weight. Indeed, for the Council, the communion of the baptized as presided over by a priest is defined on the basis of the element of territory. We can therefore use the expression "particular church" for a patriarchate and diocese or for any other similar portion of the people of God, inasmuch as the distinguishing element is not primarily that of territory; on the other hand, we can safely use the expression "local church" for the local community of the faithful, inasmuch as the distinguishing element is most particularly that of place. We must say that in a particular way, the notion of local church can be applied to the parish,[94] although this is not exclusively so, since it can also be attributed to other local communities.[95]

The definition of a parish given in the new Code is in line with the teaching of Vatican II.[96] It should then be observed that, although the territorial element is given greater emphasis with regard to the parish than to the particular church, it is not an essential element, since the Code also envisages parishes defined along personal lines according to different rites, language, or nationalities.[97]

From what we have seen, we can conclude that there are also two distinguishing elements with regard to the universal Church, the particular church, and the local church: the first is the portion of the people of God involved, which can in turn be defined by the element of territory, rite, and cultural, spiritual, and liturgical tradition; and the second is the organ of government, which is in itself an element essential to the nature of the Church, but also an accidental element of distinction. Thus, in order to have Church, there must of necessity be those who are invested with the sacred ministry and preside over the people of God, although the universal Church is distinguished by being presided over by the Supreme Pontiff and the college of bishops, the particular church by the patriarch or bishop or other similar figure, and the local church by the priest.

Hierarchical Communion as an Essential Element in Defining the Universal, Particular, and Local Churches

Having seen that hierarchical communion and ecclesiastical communion are two interrelated and interdependent elements and concepts, we must now examine the relationship between the concept and reality of hierarchical communion and those of the universal, particular, and local Church. More detailed study of this latter relationship will also give us a better understanding of ecclesiastical communion and of interchurch communion.

The concept of the Church as hierarchical communion would appear to unite the oldest Catholic tradition, which sees the Church as communion between particular churches within the one universal Church inasmuch as they have Rome as their center, with classical Catholic ecclesiology, according to which the Church tends to be defined more on the basis of its well-organized hierarchical structure.[98]

In this perspective, any contradiction between the noun "communion" and the adjective "hierarchical" disappears, since communion is not to be understood as "some vague sort of good will, but as something organic which calls for a juridical structure as well as being enkindled by charity."[99] And this does not refer only to relationships of bishops with the head of the college and with the other members, or between clergy and the order of bishops, but involves the whole Church.

Government by the successor of Peter and the college of bishops means that the communion between the baptized scattered throughout the world is the catholic or universal communion (the universal Church), in other words "the sole Church of Christ which in the Creed we profess to be one, holy, catholic and apostolic."[100] Similarly, in order for the communion between the baptized in one specific part of the people of God to be considered a "particular church" in which the Church of Christ is present, it must be governed by the patriarch or bishop, who must be in hierarchical communion with the head and the other members of the college.[101] And lastly, the local community, as a portion of the Lord's flock, can be called a "local church" when it is led by a priest who is in hierarchical communion with his bishop and thus with the whole order of bishops.[102]

According to the teaching of Vatican II, and bearing in mind what we have already said about the charismatic and institutional structure of the Church, we must observe that there is a structure of communion present in it, together with a structure of mission. And these two concepts or realities are interrelated: the Church is the communion of all those who share in the same mission, on the one hand, specifically because of the unity of the mission of salvation that the Church has received, and on the other, because only those who are united by the bond of communion in faith and charity as created by the Spirit share in that one mission. The different functions of the members of the ecclesial communion must be seen within the framework of these reciprocal relations between communion and mission, since, despite the fact that the mission is one, participation in the priesthood of Christ and in his work varies according to the diversity of charisms and ministries bestowed by the Spirit.[103] This twofold structure concerns the whole life of the Church in its totality, and if we apply it to the hierarchical structure of the Church, we can understand the relationship and the difference between the common priesthood of the faithful and the ministerial priesthood within the unity of the one priesthood of Christ, the relationship and difference between bishops and priests within the unity of the one sacred ministry, and the relationship and difference between bishops and the Supreme Pontiff within the unity of the one college of bishops. And we can also understand the bond of communion between the different particular churches, the bond of hierarchical communion with the church of Rome, and lastly the specific function and mission of the church of Rome and its bishop.

In order to reach a proper understanding of the relationship that exists between hierarchical communion and ecclesiastical communion, and hence between universal Church and particular church, and between universal and particular church on the one hand and local church on the other, we must examine the relationship between the ministry of the Supreme Pontiff and that of bishops,[104] and between the ministry of bishops and that of priests, and also the mutual obligations and rights set up by these.

There is a close link between the ministry of the Supreme Pontiff and that of bishops. The ministry of the Supreme Pontiff consists of the fact that as the successor of Peter, "the rock-foundation and the holder of the keys of the Church" as established by the Lord,[105] he is the perpetual and visible source and foundation of the unity of faith and of the communion both of bishops and of all the faithful.[106] The ministry of bishops consists of the fact that as individuals they are the visible source and foundation of unity within their particular churches that they represent, whereas as college—that is, all of them together with the Supreme Pontiff as their head—they represent the whole Church in the bond of peace, love, and unity.[107]

In virtue of the one episcopal consecration, a bond of sacramental and spiritual communion is set up between the Roman Pontiff and the bishops, and under this aspect the Roman Pontiff and the bishops are equal. However, because of the very fact that communion is, as the *Preliminary Explanatory Note 2* states, "something organic" (and something which, of its very nature, requires a structural relationship with the authority that, precisely through the exercise of its specific authority, shapes the life of that structure), a relationship of hierarchical subordination is set up between the Roman Pontiff and the bishops. In this way, the relationship of communion is necessarily a relationship of hierarchical communion. Hierarchical communion is an organic reality that is structured around the authority of the head of the communion, the Supreme Pontiff, precisely when he exercises his power as head of this hierarchical communion.[108]

The bishop is placed within the hierarchical communion through the legitimation of his episcopal consecration, which is given through a free appointment or confirmation by the Supreme Pontiff,[109] and through a pontifical or apostolic mandate in cases where the Supreme Pontiff himself does not consecrate the bishop.[110] Only a legitimately consecrated bishop stands within the hierarchical communion,[111] becomes a member of the college of bishops, and can be fully commissioned in the episcopal office.[112] In other words, a bishop is made a member of the episcopal body in virtue of his sacramental consecration and through hierarchical communion with the head of the college and the other members.[113] As a member of the college, a legitimate bishop is given a share in the supreme and full authority over the universal Church, and thus in both the governing and authentic teaching offices; the college is the subject of this authority by divine right inasmuch as it is the successor of the college of the apostles in teaching and pastoral government,[114] and the college of the apostles is constantly present in the college of bishops as it remains in communion with its head.

It can be held that as members of the college, the bishops are made partakers in the supreme and full collegial power, either directly by Christ, or, according to a more firmly based teaching in the tradition of the Church, through the Roman Pontiff who transmits—not delegates—such power to them. Even if we hold the first position (that the college of bishops receives its collegial power directly from Christ) this does not cancel the relationship of hierarchical communion between the Supreme Pontiff and all the bishops, even taken together collegially, since the college "necessarily and at all times involves a head and in the college the head preserves intact his function as Vicar of Christ and pastor of the universal Church."[115] This is seen in the fact that episcopal consecration must be legitimated by some direct or indirect act of the Supreme Pontiff in order for the bishop to be placed within the hierarchical communion and thence become a member of the college with all the relative obligations and rights. An illegitimate bishop is a true bishop but is not a member of the college of bishops and does not share in the collegial power. The two elements of consecration and hierarchical communion are equally necessary[116] in order for a bishop to enter the college and therefore for the actual constitution of the college itself. Indeed, without the head there is no college: ". . . it is not a distinction between the Roman Pontiff and the bishops taken together but between the Roman Pontiff by himself and the Roman Pontiff along with the bishops."[117] We must not ignore the fact that the supreme authority of the college over the universal Church must necessarily be full in order not to jeopardize the fullness of the power of the Roman Pontiff,[118] who always retains his primacy of authority within the college. Thus, in the absence of the authoritative action of the head, the bishops could not act as college, inasmuch as they could not be seen as college, as is clear from the very concept of the episcopal college, which "is not taken in the strictly juridical sense, that is, as a group of equals who transfer their powers to their chairman, but as a permanent body whose form and authority is to be ascertained from revelation."[119] In this way—and in this way alone—the bishops, as college, preside over the universal Church, governing and representing it.

All this means that we can state that within the Church there are two subjects holding the supreme and full power of governance and authentic magisterium in the universal Church: the Supreme Pontiff and the college of bishops,[120] although they are not completely distinct from one another, inasmuch as in the intersection of reciprocal obligations and rights between the Roman Pontiff and the college of bishops, only the former has the right to perform certain acts that are completely outside the competence of bishops either as individuals or as college (for example, convening and directing the college, approving its norms of action, approving and promulgating its decrees, legitimating the consecration of bishops[121]), while the college has no right to act independently of the head.[122] Obligations and rights of hierarchical communion are thus set up between the Supreme Pontiff and the college of bishops. These obligations and rights are established by the twofold ecclesiological relationship of communion and subordination, as based on the different charisms bestowed by the Spirit and by the ministries established in the Church through the action of the same Spirit.

From what we have seen, it is now easier to understand the definition of the universal Church given previously as the totality of the people of God, in other words, as the communion of all the baptized—a communion that, under the pastoral leadership of the Supreme Pontiff and the college of bishops in government and authentic teaching, extends throughout the world. It is thus easier to understand why, in the definition of their mutual obligations and rights, the Supreme Pontiff and the college of bishops must be seen as essential elements for the definition of the universal Church as catholic ecclesiastical communion.

The authority to govern and authentically teach a particular church is transmitted to legitimately consecrated bishops by means of their canonical mission, which is a direct or indirect exercise of the power of the head of the hierarchical communion so that they can exercise their episcopal ministry in the church entrusted to them.[123] Bishops could not establish those subject to them within hierarchical communion if they themselves did not share in the structure of hierarchical communion with the head of the college and the other members in virtue of the legitimacy of their consecration and canonical mission.[124] If bishops did not share in the hierarchical communion formed by the exercise of the power of primacy of the head of the college, their particular churches would be schismatic since they would not be in ecclesiastical communion with the church of Rome, and hence with all the other particular churches.[125] In order for a particular church to be the image of the universal Church and for the one, holy, catholic and apostolic Church to be present within it,[126] it must live within a structural relationship of subordination with the church of Rome: in virtue of the legitimacy of the bishop's consecration and canonical mission—this latter element establishing him in the office of head of the particular church—he shares in the structural relationship of hierarchical communion with the head of this communion, and thus makes his particular church share in the organic and structural reality of the ecclesiastical communion of the whole Church around its visible head. In this way—and in this way alone—the bishop represents the particular church entrusted to him.[127]

We must note that the relationship of hierarchical communion is twofold: with the head of the college and with its members. The relationship with the head of the college establishes the episcopal office in relation both to the universal Church and to the particular church.[128] And this individual bond set up between each bishop and the head of the college also means that all the bishops together are linked to the same head with the same bond. Apart from the episcopal consecration common to them all, this bond of hierarchical communion of each bishop, and of all the bishops together, with the head means that each bishop is established in a relationship of organic communion

with all the other bishops, inasmuch as apart from his consecration, the same individual relationship of the bishop with the
head of the college places him, on the one hand, in a bond of
individual communion among equals with each bishop in the
college, and, on the other hand, in a bond of hierarchical communion with all the bishops taken together who, in virtue of the
presence of the Supreme Pontiff among them as head, make up a
college.[129] This means that ecclesiastical communion is between
the particular churches and the church of Rome, and also between the various particular churches, so that their variety does
not militate against unity, but in fact expresses it,[130] and "it is in
these and formed out of them that the one and unique Catholic
Church exists."[131]

In short, we see that the bishop, in hierarchical communion
with the head of the college and its other members, and in the
definition of his obligations and rights in relation to both the
former and the latter, is the essential element for the definition
of a particular church. Indeed, the diocesan bishop has the obligation and right to govern the diocese entrusted to him "with
ordinary, proper and immediate power."[132] This obligation and
right is the source of the other obligations and rights of the
bishop with regard to the members of his particular church[133] as a
manifestation of his pastoral charity. However, the ecclesiological nature of the office of the diocesan bishop is also the
source of the obligations of the latter with regard to the Roman
Pontiff and the college. The same reality of hierarchical communion, in which the bishop must exercise the functions (munera)
received with episcopal consecration and the powers transmitted
to him together with these,[134] is what establishes and defines the
reciprocal obligations and rights between individual bishops and
the Roman Pontiff and the whole college. The fact that the one,
holy, catholic, and apostolic Church of Christ is truly present
and operative in the particular church that remains within Catholic ecclesiastical communion makes it easy to understand why
and how both the Roman Pontiff as an individual and also the
college are present in the particular church, and, for the good of
both the universal Church and the particular church, have the
right and sometimes the duty to exercise their ordinary, immediate, supreme, and full power in the particular church too,[135]
although the right of the particular church to its just autonomy
must always be respected.[136] The very nature of the reciprocal

relationships between the individual bishops can also enable us to gain a clearer idea of the care and concern bishops must have both individually and as a group toward the other particular churches.[137]

Hierarchical communion also unites the ministry of the priest closely with that of the bishop, so that the local church is defined in the context of the particular church. In virtue of the sacrament of Orders, bishops and priests are united in a sacramental and spiritual communion inasmuch as they share in the one priesthood and ministry of Christ.[138] Through legitimate priestly ordination, which is obtained by means of dimissorial letters given by the competent ecclesiastical authority, priests are established in hierarchical communion with their own bishop and with the order of bishops,[139] and together with the other priests they form a fraternity and a priestly communion[140] so as to constitute a "unique sacerdotal college" with their own bishop.[141] The Council does not use the same tone in speaking of the college of priests as it does for the college of bishops; nevertheless, by analogy, we can say that a priest is made a member of the sacerdotal college or *presbyterium* in virtue of his sacramental consecration and through hierarchical communion with his bishop and the order of bishops. We can, therefore, also state that all priests, taken as a group together with their bishop, represent the particular church and have some sort of authority over it.[142] The priestly ministry lies in the fact that priests cooperate with their own bishop and with the whole order of bishops.[143] In order for priests to be able to exercise this ministry, the canonical mission must be conferred on them by the bishop or other competent ecclesiastical authority. This mission confers the office and transmits the corresponding power of governance. The priest thus makes the bishop present in the local church, linked as he is to him by the bonds of hierarchical communion,[144] in such a way that the universal Church of Christ is truly present even in the local community.[145] As we have said, the parish is the prototype of the local church, under the leadership of the parish priest, whose office carries with it the right to govern the parish entrusted to him.[146] The exercise of this right entails the fulfillment of obligations and the exercise of rights toward both the members of the faithful[147] and the bishop.[148] The same can obviously be said of any priest who has any office in a particular church.

In short, we can conclude that the Roman Pontiff and the

college of bishops, the bishop, and the priest are essential elements for the definition, respectively, of the universal Church, the particular church, and the local church. Hierarchical communion thus plays a role of primary and fundamental importance in shaping and defining the reciprocal obligations and rights that spring up between the different sacred ministries on the basis of the twofold and simultaneous ecclesiological relationship of communion and subordination.

Conclusions

As we have repeated a number of times in the course of this study, the bond of communion in the life of the Church is not confined to the invisible and spiritual sphere, but requires a juridical form, although this must be animated by charity.[149] This juridical form and the fact that it is animated by charity must not and cannot be seen as contradictory, but rather as two aspects of a single reality in which the juridical form animated by charity exists. Indeed, since the juridical relationships between different persons in the Church and between different particular and local churches have their source in the gift of the Holy Spirit and are constituted and founded in the Eucharist, they must of their very nature be animated by charity. The Eucharist is the source, center, and summit of the whole life of the Christian community, and all the ecclesiastical ministries exercised by different people in the Church must have the Eucharist as their reference point and be ordered in view of it.[150] The ministry of the bishop and the priest in the exercise of the functions of sanctifying, teaching, and governing is defined in relation to the fact of presiding at the eucharistic celebration.[151] The bishop and the priest sanctify, teach, and govern, inasmuch as they preside at the Eucharist. However, the legitimacy of the eucharistic celebration depends on the legitimacy of the consecration of the bishop and the priest.[152] Only when the legitimate eucharistic president presides is the Eucharist legitimate; and only where the Eucharist is legitimate is there the full expression of the mystery of Christ and the genuine nature of the true Church of Christ,[153] inasmuch as the true particular church is gathered around the bishop,[154] and the local church around the priest.[155] The Eucharist is the sacrament of unity and charity between all the members of the Church and between all the churches, and it therefore produces and expresses both hierarchical communion and ecclesiastical communion.[156]

For this reason, the juridical hierarchical form necessarily has charity as its constitutive element. Charity is therefore the fundamental principle (which is necessarily expressed in juridical terms) of all social relationships—and thus of all juridical ecclesiastical relationships, whether those between equals or those of an organic and hierarchical nature between superiors and those subject to them.

It is charity that, as a gift of the Spirit, first of all constitutes communion between the baptized, both on the universal level and on the particular and local levels. Juridical relations, which are defined by laws, of themselves presume the exercise of charity. The juridical structure is already contained in the gifts of the Spirit to the faithful and is expressed in positive laws, inasmuch as the fundamental structure of the Church is a charismatic and institutional one. Thus, the juridical structure of the fundamental institutions of the Church—in other words, that of the fundamental relationships between the members of the Church, established in accordance with the different charisms and ministries, and between the particular churches—is required by the dogmatic structure of the Church itself. All this is the source of an element of major importance and one that must be borne in mind if we do not want to end up constructing a partial ecclesiology that does not correspond to the teaching of Vatican II: the source of the binding force—that is, the juridicity—of the fundamental institutions of the Church and of the norms that regulate and express them, is to be sought in the dogmatic structure of the Church.[157]

It is charity that brings about the union between faithful and pastor, and between different pastors. And universal, particular, and local communion, which is expressed in corresponding juridical forms, has its life from this union in charity. Charity, as the gift of the Spirit given in order to perform a ministry in the Church, builds up communion between the bishops and the Roman Pontiff, who presides over the universal communion of charity,[158] and between the bishops themselves. In order that this union of charity can in fact be such, it requires the hierarchical subordination of the bishops to the head of the college and its members. If there is no subordination in hierarchical commu-

nion, there is no perfection of charity. And if there is no perfection of charity, there is no fullness of Christ's action and presence, and hence the realization and manifestation of the Church
is not fully perfected. This is why

> . . . the sole Church of Christ which in the Creed we profess
> to be one, holy, catholic and apostolic, . . . constituted and
> organized as a society in the present world, subsists in the
> Catholic Church, which is governed by the successor of Peter
> and by the bishops in communion with him. Nevertheless,
> many elements of sanctification and of truth are found outside
> its visible confines. Since these are gifts belonging to the
> Church of Christ, they are forces impelling towards Catholic
> unity.[159]

Thus, a Christian community assembled around an illegitimate
bishop cannot be considered a particular church. The juridical
structure of relations between bishops and the Roman Pontiff,
like that of those between particular churches and the church of
Rome, is shaped precisely by charity, which is nourished and
expressed in eucharistic concelebration. Charity brings about
communion between particular churches; and the various juridical structures (for example, the synod of bishops, conferences of
bishops, local councils, mutual assistance) with which particular
churches are united to one another express charity.

Charity is the source of communion between priests and their
own bishop and the whole order of bishops, and between different priests. However, such charity must be exercised in hierarchical subordination; in other words, in order for charity to be fully
expressed in the particular and local church, communion of
priests with their own bishop and with the whole order of bishops
cannot be other than a hierarchical communion. If a priest was
not in hierarchical communion, the Eucharist he celebrated
would not be legitimate, and the Christian community assembled around him could not fully be called Church. In the particular and local church, too, the union of charity is nourished and
expressed by eucharistic concelebration.

It is the Holy Spirit, given by the Father through the Son,
who communicates the charity of the triune God to the Church,
and makes the communion between faithful, pastors, particular
churches, and local churches necessarily hierarchical, so that

"the universal Church is seen to be 'a people brought into unity from the unity of the Father, the Son and the Holy Spirit.' "[160]
Translated from the Italian by Leslie Wearne.

Notes

1. LG 9; 48b; SC 26a; AG 1a; GS 45a.
2. LG 4b.
3. LG 2.
4. *Ibid.*
5. LG 3.
6. LG 4a.
7. UR 2b.
8. AG 39a; LG 3, 7b.
9. UR 15a.
10. LG 7b; UR 7c; AG 39a; GS 38b.
11. UR 14a, 15a.
12. UR 15a.
13. LG 9b; UR 14a.
14. The expression "spiritual communion" does not appear in the conciliar documents, which use only the term *communio* in this first and broader sense.
15. LG 13a. See also PC 13a; DV 10a; AA 18a.
16. AG 4; LG 4, 13c; GS 32d.
17. AG 4; cf. also our article "De variis ordinibus et conditionibus iuridicis in Ecclesia," *Periodica*, 71 (1982), 379–396.
18. *PEN* 2.
19. It should be noted that even in the antepreparatory stage of the Council, the question of the relationship between the invisible-divine element and the visible-human element emerged as the fundamental problem in defining the nature of the Church. The Council Fathers discussed this point at length in the preparatory stage and in the Council Hall itself, and the evolution of this text from its beginning through to the final approval of the Constitution demonstrates the difficulties encountered and also the importance of the teaching it contains; cf. our book *"Hierarchica communio"—Significato della formula nella "Lumen Gentium"* (Rome, 1980), 6–12, 34–56, 107–125, 174–177, 181–230. The problem was clarified with the use of the concept of the Church as sacrament, mystical body of Christ, and hierarchical communion; cf. *ibid.*, 410–429.
20. LG 8a; cf. H. Muller, "De analogia Verbum Incarnatum inter et Ecclesiam (LG 8a)," *Periodica*, 66 (1977), 499–512.
21. LG 8b; Canon 204, §2.

22. *LG* 31a; Canon 204, §1.

23. *LG* 32b, c, d; GS 29a; Canon 208.

24. Canons 209–223. The sixth of the ten principles that were to guide the revision of the Code, according to the document discussed between 30 September and 4 October 1967 in the first general session of the synod of bishops, concerned the safeguarding of the rights of the person. This document stated: "Et quoniam non omnes eandem functionem in Ecclesia habent, neque idem statutum omnibus convenit, merito proponitur ut in futuro Codice ob radicalem aequalitatem quae inter omnes christifideles vigere debet, tum ob humanam dignitatem tum ob receptum baptisma, *statutum iuridicum* omnibus commune condatur, antequam iura et officia recenseantur quae ad diversas ecclesiasticas functiones pertinent" (*Communicationes*, 1 [1969], 82–83; italics in the original). Moreover, the group of consultors "De laicis deque associationibus fidelium" of the Commission for the Revision of the Code stated: "Hoc enim modo laicorum officia et iura congruam enuntiationem ac protectionem obtinebunt in toto ambitu legislationis ecclesiasticae atque ita, dum ex una parte servatur hierarchica structura quae ex voluntate Dei ad Ecclesiam pertinet, vitatur ex altera parte visio stratificata membrorum Populi Dei, quae a non paucis considerata est unus ex praecipuis defectibus systematicis in Codice nunc vigente, longe superata est a Concilio Vaticano II. Ius canonicum plene fiat oportet ius Populi Dei, ius nempe quod dirigat ac promoveat vitam totius communitatis ecclesialis, attenta non solum diversitate functionali fidelium, sed etiam eorum radicali aequalitate. Ex hoc vero consequitur ut normae Codicis concipi nequeant tamquam complectentes quosdam circulos clausos personarum aut institutionum, eoque minus uti complexus legum qui unice ordinet officia ecclesiastica, sed contra intelligendae sunt sensu communitario ac pastorali, uti ius nempe pro universa Ecclesia regitur. Iuxta hoc criterium; diversa statuta iuridica personalia continebunt solummodo iura et officia fundamentalia, quae tamen, ut vere operativa dici queant, influxum exerceant oportet in redactione ceterarum Codicis partium" (*Communicationes*, 2 [1970], 96).

25. *LG* 31a; Canon 204, §1. See also 1971 Synod of Bishops, *Ultimis temporibus* (document on the ministerial priesthood) (30 November 1971), in *AAS*, 63 (1971), 905–906.

26. *LG* 4a; 13c; AG 4; GS 32d.

27. *LG* 12b. On this point, cf. our works: "Ecclesialità della vita consacrata," in A. Longhirano (ed.), *La vita consacrata*, Collana Il Codice del Vaticano II (Bologna, 1983), 13–52; "De variis ordinibus et condicionibus iuridicis in Ecclesia" (*art. cit.*); "De Christifidelibus (cann. 204–207)," in P.A. Bonnet and G. Ghirlanda, *De Christifidelibus— Adnotationes in Codicem* (Rome, 1983), 9–17; "La vita consacrata nella struttura carismatico-istituzionale della Chiesa," in M. Augé et al., *Carisma e istutuzione—Lo Spirito interroga i religiosi* (Rome, 1983), 163–180.

28. Canons 209–223.

29. Canons 748, §1; 750; 752–754; 212, §1.

30. Canon 210.

31. Canon 209, §1.

32. The obligations to remain faithful to revealed truth, lead a holy life, and preserve communion with the Church do in fact constitute one single obligation, since, on the one hand, communion with the Church and with God is preserved only when the one true faith is professed and when charity is exercised, whereas, on the other hand, the one true faith and charity are communicated and nourished only in ecclesial communion. Moreover, as is taught in *Lumen gentium* 14b, full communion with the Church requires communion with God, inasmuch as the former does not exist only through outer institutional bonds, such as the profession of faith, the sacraments, and ecclesiastical government and communion, but also through the interior bond of grace, that is, the Spirit of Christ; cf. F. Coccopalmiero, "Quid significent verba 'Spiritum Christi habentes,' *Lumen Gentium* 14, 2," *Periodica,* 68 (1979), 253–278. It is easy to see that Canon 205 remains on an excessively "exterior" and legalistic level in expressing the concept of full communion with the Catholic Church, since, although it draws its inspiration from *Lumen gentium* 14b, it ignores the element of the invisible grace of the Spirit of Christ, which must however continue to be seen as of fundamental importance. We must, therefore, interpret this canon (and, for that matter, all the others) in the light of the teaching of the Council.

33. Canons 747, §1; 760.

34. Canon 213. With regard to the whole question of the obligations and rights of the faithful, cf. our article "De obligationibus et iuribus Christifidelium in communione ecclesiali deque eorum adimpletione et exercitio," *Periodica,* 73 (1984), 329–378; "Doveri e diritti dei fedeli nella comunione ecclesiale," *La Civiltà Cattolica,* 136/1 (1985), 22–36.

35. LG 13c, 12b.

36. LG 12b.

37. LG 31b; Canon 225, §2.

38. Canons 228, §1; 230.

39. Canons 224–227; 229, §§1, 2; 231.

40. Canons 273–289; 381, §1; 382–400; 405; 407, §3; 408, §1; 410; 436–438; 349; 353; 355–357; 331; 333, §1; 337, §1; 338; 339, §1.

41. Canons 578; 586; 590; 593; 594; 598–602; 662–672; 687; 598; 701; 712; 714–716; 719; 729; 732; 733, §2; 737–740; 741, §2; 746.

42. *UR* 20.
43. *LG* 13c; *AG* 22b.
44. *UR* 4c; 15a.
45. *OE* 4; *UR* 3a, 4d; and also *UR* 13b, 19a.
46. In the Relatio to number 15 of the Constitution on the Church, the Doctrinal Commission of the Council stated under letter D, in *AS*, III/I, 204: "*In propriis communitatibus ecclesiasticis:* haec indicatio postulatur a pluribus, dum E/583 loquitur de 'communionibus.' De Communitatibus christionis non-catholicorum loquuntur Romani Pontifices IOANNES XXIII et PAULUS VI. Elementa quae enumerantur non tantum individuos respiciunt, sed etiam communitates; in hoc praecise situm est principium motionis oecumenicae. Documenta pontificia possim de 'Ecclesiis' orientalibus separatim loquuntur. Pro Protestantibus ultimi Pontifices adhibent vocem 'communitates christianae.' "
47. *UR* 3a, 13b, 19a.
48. *LG* 15.
49. *LG* 13, 14, 15; *OE* 4, 30; *UR* 3e, 4d, 17b, 18; *GS* 92c.
50. The legitimacy of episcopal consecration is brought about either through free nomination on the part of the Roman Pontiff of the bishop to be consecrated, or through confirmation of the legitimately conducted election (Canon 377), and, apart from this, through a pontifical or apostolic mandate if the Roman Pontiff himself does not consecrate the bishop (Canon 1013). If a bishop is consecrated without a pontifical mandate (and hence, obviously, he has not even been legitimately appointed), both the bishop who carries out the consecration and the person who receives such a consecration incur an automatic (*latae sententiae*) excommunication reserved to the Apostolic See (Canon 1382). The discipline of the Eastern-rite Catholic Churches is very similar to that of the Latin Church. With regard to the draft of the new Code, the Commission for the Revision of the Code of Eastern Canon Law took its lead from the Motu proprio *De sacramentis* of 1958, which was never promulgated, but which stated in Canon 191: "Firmo iure Romani Pontificis, ordinatio episcopalis reservatur, ad normam iuris, Patriarchae vel Archiepiscopo vel Metropolitae, ita ut nulli Episcopo licet quemquam ordinare Episcopum, nisi, prius constet de competenti mandato" (*Nuntia*, 7 [1978], 65). As we can see, for legitimate consecration, mention is made only of "competent mandate" and not of "pontifical mandate," since the Eastern church operates according to the hierarchical structure of patriarchs (cf. *CICO*, Canon 216, in Motu proprio *Cleri sanctitati* [2 June 1957], in *AAS*, 49 [1957], 497), archbishops and metropolitans, who have a true power of jurisdiction over other bishops (cf. *CICO*, Canons 319, 310, 324, 326, in *ibid.*, 528–529, 530). Even so, we must bear in mind that at present the election of patriarchs, major archbishops, metropolitans, and bishops must always be approved

by the Supreme Pontiff (cf. *CICO*, Canons 235, 236, 253, 254, in *ibid.*, 502, 503, 509, 530), whereas according to the draft of the new Code for the Eastern Churches, the intervention of the Supreme Pontiff can take place either through the granting of ecclesiastical communion (patriarchs: Canons 45 and 46), or through confirmation (major archbishops: Canon 129), approval (metropolitans *sui iuris:* Canon 144), assent (bishops: Canon 150), or direct appointment (bishops: Canon 149); cf. *Nuntia*, 19 (1984), 28, 48, 52, 53. The penalty envisaged in the draft for episcopal consecration without the mandate of the competent authority is major excommunication; cf. Canon 55, §1, in *Nuntia*, 13 (1981), 78.

51. LG 21b, 22b; *PEN* 2, 4; *CD* 4a, 5; Canons 375, §2; 336.

52. Canon 1015, §1, lays down that candidates are to be ordained to the diaconate or the presbyterate by their own bishop or with legitimate dimissorial letters from him, so that, according to Canon 1383, a bishop who ordains a person who is not his subject without legitimate dimissorial letters is prohibited for a year from conferring the order, whereas a person who has received ordination in such circumstances is automatically (*ipso facto*) suspended from the order received. In the Motu proprio *De sacramentis,* in Canon 193, §3, on the legitimacy of ordination in the Eastern Churches, the provision is in line with that of the Latin church, whereas in the draft of the Eastern Code, we find that the penalty for ordinations performed without dimissorial letters is not specified; cf. *Nuntia*, 4 (1977), 94; and 13 (1981), 79. However, it is clear that the penalty envisaged for priestly ordination is lighter than that for episcopal consecration, in view of the fact that the consequences for the life of the Church are not as serious.

53. PO 7a, 15b; Canons 273, 519.

54. LG 29a; *CD* 15a. It should be stated that the diaconate has no significance for the definition of the Church, since it is not a degree of the priesthood, although it is a degree of the sacrament of orders; cf. J. Beyer, "De diaconatu animadversiones," *Periodica,* 69 (1980), 440–460.

55. LG 22b; *PEN* 3; UR 2b; AG 6a; *CD* 4a; Canon 336; LG 18b, 23a, 13c; AG 22b, 38a; Canon 331.

56. See note 51.

57. The Council speaks of ecclesiastical communion, referring always to particular churches as a whole, whereas the Code uses this expression to refer to individual baptized persons; cf. Canons 96; 316, §1; 840; 1741, §1. In two passages (*SC* 69b and LG 15), although the Council uses the term "communion" simply to refer to individual baptized persons, it does not use it in the sense of spiritual communion, but without doubt in that of ecclesiastical communion. This transfer of the concept from particular churches as a whole to individual baptized persons is easy to understand, since the particular churches that are in ecclesiastical communion are made up of all those who have been baptized, profess the whole faith, and preserve the unity of communion under the successor of Saint Peter.

58. LG 9, 13, 17, 22b; CD 10a, 23d; OT 2e; PO 11b; AG 26b.

59. LG 14b; cf. OE 2.

60. AG 4.

61. We can see from the evolution of the text of *Lumen gentium* 14b cited that "ecclesiastical government" and "communion" are identified with one another here; cf. our book "*Hierarchica communio,*" 216.

62. As regards the interpretation of conciliar teaching on the universal, particular, and local Church, cf. P. Chouinard, "Les expressions 'Eglise locale' et 'Eglise particulière' dans Vatican I," *Studia canonica*, 6 (1972), 116–161; H. de Lubac, *Les Eglises particulières dans l'Eglise universelle* (Paris, 1971); E. Lanne, "L'Eglise locale: sa catholicité et son apostolicité," *Istina*, 14 (1969), 46–66; *id.*, "Pluralisme et unité: possibilité d'une diversité de typologies dans une même adhésion ecclésiale," *Istina*, 14 (1969), 171–190; G. Nedungatt, "Ecclesia Universalis, Particularis, Singularis," *Nuntia*, 2 (1976), 75–87; J. Beyer, "Chiesa universale e chiese particolari," *Vita Consacrata*, 18 (1982), 73–87.

63. CD 10a, 23d; OT 2e; PO 11b; LG 13b, 22b; AG 26b.

64. LG 8b; UR 3a, 4c, d, 19a; OE 26.

65. LG 8b.

66. LG 48b; AG 1a; GS 45a; LG 1, 9, 59; SC 26; AG 5a.

67. See note 46.

68. Also CD 3b; AG 6c.

69. CD 3b, 11a, b, 23e, 28a; LG 23a, b, 27a, 45b; AG 19, 20a, g, 6c, d; SC 13b, 111b.

70. LG 13c; OE 2 (title), 3, 4, 16, 17, 19; UR 14a. We must remember that when we speak of a particular church in relation to its own specific discipline, liturgical customs, and so on, this includes not only Eastern-rite Churches but also Latin-rite Churches, since all particular churches, whether Eastern or Western, enjoy the same dignity; cf. OE 3.

71. OE 7b.

72. OE 10a.

73. AG 22b.

74. LG 13c, 23d.

75. UR 14a; LG 23d, 26a; AG 19d, 27a.

76. Canon 368.

77. Canon 369.

78. Canon 370.

79. Canon 371, §1.

80. Canon 371, §2.

81. A personal prelature cannot be seen as similar to a particular church, since it does not have a people of its own; in other words, it cannot be defined as a portion of the people of God under the leadership of the prelate. Indeed, the Code does not mention personal prelatures among particular churches, but deals with them in Part I of Book II under Title IV, immediately after dealing with sacred ministers, since it is to be seen as an administrative organ or institute to obtain an adequate distribution of priests or in order to perform special pastoral or missionary tasks for different regions or social categories (Canon 294). Lay people are not incorporated into the prelature, since they can simply dedicate themselves to the apostolic works of the personal prelature through specific agreements: what is involved is an organic cooperation, but one that is given from outside (Canon 296). The evolution of the canons regarding personal prelatures and especially the wish to place them in the position in which they are found within the Code confirm all this.

82. Canon 372.

83. LG 23a.

84. Ibid.

85. PO 6d.

86. LG 28b. It should be noted that once (in LG 26a) the expression *congregatio localis fidelium* is also used to indicate a diocese.

87. PO 5c; AG 15b, d.

88. PO 6d; LG 28d; AA 30c.

89. LG 28b; PO 5a.

90. SC 42a; PO 5c.

91. SC 42a.

92. LG 28b.

93. LG 28d.

94. SC 42; CD 30a; AA 30c.

95. LG 28b, d; PO 5c; AG 15b, d.

96. Canon 515, §1.

97. Canon 518.

98. P.C. Bori, *Koinonia—L'idea della comunione nell'ecclesiologia recente e nel Nuovo Testamento* (Brescia, 1972), 69–77; H. Fies, "Wandel des Kirchenbildes und dogmengeschichtliche Entfaldung," *Mysterium Salutis*, 4/1 (Einsieldeln/Zurich/Cologne, 1972), 223–285; L. Bouyer, *L'Eglise de Dieu* (Paris, 1970), Part I; A. Acerbi, *Due ecclesiologie— Ecclesiologia giuridica ed ecclesiologia di communione nella "Lumen Gentium"* (Bologna, 1973), 13–105.

99. PEN 2.

100. LG 8b.

101. LG 23a, b, 21b, 26a.

102. LG 28b; PO 7a, 6a, 15b.

103. LG 36d, 43b; AA 26, 5, 6; PO 2a; LG 10b, 41.

104. It is clear that when we speak of the ministry of bishops, or in general when we speak of bishops, we are including also the patriarchs or major bishops of the Eastern Churches.

105. LG 22b.

106. LG 18b, 23a; Canon 331.

107. LG 23a.

108. Paul VI was the first to use the expression *hierarchica communio* in an official document of the Council, in his Allocution on the Opening of the Third Session of the Council, on 14 September 1964. This speech is of major importance in interpreting the formula *hierarchica communio*, which was then used by the Council in various texts, since it was used in these texts because of the express wish of the same Paul VI. At the beginning of his speech, Paul VI speaks, within a general ecclesiological perspective, of the role of the episcopate in the Church and of the sacramental equality between Supreme Pontiff and bishops, but also of the difference between them with regard to supreme government: "Deus enim nobis inaestimabili gratiae suae munere dedit, ut in ipso crederemus, ut baptismo ablueremus, ut caritate eiusdem sacri et visibilis populi Dei compaginaremur. *Efficimus Ecclesiam*, quia eius administri sumus, scilicet sacerdotes peculiari charactere insigniti; vi cuius *in hoc officio sumus constituti, cum sacramentalem ordinationem suscepimus, quae potestates mirabiles et gravissimas contulit nobis, et sacrae Hierarchiae Ordinis nos compotes reddidit,* cuius est ministeria obire apta ad pergendum per tempora et ad propagandum in terris ipsum munus salvificum Christi. *Ecclesiam demum efficimus, quia ut Magistri fidei, Pastores animarum, Dispensatores mysteriorum Dei, illius universae partes hic agimus,* non quidem ut delegati vel delecti a fidelibus . . . sed ut Patres ac Fratres, qui *communitatum, curis uniuscuiusque nostrum commissarum, personam gerimus et ut Coetus plenarius, quem Nos,* cum omnibus vobis sociati *ut Frater vester,* iure meritoque *convocavimus qua Episcopus Romae* . . . , *qua successor* . . . *Petri Apostoli* . . . , *versus Moderator Ecclesiae Catholicae et Christi Vicarius*" (AS III/I, 141; the italics are ours). In the third part of the same speech, Paul VI explains hierarchical communion in the following terms: "Quodsi utpote Petri successor, atque hac de causa *in universam Ecclesiam potestate praediti,* Nos . . . *officio fungimur vestri Moderatoris;* hoc non eo spectat ut vestra imminuatur auctoritas. . . . Praeterea, si apostolicum munus a Nobis requirit ut, ad potestatis episcopalis perfunctionem quod attinet, aliquid Nobis reservemus, limites praefiniamus, formas statuamus, agendi rationes Ordinemus, *haec omnia* . . . *ipsum Ecclesiae universae bonum postulat, postulat unitas Ecclesiae.* . . . Haec potestatis ecclesiasticae *in unum veluti centrum ordinatio* . . . *indoli Ecclesiae respondet, quae suapte natura una et hierarchica est.* . . . Quam ob rem verba commemorare placet, quae Decessor noster Pius XII fel. rec. ad Episcoporum coetum habuit:

'Haec ergo coniunctio et congruens communicatio cum Sancta Sede non oritur ex quodam studio omnia in unum cogendi et conformandi, sed ex iure divino et ex proprio ipsius constitutionis Ecclesiae Christi elemento.' Attamen haec norma episcopalem auctoritatem nullo modo extenuat, immo robore auget, sive ea in singulis Antistitibus, sive in toto Episcoporum collegio consideratur. . . . Alio quoque argumento has catholici Episcopatus laudes confirmare placet, ut manifesto pateat quantum eius dignitati, quanto eius caritati prosint haec hierarchicae communionis vincula, quae Episcopos cum Apostolica Sede coniungunt, scilicet Sede Apostolica vobis indiget, Venerabiles Fratres! Etenim quemadmodum vobis, varias terrarum orbis partes incolentibus, ut veram Ecclesiae notam catholicam efficiatis atque ostendatis, necessario omnino est centrum et principium unitatis fidei et communionis quod in hac Petri Cathedra habetis . . ." (ibid., 147–148; the italics are ours). As can be seen, according to Paul VI, the office of the head of the college as moderator of the power of the bishops, due to the fulfillment of which all ecclesiastical power converges in a center, is of divine law, or, in other words, concerns the fundamental structure of the Church. The set of relationships between bishops and their head forms what are called the bonds of hierarchical communion, which are thus based on the exercise of the office of moderator of the head himself. It is because of hierarchical communion that bishops implement and truly express the catholicity of the Church. It is therefore clearly stated that in order for this catholicity to be expressed, the ministry of the See of Peter is needed as center and source of the unity of faith and of communion. Further, we must say that through the acts with which the bonds of hierarchical communion with the bishops are set up, the Roman Pontiff exercises the power of his primacy of jurisdiction, which is in its very nature totally different from the power of orders as received in episcopal consecration. From the sacramental viewpoint, the head and the other bishops are equal. The actions that come from the exercise of the power of primacy are essentially necessary to the life of the Church, inasmuch as they constitute the hierarchy of the Church according to Christ's wishes. Lastly, according to Paul VI, hierarchical communion must be seen as the constitutive element of the episcopal office viewed in its full theological and juridical extent, so that this office can be fully manifested and the bishop can fulfill his mission; cf. my article "De hierarchica communione ut elemento constitutivo officii episcopalis iucta 'Lumen Gentium,' " Periodica, 69 (1980), 31–57.

109. Canon 377, §1.

110. Canon 1013. It should be noted that hierarchical communion is of divine law, and is thus a necessary requirement in order for a bishop to be legitimate and to be taken up into the episcopal office (cf. LG 24b), while the acts through which the legitimation of consecration is brought about (direct nomination, confirmation, pontifical mandate) are of ecclesiastical law for the direct safeguarding of divine law.

111. Canon 1382.

112. LG 24b.

113. LG 22a; Canon 336.

114. LG 22b; Canon 336.

115. PEN 3. We must note at this point that the Supreme Pontiff receives his power of primacy directly from Christ—that is, his power as head of the whole hiarchical communion—but with legitimate election, accepted by him, together with episcopal consecration (Canon 332, §1). From the replies given to *Modi* 35 and 65, it seems clear that the doctrinal commission of the Council fully and unreservedly accepted the traditional doctrine according to which, if a person who is elected Pope but is not a bishop has the requirements to be Supreme Pontiff, immediately on acceptance of election he receives the supreme power through nonsacramental means, in other words, through direct divine mission; cf. AS III/VIII, 61, 69. Even the bishops as college do not have power over the universal Church in virtue of their episcopal consecration, but immediately from Christ through the very fact of becoming members of the college, which is, as such, the depositary of such power through the fact that the apostolic college perdures in it. The power of the head of the hierarchical communion—in other words, the whole Catholic hierarchy and the whole people of God—is not some sharing in the power of the college, but a personal power given directly by Christ so that the Roman Pontiff can perform his unique function within the college. The power of primacy is obtained by acceptance of legitimate election, although in order for it to be fully episcopal, consecration is required, and therefore such consecration is required by positive ecclesiastical law as a condition for the power of primacy to be exercised. Canon 332, §1, therefore, lays down that if the person elected lacks the episcopal character, he is to be ordained bishop immediately. The aim is to prevent any exercise of the power of primacy prior to consecration, as has happened in the course of history in the case of various deacons who were elected Pope. For this whole question, cf. our article "De natura, origine et exercitio potestatis regiminis iuxta novum Codicem," *Periodica*, 74 (1985), 136–140.

116. Cf. the Relatio to number 22 of the schema on the Church by the doctrinal commission; cf. AS III/I, 242–243; and our already cited book "*Hierarchica communio,*" 354–356.

117. PEN 3.

118. *Ibid.*

119. PEN 1; cf. *ibid.*, 4.

120. LG 22b, 25; Canons 331; 336; 330; 749, §§1–2.

121. PEN 3; Canons 333, §1; 337, §3; 338; 341; 377, §1; 1013.

122. *PEN* 1, 3, 4; Canon 336.

123. *LG* 24b; *PEN* 2. Having carried out a serious survey of the Acts of the Council, we certainly cannot say that the Council wanted to resolve the question of whether the origin of the power of governance of bishops was immediate or mediate, sacramental or not. Indeed, in response to *Modus* 200, the doctrinal commission expressly declared that by changing the revised text of number 28 of the draft of *Lumen gentium* in accordance with the request made in *Modus* 199, there was no intention of entering into the question of the origin of the power of jurisdiction of bishops (AS III/VIII, 96–97); on this matter, cf. our book "*Hierarchica communio*," 391–429. Here it is important to stress the difference between pontifical mandate and canonical mission. The pontifical mandate confers no power but simply legitimates consecration, whereas canonical mission, which is given on the assumption of the legitimacy of consecration, confers an office and therefore also transmits the power needed in order to fulfill the office. A bishop is placed in hierarchical communion through legitimate consecration and not through canonical mission. *Lumen gentium* 24b and the *Preliminary Explanatory Note* 2 do not in any way take into account the function of the pontifical mandate and, therefore, seem to attribute to canonical mission (or *canonica seu iuridica determinatio*) the function of placing bishops in hierarchical communion, and this creates confusion. In fact, through his personal power as head of the hierarchical communion, and by means of canonical mission, the Supreme Pontiff transmits the power of governance and magisterium over a particular church to a legitimately consecrated bishop. Even so, it must be clear that through divine law, it is through Christ that the bishop who is in hierarchical communion receives the power to govern and authentically teach, but that since he receives it in the Church and for the Church, it must be transmitted through this same Church, that is, through the Supreme Pontiff by means of canonical mission, in order that the divine law as to the formation and expression of hierarchical communion may be better safeguarded; cf. our article, already cited, "De natura, origine et exercitio potestatis regiminis," 134–136, 140–142, 149–164. Lastly, by distinguishing clearly between universal power directly (or even indirectly) shared by the bishop as member of the college and the specific power received by the bishop through canonical mission, it is easier to understand how a titular bishop has and exercises universal power although he has no power over any particular church, and also how a diocesan bishop who has resigned from his diocese still retains the universal collegial power. It is clear that since a bishop who breaks hierarchical communion no longer holds his office legitimately, he is no longer a member of the college, and therefore loses any power, whether universal or specific; cf. Canons 1331, §1 3°, §2 2°; 1336, §1 2°.

124. See note 51.

125. *LG* 13c, 15; *AG* 22b.

126. *LG* 23a, 26a; Canons 368, 369.

127. *LG* 23a.

128. Our article "De hierarchica communione ut elemento constitutivo officii episcopalis iucta."

129. *LG* 22b, 23a, 25a; *PEN* 3, 4; Canon 336.

130. *LG* 13c; *AG* 22b, 38a; *OE* 2.

131. *LG* 23a; Canon 368.

132. Canon 381, §1.

133. Canons 383–398.

134. *LG* 21b; Canon 375, §2. We cannot identify *munus* with power, since the conciliar text did not do so—and was, indeed, careful not to, as can be seen from an examination of the Acts of the Council rather than a superficial reading of the definitive text of *Lumen gentium* 21b. *Munus* tends more to indicate the gift of the Spirit that is received in consecration together with the character and the grace of the sacrament, and through which the bishop is fully conformed to Christ the priest, prophet, and king. Then, in order for this assimilation to the life and mission of Christ to be implemented in the life of the Church, the bishop receives powers to perform specific acts for the sanctification, instruction, and government of the people of God. The person consecrated, therefore, receives the power to sanctify, the power to teach authentically, and the power to govern. However, the individual powers are by their very nature more restricted than the *munus*, since the latter is comprehensive, encompassing the whole of the consecrated person (cf. John Paul II, Letter to All the Priests of the Church, *Novo incipiente* [8 April 1979], in *AAS*, 71 [1979], 397), whereas the former are aimed at the performance of specific acts (cf. *PO* 6a). It is the purpose of the acts that distinguishes the means of transmission of the power. With a view to the performance of sacramental acts, the means of transmission of the power of sanctification must be sacramental, whereas with a view to the performance of acts concerning the authentic confirmation of the profession of faith of the people of God and their pastoral governance, the means cannot be an indelible sacramental act but a hierarchical act. The plurality of services that must be carried out within the Church means that there is a plurality of channels through which the power to perform such services is transmitted; however, the source is one, insofar as it is Christ who sanctifies, teaches, and governs within his Church. It is therefore clear that according to the teaching of the Council, the relationship between the *munera* and the various types of power—and hence between sacramental consecration and the office of teaching authentically and governing—is very close. Consecration is a necessary precondition for the exercise of the offices and the relative

powers, and a bishop can only enter into possession of his office after consecration (Canons 379; 382, §4), in order to avoid the type of abuses that have sometimes taken place in the past. It is worth noting here that lay people can be assumed by the competent hierarchical authority to those offices that are not considered strictly clerical or hierarchical (cf. Canon 228, §1) and that this can entail the exercise of the power of ecclesiastical governance or jurisdiction, since such power is not transmitted in the Church by sacramental means but by hierarchical means (cf. Canons 129, §2; 1421, §2; 1428, §2; 1437, §1; 482, §1; 494, §3; 363, §1; 517, §2), but does not necessarily always require the exercise of such power (cf. Canons 1424; 1435; 228, §2; 1112; 229, §3). The nonsacramental origin of the power of ecclesiastical governance also provides the basis for the nature and origin of the power exercised in institutes of consecrated life, including lay ones (cf. Canons 596, 618). With regard to this whole very complex question, cf. our article "De natura, origine et exercitio potestatis regiminis," 109–134, 143–149.

135. Canons 333, §1; 336.

136. LG 23d. The fifth of the ten guiding principles for the revision of the Code as given in the document discussed between 30 September and 4 October 1967 in the first general session of the synod of bishops looked for the application of the principle of subsidiarity in canon law. The document stated: "Principium confirmat unitatem legislativam quae in fundamentis et maioribus enunciationibus iuris ciiuslibet societatis completae et in suo genere compactae servari debet. Propugnat vero convenientiam vel necessitatem providendi utilitati praesertim institutionum singularium tum per iura particularia ab iisdem condita tum per sanam autonomiam regiminis potestatis exsecutivae illis recognitam. . . . Alienum videtur a mente et spiritu Concilii Vaticanii II, salvis disciplinis Ecclesiarum Orientalium propriis, ut in Ecclesia Occidentali Statuta peculiaria adsint, quae veluti formam praebeant specificam legibus ecclesiarum nationalium. Attamen id significare non debet in legislationibus particularibus maiorem amplitudinem et autonomiam non desiderari, praesertim in iure a Conciliis nationalibus, regionalibus condendo, adeo ut aspectus peculiares ecclesiarum singularium non apparere non possit" (*Communicationes*, 1 [1969], 81). Pius XI was the first to formulate the principle of subsidiarity for civil society in his Encyclical *Quadragesimo anno* (15 May 1931), in *AAS* 23 (1931), 203. Pius XII, in his Allocution to the Cardinals on 20 February 1946, in *AAS*, 28 (1946), 145, applies the principle to the life of the Church— provided, however, that its hierarchical structure is safeguarded. We must in fact say that the application of the principle to the life of the Church can only be analogical, since the nature of the Church is different from that of civil society: power in the Church comes from above and not from the people; the fundamental structure of the Church is established by Christ himself and not by the members of society; the common good of the Church belongs to the supernatural order and not only the natural order; the duties and rights of the faithful are conferred by the Church with baptism (cf. Canon 96) and are not prior to the Church. While always safeguarding the just autonomy of individual social groups, it is more necessary in the Church than in civil society for higher authority to intervene in matters to be dealt with by lower authority, in order to safeguard and nourish the holiness and unity of the Church, whether universal, particular or local. Indeed, the Church is not made up of a confederation of particular churches but of communion between the churches, in such a way that the one holy, catholic, and apostolic Church is present in each particular church (cf. LG 23a, 26a). This explains the power of the Roman Pontiff and the college of bishops over all the particular churches. In his Allocution of 27 October 1969, in AAS, 61 (1969), 728–729, Paul IV expressly stated: "Itemque animo promptissimo sumus ad omnia legitima optata, quae patefiat, ut locorum Ecclesiis pleniorem in modum concedantur ac probentur propriae notae peculiaresque necessitates et postulata, bene apteque in rem deducto principio 'subsidiarietatis,' ut aiunt: quod sane principium postulat procul dubio ut cogitatione et re penitus usque intellegatur atque illustretur, Nosque idem in sua praecipua significatione prorsus admittimus: Attamen haudquaquam fieri potest, ut hoc principium cum quadam illius 'pluralismi' postulatione confundatur, qui Fidem, morum legem et primarias Sacramentorum, necnon liturgiae et canonicae disciplinae formas laedat, eo potissimum spectantes ut necessaria unitas in universa Ecclesia servetur." On the basis of these reflections, instead of speaking of the application of the principle of subsidiarity to the life of the Church, maybe it would be better to speak of the necessary coordination between universal law and particular law, and between common law and specific law, so that the diversity of the particular churches within the unity of the universal Church is better safeguarded, together with the special characteristics of the rights of the faithful and the possibility of appeal to higher authority; cf. J. Beyer, "Le nouveau Code de Droit canonique—Esprit et structures," *Nouvelle Revue Théologique*, 106 (1984), 369–370.

137. LG 23, 25; CD 2b, 3, 36, 37; Canons 431, §1; 434; 447.

138. LG 28a, 41b; PO 2b, 5a, 7a, 10a; CD 28a, 15a. As concerns the sacramental power or power of Orders, we cannot say that from the ontological point of view there is any real difference between bishop and priest, since the difference is found on the level of the fullness of the *munus* sacramentally received and of the exercise of sacramental power or power of Orders, as well as that of the power to teach authentically and to govern, which is transmitted by legitimate authority in

order to perform different ministries in the Church. On this age-old question, cf. J. Beyer, "Nature et position du sacerdoce," *Nouvelle Revue Théologique*, 76 (1954), 356–373; H. Müller, "De differentia inter Episcopatum et Presbyteratum iuxta doctrinam Concilii Vaticani Secundi," *Periodica*, 59 (1970), 599–618; and our own article "Episcopato e Presbiterato nella *Lumen Gentium*," *Communio*, 59 (September–October 1981), 53–70.

139. PO 5a, 7b, 15b; Canon 273.

140. LG 28c, 41c; PO 8a; Canon 275, §1.

141. LG 28b; PO 8a; CD 28a.

142. PO 7b stated that a commission or senate of priests should be set up to represent the body of priests (or *presbyterium*); through its advice, this commission or senate "could effectively help the bishop in the management of the diocese." It can be called the "presbyteral council" or "council of priests." Although it was then ruled that this council should have a consultative vote, it was accepted that it could have a deliberate vote where this is laid down by universal law or in individual cases where the bishop grants this; cf. the circular letter of the Sacred Congregation for the Clergy, *Presbyteri sacra* (11 April 1970), 9, in *AAS*, 62 (1970), 463–464. Canon 500, §2, states that "the presbyteral council enjoys only a consultative vote," that the diocesan bishop is to listen to it in matters of major importance, but that he needs its consent only in cases expressly defined by law. We must remember that even when it does not have a deliberative vote, any council always indirectly shares in government, because it assists authority in the decision to be taken and thus in some way also shares in the order that is given.

143. LG 28b; PO 2b.

144. LG 28b; SC 42a; CD 15a; PO 5a.

145. LG 26a.

146. Canons 515, §1; 519.

147. Canons 528–535.

148. Canon 515, §1.

149. PEN 2.

150. LG 11a; PO 5a; Canon 897.

151. LG 10b, 17, 26b, 28a, 41c; CD 11a; PO 5a, c.

152. LG 26b, 28b; SC 42a; Canons 899, §§1–2; 900.

153. SC 2; Canon 897.

154. SC 26a, 41b; CD 11a; Canon 369.

155. LG 28d; Canon 515, §1.

156. SC 47; LG 3a; UR 2a; SC 7a; PO 7a, 8a; UR 4c, 15a.

157. F. Coccopalmeiro, "De conceptu et natura iuris Ecclesiae animadversiones quaedam," *Periodica*, 66 (1977), 447–474; and our article "De variis ordinibus." As concerns the relationship between Eucharist and law, cf. P.A. Bonnet, "Eucharistia et ius," *Periodica*, 66 (1977), 583–616.

158. *LG* 13c; *AG* 22b.

159. *LG* 8b.

160. *LG* 4b.

CHAPTER 32

The Significance of
the Vatican II Declaration
that the Church of Christ
"Subsists in"
the Roman Catholic Church

Francis A. Sullivan, S.J.

Summary

The purpose of this article is to investigate what Vatican II meant by the "subsisting" of the Church of Christ in the Catholic Church, and what ecclesial reality it acknowledged in other Christian communities. The conclusion reached is that "subsists in" means that it is in the Catholic Church alone that the Church of Christ continues to exist with all those properties and structural elements that it cannot lose, while at the same time the Council recognized that outside the Catholic Church, there are not merely "elements of Church," but there are "particular Churches," by whose celebration of the Eucharist the Church of God is built up, and there are ecclesial communities that are analoguous to particular churches, inasmuch as the one Church of Christ is somehow also present and operative in them for the salvation of their members.

———
———

Just twenty-five years ago, before the opening session of the Second Vatican Council, there was no doubt about what was meant when one said: "The Church of Christ is the Roman Catholic Church." ("Roman" here means "in communion with Rome," and, of course, includes the Eastern Catholic Churches). Pope Pius XII had made it perfectly clear, both in *Mystici Corporis*[1] and in *Humani generis*,[2] that the Mystical Body of Christ, the Church of Christ, and the Roman Catholic Church were one and the same thing.

After Pope John XXIII had announced the convocation of the Second Vatican Council, a Preparatory Theological Commission was formed in 1960, with Cardinal Ottaviani, Prefect of the Holy Office, at its head, and Father Sebastian Tromp, chief collaborator in the writing of *Mystici Corporis*, as its secretary. From the texts produced by this commission, one can safely judge that the expectation of its members, carefully picked by the Holy Office, was that the bishops gathered at the Council would in no case depart from the official teaching of the Popes. It seems clear that they saw the role of the Council as turning into conciliar doctrine what was already papal teaching.

Hence, it is no surprise when we find the following statements in the *schema De Ecclesia* presented by this preparatory commission to the Council in its opening session of 1962: "The Roman Catholic Church is the Mystical Body of Christ . . . and only the one that is Roman Catholic has the right to be called Church."[3]

Among the criticisms that were made of this schema during the week that it was discussed by the Council,[4] one that was heard a number of times concerned this exclusive identification between the Mystical Body and the Catholic Church.[5] As is well known, the frosty reception given to the whole schema was enough to convince the leadership of the Council that it should be quietly withdrawn without even being put to a vote. So, during the spring and summer of 1963, a new *schema de Ecclesia* was prepared, which, it must be said, did incorporate quite a lot of material from the previous one, while differing a great deal from it in tone and general approach.

On the question we are dealing with, the new schema followed the previous one in asserting that the one and only Church of Christ is the Roman Catholic Church; but it added the significant admission that "many elements of sanctification can be found outside its total structure," and that these are "things properly belonging to the Church of Christ."[6] This last

phrase at least implied that such "elements of sanctification" as
are to be found outside the Catholic Church are ecclesial in
nature; and that suggests that there is at least something of
church beyond the limits of the Catholic Church.

This is the schema that was discussed for the whole month of
November 1963, and on which the bishops submitted their *modi*,
or proposals for emendation. In the interval between the session
of 1963 and that of 1964, a very considerable revision was made
of the *schema de Ecclesia*, and it was while the Theological Commission was preparing the revised text that the question was
raised within the commission itself as to the consistency of maintaining on the one hand that the Church of Christ was simply
identified with the Catholic Church, and then admitting that
there were "ecclesial elements" outside of it. The solution arrived
at was to change the text from saying that the Church of Christ *is*
the Catholic Church to saying that it *subsists in* it. The official
explanation given to explain this change to the bishops was "so
that the expression might better agree with the affirmation about
the ecclesial elements which are found elsewhere."[7] Unfortunately for the commentators, no further elucidation was offered
as to the precise sense in which the word "subsists" was intended
to be taken.

The one fact that is absolutely certain is that the decision no
longer to say "is"—a decision ratified by the vote of the Council—
is a decision no longer to assert such absolute and exclusive identity between the Church of Christ and the Catholic Church as had
been claimed by the previous *schemata*. The fact that the "many
elements of sanctification and of truth"—these last words added by
the commission at the same time—are explicitly recognized as
"ecclesial" in nature, evidently suggests that there must be something of church out there. There would have been no point in
making this change if the new term "subsists in" were to be understood in the same exclusive sense that had been affirmed by the
simple copulative "is."

Practically all commentators have seen in this change of wording a significant opening toward the recognition of ecclesial reality in the non-Catholic world.[8] But much remained to be clarified, and I would venture a guess that more ink has been spilled
on the meaning of "subsistit" than on any other single word in
the documents of Vatican II. I would distinguish three questions
that need to be answered, and to which I shall address myself:

1. What is the significance of this change from "is" to "subsists in" for our thinking about the Catholic Church?
2. What is its significance for our thinking about other Christian communities?
3. What is its significance for our thinking about the universal Church of Christ?

The first point I would make is that none of these questions can be given a satisfactory answer on the basis of this one text of *Lumen gentium* alone. What we are seeking is the "mind of the Council" about some of the most basic questions relating to what the Decree on Ecumenism calls "the Catholic principles of ecumenism."[9] The people working on the *schema de Ecclesia* were very much aware of the fact that at the same time a *schema de oecumenismo* was being prepared, and it was their intention to leave the ecumenical aspects of ecclesiology to be handled in that decree.[10] Actually, these two documents were promulgated on the very same day, 21 November 1964. In the allocution that he gave on that occasion, Pope Paul VI, in addressing himself especially to the non-Catholic observers, made the explicit point that the doctrine on the Church in *Lumen gentium* was to be interpreted in the light of the further explanations given in the Decree on Ecumenism.[11] So we shall seek the answers to our questions in both of these documents and in the official *relationes* given by the respective commissions to the Council Fathers.

Significance For Our Thinking
About the Catholic Church

We begin our first question by asking: How is the word "subsists" to be understood? The *relatio* that I have already quoted as giving the reason for the change gives us no further light on the way they intended "subsists" to be taken. However, the commission also provided a *relatio* that briefly summarized the contents of each paragraph of Chapter I. The second paragraph of number 8, in which our phrase occurs, was summarized as follows: "Ecclesia est unica, et his in terris adest in Ecclesia Catholica, licet extra eam inveniantur elementa ecclesialia" ("There is but one Church, and on this earth it is present in the Catholic Church, although ecclesial elements are found outside of it").[12] Here the

word that corresponds to "subsistit in" is the very simple "adest
in." This, I think, is a good reason for not following those commentators who have interpreted the word "subsistit" in the light
of a philosophical notion of *subsistentia*. [13] One went so far in this
direction as to suggest that the Catholic Church is to other
Christian communities what *esse subsistens* (the divine Being) is
to created beings. [14] Another philosophical approach is to imagine that the Church of Christ is being thought of here as a kind
of "platonic idea" that has its "concrete form of existence" in the
Catholic Church. Some German translations actually lend themselves to such an interpretation. [15]

However, most commentators, and I believe rightly, reject the
idea that "subsists" is being used here in any such technical
philosophical sense. [16] It is a good working rule that, in the absence of clear indications to the contrary, terms used in conciliar
documents are meant to be taken in the ordinary sense that the
word has in common usage. If you look up the word *subsisto* in a
Latin lexicon, you find that the primary meaning is "to stand
still, to stay, to continue, to remain," etc. That such is actually
the correct meaning of the word in our passage is confirmed both
by the context and by other places in the conciliar documents
where the same word occurs.

If you read the whole paragraph (8b), you see that the Church
of Christ that is said to subsist in the Catholic Church is not an
ideal church, needing to be concretely realized in this world, but
is the historical church of the New Testament: the church that
Jesus entrusted to Peter and the other apostles to be propagated
and governed. It makes excellent sense to say that this church
continues to exist, and that it is still to be found in the Catholic
Church, the one, namely, that is governed by the successors of
Peter.

Other passages confirm this interpretation of the word "subsist," especially two that occur in the Decree on Ecumenism. In
number 4c, we are told that "the unity which Christ gave to his
Church can never be lost, and it *subsists* in the Catholic
Church." Later, in number 13b, the Decree speaks of the Anglican Commission as one of the separated Christian communities
in which Catholic traditions and institutions "ex parte subsistere
pergunt" (at least in part continue to exist).

But the all-important question, on which we are seeking the
mind of the Council, is still to be answered: Namely, *how*, in

exactly what way, does the Church of Christ subsist in the Catholic Church? I believe the answer to this question is found in the Decree on Ecumenism. Number 2 of this decree gives us the best description to be found anywhere in the documents of the Council, of the kind of unity that Christ gave to his Church. There we see that while it is essentially a communion of faith, hope, and love, whose principal cause is the Holy Spirit, the Church is also intended to be visibly united in the profession of the same faith, the celebration of the same sacraments, in the fraternal concord of one people of God. In order to bring about and maintain such unity, Christ endowed his Church with a threefold ministry of word, sacraments, and leadership, first entrusted to the apostles with Peter at their head, and then continued in the college of bishops under the Pope.

If we keep in mind this description of the unity that Christ gave to his Church, we can see how significant is the statement in the same Decree, number 4c: "We believe that the unity with which Christ from the beginning endowed his Church is something it cannot lose; it subsists in the Catholic Church, and we hope that it will continue to increase until the end of time."

What follows explicitly from this profession of faith on the part of the Council—this is without doubt the force of the opening words: "we believe"—is that the Church of Christ subsists in the Catholic Church with that unity, both spiritual and visible, described in UR number 2. Neither the separation between East and West in the eleventh century nor the divisions of Christianity since the sixteenth century has meant the loss of such unity. It subsists; it is still to be found intact in the Catholic Church. This does not mean that there is no ecclesial unity at all to be found in other Christian churches, nor indeed that there is no real, though imperfect communion still binding all the baptized and their communities together. But the Decree goes on to say, with complete frankness, that our separated brethren and their churches do not enjoy the kind of unity that Christ intended his Church to have. Such unity subsists in the Catholic Church, and in it alone (UR 3e).

What I believe follows implicitly from this is that it is the mind of the Council that the Church of Christ subsists in the Catholic Church not only with the unity that Christ intended his Church to have, but with all its inalienable properties intact. To say that the Church of Christ subsists means that it still exists with all those gifts with which Christ endowed it. To say that it subsists in the Catholic Church means that it is in the Catholic Church that it is to be found still existing with all its essential properties: its oneness, holiness, catholicity, and apostolicity. This does not mean, of course, that they are found there in a state of eschatological perfection. We have already seen the Council express its hope that the unity of the Church will continue to increase until the end of time. *Lumen gentium* 48c describes the Church in this world as endowed with a holiness that, while real, is still imperfect. *Unitatis redintegratio* 4, 10 admits that the divided state of Christianity hinders the Church from achieving the fullness of its catholicity. But, while imperfectly achieved, these are properties that the Church of Christ can never really lack. To say that the Church of Christ subsists in the Catholic Church then means that it continues to exist there with all those gifts that it can never lose.

Another statement of the Decree on Ecumenism that suggests the mind of the Council on our question is the assertion: "It is through the Catholic Church alone that the whole fullness of the means of salvation can be obtained" (UR 3e). This does not mean that there are not many such means of salvation present and effectively used in other Christian churches and communities; this is explicitly recognized in the same context. But, at the same time, it is said, in general, of the separated communities, that "we believe they suffer from defects" in this regard. From this it follows that it is in the Catholic Church alone that the Church of Christ subsists with that fullness of the means of salvation that Christ entrusted to the apostolic college.

To sum up: I believe we have a clear answer, in the Decree on Ecumenism, to the question as to how the Council intends us to understand the statement that the Church of Christ subsists in the Catholic Church. It means that the Church of Christ has continued and will continue to exist until the end of time with all its inalienable properties and with all the means of salvation with which Christ endowed it, and it is precisely in the Catholic Church that it continues *so* to exist.

Of course it must be kept in mind that this is a question of institutional integrity: of fullness of the means of salvation; or, to put it another way, we are talking about the Church as *sacramentum*, not as *res sacramenti*. There is no question of denying that a non-Catholic community, perhaps lacking much in the order of sacrament, can achieve the *res,* the communion of the life of Christ in faith, hope, and love, more perfectly than many a Catholic community. The means of grace have to be well to achieve their full effect, and the possession of a fullness of means is no guarantee of how well they will be used.

I would also like to point out that I do not think that the interpretation that I propose as corresponding to the mind of the council as to *how* the Church of Christ subsists in the Catholic Church would certainly follow from the mere use of the word "subsistit" in *LG* 8. The word "subsistere" by itself does not necessarily connote such structural integrity as is claimed for the Catholic Church. In fact, the Council used the same word, with the qualifier "ex parte," "partially," or "incompletely," when it said that certain Catholic traditions and institutions "subsist" in the Anglican Communion (*UR* 13b). This has to be kept in mind if the question is raised whether the Church of Christ can be said to "subsist" also in other Christian churches. I would say that if such language is to be used, care must be taken to qualify the statement in some such way as the Council itself qualified its statement about the Catholic traditions that "subsist" in the Anglican Communion.[17]

Another point that seems important to make is that the Council surely means to say that the Church of Christ subsists in the Catholic Church with such structural or institutional integrity that it cannot lack an authoritative magisterium capable of settling dogmatic questions in a definitive and eventually infallible way. The thesis of a recent book by the Basque Jesuit Luis Bermejo, *Towards Christian Reunion,*[18] is that the dogmatic decisions of the Western Catholic Councils, and specifically those of Vatican I, have no claim to infallibility, because the Church of Christ is no longer exclusively identified with the Roman Catholic Church, and therefore only a truly ecumenical consensus of the whole Christian world would enjoy the privilege of infallibility. The problem is that Bermejo builds his thesis on the dropping of the word *est*—which does mean abandoning the exclusive identification of the Church of Christ with the Catholic Church—but he never seriously examines the question as to what the Council meant by its alternative assertion: that the Church of Christ subsists in the Catholic Church. He does not consider the implications of the Council's statement that the unity that Christ gave to his Church cannot be lost and that it subsists in the Catholic Church. If the unity of the Church is essentially its unity in faith, then the Church can never lack the effective means to promote and safeguard such unity, and this ultimately involves its capacity to settle questions about faith definitively and with a divine guarantee of truth in its ultimate decisions.

Significance for Our Thinking
About Other Christian Communities

We come now to our second question: What is the significance of the change from "is" to "subsists in" for our thinking about the rest of the Christian world? It hardly has to be said that we cannot depend for our answer to this question on the statement of *LG* 8 alone, which speaks of the presence of elements of sanctification and truth outside the Catholic Church: elements which are said to be gifts properly belonging to the Church of Christ.

At this point, it seems necessary to consider the interpretation that the Congregation for the Doctrine of the Faith (CDF) has given of this text in the *Notificatio,* which it recently published concerning Leonardo Boff's book, *Church Charism and Power.* [19] In criticizing the statement of Boff to the effect that the Church of Christ subsists also in other Christian churches, the Congregation offered the following interpretation of the mind of the Vatican Council (I quote the Italian, which is the official version, published in the *AAS*)[20]: "Il Concilio aveva invece scelto la parola 'subsistit' proprio per chiarire che esiste una sola 'sussistenza' della vera Chiesa, mentre fuori della sua compagine visibile esistono solo 'elementa Ecclesiae' che— essendo elementi della stessa Chiesa—tendono e conducono verso la Chiesa Cattolica (*LG* 8). Il Decreto sull'Ecumenismo esprime la stessa dottrina (*UR* 3–4), la quale fu di nuovo precisato nella Dichiarazione *Mysterium Ecclesiae* n. 1" (*AAS,* 65, 1973, 396–398).

I must confess that I am not sure how to translate the phrase: "esiste una sola sussistenza della versa Chiesa"; taken literally, it would mean: "there exists only one subsistence of the true Church." In any case, what does seem clear is that the CDF is interpreting the Council to mean that the Church of Christ subsists in the Catholic Church in so exclusive a way that outside of her limits there can be found *only elements* of Church.

My first observation is that while in this context the Council *mentions* only elements, the conciliar text certainly does not say "*only* elements"; the word in the text is *plura* (many), not *solum*. Secondly, it is a fundamental principle of exegesis that one judges the meaning of a text in the light of the whole document, and we have already quoted Pope Paul VI to the effect that the doctrine about the Church in *Lumen gentium* is to be understood in the light of the explanations given in the Decree on Ecumenism. The CDF claims that its interpretation of the text is confirmed by the Decree. With all due respect, I do not see how one can justify such a claim.

But, before looking at the Decree on Ecumenism, there is an important text of *Lumen gentium* itself that sheds light on this question. In number 15, *LG* describes the many ways in which the Catholic Church is linked or joined with non-Catholic Christians. It declares that these Christians, consecrated to Christ by their baptism, also recognize and receive other sacraments *in their own churches and ecclesiastical communities*. It is particularly noteworthy that this phrase was added to the text, as the official *Relatio* tells us, in response to many requests of the bishops. This *Relatio* goes on to say: "The elements which are mentioned concern not only individuals but their communities as well; in this fact precisely is located the foundation of the ecumenical movement. Papal documents regularly speak of separated Eastern 'Churches.' For Protestants recent Pontiffs have used the term 'Christian communities.' "[21]

It is obvious that the Conciliar Theological Commission did not share the view that outside the Catholic Church there exist *only elements* of Church.

What is to be said of the claim that the interpretation of the CDF is confirmed by the Decree on Ecumenism? I do not see how such a claim can stand up against the explicit recognition of the salvific role not only of the ecclesial elements and "sacred actions of the Christian religion" found among our separated brethren (*UR* 3b–c), but also of their churches and ecclesial communities *as such* (*Ipsae Ecclesiae vel communitates*). *Unitatis redintegratio* 3d declares that these "are by no means deprived of significance and importance in the mystery of salvation, for the Holy Spirit has not refrained from using them as means of salvation."

It did not escape the notice of some less ecumenically minded bishops that this text was clearly attributing a salvific role not just to the sacraments that might be found in non-Catholic communities, but to these churches and communities as such. This occasioned a *modus* proposing that the text be amended to say rather: "In these communities means of salvation are preserved which the the Holy Spirit has not refrained from using, etc." The response of the Commission is as follows: "Wherever valid means of salvation are being used, which, as social actions, characterize those communities as such, it is certain that the Holy Spirit is using those communities as means of salvation."[22]

Finally, the whole of Chapter III of the Decree on Ecumenism would have to be dropped if it were true that outside the Catholic Church there can be found nothing but "*elements* of the church." The very title of this chapter makes this clear: it reads: "Churches and Ecclesial Communities separated from the Roman Apostolic See." In the first part of this chapter, entitled "The special position of the Eastern churches," these churches, while not in full communion with Rome, are certainly recognized as "particular churches" in a theological, and not merely conventional sense of the term.[23]

What about the others that are called "ecclesial communities"? The distinction is based on what may be called a principle of "eucharistic ecclesiology," that is, there is not the full reality of Church where there is not less full reality of the Eucharist.[24] However, the very term "ecclesial" suggests a recognition that these communities have an ecclesial, that is, churchly character. The *Relatio* that explains the use of these terms puts it as follows:

> It must not be overlooked that the communities that have their origin in the separation that took place in the West are not merely a sum or collection of individual Christians, but they are constituted by social ecclesiastical elements which they have preserved from our common patrimony, and which confer on them a truly ecclesial character. In these communities the one sole Church of Christ is present, albeit imperfectly, in a way that is somewhat like its presence in particular churches, and by means of their ecclesiastical elements the Church of Christ is in some way operative in them.[25]

In other words, while the Council did not hesitate to speak of the separated Eastern Churches as "particular churches" without qualification, it was the mind of the Commission that the western communities that lack the full reality of the Eucharist—without attempting to decide which ones these were[26]—still have a truly ecclesial character, and are at least analogous to particular churches of the one Church of Christ.

Significance for Our Thinking
About the Universal Church of Christ

This leads us to our final question: How then are we to think about the universal Church of Christ? As far as the Eastern Churches are concerned, which Pope Paul VI repeatedly referred to as "sister churches,"[27] one very significant statement is that "by the celebration of the Eucharist of the Lord in each of these Churches the Church of God is built up" (UR 15a). I do not know how one could take the term "Church of God" here to refer exclusively to the Catholic Church. And if that is impossible, then it must mean that there is one Church of God that embraces the particular churches of both East and West, even though at present they are not in full communion with one another.

Can it be said that the universal Church in some way also embraces the "ecclesial Communities"? If we understand the universal Church as essentially the communion of the particular churches "in which and from which the universal Church has its existence" (LG 23 a), and if one accepts the fact that in the actual state of divided Christianity, both these terms, "communion" and "churches," admit greater or less fullness, I believe that one can think of the universal Church as a communion, at various levels of fullness, of bodies that are more or less fully churches. Such a view is by no means identical with the one excluded by the Declaration Mysterium Ecclesiae, which insists rightly that "we cannot imagine that Christ's Church is nothing more than a collection (divided, but still possessing a certain unity) of churches and ecclesial communities."[28] The Church of Christ is certainly something more than any such "collection" (summa); it is a real communion, realized at various degrees of density or fullness, of bodies, all of which, though some more fully than others, have a truly ecclesial character.

I am convinced that such a view is consistent with our belief that we belong to that Church in which alone the one true

Church of Christ subsists with all those properties and structural elements that are gifts of Christ to his Church, and which, by his enduring grace, it can never lose. It is in this sense, I submit, that we must interpret the remark made in a response to a proposed emendation of the Decree on Ecumenism, where the objection was raised that the text seemed to include the Catholic Church among the "many Christian communities that present themselves to men as the true heritage of Jesus Christ" (UR 1a). The reply of the Commission was: "Here simply a matter of fact, obvious to all, is described. Later on it is clearly affirmed that only the Catholic Church is the true Church of Christ."[29] The only statement in the Decree on Ecumenism that seems to be the one intended in that response is: "For it is through Christ's Catholic Church alone, which is the all-embracing means of salvation, that the fullness of the means of salvation can be obtained." (UR 3e). In other words, by the "true Church of Christ" is meant that church that has preserved the fullness of the means of salvation; and this is certainly affirmed of the Catholic Church alone. But we are no longer making the same exclusive claim that was typical of pre-Vatican II Catholic ecclesiology.

Similarly, one can hardly take the statement in the Decree on the Eastern Catholic Churches that describes the "Holy Catholic Church as the Mystical Body of Christ" (OE 2) in the same sense in which Pius XII in Mystici Corporis simply and exclusively identified the Mystical Body with the Roman Catholic Church. The change of attitude that took place during Vatican II regarding the ecclesial status of non-Catholic communities is dramatically evident in the new policy laid down in the same Decree concerning communicatio in sacris with the Orthodox. Here, "in order to promote closer union with the Eastern Churches separated from us," a policy of reciprocal sharing of Eucharist and other sacraments is not only permitted but encouraged between Catholics and members of the separated Eastern Churches (OE 26–29).

To sum up: the point of this article has been to show that, beginning with the change of wording from est to subsistit in, the Second Vatican Council introduced a way of thinking about the Catholic Church and about the other Christian Churches that is substantially different from the view put forward in the schema De Ecclesia drawn up by the Preparatory Commission and presented to the Council Fathers in the opening session of 1962. No subsequent statement can be a correct interpretation of the mind of Vatican II if it means a return to the exclusive claim made in that *schema* that only the one that is Roman Catholic has a right to be called Church.

Notes

1. *AAS*, 35 (1943), 221 ff.
2. *AAS*, 42 (1950), 571.
3. *AS*, I/4, 15.
4. 1–7 December 1962; *AS*, I/4, 126–391.
5. Thus, Cardinal Liénart, *AS*, I/4, 126–127; Bishop De Smedt, *AS*, I/4, 142–144; Cardinal Bea, *AS*, I/4, 228.
6. *AS*, II/1, 219–220.
7. *AS*, III/1, 177.
8. G. Philips, *L'Église et Son Mystère au IIe Concile du Vatican*, vol. I, 119; C. Butler, *The Theology of Vatican II* (London, 1967), 61; Y. Congar, "Le développement de l'évaluation ecclésiologique des Églises non catholiques," *Rev. Droit can.*, 25 (1975), 215–216; J. Feiner, in *Commentary on the Documents of Vatican II* (Herder, Vol. II), 69; A. Grillmeier, in *Commentary on the Documents of Vatican II*, vol. I, 150; E. Fischer, *Kirche und Kirchen nach dem Vatikanum II* (Munich, 1967), 79–80; H. Fries, "Church and Churches," in R. Latourelle and G. O'Collins (eds.), *Problems and Perspectives in Fundamental Theology*, (New York/Ramsey, 1982), 317; A. Dulles, "The Church, the Churches and the Catholic Church," *TS*, 33 (1972), 211; A. De Halleux, "Les principes catholiques de l'eocuménisme", *Rev. Th. Louv.*, 16 (1985), 320–322.
9. This is the title of Chapter I of the Decree on Ecumenism. The change from the earlier title, "On the Principles of Catholic Ecumenism," involved the recognition of the fact that there is not a specifically Catholic ecumenism.
10. G. Dejaifve, "La Magna Charta de Vatican II: La Constitution 'Lumen Gentium,' " *NRT*, 87 (1965), 8; J. Willebrands, "The Ecumenical Movement, Its Problems and Driving Force," *One in Christ*, 11 (1975), 218.
11. *AAS*, 56 (1964), 1012–1013.
12. *AS*, III/1, 176.
13. Thus, G. Baum interprets *subsistit in* to mean that the Church of Christ is "realized and embodied in the Catholic Church"; it is the "realization of the Church of Christ on earth," in "The Ecclesial Reality of the other Churches," *Concilium*, 4/1 (1965), 38.
14. See, in this sense, F. Ricken, "Ecclesia . . . universale salutis sacramentum," *Scholastik*, 40 (1965), 373.

15. The standard German translations are "ist verwirklicht in" or "hat ihre konkrete Existenzform in." See the critique of these translations by W. Dietzfelbinger in "Die Grenzen der Kirche nach der dogmatischen Konstitution 'De Ecclesia,' " *Kerygma und Dogma*, 11 (1965), 169; and by E. Fischer in *Kirche und Kirchen nach dem Vatikanum II*, 78.

16. A particularly authoritative rejection of such an interpretation is given by J. Willebrands in "The Ecumenical Movement," *One in Christ*, 11 (1975), 219. Others who reject it are A. Dulles, art. cit., 211, M.J. Le Guillou, art. "Church," *Sacr. Mundi*, I, 324; P.W. Scheele, "Das Kirchensein der Getrennten," *Catholica*, 22 (1968), 30.

17. I would say that when Leonardo Boff, in his book *Church: Charism and Power*, says that the Church of Christ may subsist also in other Christian Churches, the context does supply the needed qualification. See the English translation, published by the SCM Press, London, 1985, p. 75, where the translator has used the expression "may be present in" instead of "subsists in." I believe that this is a good rendition of the sense of the original, in its context.

18. Luis M. Bermejo, S.J., *Towards Christian Reunion. Vatican I. Obstacles and Opportunities*, Jesuit Forum Studies 2 (Anand, India, 1984).

19. Leonardo Boff, *Church: Charism and Power*, translated from the original Portuguese, *Igreja, Carisma e Poder* (Petropolis, Brazil, 1981).

20. AAS, 71 (1985), 758–759.

21. AS, III/1, 204.

22. AS, III/7, 36.

23. See UR 14–18, and the *Relatio* that replies to an objection to such use of the term "Churches." The objection was "Ecclesia non datur nisi una, nempe Catholica; communitates non-catholicae proprio sensu nequeunt vocari Ecclesiae." The response was "Duplex expressio 'Ecclesiae et communitates ecclesiales' seu seiunctae a Concilio approbata legitime omino adhibetur. Una quidem est Ecclesia universalis; plures vero Ecclesiae locales et particulares. Solemne est in Traditione Catholica communitates orientales seiunctas vocare Ecclesias—locales sive particulares utique—et quidem sensu proprio. Concilii non est investigare et determinare quaenam inter alias communitates vocandae sint Ecclesiae sensu theologico" (AS, III/7, 35).

24. It is surely significant that in UR 22c, the Council does not use the term "Churches and ecclesial communities," but only "ecclesial communities," as the subject of the sentence in which it denies the presence of the "genuine and total reality of the Eucharistic mystery" because of the "lack of the sacrament of Orders." That this was the mind of the Commission in making this distinction is also clearly indicated in its *Relatio*, AS, III/2, 335, where it recognized the propriety of speaking of the Orthodox and Old Catholic "Churches," precisely because they had preserved valid orders and the full reality of the Eucharist.

25. AS, III/2, 335.

26. See the *Relationes*, AS, III/4, 13, and III/7, 35.

27. See E. Lanne, "Eglises-soeurs. Implications ecclésiologiques du *Tomos Agapis*," *Istina*, 20 (1975), 47–74.

28. AAS, 65 (1973), 398.

29. AS, III/7, 12.

CHAPTER 33

The *Ecclesiae Sui Iuris* in the Revision of Canon Law

Ivan Žužek, S.J.

Summary

The identification made between the terms *Ritus* and *Ecclesia particularis* in the conciliar Decree *Orientalium Ecclesiarum* led to some deep reflection on these concepts. After laborious and lengthy research and study, which is described in this article, more or less complete clarification is reached, on the basis of which we can clearly distinguish between *Ritus*, which is defined as the *patrimonium liturgicum, disciplinare, spirituale et theologicum* and *Ecclesia sui iuris*, which indicates a hierarchically organized community of the faithful to which this heritage belongs. The article then describes the juridical structures of various *sui iuris* Churches and the differences in their *patrimonium rituale*, with a view to a better understanding of the canonical norms relating to these (for example, Canons 111 and 112).

In the schema *De Ecclesiis orientalibus*, which was drawn up in 1963 by the relative commission for the Second Vatican Council, the Eastern Catholic Churches were no longer described by the word *Ritus*, as they had been in the 1917 Code of Canon Law and in the Motu proprio *Cleri sanctitati* of 1957, but by the expression *Ecclesiae particulares*. Those who then expressed the wish to retain the word *Ritus* in the sense of *Ecclesia orientalis* received a decided negative response, emphasizing that first of all "deberet dari clara definitio termini ritus."[1]

However, the schema itself was not always in line with this view,[2] although the decision not to use the word *Ritus* except in the sense of the *liturgia, ecclesiastica disciplina et patrimonium spirituale* (OE 3) typical of the various Eastern Churches permeates the whole of this first draft.

Very few voices were raised against this in the Council Hall, and few are found among the written votes.[3] Even so, in the first vote, articles 2–4 of the schema, which were the most important in this connection, did not receive the necessary two-thirds,[4] one of the main reasons undoubtedly being the terminological discrepancy between this schema and the schemata of the Dogmatic Constitution *Lumen gentium* and the Decree *Christus Dominus*. In these two documents, the expression *Ecclesia particularis* simply indicated a diocese—as it does in the promulgated text—while the Eastern Churches were called *coetus Ecclesiarum particularium,* or even *Ecclesiae locales* (LG 23). Out of those who gave the *placet iuxta modum* (719 out of the 2170 who voted) about fifty, although *diversimode,* wanted the word *Ritus* to be introduced into the schema as an equivalent of *Ecclesia particularis,* or the use of other terms, such as *coetus Ecclesiarum particularium.*[5] The subcommission that examined these proposals minimized possible disagreements: ". . . nihil obstat, quod in aliis schematibus etiam dioecesis vocatur Ecclesia particularis." Nevertheless, the subcommission accepted the use of both terms, speaking "De Ecclesiis particularibus seu Ritibus."[6] This was then the definitive decision taken by the entire commission, with the following explanation:

Ob difficultates in usu dictionis Ecclesiae particulares, opportunum visum fuit dictionem hanc aequiparare aliae, nempe Ritibus, quae hucusque in usu est, tum canonico cum quotidiano, tum etiam in ipso schemate, proposito; hoc modo maior claritas obtinetur tuam quoad alia schemata, tum quoad usum quotidianum; ubi dictio ritus sensu liturgico adhibetur, id clare notatur.[7]

There is thus no doubt that the only reason for this reversal of the previously mentioned decision was the need for greater consistency with the schemata of *Lumen gentium* and *Christus Dominus*. Even so, it is significant that despite everything, the relative commission did not give up speaking of *Ecclesiae particulares* in the sense of entire Eastern Churches, some of which (at least *de iure*) are not only *coetus dioecesium* but also *coetus metropoliarum*. It should, however, be pointed out that although the return to a less technical term such as *Ritus* for whole Eastern Churches is of some help in daily use, it does not contribute to the clarity of the conciliar texts. Indeed, the variation in meanings of this term, which was already visible in the schema, is compounded to the point that in the promulgated text of the Decree *Orientalium Ecclesiarum* it is necessary to define the precise meaning, article by article, on the basis of the context.[8]

It is not surprising that the whole vast question of the concepts of *Ritus* and *Ecclesia particularis* as used in the conciliar Decree *Orientalium Ecclesiarum* was one of those that attracted greatest attention from the Commission for the Revision of the Code of Eastern Canon Law and necessarily concerned the Commission for the Revision of the Code of Canon Law of the Latin Church, too, apart from the so-called *Coetus mixtus de lege Ecclesiae fundamentali*. If we have now reached a large degree of agreement on these concepts, as is already expressed in part in the Code of Canon Law of the Latin Church, this is the result of a laborious process, and it will be helpful to take a brief look at this process, not only to provide an historical record and greater understanding of the canons of the Code promulgated in 1983 with regard to the *Ecclesiae rituales sui iuris*, but above all in order to make the present work of codification with regard to the Eastern *Ecclesiae sui iuris* more comprehensible—and also, it is to be hoped, the whole future Code of Eastern Canon Law.

A first proposal regarding the word *Ritus* was put forward by the Faculty of Canon Law of the Pontifical Oriental Institute at the beginning of 1973, within the framework of the proposed "Norms for the Verification of Eastern Canon Law," drawn up by the same faculty on the invitation of the Pontifical Commission for the Revision of the Code of Eastern Canon Law.[9] The faculty proposed that "the concept of rite should be reexamined and should be reserved solely for rites in the liturgical sense, as is more natural and more commonly used," and then added the following:

Today there is no longer any need to call particular Churches "Rites" because there is no longer any danger of confusion between the one universal Church and the particular Churches, of which there are many.

Such terminology has already been used in the two last Motu proprio of Pius XII, *Sollicitudinem nostram* (6 January 1950, in *AAS*, 42 [1950], no. 1) and *Cleri sanctitati* (2 June 1957, in *AAS*, 49 [1957], 433–603), which speak of *Ecclesiae orientales* and not of only one *Ecclesia orientalis*. Similarly, the *Sacra Congregatio Orientalis* is now called the *Sacra Congregatio pro Ecclesiis Orientalibus* (Paul VI, *Regimini Ecclesiae*, 41, in *AAS*, 59 [1967], 899). The conciliar Decree *Orientalium Ecclesiarum* lays down the same course, first referring to the *particulares Ecclesiae seu ritus*, and then using only the former term. Furthermore, the ecumenical atmosphere demands this, inasmuch as non-Catholic orientals never speak of "Rites" but only of "particular Churches."[10]

Although the faculty knew that *Lumen gentium* and *Christus Dominus* use the term *Ecclesiae particulares* for dioceses, it was aware of the whole problem surrounding the word *Ritus*,[11] and asked that the Eastern codification remain faithful to the terminology used in the conciliar Decree *Orientalium Ecclesiarum*, that is, in referring to the reality that today we call *Ecclesiae sui iuris*.

After a first examination by the members of the Commission for the Revision of the Code of Eastern Canon Law, and after it had been revised by an appropriate group of consultors of the same commission, this proposal of the Faculty of Canon Law of the Pontifical Oriental Institute was formally submitted for the approval of the members, who met in March 1974 with the aim of drawing up "guidelines for the revision of the Code of Eastern Canon Law." The final outcome was the following concise instruction: "The concept of Rite should be reexamined and agreement should be reached on a new terminology to indicate the various particular Churches of the East and West."[12]

As can be seen from the prudent formulation of this "guiding principle," the members of the commission avoided giving reasons, and called for further study of the word *Ritus*, although they also asked that the "particular Churches," including the Latin Church, should be indicated with the same name. In other words, they did not want there to be any discrepancy in terminology between the Latin and Eastern Codes, as there is between *Orientalium Ecclesiarum* and *Lumen gentium*, or even between *Orientalium Ecclesiarum* and *Christus Dominus*.

It was clear that after fresh study of the term *Ritus*, such a plan

could only be carried out in collaboration with the Pontifical
Commission for the Revision of the Code of Canon Law of the
Latin Church. The prospects for such collaboration were rosy
because, following the wishes of the Holy Father, a *Coetus mixtus
de lege fundamentali* was set up during this same meeting of the
members of the Commission for the Revision of the Code of
Eastern Canon Law.[13] It was known that in the schemata of this
Code, the expression *Ecclesiae particulares* was reserved for dioceses, and therefore in the *Coetus mixtus* of the members of the two
commissions, a fresh examination of the whole question of the
word *Ritus* was clearly necessary. It is a good thing to emphasize
the fact that it was also difficult for the orientals to accept the
expression *Ecclesiae peculiares* that appeared in the second canon
of the schema of the same Code, but in a context that made their
relative autonomy extremely clear. This canon read as follows:

> Variae Ecclesiae particulares in plures coniunguntur coetus
> organice constitutos, quorum guidem praecipui sunt Ecclesiae
> peculiares secundum ritum, disciplinam atque propriam, infra
> supreman Ecclesiae auctoritatem, hierarchicam ordinationem
> praesertim inter se distinctae, videlicet Ecclesia latina et
> variae Ecclesiae orientales aliaeque quae suprema Ecclesiae
> auctoritate, constituuntur; quae omnes, salva quidem fidei
> unitate et unica divina constitutione Ecclesiae universae,
> propria gaudent disciplina, proprio liturgico usu atque proprio
> theologico spiritualique patriomonio.[14]

Within the Commission for the Revision of the Code of Eastern Canon Law, the canons *De ritibus* were entrusted to the study
group *De normis generalibus*. During the two years following 1974,
after an in-depth reexamination of the previously mentioned
concepts and a number of discussions, this group came to the
conclusion that the concept of *Ritus* must be separated from that
of *Ecclesia particularis*, in the sense used in the conciliar Decree
Orientalium Ecclesiarum, and that they should no longer be used
as synonyms (*Ecclesiae particulares seu Ritus*): the word *Ritus*
should only be used for the whole "patrimonium liturgicum,
disciplinare, spirituale et theologicum" (*OE* 3) of an *Ecclesia
particularis*, whereas the latter expression should mean a "coetus
fidelium hierarchia ad normam iuris iunctus, quem uti sui iuris
agnoscit Romanus Pontifex vel Oecumenica Synodus."[15]

A particularly convincing argument in support of this proposal of the above-mentioned *Coetus de normis generalibus* came to light in the course of the revision of the canons regarding the assignment of a baptized person to a specific Church, that is, to a clearly defined and hierarchically organized *coetus fidelium,* in such a way that through baptism itself, each baptized person becomes juridically subject to a specific *Ordinarius loci*—called the *Hierarcha loci* in Eastern law. However, membership of the ritual heritage or tradition of this *coetus fidelium* is only a consequence of such assignment and cannot per se be defined juridically—indeed, in the depths of people's hearts, there may be a lack *quod Deus avertat*—although it is presumed and called for on the juridical level so far as its outward manifestations are concerned.

As a result of this, the canons *De ritibus* were divided into two clearly distinct sections, *De ritibus servandis* and *De ascriptione alicui Ecclesiae particulari,* with the following introductive canon:

1. Nomine ritus, hoc in Codice, nisi aliud constet, intelligitur patrimonium liturgicum, disciplinare, spirituale et theologicum, fundatum in traditionibus Alexandrina, Antiochena, Constantinopolitana, Chaldea et Armena, et legitime evolutum conditionibus populorum, quod modo fidei vivendae uniuscuiusque Ecclesiae particularis proprio exprimitur.

2. Nomine Ecclesiae particularis, hoc in Codice, intelligitur coetus fidelium hierarchia ad normam iuris iunctus, quem uti sui iuris expresse vel tacite agnoscit Romanus Pontifex vel Oecumenica Synodus.[16]

As can be seen from this text, there was still a conviction within the Commission for the Revision of the Code of Eastern Canon Law that the Eastern Churches should be called *Ecclesiae particulares,* while another expression was sought for dioceses, although the latter were, of course, still called *Ecclesiae.* This appears very clearly from the brief but incisive work of G. Nedungatt, which was published in *Nuntia 2,* and which shows that the study group *De normis generalibus* "wittingly or unwittingly" (p. 84) followed "the long and widespread Latin Scholastic tradition." Indeed, it seems to be proven that this tradition contains the following "triad," to use the words of J. Donat, which are cited in the work of Nedungatt:

Suppositio universalis est usus termini pro omnibus in eius extensione contentis, e.g., Christus redemit homines *omnes*.

Suppositio particularis est usus termini pro parte extensionis, e.g., homines *aliqui* crucifixerunt Deum suum. . . .

Suppositio singularis est usus termini pro determinato individuo, e.g., homo (*Adamus*) nos perdidit, homo (*Christus*) nos redemit.

It is not difficult to see that the term *Ecclesia particularis* as expressing a certain juridical unity but also the pluralism of the *Ecclesiae singulares* that are part of a specific Eastern Church, takes its place naturally between the term *Ecclesia universalis* in the sense of the whole Catholic Church and the term *Ecclesia singularis* as referring to a specific diocese. And the fact that in its definition of a diocese (referred to in the drafts of the Eastern Code as an *eparchia*), the Commission for the Revision of the Code of Eastern Canon Law does not indicate it with the term *Ecclesia particularis*, but has until now called it an *Ecclesia singularis*,[17] in fact comes from the conviction that this usage is the most convenient. Nevertheless, it should be noted that this difference between the Latin and Eastern Codes could be eliminated in the light of what may be said—at least for reasons of convenience if not because of any certainty—to have found the best formulation.

It is therefore very easy to see why, at the very first meeting of the *Coetus mixtus de lege Ecclesiae fundamentalis* (23–26 April 1974), and with a view to reaching agreement on a new terminology to be used to describe both the Eastern and Western Churches, "unus Consultor nomine Consultorum orientalium" of the *Coetus mixtus de lege Ecclesiae fundamentali*, proposed that the use of the term *Ecclesia particularis* or *peculiaris* be reexamined inasmuch as the *Lex Ecclesiae fundamentalis* was to be determining for both Eastern and Western Codes.[18] And, given the already advanced stage of the drafting of this *Lex*, it is also easy to understand that this proposal immediately ran into considerable difficulties. It was at once pointed out by the chairman of the *Coetus* that the terminology of this draft "probata iam est ab Episcopis universae Ecclesiae, qui interpellati fuerunt quoad primum schema LEF."[19]

This question was formally reexamined almost two years later, in the meeting of the *Coetus mixtus* on 23–27 February 1976, when the Cardinal President of the Commission for the Revision of the Code of Eastern Canon Law, who was also the vice president of the *Coetus mixtus*, proposed: "ut: a) in Ecclesia latina adhibeatur tantum vox 'diocesis'; b) in Ecclesiis orientalibus expressio 'Ecclesia particularis' designet Ritum," whereas the Cardinal president of the *Coetus mixtus* itself disagreed, because "in Const. 'Lumen gentium' et in Decr. 'Christus Dominus' semper dicitur 'Ecclesia particularis' seu 'dioecesis,' quae igitur habenda est ut terminologia aim fixa; praterea sunt 'Ecclesiae particulares'—Administrationes apostolicae, Praelaturae, Abbatiae, etc.—quae dici nequeunt dioeceses." Moreover, referring to the proposal, which was also made in the *Coetus mixtus*, to use the term *Ecclesiae singulares* for dioceses, the Cardinal president added: "Ecclesiam universalem cue praeest Romanus Pontifex, constare Ecclesiis particularibus, quae Episcopis regendae committuntur. Distinctio viget non inter singularem et universalem, sed inter particularem et universalem."[20]

However, because of the different terminology of conciliar texts and the conviction that *particularis* can conveniently be placed between *universalis* and *singularis* and that no difficulty is created by the fact that the universal Church "constat Ecclesiis singularibus, quae Episcopis regendae committuntur," not everybody will agree with the arguments given. Even so, when they read what has become public knowledge on the events of this session—which can be described as "historic" for a number of reasons—anybody can understand that it really was a good idea to stop calling the Eastern Churches *Ecclesiae particulares* and that another term had to be found for them other than those used in the three conciliar texts mentioned. The choice was *Ecclesiae rituales sui iuris*, with twenty-three *placet* and five abstentions.[21] This corresponds very well both with the law now in force for Eastern Catholics (Canon 303 of the Motu proprio *Postquam apostolicis litteris*) and with the previously mentioned draft of the first canon *De ritibus*, in which these Churches are called *coetus fidelium . . . sui iuris*. It should be inferred that the Latin Church itself is one of the *Ecclesiae rituales sui iuris*.

In the second canon of the *Lex Ecclesiae fundamentalis*, which was being drafted at that time, we therefore find (in paragraph 2) that

. . . variae Ecclesiae particulares in plures coniunguntur coetus organice constitutos, quorum quidem praecipui sunt Ecclesiae rituales sui iuris . . . , videlicet Ecclesia latina et variae Ecclesiae orientales aliaeque quae, suprema Ecclesiae auctoritate probante, constituuntur.[22]

This same approach was then adopted by the Commission for the Revision of the Code of Canon Law of the Latin Church, as can be seen in Canons 111 and 112 of the Code promulgated in 1983, and it is also the line followed by the Commission for the Revision of the Code of Eastern Canon Law, with a reservation as to the word *ritualis*, which (at least in the context of the Eastern Code) is considered superfluous and counterproductive when speaking of *Ecclesiae sui iuris*, especially since there are different *Ecclesiae sui iuris* belonging fundamentally to the same *Ritus*.

Thus, with one exception, the various traditions or *Ritus generici* are concretized in various churches *sui iuris*, which are distinguished from one another not so much because of their position as *rituales* but precisely because they are *sui iuris*—in other words, hierarchically organized under one of the forms of "special status" approved by the supreme authority of the Church. At the present stage of the work of the Commission for the Revision of the Code of Eastern Canon Law, the following such forms are envisaged:

1. Churches with a status of *Ecclesiae patriarchales*.
2. Churches with a status of *Ecclesiae archiepiscopales maiores*.
3. Churches with a status of *Ecclesiae metropolitanae sui iuris*.
4. *Ceterae Ecclesiae sui iuris*, some of which are *de facto* made up only of one diocese or even of a single *exarchia*, although at least potentially they are capable of developing into one of the other three forms.

The following overall description of an Eastern Catholic Church appears in *Seminarium*:

An Eastern Catholic Church is a part of the universal Church which lives the faith (liturgy, spiritual heritage, discipline) in a manner corresponding to one of the five great Eastern traditions (Alexandrian, Antiochene, Constantinopolitan, Chaldean, or Armenian) and which contains or is at least capable of containing as its lesser components various diocesan communities hierarchically gathered under the leadership of a common head (patriarch, major archbishop, metropolitan) who is legitimately elected and is in communion with Rome, and who, with his own synod, is the highest forum for all the administrative, legislative and juridical affairs of these communities, within the framework of the law common to all the Churches, which is laid down in the canons approved by Ecumenical Councils or the Roman Pontiff, while always retaining the right of the latter to intervene in individual cases.[23]

The exception mentioned is the Armenian Church, which has patriarchal status, and is the only church belonging to the Armenian *Ritus*. Two churches belong to the *Ritus alexandrinus:* the first, the Coptic Church, is of patriarchal status, whereas, according to the juridical forms listed but not yet in force, the Ethiopian Church would have metropolitan status. Three churches belong to the *Ritus antiochenus:* the Maronite Church and the Syrian Church, which are of patriarchal status, and the Malankar Church, which (again according to the listed proposed forms) would have metropolitan status. Two churches belong to the *Ritus chaldaeus:* the Chaldean Church, which is of patriarchal status, and the Malabar Church, which at present has its own organization, similar to that of an episcopal conference. Twelve churches *sui iuris* belong to the *Ritus byzantinus:* the Melkite Church is of patriarchal status, the Ukrainian Church has the status of a major archbishopric, while for the Byelorussian, Bulgarian, Greek, Italo-Albanian, Romanian, Ruthenian, Slovak, Hungarian, Russian and Yugoslavian Churches, it will not be difficult to find the category corresponding to their present status among the forms envisaged in the schemata of the future Code of Eastern Canon Law. It must always be remembered that the only authority that lays down the type of status *sui iuris* of a given Eastern Church is the supreme authority of the universal Church, that is, the Pope or an Ecumenical Council, and that this authority alone has the right to change such a status, either by upgrading (eparchia, metropolitanate, major archbishopric, patriarchate) or by downgrading, even to the extent of suppressing an *Ecclesia sui iuris*.

It is worth observing here, as regards the Latin Church, which is also an *Ecclesia ritualis sui iuris,* as is clear from Canons 111 and 112 of the 1983 Code of Canon Law, that its nature is such that it cannot be fitted into any of the juridical forms listed, even though the titles of the Roman Pontiff include that of "patriarch." If we speak of the Roman Pontiff as "Patriarch of the West" and the Latin Church as the "Patriarchate of the West," we must always remember that within the primatial power conferred by Christ on Peter and his successors, it is not possible to make *adequaetae distinctiones* between his powers as Bishop of Rome, Archbishop and Metropolitan of the Province of Rome, Primate of Italy, and Patriarch of the West. It is therefore impossible for the structure of the Latin Church to be equal or analogous to an Eastern *Ecclesia patriarchalis*, in which (in view of the fact that it is not a structure *iuris divini* but only *iuris ecclesiastici* even if *Divina autem Provindentia—LG* 23) the patriarch is ascribed only a power limited *ad normam iuris* and quite frequently conditional on the *consensus* of a synod of bishops, which has its own specific powers—which may even be exclusive, such as those concerning legislative power for the whole patriarchate.

From what we have seen, it is easy to understand that it is particularly helpful for the Catholic Church to have two Codes of Canon Law, one for the Latin Church and one for all the Eastern Churches, despite the ritual differences there may be among the latter. Although the five great Eastern traditions differ considerably as regards their *patrimonium liturgicum*, they seem to differ much less as regards their *patrimonium spirituale et theologicum*. As far as their *patrimonium disciplinare* is concerned, both regarding the hierarchical structure of the churches *sui iuris* and the various other sections of canon law, there is a good basis for holding that it is substantially the same for all five of the great Eastern traditions.

Indeed, at the basis of their discipline, all the Eastern Churches have the same "sacred canons," which were listed in the second canon of the Council in Trullo, and are still formally in force today for the Orthodox Byzantine Churches without exception, although *per economia* some of them may not be considered applicable to the circumstances of contemporary life. As regards the non-Byzantine Churches, the same thing can be seen, with the exception of the canons of the Council of Chalcedon and those of the Council in Trullo—since these churches do not recognize these two Councils; it can be said that these churches still observe the Prechalcedonian Code, made up of a little over 500 canons, whereas the Trullan Code, which is valid for the Byzantine Churches, has roughly 635, with slight variations due to the different systems of numbering the canons used in different canonical collections.[24] The *Ritus* in the sense of the *patrimonium disciplinare* is therefore basically the same for all the Eastern Churches, although, for the benefit of legitimate pluralism, it has been diversified into as many *iura particularia* as there are *Ecclesiae sui iuris*, for those matters not treated in the sacred canons and for the practical application of these canons to the lives of the individual churches.

It also seems helpful to add that the previously mentioned common Code was promulgated for all the churches by an Ecumenical Council, and it should therefore be considered open to modification only on the part of the supreme authority of the universal Church. This is a nonnegotiable point both for the Orthodox Churches and for the Eastern Catholic Churches and, therefore, in view of the *sui iuris* status enjoyed by these churches, there is no way in which they can call for their own *codex iuris canonici*—since in order to be their own, it would have to be promulgated by them. Indeed, it is beyond doubt that, at least from the Council of Nicaea (A.D. 325) on, there has never been an *Ecclesia sui iuris* that was not obliged to observe the sacred canons that the supreme authority of the universal Church promulgated for it too.

If the Commission for the Revision of the Code of Eastern Canon Law already had very clear ideas in 1975, the Commission for the Revision of the Code of Canon Law of the Latin Church did not reach similar clarity until later. In 1975, the Eastern *Coetus de normis generalibus*, which had the task of reviewing the canons *De ritibus*, had already made the following three points:

1. *Ritus* means the *patrimonium liturgicum, disciplinare, spirituale et theologicum*.
2. The baptized belong not to a *Ritus* but to an *Ecclesia sui iuris*, which at that time was still called an *Ecclesia particularis*.
3. The person *baptizatus est aut baptizare debuisset* must belong not to that Church *cuius caerimoniis*, but to the one to which his father belongs in the case of the baptism of children, or to the one freely chosen by an adult being baptized, not to mention other cases of an *ascriptio alicui Ecclesiae sui iuris*.[25]

Following the decision of the *Coetus mixtus de lege Ecclesiae fundamentali* in February 1976, and following an exchange of opinions between the two commissions, which can be read between the lines of what has actually been published in this connection,[26] in October 1979, the Commission for the Revision of the Code of Canon Law of the Latin Church accepted the first two points in substance. As a result, Canon 15 of the schema *De populo Dei,* which until then had been very similar to Canon 98 of the 1917 Code ("Inter varios Ecclesiae ritus ad illum quis pertinet cuius caerimoniis . . . ," etc.), took the new approach into account and was amended as follows: "Inter varias Ecclesias rituales sui iuris ad illam quis pertinet in qua ad normam iuris baptizatus est aut baptizari debuisset."[27] This text appears in Canon 109 of the 1980 draft of the whole Code, where it has been further improved in its second part (". . . ad illam baptizatus pertinet in qua ad normam iuris baptizandus erat").

It is clear from this that the third point had not yet been accepted, because the canon was still closely linked to the concept of the *norma iuris* determining the *Ritus* in which baptism must be administered. Although the wording of this *norma iuris* was improved in the schemata of the Code, the substance itself remained basically the same as Canon 756 of the 1917 Code: "Adultus baptizetur ritu libere ab ipso electo," while "infans baptizetur ritu parentum."[28] As a result, in the 1980 schemata of the Code (the equivalent canon was numbered 806), the rather curious tension found in the 1917 Code and in the law still in force in the Eastern Catholic Churches[29] had not yet been eliminated; thus, in order to know the *Ecclesia* to which a child will belong, one must know the *Ritus* with which he will be baptized, and in order to know this, one must know the *Ecclesia* to which his parents belong—and all this in order to reach a final conclusion that the child will in any case belong to the parents' *Ecclesia.*

Furthermore, in Canon 109 of the 1980 schema of the Code, there was another more serious inconsistency which may have been excusable in the 1920s, when there was still no Code of Eastern Canon Law, but not in an up-to-date Code that declares that it concerns *unum Ecclesiam latinum* (Canon 1). However, the canon still had the tone of a *lex Ecclesiae catholicae universae,* to avoid using the expression *lex universalis* here, which is so common in the Code promulgated in 1983, although it is used in

the latter in the restricted sense of a *lex* concerning the whole
Latin Church and only the Latin Church.

It is, therefore, not surprising that *aliquis Pater,* who must have
been well aware of the work of the Commission for the Revision
of the Code of Eastern Canon Law, made the following observation on Canon 109 of the 1980 schema:

> De adscriptione Ecclesiae latinae (cann. 109 et 806) different
> canones utriusque Commissionis. In Can. 109 substantialiter
> eodem modo ac in C.I.C. a. 1917 adscriptio alicui Ecclesiae
> concipitur, hoc est uti ius Ecclesiae universae determinans.
> Non est Ecclesiae latinae statuere quidquid de adscriptione
> Ecclesiis Orientalibus, nec est Ecclesiae Orientalis cuiusdam
> vel Codicis orientalis quidquid statuere de adscriptione Ec-
> clesiae latinae vel de licentia data latinis transmigrandi ad
> alium ritum.[30]

The observation was accepted and the canon reformulated in
such a way as to start with "ad Ecclesiam pertinet latinam
baptizatus qui in ea ad normam iuris baptizandus erat."[31] There is
a very clear wish not to make laws for the orientals in the Code of
Canon Law of the Latin Church.

Even so, formulated in this way, the text still retained the
reference to the *norma iuris* that laid down who *in Ecclesia latina
baptizandus est,* which was contained in Canon 806 of the 1980
schema, and as a result, the relative difficulty mentioned above
was not eliminated. Indeed, *aliquis ex Patribus* (it is left to the
reader to identify him with the *aliquis Pater* mentioned before)
had the following observations to make on Canon 806:

> Vox "ritus" refertur in canone ad caerimonias liturgicas, ut
> videtur. Si ita, vix loqui possumus de "caerimoniis liturgicis
> parentum," vix dicere possumus quod "parentes ad diversas
> caerimonias liturgicas pertinent" etc. Si vero "vox ritus" sig-
> nificat etiam in hoc canone "Ecclesiam ritualem sui iuris,"
> haec magis expresse dicenda sunt.

This observation was not accepted, thanks to a line of argument that could be described as *ad hominem,* presuming that the
proposer was referring to the schemata of the Eastern Code,
inasmuch as it was stated that "in can. 18, §1 schematis can-

onum 'de cultu divino et praesertim de sacramentis' a
P.C.C.I.C.O.R. exarati vox 'ritus' eodem utitur sensu ac in
nostro schemate."[32] Although it was in fact comprehensible, this
argument lost its validity at the beginning of June 1981 when the
relative Eastern *Coetus a studiis* reformulated the canon in question in the opposite manner, that is, in such a way that it should
refer to the canons *de ascriptione alicui Ecclesiae sui iuris* and not
vice versa. The canon in question was reduced to the following
text: "Proles baptizari debet ritu Ecclesiae cui ad normam canonis
NN 'De ritibus' ascribenda est."[33]

However, Canon 806 had disappeared from the Code promulgated in 1983, while the two canons dealing with the *adscriptio
Ecclesiae latinae* (Canon 111), or, with reference to the "Latins,"
of the *adscriptio alii Ecclesiae rituali sui iuris* (Canon 112), say
everything *in recto* without any reference to the canons on baptism, precisely in accordance with the approach followed since
1975 by the Commission for the Revision of the Code of Eastern
Canon Law. Through these efforts—and also thanks to improve-
ments in wording—these two canons have helped to improve
understanding between East and West.

Translated from the Italian by Leslie Wearne.

Notes

1. AS, III/IV, 498, em. (= emendatio) 8; cf. also 501, em. 38 and
45; 502, em. 56; 507, em. 92 and 103.

2. AS, III/V, 745, "Appendix" art. 11.

3. AS, III/V, 36; written votes from p. 759.

4. AS, III/V, 269 and 279, General Congregation 106 of 21 October 1964.

5. AS, III/VIII, 561—31 Fathers ask that the actual title of the
schema speak *De ritibus*; 564—8 Fathers ask for greater consistency with
other schemata; 565—one Father wants the use only of the word *Ritus*
with no mention *De Ecclesiis—quia Ecclesia est unica*; 9 Fathers want the
terms *coetus Ecclesiarum* as in *Lumen gentium*; 563—various proposals,
including the suggestion that mention should be made *de patriarchatibus,
de Ecclesiis patriarchalibus, archiepiscopalibus maioribus seu metropolitanis.*

6. AS, III/VIII, 563–564.

7. AS, III/VIII, 558.

8. Thus, for example, in article 6, this term means only liturgy, as
opposed to discipline; in article 3, it means the complex of *liturgia,*

ecclesiastica, disciplina et patrimonium spirituale; in articles 2, 3, and 10, it is equivalent to the *Ecclesia particularis;* in the context of article 4, *proprium retineant ritum,* the term does not indicate what was intended— in other words that they remain juridically ascribed to their own Church *sui iuris;* in article 7, the *vel ritus* is ambiguous (cf. *Nuntia* 6, 17–18) and what is intended is clear only from the words *ad normam iuris;* in article 16, the *loca sui ritus* appear in the sense of *loca* where a bishop is *hierarcha loci,* while in article 21 the terms *regio vel territorium proprii ritus* have the strictly juridical meaning of Canon 303 of the Motu proprio *Postquam apostolicis litteris* (*territorium ritus* is that territory where *saltem exarchia erecta est*).

9. The proposal is made public in a photostat issue of *Nuntia,* that appeared in November 1973 in only 400 copies. See pp. 20–33.

10. *Ibid.,* 30.

11. The whole problem referred to here was well dealt with in the book of W. Bassett, *The Determination of Rite* (Rome, 1967), where the whole bibliography dealing with this question is listed.

12. *Nuntia* 3, 7.

13. The *Coetus mixtus de lege Ecclesiae fundamentali* had Cardinal P. Felici as its president, and he was director of the revision of the CIC, while the vice president was Cardinal J. Parecattil, who is still president of the Commission for the Revision of the Eastern Code. Among the names of the other thirty-three members of this *Coetus,* apart from I. Mansourati (vice president) and I. Žužek (then prosecretary of the latter commission), nine consultors of the same commission can be noted: M. Brini, G. Amadouni, P. Rai, E. Eid, J. Sarraf, I. Malak, P. Podipara, S. Mudryj, G. Řezáč. The whole list can be found in *Communicationes,* 1 (1974), 59–60; see also *Nuntia* 1, 19.

14. *Communicationes,* 1 (1976), 80–81.

15. *Nuntia* 3, 45, Canon 1.

16. *Ibid.*

17. *Nuntia* 9, 5, Canon 1; *Nuntia* 19, Canon 145.

18. *Communicationes,* 2 (1976), 81.

19. *Ibid.,* 82.

20. *Communicationes,* 2 (1977), 298.

21. *Ibid.,* 299.

22. *Communicationes,* 1 (1980), 31.

23. Ivan Žužek, "Che cosa è una Chiesa, un Rito orientale?" *Seminarium,* new series 15 (April–June 1975), 276.

24. The Prechalcedonian Code: First Council of Nicaea, 20 canons; First Council of Constantinople, 7 canons; Council of Ephesus, 3 canons; Canons of the Holy Apostles, 85 canons; Synod of Ancyra, 25 canons; Synod of Neocaesarea, 15 canons; Synod of Gangra, 20 canons; Synod of Carthage, 133 canons; Dionysius of Alexandria, 5 canons; Gregory of Neocaesarea, 11 canons; Peter of Alexandria, 15 canons; Athanasius of Alexandria, 5 canons; Basil of Caeserea, 96 canons; Gregory of Nyssa, 8 canons; Gregory of Nazianzus, 1 canon; Amphilochius of Iconium, 1 canon; Timothy of Alexandria, 29 canons; Theophilus of Alexandria, 14 canons; Cyril of Alexandria, 8 canons; Cyprian of Carthage, 1 canon. The Trullan Code also contains: Council of Chalcedon, 30 canons; Council in Trullo, 102 canons; Gennadius I of Constantinople, 1 canon.

25. *Nuntia* 3, 44–53.
26. *Communicationes*, 1 (1980), 70–74.
27. *Ibid.*, 74.
28. *Communcationes*, 1 (1981), 216, Canon 20.
29. Motu proprio *Cleri sanctitati*, Canon 6.
30. *Communicationes*, 2 (1982), 2, 141.
31. *Ibid.*, 142.
32. *Communicationes*, 2 (1983), 2, 178.
33. *Nuntia* 15, 17.

CHAPTER 34

Ecclesiological Issues in the Lutheran–Catholic Dialogue (1965–1985)

Jared Wicks, S.J.

Summary

Following the promulgation of Unitatis redintegratio, the Catholic Church has entered vigorously into bilateral dialogues. With the Lutheran churches, an international Study Commission (1967–1971) issued a first joint analysis of Lutheran–Catholic agreements and differences in the "Malta Report" of 1972. Regional dialogues in the United States and Germany have further clarified this relationship, and a world-level Joint Commission (1974–1984) substantively promoted Lutheran–Catholic reconciliation through declarations on the Eucharist, ministry, and phases, and forms of Church unity. Among the ecclesiological themes treated, attention now needs to concentrate on clarifying the following: (1) What kinds and how much diversity of doctrine and structure can coexist with the bond of ecclesial communio? (2) What is the present ecclesiological status of the Lutheran churches while they remain detached from Catholic unity?

At the Second Vatican Council, the Decree on Ecumenism, Unitatis redintegratio, inaugurated a new phase in the life of the Catholic Church. There was, for all practical purposes, no previous Catholic tradition of officially sanctioned ecumenical action on the world level when this decree was promulgated on 21 November 1964. This date, in effect, signals the Roman Catholic entry into a movement that Church leadership had viewed with wariness and even hostility before the Council.[1]

The Climate of Dialogue

Two decades after Vatican II, ecumenism has clearly become a significant dimension of Catholic life. One can survey a broad panorama of ecumenical efforts and events in which Roman Catholics have contributed in official capacities. Relations with the World Council of Churches have begun and are being intensified, especially through the official Joint Working Group.[2] Catholic theologians collaborate as members of the Faith and Order Commission. On local and regional levels, a host of common efforts and joint dialogues with other churches have developed.[3]

Since 1978, many of the pilgrim visits of Pope John Paul II have included encounters and exchanges with leaders of Christian bodies not in communion with the Roman See. On 12 June 1984, the Pope visited the headquarters of the World Council in Geneva and gave this testimony:

> The simple fact of my presence here among you . . . is a sign of this will for unity. From the beginning of my ministry as Bishop of Rome, I have insisted that the engagement of the Catholic Church in the ecumenican movement is irreversible and that the search for unity was one of its pastoral priorities.[4]

Similarly, the *Relatio Finalis* of the 1985 Extraordinary Synod of Bishops declares,

> After these twenty years we can affirm that ecumenism has inscribed itself deeply and indelibly in the consciousness of the Church. We bishops ardently desire that the incomplete communion already existing with the non-Catholic churches and communities might, with the help of God's grace, come to the point of full communion.[5]

Some of the most promising results of Catholic engagement in ecumenism since Vatican II have come from the bilateral dialogues with particular Christian bodies. The Council itself had called for such exchanges, giving in the Decree on Ecumenism two descriptions of these conversations between representatives of Christian communities now detached from one another. In dialogues between competent experts,

> each explains the teaching of his communion in greater depth and brings out clearly its distinctive features. Through such dialogue, everyone gains a truer knowledge and more just appreciation of the teaching and religious life of both communions (UR 4).

The Council went on to recommend that this understanding of and appreciation of other Christians should develop through exchanges on problematic points by experts. These are foreseen as valuable instruments of clarification.

> From dialogue of this sort will emerge still more clearly what the true posture of the Catholic Church is. In this way, too, we will better understand the attitude of our separated brethren and more aptly present our own belief (UR 9).

Two decades after these recommendations were formulated and approved by the Council, bilateral dialogues are underway, as of early 1986, between representatives named by the Vatican Secretariat for Promoting Christian Unity and other representatives named by nine worldwide bodies of other Christians. Through these joint commissions for dialogue, the Catholic Church is engaged officially with the Orthodox, Old Catholics, Anglicans, Lutherans, Reformed or Presbyterians, Methodists, Disciples of Christ, Pentecostals, and Baptists. In addition to these "world-level" exchanges, numerous national dialogues, with Catholic participants being named by national episcopal conferences, have also been undertaken with these same bodies of separated Christians.[6]

A detailed review and assessment of all these exchanges would produce a remarkable volume of evidence for the new ecumenical atmosphere created by the commitment made by the Second Vatican Council. In addition to climatic or attitudinal changes, the dialogues also register significant advances toward making explicit the agreement in faith that is needed for the restoration

of communion between Christian bodies now detached from one
another. Where Vatican II envisaged the exchange of accurate
information, the dialogues have in fact moved on from this starting point to notable moments of discovery of proximity, communality of intention, and even consensus on points where different
doctrinal languages and styles of thought had earlier concealed
similarity of conviction. Not all the divisive issues of doctrine
and Church order have been confronted in the dialogues, but on
numerous issues the joint commissions have demonstrated a degree of agreement that raises the question whether the remaining
differences in these areas are such as to justify continued divisions between the churches.

We will, in this essay, examine certain selected aspects of one
bilateral dialogue, that between Roman Catholics and Lutherans, in order to exemplify ecumenical progress since Vatican II.
This consists in sustained joint reflection on what our now separated communions hold in common, in astute assessment of
points of discord, and, most recently, in a promising joint attempt to envisage the steps by which visible unity can be established between the Roman Catholic Church and the Lutheran
churches of the world. Ecumenism, in its Lutheran–Catholic
form, has passed beyond the stage of "getting to know you," as
proposed by Vatican II, and is at present beginning to "face
unity"—according to the document issued by the world-level
Lutheran–Catholic Joint Commission in 1985.[7] Here we will
report the main steps in this advance, reflecting especially on the
ecclesiological issues that have come to the surface in these
twenty years of dialogue.

Preparing for Dialogue

The Lutheran–Catholic ecumenical dialogue at the world
level grew out of the presence of official observers named by the
Lutheran World Federation at all four sessions of Vatican II.
Reciprocally, Roman Catholic observers attended the Fourth Assembly of the World Lutheran Federation at Helsinki, in July–
August 1963. It was the Lutheran observers at Vatican II who
recommended to the Federation that it explore the possibility of
continuing and eventually intensifying official relations with the
Catholic Church.[8]

A first joint consultative working group of fourteen members—seven from each side, including bishops, churchmen, and theologians—held meetings in August 1965 and April 1966 to plan for future dialogue. The working group drew up an itemized list of topics to indicate the points where one might assume there would be serious differences between Catholics and Lutherans. The dialogue should strive to clear away misunderstandings by offering a more authentic perception of the religious concerns underlying the respective doctrinal traditions. The retracing of past history was not the main task, but instead a contemporary encounter that would take account of today's world view and an up-to-date understanding of Scripture. Seven principal areas were noted, with particular topics added to each to suggest the possible configuration of the issues for dialogue:

1. The word of God: the authority of and interpretation of Scripture; Scripture and Tradition; divine revelation and the Creeds.
2. The presence of Christ in the Church: baptism, the Eucharist, the priesthood of believers, authority and ministry in the Church, the purity of the gospel and the fullness of the Church.
3. Christology: the saving role of the humanity of Christ; *solus Christus* and human cooperation; the implications of marian doctrine; anthropology and the cosmic implications of christological doctrine.
4. Pneumatology: the presence of the Spirit in the Church; Spirit and institution, charism and ministry; sin and temptation in and of the Church itself; the role of law in the Church.
5. Justification and sanctification: law and gospel; the meaning of sin; baptismal faith and justification; the sacramental means of grace.
6. Renewal and reform: the meaning of the Reformation; the significance of Luther's teachings for Catholics; self-criticism on the Lutheran side; permanent and changeable elements in the Church.
7. Missionary and pastoral problems: common efforts in world mission; theology of marriage; Lutheran–Catholic mixed marriages; religious liberty.[9]

The 1965–1966 Working Group recommended that the Holy See and the Lutheran World Federation appoint two joint commissions to tackle these problematical issues. One commission should deal with a panoramic range of topics under the rubric, "The Gospel and the Church," while another mixed group should focus specifically on the doctrine of marriage in the Catholic and Lutheran traditions and on the problems connected with mixed marriages.[10]

The Commission on "The Gospel and the Church," 1967–1971

The recommended dialogue on marriage was not implemented immediately, but the joint Lutheran–Catholic Study Commission was formed to deal with "The Gospel and the Church." Seven Catholic and seven Lutheran members—exegetes and systematic theologians mainly—were named and began their work in November 1967. The title of the Commission deftly linked paramount values of the two traditions: for Lutherans, the liberating announcement in the gospel of God's saving grace to sinners in Christ; for Catholics, the shared life of those gathered by Christ and his Spirit into the visible community of the Church. The Commission's work, however, would show that neither gospel nor Church was a concern belonging exclusively to only one of the partners in dialogue.

The work of the Study Commission bore a scholarly complexion, marked by exegetical citation and biblical theology, by historical lights on traditional doctrines, and by systematic proposals on how to view doctrine and Church practice today. For each of the five week-long sessions, from 1967 to early 1972, papers were prepared and then discussed by members of the Commission and by invited experts.[11] A committee drew up the "directions and results of the discussions" and this provided the raw material for a concluding document.[12]

The Commission did not tackle traditional points of Lutheran–Catholic divergence in a direct manner, but instead chose a biblical starting point. For the 1967 meeting, four New Testament experts submitted papers on the earliest Christian proclamation of the gospel and on the normative role of this original message even within the New Testament. The discussions revealed the existence of a central complex of agreements, around which differences emerged. The problems concerned the criteria of valid traditions in the Church, the immutable character of Catholic dogmatic declarations, and the Lutheran concentration of the meaning of the gospel of Christ almost exclusively in the Pauline doctrine of justification by faith alone.

But the two main agreements registered in this first session both demonstrated the ecumenical fruitfulness of the teachings of Vatican II. First, the participants were one in recognizing the priority of the gospel or kerygma of God's saving action over both Tradition and Scripture. This conviction, expressed by Vatican II in *DV* 7–9, changes notably the terms of the centuries-long dispute over Scripture and Tradition. Second, the teaching of the Council in *DV* 10 expresses a conviction common to both Catholics and Lutherans, namely, that the Church and its authoritative teaching are to render a docile service to the word of God in promoting its integrity and vitality today. Church authority can exercise no mastery over the word of God, but the gospel has a normative standing over the Church.[13]

The 1968 working session of the Study Commission turned to the consideration of "the world" as the situation in which the gospel must be proclaimed ever anew. One perceives the influence on the Commission of the concern enunciated at the beginning of Vatican II's Pastoral Constitution on the Church in the Modern World: "*Hominis enim persona salvanda humanaque societas instauranda*" (*GS* 3). The discussions of the four papers revealed that the modern world poses basic questions to both Churches and that both sense the need to promote human reconciliation, justice, and peace—by both words of advocacy and practical action. There was no hesitancy, however, in saying together that the gospel of Christ does *not* arise from the world in a modernistic manner as the articulation of secular experience. Also, the message of redemption, while affecting the public sphere of life, does offer more than simply the rehabilitation of a creation defaced by sin.

Prevalent in the second session was the sense of being together in the face of a complex common challenge. But the papers, on one point revealed a significant ecclesiological difference. Walter Kasper's reflections on the world as the *locus* of the gospel built on the foundational significance of faith in the Incarnation of the Son of God. This means that revelation occurs amid historical contingency, as *DV* 4 describes it, but is wholly God's own revelation of himself in an absolute promise for the world.[14]

But the Lutheran Per E. Persson came to question, in the subsequent paper, whether Catholic ecclesiology was on a sound foot-
ing in its preference for thinking about the Church in terms of its
analogy with the Incarnation. Rather than stressing the union of
divine and human elements in the Church would it not be more
true to the gospel to articulate the nature of the Church from the
kerygma of Jesus' Cross and Resurrection, that is, from the Easter
victory of God's love over human enmity and sin.[15]

Ecclesiology was under indirect treatment in 1969, when the
Joint Study Commission took up four papers on Church structures and ministry. The dialogue group first faced the exegetical
and historical evidence for structural variety in the churches of
the Apostolic age and for the only gradual emergence of the
presbyteral–episcopal system as the normative form of ministry.[16]
In response, members on both sides reacted against drawing any
conclusions that would dissolve the Church into a welter of
unbinding contingencies. For the gospel itself calls forth structures of service in order to assure its ongoing actualization both
on mission and in communities of faith. Thus, ministerial office
is of fundamental importance for service of the message by which
the Church lives.[17]

Two papers on ministerial office, also discussed in 1969, represented a breakthrough for the Commission. The background
here is the view, expressed in *UR* 22, that Protestant communities suffer the lack (*defectus*) of the sacrament of Orders and
consequently have not preserved a fully authentic and integral
celebration of the Eucharist. Thus, treatment of respective doctrines of ministry, of the practice of ordination, and of apostolic–
episcopal succession is critical in any dialogue seeking to serve
the establishment of *communio* between the Catholic Church
and a presently detached Protestant body.

From the Lutheran side, George Lindbeck related how the
official Lutheran confessional documents do not derive ecclesial
ministry from the priesthood of all believers, in contrast with the
way some statements of Luther seem to portray the genesis of
ministry. The Confessions maintain instead a type of "divine
institution" of ministry, because Jesus Christ wills that his gospel
be preached in word and actualized in sacrament for eliciting and
sustaining justifying faith. Lindbeck also pointed out that Lutherans have the functional equivalent of a ministerial *character
indelibilis*, because no Lutheran Church practices reordination in

the case of a person returning to ministry after a time away from such pastoral service.[18]

Edward Schillebeeckx gave a complementary account of the Catholic view of the character imparted by ordination, stressing the irrevocable placing of the minister in a special service group in the Church. The priest or bishop, by the office imparted, can then speak in the name of the exalted Christ "over against" the community of faith. Although the minister is a member of the community of the Church, he also takes the initiative in transmitting to the community words and signs of grace that do not arise out of the community. At this fundamental level, the Lutheran and Catholic traditions agree.

Even more significant for the course of the dialogue was Schillebeeckx's discussion of the validity of ministerial office. He submitted that a valid ministry is one that serves the fidelity of an ecclesial community to the apostolic faith. Differences of structuring in ministry and of modes of transmission are secondary to the authenticity of the Church served by its ministry. Because Vatican II has to an extent acknowledged the apostolic and ecclesial reality of the presently detached churches (LG 8, 15; UR 3, 19–23), the Catholic Church has also, to the same degree, implicitly accepted the validity of the ministerial office in those churches. Although this ministry is not derived from the historic episcopate, and is charismatic in origin, its validity can still be maintained.[19]

Schillebeeckx's position on validity was innovative, but not idiosyncratic, in the dialogue of 1969. He brought to bear on Lutheran–Catholic relations a thesis that was developing then from a variety of viewpoints—historical, sacramental, and canonical.[20] Within the Study Commission, the question was moved whether a recommendation could be made asking for official Roman Catholic recognition of ministry in the Lutheran churches. This brought with it, eventually but naturally, the issue of eucharistic hospitality between the Churches and the formal adoption of a policy permitting intercommunion.

The discussion of 1969 on Church structures continued through four papers on Church law and Christian freedom in the 1970 session, while the treatments of ministry by G. Lindbeck and E. Schillebeeckx led naturally to three 1971 papers on recognition of ministries and the advisability of a new discipline on intercommunion.

Under the broad rubric of "Gospel and Church Law," the 1970

session of the Study Commission led to clarifications of long-term significance for the Lutheran–Catholic dialogue. The Lutheran theologian W. Lohff argued that notwithstanding certain risks of misunderstanding, the theme of "Christian freedom" is the best comprehensive espression in our day for the saving gift conferred by Christ. Complementing Lohff's systematic exposition, the Catholic exegete H. Schürmann showed that St. Paul's teaching can well be seen as centered in the message of freedom: "For freedom Christ has set us free!" (Gal. 5:1).[21] Early in his paper, Lohff observed that in the light of recent Roman Catholic studies, the classic Roman Catholic–Lutheran controversy over justification seems to be essentially settled. There is now a central agreement on the fundamental points of justification doctrine, while ongoing differences continue regarding (1) the place or rank of this doctrine in the larger body of Christian truths, and (2) the consequences following from the gratuity of God's salvation and the certainty of faith for institutional structures in the Church.

The theme of institutionalization in Christianity was central in 1970, for which the Commission had a solid basis in H. Schürmann's exposition of the communitarian matrix of graced freedom in St. Paul. "The Jerusalem above is free and she is our mother" (Gal. 4:26). Thus, one receives eschatological freedom only along with other citizens of this city and other children of this mother. In such a social context, during our time of ongoing pilgrimage, there are ordinances that stand in the service of the exalted Christ.[22] The Commission agreed on the rightfulness of such structures of visible Church life, but two Lutheran concerns brought to expression aspects of ecclesiological dissensus.

W. Lohff again asserted the supremacy of the gospel of gratuitous salvation as a critical criterion against Church structures. Scripture provides a means of direct encounter with the truth of the apostolic message, and thus faith is not dependent on Church office for the guarantee of true preaching and right sacramental administration, as the Catholic tradition maintains. The grace and truth of the gospel are accessible and then can serve as the litmus in testing traditions and structures of ministry, hierarchical authority, and Church law.[23] Once again, the Commission faced a significant difference over the criterion of authentic Church life and over the manner in which the structures of ministry are legitimated as a genuine service of the Lord of the Church and of his Spirit.

A second type of Lutheran objection to Roman Catholic institutionalism arose in the discussion following S. Kuttner's exposition of the genesis, nature, and binding force of Catholic canon law.[24] The paper alerted the Commission members to the work then in progress on a new Code of Canon Law. Some Lutheran members questioned the propriety of a single codification of law for a major part of the Church, seeing here a centralizing threat to legitimate diversity in the local churches. The Catholic participants in the discussion pointed out how a single codification of law for the universal Church was coherent with an ecclesiology in which Church order is anchored in a single worldwide college of bishops unified around the Pope. Thus, the Lutheran rejections and reservations about the papacy ultimately constitute the root of differences between the two traditions on a range of issues concerning Church order and its regulation.[25]

Although it was conscious of these differences, the bilateral Study Commission was by 1970 convinced that its working sessions had uncovered significant areas of agreement on salvation and justification, word and sacraments, and Church and ministry. The question therefore gained momentum whether partial visible fellowship could not be established between the Catholic and Lutheran Churches. The initial steps would be (1) mutual recognition by each Church that the other Church has a valid Christian ministry, and (2) the sanctioning of limited intercommunion. Thereby the awareness of important matters of consensus would not remain with a select band of theologians but would find articulation all through the Churches. Even more importantly, it would be expressed and sealed on occasion by sacramental sharing in the body and blood of Christ. The session of 1971 was given over to direct treatment of these two critical and delicate issues.

Walter Kasper unrolled the problem of a Catholic recognition of Lutheran ministerial office.[26] Can those who are not *rite ordinati* (DS 1777) possibly be acknowledged as exercising true Christian ministry? Kasper argued first on historical and strictly dogmatic grounds that the issue should be considered an open question. First, cases of priests ordaining other priests are found in history and the practice received some theological backing (Huguccio, G. Vasquez). Second, the Lutheran churches have maintained from the beginning a "presbyterial succession," by the ordination of new pastors by already ordained ministers.

Third, the widely held view that Lutherans lack valid Orders, expressed in *UR* 22, is not a conclusion following necessarily from the relevant canon of the Council of Trent (DS 1777). An approach toward recognition of ministry among Lutherans has a good basis in the agreements on the nature of ministry and ordination already ascertained by the Study Commission. But the immediate approach to the question should be ecclesiological, according to Kasper, that is, it should be based on the recognition of apostolic faith and its fruits among Lutherans, and move to consider how these gifts are present precisely because of the service their ministers render with the means of Christ's grace and truth. Recognition of ministry would in the end be a matter of discernment of spirits, as those who know the now detached community ask whether the Spirit of God has not in fact broken in and is continuing to make itself felt through the structures of service by which these Christians are formed and live in the Lord.

The 1971 agenda also included the topic of eucharistic hospitality and intercommunion between Catholics and Lutherans. The two papers on the topic constituted a sharp divergence over the existing prohibitions, especially on the Catholic side, of eucharistic sharing by and with other Christians.[27] In addition to the debate set up by the papers' central theses, there was long-term significance in the notably diverse approaches by which the papers on intercommunion attacked this particular issue. An important Catholic–Lutheran difference became clear that would need more extensive clarification if the reconciliation of the Churches was to be placed on a solid foundation.

The Lutheran theologian Vilmos Vajta intervened as a forceful advocate of change in the existing discipline by which one Church excluded members of other churches from participation in its eucharistic communion. The earthly Jesus set a contrary example by feeding the multitudes, by generously granting table fellowship to sinners, and by his parables stressing God's all-inclusive invitation to the eschatological banquet. The Churches' Eucharist, consequently, must be an unconditional offer of grace that is generous and nondiscriminatory, under pain of being untrue to the very meaning of Jesus' original institution.[28] The Lord's Supper in the Churches must express the gospel of unconditioned grace and not impede the work of salvation by juridical obstacles. Traditional norms of institutional membership should not block access to Christ's own means of grace, in this case, to the meal in which he brings men and women into saving communion with himself. Vajta insisted that the official discipline of exclusion by the Catholic Church was tantamount to laying the severe penalty of excommunication upon members of other Christian bodies. It must give way to a practice more in accord with the known Christian character of others and with the nature of the eucharist itself.

Whereas Vajta argued directly from Christ's institution of his chosen means of grace, Jan Witte sketched a carefully crafted Catholic ecclesiology. In the end, Witte was quite reserved toward wide eucharistic hospitality. The Lutheran paper had focused sharply on Christ's gift to the sinner for his salvation, while the Catholic presentation looked first to the nature of the community that engages in the eucharistic celebration.

For Witte, one must indeed define the church as the *communio* of believers united in Christ through the Holy Spirit. But sound ecclesiology requires more. One must go on to specify the eschatological orientation of this community, which now looks ahead in hope toward a definitive unity freed of all divisions. Also, the *communio* is sacramental in character, and thus even now an effective sign, especially in the Eucharist, of the peace and unity of the New Age. One must further take account of the historical nature of the community of God's people, in which members must repeatedly respond in freedom to God's word and call. The *communio* of Christ's Church is, therefore, beset by defects, imperfections, and threats as the community moves through history. Especially scandalous at present is the side-by-side existence of ecclesial bodies detached from one another.

Witte underscored that a Protestant church is not just a congeries of "elements of sanctification and of truth" (*LG* 8), but instead a meaningful configuration of an ecclesial nature in which the one *communio* in Christ realizes itself. Among the churches, the special Roman Catholic vocation is to manifest amid flaws the fullness of ecclesiality, that is, of revealed truth, of sacramental life, and a unified structure of pastoral ministry culminating in the papacy. Other churches realize visible ecclesiality in analogous manners, but the degree of this realization has not yet been ascertained in particular cases. Ecumenical ecclesiology has not yet worked out the analogy of ecclesial reality as this comes to expression in Catholic, Orthodox, and Protestant Churches. One may not simply assume the three essential elements of professed faith, sacraments, and ministry. To be sure, mutual eucharistic hospitality can only be practiced after mutual recognition of ministry, but even more than this is needed. So it would be precipitous at present to move to the supreme expression of ecclesial community, that is, our oneness with each other in the eucharist of the glorified Lord as he makes present his saving death and resurrection.

The clash between the positions of Vajta and Witte made it evident that the Study Commission harbored within itself widely differing approaches to the mystery of eucharistic sharing in the Church.

The Lutheran–Catholic Dialogue in America, 1965–1970

The international Study Commission's 1969–1971 discussions of recognition of ministry and intercommunion were being influenced by the results of the Lutheran–Catholic bilateral dialogue in America, which had begun in 1965. With members named by the United States Bishops' Committee for Ecumenical and Interreligious Affairs and by the USA National Committee of the Lutheran World Federation, the American dialogue had published the outcome of its discussions of the following topics by 1971:

1. The Nicene Creed as Dogma of the Church (1965).
2. One Baptism for the Remission of Sins (1966).
3. The Eucharist as Sacrifice (1967).
4. Eucharist and Ministry (1970).[29]

The first two American discussions yielded a clear sense of Catholic–Lutheran communality in basic beliefs about God, Christ, and baptismal initiation into the Church. Differences surfaced over the role of the Church's magisterium in relation to Scripture and over the irreformable character of dogma. The third topic showed a significant consensus on the eucharistic Real Presence of the Body and Blood of Christ precisely as the once-for-all saving sacrifice to the Father. Agreement was ascertained concerning the worshiping community's consent to Christ's offering in its own grateful oblation of praise to God. However, discussion of the Eucharist also identified a series of unresolved differences, for example, the propitiatory offering of

Christ in the Mass, private masses and stipends, devotion to the reserved sacrament, and transsubstantiation as an explanation of the Real Presence.[30]

After a March 1968 session on eucharistic hospitality and intercommunion, the American dialogue gave sustained attention to the doctrine of the ministry in the two Churches. Policies on admission to Holy Communion, it became clear, could not be determined solely on the grounds of belief in Christ's presence and sacrifice. The doctrine of ministry and ordination is also essential, since agreement to practice eucharistic hospitality by its nature entails mutual acknowledgment of the validity of the ministry of those presiding at the eucharistic liturgies of the Churches.

The work of the world-level Study Commission was most directly affected by the "Statement" on eucharist and ministry issued in 1970 as the fruit of the fourth American dialogue.[31] Detailed historical investigations had clarified the origins of the different emphases of the two traditions, namely, Catholic succession in ministerial office by the continuity of the episcopate, and Lutheran succession in apostolic faith and doctrine (15). There was substantial agreement on ordination as the sacramental act that sets a person apart once and for all for ministry in the Church (16–18). The Lutheran participants acknowledged that Roman Catholic priests celebrate a valid Eucharist, but they cautioned that other issues had to be clarified and resolved before the two Churches could establish pulpit and altar fellowship (30–32).

The American Catholic participants in the dialogue gave a carefully ordered account of the reasons that called for a Catholic reappraisal of the eucharistic ministry of Lutheran pastors (38–53). Early data shows variation in the types and structure of Christian ministry. The reservation of priestly ordination to bishops may not derive from the divine institution of the sacrament of Orders. Priests have ordained other priests, and the Lutheran churches have a "presbyterial succession." Lutherans have a recognizable ecclesiality and stand in continuity with the apostolic faith enshrined in the Nicene Creed. The tridentine declaration against the legitimacy of Protestant ministers is open to various interpretations, including that of being only a declaration of canonical illegitimacy. Consequently, the Catholic members of the dialogue formulated this request:

We see no persuasive reason to deny the possibility of the Roman Catholic Church recognizing the validity of this Ministry [in Lutheran churches]. Accordingly, we ask the authorities of the Roman Catholic Church whether the ecumenical urgency flowing from Christ's will for unity may not dictate that the Roman Catholic Church recognize the validity of the Lutheran Ministry and, correspondingly, the presence of the body and blood of Christ in the eucharistic celebrations of the Lutheran churches (54).

The Malta Report, 1972

At the time the American request was published, the international Study Commission was working to formulate the results of its five-year dialogue. The concluding meeting was held at San Anton, Malta, in 1971, and so the document, released officially in 1972, is known as the "Malta Report."[32]

The report was submitted both to the Catholic and Lutheran Churches for wide discussion (12) and to "appropriate Church authorities" for the clarification and improvement of official relations between Lutheran churches and the Roman Catholic Church (13). Improvement can build on the "noteworthy and far-reaching consensus" reached by the Commission members on the meaning and transmission of the gospel in the world (8, 47–50).

The Malta Report gathers into one text the agreements, convergences, and unresolved issues that surfaced in the Study Commission meetings of 1967–1971. Its starting point is the early and ever-timely Christian kerygma:

> There was consensus that the Gospel rests fundamentally on the witness to the Easter event. What God has done for the salvation of the world in Jesus Christ is transmitted in the Gospel and made present in the Holy Spirit. The Gospel as proclamation of God's saving action is therefore itself a salvation event (16).

The foundation and center of the gospel "is constituted by the eschatological saving act of God in Jesus' cross and resurrection" (24).

The Commission does not hesitate to affirm the development

in our day of "a far-reaching consensus . . . in the interpretation of justification" (26), but it also notes that differences arise when Lutherans and Catholics assess the place of justification in the hierarchy of truths (28) and when Lutherans subject all ecclesial traditions and institutional forms to the evaluation criterion of the unconditioned grace of the gospel (29).

The contemporary world provides the living and changing matrix in which institutionalized Church orders are actualized in law (33) and in which the gospel itself is articulated.

> The Gospel . . . becomes the *viva vox evangelii* only when it is formulated and expressed through the power of the Holy Spirit in reference to the ever new questions raised by men of to-day. . . . It is this very world which to a certain extent en-riches us with a deeper understanding of the fullness of the Gospel (43).

An ecclesiology of notable adaptability seems imperative.

As the Malta document begins its report on ministry in the Church, a footnote calls attention to the more extensive treat-ment of ministerial office in the papers and statement of the American dialogue, *Eucharist and Ministry*. A special accent, however, is perceptible in the Malta Report's movement from the gospel and justification to the position and correct under-standing of ministerial office:

> It is here that the question of the gospel in and over the church becomes concrete. What, in other words, are the con-sequences of the doctrine of justification for the understanding of ministerial office (47)?

It is agreed that ministry is not an arbitrary enactment posited beside Christ's saving work: ". . . the ministry of reconciliation belongs to the work of reconciliation" (48). From early on, this ministry was both apostolic and charismatic, with a variety of congregational orders of ministry being reflected in the New Testament. Because the Church lives in a changing world, its structuring of ministerial office rightly undergoes change and development, and the churches of our own time to an extent manifest particular developments of different New Testament congregational and ministerial patterns (55–56).

The report gives a concise review of historical and theolgical data on apostolic succession, ordination, and legitimacy of ministry (57–62), and this leads to a twofold request for action by the respective Churches. The Catholic members of the Study Commission ask that Vatican II's recognition of the ecclesial character of the detached communities (UR 3–4, 19) be now complemented by an official consideration of Lutheran ordinations and ministry. This should weigh what is known about charismatic gifts, the emergency situation of the first Lutheran ordinations, presbyterial succession, and the present succession of Lutherans in apostolic teaching. Thus, the Catholic Church should "examine seriously the question of recognition of the Lutheran ministerial office" (63).[33] Conversely, the Lutheran members say that their churches should also examine making explicit the recognition of Roman Catholic office that is implied by Lutheran doctrine and by present Lutheran perceptions of Catholicism (64).

A final section of the Malta Report addresses two specific aspects of Church unity. First, papal primacy is clearly a subject of continuing interconfessional controversy. But the Lutheran members of the Commission admit the importance of a ministry specifically devoted to the unity of all local churches. Still, though, they cannot affirm that such an office is constitutive, and thus necessary, for the Church of Jesus Christ. Historical studies and development of Catholic doctrine, for example, on episcopal collegiality, set the papacy in a new light, but a serious unresolved issue remains between Luterans and Roman Catholics (66–67).

A final topic was intercommunion. Was it possible that the bond of a common baptism—and the extent of agreement already ascertained—could lead to eucharistic hospitality? Catholics admit that the one Church of Christ is actualized in an analogous manner also in the presently detached churches, and so that the baptized members of these churches are invited in principle to the Eucharist of Our Lord (71). The Lutheran emphasis falls on Christ's gift of saving communion with himself in the Lord's Supper, and so they sense an inner contradiction when some baptized believers are excluded from participation in Communion (72).

And so the Commission concluded its report with a call for a specific, although quite limited, change in the current official discipline of the two Churches:

A process of gradual rapprochement is necessary in which various stages are possible. At present it should already be recommended that the Church authorities, on the basis of what is already shared in faith and sacrament, and as sign and anticipation of the promised and hoped-for unity, make possible occasional acts of intercommunion as, for example, during ecumenical events or in the pastoral care of those involved in mixed marriages. Unclarity concerning a common doctrine of the ministerial office still makes for difficulties in reciprocal intercommunion agreements. However, the realization of eucharistic fellowship should not depend exclusively on full recognition of the offices of the ministry (73).

Events showed, however, that four of the seven Catholic members of the Study Commission were not satisfied with this recommendation of a change on intercommunion. The Malta Report thus bears the shadowy distinction among ecumenical consensus texts of being accompanied by "special statements," in which members express their reservations about selected points of the document. The four Catholic members found it wrong to bypass mutual recognition of each Church's ministerial office before opening the way to mutual eucharistic hospitality. However, two of these four members still felt that more "limited" and "occasional" admission to eucharistic sharing could nonetheless be recommended to Church authorities.[34] But two other Catholic members were strongly opposed to any permission for Catholics to share Holy Communion where the ministry of the eucharistic celebrant had not been officially recognized.[35]

Reflections on the First Phase of Dialogue, 1965–1972

From our later perspective, the first phase of Catholic–Lutheran dialogue after Vatican II has the character of pioneering theological service of the Churches by gifted and conscientious thinkers. The papers submitted in the course of both the world-level dialogue from 1967 through 1971 and the regional dialogue in America from 1965 through 1970 were insightful and still prove rewarding upon rereading. Our report has shown their richness as we narrated the work of the Study Commission.

Critical attention, however, is inevitably drawn to the Malta

Report. Its programmatic character has been underscored by the steps taken in the further course of the dialogue. The very limitations evident in the report gave a special urgency to certain items on the Lutheran–Catholic ecumenical agenda. Four of these limitations can be mentioned.[36]

First, we already pointed out the deep cleft between V. Vajta and J. Witte on the Eucharist. Plausibly, the Lutheran intensity of focus on Christ's present gift and grace could be comprehended within a Catholic eucharistic vision of ecclesial worship. But the two approaches would first have to come together in serene and sustained dialogue.

Second, from a Catholic perspective, the transition in the Malta Report, No. 47, from justification to ministry is not satisfying.[37] Such a transition reflects the movement of the Augsburg Confession from the gratuity of justification, in Article 4, to the office of the ministry, as God's chosen means for eliciting justifying faith (Art. 5). But the report does not do justice to the ecclesiological considerations that for Catholics have an identity of their own alongside of justification doctrine and that profoundly influence a correct understanding of ministry.

Third, the case made in the American fourth dialogue and in Malta Report Nos. 57–63 for valid ministry outside episcopal succession had in 1971 not yet stood the test of scrutiny by the broader Catholic theological community. The themes and arguments recommended for consideration were not without persuasive force, but on such a critical issue, a lengthy sounding would have to be taken. The proposal was also weakened by the absence at the time of a fully satisfying demonstration of the precise ecclesiological character to be ascribed on Catholic principles to the detached Lutheran churches of the world.[38]

Finally, in terms of the broad thematic set before the Study Commission, "The Gospel and the Church," the report of 1972 is in the end far more informative on the Christian gospel than on the Church of believers in Christ. A whole series of themes freshly articulated in *Lumen gentium* offer themselves for discussion and ecumenical clarification. How much Lutheran agreement would be forthcoming on the Church as a living corporate object of the Holy Spirit's teaching and sanctifying work (*LG* 3, 12, 39–42)? How do Lutherans see the ongoing union of Christ the head and his ecclesial body (*LG* 7), the composite unity of invisible and visible ecclesial realities (*LG* 8), the interaction of community and individual in salvation (*LG* 9), and the relation between particular churches and the one Church of Christ (*LG* 26)? Does the Church have a corporate identity, a communal faith, and an intrinsic role in God's revelation of himself?[39] All of these topics, formed here as ecclesiological questions, impinge upon a person's thinking both about the goal of dialogue and about ministry, mutual recognition, and intercommunion.

A Decade of Progress, 1973–1983

In swift review, we will indicate how the Catholic–Lutheran dialogue advanced in substantial ways in the decade following the Malta Report. Important lacunae were filled through four major study documents.

In 1973, the American dialogue was already moving toward placing the discussion of the papacy on a better basis than given in Malta Report Nos. 66–67. In 1970, an American biblical task force was commissioned to clarify the images and roles of the Apostle Peter in all relevant documents of the New Testament.[40] Thus, the subsequent development of the papal office could be studied by the dialogue commission in terms of its consistency with the "Petrine function" sketched by the Apostolic Church. A convergence text of 1974 explained where the American Catholic–Lutheran dialogue stood regarding "Different Attitudes Toward Papal Primacy," in a common statement that was then followed in the text by different reflections of the Lutheran and Catholic participants.[41] A notable result at this stage was the discovery of common ground in the awareness that the Church needs a specific ministry that serves and promotes its worldwide unity and universal mission.

Undaunted by the hazards of raking up old and bitter controversy, the American dialogue went on in 1974 to 1978 to treat "Teaching Authority and Infallibility in the Church."[42] Lutherans also, it was discovered, believe that God protects the Church from definitive error on issues of vital importance in his revelation of himself. The Catholic starting point, however, is in Trent's subtle and Vatican II's more articulated statement of the primacy of the gospel over its means of transmission, Scripture, Tradition, and Church teaching (DS 1501, 1506; *DV* 7–10). Today, an accentuated awareness of the diversity of cultures

makes it imperative that the Church can officially reformulate its
message in new situations—a task for which a charismatically
graced office can be an acceptable part of the Church's structure.

While the American dialogue was attending to ecclesial structures of unity, universal mission, and the mediation of doctrine,
a new phase of the world-level dialogue took up issues of the
Church's sacramental life. A reconstituted Lutheran–Catholic
"Joint Commission" concentrated on two subjects whose urgency
was sufficiently evident: the Eucharist and ministerial office in
the Church.

First came the widely discussed convergence text of 1978 on
eucharistic doctrine and worship. [43] Here the Joint Commission
appropriated key insights of other ecumenical treatments of the
Lord's Supper, such as those produced by the Group of les
Dombes, the Faith and Order Commission, and the Anglican–
Roman Catholic International Commission. But the Joint Commission put its own stamp on the topic by organizing a common
witness around liturgical expressions: "mystery of faith"; "through,
with, and in Christ"; "in the unity of the Holy Spirit"; "glorification of the Father"; "for the life of the world"; and "with a view to
future glory." Only then were traditionally controverted issues
faced and present Catholic–Lutheran proximity measured: the
Real Presence (common confession, with differences in theology
of varying seriousness, 48–55), sacrifice ("growing convergence,"
61), the eucharistic ministry ("significant convergences," 68),
and the liturgical form of the Church's celebration. The last-
named topic occasioned a respectful exchange of requests between
the two sides, for example, that Catholics avoid private celebration of the Mass, and that Lutherans forge a closer link between
word and sacrament (76). Just seven years after the clash of different approaches in Malta, a liturgical framework had become a
fruitful context of Catholic–Lutheran agreement and convergence on the Eucharist. [44]

A second major advance recorded by the international Joint
Commission came in its 1981 document on ministry. [45] The previous statement on the Eucharist noted important unresolved questions concerning the minister of the Eucharist. [46] But the 1981
declaration was not narrowly focused on problem-solving, even
though it did speak a quite technical language for a work of its
genre. It gave a brief account of God's saving action and its
communication in history. "The Church is the recipient of salva-

tion in Christ, and is at the same time sent with the authority of Christ to pass on the received salvation to the world" (12). Jesus Christ acts in the ministries instituted among the people of the new covenant (21). Historical issues are clarified regarding the occasion and precise content of Reformation polemics and Lutheran constructive positions on priesthood, the proclamation of the gospel, and episcopal ministry (13, 26–29, 42–43).

In one respect, *The Ministry in the Church* marks a noteworthy shift in the self-understanding of the goal of a dialogue on doctrine. After showing how Lutherans restructured the episcopal function in the Church and then how Catholic doctrine distinguishes between bishop and presbyter, the statement continues with a conditional sentence:

If both churches acknowledge that for faith this historical development of the one apostolic ministry into a more local and more regional ministry has taken place with the help of the Holy Spirit and to this degree constitutes something essential for the Church, then a *high degree of agreement* has been reached (49).

Thus, the Joint Commission raises the question of subsequent reception and approval of their work by the respective Churches. The Commission does not assert its findings definitively, but after scouting the terrain draws back to wait for their Churches to occupy the common ground surveyed by the Commission's theological historians and scholars.

The Ministry in the Church holds that eucharistic fellowship between Catholic and Lutheran Churches depends essentially upon mutual recognition of ministries (74). Ecumenical theology has raised the question whether the *defectus* Catholics see in Protestant orders (*UR* 22) is a partial defect or a complete absence. On Catholic principles, it could be just the fact of being outside historic succession, while not precluding the exercise of essential ministerial and ecclesial functions (77).

What, though, is to be done? *The Ministry in the Church* does not call for a single declaration or a series of remedial actions focused narrowly on ministry itself. The resolution should instead be part of a broader ecclesial development, which the Commission then sketches concisely.

The only theologically meaningful way of solving this question is through a process in which the Churches reciprocally accept each other. From this standpoint, the acceptance of full Church communion would signify also the mutual recognition of ministries. The precondition for such acceptance of full Church communion is agreement in the confession of faith— which must also include a common understanding of the Church's ministry—, a common understanding of the sacraments, and fraternal fellowship in Christian and Church life.

Such a recognition can only come about gradually. The various stages lead from a mutual respect of ministries through practical cooperation to full recognition of the ministry of the other Church which is identical to the acceptance of Eucharist fellowship (82–83).[47]

Thus, dialogue on ministry led to the specification of three elements of visible community and pointed to the needed stages of a lived process of ecclesial growth into unity. *The Ministry in the Church* is, therefore, a major contribution to the discussion of viable models for the ecclesial "reintegration of unity."

Further Advances, 1983–1985

In an uncommonly short span of time, the Catholic–Lutheran ecumenical dialogue has recently made strides toward full clarity over doctrinal differences and to a new and helpful way of thinking concretely about future unity. We will note three major works recently published in different sectors of the dialogue.

In 1983, the American Lutheran–Catholic dialogue completed its seventh round and published a lengthy consensus-and-convergence statement, resulting from five years of work, on justification.[48] At long last, the dialogue has tested and verified the assertion of the Malta Report of a developing consensus on the doctrine of justification. Finally, a set of Martin Luther's deepest and dearest convictions have been laid on the table for ecumenical reassessment: faith alone, the rejection of all works-righteousness, the bondage of the will, forgiveness and righteousness *propter Christum,* and consolation for anxious consciences. On this critical point of Lutheran self-understanding, dialogue has sought to advance to a common confession of faith that would then for Lutherans lead practically of itself to basic agreement on sacraments and ministry.

The American statement of 1983 is built around a fundamental affirmation about God's salvation and faith in Christ. It expresses a conviction claimed to be shared by both Lutherans and Roman Catholics:

> Our entire hope of justification and salvation rests on Christ Jesus and on the gospel whereby the good news of God's merciful action in Christ is made known; we do not place our ultimate trust in anything other than God's promise and saving work in Christ (4, 157).

Such a common fundamental conviction is not identical with full agreement on human freedom, grace, justification, faith, and the role of the Church in salvation. But it serves well as a common basis on which to stand while reconsidering the old controversies. The shared affirmative gives motivation for seeking to understand the concerns leading others to draw conclusions different from one's own. Their thinking too stands in relation to a valued part of one's own faith in God.

Part I of the text gives an informative review of Augustinian, medieval, Reformation, and tridentine teaching on justification (5–63). A survey of recent developments among Catholics and Lutherans (73–93) concludes with a new Lutheran approach, a "hermeneutical perspective" on the proclaimed word and its effect in the self-understanding of a person gifted with faith (88–93).[49]

In Part II, six topical sections examine the clash of the two traditions, noting some common ground, but stressing more the contrasts arising from the diversity of Lutheran and Catholic concerns and thought patterns (94–121). Lutherans see doctrine and theology taken into the service of a spiritual project: the uncompromising exclusion of reliance on self for salvation. So they emphasize God's forensic act, something wholly his own, by which he declares sinners righteous because of Christ. But Catholic thought wants to secure the effectiveness of God's saving work, and so it insists on themes such as healing, renewal, and sanctification. Lutherans see the ascription of "merit" to the deeds of the righteous as derogating from the unconditionally salvific character of God's word and deed, whereas Catholics are concerned to maintain the real presence of the Holy Spirit who initiates and fosters growth unto eternal life through the good works of those now "in Christ."[50]

A telling observation near the end of Part II gives voice to Lutheran discomfort with the role Catholics usually attribute to the Church in justification, sanctification, and salvation (119). To be sure, Lutherans want to stress the sacramental means of grace and want to avoid religious individualism. But does not Catholicism derogate from God's gratuitous and unconditioned gift when it makes ecclesial realities, "rites and orders," necessary conditions in the mediation and reception of God's salvation? This probing question, echoing the Malta Report, No. 29, is left suspended in the midst of the American statement—ominously, it would seem. Ecclesiology intrudes once again to upset the calm equilibrium of dialogue.

Part III first gives a reading of the biblical data as the Catholic and Lutheran partners in dialogue make a first move toward "reconstruction."[51] The dialogue was refreshed by its biblical study and states with becoming modesty, "The biblical witness to the gospel of God's saving work in Christ is richer and more varied than has been encompassed in either traditional Catholic or Lutheran approaches to justification" (149).

In its final summation, the statement first registers an incomplete convergence on a theme recurrently present in the post-Vatican II Lutheran–Catholic dialogue: the application of truths about justification as criteria of authenticity of the Church's proclamation and practice.[52] Two labored paragraphs (153–154) try to render an account of this thorny issue, but in reality they only point to other issues that remain unresolved, such as (1) the doctrines of purgatory, veneration of saints, and the papacy; (2) the widely misunderstood but still cited "hermeneutical perspective" on justification; and (3) the influence of "differences in thought structures" in formulating doctrines.[53]

But in contrast with these outlying problems, a final consideration of justification in itself yields a list of important convergences. There follows a listing of twelve points that constitute "a very significant agreement" (155) on justification itself: its source in Christ, its dire necessity in our fallen humanity, its effectiveness, its mediation by word and sacrament, its dynamism toward good works, its precariousness in this life, and its culmination in God's final reward and gift (156).

A second recent dialogue document, treating Catholic–Lutheran church fellowship in word and sacrament, was issued in 1984 by an official bilaterial working group in the German Federal Republic.[54] Seven Catholic and seven Lutheran representatives worked nearly eight years, ranging widely in their discussions. They have produced what ranks today as the best panoramic view of Lutheran–Catholic doctrinal and ecclesial differences. Study of *Kirchengemeinschaft in Wort und Sakrament* will be bracing for anyone given to ecumenical euphoria, because the document takes stock forthrightly of the remaining and outstanding points of divergence between the two doctrinal traditions. In fact, the final point made is a warning against unrealistic hopes of an early establishment of full Church fellowship between the now divided Churches (88).

Structurally, this new treatment of Catholic–Lutheran Church relations moves through the classic three areas in which mutual recognition must occur: confession of faith (10–19), sacramental and liturgical celebration (20–55), and the office of ministry (56–76). A report on its ample inventory of settled agreements and still controverted issues would burst the limits of the present report. But three aspects are particularly relevant.

First, when the German dialogue document does ascertain an enduring difference between Catholic and Lutheran doctrine, on occasion it also ventures an explicit assessment that the difference is not so serious as to be "Church divisive." For example, both traditions insist on the body and blood of Christ being really present as the gift of Holy Communion. But the dogmatic accounts of this presence differ, with Catholics teaching a change of substance and Lutherans the co-presence of Christ and the elements. But the 1984 statement judges that such a difference is not in itself an obstacle to Church unity (34). Also, the Catholic application of sacramental categories and principles to ordination, which Lutherans do not do, may well not be of itself divisive (66). Further, the differences over confirmation, penance and absolution, marriage, and anointing of the sick are of very different doctrinal weight in relation to Church fellowship (50).

This aspect of ecumenism needs further concentrated study. Our goal is no doubt a particular form of "reconciled diversity" between Church bodies that will not simply dissolve as they enter into communion with each other. The reconciliation will entail mutual acts of recognition of the Christian and apostolic character of each other's confession of faith, sacramental life, and pastoral ministry. But what forms of diversity can then coexist with such recognition and consequent fellowship? How much diversity can really be reconciled?[55] Increasingly, ecumenical exchanges will have to think more concretely about what would impede a living bond of communion between the now separated bodies. At some point in time, Church leadership on both sides will have to take a magisterial stand on this issue of pluriformity in unity.

Second, *Kirchengemeinschaft in Wort und Sakrament* reaffirms the role of theology in ecumenical work (77–81). Church fellowship is not simply doctrinal rapprochement, but such a basis is essential. Theology, thus, has a key role in ascertaining the agreements that make Church fellowship possible and in reexamining traditional differences in the light of today's biblical and historical knowledge. *Kirchengemeinschaft in Wort und Sakrament* deems desirable a more robust attitude to questions of truth and falsity in ecumenical dialogue. Its authors voice their dissatisfaction with dialogues that only ascertain communality and proximity instead of reaching agreement in binding doctrine. "Convergences" may be registered, but they do not suffice for ecumenical understanding between the Churches (80).

But what more has theological dialogue between Lutherans and Catholics still to do? This is the third area of special pertinence of *Kirchengemeinschaft in Wort und Sakrament*. For it points to areas of ecclesiology now in need of collaborative treatment:

> We agree that important themes of our respective understandings of the Church, which we have not explicitated here, need further clarification. We think especially of the relationship between the hiddenness of the true Church in history, as maintained by the Reformers, and the Church's visibility in history, which both Catholic and Lutheran theologies teach (80).

This area, however, is not just pointed out in the 1984 German statement for a dense opening section sketches key themes of ecclesiological agreement. Jesus Christ is the one foundation (1), and the Church has firm roots in the Christ event as a whole (2). Life in the Church is a way of conformity to Jesus' living, walking, suffering, and passing to glory (3). It is fellowship in the

Holy Spirit by whom the Church becomes an ever-new event (5–6).

Tensions, however, arise as Catholic and Lutheran ecclesiologies render their respective accounts of the relationship holding between the visible, institutional form of the Church and the hidden, spiritual reality of the Church that we grasp and confess in faith (9). Does the organization of the pastoral ministry have a single and presently definitive form? What importance is to be ascribed to apostolic succession in the episcopate? Is "hierarchical communion" (*LG, Nota praevia; CD* 4; *PO* 7, 15) the anchor to which fellowship in faith and sacrament are inseparably linked?

With these questions, the introductory section of *Kirchengemeinschaft in Wort und Sakrament* has pointed in its way to the ecclesiological area as the next major *locus* on the Lutheran–Catholic ecumenical agenda. Other ways of formulating the issue are surely possible, for example, by focusing on Scripture in the Church and asking what role the Church as such has in mediating God's revelation today. Or one could take an anthropological starting point, probing then into the place of community and into communal influences on the existence of the Christian. Whatever the line of approach, however, ecclesiology is undoubtedly of the order of the day in Catholic–Lutheran ecumenism.

Consonant with the ecclesiological turn indicated for the immediate future in Catholic–Lutheran dialogue, a document of the world-level Joint Commission was issued in 1985, which focuses sharply and intently on how Church fellowship might in fact be realized between Lutherans and Catholics.[56] The Commission has broken through to a new kind of bilateral work by venturing to name a series of steps for approaching full visible communion between the Catholic Church and the Lutheran churches of the world.

Facing Unity names six essential elements in a future Lutheran–Catholic reconciliation (47–49): fundamental agreement in the apostolic faith will be ascertained and confessed; diversity in piety and theology will remain; mutual condemnations will cease; a common sacramental and liturgical life will grow; structures will be created for joint action of both local and worldwide scope; church leadership will be coordinated in a structure of joint exercise of ecclesial *episcopē*. The model guiding the

thinking of *Facing Unity* is that of "unity in reconciled diversity"
(31–34, 47, 61–66, 84). Reconciliation does not aim at eliminating the pluriformity of diverse spiritual and theological patrimo-
nies, which will mutually enrich member churches in a future,
more universal *communio*.

An important orientation point is Pope Paul II's assertion that
beyond the partial agreements on particular truths, there exists
even now between Catholics and Lutherans "agreement on the
fundamental and central truths" (51).[57] *Facing Unity* lists the
major areas of present consensus in faith (57–60), including "a
basic though not complete consensus in the understanding of the
Church (57). It is frankly admitted that for Lutherans, the recent
Catholic dogmas on Mary and the papacy go beyond what seems
justified by Scripture (66). But still a concrete step of rapprochement is possible now, and is urgently necessary. The past
doctrinal anathemata that still traumatize Catholic–Lutheran relations should be reviewed carefully, leading to a declaration,
where justified, that the condemnations are now meaningless in
view of the present doctrines of the Churches and our present
state of mutual understanding (67–69).[58]

Facing Unity then calls for the two Churches to commit themselves to realizing a structured form of unity and common ministry (86–93), even though this is beyond immediate realization.
Facing this difficulty, the document moves into hitherto unex-
plored ecumenical territory as it begins (117) to sketch the process by which presently detached church bodies could move toward realizing fellowship in the exercise of the pastoral ministry.
Church leadership would first be exercised in a formally coordinated manner (120–122), leading to an initial act of mutual
ecclesial recognition based on consensus in faith, sacramental
life, and understanding of ministry (123–126). This would be a
transitional act, which for Catholics would entail an affirmative
acknowledgment of the Church of Jesus Christ in Lutheranism
but not necessarily the fullness of ecclesiality (124). Upon recognition, a phase of common exercise of episcopal ministry would
begin, leading to collegiality (127–131).

The critical transition that would seal Lutheran–Catholic fellowship would be the concelebrated ordination of new pastoral
ministers by bishops already exercising a collegial *episcopē* in a
given region (132–141). Thus, a common ministry would result,
after the phases of joint exercise of leadership, mutual recogni-

tion, and episcopal collegiality. A liturgy of ordination, thus, by commissioning a body of pastors for a united Church, would enact a climactic sign of God's grace of unity. It would signal the presence in the Church of a body of ministers who would be most concerned with fostering the apostolic faith and sacramental life of the Church of Christ in its new configuration of reconciliation.

This review of some main proposals of *Facing Unity* indicates how the Joint Commission has moved dramatically beyond the earlier work devoted to ascertaining areas of agreement and convergence in doctrine, worship, and polity. The programmed steps are concerned with visible unity, thus counteracting tendencies to spiritualize the ecumenical goal, by a species of ecclesiological docetism, or to project it into an eschatological future wholly beyond our planning and effort. It is a great gain to have a coherent scenario of development toward ecclesial reintegration of unity between two detached traditions. *Facing Unity* has creatively thought out a plausible future, which will be of considerable help in the time of labor, earnest prayer, and struggle that surely lies ahead.

Conclusion

This dialogue has advanced in numerous and varied ways to new clarity and a new concretization of the Catholic–Lutheran unity we seek. Further progress should now be sought in the ecclesiological field; but for this, numerous themes, formulations of problems, and tentative solutions have already surfaced in two decades of dialogue.

The critical issues of the next stage would seem to cluster around two poles. First, the problem of pluriformity in unity. What kinds of diversity are acceptable between Churches linked by the bond of communion? How much disparity in doctrine, sacramental life, and ministerial structures can obtain between Christian bodies that acknowledge each other's authenticity within the network of visible unity. *Unitatis redintegratio* 11, on the "hierarchy of truths" is one possible starting point, but today the work especially of Yves Congar provides many valuable considerations that need to be taken up into a fuller biblical, historical, and systematic account of ecclesial pluriformity.[59]

Second, there is the recurrent problem of how the analogy of

ecclesiality is realized in the presently detached churches with
their own social cohesiveness.[60] Lutherans rightly expect that
account be taken of their unified configuration of the "elements
of sanctification and truth" (LG 8) by which they live as Christians. Preliminary to any recognition of ministries and sacraments, one must define the positive though limited role of the
formed and formative communities in which these ministers
preach and preside at sacramental celebrations.

Notes

1. A good brief account of the ecumenical movement, and of
official Catholic attitudes to it, is P. Neuner, *Kleines Handbuch der
Ökumene* (Düsseldorf, 1984), translated into Italian as *Breve manuale
dell'Ecumene*, Giornale di teologia 162 (Brescia, 1986). In the latter
edition, see esp. pp. 86–136.

2. A noteworthy product of this collaboration is the fifty-page
study document, *Common Witness* (Geneva, 1982), prepared for the
Joint Working Group to document the manifold ways in which Christians of different confessions are joining to give witness to Christ and
advocate protection of human values, as they confront oppression, plan
to educate youth, join in Bible study, and serve the sick and dying.

3. A brief but suggestive overview is given by J.M.R. Tillard,
"Oecuménisme et Eglise catholique. Les vingt ans du Décret sur
l'oecumenisme," *NRT*, 107 (1985), 43–67, under the subtitle, "Les
acquis definitifs: l'action en commun," pp. 44–49. Informative chroni-
cles of ecumenical activities, with documents, are given regularly in the
periodicals *Irénikon* (Chevtogne, Belgium), *One in Christ* (Turvey Ab-
bey, England), *Unitas* (Rome), and—since 1983—*Studi ecumenici* (Ve-
rona, Italy). The activities of the Vatican Secretariat for Promoting
Christian Unity are reported in the parallel English and French issues of
the Secretariat's *Information Service/Service d'information*.

4. *Information Service*, 55 (1984), 39. Especially noteworthy were
the Pope's meeting with German Protestant leaders in Mainz, 17 November 1980, and his participation in the ecumenical liturgy with
Anglican churchmen at Canterbury Cathedral, 29 May 1982.

5. *L'Osservatore romano* (10 December 1985); my translation from
the Documentary Supplement of this issue, p. IV.

6. The immense literature of news reports, documents, and analy-
ses generated by the dialogues is conveniently listed in J. F. Puglisi and
S.J. Voicu, A *Bibliography of Interchurch and Interconfessional Theological
Dialogues* (Rome, 1984), distributed by the Centro pro unione. Annual

supplements appear in the *Bulletin* of the Centro (via S. Maria dell'Anima, 30–00186 Rome).

7. "Facing Unity," *Information Service*, 59 (1985), 44–72; also published in English in booklet form by the Lutheran World Federation, Geneva, and in German as *Einheit vor uns* (Paderborn/Frankfurt, 1985).

8. "Le rapport du group mixte de travail, Église catholique et la Fedération luthérienne mondiale," *Documentation catholique*, 63 (1966), 1691–1698, giving the report of Bishop Johannes Willebrands, then Secretary of the Secretariat for Promoting Christian Unity, in columns 1691–1693.

9. *Ibid.*, 1696–1698.

10. *Ibid.*, 1695.

11. The papers have been published in H. Meyer (ed.), *Evangelium—Welt—Kirche* (Frankfurt, 1975). Among the contributors were Hans Conzelmann, Krister Stendahl, Joseph Fitzmyer, Walter Kasper, Johannes Baptist Metz, Heinz Schürmann, Stephan Kuttner, and Johannes Witte. A good retrospective view of this phase of the dialogue is H. Meyer, *Luthertum und Katholizismus im Gespräch*, Ökumenische Perspektiven 3 (Frankfurt, 1973).

12. One can follow the development of the discussion from 1967 through 1970 in H. Meyer and A. Hasler, "The Joint Lutheran/Rome Catholic Study Commission on 'The Gospel and the Church,' " *Lutheran World*, 16 (1969), 363–379, and 18 (1971), 161–187. Doctors Meyer and Hasler assisted the Commission from the staffs of the Lutheran World Federation and the Vatican Unity Secretariat, respectively.

13. J. Fitzmyer cited *DV* 10 in his paper, "The Kerygmatic and Normative Character of the Gospel," in H. Meyer (ed.), *Evangelium—Welt—Kirche*, 111–128, on p. 123. P.E. Persson noted explicitly the agreement ascertained on this point (*ibid.*, 149). At a later stage of the post-Vatican II dialogue, the Catholic–Lutheran dialogue in the USA gave a constructive and creative account of church doctrine and the ecclesial magisterium. P.C. Empire et al. (eds.), *Teaching Authority and Infallibility in the Church*, Lutherans and Catholics in Dialogue VI (Minneapolis, 1980). Even in the late 1960s, one could recall H. de Lubac's word to Protestants fearful that the Catholic magisterium places itself above Scripture and claims to judge the word of God. According to de Lubac, it is not Scripture that needs a rule or a higher light of interpretation, but our human glosses. Our Scripture interpretations—these need discerning evaluation by the church. *La Révélation divine* (Paris, 1983³), 182, reprinted from the Preface to R. Schutz and M. Thurian, *La Parole vivante au Concile* (Taizé, 1966).

14. W. Kasper, "Die Welt, der Ort des Evangeliums," in H. Meyer (ed.), *Evangelium—Welt—Kirche*, 131–145, esp. 135–138.

15. P.E. Persson, "Die Welt, das Ziel des Evangeliums," in *ibid.*,

157–158. Vatican II's formulation in *LG* 8 locates the point of comparison between the Church and the Incarnation in the instrumental service rendered by the visible Church to the Spirit of Christ. This is
analogous to a similar relationship of instrument to primary agent obtaining between the human nature of Christ and the divine word that
assumed this nature.

16. H. Conzelmann, "Die Vielfalt der neutestamentlichen Kirch-
enstrukturen und die Frage ihrer Einheit," in H. Meyer (ed.),
Evangelium—Welt—Kirche, 203–211, and W. Burghardt, "Church
Structures in Historic Development," in *ibid.*, 213–261.

17. This conviction, present in the Commission, is reported by H.
Meyer and A. Hasler, "The Joint Lutheran/Roman Catholic Study
Commission," *Lutheran World*, 18 (1971), 162–165.

18. G. Lindbeck, "Doctrinal Standards, Theological Theories, and
Practical Aspects of the Ministry in the Lutheran Confessions," in H.
Meyer (ed.), *Evangelium—Welt—Kirche*, 263–283. Also published,
with a new two-page introduction and added notes, as "The Lutheran
Doctrine of Ministry: Catholic and Reformed," *TS*, 30 (1969), 588–
612. To his report on Lutheran doctrine, the author added an informative reflection on the modern crisis of confidence among Lutherans
over being able to identify the living word of Christ by the norm of
Scripture as the latter is interpreted today. Regarding the Catholic
Church, however, he cautioned that the present rapprochement still
seems threatened by the Catholic commitment to seeing the authenticity of word and faith guaranteed by the legitimacy of Church teaching
office, instead of office being guaranteed by the word it teaches.

19. E. Schillebeeckx, "The Catholic Understanding of Office in
the Church," in H. Meyer (ed.), *Evangelium—Welt—Kirche*, 285–306.
The article also appeared in *TS*, 30 (1969), 567–587.

20. J.E. Burns, "The Unity of the Church and its Ministry," *The
Ecumenist*, 3 (1964–1965), 21–23. F.J. van Beeck, "Proeve van een
ecumenischen beschouwing over de sacramenten," *Bijdragen*, 26 (1965),
128–179 and "Towards an Ecumenical Understanding of the Sacraments," *JES*, 3 (1966), 57–112; W. Kasper, "Der ekklesiologischen
Charakter der Nicht-katholischen Kirchen," *TQ*, 145 (1965), 42–62;
G.H. Tavard, "The Function of the Minister in the Eucharistic Celebra-
tion: An Ecumenical Approach," *JES*, 4 (1967), 629–649; J.M.R.
Tillard, "Le *votum eucharistiae*: L'Eucharistie dans la rencontre des Chrétiens," in *Miscellanea Liturgica in onore di Sua Eminenza il Cardinale G.
Lercaro*, II (Rome, 1967), 143–194; M. Villain, "Can There Be Apos-
tolic Succession outside the Continuity of the Laying-on of Hands?"
Concilium, 4 (1968), No. 4, 45–53 (also published in the Dutch, French,
German, Italian, Portuguese, and Spanish editions of *Concilium*).

21. W. Lohff, "Die christliche Freiheit als Kontroverspunkt und gemeinsames Problem für Lutheraner und Katholiken heute," in H. Meyer (ed.), *Evangelium—Welt—Kirche*, 379–395, and H. Schürmann, "Freiheit und Ordnung. Die Freiheitsbotschaft des Paulus—Mitte des Evangeliums?" in *ibid.*, 309–351. A sizeable portion of Schürmann's paper (pp. 337–351) is an appendix giving six theses on the foundation in Paul for Church order and Church law.

22. Characteristically, Schürmann spoke of the Spirit taking hold of certain earthly realities, compenetrating them with his presence, and thus making some of them at least into constitutive instruments for the Lord's work in the community of the new covenant (*ibid.*, 341).

23. W. Lohff, "Die christliche Freiheit," 383–386. Pointedly formulated: "Die reformatorische Lehrverkündigung ist deshalb getragen von dem Vertrauen in die unmittelbare Wahrheitsmacht des apostolischen Evangeliums, das durch die kirchliche Verkündigung immer neu vernommen wird. Begründet wurde dieses Vertauen durch die Erforschung der Heiligen Schrift, in der man das Evangelium eindeutig zu vernehmen gewiss war. . . . Ist aber ein unmittelbarer Zugang zum Evangelium der Schrift eröffnet, dann sind kirchliche Traditionen und Institutionen an der Schrift darauf hin zu prüfen, inwiefern sie diesem Evangelium dienen. Alle kirchlichen Institutionen und Traditionen unterstehen deshalb dem Kriterium, ob durch sie rechte Verkündigung des Evangeliums möglich wird. Sie sind an diesem Kriterium immer wieder zu prüfen" (*ibid.*, 384).

24. S. Kuttner, "Gospel and Law in the Roman Catholic Church," in *ibid.*, 367–377.

25. This formulation of the controversy is reported in H. Meyer and A. Hasler, "The Joint Lutheran/Roman Catholic Study Commission," *Lutheran World*, 18 (1971), 182–184.

26. W. Kasper, "Zur Frage der Anerkennung der Ämter in der lutherischen Kirchen," in H. Meyer (ed.), *Evangelium—Welt—Kirche*, 399–414; also in *TQ*, 151 (1971), 97–109. There was no need for a lengthy justification of a Lutheran recognition of Roman Catholic ministry, because the fundamental agreement on the priority and content of the gospel was for Lutherans a certification that Catholic ministry stands in the service of Christ's truth and grace.

27. V. Vajta, "Die Annahme des Menschen im Abendmahl," in H. Meyer (ed.), *Evangelium—Welt—Kirche*, 415–436, and J. Witte, "Thesen über die Kirche im Zusammenhang mit dem Interkommunionsfrage," in *ibid.*, 437–455.

28. "Das Abendmahl ist von dem gekreuzigten und verherrlichten Herrn den Menschen geschenkt worden, damit sie in seine Gemeinschaft aufgenommen und darin errettet werden sollen. Eine Abendmahlsfeier, von der Menschen ferngehalten werden, erfüllt deshalb schon in ihrem Ansatz die ihr vom Herrn gestellte Ausgabe nicht.

Abendmahl ist Annahme," in Vajta, "Die Annahme des Menschen im Abendmahl," 418.

29. The papers presented at the semiannual meetings and the concluding statements were published by the two sponsoring bodies in a series of booklets, *Lutherans and Catholics in Dialogue*, I–IV. They have been reprinted, with volumes I–III joined in single volume, by the Augsburg Press of Minneapolis.

30. The third American dialogue, on eucharistic sacrifice, was studied at length in K.W. Irwin, *American Lutherans and Roman Catholics in Dialogue on the Eucharist: A Methodological Critique and Proposal*, Studia Anselmiana 76 (Rome, 1979). Irwin faults the dialogue principally for not developing the major significance of liturgy, liturgical practice, and piety for eucharistic doctrine. Such study, for instance, of recent liturgical developments yields a quite positive outcome: "Indeed the reform of the eucharistic liturgy in both the Roman Catholic Church and the Lutheran Churches in North America show a remarkable consensus on the eucharist" (*ibid.*, 120).

31. "Eucharist and Ministry: a Lutheran–Roman Catholic Statement," in *Eucharist and Ministry*, Lutherans and Catholics in Dialogue IV (Washington/New York, 1970), 7–33. The statement was also published in *TS*, 31 (1970), 712–734. In French, *Istina*, 18 (1973), 475–495. In German, *Um Amt und Herrenmahl: Dokumente zum evangelisch/römisch-katholischen Gespräch*, Ökumenische Dokumentation 1 (Frankfurt, 1974), 71–102. In Spanish, *Diálogo Ecuménico*, 9 (1974), 57–84. Subsequent references in my text are to the numbered paragraphs of the statement.

32. The English translation appeared in *Lutheran World*, 19 (1972), 259–273, and in H. Meyer and L. Vischer (eds.), *Growth in Agreement*, Ecumenical Documents 2 (New York/Geneva, 1984), 168–189. In French, H. Legrand and M. Meyer (eds.), *Face à l'unité* (Paris, 1986), 21–59. In Italian, S.J. Voicu and G. Cereti (eds.), *Enchiridion oecumenicum: documenti del dialogo teologico interconfessionale*. Vol. 1, *Dialoghi internazionali, 1931–1984* (Bologna, 1986), 554–588. The German original is in H. Meyer, H.J. Urban and L. Vischer (eds.), *Dokumente wachsender Übereinstimmung* (Paderborn/Frankfurt, 1983), 248–271. Subsequent references will be to the numbered paragraphs of the report.

33. Statements made later by two members of the Commission, H. Schürmann and H. Conzelmann, questioned the propriety of this recommendation in view of the inner-Lutheran differences over the doctrine of the ministry and ordination [*Lutheran World*, 19 (1972), 272–273]. When G. Lindbeck published his paper on ministry, he had added the caveat that, for many, Luther's own teachings were more influential than the Confessions from which he, Lindbeck, worked.

The variety of interpretations of Luther's idea of ministry could thus lead some to see Lindbeck's presentation "an incomplete account of the Lutheran position." Cf. "The Lutheran Doctrine of the Ministry," *TS*, 30 (1969), 589.

34. Statements of H. Schürmann and J. Witte, *Lutheran World*, 19 (1972), 272. Later, Schürmann called attention to the Malta Report's own list of fundamental points disputed between Catholic and Lutherans that the Commission had not treated: faith/sacrament, nature/grace and law/gospel, magisterium, and Marian doctrine (9). In this light, Schürmann was surprised that the Commission's majority felt justified moving on to recommend intercommunion ["Die Arbeit und der Bericht der evangelisch-katholischen Studienkommission 'Das Evangelium und die Kirche,' " *Theologisches Jahrbuch 1974* (Leipzig, 1974), 516–542, at 531].

35. Special statement of H. Martensen and A. Vögtle [*Lutheran World*, 19 (1972), 272].

36. The 1981 document on ministry issued by the Study Commission's successor, the Roman Catholic/Lutheran Joint Commission, opens with a reference to the problems the Malta Report could not deal with, or which it treated in insufficient detail, or which later evaluations by both Lutherans and Catholics have said need further work. *The Ministry in the Church* (Geneva, 1982), 3.

37. Earlier, the Malta Report itself had indicated that it was still questionable whether both sides would agree on the implications for the life of the church flowing from agreement on justification (No. 28). Such an unresolved question was a weak starting point for treating ministry.

38. Even in 1986, this does not seem to have been done satisfactorily. The International Theological Commission approached the subject in Chapter 9 of *Themata selecta de ecclesiologia*, CTI Documenta 13 (Vatican City, 1985), 50–53, but it did not advance the special issue of specifying the ecclesiality of the detached communities in their own social unity and particularity. More can surely be done than simply repeat that outside visible Catholic unity there exist "non solum plures veri christiani, sed plura principia vitae et fidei vere christiana" (52). The Congregation for the Doctrine of the Faith has further obscured the matter by its questionable interpretation of *LG* 8 to the effect "che esiste una sola 'sussistenza' della vera Chiesa, mentre fuori della sua compagine visibile esistono solo 'elementa Ecclesiae.' " *Notificazione sul volume "Chiesa: carisma e potere" del Padre L. Boff, O.F.M.* (Vatican City, 1985), 6. Cf. the contribution of Francis A. Sullivan to this volume.

39. Cf. the stimulating passage on the Church as historical subject in Chap. 3 of the International Theological Commission's *Themata selecta de ecclesiologia*, 18–23.

40. The results came out in R. E. Brown et al. (eds.), *Peter in the New Testament* (Minneapolis/New York, 1973). In French, *Saint Pierre dans le Nouveau Testament*, LD 79 (Paris, 1974). In German, *Der Petrus der Bibel* (Stuttgart, 1976). In Spanish, *Pedro en el Nuevo Testamento* (Santander, 1976).

41. P.C. Empie and T.A. Murphy (eds.), *Papal Primacy in the Universal Church*, Lutherans and Catholics in Dialogue V (Minneapolis, 1974), containing the text and the study papers discussed in the course of the dialogue. The convergence text itself appeared as well in *One in Christ*, 10 (1974), 276–316. In French, *Documentation catholique*, 71 (1974), 373–380. In Italian, *Il Regno*, 19 (1974), 567–572. In German in G. Gassmann and H. Meyer (eds.), *Das kirchenleitende Amt*, Ökumenische Dokumentation 5 (Frankfurt, 1980), 49–97. In Spanish, *Diálogo Ecuménico*, 11 (1976), 323–359.

42. P.C. Empie et al. (eds.), *Teaching Authority and Infallibility in the Church*, Lutherans and Catholics in Dialogue VI (Minneapolis, 1980), containing the text and study papers contributed to the dialogue. The convergence statement also came out in *TS*, 40 (1979), 116–166, and *One in Christ*, 15 (1979), 114–169. In German, G. Gassmann and H. Meyer (eds.), *Das kirchenleitende Amt*, 97–172.

43. *Das Herrnmahl* (Paderborn/Frankfurt, 1979). Just four years after it first appeared, this booklet was in its eleventh printing. In English, *The Eucharist* (Geneva, 1980). In Italian, *La cena del Signore* (Turin, 1983). These booklets add to the common statement a series of texts in use at Catholic and Lutheran eucharistic worship and six supplementary studies by V. Pfnür and H. Meyer. The convergence text also appeared in English in the Secretariat for Promoting Christian Unity's *Information Service*, 39 (1979), 22–35; in *Origins*, 8 (1979), 465–478; in *One in Christ*, 15 (1979), 249–273; and in H. Meyer and L. Vischer (eds.), *Growth in Agreement*, 190–214. In French, in the Unity Secretariat's *Service d'information*, 39 (1979), 23–36; and in H. Legrand and H. Meyer (eds.), *Face à l'unité*, 61–138. In German, H. Meyer et al. (eds.), *Dokumente wachsender Ubereinstimmung*, 271–295. In Italian, S.J. Voicu and G. Cereti (eds.), *Enchiridion oecumenicum*, vol. 1, 589–653. In Spanish, *Diálogo Ecuménico*, 14 (1979), 387–413. Further references in this paragraph will be to the numbered paragraphs of *The Eucharist*.

44. J.F. Puglisi and S.J. Voicu list thirty published reflections on and reactions to *Das Herrnmahl/The Eucharist. A Bibliography of Interchurch and Interconfessional Dialogues*, 160–161. Two recent works that advance the discussion are K. Lehmann and E. Schlink (eds.), *Das Opfer Jesu Christi und seine Gegenwart in der Kirche*, Dialog der Kirchen 3 (Freiburg/Göttingen, 1983); and J. Reumann, *The Supper of the Lord: The New Testament, Ecumenical Dialogues, and Faith and Order on Eucharist* (Philadelphia, 1985).

45. *Das geistliche Amt in der Kirche* (Paderborn/Frankfurt, 1982). In English, *The Ministry in the Church* (Geneva, 1982). These booklets add to the common statement a compilation of Catholic and Lutheran ordination liturgies and supplementary studies on the admission of women to the Ministry and on "One Mediator" (the last by Yves Congar). The common statement also appeared in English in *Origins*, 12 (1982), 295–304; and in the Unity Secretariat's *Information Service*, 48 (1982), 12–29; and in H. Meyer and L. Vischer (eds.), *Growth in Agreement*, 248–275. In French, in the Unity Secretariat's *Service d'information*, 48 (1982), 14–32; and in H. Legrand and H. Meyer (eds.), *Face à l'unité*, 195–279. In German, in H. Meyer et al. (eds.), *Documente wachsender Übereinstimmung*, 329–357. In Italian, in S.J. Voicu and G. Cereti (eds.), *Enchiridion oecumenicum*, vol. 1, 702–742. In Spanish, in *Diálogo ecumenico*, 17 (1982), 71–104. Further references in our text are to the numbered paragraphs of *The Ministry in the Church*.

46. After indicating the convergences ascertained on the basis and function of ministry and on ordination, these questions were said to need answering. "It must be asked, among other things, how the Lutheran churches regard a Eucharist celebrated without an ordained minister. It must also be asked, in view of the Lutheran interpretation and practice of ordination, how the Roman Catholic Church evaluates the Eucharist celebrated in the Lutheran church. What needs to be clarified, then, is the importance and ecclesiological ordering of the ministry, and what consequences it has for the structure of the church." *The Eucharist*, 24 (No. 68).

47. Particularly significant is the three-part notion of community: confession of faith, sacraments, and fellowship in ministry and Church life. As far as I can see, this triad was first set before the Study Commission by J. Witte at the end of his 1971 "Thesen über die Kirche in Zusammenhang mit dem Interkommunionsproblem," in H. Meyer (ed.), *Evangelium—Welt—Kirche*, 453. Earlier, Witte cited UR 22, on the dynamic orientation of Baptism, in this vein (*ibid.*, 444). By 1981, the triad, Word/Sacrament/Ministry, had become central in the work of the Joint Commission, as it thought about the goal of unity and its mediation in this world. Cf. the summary paper "Ways to Community," issued in 1980, Nos. 14–23, in the Unity Secretariat's *Information Service*, 46 (1981), 66–67.

48. "Justification by Faith," *Origins*, 13 (1983), 277–304. In French, *Documentation catholique*, 82 (1985), 126–162. In Italian, *Il Regno*, 29 (1984), 162–190. A further English publication is in the volume containing sixteen background papers discussed over the five years of dialogue, H.G. Anderson et al. (eds.), *Justification by Faith, Lutherans and Catholics in Dialogue VII* (Minneapolis, 1985). The following references in this section will be by the paragraph numbers of the statement.

49. Later this hermeneutical perspective is said to heighten tension with Catholic views (154). Some critical questions arise here. (1) The term "hermeneutical" seems more to obscure than to define what is meant. (2) Does a viewpoint largely forgotten in Lutheranism and even now often not understood (93) really belong in a dialogue between churches identified by the faith they confess and the doctrine they officially teach? (3) Has the perspective been sufficiently examined with a view to bringing out its connections with Catholic doctrine? The heart of this teaching seems to be the efficacy of a word of grace "that announces the death and resurrection of Jesus Christ. God's word does what it proclaims" (88). Luther found such a word preeminently in absolution, baptism, and the eucharistic words of institution. In the pastoral context of affirming God's consoling and reliable grace for the benefit of anguished consciences, Luther gave a new twist to the traditional thesis on a sacrament as *signum efficax* by depicting *fides* as the grace-effect of such words. Cf. J. Wicks, "Fides sacramenti—Fides specialis. Luther's Development in 1518," *Gregorianum*, 65 (1984), 53–87. (4) It is not so that Luther's exclusion of *liberum arbitrium* from justification followed from his insight into the efficacy of the sacramental word (91, 154). The doctrine of the will's bondage emerged in Luther's anti-Pelagian and anti-Occamist arguments in university lectures and disputations, not in his pastoral instruction. One can see this by comparing Luther's pastoral instructions of late 1519 on preparing to die and on Penance, Baptism, and Holy Communion, with the disputatious rejection of *liberum arbitrium* in No. 36 of *Assertio omnium articulorum* (1520). The former works are ingeniously centered on the efficacious word and *fides sacramenti*, a conception that does not of itself decide whether or not human freedom has a role in personally appropriating or declining the word's saving gift.

50. The discussion of merit can be illumined by the radical difference in thought forms: Lutheran dialectic, involving schemes of totality and exclusive alternatives, contrasts with Catholic participation, involving schemes of analogy, dependence, and conformity. Cardinal Cajetan was lucid on the latter in his 1532 work *De fide et operibus*, Chap. 12. Cf. his *Opuscula omnia* (Lyon, 1581), 291b–292a; translated in J. Wicks (ed.), *Cajetan Responds* (Washington, 1978), 237. On Cajetan's theology, we now have an impressive monograph: B. Hallensleben, *Communicatio. Anthropologie und Gnadenlehre bei Thomas de Vio Cajetan* (Münster, 1985). Cajetan's inclusive, participatory thinking emerges especially in the sections on causality and analogy (94–108) and on divine-human collaboration and *meritum* (401–423).

51. As in the fifth American dialogue, on papal primacy, so also in the most recent one, on justification, a special volume of biblical analysis was prepared in advance: J. Reumann, *"Righteousness" in the New Testament*, with responses by J. Fitzmyer and J. Quinn (New York/ Philadelphia, 1982).

52. In the first meeting of the world-level Study Commission in 1967, the paper by H. Conzelmann on tradition in the New Testament gave rise to a lively argument over the criterion of valid tradition. H. Meyer and A. Hasler, "The Joint Lutheran/Roman Catholic Study Commission on 'The Gospel and the Church,' " *Lutheran World*, 16 (1969), 367–369.

53. The American dialogue is now (1986) engaged in treating the role of Mary and the saints, while a reconstituted world-level Commission is taking up the Church's place and role in salvation.

54. *Kirchengemeinschaft in Wort und Sakrament* (Paderborn/ Hanover, 1984), a booklet of 110 pages, giving a text in 88 numbered paragraphs to which we refer subsequently in our text.

55. The best-known recent proposal speaking to this point is H. Fries and K. Rahner, *Einigung der Kirche—reale Möglichkeit*, Quaestiones Disputatee 100 (Freiburg, 1983). Their innovative recommendation of "epistemological tolerance" would admit some dogmatic differences around the perimeter of common assent to Scripture and to the Apostles' and Nicene Creeds. But official assent could in cases be withheld regarding the dogmas going beyond the fundamental truths. Tolerance, though, is limited by the exclusion of direct contradiction by one church of what another church in communion teaches as decisive for salvation. The grounds for this recommended tolerance of dogmatic diversity deserve careful examination. Special attention should be given to the performative character of doctrine, and to asking whether Scripture and the ancient Creeds suffice for action together in our world.

56. *Facing Unity. Models, Forms and Phases of Catholic–Lutheran Church Fellowship* (Geneva, 1985). Also in the Unity Secretariat's *Information Service*, 59 (1985), 44–73. The parallel German text is *Einheit vor uns* (Paderborn/Frankfurt, 1985). In French, in the Unity Secretariat's *Service d'information* 59, (1985), 45–77; and in H. Legrand and H. Meyer (eds.), *Face à l'unité*, 295–387. In Italian, in S.J. Voicu and G. Cereti (eds.), *Enchiridion oecumenicum*, vol. 1, 752–827. In our text, we refer to the numbered paragraphs of *Facing Unity*.

57. The Pope's words were spoken during his visit to Germany in 1980, and have their original context in the commemoration of the Augsburg Confession of 1530. The statement gave rise to controversy, as some, such as the Lutheran theologian Eilert Herms, were provoked into declaring and demonstrating an allegedly unreconcilable fundamental *dissensus* between Catholics and Protestants. Cf. E. Herms, *Einheit*

der Christen in der Gemeinschaft der Kirchen (Göttingen, 1984). The problematic is conveniently surveyed—including a report on Herms' strained view of unity in dissent—in H. Meyer, "Différence fondamental, Consensus fondamental," *Irénikon*, 58 (1985), 163–179; with a German version in *Ökumenische Rundschau*, 34 (1985), 347–359.

58. A working group of Catholic and Protestant theologians in West Germany, under the coleadership of Bishop Karl Lehmann and Prof. Wolfhart Pannenberg, has just completed a study of the sixteenth-century doctrinal condemnations. A significant reassessment seems possible on a broad front. See the prepublication analysis of March 1986: "Auf dem Weg zu einer immer stärken verbindenden Gemeinschaft," *Herder Korrespondenz*, 40 (1986), 135–142.

59. Cf. especially Y. Congar, *Diversités et communion. Dossier historique et conclusion théologique*, Cogitatio Fidei 112 (Paris, 1982). In English, *Diversity and Communion* (London, 1984). In Italian, *Diversità e comunione* (Assisi, 1983).

60. Two recent articles emphasized this unfinished theological task. J.M.R. Tillard, "Oecuménisme et Eglise catholique," *NRT*, 107 (1985), 43–67, at 56–59. A. de Halleux, "Les principes catholiques de l'oecuménisme," *RTL*, 16 (1985), 316–350, at 318–326.

CHAPTER 35

The Eucharist Makes the Church
The Ecclesial Dimension of the Sacrament

Gerardo J. Békés, O.S.B.

Summary

While the Church celebrates the Eucharist, it is the Eucharist that makes the Church. Indeed, the eucharistic celebration makes the mystery of salvation sacramentally present, and it is this presence that creates the ecclesial community as a divine and human communion: divine, with the Father through Christ in the Spirit; and human, with our brothers and sisters as they share in the mystery. This ecclesiological significance of the Eucharist, which was only recently rediscovered by theologians, appears in the documents of the Council and is one of the main themes of ecumenical dialogue.

———
———

The central consideration around which all the reflections of the Council took place was that of the Church, with its nature and mission, its multiple functions, and its different relationships with the world. The Council devoted no systematic treatment to the Eucharist, and especially not to its doctrinal aspects, although a quick glance at any analytical index is enough to demonstrate the presence of the sacrament in the conciliar texts, even if such references are mainly in connection with the Church. The fundamental text in this connection is found in number 26 of *Lumen gentium,* and in view of its fundamental importance we give it here almost in full:

This Church of Christ is really present in all legitimately organized local groups of the faithful, which, insofar as they are
united to their pastors, are also quite appropriately called
churches in the New Testament.[1] For these are in fact, in
their own localities, the new people called by God, in the
power of the Holy Spirit and as the result of full conviction
(cf. 1 Thess. 1:5). In them the faithful are gathered together
through the preaching of the Gospel of Christ, and the mystery of the Lord's Supper is celebrated. . . . In these communities, though they may often be small and poor, or existing in
the diaspora, Christ is present through whose power and influence the one, holy, catholic and apostolic Church is constituted.[2] For "the sharing in the body and blood of Christ has no
other effect than to accomplish our transformation into that
which we receive."[3]

This text makes three statements that constitute the basis of
our subject: (1) the Church of Christ is present in every legitimate local assembly of Christians, which are also called churches
in the New Testament; (2) these local churches are assembled
through the preaching of the gospel, and in them, under the
sacred ministry of the bishop, the Eucharist is celebrated; (3) in
such eucharistic celebrations, through participation in the body
and blood of Christ, these local churches become the body of
Christ, which is the one, holy, catholic and apostolic Church.
    These same ideas are also substantially confirmed in the Con-
stitution Sacrosanctum concilium. In number 26, it is stated that
the liturgical celebrations that take place in local churches are
ecclesial and communitarian by nature, and that, carried out
under the leadership of the bishop, they show forth the unity of
the people of God. And number 41 expands on this statement in
more practical terms, saying that the principal manifestation of
the Church is found in the sharing of the people of God in the
same liturgical celebrations, and especially in the same Eucharist, over which the bishop presides, with his college of priests.
    In number 42, this liturgical and sacramental view of the
diocese as a local church that is a manifestation of the universal
Church is also extended to more limited liturgical assemblies.
Since the bishop cannot always preside in person over the assemblies of the faithful everywhere in his diocese, local communities
must of necessity be formed, and among these parishes, under the

leadership of a pastor who represents the bishop, have a preeminent but not exclusive place. *Sacrosanctum concilium* states that, in turn, all such communities, even more limited ones made up solely of religious or lay people, "represent the visible Church constituted throughout the world."

These conciliar texts, together with others that can easily be found by consulting any analytical index, express clearly enough the very close relationship between eucharistic celebration and the existence of the Church. We believe that on the basis of this relationship, it is possible to state that the local church that celebrates the Eucharist is an authentic manifestation of the Church of Christ, because the local assembly in fact becomes the one, holy, catholic, and apostolic Church in this celebration.

In view of this fact, we now have the task of explaining the biblical and theological basis for these conciliar statements. And, unlike the Council and most commentators, with this end in mind, we shall not proceed from the top downwards, in other words, from the universal Church to the local church, but rather from the base upwards, in other words from the local communities to their universal communion. First, however, we shall try to understand the Eucharist in its paschal origins, so that on the basis of the sources we can then explain its function in forming ecclesial communities and the universal communion of these communities.

The Origins of the Eucharist: The Passover Meal as Constitutive of the Ecclesial Community

In order to understand the relationship between the Eucharist and the community that celebrates it, we must go back to its origins in the celebration of the Last Supper by Jesus with his disciples, and further back still to the origins of this meal in the actual Old Testament Passover meal, which, in the words of a recent author, N. Füglister,[4] demonstrates "an extraordinary structural similarity" with it (169).

The Characteristics of the Old Testament Passover Meal

The Passover meal of the old covenant is a liturgical rite that represents the core of the Passover celebrations as laid down in

Chapter 12 of Exodus. The theme of the celebration is, of course, the liberation of the people of Israel from slavery, and the creation of the liberated people, specifically through the covenant, as the holy and priestly people of God. The liturgical rite of the meal summarizes and expresses this meaning. Füglister explains that in this meal,

> . . . looking to the past, God is glorified, and, looking to the future, full of hope, the people meditate on God's great action of salvation which is the basis, symbol and pledge of present and future paschal salvation: the liberation from Egyptian slavery (143).

All the other elements of the passover celebration

> . . . are in some way seen in relation to this commemorative celebration: the lamb is sacrificed with a view to the meal; the blood is sprinkled for those who will eat the meal together, and the unleavened bread, the wine and the bitter herbs, as constitutive elements of the meal, take on their meaning during the liturgy of the passover meal (*ibid.*).

Now the main characteristic of this rite lies in its nature as a sacred meal, or, to put it more precisely, as a ritual meal of a sacrificial nature. Füglister explains this feature by providing a detailed analysis of the sacrificial significance of the paschal lamb that it is eaten precisely as sacrificial food during the supper (51–81).

As far as our particular subject is concerned, it is very significant that this meal is attributed with "the *power* implicit in it and expected from it, *of forming a community*" (143). Indeed, our author goes on to explain that sharing the same food with another person signifies sharing in the same vital energy, and therefore entering into a communion of life with him, which is a personal communion of friendship and trust. Thus, each shared meal creates a sort of fraternal communion. Further, what applies to relations between men applies also to the relationship between man and his God: ". . . on the occasion of the sacred meal he [man] enters into a special relationship and close communion with the divinity" (144).

In order to evaluate this statement correctly, we must consider the sacrificial character of the meal. In virtue of the sacrifice itself, the sacrificed lamb is given to God, so that in the sacred meal, those taking part share in what belongs to God. Füglister therefore concludes that "in the Old Testament, which is in line here with the cultic conceptions common in the ancient world, the sacred meal is in fact a *communio* or a sacramental," in other words, a symbolic sacramental sign of the communion of man with God and with his brethren, and thus a sign that creates and further shapes the community. In our case, this sign is the Passover meal that creates or renews the community of the holy people of God.

What is the source of the power inherent in this meal? What makes it so effective? The answer lies in the actual nature of the celebration, which is described in Exodus as a *memorial*: "This day shall be for you a memorial day [*le-zikkaron*], and you shall keep it as a feast to the Lord; throughout your generations you shall observe it as an ordinance for ever" (12:4; cf. 13:9).

The celebration of the Passover and its core, the paschal meal, are (indeed, like all the feasts of the Israelites) therefore of a commemorative or anamnetic nature, as is expressed in the term "memorial" (or "anamnesis").

As far as the overall significance of the memorial is concerned, Füglister notes the twofold sense of the term: "It refers at the same time to the Lord and to the Israelites, so that both the Lord and Israel can be both subject and object of the remembrance" (158). This twofold quality is of major importance in understanding the power and efficacity of the sacrificial meal of the Passover as regards the formation of the community of the people of God. Füglister explains that

. . . on passover night not only does Israel remember the Lord and his salvific actions, but the Lord also remembers Israel and his faithful servants. In both the biblical and late-Jewish approaches, the fact that God remembers means that God makes himself present and that his salvation is accomplished (161).

In the "memorial" God and his salvation, therefore, become present, and since this memorial is also a sacrificial meal, Israel enters through it into communion with God, and is created as a new community of the holy and priestly people of God.

However, the Passover celebration is not only of an anamnetic nature, but can "become a *prophetic sign* for the future, and a guarantee of final salvation" (161). The Passover meal has a decidedly joyful aspect, in that it expresses the joy of living in communion with God and is seen as "a foretaste of the salvific meal of the end of time" (146)—in other words, the great messianic and eschatological feast.

To summarize as concerns our subject, we can say that the Old-Testament meal is a sacrificial meal of an anamnetic and eschatological nature, which has the power actually to create the community of the holy and priestly people of God, because as memorial it "recalls" the Lord and his salvific action of the past, and, in virtue of the "memory" of the Lord, the divine salvation worked in the past is performed in it in the present, while the fulfillment of eschatological salvation is foretold in it as prophetic sign. The Passover meal is thus the liturgical and sacramental rite in which communion between God and Israel, and among the Israelites themselves, is brought about: in it, Israel is truly created as the holy and priestly people in covenant with God.

The Last Supper and the Eucharistic "Memorial"

The Last Supper of the Lord, and the eucharistic celebrations of the apostolic Church after his resurrection show a "strange structural similarity" with the Old-Testament Passover meal: "All the essential elen.ents of the Old-Testament Jewish passover liturgy are still found in the Christian eucharistic celebration" (169), which is seen as a sacrificial meal of an anamnetic and eschatological nature, and encompasses proclamation, instruction, praise, thanksgiving, and prayer. Thus, "in its structure and thematic content, the New-Testament eucharistic celebration corresponds broadly to the Jewish Old-Testament passover celebration" (335).

It is not, of course, our task to enter into details of exegetical and theological research into the New-Testament texts in order to bring out this similarity. This research has already been carried out in masterly fashion by Füglister and by others who are meticulously cited in his book. Nevertheless, there is one essential aspect of this similarity that directly concerns our subject inasmuch as it involves the capacity to create community. As in the old covenant, this aspect is the anamnetic nature of the meal as *memorial* of God's salvific action, and we shall explain this briefly.

Jesus celebrates the Last Supper with his disciples as an Old-Testament Passover meal of an anamnetic nature. Even so, the absolutely novel element in this celebration is the presence of a new content and a new meaning. Within the framework of the old meal, Jesus presents a new salvific action on God's part and institutes a new memorial of this action. Substituting himself, so to speak, for the sacrificed lamb, he takes the bread and distributes it to his disciples, identifying it with his body, which is to be sacrificed for our salvation; and after the meal he takes the cup of wine and distributes it to them, identifying it with his blood, which is also to be poured out for us. In this way, the Lord foreshadows his sacrificial act, the new divine act of salvation that will be accomplished on the cross.[5]

The divine action of New-Testament salvation basically consists, on God's part, in "giving his Son" for the salvation of the world, and, on Christ's part, in identifying himself with this divine action, in "giving himself" to God as a perfect gift carried out on the cross. God's action and the corresponding action of Christ are two aspects, divine and human, of the one salvific action with which God reconciled the world to himself (cf. 2 Cor. 5:18–19) and opened the way to salvation for mankind.

Now, this salvific action, as concretized in the sacrifice of Jesus, is anticipated in the Last Supper in the symbolic and sacramental action of "giving his body" and "pouring out his blood." In this way, the eucharistic celebration of the Last Supper becomes the anticipation in symbolic and sacramental signs of the sacrifice of the cross. The Eucharist is therefore a *sacramental sacrifice*. Moreover, the sacramental signs are received by those sharing in the meal, so that the sacramental sacrifice becomes a sacramental meal that means they share in the sacrifice. The Eucharist is therefore also a *sacrificial meal*. And lastly the disciples are ordered to do the same "in memory" (*eis anamnesin*) of the Lord. Thus, the sacramental celebration of the sacrifice of Jesus and the meal that makes us share sacramentally in this sacrifice were instituted in advance at the Last Supper as anamnetic celebration, in other words, as the memorial of God's salvific action that was to be carried out through the Lord's passion. The *memoria passionis*, therefore, constitutes the new content and meaning of the Eucharist as New-Testament Passover celebration.

In this way, what has been said of the Old-Testament memorial also applies to the New-Testament memorial.

The eucharistic celebration is carried out not only in order that believers should remember Jesus and his salvific action, but also in order that God should remember Christ and Christians so as to implement in the present the salvation that has its basis in the past, that is, in the salvific action that took place once and for ever (169).

At the same time, this memorial also becomes a *prophetic sign* of the Lord's Parousia and of the eschatological fulfillment of his salvation. "For as often as you eat this bread and drink the cup, you proclaim the Lord's death until he comes" (1 Cor. 11:26).

To summarize what we have said thus far, the Eucharist instituted at the Last Supper is a *memorial* of God's salvific action as performed through Christ's passion. This memorial is a sacrificial meal that sacramentally performs the Lord's gift of himself in order to enable his disciples to share in it and to provide them with a prophetic sign of his Parousia and of the eschatological fulfillment of salvation.

The Eucharistic Memorial and the Christian Community

The Old-Testament Passover meal was a community celebration, and in this connection Füglister observes that

. . . in all three historical configurations assumed by the celebration of the passover (the "Egyptian" passover, the deuteronomistic passover celebrated in the Temple, and the postbiblical late-Jewish passover) two different communities are seen as participating in the passover meal. These are superimposed but are linked to one another: on the one hand, the little domestic community, and on the other the great community of the people (149).

The family or domestic community can be seen primarily in the celebration of the so-called "Egyptian" passover, which is predeuteronomistic and is described in Chapter 12 of Exodus. In the period of the Deuteronomist, this celebration is centralized in the Temple and becomes the foremost feast of Israel, as the memorial celebration of the liberation from slavery and the constitution of Israel as the people of God. An intermediate approach is found in the late-Jewish period, with the lamb being sacrificed in the Temple, while the meal takes place in the domestic community.

The Lord's Last Supper was a domestic meal in the community of his disciples, and the early Christian communities also "broke bread in their homes" (Acts 2:42, 46; 20:7). Paul, in turn, stresses the communitarian nature of the celebration of "the Lord's supper" (1 Cor. 11:17–34), and the reason is clear: the Passover meal has always been a community act, and it is the Christian community that celebrates the Eucharist.

However, we may wonder whether the reverse is not even truer: before the Church celebrates the Eucharist, is it the Eucharist that constitutes the Church?

It would appear that this is precisely what Paul is saying when he speaks of the Eucharist as a participation in the sacrificial meal of the Lord:

> The cup of blessing which we bless, is it not a participation in the blood of Christ? The bread which we break, is it not a participation in the body of Christ? Because there is one bread, we who are many are one body, for we all partake of the one bread (1 Cor. 10;16–17).

According to this text, all those who share in the bread/body and wine/blood of the Lord form one single body—that of Christ—so that this body can be said to be constituted by the Eucharist. *Lumen gentium* 3 has the following to say in this connection:

> As often as the sacrifice of the cross by which "Christ our Pasch is sacrificed" (1 Cor. 5:7) is celebrated on the altar, the work of our redemption is carried out. Likewise, in the sacrament of the eucharistic bread, the unity of believers, who form one body in Christ (cf. 1 Cor. 10:17) is both expressed and brought about.

These biblical and conciliar statements of an ecclesiological and sacramental nature are obviously based on the soteriological foundation of reconciliation. It is our faith—as has also been explained—that through the sacrificial act of Christ, God has reconciled the world to himself, offering man communion of life

with himself and fraternal communion with his fellows. This reconciliation, as the work of God, is objectively real. The question is
then that of how this divine reality becomes subjective reality in
the personal life of man. It obviously does not do so without some
at least representative personal act of faith and without Baptism,
which is closely linked to this (*fidei sacramentum*). Justified
through faith and Baptism, through the Spirit of Christ the Christian enters into living contact with the Lord; sharing in his salvation, he becomes a member of the community of the people of God
which is the body of Christ, the Church. "For by one Spirit we
were all baptized into one body" (1 Cor. 12:13).[6]

To summarize what we have said here, by means of faith, the
Spirit of Christ unites the believer to the body of the Church, in
which the salvific act of Christ is constantly made present
through the eucharistic memorial. Participation in the eucharistic memorial in turn reconciles, or, to put it more precisely,
accomplishes the reconciliation of the Christian with God, and
through Christ the Savior and his Spirit creates or effects permanent communion with the Father and with all those who belong
to Christ. Here we have the essence of the Church: in a vertical
sense, it is divine communion, through Christ in the Spirit with
the Father, and, in a horizontal sense, it is human and ecclesial
communion with all those who live in divine communion. This
divine and human communion is the theandric unity of Christ as
brought about mystically in his body, which is the Church.

Even if it is true that Church makes the Eucharist, it is therefore still more profoundly true that the Eucharist makes the
Church, inasmuch as it is through the Eucharist that the communion between God and man—the very mystery of divine
redemption—is made sacramentally present and constantly accomplished within the Christian community.

The Eucharist: Local and Universal Communion

As the New-Testament Passover meal, the Eucharist is one of
the factors that formally constitute the Christian community as
Church. This statement, which flows from our foregoing reflections, obviously refers to local communities, since the Eucharist
must of necessity be celebrated locally in a specific community.

To continue with the development of our subject, we must

now consider the sense in which the above statement can be applied to the universal Church. Can we truly say that the Eucharist is a constitutive factor for the universal Church?

In order to answer this question, we must first of all define the local church and its relationship to the universal Church, and then on the basis of this relationship, we can consider the sense in which the Eucharist celebrated in local churches can constitute the communion of these churches, and thus the universal Church itself.

The Relationship Between the Local Church and the Universal Church

The relationship between the local church and the universal Church was clearly defined in the Council. According to the fundamental principle, as cited in our introduction, the Church of Christ, on the one hand, is present "in all legitimately organized local groups of the faithful, which, insofar as they are united to their pastors, are also quite appropriately called churches in the New Testament"; on the other hand, in these local communities, which are often small and poor, "Christ is present, through whose power and influence" they are gathered into the one, holy, catholic, and apostolic Church (cf. LG 26).

In this text, the Church is considered under three aspects: first, without any specific concretization, as the community of Christ's faithful; second, as the gathering of the faithful in the local assemblies or churches; and third, as the uniting of the local churches in the universal Church. The Church of Christ, taken in a general sense, is therefore present on two levels: the concrete local level, and the universal, and in a certain sense abstract, level.

In order to understand the relationship between these two levels, we must first of all note the criteria for the authentic presence of the Church of Christ, which are clearly given in this same conciliar text: the first is the preaching of the gospel; the second, the celebration of the Lord's Supper; and the third, the fact of being "under the sacred ministry of the bishop," which guarantees the apostolic authenticity of the first two elements.

These criteria obviously do not all have the same function in the constitution of the local church. The first two, taken generically as doctrine of the faith and sacramental participation in salvation, represent the material element or actual content of "existence as Church," in other words, the continuity of the *paradosis,* which is faithful continuation of the traditional teaching of the apostolic faith together with the *apostolica vivendi forma.* However, the third criterion is the formal element or the structure, in other words, the succession in the apostolic ministry, the *diadoche,* as the visible sign and guarantee of the apostolic authenticity of the *paradosis.* The succession must obviously be understood in line with the thought of the Council, in other words, not in an individualistic sense, but in a collegial one, as the fact of being a member of the college of bishops that is the successor of the college of the apostles. In this way, *paradosis* and *diadoche* are mutually complementary and together form the apostolicity—or apostolic authenticity—of the local churches. To use a happy phrase of J. Ratzinger: "Succession is the form of tradition, and tradition is the content of succession."[7]

Therefore, wherever the ecclesial situation corresponds to these criteria, the Church of Christ is fully present. Along these lines, in an intervention at the Council, E. Schick, Auxiliary Bishop of Fulda, highlighted the nature of the local church and its relationship to the universal Church:

> Thus, in theological terms, the parish, or indeed any community of Christ's faithful in a specific place which is accustomed to gather for the celebration of the Eucharist, is itself "Church" according to the New Testament. It is not merely some administrative "section" of the Church, but is a true representation and manifestation of the universal Church. In such a representation not only a part but the whole Christ [*totus Christus*] who is Lord of the Church lives, gives life, and activates that mystery by which the universal Church comes to its true self. . . . Both the local Church gathered together through the word of God and the body of Christ, and the universal Church are thus two integral elements [or "poles"] of one and the same reality which is the Church.[8]

To be still more exact, we would note two limitations, one for the local church and the other for the universal Church, which protect us from the danger of interpreting this relationship wrongly. On the one hand, the local church is not an administrative section or a province of the universal Church; and, on the other, the universal Church is not an association or confederation of local churches, but is in some way greater than the sum total of the latter.[9] The relationship between local church and universal Church cannot be defined better than through two terms used by Bishop Schick, "representation" and "manifestation," which are, moreover, synonymous or equivalent with those found in the Council texts (cf. LG 26; SC 26, 41, 42; and AG 20, 37). Since the local church is thus a representation and manifestation of the universal Church, the whole ecclesial force of the Church of Christ is present and manifested in it. Rahner uses other words to express the same concept: ". . . a local church is not brought about by an atomizing division of the world-territory of the universal Church, but by the concentration of the Church into her own nature as 'event.' "[10] And to conclude, we would quote some summarizing words from Ratzinger:

> . . . the Church is realized immediately and primarily in the individual local Churches which are not separate parts of a larger administrative organization but rather embody the totality of the reality which is "the Church." The local Churches are not administrative units of a huge apparatus but living cells, each of which contains the whole living mystery of the one body of the Church: each one may rightly be called *ecclesia*. We may then conclude that the one Church of God consists of the individual Churches, each of which represents the whole Church.[11]

Which Is the Local Church Constituted by the Eucharist?

Which is the Christian community that corresponds to the criteria just given? Where do we find those elements on the basis of which a community can be called Church?

In the text cited, Bishop Schick also considers the local church to be the parish—or indeed any Christian community in which the Eucharist is celebrated. And many authors, such as Bardoni, Cunnane, Kress, Latourelle, and Marranzini, share his opinion. Rahner, however, distinguishes between local church and local liturgical assembly, basing this distinction on the need for the presence of the whole ecclesial reality: a community is called Church not only because of the celebration of the Eucharist (and the other sacraments) and the preaching of the gospel, but also because of the bishop, who guarantees the apostolic authenticity of these elements. Rahner, therefore, holds that only the diocese can be called a local church, and that the title cannot be applied to a parish or other community that celebrates the Eucharist.[12]

The conciliar Decree *Christus Dominus* 11 also speaks along similar lines:

> A diocese is a section of the People of God entrusted to a bishop to be guided by him with the assistance of his clergy so that, loyal to its pastor and formed by him into one community in the Holy Spirit through the Gospel and the Eucharist, it constitutes one particular church in which the one, holy, catholic and apostolic Church of Christ is truly present and active.

And the new Code of Canon Law, in turn, has the following to say: "Particular churches in which and from which exists the one and unique Catholic Church are first of all dioceses" (Canon 368), whereas the parish is seen as "a definite community of the Christian faith established on a stable basis within a particular church" (Canon 515).

So which is the local church: the diocese or the community that celebrates the Eucharist? The question does not seem a valid one to us. It is certainly true, on the one hand, that the presence of the bishop, who represents succession in the apostolic ministry, belongs to the fullness of the ecclesial essence.[13] On the other hand, all the authors who speak of the parish or even smaller community as the local church take it for granted that any such community is, through a member of the *presbyterium* of the diocese, "under the sacred ministry of the bishop." Thus, any community that celebrates the Eucharist, as presided over by the bishop or a member of his clergy, is celebrating it legitimately, with the result that the salvation of Christ and the communion between God and men take place within it, which in turn means that the community becomes Church. And thus, says Rahner, "the Eucharist as an event in a place not only occurs in the Church; the Church herself becomes in the fullest sense an event only in the local celebration of the Eucharist."[14]

In What Sense Is the Universal Church Constituted by the Eucharist?

We are left with a last question: How is it that the Eucharist celebrated in local communities can constitute the universal Church?

The answer presupposes a correct concept of the universality of the Church, according to which, from the ecclesiological point of view, its essential property is nothing other than its catholicity. As Y. Congar and others have pointed out,[15] this third essential property of the Church, as professed in the Niceno–Constantinopolitan Creed, is not primarily a quantitative concept. Its translation with the term *universalis* does not do full justice to the original sense. Indeed, viewed in its original perspective, it is neither an ethnic–geographic concept (all the people of all the continents), not an historical one (for all the ages of human history), nor yet a sociological one (for all human categories), because in none of these perspectives even today could the Church—except maybe in potential—be called "catholic." However, if it is understood in its original sense as a qualitative concept, catholicity is a reality that was already present in the tiny flock of the apostolic community. The term *kath'olon* in fact expresses wholeness, totality, fullness, so that *katholike* as a quality of the Church means that the divine salvation is fully present in the Church. This is expressed in the Pauline and Johannine term *plerōma,* inasmuch as "the fullness of God" (Col. 2:9; 1:19) and particularly the Father's love is present in the person of Christ, and it is in turn this fullness that, through the Spirit, fills the body of Christ, which is the Church (Eph. 1:23). Since the incarnate only begotten Son is "full of grace and truth," "from his fullness have we all received, grace upon grace" (Jn. 1:14, 16). Catholicity, therefore, originally means this fullness of divine salvation, in other words, the divine–human communion that is brought about in the very person of Christ, and that is communicated to the Church as its essential quality through the Spirit.

Now, this essential catholicity is truly brought about in the local church that legitimately celebrates the Eucharist. In this celebration as presided over by the bishop or a member of his clergy, the catholicity of the Church of Christ is made present within the community, or, in other words, the divine salvation becomes present in its fullness, and communion between God and men is brought about; and in this way the local community truly becomes Church. When the local church represents and manifests the catholicity of the Church of Christ in this way, it also manifests its own essential identification with all the other local churches that also legitimately celebrate the same Eucharist. The catholic communion (*koinonia*) of the churches—the one, holy, catholic, and apostolic Church of Christ—is therefore truly brought about in the eucharistic celebration. It is thus the Eucharist as presence of the mystery of salvation "by which the unity [and the universality] of the Church is both signified and brought about" (*UR* 2).

Lastly, we must say a word about the ecumenical aspect of this eucharistic view of the local church and of the communion of the churches. This approach, which is reflected in the documents of the Council, permeates the whole Catholic–Orthodox document, *The Mystery of the Church and of the Eucharist in the Light of the Mystery of the Holy Trinity,* [16] and is also clearly expressed in the Lima document of the World Council of Churches, *The Eucharist,* [17] and in the Catholic–Lutheran document, *The Lord's Supper,* [18] as we attempted to show in a recent work. [19]

Translated from the Italian by Leslie Wearne.

Notes

1. Cf. Acts 8:1; 14:22–23; 20:17 *et passim.*

2. Cf. St. Augustine, *Contra Faustum* 12, 20, in *PL,* 42, 265; *Serm.* 57–7, in *PL,* 38, 89.

3. St. Leo the Great, *Serm.* 63, 7, in *PL,* 54, 357C.

4. N. Füglister, *Il valore salvifico della pasqua* (Brescia, 1976); henceforth, we shall indicate the page number in parenthesis within our text.

5. A recent book on this subject, with bibliographic information: F.X. Durrwell, *L'eucaristia sacramento del mistero pasquale,* Teologia 32 (Rome, 1982).

6. Cf. J. Hamer, *La Chiesa è una comunione* (Brescia, 1983), 32–44.

7. J. Ratzinger, "Primacy, Episcopate and Apostolic Succession," in K. Rahner and J. Ratzinger, *The Episcopate and Primacy,* Quaestiones disputatae 4 (New York, 1962/1963), 54. As regards the relationship between word and sacrament (*paradosis*) on the one hand, and ministry

(*diadoche*) on the other, cf. J. Ratzinger, "Das geistliche Amt und die Einheit der Kirche," *Catholica*, 17 (1963), 178: ". . . von den drei Komponenten Sakrament-Wort-Amt die dritte den beiden ersten ungleichartig ist: Die beiden ersten *begründen* die Einheit, die dritte *bezeugt* sie. In scholastischer Sprachweiss könnte man sagen: Die beiden ersten sind *Ursache*, das Amt ist der *Bedingung* der Einheit. . . ."

8. AS II/II, 397.

9. Cf. J. Hamer, "Chiesa locale e comunione ecclesiale," in A. Amato (ed.), *La Chiesa locale: Prospettive Teologiche e Pastorali* (*Conferenze della Facoltà Teologica Salesiana, 1975–1976*) (Rome, 1976), 37.

10. K. Rahner, "The Episcopate and Primacy," in Rahner and Ratzinger, *The Episcopate and Primacy*, 27.

11. J. Ratzinger, "The Pastoral Implications of Episcopal Collegiality," *Concilium*, 1/1 (January 1965), 22.

12. K. Rahner, "Über den Episcopat," in E. Fincke (ed.), *Das Amt der Einheit. Grundlegendes zur Theologie des Bischofsamtes* (Stuttgart, 1964), 273.

13. Cf. St. Ignatius of Antioch, *Phil.* 4, in *PG*, 5, 822–823.

14. Rahner, "The Episcopate and Primacy," 26. Cf. *ibid.*: "Therefore the celebration of the Eucharist is the most intensive event of the Church. For by this celebration Christ is not only present in the Church's liturgical solemnity as the Redeemer of his body, as the salvation and lord of the Church; but in the Eucharist the union of the faithful with Christ and with one another is also most tangibly visible, and at the Holy Table is most interiorly realized."

15. Y. Congar, "La cattolicità della chiesa," *Mysterium Salutis*, 7 (Brescia, 1972), 577–605; cf. W. Beinert, *Um das dritte Kirchenattribut I–II*, Koinonia 5 (Essen, 1964).

16. Secretariat for Promoting Christian Unity, *Information Service*, 49/2–3 (1982), 107–112.

17. *Baptism, Eucharist and Ministry*, Faith and Order Paper 111 (Geneva, 1982), 10–17.

18. *Origins*, 8/30 (11 January 1979), 1 and 467–477.

19. G.J. Békés, *Eucaristia e Chiesa. Ricerca dell'unità nel dialogo ecumenico*, Liturgia fonte e culmine 2 (Rome/Casale Monferrato, 1985); cf. also B. Forte, *La chiesa nell'eucaristia. Un ecclesiologia eucaristica alla luce del Vaticano II* (Naples, 1975).

PART VI

THE VIEW
OF
HUMANITY

CHAPTER 36

Human Beings
and Their Search for God

The Doctrine of the Magisterium of the Church
Between Vatican I and Vatican II

Félix-Alejandro Pastor, S.J.

Summary

The article covers the following topics: The traditional teaching of the magisterium of the Church on "the problem of God." From the conflict between rationalism and fideism in Vatican Council I to the dialectic between transcendence and history in Vatican Council II. From man as the image of God to the image of God in man. Knowledge of God through creation and through revelation in salvation history. The search for God in the religious experience of the mystical religions and the monotheistic religions. The problem of atheism as the negation of God. "Evangelical preparation" and the salvific will of God. Transcendence and history. The theoretical and practical meaning of the first article of faith.

The theological question of humanity's search for God, as possibility or as reality, as act of believing or content of belief, has always had an important place in ecclesial thought. Throughout the centuries, various models of understanding have succeeded one another in finding favor with the various theological schools. Apophatism and cataphatism, fideism and rationalism, spiritualism and immanentism have been the most persistent themes in developing the fundamental religious question of the search for and recognition of God, in light of existing conditions, internal logic, and formal linguistic structure, and the theoretical and practical meaning they assume for the ecclesial community and the individual believer. The human desire to affirm the divine reality, to know it and to give it a name, seems destined to yield to various temptations: idolatrous anthropomorphism or escape into irrationality, intellectualist rationalism or fideist voluntarism, illusory titanism or surrender to superstition. The objective of this essay is to discuss the theological problem of the human search for God, as possibility or as reality, as act or as substance, by analyzing the most relevant statements of the magisterium of the Church, particularly those having reference to the first article of faith as it has been formulated by ecclesiastical orthodoxy in its creeds, definitions, and declarations. Study of the traditional doctrine will enable us to understand better the originality and meaning of the doctrinal *aggiornamento* brought about by Vatican II in its desire to proclaim the divine message of the gospel with greater efficacy to contemporary humanity.[1]

The Creator and the Creature

In direct compliance with the gospel and as expressions of belief, expressions of faith abound in the catechumenal and baptismal ceremonies of the Church on the occasion of the reception of the "Sacrament of the faith." In the liturgy of the Easter vigil, the explanation of the creed preceded the baptismal action. In the profession of faith, the catechumen had to declare first of all faith in the "one God, Father almighty, creator of heaven and earth."[2] In this, we find the echo of the apostolic faith, the first statement of which refers always to the one God, creator and Father, not only in the baptismal formulas, but also in the liturgical doxologies and eucharistic anaphoras. The entire life of the praying community has as the ultimate point of reference of the ecclesial prayer the Father and his divine kingdom in the economy of salvation. The same is true in the prayers of benediction and of postbaptismal anointing, in the confirmation of the baptized, in the laying on of hands, whether in the reconciliation of penitents or in the rites of ordination to the ministry.[3]

In all the creeds of the ancient Church, from the most archaic formulas to the most elaborate, faith in one God, Father and Creator, is always affirmed as the first article of faith. The same applies to the Apostles' Creed and to the synodal creeds of Nicaea and Constantinople.[4] Also important are the repeated affirmations of "divine sovereignty" coexisting with the hypostatic trinity and the interpersonal equality in the one undivided divine essence.[5] Of equal relevance appears the antiorigenist synodal declaration condemning every negation of the divine infinitude and incomprehensibility, and thus reaffirming a primordial apophatism in language regarding God as infinite and incomprehensible.[6] The language of ecclesial orthodoxy first declares its faith in the one God, Father almighty, creator of all that is visible and invisible in the universe, thus identifying, against all gnostic dualism, God the creator and provider of the old covenant with the merciful Father of the new covenant. The incomprehensible and infinite God, ungenerated and eternal, omnipotent creator, is identified with the holy Father of the eternal divine Son, active inspirer of the paraclete Spirit, omniscient judge of history. God the Father is thus proclaimed the beginning without beginning of the intradivine "immanent" life, and the origin without origin of the salvifical-historical "economy."[7]

In the Latin West, the magisterium of the Church constantly reproposes the first article of the faith, defending it against all heretical interpretations, whether dualistic or pantheistic. Thus, the Councils of Quiercy (851) and Valence (855) refuted various errors concerning divine foreknowledge and predestination, which undermined faith in divine justice and goodness by supporting the heretical doctrine of John Scotus Erigena on the theological necessity of evil because it is known by the divine foreknowledge and decreed by the divine predetermination.[8] For its part, the Council of Sens (1140) rejected as heretical certain propositions of Peter Abelard regarding "theological optimism," according to which God could not have made a better world than the one he made, just as it rejected the assertion of any necessity in divine action that God himself could not escape from even as regards evil.[9] Similarly, in 1148, the Council of Reims adversely criticized the theological language of Gilbert de Poitiers, who made a real distinction between the divine essence, as substance or nature, and the divine Trinity as tripersonal reality.[10]

The Albigenses and the Cathars repeated the heretical asser-

tion of a divine theological dualism, making a distinction between a God creator, principle of evil, and a God savior, principle of good, and thus irremediably separating the old from the
new covenant. Against this assertion, the Fourth Lateran Council (1215) reaffirmed the unicity of the divine sovereignty, professing faith in "a one and unique true God, eternal, immense
and immutable, incomprehensible, omnipotent and ineffable."[11]
The analogy theory of this Council seems particularly relevant as
an attempt at mediation between a theology of identity and a
theology of difference. The Council posited between Creator and
creature a dialectic of likeness and difference, in which the difference is always greater, and it thus took a position close to the
moderately apophatic position.[12] On the other hand, the Council not only had to combat the dualist heresy, which made too
great a distinction between God as Creator and as Savior, as if
there were two different divine principles, but it had also to
reject the pantheistic doctrine of Amalric of Bène, who identified the creature with the Creator and God with the totality of
the universe.[13]

The Second Council of Lyon (1274) reaffirmed this same doctrine regarding the divine unity and uniqueness against all theological dualism and all cosmical-diabolical pessimism.[14] John
XXII condemned various propositions on the eternity, unity, and
goodness of God contained in the writings of Master Eckhart
(1329). The paradoxical language and apophatic ideas of the
Eckhartian theology seemed to infer the eternity of the world,
the absolute unity of God in both his substantial and his personal
reality, and an impossibility of speaking of the divine goodness.[15]
The Council of Florence (1442) confirmed the doctrine of the
unity of the divine sovereignty, which had been previously affirmed by the magisterium of the Church.[16] For its part, the
Council of Trent renewed its profession of faith in the creed of
Nicaea-Constantinople (1564), with the twofold intention of
restoring ecumenical unity and of remaining faithful to the tradition of the Latin Church.[17]

Through these professions of faith, theological definitions,
and dogmatic statements, the magisterium of the Church reaffirmed the faith of the Catholic Church, proclaiming its convinced faith in a profound identity between the mysterious God,
Creator and provider, who is manifested in the Old Testament,
and the God revealed in the New Testament as Lord of salvation

history and merciful Father. The magisterium at the same time affirmed the insurmountable difference between the Creator and the creature, between God and the world. Furthermore, the divine transcendence in a creational and salvific immanence was affirmed, which emphasized on the one hand the incomprehensible and ineffable divine holiness, and on the other the divine presence and activity in creation and in history. Finally, the magisterium opposed all language that could undermine faith in divine justice and divine goodness, whether with regard to divine foreknowledge and predestination or to created reality.

Reason and Faith

During the first millennium, the danger for the Christian faith regarding the first article of the creed came particularly from a temptation to accept a divine diarchy, splitting the Father's sovereignty into a twofold supreme principle of evil and of good, of darkness and of light, of creation and of salvation, of the old covenant and the new. During the second Christian millennium, and especially from the beginning of the modern era, the danger of denying the first article of faith came also from a loss of consciousness regarding the difference between Creator and creature, the infinite and the finite, God and world. This comes down to an acceptance of pantheizing monism, whether of a spiritualistic and idealistic or of a materialistic and naturalistic kind, which turns ultimately into nihilism and atheism.

On the other hand, the model of the profound integration of contemplative reason with religious faith, which characterized Christian Platonism, and which was replaced with the model of a moderate subordination of scientific reason to faith, which characterized Christian Aristotelianism, has in the modern era become the model of an exaggerated subordination of the critical and governing reason to a heteronomously conceived faith, such as fideist traditionalism, or, on the contrary, and with equal lack of proportion, to subordination of theonomous faith to the control of critical reason, as in idealist rationalism.

That is the reason why the magisterium must, in its declarations, reject both fideism and rationalism and affirm once more the theological wisdom of a profound integration of the demands of faith with rational method. And, in fact, during the pontificates of Gregory XVI and Pius IX, both the fideistic errors of L.E. Bautain and A. Bonnety[18] and the Catholic rationalism of A. Günther and I. Froschammer were rejected.[19] The magisterium in like manner had to repulse the tendency toward pantheism in its various forms, whether absolute or essential, evolutive or emanantist, by defending the substantial difference between the divine reality and the created world, and also the divine freedom in its creative and provident activity. For this reason, in the period of Pius IX, both pantheism and pantheizing ontologism, as well as every denial of freedom in the divine creative act, were rejected as errors contrary to faith.[20]

In this religious and cultural context, the magisterium of Vatican I in its dogmatic constitution on the Catholic faith (1870) acquires particular importance as regards its rejection as heretical errors of atheism and pantheism, agnosticism and deism, fideism and rationalism.[21] The Council also reaffirmed the identity and reality of God and his essential difference from the world, thus confirming the religious language of biblical revelation and of the Catholic theological tradition.[22] We must acknowledge the particular importance of the conciliar teaching on the real possibility of affirming knowledge of the existence of God from what is known of created reality by the "natural light of human reason," as well as from what is known from revelation by the light of faith.[23] However, the conciliar constitution did not indicate a particular preference for any one model of understanding, nor was it oriented toward a single philosophical-religious system or toward a specific theological method. It accepted rather the theory of the connaturalness or spontaneity of human religious feeling, which is typical of the patristic tradition; the apophatic theory of the divine transcendence and mystery, which is typical of Christian Platonism, and the cataphatic theory of the possibility of asserting knowledge of the divine reality through causality, which is typical of scholastic Aristotelianism.[24]

Faced with the modern challenge of unbelief and atheism, the traditional doctrine of the Church's magisterium concerning the affirmation of God's existence in the light of the first article of faith has had to deal first with the question of the possibility of overcoming nihilism and materialism, together with unbelief and religious indifferentism, by condemning theoretical atheism and every negation of Christian monotheism.[25] An alternative action taken by the magisterium of the Church has been the assertion of the possibility of "natural theology," which is also not identified with a particular school of philosophy. Thus, under Pius X, at the time of the modernist crisis (1907–1910), the papal teaching reaffirmed the possibility of natural theology to overcome the view of religiosity reduced to the immanentism of subjectivity and the individualism of the interior conscience, and it indicated that the way divine reality is to be demonstrated is through causality.[26] Later, when Pius XII took a position in the ecclesial debate on the "new theology" (1950), although he acknowledged that modern mentality has difficulty accepting a "natural theology," he again propounded the traditional thesis of the real possibility of knowing God by the natural light of reason and of reaching an acceptance of his existence as a reality both unique and transcendent, absolute and personal.[27]

However, the condemnation of theoretical atheism and the presentation of a rationally legitimate theism are not equivalent to acceptance of an extreme cataphatism or of theological rationalism. The Church's magisterium is always based on a notion of God as absolute mystery, transcendent and personal, incomprehensible and ineffable both in his reality and in his salvific self-revelation. Likewise, its affirmation of a "natural knowledge" of God as a precondition for the act of faith, an affirmation that rises above extreme traditionalism and fideism, does not signify any denial of the positive influence believing tradition has had in developing the response of faith. Still less does it signify a denial of the religious utility of the Christian revelation, including its moral necessity, so that truths concerning the religious attitude and moral behavior of human beings may be universally known and accepted with certainty and without error.[28] In like manner, the affirmation by the magisterium of possible culpability in atheism does not imply any exclusion from the mysterious divine salvific providence of those who without fault do not know God and search for him in their own way.[29]

The Search for God

Vatican II concerned itself in various documents with the theoretical and practical question of the human search for God. For example, the subject of the Dogmatic Constitution on Divine Revelation, *Dei Verbum* (1965), is the mystery of the God of revelation and of the faith, who out of his divine goodness and wisdom,, wished to reveal himself personally and to manifest his plan of salvation. The merciful and invisible God thus speaks to human beings and invites them to a mysterious participation in his life and in his infinite beatitude through words and deeds throughout the history of revelation and salvation that culminated in Christ, mediator and plenitude of that same eschatological salvific revelation.[30] The God of creation gives us a perpetual testimony of himself through created works. To all those who persevere in doing good, the God of salvation offers eternal life. The God of revelation always manifested himself to humanity, particularly in the history of the election of and covenant with the People of the Promise, as the one living and true God, creator of the world and just judge of history, provident Father, holy and merciful.[31] This revelation found its culmination in the manifestation of his eternal Son, divine word made flesh for our teaching and salvation, and, finally, with the mission of the divine Spirit, witness of the divine solidarity and present, to deliver us from evil and give us eternal life.[32] Moved by the light and grace of the Holy Spirit, humanity must give a free and total consent of will and reason to the Father who reveals himself in the Son, Jesus Christ.[33] The divine plan is revealed in the divine communication of self and of the salvific will. God, beginning and end of the universe, foundation of being and of knowing, offers in the divine revelation a knowledge of himself that is universal and readily available, infallible and certain.[34]

However, Vatican II not only affirmed the real possibility of the natural knowledge of God, but it took note also of the reality of religious knowledge and the existence of experience of the sacred as a constant search for the divine that probably has its most significant forms of expression in the great historical religions, whether in the living of a mystic and apophatic moment of the divine mystery or in living in the prophetic revelation and the faith of Abraham. Indeed, one of the merits of the conciliar Declaration on the Relation of the Church to Nonchristian Religions, *Nostra aetate* (1965), was that it called to the attention of Christians the theological value of the religious experience of God as provident Creator and merciful Father. In religious experience, human beings are really debating the greatest existential questions, those concerning being and living, good and evil, suffering and happiness, religious fear and desire for God.[35] The conciliar magisterium recognizes the presence of numerous cultural, moral, and spiritual values among the followers of non-Christian religions, in which they find a way of purification and a mystical refuge in God, the path to a liberation from worldly passions and a supreme illumination of the soul.[36] Furthermore, in the great monotheistic religions, such as Islam and Judaism, the one God is adored who is existing and living, provident Creator, protector of Abraham and almighty and merciful Lord of the covenant of salvation in history, which was to reach its culmination in the coming of Christ.[37]

In the Pastoral Constitution on the Church in the Modern World, *Gaudium et spes*, an important reference is made to the problem of atheism, in which the seriousness of the phenomenon as an explicit denial of the human search for God is remarked upon. Humanity's loss of a consciousness of transcendency condemns it to be like an unsolved problem.[38] However, the magisterium of the Church comments that frequently what is denied is more a perverse and false caricature of the divine than the "God of the Gospel."[39] The situation of those who seem to have lost even religious uneasiness, or who give unlimited value to the perishable goods of the earth, is more tragic. In other cases, where a heteronomic conception of the need for religion is involved, there is not so much an intention of denying the existence of God as of affirming humanity in its responsible autonomy and defending its legitimate emancipation from all kinds of unjust oppression.[40] Nevertheless, the pursuit of an historical liberation is not infrequently limited to a merely earthly horizon, with actions that are confined to the social, economic and political spheres. Although the Council alludes to possible moral guilt in atheism, it does not go deeper into this problem. It does not fail, however, to recognize that some share of responsibility for the unbelief of atheists is attributable to certain theoretical and, more important, practical failures of believers in practicing their religion inconsistently.[41] In any event, religion should not furnish a reason or a pretext for indifference on the part of the believer relative to the problems of justice among people, nor for an irresponsible detachment from historical problems. However, neither should involvement in the struggles of human life lead to neglect of the tremendous dimension of religious concern,[42] nor of human openness to the transcendence and to the God of faith.

The problem of the possibility of an inculpable atheism, in the theoretical sphere or the reflex conscience, which accompanies a practical theism in moral life, also finds an echo in the Dogmatic Constitution on the Church, *Lumen gentium* (1964). Whoever lives an upright life, even without reaching an explicit knowledge of God, is not excluded from salvation, since moral goodness does not come "without divine grace," and the elements of truth and goodness present in such a way of life represent a real "evangelical preparation."[43] But the possibility of a theoretical inculpable atheism cannot be extended to the practical area, since the values of morality and justice, of truth and goodness, are part of humanity's deepest being, and their negation cannot occur without fault. The Council made no pronouncement as to the possibility of remaining for a long period in a state of theoretical atheism. In the past, this hypothesis was denied, but at present there is little agreement on the subject because of the diversity and complexity of situations from the cultural and personal points of view.[44] The Decree on the Missionary Activity of the Church, *Ad gentes* (1965), also states that God in a mysterious way can attract to the faith people who, without fault, do not know the gospel. This corollary is derived from God's universal salvific will.[45]

Revelation and Mystery

Vatican II, in its constitutions, decrees, and declarations, manifests its continuity with the preceding ecclesial magisterium by reaffirming the Christian profession of faith in the one revealed and mysterious God. In contrast with other periods, the conciliar magisterium did not have to repulse a division of the divine sovereignty of the Father into a divine antithetic and supreme diarchy of the principles of evil and good, matter and spirit, creation and grace, old covenant and new covenant, because all of that was obsolete. The rebuttal of heretical doctrine concentrated rather on criticism of atheism as minimizing the mystery of humanity and hence the mystery of God.[46] The conciliar magisterium always preserved the uniqueness of the sovereignty of the one living and eternal God, Father Almighty, uncaused cause of the intradivine life, origin without origin of the created universe and of salvation history, absolutely different and distinct from the created world.[47]

The Christian religious experience takes as a given the insurmountable dialectic of religion and mystery, communication and ineffability, transcendence and history, unconditionality and personality. Every methodological dilemma that stubbornly proposes as antithetic alternatives a mystic theology of the divine transcendence or a moral theology of involvement in history helps to impoverish the richness of the Christian religious act by doing away with the tension between contemplation and ethics, liturgy and prophecy, theory and practice. The methodology of Christian theology can only follow the way of dialectical synthesis, in which religious reason meets intelligent faith. The ecstatic and contemplative reason adores the divine mystery, transcendent, absolute, infinite, eternal, and holy: faith, obedient to the gospel revelation of a just God and merciful Father, confesses the glory of the divine design of a universal salvific will in the mysterious epiphany of the cross and of grace. Christian theology is thus born as religious intelligence that searches for faith in order then to transform itself into the theological faith that seeks its own intelligibility. That is why, finally, theology is as it were a noble dialectical theory of the believing reason.[48]

From this insurmountable tension between the incomprehensibility of the divine mystery and the will to assert God's existence arises the fundamental problem of Christian theological language, the ultimate reference point of which is always the ineffable God. Consequently, every affirmation of faith must in some way reconcile in a corrective way cataphatic propositions and apophatic silence. The God of faith is linguistically ineffable, cognitively incomprehensible, ontologically transcendent, and personally elusive in his liberty.[49] Linguistic forms, which are finite and limited, do not succeed in expressing fully the absolute, unconditioned, and infinite content of the divine message and of the divine mystery. Hence, every affirmation about God must be expressed in an analogical and paradoxical language. In the analogy of being, the paradoxical is presented as an objective and insuperable tension between finite and infinite, the conditioned and the unconditioned.[50] In the analogy of faith, the paradoxical appears as unquestionable subjective tension between grace and sin, the astonishing revelation of infinite mercy and of the unmerited justification of the sinner.[51] In the analogy of symbols or of images, the paradoxical is also inevitable, since man is a theomorphic symbol of the divine reality, inasmuch as

he is created in the image of God[52]; but, in like manner, as a filial
image of the eternal Father and an expression of his divine self-
communication, the word incarnate, Jesus Christ, is a real symbol of the divine goodness.[53]

Faithful to the tradition of the Church, the conciliar magisterium has once more defended the real possibility of asserting
God's existence as a fact of universal religious experience. God
affirms himself in human existence as the foundation of being
and knowing through the light of religious reason and of faith
obedient to divine revelation. Through reality that is contingent
and immediate, relative and finite, absolute and ultimate reality,
unconditioned and infinite, may be sought and known, recognized and affirmed.[54] The search for the eternal and incomprehensible God is fulfilled in time, which is blessed with both
natural revelation and positive revelation. The mysterious God
searched for by religious reason reveals himself as the same and
identical God of the gospel, who is obeyed in faith. The mysterious God, uncaused foundation of and necessary reference point
of all contingent and caused reality, reveals himself as the God of
the covenant and the compassionate Father of salvation history.
The God *in se* reveals himself in the God *extra se*.[55]

Again, following Christian tradition, the conciliar magisterium affirms that the God of revelation and of faith is at the same
time absolute reality and personal reality. As absolute, God manifests himself as the most real and all-perfect being, wholly unique
and infinitely holy. He reveals himself also as the eternal living
being, omnipresent in his glory and majesty, his divine presence
being a spiritual and personal reality.[56] As personal reality, God
is seen as infinitely intelligent and free, omniscient in his wisdom, and omnipotent in his goodness, just in his judgment and
in his justice, merciful in his purpose, both in the order of creation and, above all, in the order of salvation.[57] God thus reveals
himself as omnipotent Creator in his mysterious and holy providence; as faithful Lord in his universal covenant of salvation; as
just king in his divine cosmical and historical sovereignty; as
compassionate Father full of mercy and goodness. However, this
transcendent and metacosmical God is identical to the faithful
Lord of the historical covenant. Similarly, the holy and eternal
king is identical to the bountiful Father of the eschatological
epiphany of divine grace.[58]

Consequently, in the light of the first article of faith, in the Christian religious act of affirming God's existence, as a fundamental numinous moment, there is synthesized dialectically both the sacramental and epiphanic, the mystic and ecstatic dimension of the religious experience of God as absolute and transcendent, and the moral and critical, the prophetic and evangelic dimension of the experience of the grace of a God who is personal and near, and who communicates himself eschatologically in the history of Christian salvation. To this irruption of the unconditioned into the sacred, as a theophany of the divine holiness, a response is given of mystical adoration of the glorious presence of the Eternal.[59] However, associated with the manifestation of the marvelous moment of numinous experience is an unconditioned exigency of divine justice, as absolute moral imperative and as tension relative to an unconditional awe.[60] In the insuperable dialectic between mystical identity and ethical difference, this tension can be resolved only, in an unhoped for and surprising way, in the divine paradox of a theology of the cross and of grace.[61] In this way, a complex structure of the believing religious act is indirectly confirmed through existential confrontation with the divine mystery searched for in his ineffable holiness and eternal presence, recognized in his just wisdom and in his compassionate faithfulness.[62]

History and Transcendence

The response to man's search for God as ultimate term of the religious act is found in a particular formulation in the first article of the Christian faith. In accordance with ecclesial Tradition, the conciliar magisterium tried, both in Vatican I and most particularly in Vatican II, to synthesize in a dialectic of identity and difference, the conflicting demands of revelation and mystery, transcendency and history, unconditionality and personality. Between the Creator and the creature, between God and the world, there is a qualitatively infinite difference.[63] Between the mysterious and provident God of creation and the Lord revealed in the history of salvation as Father of goodness, there is a profound and absolutely unique identity.[64]

On his part, the mysterious, incomprehensible, and ineffable

God manifests himself in the works of creation and in the moral conscience, in the religious sentiments of piety and adoration, and, above all, in the experience of revelation and of faith. However, out of the dialectic of identity between revelation and mystery, there comes an extremely important conclusion—the hidden and mysterious God groped for by religious reason is the same and identical God revealed and obeyed in faith. In other words, the veiled God who dwells in the inaccessible light of mystery, foundation and abyss of contingent reality, is the very same God revealed in the history of salvation as merciful Father. The incomprehensible and eternal God becomes known as Father in the privileged time of revelation and grace.[65]

Likewise, the transcendent and distant God becomes immanent and near in history. The metacosmical God of creation reveals himself as the God in the history of salvation. The God of the covenant with Israel is also the God of nations and the God of creation and of Christian hope. God is one, unique and absolutely singular. The self-evident truth of monotheism keeps all its force in proclaiming the absolute divine sovereignty over nature and history, over mysticism and morality. God manifests himself therefore as being at the same time both absolute and personal. On the one hand, God appears as numinous reality, unconditioned and infinite; on the other, he reveals himself as also the basis for invincible trust and uncontainable religious awe.[66]

For this reason, the divine reality can never be a matter of indifference to man, not only relative to his experience of the transcendent ontological relationsihp, but also to his consciousness of a fundamental moral imperative. The created subject searches for God not only as an absolute object, but above all as infinite subject of absolute power, truth, and goodness. In the eschatological epiphany, the mysterious God reveals himself as compassionate Father; the unique and eternal, infinite and ultimate reality manifests itself as extremely intimate and personal, singular and proximate. Thus, the Christian creed must always begin by professing, as the first proposition of faith, the supreme identity between the one God, almighty creator, and the holy Father, omnipresent ally, paradoxical hope of concrete existence.[67]

The mysterious and transcendent God who reveals himself and intervenes in his immanence in creation and salvation as providence and grace arouses in the redeemed creature a mystic awe and paradoxical love, profound dependency and mysterious communion, filial religiosity and fraternal compassion. The Christian theory of the divine mystery thus ends in a believing practice of justice and goodness. In like manner, the search for the God of religion ends in the adoration and service of the God of the gospel of the kingdom, who is the Father of love and of hope. The revelation of the divine sovereignty announces a hope anticipated in time and consummated in the kingdom of God. But the Christian utopia is not limited to the horizon of the temporal, although it implies it in some way, nor does it dissociate itself from personal conversion or from community reconciliation.[68]

Since Christians have been invited to transform the world by seeking a profound interpenetration between the unconditioned values of the kingdom of God and the conditioned reality of history, the Christian imperative of fraternity and hope must find room for involvement in social reality, so as to promote a deep renewal of the temporal order in accordance with the values of the gospel. Faith cannot therefore remain indifferent to efforts made to transform the world in a positive way.[69] The dialectical tension between unity and difference, between commitment in history and the coming of the kingdom, will not be resolved by contemplative immobility, but will find its proper sphere of action in the concrete reality of human existence and the social community. Indeed, the tension between the unlimited scope of the demands of the kingdom and the limited realizations of history will not be resolved by having an impassable hiatus, nor by a total identification either.[70] Between the kingdom of God and human history, or between faith and politics, there can be neither confusion nor identity, nor yet indifferent separation in a stoical manner. The ecclesial community, prophetically bearing witness to the demands of the kingdom and to the power of the gospel, cannot fail to show its solidarity with the poor and oppressed.[71] The prophetical denouncement of injustice and the eschatological announcement of the gospel are the two edges of the sword of the word entrusted to the community of the disciples of Jesus.

Hence, the teaching of Vatican II is seen to be fully consistent with the intentions originally indicated by the Council Fathers themselves, those of responding to the wishes of people who "search for God," and at the same time to bear witness to the

Father's love, shown in the gift of the Son and in the gift of the
Holy Spirit, for our reconciliation and sanctification in love,[72]
but also to be solicitous preferentially for the poorest and humblest, and to collaborate with the divine salvific, eschatological,
and historical will.[73]

Translated from the Spanish by Louis-Bertrand Raymond and
Edward Hughes.

Notes

1. R. Aubert, Vatican I (Paris, 1964); A. Vanneste, "Le problème
de Dieu de Vatican I à Vatican II," RClerAfr, 22 (1967), 234–251; H.J.
Pottmeyer, Der Glaube vor dem Anspruch der Wissenschaft (Fribourg,
1968); J. Alfaro, "La Costituzione Dei Filius del Vaticano I e le sue
ripercussioni sul Vaticano II," Oss.Rom. (7 December 1969); H.
Brouillard, "Le concept de révélation de Vatican I à Vatican II," in J.
Audinet et al., Révélation de Dieu et langage des hommes (Paris, 1972),
35–49; E. Klinger and K. Wittstadt (eds.), Glaube im Prozess. Christsein
nach dem II. Vatikanum, Für Karl Rahner (Fribourg, 1984).

2. Irenaeus, Ad Haer, I, 10, 1 (PG 7, 549); Tertullian, Apolog., 17
(PL 1, 375); Origen, C. Celsum, I, 23 (PG 11, 701); Cyril Hier.,
Catech., 4, 4 (PG 33, 457); Augustine, De vera relig., 25, 46 (PL 34,
142).

3. Clement of Rome, Ad Cor., I, 58, 2 (Funk I: 1972); Justine,
Apolog., I, 65 (PG 6, 428); Ambrose, De myster., 7, 42 (PL 16, 402).

4. DS 1–6, 10–11, 40–42, 60, 125, 150.

5. DS 13–19, 25–30, 71–76.

6. DS 410.

7. DS 139, 441, 451, 490, 525, 617.

8. DS 623, 626, 627, 633.

9. DS 726, 727.

10. DS 745.

11. DS 800.

12. DS 806.

13. DS 808.

14. DS 851.

15. DS 951–953, 973–974, 978.

16. DS 1330–1336.

17. DS 1862.

18. DS 2751, 2755, 2756, 2765, 2768, 2811–2814.

19. DS 2828–2829, 2853–2857.

20. DS 2841–2847, 2901–2905.

21. R. Aubert, "La Constitution 'Dei Filius' du Concile du Vati-

can," in *De doctrina councilii Vaticani Primi* (Rome, 1969), 46–121; J.M.G. Gomez-Heras, "Sapientia in mysterio," "El misterio de fe y su inteligencia racional según el Vaticano II," *Burgense*, 10 (1969), 111–174; V. von Kantfenbach and G. Müller (eds.), *Reformatio und Confessio* (Berlin, 1965), 231–243.

22. DS 3001–3003, 3021–3023.

23. DS 3004–3005, 3026–3028.

24. M. Chossat, "Dieu I," *DTC*, 4, 839–842.

25. DS 3021.

26. DS 3420, 3275–3277, 3538.

27. DS 3875, 3892.

28. DS 3001; cf. 3005, 3028.

29. DS 3869–3872.

30. R. Latourelle, "La Révélation selon la Constitution *Dei Verbum*," *Gregorianum*, 47 (1966), 5–40; H. de Lubac, "Commentaire du préambule et du chapitre I," in *La révélation divine* (Paris, 1968), 157–302; N. Silanes, "Trinidad y revelación en la *Dei Verbum*," *Est. Trin.*, 17 (1983), 143–214.

31. "Placuit Deo in sua bonitate et sapientia Seipsum revelare et notum facere sacramentum voluntatis suae" (*DV* 2); ". . . erudivit ad Se Solum Deum vivum et verum, providum Patrem et judicem justum agnoscendum" (*DV* 3).

32. "Nulla jam nova revelatio publica expectanda est" (*DV* 4).

33. "Deo revelanti praestanda est oboeditio fidei" (*DV* 5)

34. "Deus Seipsum atque aeterna voluntatis suae decreta circa hominum salutem manifestare ac communicare voluit" (*DV* 6).

35. J. Goetz, "Summi Numinis vel etiam Patris," in *L'Eglise et les missions* (Rome, 1966), 51–63; K. Rahner, "Uber die Heilsbedeutung der nichtchristlichen Religionen," in *Evangelizzazione e culture* (Rome, 1976), I, 295–303; H. Wandelfels, "Theologie der nichtchristlichen Religionen. Konsequenzen aus *Nostra aetate*," in *Glaube im Prozess* (Fribourg, 1984), 757–775.

36. ". . . illud ultimum et ineffabile mysterium quod nostram existentiam amplectitur" (*NA* 1); ". . . perceptio illius arcanae virtutis quae cursui rerum et eventibus vitae humanae praesens est" (*NA* 2).

37. ". . . unicum Deum adorant, viventem et subsistentem, misericordem et omnipotentem, Creatorem caeli et terrae" (*NA* 4); ". . . populi omnes una voce Dominum invocabunt" (*NA* 4); "Deum omnium Patrem invocare" (*NA* 5).

38. T. Fornoville, "La Constitution 'L'Eglise dans le monde de ce temps' en face de l'athèisme," *Studia Moralia*, 4 (1966), 263–290; R. Belda, "La Iglesia frente al ateismo moderno," in *Estudios sobre la Constitución Gaudium et Spes* (Bilbao, 1967), 45–59; P. Ladrière, "L'athéisme au Concile Vatican II," *ASocRel*, 32, (1971), 53–84.

39. "Alii Deum sibi ita effingunt, ut illud figmentum, quod repudiant, nullo modo Deus sit Evangelii" (*GS* 19).

40. ". . . optatum autonomiae hominis eo usque perducit ut contra qualemcumque a Deo dependentiam difficultatem suscitet" (*GS* 20).

41. ". . . dictamen conscientiae suae non secuti, culpae expertes non sunt" (*GS* 19).

42. "Omnis homo interea sibi ipsi remanet quaestio insoluta, subobscure percepta" (*GS* 21).

43. "Neque ab aliis, qui in umbris et imaginibus Deum ignotum quaerunt, ab hujusmodi Deus ipse longe est" (*LG* 16).

44. K. Rahner, "Atheismus," *SM* I, 375.

45. "Etsi ergo Deus viis sibi notis homines Evangelium sine eorum culpa ignorantes ad fidem adducere possit" (*AG* 7).

46. "Ecclesia vero, etiamsi atheismum omnino reiicit" (*GS* 19).

47. "Aeternus Pater, liberrimo et arcano sapientiae ac bonitatis suae consilio, mundum universum creavit, homines ad participandam vitam divinam elevare decrivit" (*LG* 2).

48. ". . . adjuventur ad perspiciendos nexus qui intercedunt inter argumenta philosophica et mysteria salutis quae in theologia superiore lumine fidei considerantur" (*OT* 15).

49. "ineffabile mysterium" (*NA* 1); "ex ineffabili misericordia" (*NA* 4); "ineffabilem Dei benignitatem" (*DV* 13); "ineffabilis Ipsius consilii" (*GS* 343).

50. "ad infinitam pulchritudinem divinam" (*SC* 122); "infinite superat" (*AG* 13).

51. "in Jesu Christo justificati" (*LG* 40); "justificati ex fide" (*UR* 3).

52. "ad imaginem et similitudinem" (*AA* 7); "ad imaginem Dei creatos" (*NA* 5)

53. "imago Dei invisibilis" (*LG* 2; *GS* 22).

54. *DV* 6; cf. DS 3004; *GS* 12: "capacem suum Creatorem cognoscendi et amandi."

55. *DV* 2, 6; cf. DS 3005.

56. "solus Sanctus" (*PO* 5); "secreta Dei praesentia" (*AG* 9, cf. 15).

57. *LG* 15: "in Deum Patrem omnipotentem"; *DV* 15: "Deus justus et misericors."

58. *DV* 3: "solum Deum vivum et verum, providum Patrem et judicem justum."

59. "ad gloriam Dei" (*LG* 16); "ad gloriam Patris" (*AG* 7).

60. *LG* 9: "Deo acceptus est quicumque timet Eum et operatur justitiam."

61. *LG* 13: "gratia Dei ad salutem vocati"; *LG* 56i: "omnipotentis Dei gratia."

62. *SC* 6: "fiunt veri adoraorees, quos Pater quaerit"; cf. *AG* 3.

63. DS 3001: "re et essentia a mundo distinctus"; "ineffabiliter excelsus."

64. *DV* 14: "tamquam unicum Deum verum et vivum."

65. GS 41: "Etsi enim idem Deus sit Salvator qui et Creator."

66. *Ibid.*: "idem quoque Dominus et historiae humanae et historiae salutis."

67. *SC* 6: "Aeterno Patri"; *LG* 2: "Aeternus Pater"; *DV* 3: "providum Patrem"; *AA* 4: "Deo et Patri"; *NA* 5: "Patrem invocare"; *GS* 92: "Pater principium omnium"; *AG* 2: "Principium sine principio."

68. GS 39: "His in terris Regnum jam in mysterio adest."

69. *AA* 7: "Circa mundum vero consilium Dei est, ut homines concordi animo ordinem rerum temporalium instaurent jugiterque perficiant."

70. GS 39: "Ideo, licet progressus terrenus a Regni Christi augmento sedulo distinguendus sit, inquantum tamen ad societatem humanam melius ordinandum conferre potest, Regni Dei magnopere interest."

71. LG 8: "(Ecclesia) in pauperibus et patientibus imaginem Fundatoris sui Pauperis et patientis agnoscit, eorum inopiam, sublevare satagit."

72. "Nuntius ad universos homines Summo Pontifice assentiente a Patribus missus ineunte Concilio Oecumenico Vaticano II," (20 October 1962); *AAS, 54,* (1962); 822–823.

73. *Ibid.,* 823–824.

CHAPTER 37

Humanity in the Light of Christ in the Second Vatican Council

Luis Ladaria, S.J.

Summary

The Second Vatican Council, in GS 22, asserts that the mystery of humanity takes on light in the mystery of the incarnate word. This basic principle of the Council's anthropology is elaborated upon mainly in the first part of the pastoral constitution. Although it did not develop all the facets of this central assertion, we can say that the Council, in substance, has remained consistent with it.

———

———

Vatican II did not expressly dedicate one of its documents to the mystery of humanity. But the Pastoral Constitution on the Church in the Modern world, *Gaudium et Spes,* is especially concerned about humanity. It is declared in GS 3: ". . . the pivotal point of our total presentation will be man himself, whole and entire, body and soul, heart and conscience, mind and will." And it could not have been any other way: the problems of the modern world on which the Church wants to shed light are the problems of humanity. These should be approached from the anthropological point of view, and will be solved according to one's vision of humanity. God wants to save humanity in all its personal and social dimensions and the Church shares "the joys and hopes, griefs and anxieties of the men of this age" (GS 1). This solidarity with humanity does not originate from outside:

the Church and the Christians are part of the world; they live the conditions and situations lived by the rest of humanity; they share the good fortune and misfortune of all humanity.

The vision of humanity, as expounded in the first chapters of *Gaudium et spes,* is the most exhaustive we can find in the Council's documents. I do not attempt to examine all the aspects of the Council's anthropology,[1] limiting myself to investigate how the Council determines Christ's relationship with man, mainly in the Constitution *Gaudium et spes,* but also in the other documents of the Council, so as to verify to what degree they reflect the doctrine put forward in GS.

Christ and Humanity in the Constitution *Gaudium et spes*

As pointed out, GS 3 specifies that humanity will be the pivotal point of the statements that follow. And, in this same passage, it is mentioned that there is a divine seed (*divinum quoddam semen*) in humanity; and the Church proclaims its existence by making known its most eminent vocation. At this early stage, no reference has been yet made to Christ: the first one can be found in 10, 2, in the conclusion of the introductory statement, in which the Council reaffirms the intention to answer humanity's deeper questions. Christ alone, dead and risen for us, can give us, through the Holy Spirit, the moral strength we need to measure up to our destiny. He alone can make our salvation possible. It is then specified:

[The Church] likewise holds that in her most benign Lord and Master can be found the key, the focal point, and the goal of all human history. She also maintains that beneath all changes there are many realities which do not change and which have their ultimate foundation in Christ, who is the same yesterday, today, and forever (Heb. 13:8). Hence in the light of Christ, the image of the unseen God, the firstborn of every creature (Col. 1:15), the Council wishes to speak to all men in order to illuminate the mystery of man and to cooperate in finding the solution to the outstanding problems of our time.

We must briefly dwell on the program contained in this text. Besides illuminating the mystery of humanity, the Church wishes to collaborate in solving the problems of our age. We must keep in mind the practical, "pastoral" dimension of GS, even though it will not always be highlighted in the following pages. In stating its intention to shed light on the mystery of humanity, the Council implicitly invites us to pay attention to Christ as foundation of that which does not pass away and therefore is the key, focal point, and goal of history. Christ is also the foundation of the essence of humanity, whose mystery is to be illuminated. It is not specified yet how Christ sheds his light on the mystery of humanity. But Christ's titles, quoted from Col. 1:15, refer to his condition as foundation (a theme already mentioned) and as revealer (which is discussed in No. 22). Everything, including humanity, is oriented toward Christ and finds in him its foundation. All history is interpreted with a christological key, even though, especially with regard to creation, this idea is merely suggested.

To understand the significance of this text, we have to recall the method followed in the "Introductory Statement." The direct starting point is not the truth of faith, but the experience of human beings of our age that is common to believers and unbelievers: the signs of the times question all and are lived by all. And, finally, Christ appears as the Christian answer to all these questions. Hence, the fact that the mystery of Christ is not mentioned from the beginning does not mean that it was not always kept in mind. In all four chapters of the first part of GS, the same method is followed. The question of humanity asked in No. 3 must be answered, according to No. 10, in the light of Christ.

In No. 11, the introduction to the first part, just as in No. 12, the beginning of the chapter dedicated to the dignity of the human person, the question is again asked: "What is man?"[2] But, in contrast to the "Introductory Statement," the answer comes from divine revelation and is given gradually, starting with the Old Testament. According to Genesis 1:26 (cf. Wis. 2:23), human beings were made in God's image.[3] By this the Council means two things: human beings are capable of knowing and loving their creator; and they were appointed masters of all earthly creatures so that they might subdue them and use them to God's glory. The dignity of humanity and its condition as God's image are clearly connected. The citation of Psalm 8:5–7 emphasizes the prominent place held by humanity within the universe. The social nature of human beings, which is not linked to the theme of the image, also corresponds to God's design as creator. This paragraph on human beings as God's image concludes with a reference to the goodness of creation, which is crowned by the appearance of human beings. An answer to the question of the nature of humanity, mainly based on the Old Testament, has taken shape. A purely inductive method was not used; what is central to faith in Christ was not put forward. But, we know that from the very beginning, the Council had Christ in mind.

The chapter dedicated to the dignity of the human person draws its inspiration from the Bible, without this time confining itself to the Old Testament or renouncing the language of practical experience. It speaks, in No. 13, of sin that distorts God's image in humanity and puts it into disharmony with itself, with others, and with all created things. In this number and in the following ones dealing with the unity between humanity's body and soul, its intelligence and wisdom, its moral conscience and liberty, and the mystery of its death, nothing can be found that might direcly interest us. It contains no reference to Christ, except in No. 18, where mention is made that we owe our hope to live forever to the redemption and resurrection of Jesus.[4] In No. 17 it is mentioned that "authentic freedom is an exceptional sign of the divine image within man"; God has willed that human beings be left "in the hands of [their] own counsel" (Sir. 15:14), so that they can seek their creator spontaneously; the theme of the image reappears, but without referring to the New Testament. From Nos. 18 to 21, the text deals with atheism and the attitude of the Church towards this phenomenon, and serves as an introduction to No. 22, in which a link is explicitly made between Christ and what has been exposed up to that point. We do know that the Council meant to illuminate the mystery of humanity; but, after all, since the Council's formal answer is based on divine revelation, we do not understand why the reference to Jesus was deferred to the end.

But, first, let us examine what GS 22 says about the light shed by Christ on the mystery of humanity. This highly theological text undoubtedly contrasts with the timidity of GS when it touches on questions more strictly theological.[5] Moreover, the idea that forms the basis of this paragraph did not emerge unexpectedly. That the christological foundation of anthropology be mentioned

was a wish many times expressed in the Council halls.[6] The text
we now have adequately meets these wishes and expectations.
The following is the content of the first paragraph of No. 22:

> The truth is that only in the mystery of the incarnate Word
> does the mystery of man take on light. For Adam, the first
> man, was a figure of Him who was to come, namely, Christ
> the Lord. Christ, the final Adam, by the revelation of the
> mystery of the Father and His love, fully reveals man to man
> himself and makes his supreme calling clear. It is not surpris-
> ing, then, that in Him all the aforementioned truths find root
> and attain their crown.

To begin with, we can focus attention on the last sentence.
All that was said in the first chapter about humanity and its
dignity finds meaning in faith in Christ. Thus, only from what
has been said concerning Christ can we understand and interpret
what up to now has been pointed out. After all, whatever has
been asserted of humanity was eminently affirmed of Christ. And
although the Council's intention is unequivocal, we may nevertheless ask if the Council has put into practice, with consistent
rigor, the principles here mentioned.

The last sentence of the paragraph, which gives us a key to
interpret not only what has already been declared, but also what
will be subsequently stated, is in accordance with what has been
affirmed in the preceding lines. What in No. 10 still remained
somewhat obscure is here most clearly expressed. The Council
talks about humanity in the light of Christ, not only because
everything takes on light in Christ, but because in the incarnate
Son, we find out what humanity is and to what end it is called.
The light in question here does not come from outside, but from
the very reality of Christ's life. Adam is the figure of the Son to
be incarnate. The reader will find in a footnote Tertullian's
commentary on the subject, which is rich in meaning.[7] One
could find in Irenaeus passages expressing the same idea: the first
human being, fashioned by God's hands from the silt of the
earth, is already the image of Christ to be incarnate.[8] Adam does
not explain Christ: Christ explains Adam. Thanks only to Christ
only we are able to know humanity. The revelation of humanity's nature is given together with the revelation of the Father;
humanity is therefore the inseparable consequence of revelation.

By revealing the Father's love to us and thus revealing himself as the Son, Christ reveals through his life humanity's vocation: from the very beginning we were called to be in communion with God, to be his children in the Son. It follows from what the Council has declared in the beginning of this paragraph that the Son, in his human life, makes God's design on humanity known to us. This declaration goes back to the earliest period of Christian tradition, although we must admit that of late this insight has been obscured by an overemphasized distinction between the natural and the supernatural order.[9]

The second paragraph of No. 22 again quotes Col. 1:15, which appeared in No. 10: Christ, "the image of the invisible God." He who revealed God to us is also the perfect human being (not simply a perfect human being). Precisely because he is the Son of God, revealing God to us through his perfect humanity, he in turn reveals humanity's vocation to us: hence, the gospel makes sense by insisting on following Jesus. Further on, we are told that Christ restores in human beings the divine likeness that had been disfigured from the first sin onward.[10] Although the first paragraph might suggest it, no mention is made that the original image and likeness that have been altered by sin have some connection with Christ: we will have to come back to this point. The human nature that Christ has taken on was not absorbed by his divinity; likewise our human nature, by coming into contact with Christ, does not disappear nor become diminished. On the contrary, it is exalted to its supreme dignity. The Council then tells us that through his incarnation, Christ has joined himself to all humanity. Once more here we have a statement inspired by the Church's great tradition: in some way, all humankind has been assumed by the Son.[11] But the Council, in contrast to the Fathers of the Church, did not remain on the ontological level, but entered into the existential and practical levels of human life[12]: "He worked with human hands, and loved with a human heart. . . . He has truly been made one of us, like us in all things except sin" (Heb. 4:15).

The third paragraph focuses on Christ who abandoned himself to death for our sins. Here the solidarity of Jesus with us, which was mentioned previously, reaches its ultimate goal: not only life, but also death attains new meaning in the person of Christ.

The fourth paragraph, from our standpoint, is particularly significant: it must be considered in connection with the second paragraph, which spoke of Christ, God's image, and restoring our disfigured divine likeness. In this paragraph, it is clearly stated that the Christian is conformed to the likeness and image of Christ. But this time, the theme of the image emerges as interpreted in the light of the New Testament and with explicit reference to Christ. In a footnote, the Council alludes to Romans 8:29 and Colossians 3:10–14; but we deplore the absence of a reference to 1 Corinthians 15:45–49, which might have linked together protology and eschatology. Indeed, in the first paragraph, the christological dimension of God's image in humanity from the very beginning is acknowledged only implicitly. And this point is not further clarified in paragraph No. 2, where restoring the likeness is discussed. It is however very clearly emphasized that the conformity of the Christian to Christ's likeness and association with the paschal mystery fulfill God's original design for humanity.

This same idea is expressed with even greater force in the following paragraph, which mentions that what has just been said "holds true not only for Christians, but for all men of good will in whose hearts grace works in an unseen way." All are called to be united with Christ, since Christ died for all and "since the ultimate vocation of man is in fact one and divine." Again Christ's universal redemption is stated, but with more emphasis on redemption and eschatology than on creation. From these premises, we can conclude that "we ought to believe that the Holy Spirit in a manner known only to God offers to every man the possibility of being associated with the paschal mystery."[13] All men are called to be saved and associated with the life of the dead and risen Jesus. The mention of the Holy Spirit is indeed most appropriate: in him we conform to Christ and are incorporated into his life and death. Something would have been indeed missing in a text so rich in christological inspiration if the Spirit who carries through the Son's work had been forgotten.

The last paragraph insists on the greatness of the mystery of humanity, of its supernatural and unique vocation: such light has to come from Christian revelation. In Christ, light is shed on the mystery of sorrow and death. By rising from death, he lavished life upon us "so that, as [children] in the Son, we can cry out in the Spirit: Abba, Father!" The Trinitarian dimension of our salvation is made patent in this text, which is definitely inspired by Saint Paul (cf. Rom. 8:15, Gal. 4:6). Humanity reaches its

fulfillment when, through the work of the Holy Spirit, it partici-
pates as children in the Son in the unique relationship between
Jesus and his Father. Thus, salvation takes on a community
dimension, an insight that the Council brings to the fore in
Chapter 2.

Having said this, there is every good reason for insisting on the
importance of GS 22. In Jesus, we find our true identity. From
Christ alone Christian anthropology receives its definitive illumination. Thus, the incarnation cannot be viewed as the more or
less extrinsic culmination of a natural or created order that is
turned in on itself.

Chapter 2 of the first part of GS is dedicated to the human
community: following the method used in Chapter 1, Christ is
expressly mentioned only toward the end. On several occasions,
the theme of humanity's dignity as God's image does emerge, but
without mention of Christ (GS 24, 26, 29). In No. 24, it is
pointed out that "man is the only creature on earth which God
willed for itself." Number 32, which concludes Chapter 2, repeats some ideas of No. 22, and applies them to humanity's social
nature:

> This communitarian character is developed and consummated
> in the work of Jesus Christ. For the very Word made flesh
> willed to share in the human fellowship. He was present at the
> wedding of Cana. . . . He revealed the love of the Father and
> the sublime vocation of man. . . . He sanctified the human
> ties, especially family ones, from which social relationships
> arise. He willingly obeyed the laws of his country. He chose to
> lead the life proper to an artisan of His time and place.
>
> In his preaching He clearly taught the sons of God to treat
> one another as brothers. . . . He commanded His apostles to
> preach to all peoples the gospel message so that the human
> race might become Family of God, in which the fullness of the
> Law would be love.
>
> As the first-born of many brethren and through the gift of
> His Spirit, He founded after His death and resurrection a new
> brotherly community composed of all those who receive Him
> in faith and love. This He did through His Body which is the
> Church. There everyone, as members one of the other, would
> render mutual service according to the different gifts bestowed
> on each.

This solidarity must be constantly increased until that day on which it will be brought to perfection. Then, saved by grace, men will offer flawless glory to God as a family beloved of God and of Christ their Brother.[14]

As we mentioned, there is here an echo of the ideas contained in No. 22. In solidarity with all men, Jesus participated in various social classes. He thus revealed the love of the Father and the vocation of humanity in terms of brotherhood. God's design for humankind consists in its being united to Christ and to His Body which is the Church. One might well ask if Christ and the divine design of union with him represent the first and original link between men, or if a preexisting solidarity, based on whatever other factor, finds in Jesus its perfection.[15] As we have pointed out regarding No. 22, the link between creation and Christ still remains somewhat obscure here.

Chapter 3 of the first part of GS once more saves until last (and, this time, in No. 3B, which is the next to last paragraph) the christological statement. Here again we must point out the mention of creation of humanity as God's image without reference to Christ (No. 34). However, No. 38 adds some ideas that had not previously been expressed: "God's Word, through whom all things were made, was Himself made flesh and dwelt on the earth of men. Thus He entered the world's history as a perfect man, taking that history up into Himself and summarizing it." He is the one who made that history and that world which he assumed and summarized: the unity between the order of creation and the order of redemption comes from Christ. He is the perfect human being, as stated in No. 22. And, as the perfect human being, he teaches us the love of the Father and at the same time reveals to us that human beings find their perfection in love. Thus, with a few variants, the ideas of Nos. 22 and 32 are repeated. Jesus revealed to us the love of the Father through his concrete life, death, and resurrection. And, through the gift of the Spirit, he makes the heart of humanity capable of loving.

Chapter 4 of the first part, dealing with the Church's mission in the world, once more states the nature of humanity in the light of Christ: "Since it has been entrusted to the Church to reveal the mystery of God, who is the ultimate goal of man, she opens up to man at the same time the meaning of his own existence, that is, the innermost truth about himself" (GS 41,

1). The revelation of God and the truth about humanity are linked to Christ's message. Humankind's aspirations, as are mentioned further on, are answered only in God: that is why it never can be absolutely indifferent to the problem of religion. Humanity will always question itself about the meaning of life and death. The very existence of the Church reminds it of these problems: "But only God, who created man to His own image and ransomed him from sin, provides a fully adequate answer to these questions. This He does through what He has revealed in Christ His Son who became man" (GS 41, 1). We recognize here the idea that Christ reveals the being of humankind. For the third time, we are told that Jesus is the perfect human being: by following Christ, a human being perfects its own being. And, once more, mention is made of the creation of human beings in the image of God without reference to Christ, although the latter is suggested by the context. And later on it is declared:

For though the same God is Savior and Creator, Lord of human history as well of salvation history, in the divine arrangement itself the rightful autonomy of the creature, and particularly of man, is not withdrawn. Rather it is re-established in its own dignity and strengthened in it (GS 41, 6).

Here the unity between creation and salvation is strongly emphasized, but once more no express reference to Christ is made.[16]

Number 45, with which both Chapter 4 and the first part of GS end, again presents Christ as the center of humankind and as the goal of history:

God's Word, by whom all things were made, was Himself made flesh so that as perfect man He might save all men and sum up all things in Himself. The Lord is the goal of human history, the focal point of the longings of history and of civilization, the center of the human race, the joy of every heart, and the answer to all its yearnings. He it is whom the Father raised from the dead, lifted on high, and stationed at His right hand, making him Judge of the living and the dead. Enlivened and united in His Spirit, we journey toward the consummation of human history, one which fully accords with the counsel of God's love: "To re-establish all things in Christ, both those in the heavens and those on the earth" (Eph. 1:10).

For the fourth time, Christ is said to be the perfect person. It is also said that the incarnation is oriented to the consummation and redemption of all in him; Jesus is the goal of history toward which all things are converging. He is the center of the human race: this expression is not explained, although No. 10 already spoke about Christ as the center of history in an context referring to creation and its eschatological consummation. In the present, immediate context, reference seems to be made only to the latter, although, at the beginning of the paragraph, mention is made of Jesus' mediation in creation.[17]

By and large, we can say that this first part of GS sheds considerable light on the subject of our paper, and thus achieves the goal of treating humanity in the light of Christ. The anthropology presented to us here finds in christology both its foundation and culmination. Through his life, Jesus has revealed to us the true vocation of humanity, by manifesting to us the paternity of God. These two themes are thus closely linked. Their logical connection originates in the divine filiation of Jesus, which He also lived as a man. That is why Jesus is the perfect person; insofar as we follow him, we become more human. History and salvation, which is found only through incorporation into his body, are making their way toward Him.

Humanity's definite vocation is its divine vocation: therefore, we must refer to Christ so as to understand not only the Christian but also humanity in general. Yet, we cannot help noticing that in the majority of passages dealing with human beings as created in the image of God no reference is made to Christ.[17] Were we called to reproduce the image of Christ from the very beginning of creation? As we have discovered, we are provided with all the elements required to answer affirmatively, but without total clarity. Likewise, the mediation of Christ in creation seems to be mentioned at least three times (Nos. 10, 38, and 45). Yet, in one passage in the second part of GS dealing with creation and redemption, allusion is made to Christ only in his relationship to the latter: "[In the human person] the values of intellect, will, conscience, and fraternity are pre-eminent. These values are all rooted in God the Creator and have been wonderfully restored and elevated in Christ" (GS 61). But somewhat earlier, in GS 57, which discusses the creative wisdom of God which probably refers to Christ, it is added that: "[The Word of God] before becoming flesh in order to save all things and to recapitulate them in Himself, was in the world already as '*the true light that enlightens every man*' " (Jn. 1:9).[19]

The final editing of the passages of the Constitution is not always successful: all statements do not perfectly match, even those that are relatively near each other. The intricate process of composing the text without doubt explains many of these discrepancies. Nevertheless, the text positively asserts the divine and unique vocation of all men in Christ who, by revealing to us the love of the Father, teaches us our true identity before God. The mystery of man is clarified only through the mystery of the word incarnate.

Christ and Humanity
in the Other Documents of the Council

Obviously, we cannot expect to find that these other documents systematically discuss the problem we have before us. But the various allusions we find in them allow us to establish to what extent the governing ideas of *Gaudium et spes* have been repeated.

Some of the themes familiar to us reappear in AG 8: "By manifesting Christ, the Church reveals to men the real truth about their condition and their total vocation. For Christ is the source and model of that renewed humanity . . . to which all aspire." Once more the Council did not go beyond what is declared in GS: the relationship between Christ and creation stays in the background.

Apart from GS, few allusions are made to the human condition of being image of God. The following is of significance to me:

> We cannot in truthfulness call upon that God who is the Father of all if we refuse to act in a brotherly way toward certain men, created though they be to God's image. A man's relationship with God the Father and his relationship with his brother men are so linked together that Scripture says: "He who does not have love does not know God" (1 Jn. 4:8) (NA 5).

The whole context of this passage tells us about Christ; moreover, the divine filiation and fraternity between people are based on Christ.[20] To recognize not only God but also Christ in one's brother is part of the authentic teaching of the New Testament. It is nevertheless a fact that the theme of humanity as God's image has not been directly linked to Christ. In another passage, we read that God's face and presence reveal themselves in those who with greater perfection are transformed into the image of Christ.[21]

Such indeed is the vocation of humanity. The context of this statement is found in Chapter 7 of *Lumen gentium* on the eschatological nature of the Church. Here the centrality of Christ is more clearly expressed in relation to the consummation of the world and of humankind than in relation to their origin. But, in No. 3 of *LG* 3, we are told: "All men are called to this union with Christ, who is the light of the world, from whom we go forth, through whom we live, and towards whom our journey leads us." Therefore, Christ is the origin and term of humanity, his beginning and end. The content of these statements is not explained further.

The centrality of Christ is often brought to light in connection with two more points. First, the Council very often repeats that the vocation of person, as a child of God, is incorporation into Christ and life in him.[22] Second, it is emphasized that humanity fulfills this vocation inasmuch as it incorporates itself into the Church, Body of Christ, who is on the move toward the ultimate plenitude; all persons without exception are called to the union with Christ, head of the Church.[23]

Conclusion

In spite of the vacillations we have noted, the Second Vatican Council teaches God's single design for humanity that, in the person of Christ, Lord of history, finds its unique foundation. In no case were the order of creation or of humanity said to be perfect and complete in themselves, without any intrinsic relation to Jesus. Many times, we have pointed out how the preeminent role played by Christ in creation has not the same appeal it has with regard to the reconciliation and salvation of humanity. Perhaps the Council wanted quite logically to avoid taking sides with a particular school of theology on questions traditionally debated in the Church; perhaps this diversity of opinions and mentalities also did not make it possible to further elucidate certain points. Nevertheless, the Council has marked out a path that seems to be sufficiently unequivocal. Theology can take this path with more confidence than some of the passages we have discussed may, at first glance, have suggested. In my opinion, this view is confirmed by the abundant fruits that Catholic theology has reaped, since the closing session of the Council, by following this path. The study of humanity, which starts from the one whose image since the beginning it has been called to reproduce, has lost nothing of its great relevance. The results of humanity's quest are not thereby minimized nor are the questions that are still of concern and await a solution declared to be without importance. Much less—and in this respect the conciliar texts are clear—are the differences put aside between Christians and non-Christians as well as nonbelievers. On the contrary, any unselfish effort or legitimate aspiration noticed in humanity receives a new illumination. In short, if one believes that in the human being a divine seed is dwelling, a transcendental dimension coming from within humanity is acknowledged.

Translated from the Spanish by Louis-Bertrand Raymond.

Notes

1. One can refer to the numerous commentaries on the Constitution: e.g., A. Herrera Oria (ed.), *Comentarios a la constitución Gaudium et Spes sobre la Iglesia en el mundo actual*, BAC 276 (Madrid, 1968); Y.M.-J. Congar and M. Peuchmard (eds.), *L'Église dans le monde de ce temps*, 3 vols. (Paris, 1967); G. Baraúna (ed.), *L'Église dans le monde de ce temps*, 2 vols. (Bruges, 1967–1968); *LTK, Das zweite Vatikanische Konzil. Konstitutionen, Dekrete und Erklärungen* III (Fribourg, 1968), 241–592; *La costituzione pastorale sulla Chiesa nel mondo contemporaneo* (Turin, 1968).

2. The Council often mentions the "vocation" of man; his being is called to perfection: GS 3, 10, 11, 13, 18, 19, 22, etc.

3. No mention is made of the "resemblance"; No. 22 points out that Christ has restored it. Do we have here an allusion to the distinction made by the Fathers of the Church between the image given at the beginning and the eschatological resemblance?

4 No. 14 speaks about the immortality of the soul, but without linking the two statements.

5. J. Ratzinger, *LTK, Das zweite Vatikanische Konzil III*, 350: "Der

sonst theologisch etwas zurückhaltende Text unserer Konstitution gewinnt hier eine betrachtliche Höhe und wird wegweisend für die Richtung des theologischen Denkens in unserer Situation."

6. Cf. *Acta Synodalia Sacrosancti Concilii Oecumenici Vaticani II*, v. III, V (Vatican City, 1975), 232, 237, 273, 300–301, 387, 501; also AS IV, I (1976), 449–570; IV, II (1977), 382, 407, 423, 637, 775, 915. In one of his reports (IV, I, 555), Bishop Garrone said: "Homo enim dicere est ac Christum evocare."

7. *De carnis res*, 6: "Quodcumque limus exprimebatur, Christus cogitabatur homo futurus" (*PL* 2, 282; *CSEL* 47, 12–13, 33).

8. Cf. A. Orbe, *Antropologia de san Ireneo*, BAC 286 (Madrid, 1969), 99–105; and also in note 19.

9. Some Fathers of the Council insisted on this distinction: AS III, V, 215, 516; IV, II, 368.

10. Refer to what has been said in note 2.

11. For example, Clement of Alexandria, *Ped.* II, 20, 1 (*GCS*, 12, 168); St. Gregory Nazianzus, *In Cant.* h. II (*PG* 44, 802).

12. This asserted with good reason by J. Ratzinger, *Das zweite Vatikanische Konzil III*, 350.

13. Cf. *LG* 16.

14. *GS* 42; 78 also speaks about Christ and the human community. Other texts in note 23.

15. Bishop Garrone said in his report, AS IV, I, 556, "in quo [Christo] fundatum quidquid solidaritatis humanae nomen legitime habet." Cf. Y.-J. Congar, in Y.M.-J. Congar and M. Peuchmard (eds.), *L'Église dans le monde de ce temps* II, 326.

16. The transformation of this text is interesting: in the project of 21 September 1965, it said: "in praesenti ac 'definitiva' oeconomia ordo redemptionis in se ordinem creationis includit" (AS IV, I, 469); the *Relatio* (*ibid.*, 556) used the same words.

17. Y.M.-J. Congar, in *L'Église dans le monde de ce temps* II, 326, says about this passage: "Il [le Christ] a été mis au milieu de cette histoire comme un nouveau principe d'existence par lequel la création peut ráliser son sens dernier."

18. In the *Relatio* on the project of September, it is said: "Plures [Patres] . . . insistunt in veritate 'biblica' circa hominem creatum ad imaginem Dei, cujus dignitas in Christo restauratur" (AS IV, I, 530). Some Fathers saw the christological perspective more clearly (AS IV, II, 382, 637, 775), but their opinion was not accepted in the text. J. Corbon, "La Constitution du point de vue de la théologie orientale, in G. Baraúna (ed.), *L'Église dans le monde de ce temps* II, 702–704, mentions this limitation in *GS*.

19. In the footnote, allusion is made to St. Irenaeus, *Adv. Haer.* II, 11, 18; 16, 6; 21, 10; 22, 3; Sagnard (ed.) (*SC* 34) 200, 290–292, 370–

372, 378. The last passage is interesting: "Unde et a Paulo *typus futuri* (Rom. 5:14) dictus est ipse Adam, quoniam futuram circa Filium Dei humani generis dispositionem in semetipsum Fabricator omnium Verbum praeformaverat, praeformante Deo primum animalem hominem videlicet uti ab spiritali salvaretur." On this question, cf. B. Lambert, "La problématique générale de la constitution pastorale," in Y.M.-J. Congar and M. Peuchmard (eds.), *L'Église dans le monde de ce temps* II, 131–170; esp. 161–166.

20. As stated in GS 92, 93.

21. *LG* 50. Romans 8:29 is quoted without commentary in *LG* 2.

22. Among other passages, in *LG* 3, 6, 7, 9, 11, 31, 40, 42, 48–51; *DV* 2; *SC* 6; *AG* 3.

23. *LG* 1–3, 6–7, 13, 32, 48–51, 52; *SC* 2, 48; *PO* 22; *AA* 17, 18; *AG* 1, 3, 6–7; *UR* 2–3, etc.

CHAPTER 38

Anthropology of
the Christian Vocation
Conciliar and Postconciliar Aspects

Luigi M. Rulla, S.J.; Franco Imoda, S.J.,
and Sister Joyce Ridick, S.S.C.

Summary

Following an invitation of the Second Vatican Council (*Gaudium et spes*, No. 62), the present essay offers a critical evaluation of the first three chapters of Part I of *Gaudium et spes* in terms of an anthropology that is modern and *interdisciplinary*. Such an interdisciplinary approach makes it possible to attain a more concrete vision of the human person, both doctrinal and pastoral, and to provide the general outline of an anthropology that is more complete, more explicit, and so more realistic and more useful in pastoral terms.

Premises

The title of the present contribution directs the reader's attention to a document of the Second Vatican Council, namely, *Gaudium et spes* (GS); and, indeed, the whole theological approach of this document of the Council gives special prominence to *the theme of anthropology*.

In its intention of communicating with the world of today, the Council desires above all to establish a dialogue with "all men of good will in whose hearts grace works in an unseen way" (GS, No. 22, second-last paragraph). Further, this dialogue is focused on the idea of *humanitas*. This point is clearly stated in the third article and then repeated a number of times in the course of the document. Thus, for example, No. 11, introducing Part I, declares that "The People of God believes that it is led by the Spirit of the Lord . . . [and] labors to decipher authentic signs of God's presence and purpose," and then states that "faith throws a new light on everything, manifests God's design for man's total vocation, and thus directs the mind to *solutions which are fully human*" (first paragraph; emphasis added). Likewise, the same eleventh article, in its third paragraph, affirms that in the teachings of GS, "the Church will show its religious, and by that very fact, its supremely human character."

In a certain sense, that is in a *broad* rather than specific sense, GS can be described in terms of a dialogue of the Church with the world regarding who and what the human person is, in his or her integral vocation.

How, and to what extent, did GS come to propose the general lines of this anthropology in the Christian vocation? In seeking to offer at least a partial answer to this complex question, it is best to proceed in successive steps that are also meant to indicate the perspectives of the present contribution.

First, it is well to recall the words of John XXIII, who conceived the Council and was its first Father, that "the Ecumenical Council is above all the work of the Holy Spirit."[1]

Nevertheless, as pointed out by John Paul II in his talk at the time of the Sunday Angelus on 6 October 1985,[2] the Fathers of the Council translated "the words of God into human language. This expression, insofar as it is human, may be incomplete and remain open to increasingly exact formulation," while "at the same time it is authentic, because it contains just what the Spirit 'said to the Church' at a given moment in history." Such more exact formulations must retain their bond to the authority of the magisterium of the Church.

At this point, it is important to stress the significance of the brief note placed at the start of GS, indicating the theological qualification of this document. It should be remembered that this note is indisputably part of the text, and was approved as such by the Council when it voted to accept GS as a whole.

Now this note states that in Part I of GS, "the Church develops her teaching on man, on the world which is the enveloping context of man's existence, and on man's relations to his fellow men." In Part II, "the Church gives closer attention to modern life and human society; special consideration is given to those questions and problems which, in this general area, seem to have a greater urgency in our day"; the note goes on to point out that these aspects of the second part are more likely to be linked to "changeable circumstances." One might say that it is the first part that discusses the theme of anthropology in *a more specific and narrow sense*; this point is made by commentators such as Semmelroth[3] and Mouroux.[4] This applies in particular to the first three chapters, which present the general lines of an anthropology.

But these are only the general lines of an anthropology, and further, as noted by Lambert,[5] many points in GS remain implicit and schematic, as indications and orientations toward a new Christian vision of anthropology. This line of thought is expressed also by other writers, who stress the important point that the elaboration of a Christian anthropology is still a necessity. Thus, in conclusion to a large collection of essays on *Lumen gentium*, Y.M.-J. Congar writes that "many values reaffirmed by the Council will find their proper place and foundation only in a Christian anthropology"[6]; and Congar, who was a *peritus* at the Council, adds that even Schema XIII of GS stands in need of a fuller doctrine on Christian man. That GS has provided dynamic seeds for growth toward a Christian anthropology is also made clear by another *peritus*, C. Moeller, in his conclusion to a history of GS,[7] and by G. Alberigo in his discussion of GS in its relation to the overall teaching of the Council.[8]

It is after all well known that GS had a history that passed through various drafts and formulations expressing different currents of thought. One may recall the text of May 1963, the draft of Malines of September 1963, the "Zurich text" of early 1964, and the text of Ariccia (1965). Limits of time at the conclusion of the Council did not permit a full implementation of the vital exhortation of John XXIII, to seek more effective forms of expression for the perennial doctrine of the *depositum fidei*, including use of "recent studies and findings of science, history, and philosophy" (cf. GS, No. 62, par. 2). As regards these "recent studies and findings of science," it should be noted that research and comment since the Council have given more emphasis to the sociological than to the psychological-anthropological aspect of understanding the human person.

Purpose and Limitations

Confined space requires that the present contribution be inevitably limited both in purpose and method.

Its point of departure is found in some of the basic goals proposed by GS. First of all, we hope to offer a brief and partial contribution in the sense of the doctrinal and pastoral intent of GS as expressed in the prefatory note: "the pastoral Constitution *On the Church in the Modern World . . .* is called 'pastoral' because, while resting on doctrinal principles, it seeks to express the relation of the Church to the world and modern mankind."

Farther on, then, in No. 62, referring to the desire expressed by John XXIII in his *Opening Speech to the Council,* GS gives clearer expression to these doctrinal and pastoral intentions, indicating also some means for their attainment. At the start of the second paragraph of No. 62, referring primarily to the aspect of doctrine and its relation to faith, it is stated that ". . . recent studies and findings of science, history, and philosophy raise new questions which influence life and demand new theological investigation." In the following paragraph, dealing primarily with the pastoral aspect, one reads, "In pastoral care, appropriate use must be made not only of theological principles, but also of the findings of the secular sciences, especially of psychology and sociology. Thus the faithful can be brought to live the faith in a *more thorough and mature way*" (emphasis added).

The present study is (within its limits) directly intended to contribute to this discussion and integration of the theological principles, doctrinal and pastoral, of GS. This discussion and integration will be carried out by comparing the contribution of GS with that of an anthropology that is Christian, interdisciplinary, and modern, that keeps in mind and seeks to integrate the three approaches to the human person suggested in No. 62 of GS, those (respectively) of a theological, a philosophical, and a psychosocial anthropology. Concretely, we intend to offer a brief commentary and an exploration in depth of *some* of the articles of GS taken from that part of the document that is more specifically anthropological, namely, the first three chapters of Part I. Commenting on these articles will make possible a brief development of this document of the Council, by way of postconciliar reflections, observations, and research based on an anthropology that is Christian, interdisciplinary and modern, of the kind, then, that was urged in No. 62 of GS.

This commentary on, and comparison between, the contribution of the Council and possible subsequent efforts of an interdisciplinary kind has a number of purposes. The first is that of highlighting certain aspects of the anthropological scheme of GS that converge with the project and to the already referred to research findings of the postconciliar and interdisciplinary anthropology. The second is that of a critical evaluation of the work of the Council, indicating not only its positive aspects, but also omissions, and expressions that remain less than clear, especially for the purpose of adequate pastoral care. The third is to make explicit some points that remain implicit in GS. Finally, our fourth purpose is a deeper exploration of some aspects of GS, whose richness was perhaps not fully appreciated at the time of the Council, by introducing new aspects suggested by the interdisciplinary anthropology already mentioned, which has been worked out since the Council.

This newly developed interdisciplinary anthropology has been presented in two recent volumes.[9] The interdisciplinary character of these two books* is due to the fact that the anthropological vision of the Christian vocation that they discuss has a threefold basis, in an anthropology derived from biblical theology that then converges with the insights of philosophical anthropology and also with those of a scientific psychosocial anthropology, as explained in *Vol. 1*; and also with the observations and research findings (dealing with concrete existential situations) that are presented in *Vol. 2*. This research involved a study of several hundred persons of either sex, in the U.S., who had entered either houses of priestly or religious formation, or else Catholic colleges. It is worth stressing that both the formulation of this interdisciplinary anthropological theory, and the related research findings that provide its existential confirmation, are based on principles and methods that, being of a transsituational and

---

*For brevity, these two works are referred to simply as *Vol. 1* and *Vol. 2*.

transtemporal nature, permit an application to any and every culture (cf. *Vol. 1*, sec. 9.4.2.).

Obviously, in the present context, we can discuss only a *few* of the points made in *Vol. 1* and *Vol. 2*, and that only by way of brief references to these works. For a *fuller and more precise* interpretation of the points involved, the reader is referred to the original texts by way of the references made in the course of the present study.

The discussion develops in three parts, which correspond respectively to Chapters 1, 2, and 3 of Part I of GS, and, in dealing with these chapters, considers only some of the articles, those that are more pertinent to the purpose of this study. It is worth recalling that Part I of GS bears the title "The Church and Man's Calling"; and further that its first three chapters deal primarily with anthropology, and so with humankind as considered from three different viewpoints: as a person with the dignity of an individual standing in relation to God (Chapter 1); as a person related to the society of other persons (Chapter 2), and as related to the material world of earthly realities in which the person must act in the historical development of his or her humanity (Chapter 3).

The Dignity of the Human Person

In discussing the anthropology of the Christian vocation in terms of the purposes and limits of the present essay, the following articles of Chapter 1 merit attention: 12–17, 22. They discuss the image of God in humanity, the deformation of this image due to sin, different levels in the human personality, and finally the renewal, in the Risen Christ, of the human person as the image of God.

In terms of an anthropology of the Christian vocation, the articles listed can be divided up into two groups: Nos. 12–14 as dealing with the *basic constitutive elements* of an anthropology of vocation; then Nos. 15–17 as dealing with the *manifestations* of these basic constitutive elements, manifestations that highlight fundamental anthropological motivations of the Christian vocation, these in turn having their beginning and their end in Christ (No. 22).

Article No. 12: The Human Person as Made in God's Image

A comment, and a comparison of this article with *Vol. 1* and *Vol. 2* of our own study, suggests the following observations.

First, the second paragraph emphasizes the polar tension, the contradiction between greatness and misery ("the call to grandeur and the depths of misery," as we read at the end of No. 13) that mark every person, and that find expression in so many social happenings. The human person is described as a being who is divided in himself or herself. At the same time, this division does not make it impossible to recognize the dignity and the high vocation of the human person. The text of GS (cf. par. 3) promises to offer solutions, provided by divine revelation, to this *inner dialectic* in the human person, "so that man's true situation can be portrayed and his defects explained." But it seems that the biblical answer actually given might have been more complete.

Indeed, the answer just mentioned is not sustained in the rest of this article, and is present only partly in other articles. Thus, for example, No. 10 speaks of humanity as divided in itself, using Romans 7:13–25 as a biblical reference. But, as recent exegesis has shown, humanity as described in the seventh chapter of *Romans* is not *homo lapsus et redemptus* (man as fallen but also as redeemed by Christ), but *homo lapsus;* see, for example, the work of Lyonnet, *Let étapes de l'histoire du salut selon l'Epître aux Romains* (Paris, 1969), which is discussed in *Vol. 1*, Sec. 9.3.2, other authors also being cited. Furthermore, the dialectic of Romans 7:13–25 is a *conscious* dialectic. The same observations can be repeated with regard to man as "out of harmony with himself" (GS, No. 13, par. 2), which also has Romans 7:13–25 as its biblical background. Likewise, the division within the human person described in the first paragraph of No. 13 cites Romans 1:21–25, which has to do with the *conscious* dialectic between virtue and sin.

Now, as explained in Sec. 9.3.2 of *Vol. 1* calling on other biblical texts (such as Gal. 5:16–17, which deals with humanity as *lapsus et redemptus,* as fallen *and* as redeemed by Christ), it is important to recognize that the two types of dialectic (or two "dimensions") are present in the human person. The first dialectic or dimension refers to the division within the person that is characterized by the opposition existing, to a greater or lesser extent, between his or her ideal self and his or her actual self, that is to say, between what the person wants to be or to do and what the person actually is and does. This is a *conscious* opposition (cf. Gal. 5:16), and can be designated as the dimension that *disposes* the person to virtue or to sin.

But, in addition to this dimension or dialectic, there also exists in the *normal* (nonpathological) person a second dimension or dialectic. In this second dialectic also (cf. Gal. 5:17), there is an opposition between the person's actual self and ideal self, to a greater or lesser extent. But the *ideal* self is only what the person *wants to do;* it is only an *aspiration* rather than a decision of the will, or, in other words, a dynamic tendency in the will rather than a conclusion that has been reached; and since responsibility and deliberation are lacking, this dialectic in the second dimension is not sinful. Further, in this second dimensions, the *actual* self involves the action of forces that are largely *unconscious* (and are opposed to the good to which one *aspires*); and since these forces are unconscious, deliberation and responsibility are not involved. Accordingly, this second dimension *disposes* the person to nonculpable error, or, in other words, imposes a limitation on the person's *effective* freedom in the sense of leading not to the real good, but only to an apparent good (of the kind spoken of by St. Ignatius of Loyola in the *Spiritual Exercises*). Clearly, this disposition affects different people to different degrees, and the aspects of the personality that are affected also vary from one person to another.

Still, the lure of the apparent good related to this second dimension is a part of human "misery" (cf. *Vol. 1,* Sec. 9.3.2), and this point finds abundant support in the convergence of the many research findings presented in *Vol. 2.* These findings show, above all, the existence of three dimensions in the person that are qualitatively distinct; they further reveal that the second dimension can influence the living of vocation in many different ways, notably as to perseverance in vocation and the internalization or assimilation of the values of Christ and (in consequence) the person's apostolic effectiveness, having also an indirect effect in the area of chastity, etc. (see *Vol. 1,* Sec. 9.3.2 and *Vol. 2,* Sec. 9).

It should be clearly noted that the dialectic of the second dimension is present in every single person, to a greater or lesser extent but always to some extent, as one of the expressions of his *concupiscence.* After all, the Council of Trent (Session V: *Decree on Original Sin,* 5) teaches that while concupiscence, which comes from sin (original sin) is not itself sinful, yet it inclines one to sin.

It is also in principle possible that a third type of dialectic (that between normality and pathology, referred to as the third dimension) can influence the living of vocation, but this is not the general case; cf. *Vol. 1,* pp. 181–189 and Sec. 10.3.4, also *Vol. 2, passim.*)

We agree with Delhaye[10] that the biblical bases of human dignity that are invoked in GS are guidelines to thought and not a well-developed theology more or less colored by philosophy; yet these bases, considered from our present viewpoint, might have been chosen with more precision, or at least with more completeness, taking account of recent research in biblical theology and in existential anthropology.

Nevertheless, GS has made an important contribution: it has proposed a vision of the human person that is *fundamentally dialectical,* and in terms of a dialectic that affects the person's Christian vocation.

A second observation regards the third paragraph of No. 12, in which humanity is described as having been created "to the image of God" (Gen. 1:26). But as noted by Ratzinger,[11] the ideal of humanity as the image of God is, in the Old Testament, rather indeterminate in content. It finds its full meaning only when this doctrine of humanity as the image of God is transferred to Christ as the definitive Adam. Therefore, the doctrine of humanity as "in God's image" should not be confined to a theology of creation, since the teaching of the New Testament deals more with the future than with the origin of man. Accordingly, this status of the person is not to be understood as a static gift, but rather as a motivational thrust toward the person's self-transcendence (cf. *Vol. 1,* Secs. 9.1 and 9.3.3). Furthermore, if the doctrine of man as God's image is understood only as a theology of initial creation, the theology itself is impoverished; indeed, in a Christian theology of creation, the beginning, or "Alpha," is fully understood only in the light of the end, or "Omega." A human person is the image of God to the extent that he or she directs himself or herself toward God and transcends himself or herself; for St. Augustine (*De Trinitate,* XIV, 8, 11), the image of God in humanity is to be interpreted as a capacity for God, as the possibility of knowing and loving God. Number 12 of GS notes this capability of the human person at the start of the third paragraph, but does not mention the concept of the *possibility of self-transcendence* on the part of the person, toward a love that is centered on God.

This notion of the possibility of humanity's transcending itself in theocentric love is basic for understanding the process by which the Christian vocation begins, develops, and grows. This point is discussed at length in *Vol. 1*, as for instance in Sec. 7.3.2 (in which theocentric self-transcendence is distinguished from two other kinds of self-transcendence, namely, the kind that is only egocentric and the kind that is merely sociophilanthropic), and in Secs. 9.2.1 and 9.3.1 (in which, drawing on Gal. 5:13–14, it is shown that the Christian vocation is a call to freedom for self-transcendence in a love that is centered on God). The existential proofs in *Vol. 2* give repeated confirmation to the importance of this theocentric self-transcendence in vocation.

One might say that the contribution made in our own *Vol. 1* and *Vol. 2* serves to make explicit what is implicit in the anthropology of GS regarding theocentric self-transcendence as a possibility or capacity that is basic to the anthropology of the Christian vocation. Further, *Vol. 1* and *Vol. 2* develop and confirm what is implicit in GS, namely, that human motivation is fundamentally a teleological and axiological motivation centered on self-transcendent values, in other words, on values that are moral and religious, as distinct from natural values (see, for example, *Vol. 1*, Sec. 8.2.2 and *Vol. 2*, Sec. 4).

The fourth paragraph of No. 12 states, "But God did not create man as a solitary. For from the beginning 'male and female he created them' (Gen. 1 :27). Their companionship produces the primary form of interpersonal communication. For by his innermost nature man is a social being, and unless he relates himself to others he can neither live nor develop his potential."

This part of No. 12 makes two very important points. The first can be presented thus: a person, "created to the image of God" (No. 12, par. 3, citing Gen. 1:26), is the very same person that "God did not create . . . as a solitary, but from the beginning 'male and female he created them' " (No. 12, par. 4, citing Gen. 1:27). As noted by the two *periti* of the Council (Delhaye,[13] and also Ratzinger[14]), humanity's likeness to God is linked in this article to the existence of humanity as male and female, or in other words with sexuality. But this connection of human sexuality to the human creature's likeness to God involves the fact that human sexuality goes beyond the merely natural phenomena of reproduction, rising to the level of dialogue in psychological and spiritual love, and accordingly to the level of a love that involves the *whole* person. After all, as noted by Alszeghy[15] and Mouroux[16] in their comments on the twelfth article of *GS*, humanity as the image of God is an essential and living relationship to God, a relationship that is singularly complete and profound, one of dialogue with God (see *Vol. 1*, Sec. 2). Therefore, human sexuality involves *theocentric* self-transcendence by the *whole* person.

This point has been confirmed by the research findings given in *Vol. 2*, Sec. 8.2: human sexual maturity is related to maturity in terms of two *primary* predictors of the person, namely with the Index of Developmental Maturity of the person *as a whole* and also with the person's maturity on the second dimension.[17] Note that, as appears repeatedly in the course of *Vol. 2* (see in particular the reflections and research findings of Secs. 3, 5, 6, and 8.1), these two primary predictors act as motivational dispositions that are important for the internalization or assimilation of self-transcendent values, and so are dispositions that are important for the self-transcendence, centered on God, which characterizes authentic love.

But it is well to observe at once (following Ratzinger[18]) that humanity's likeness to God comes before the sexuality to which it is related. In Ratzinger's words, "the likeness to God in sexuality is prior to sexuality, not identical with it. It is because the human being is capable of the absolute Thou that he is an I who can become a Thou for another I. The capacity for the absolute Thou is the ground of the possibility and necessity of the human partner" (*ibid.*, p. 122.). Therefore, religion cannot be reduced to an identification with human solidarity.

This last point leads us to the second important statement of No. 12: the union of man and woman "produces the primary form of interpersonal communion. For by his innermost nature man is a social being, and unless he relates himself to others he can neither live nor develop his potential." As observed by Delhaye,[19] "the text recognizes sexuality as *one* of the bases of man's social being, not only on the level of husband-and-wife, but also in a much more general sense" (p. 269, emphasis added and translation supplied). This reality emerged also in our own research on a psychosocial level considering a *secondary* predictor of sexual maturity; the Index of Psychosexual Development discussed in Sec. 8.2 of *Vol. 2*. This is an element in the personality that is correlated, as a disposition, with sexual weaknesses; accordingly, not only can social relationships easily activate the dynamisms of the Index of Psychosocial Maturity, but they can also, by way of these dynamisms, lead to the emergence or nonemergence of sexual weaknesses. Without subscribing to the pansexualism of which Freud is sometimes accused, one must still recognize the motivating force of sexuality as *one* of the components of social interaction.

Regarding this secondary predictor (the Index of Psychosexual Development), it is necessary to add two points of vocational anthropology that are interconnected, and that emerge from the research findings of *Vol. 2* (Secs. 8.2.4 and 8.2.7). First, the Index of Psychosexual Maturity has a range of action in the dynamic of the person that is more limited than that of the Index of Developmental Maturity of the person as a whole, or than that of the person's second dimension, although it is correlated to these. Second, there is a statistically significant difference between the Index of Psychosexual Development and in the Index of Interpersonal Orientation (which indicates the person's *capacity* for relationships to others, which are self-transcending and centered on God). These two indices are not identical, although there can be an *indirect* reciprocal influence between them. In other words, a person's social orientation is a factor that *can easily* combine with sexuality in such a way as to lead to situations, genital or otherwise, which do not necessarily coincide with the ultimate end of a love that is self-transcending and theocentric, the end that is proper to the human person.

What has been said by way of comment on par. 4 of No. 12 offers two contributions. First, it makes more explicit some of the anthropological statements of the Council, especially with a view to their pastoral application. Indeed, as far as sexuality is concerned, the "notional" knowledge coming from revelation has been in part translated into "real" and experimental knowledge of a concrete and existential kind, in other words, into a knowledge that is useful for the pastoral care of individual persons and of their relationships with others. Second, our comments on par. 4 of No. 12 lay a philosophical and theological foundation for the factors of psychosocial anthropology that form the basic hypothesis of Sec. 8.2 of *Vol. 2;* according to this hypothesis, psychosexual relationships to others can be lived in a mature way only if they are also lived as self-transcendence in a theocentric love.

Article No. 13: Sin

As a premise to the discussion that follows, it is well to recall briefly the notion of sin proposed at the very beginning of No. 13.

GS uses two expressions to express this notion of sin. First and above all, man's sin lies in "set[ting] himself against God" and in seeking "to find fulfillment apart from God." The second expression reads: "Although he knew God, he did not glorify Him as God, but his senseless mind was darkened and he served the creature rather than the Creator. (Cf. Rom. 1:21–25.)"

As one may notice, these two expressions stress two different aspects of a single reality: sin is alienation from God, and a rejection of the ultimate purpose for which the human person was created, that of self-transcendence toward a love centered on God (see *Vol. 1,* Sec. 9.3.1). Common to these two aspects of sin is an alienation from God as the ultimate object of a person's love. For this reason, the Council can state (at the end of par. 2 of No. 13) that "man has disrupted also his proper relationship *to his own ultimate goal.* At the same time he became out of harmony with himself, with others, and with all created things" (emphasis added). This is the perspective in which to consider the sexual weaknesses discussed in Sec. 8.2 of *Vol. 2* (mentioned also in Rom. 1:21–25, which the Council cites in No. 13.) For such weaknesses are an alienation from the goal of a love that is theocentric and self-transcending, this in turn being the formal principle of the two *primary* predictors of sexual weaknesses: the Index of Developmental Maturity of the person as a whole, and also maturity/immaturity on the second dimension (cf. p. 413).

Following the suggestion of No. 13, which in citing Romans 1:21–25 uses sexual weaknesses as an *example of sin,* one can formulate the following general reflections on the anthropology of vocation. For in these terms, one can understand how the central *dialectics* not only of the person's first dimension, but also of the second dimension, and sometimes of the third (each dimension being qualitatively distinct from the others), as reflected in the two primary predictors mentioned, can have a debilitating effect on the person's will and *incline* it to sin, as exemplified in sexual weaknesses; the research findings given in Sec. 8.2 of *Vol. 2* confirm this possibility for those who are immature in terms of the two primary predictors used. This point is implicitly made in No. 13 in two other places. At the beginning of the third paragraph, we read, "Therefore man is split within himself. As a result, all of human life, whether individual or collective, shows itself to be a dramatic struggle between good and evil, between light and darkness." In its final paragraph, this article deals implicitly with the dialectic between "the call to grandeur and the depths of misery [which] are both part of human experience."

With specific reference to sexual weaknesses, it seems possible that a debilitating effect leading to these can come also from the factors making up the Index of Psychosocial Maturity (which is the secondary predictor of such weaknesses.) As will emerge in discussing No. 14, the Index of Psychosocial Development is also an expression (along with the first and second dimensions, and sometimes the third) of the unity of body with spirit in the human situation, so that the components of this Index can act as a debilitating factor leading to sexual weaknesses, when this Index reveals immaturity. Paragraph 2 of No. 14 seems to point to this possibility: "wounded by sin, man experiences rebellious stirrings in his body. But the very dignity of man postulates that man glorify God in his body (cf. 1 Cor. 6:13–20) and forbid it to serve *the evil inclinations of his heart*" (emphasis added). The research findings of Sec. 8.2 of *Vol. 2* confirm the possibility of a debilitating action on the part both of the primary factors (reflected in the Index of Developmental Maturity, which includes the three dimensions, and especially the second) and of the secondary factor (reflected in the Index of Psychosexual Development), in those persons who are *immature* in terms of these predictors.

Therefore, it seems that the various statements contained in the two preceding paragraphs, concerning a debilitating function of the three dimensions (and, as regards sexual weaknesses, *also* of the Index of Psychosexual Development) on the person's will, so as to incline it to sin, can be interpreted as statements dealing with four different characteristics of *human concupiscence*. (On this relationship of the first and second dimensions to concupiscence, see *Vol. 1*, Sec. 9.3.2.) One can stress at this point the importance of the *unconscious* as a constitutive component of human concupiscence, in that the unconscious is specifically present in the second dimension (and sometimes in the third) in such a way that it can be in opposition to vocational ideals.

Given these facts, the reflections and research findings of Vol. 1 and Vol. 2 offer a contribution to the doctrine of concupiscence, explaining in part the psychodynamic components of concupiscence itself, in terms of a scientific psychosocial anthropology.[20]

These reflections and psychosocial findings accordingly amount to a contribution, both pastoral and scientific, to a more concrete and existential understanding of the components and the action of human concupiscence, as these are found to be existentially present in *individual* persons; and also specify some of the factors of the "depths of misery" discussed, along with the "call to grandeur," in the last paragraph of No. 13 of GS.

Analysis of No. 13 of GS suggests three other brief pastoral applications, as follows:

Delhaye[21] observes that the Council "invites us to separate original sin less from actual sin," in other words, the sin of nature (otherwise, never explicitly discussed by the Council) from the person's actual sin. On the other hand, as also noted by Delhaye, GS "does not make a distinction between the sin of nature and personal sins" (*op. cit.*, p. 270). Analogous observations are made by Ratzinger[22] in his commentary on No. 13. The discussion of No. 13 in the preceding pages of this essay follows the same line of thought, at least in the sense of a lesser separation between original and actual sin.

But this invitation of the Council, to make less of a separation between original sin and actual sin, is frequently misunderstood and misinterpreted in a pastoral practice that tends to deny in a very facile way the existence of personal sin, especially in the sexual area. There exists a tendency to deny all guilt, for example, in masturbation, in premarital sex, in homosexuality, and in heterosexual friendships that are clearly not oriented to the ultimate goal of the human person; and so on. Research findings suggest, on the contrary, that there is a whole range of degrees of moral responsibility, to be judged by norms that should be applied case by case; but that the instances of a true absence of responsibility make up only a small percentage (see Vol. 2, Sec. 8.2.7, regarding cases of severe pathology in the third dimension).

In consequence, one observes in contemporary society a weakening of the sense of sin. According to Alszeghy,[23] another cause of this fading of the sense of sin lies in the fact that too often sin was considered almost exclusively as a transgression of ethical norms. Now, apart from the fact that in certain circumstances such transgression is not accompanied by true responsibility, there remains the more important fact of the true sense of such ethical norms having been forgotten: their religious meaning in terms of alienation from God.

With more direct reference to violations of chastity and the weakening of the sense of sin, it would perhaps be pastorally helpful to emphasize the positive aspect of chastity rather than the negative, stressing the notion of self-giving to the Divine Other and to the human other, a notion implying also the idea of renunciation. Keeping in mind the teaching of GS on the basic unity of the human person, to be seen in No. 14, one can understand that to "pommel my body and subdue it" (1 Cor. 9:27) does not mean "hating one's own flesh" (Eph. 5:29), but rather recognizing its real worth in directing it to its true destiny. Chastity is a sacrifice precisely because it is a renunciation of something that is not obscene or unworthy, but beautiful and good, which is given to the Divine Other and the human other, in a way corresponding to the state of Christian life that the person has chosen.

Number 13, dealing with sin, in its present form (Text 6) was added to Text 5 in order to correct the earlier vision expressed in Text 5 (the Ariccia Text), a vision of the human person that was optimistic and one-sided. But, as observed by Ratzinger,[24] this article retains the basic vision of the Ariccia Text, "which was essentially specified by a redemption which has already taken place" (see Ratzinger, *ibid.*, p. 124). In its present form, No. 13 does not allow itself to be hypnotized by the theme of sin, and so does not exaggerate this theme, but adopts a positive and realistic view (Ratzinger, *ibid.*) Still, Text 6 has toned down the position of Text 5, "sometimes in a way which may easily tend to give a slightly semi-pelagian impression" (Ratzinger, *op. cit.*, p. 124).

If this is a real possibility, then another possibility follows: that of misunderstanding and misinterpreting the Council on this point, in terms of a semipelagian view. Concretely, with respect to the powers of man in the face of sin, a semipelagian view can take shape, with diminished recognition of the importance of grace, of prayer, and in particular of the Sacrament of Reconciliation. The striking falloff in the reception of the Sacrament of Reconciliation since the Second Vatican Council may have *one* of its causes in such a misunderstanding of the Council, resulting in an overestimation view of the person's resources in dealing with sin; in other words, an excessively optimistic vision of the human person, resembling that of the "humanistic" anthropologies described in Sec. 9.3.1 of *Vol. 1.* The strength of concupiscence tends to be underestimated, while according to the Council of Trent (cf. Session V, *Decree on Original Sin,* 5), concupiscence comes from sin, is not itself sin, but inclines to sin. This influence of concupiscence is in the same line as the reflections and research findings referred to in our initial discussion of No. 13 of GS (cf. also No. 14).

A further pastoral point is also worthy of note, namely that No. 13 offers an excellent example of the efforts made by the Council in producing GS to show the convergence between Revelation and human experience in a Christian anthropological view. All three paragraphs of the article, in different ways, stress the value of such a convergence in explaining the dialectic between the grandeur and misery of the human person, as this can be concretized in the three dimensions explained in *Vol. 1* and existentially confirmed in *Vol. 2.* .

In the words of the final paragraph of No. 13, "The call to grandeur and the depths of misery are both a part of human experience. They find their ultimate and simultaneous explanation in the light of God's revelation." Ratzinger comments on this convergence of faith with human experience in the following statement: "Only if faith throws light on experience and proves to be the answer to our experience, can talk about man's humanity lead to talk about God and with God" (*op. cit.,* p. 126). As stated in the last paragraph of our *Vol. 1,* this convergence and complementarity of a biblical-theological approach with an anthropological and existential approach can be pastorally helpful and is to be favored. It is precisely this that GS has done, at several points in the text.

Article No. 14: The Makeup of Humanity

This article deals with the makeup of humanity and begins at once with the basic statement that "Though made up of body and soul, man is one." The Council wishes to stress this unity of the human person, and avoid any form of dualism, such as has some-times appeared in other theological approaches, which, follow-ing a Greek tradition (cf. *Vol. 1*, Sec. 7.1), thought of a person mainly as a composite of two substances, body and soul, united with each other. In contrast, the Council follows the biblical orientation of contemporary theology and accordingly empha-sizes the unity of the existential person, who has a "bodily compo-sition" and also "interior qualities." In the former, the person "gathers to himself the elements of the material world"; and in the latter, the person "outstrips the whole sum of mere things" (No. 14). One may recall that earlier, in Text 4 of GS, the article on the body dealt solely with "the dignity of the human body," whereas the following article concerned solely "the dig-nity of the soul and particularly of the human intellect" (cf. Ratzinger[26] and Mouroux[27]): this left the door open to a dualism of body and soul. In Text 5 of GS, "the whole constitution of man" was included in No. 14 in order to avoid any suggestion, even external, of dualism; the human body and the human soul are not merely juxtaposed, but are the two components of an organic whole, and a person may not despise his or her bodily life, but "is obliged to regard his body as good and honorable since God has created it and will raise it up on the last day" (No. 14, par. 2).

Yet, as noted by Ratzinger in the same commentary, while the doctrine of the unity of body and spirit in the human person is clearly affirmed by the Council, one still notes the lack of a new way of *giving adequate expression* to this unity so as to go beyond the schematism of body–soul dualism. Ratzinger (*op. cit.*, pp. 127–130) sees the concept of *interioritas* used in par. 3 as a way of reaching a new mode of expressing the unity of body and spirit, and suggests returning for this purpose to the theology of the interior life presented by St. Augustine.

According to Ratzinger (p. 128), dualism is overcome by "the biblical concept of the *heart* which for Augustine expresses the unity of interior life and corporeality" (emphasis added). Thus, one would attain a true *theology of the body* that conceives "the body as a human body, describing it in its humanity as the corporeal embodiment of mind and spirit, the way in which the human spirit has concrete existence" (*ibid.*, p. 129). One would then have a theology of the unity of the person as spirit in body and body in spirit. In this context, Ratzinger refers to the analogous thinking of many authors such as Guardini, Pascal, Metz, K. Rahner, G. Marcel; cf. also the comment on the word "heart," by J. de Fraine and A. Vanhoye, in *La Bibbia*, p. 1117.

Our *Vol. 1* and *Vol. 2* have followed the same line of thought as was advanced by St. Augustine for expressing the unity of body and spirit in the human person. Suffice it to recall the brief discussion in Sec. 7.1 of *Vol. 1* and (above all), the conceptualization, also in *Vol. 1*, of the three dimensions as three *habitual dispositions* in human motivation, each of which includes the three levels of psychic life: the psychophysiological, the psychosocial, and the spiritual–rational levels (see *Vol. 1*, Sec. 7.2 and note 96). Also relevant is Sec. 8.2 of *Vol. 2*, in which research findings show that the three dimensions are an important part of the two primary predictors of sexual weaknesses (see p. 412). In the same line, one may recall that the three levels of psychic life are present also in several of the components of the Index of Psychosexual Development, so that also the secondary predictor of sexual weakness is antidualistic. Therefore, as to the way of expressing the antidualistic doctrine on humanity affirmed by GS in No. 14, our *Vol. 1* and *Vol. 2* make a contribution to the elucidation of this doctrine of the Council in terms of a scientific psychosocial anthropology. Such an approach makes possible an understanding and a pastoral care of *individual* persons in their concrete existential situations.

While Nos. 12–14 present some *basic constitutive elements* of an anthropology of the Christian vocation, Nos. 15–17 deal with *manifestations of these elements,* manifestations that highlight basic anthropological motivations of vocation. These latter three articles deal with the human person's capacity for the truth, for the good, and for freedom.

Article No. 15: The Dignity of the Mind; Truth; Wisdom

What strikes one in this article is the absence of two implications of the doctrine on a person as the "image of God" of No. 12; these involve the two concepts of "person" and of "love" and the problematic related to these.

Isolated elements regarding the concept of person and related

modern philosophy are found in the first two chapters of Part I of
GS, but they are *not developed*. Some consequences of this lack
are worth noting.

The concept of person is the central link between doctrine
concerning humanity and doctrine concerning God. This concept is a product of Christianity, worked out in the attempt to
solve theological problems, both Trinitarian and christological
(Ratzinger[28]). It is due to the concept of the person as a being
gifted with infinite worth and absolute value as an image of God,
created directly by God, that all the rights of the human person
can be affirmed, and all forms of discrimination, based on sex,
race, age, language, power, possessions, cult, or whatever, become illegitimate, unjust, and odious. The concept of person
makes it possible to develop a humanism and an anthropology
that are truly universal and Christian. This concept affects not
only anthropology as interpersonal, but also makes possible an
interpersonal Christian anthropology in which all persons are
equally worthy of esteem, respect and love, especially the poorest
and the weakest, and even one's enemies.

The concept and the philosophy of *love* also lacks development in the basic doctrine on humanity presented in No. 15.
The reason for this omission probably lies in the fact that it was
decided to move this whole problematic to Chapter 2 of Part I,
"The Community of Mankind." This possibility seems confirmed
by the fact that statements pertinent to this problematic were
removed, for this reason, from Article 12 of Text 5 (cf. *Relatio*,
B, p. 28).

In *Vol. 1*, we have sought to develop these concepts of the
person (or "self") and of love, and the related philosophy (see
Sec. 7, 8, 9.3.1, and 9.3.2), whereas in *Vol. 2* (Sec. 8.1), the
reader may find confirmation that the intrapersonal anthropology of *Vol. 1* lies at the basis of relationships with others that are
lived in self-transcendence centered on God.

As a result of these omissions regarding the notions of person
and love, No. 14 deals only in an *implicit* way with the theme of
the person's capacity for *self*-transcendence towards theocentric
love. This theme is dealt with especially in the second and third
paragraphs, but is viewed rather in the context of an Augustinian
discussion of the themes of knowledge and wisdom.

Number 15 does in fact affirm that the activity of the human mind is not just the kind of knowledge that is limited and confined to external phenomena, or to outer appearances that can be perceived by the senses. The human mind, as *wisdom*, reaches beyond the phenomena to what cannot be perceived by the senses, attaining to profound and genuine realities, so that the mind is drawn "to a quest and a love for what is true and good. Steeped in wisdom, man passes through visible realities to those which are unseen." This is the possibility of self-transcendence toward a love centered on God, which is present in the human person; it is discussed at length and in an explicit way in *Vol. 1* (see Secs. 7–9) and studied existentially in *Vol. 2* (see, Secs. 5 and 8); and it is, after all, the highest expression of the dignity of the human person.

Number 15 not only discusses the positive effects of such wisdom, but touches also (in par. 4) on the question of resistance to wisdom, in calling attention to the need of "wiser men," and in stressing (in par. 5) the need for the Holy Spirit, for whom there is no substitute, so that the human possibility of theocentric self-transcendence can be realized in faith.

A more explicit discussion of possible forms of resistance to wisdom would have been helpful. Humanity's approach to the truth, to the good, and to love involves the commitment of the whole person, and accordingly requires an anthropology that takes note not only of the person's capacities of cognition and willing, but also takes sufficient account of capacities that are emotional affective or relational, like those involved in the dispositions of the first dimension, and also unconscious ones, like those of the dispositions of the second dimension, and sometimes of the third. After all, "self-transcendence is the achievement of conscious intentionality" (Lonergan[29]) and is, therefore, vulnerable to the possible action of the conscious resistances of the first dimension, as also to the subconscious resistances of the second dimension (and sometimes of the third), resistances that affect the person's effective freedom to pursue self-transcendent values, that is, moral and religious values. We have attempted to develop this theme in *Vol. 1* (Secs. 7–9) and *Vol. 2* (Secs. 5–9) and so to penetrate into the depth and the implications of the conciliar text, which speaks of such resistances and difficulties lying in the way of self-transcendence, but in a way that is perhaps incomplete.

At this point we can note that, in its fourth paragraph, No. 15

emphasizes that "our era needs such wisdom more than bygone ages" (see the relevant reflections in *Vol. 1*, Sec. 10.4.3). For this reason, GS states in No. 11 that the Church helps humanity to recognize what is right in its present aspirations, but also to discern those that are distorted "by the taint in man's heart" so as to be "wrenched from their rightful function," and "in need of purification" so that they can be related "to their divine source." And after all, wisdom (*sapientia*) aims at an axiology or hierarchy or scale of *objective* values, in terms of which a person is *called,* and engaged with his or her *whole* person. Therefore, a better knowledge of the human person, expressed in a *more complete* anthropology, can be helpful in favoring the collaboration of the human person with the primary action and initiative of divine grace, as desired by God himself.

Article No. 16: The Dignity of the Moral Conscience

This article reaffirms the transcendent and objective character of conscience: "For man has in his heart a law written by God," and this law "can when necessary speak to his heart more specifically: do this, shun that." Conscience accordingly does not create a moral order, but recognizes values and general objective moral norms established by God. "Conscience is the most secret core and sanctuary of a man. There he is alone with God, whose voice echoes in his depths." The principle of that life to which conscience calls us is the love of God and our neighbor. But the root of conscience lies in the radical thrust that orients the human person to God as the person's goal: conscience is therefore linked to the person's self-transcendence toward a theocentric love of the Divine Other and the human other.

The characteristics ascribed to conscience in this article, as just reported, correspond to those presented more explicitly in discussing the person's *call* to the self-transcendence of a theocentric love (see *Vol. 1*, Sec. 7.3.2, especially for the contribution of de Finance).

Still, it is helpful to offer some critical observations on the *formulation* of this article. First, as remarked in the preceding paragraph, the article might have formulated more explicitly the elements characterizing the *call* of conscience, its urging to do this or to shun that.

Second, the article does not take sufficient note of the different forms of psychosocial conditioning that can influence the freedom and objectivity of conscience, as conscience actually exists in the individual and existentially concrete person.

Volume 1, starting from the fact that there exists in the human person the possibility or capacity of theocentric self-transcendence and the *call* to go beyond the self in a theocentric love of God and neighbor, points out (cf. Sec. 8.4.2 with Fig. 1, Sec. 8.4.3 and *passim*) that the freedom for such self-transcendence can be limited to a greater or lesser degree by psychosocial conditioning, in other words, by the habitual dispositions of the individual, which make up his or her three dimensions or central dialectics: the conscious first dimension of virtue or sin (especially in the case of a conscious negligence in the pursuit of the truth and the good, or of "habitual sin," as mentioned at the end of No. 16); the *subconscious* second dimension of possible nonculpable error or (in other terms) of the real or apparent good; and sometimes the third dimension of normality versus pathology, mild or serious.

Note that pathology that is *not serious* does not in general attract self-transcendent values—moral or religious—in a direct and primary way (cf. *Vol. 1*, Sec. 8.2.2), affecting rather those values that are natural (such as economic or aesthetic values, etc.), and yet may in some cases affect self-transcendent values by way of an effect on the second dimension (cf. *Vol. 1*, Sec. 8.5.3). But pathology that is *serious* places limitations on conscience; these arise from notable difficulties in understanding and willing. The research findings of *Vol. 2* confirm the fact that the three dimensions can, in different degrees and ways, influence the person's freedom for theocentric self-transcendence. Our own research does not deal with severe pathology, since this was not represented in the sample studied.

Third, No. 16 does not seem to take sufficient account of the existence of limitations on the effective freedom of the person that can affect the objectivity of conscience. It is at the same time important to note that such possible limitations on effective freedom do not diminish the objectivity of conscience itself in the case of the habitual dispositions of the first dimension (arising, for example, from strong desires) that remain conscious and do not undermine the moral responsibility of the person, as long as his or her conscience has been formed on the basis of adequate information. On the other hand, one should not forget the *possi-*

ble negative influence of the second dimension upon the first dimension; it is true that this is an *indirect* influence, meaning an influence that does not diminish the person's responsibility regarding his or her dispositions in the first dimension; and yet the action of the second dimension can be a factor that indirectly debilitates the person's spiritual life and *inclines* him or her to sin (see *Vol. 1*, Sec. 9.3.2) or to religious indifference, something to be found at present on a worldwide scale (see *Vol. 2*, Sec. 9.7, and the "Final Relation" of the Synod of Bishops of 1985 on the Second Vatican Council, point I.3).

One can conclude No. 16 cannot be criticized for its basic stress both on the "objective norms of morality" and on the fact that the law of conscience "is fulfilled by love of God and neighbor," a fulfillment depending on the Holy Spirit (cf. Rom. 5:5). Yet, following Ratzinger,[30] we can note these three points: incompleteness in dealing with the concrete form of the claims of conscience, an inadequate vision of the positive or negative influence of psychosocial factors on conscience, and insufficient account taken of the limits of conscience.

The anthropology of the Christian vocation proposed and verified in our *Vol. 1* and *Vol. 2* attempts to overcome, at least partly, these three limitations on the way the teaching of No. 16 is presented, in terms of the observations and research findings reported before. Moreover, these observations and findings offer a *more complete* vision of the anthropological reality of the human conscience, especially as regards the *possible* indirect influence of the second dimension on conscience, and sometimes of the third dimension, without diminishing the moral responsibility connected with the first dimension.

In par. 3, No. 16 speaks of the conscience that errs from invincible ignorance. Depth psychology indicates that we can distinguish two ways in which conscience can so err. In general, we can say that both of these ways leave intact the dignity of conscience and the possibility of salvation. Yet it will be pastorally helpful to note that the two kinds of error have different origins.

The first kind of erroneous conscience is present when one acts on account of a conscious motivation, which seems not to be mistaken, but is indirectly misled by an erroneous motivation in the second dimension (and sometimes the third), which inspires and sustains conscience, but which is opposed to the objective values of vocation; unconscious motives, such as repressed emotional experiences of the past, can mislead us, partly or totally, regarding *the meaning of the present situation*, without our being aware of this (cf. the research findings cited in *Vol. 1*, Sec. 9.4.2, under the heading "The Dialectics of the Self"). Sometimes, however, this first form of a conscience that errs from invincible ignorance may involve guilt *in causa*; for there may indeed have been, in the past, a sense of conscious culpability due to some weakness that has been habitually yielded to, this sense of guilt having then, in the course of time, been deeply repressed and rendered unconscious, resulting in a conscience that errs from invincible ignorance, which can, however, involve to some extent a culpability *in causa*.

The second way in that conscience can err from invincible ignorance does not depend on unconscious motivation, but on a lack of correct information concerning a problem. Such a lack of correct information can have many causes, these being for the most part of a sociocultural nature. Yet, one should distinguish this kind of conscience in a *state* of invincible ignorance from a conscience in a state of ignorance that is "affected" or willed, or at least accepted *in causa*.

Regarding the conscience that errs from invincible ignorance, Lonergan[31] follows a line of thought that greatly reduces the old problem of the salvation of non-Christians (cf. *Vol. 1*, Sec. 9.3.1.b, "Self-transcendence of love and faith").

According to Lonergan, there are two kinds of knowledge: knowledge of facts and of values, and knowledge that is born of love. Knowledge of facts and generally of values precedes love (*nihil amatum nisi praecognitum*). In contrast, when knowledge is born of love, love precedes the knowledge of facts and of values. This second kind of knowledge is present in two situations: when persons fall in love, and when the person is flooded with the love that God gives as a gift.

For Lonergan (*ibid.*), knowledge of facts is obtained by the use of "reason," that is, by the set of operations of the first three levels of cognitive activity, namely those of experience, understanding, and judgment. But knowledge born of love is attained by way of the discernment of value and the judgments of value of a person who has been flooded with love. If this love is the love of God poured into human hearts, one has the knowledge that is born of *religious* love: that is to say, faith. When considered in this way, the problem of the salvation of non-Christians loses some of its complexity. But still, for Christians or non-Christians, the fact always remains that a proper discernment of spirits is necessary to determine if the love really comes from God or from human factors, which can also be unconscious and opposed to the Christian vocation (cf. St. Ignatius of Loyola, *Spiritual Exercises*, n. 336).

Article No. 17: The Excellence of Liberty

This article intends to offer a basis for the concept of freedom, and it does this in various ways. First of all, it affirms the value of freedom itself and bases this on faith: "authentic freedom is an exceptional sign of the divine image within man," and it should be the means that a person uses to seek spontaneously for his or her Creator, and "through loyalty to Him," "come freely to utter and blissful perfection."

Second, and in consequence, the dignity of the human person as an image of God requires that the person decide to be himself or herself, acting "according to a knowing and free choice," and not "from blind internal impulse nor from mere external pressure." This pairing of internal impulse with external pressure is interesting, for, after all, the external manipulation of the person by modern society (e.g., by the mass media) is possible insofar as such manipulation can appeal to the internal impulses of the person, conscious or subconscious.

Third, the person must *pursue his goal* by a free choice of what is good. Human freedom is freedom *for* this goal, and, as has been seen, it should find its expression as self-transcendence toward a theocentric love of the Divine Other and the human other. Freedom is, therefore, freedom *for a commitment of the whole person* to such self-transcendence, and not for a flight from specific commitments; it should not be merely freedom as self-determination, but self-affirmation in the sense of commitment to theocentric love (cf. *Vol. 1*, Sec. 9.3.1, under the subheading "Being Free for Self-Transcendent Love"); the person must affirm his or her own liberty in orienting this to God.

Fourth, the Council admits that human freedom has been really "damaged by sin," so that the human person needs the help of grace to be able to direct his or her life toward God.

Finally, the Council expressly teaches that *all* persons are morally responsible before God for the good or evil that they have done.

These five points of this article are important. Yet one can accept Ratzinger's comment[32] that they might have been more critically analyzed and developed. Let us now examine some possible additional contributions, seeking to integrate these with the postconciliar efforts of *Vol. 1* and *Vol. 2*.

A first observation that can be made has a historical and doctrinal origin. Text 4 of this article had been justly criticized for making a confusion in identifying the philosophical idea of freedom of choice with the saving gift of freedom conferred by Christ in the New Testament. As a reaction, the next text of this article eliminated all christological reference to the New Testament or to the teaching of the New Testament on freedom. Thus was lost an opportunity of showing the convergence between the Christian message of the New Testament and what is characteristic of the human person as such; and as a result, there is lacking a Christian and interdisciplinary convergence (like that attempted in the two volumes we have cited) between theology, philosophy, and social psychology (cf. especially *Vol. 1*, Sec. 9).

A second observation lies in the same line. Number 17 employs two biblical texts: Ecclesiasticus [Sirach] 15:14 and 2 Corinthians 5:10. Regarding the latter text, the "tribunal of Christ" of which Paul speaks has tacitly been changed in No. 17 into a "tribunal of God," thus (as Ratzinger notes, *op. cit.*) transferring the text from the perspective of faith to that of natural theology.

The same must be said of the text Ecclesiastes 15:14, by which a passage is effected not only to natural theology, but to natural ethics, and moreover, to a trend in late Jewish wisdom theology (of the second and third centuries B.C.) that was marked by *ethical optimism*. It should not be forgotten that this optimism was criticized in two other wisdom books, namely, Job and Qoheleth (Ecclesiastes).

Further, and still dealing with Ecclesiastes 15:14, we can recall that this is a moralistic reinterpretation of Deuteronomy 11:26ff., which in turn is placed in a new framework in Jeremiah 21:8, that of the concrete situation of Jerusalem under siege. Now, regarding the way in which Ecclesiastes 15:14 gives a moralistic reinterpretation of Deuteronomy 11:26ff., we must keep in mind that the text of Deuteronomy is entirely determined by the theology of the *Old* Covenant, for in this text, God addresses Israel as the representative of humanity and Israel was not able to observe this Covenant (cf. Acts 15:10). It is further to be remembered that Christ obtained for us the promise of the Spirit and of eternal life not through freedom in fulfilling the mosaic law of the Old Covenant, but by dying as a transgressor of this very Law (Gal. 3:12ff.).

In conclusion, we can say that Ecclesiastes 15:14 has in Article 17 of GS been torn from its historical context in the history of revelation so as to become the support of a philsophical doctrine of freedom. But this, in the words of Ratzinger, "represents not only an unhistorical reading of Scripture but also an unhistorical and therefore unreal view of man" (*op. cit.*, p. 138). Therefore, the general teaching on freedom developed in No. 17, at least in its *terminology*, cannot stand up either to the criticism of biblical theology or to that of the human sciences (such as philosophical anthropology or scientific psychosocial anthropology).

As to criticism from biblical theology, two points can be noted. First, as Ratzinger (*ibid.*) remarks, the text of No. 17 uses anodyne formulas, of unjustified optimism, which sound pelagian or semipelagian. The following passage of No. 17 serves as an example of pelagian *terminology*:

"Man . . . emancipating himself from all captivity to passion . . . pursues his goal . . . and procures it for himself through effective and skillful action, apt means to that end"; and as an example of semi-Pelagian terminology, the statement that grace is only a help to bring "the relationship with God into full flower" [*plene actuosam*].

Second, the deep dialectics that exist in the human person and make his freedom limited and imperfect are not taken into consideration. In *Vol. 1* (Sec. 9.3.1), by way of a commentary on Galatians 5:3–14, the person's call to freedom for the self-transcendence of theocentric love is highlighted; but then (in Sec. 9.3.2) attention is also called to the deep dialectics of the first, the second, and *sometimes* the third dimension, with which the human person must struggle continuously, even after being redeemed, in order to respond to the divine call (see the comments there on Gal. 5:16–17 and Rom. 12:2).

As to criticism arising from anthropology, philosophical or scientific and psychosocial, we can refer to Secs. 7, 8, 9.2, and 10, along with Fig. 1, of *Vol. 1*, which present repeated reflections and examples of the conscious and subconscious limitations upon the person's *effective* freedom for the self-transcendence of theocentric love, analyzing the various factors (especially the three dimensions) that intervene in the psychodynamic process of such limitations in the human person. The freedom of the Christian is, after all, both liberty and liberation; its beginning is a gratuitous gift of Christ, but it is also an object of conquest. Christian freedom is a capacity given to us by God to stand before Him as partners in the New Alliance (cf. Jer. 31:31 and Ez. 36:26). The reflections and research findings of *Vol. 2* go to confirm the existential reality of these limitations upon effective freedom, and show that they are present, to a debilitating degree, in 60 to 80 percent of persons. These limitations on freedom affect practically all the steps in the journey of vocation, such as its beginning, perseverance, growth in the internalization of self-transcendent values, vocational crises, the influence of formation, the influence of the environment in general, and the life of relationships with others, including the psychosexual area (cf. *Vol. 2*, Secs. 3 to 9).

All of these anthropological contributions, theological, philosophical and psychosocial, set in relief the basic function of freedom in Christian vocational growth toward "the freedom of the children of God." They go to show how true is the opening statement of No. 17, "Only in freedom can man direct himself towards goodness." There is a close connection between freedom and self-transcendence toward a love that is centered on God; after all, the Christian vocation is a call *to freedom for the self-transcendence of theocentric love,* of which Galatians 5:13–14 speaks (cf. *Vol. 1*, Sec. 9.3.1).

On the other hand, in the face of such converging interdisciplinary anthropological contributions, the *terminology* of some of the expressions used in No. 17 sounds anodyne and even flattering as regards human freedom; consequently, it is ambiguous and can easily be open to interpretations that are falsely optimistic concerning the reality of the human person. Many applications of the Council's teaching made by institutions or persons, in various areas such as that of priestly or religious formation, or the pastoral treatment of moral questions, as in the sexual area, have followed a line of unjustified optimism; an optimism that not only misinterprets and misapplies the thought of the Council, but also fails to correspond to the reality of the human person. As to this reality, beyond the contributions of interdisciplinary anthropology referred to before, we can mention the various manifestations of hedonism, egoism, social injustice, violence or the violation of human rights, which we must sadly recognize in the daily life of no small part of society (cf. the Synod of Bishops on the Second Vatican Council, Final Relation, in II, D, 1).

GS itself states that "The truth is that the imbalance under which the modern world labors are linked with that more basic imbalance rooted in the heart of man" (No. 10), and that "man is split within himself," so that "the call to grandeur and the depths of misery are both a part of human experience" (No. 13). Similarly, the Synod of Bishops on the Second Vatican Council (1985) takes ". . . note of a partial and selective reading of the Council, as also of a superficial interpretation of its doctrine in one way or another" (Final Relation, I, 4).

Christ as the New Person

One cannot conclude a discussion of the general lines of an anthropology of the first chapter of Part I of GS without at least recalling the basic truth expressed in No. 22: as Karl Rahner[33] puts it, christology is the end and the beginning of anthropology. Christ is the new Adam, the eschatological image of God; and "by the revelation of the mystery of the Father and His love, fully reveals man to man himself and makes his supreme calling clear." Christ grounds and animates our being without becoming in the least confused with it.

After these initial statements, the article passes on to the three basic mysteries of christology: the incarnation, the cross, and the resurrection, presented in terms of their anthropological function. In Christ, people find their existence and life, their victory over sin and death, the love of God and the love of neighbor. In brief, Christ is the image in which humanity is created and re-created.

The final thought of this article deserves note: our incorporation in Christ, by means of which we become children in the Son. This is the idea of the theocentric self-transcendence of humanity, which is not made to remain in itself, but to go beyond and above, so that humanity possesses itself fully when with the help of Grace it transcends itself and "can cry out in the Spirit: Abba, Father!"

The Community of Humanity

Premises

Humanity was created to the image of God (Gen. 1:26); but this being the image of God has its psychodynamic aspect in the human capacity or possibility of transcending oneself toward God, to know him and to love him (cf. *Vol. 1*, 9.3.3); and, as St. Augustine says (*De Trinitate*, XIV, 8, 11), a person is the image of God insofar as he or she orients himself or herself to God, while he or she deforms his or her likeness to God insofar as he or she distances himself or herself from God.

Now this human capacity to relate to the absolutely Other grounds the possibility and the necessity of human partners. But a person has not been constituted solely in relationship to any human partner. "On the contrary, the circle of human solidarity is open to a third, who is wholly other, God. . . . Man stands in immediate relation to God, he does not merely have to do with God indirectly through his work and his relations with his fellow-man. He can know and love God himself" (see Ratzinger,[34] pp. 121–123). One can say that human fraternity presupposes a theocentric self-transcendence that corresponds to what the human person is, and gives the person full self-possession in giving himself or herself totally to the other (cf. *Vol. 1*, 9.3.1).

On the other hand, as Guardini[35] observes, God has so arranged it that the human person passes through creatures (persons and things) to reach the Creator. God "has placed man within an order, an order of things, of other persons, of pre-existing realities and of happenings. This order is the will of God and may not be skipped over" (*ibid.*, p. 97). As it is true that one does not come directly to the living God except by way of Christ, so it is also true as a general rule (one that accordingly admits exceptions) that God wishes persons to come to him without bypassing the world that he has created.

But Christian maturity (cf. Gal. 2:20) consists in being related to creatures not in a merely egocentric self-transcendence nor in a merely social-philanthropic self-transcendence, but in a self-transcendence that is also theocentric and christocentric. As explained in *Vol. 1* (cf. Sec. 9.3.1), love of God and love of neighbor are a single love, which is in the last analysis theocentric. For after all, the gift of self in love should be made for the good or the theocentric value of the giver and of the receiver;

and only if it is, in the last analysis, motivated by a *theocentric* self-transcendence, rather than an egocentric or social-philanthropic self-transcendence, will the gift of self in love lead to the realization of both the persons involved (cf. Vol. I, 7.3.2). Further, the gift of self should be *total*, made with all one's heart, with all one's soul, with all one's mind and with all one's strength (Mt. 22:37–39), so that one loses one's life for the Divine Other and the human other (Lk. 17:33).

GS discusses the relationships that the person establishes with other persons in the second chapter of Part I, dealing with "The Community of Mankind." The third chapter of Part I then takes up the relationship of humanity with the realities of this world, under the title of "Man's Activity throughout the World." In the discussion that now follows, the second and third chapters are taken separately.

The contribution to understanding these two chapters of GS, provided by the interdisciplinary anthropology of *Vol. 1* and *Vol. 2*, worked out after the Council, is founded on a *basic hypothesis*. This basic hypothesis deals with the anthropological conditions that can function as *dispositions* to the primary action of grace in favoring the actuation of the two characteristics of the gift of self in relation to creatures that have been mentioned: its being a gift centered on God and its being a total gift.

According to this hypothesis, those individuals who show a greater *existential* maturity, as expressed in the person's Index of Developmental Maturity (cf. p. 412 and note 17), *together with* a greater degree of effective freedom for self-transcendence in the second dimension, are those who should be more free to live out their relationships with creatures as theocentric self-transcendence rather than as a self-transcendence that is only sociophilanthropic or egocentric.

Such better dispositions in relating to creatures, which tend to favor a self-transcendence that is centered on God and also favor totality in self-giving, are indicated by a specific *sub*structure that is part of the second dimension of these persons; this substructure reflects their capacity for interpersonal orientation, and is accordingly named the Index of Interpersonal Orientation (cf. *Vol. 2*, Sec. 8.1). This index makes it possible to distinguish between persons who are mature in their relations with others and those who are immature. Those who are mature are, in their interpersonal relations, prevalently oriented toward theocentric self-transcendence, that is, toward self-transcendent values, moral or religious; whereas those who are immature are prevalently oriented toward a self-transcendence that is sociophilanthropic or egocentric, that is, toward natural values.

The research findings of Vol. 2 (see Secs. 8.1.3–8.1.5) confirm both the validity of the basic hypothesis formulated and the validity of the Index of Interpersonal Orientation for distinguishing those who are mature in their relations with creatures from those who are immature.

Chapter II and Observations on Those Who Are Mature

The *anthropological* viewpoint of the present contribution is focused on relations with others that are lived as a self-transcendence centered on God. This viewpoint has a number of points of convergence, at least in terms of the principles stated, with important characteristics of the second chapter of Part I of GS.

First, following Haubtmann[36] and Semmelroth,[37] it should be said that in the mind of the redactors and of the commission responsible for GS, the first three chapters of the first part make up a unified whole whose attention is centered on persons in their interiority rather than on social problems; these chapters deal above all with *anthropology,* and so with the human person considered in terms of three different approaches: the person as having the dignity of an individual related to God (Chap. I); the person in relation to the community of mankind (Chap. II), and in relation to the material world of earthly realities in which the person must act in order to develop his or her own humanity (Chap. III). These three approaches to an anthropology, both theological and philosophical, seem to be very helpful in the effort to understand the maturity of the individual person in terms of a concrete existential anthropology. They correspond, in fact, to the three approaches followed in Vol. 2, in studying the maturity of the individual in the concrete existential situations of life, using the Index of Developmental Maturity. So this index seems to have solid theological and philosophical bases, and at the same time it highlights those areas of the personality that are particularly important in studying individuals and in seeking to give them pastoral help.

Second, Chapter II of GS does not recommend concrete solutions on the level of social institutions, but states that *there can be no social order* in keeping with Christian (and, therefore, human) thought, unless certain basic values and orientations are respected, these having their primary source in God, and *corresponding to the divine vocation of the integral human person*. These theological and philosophical approaches of GS match the approaches to an interdisciplinary anthropology as formulated in *Vol. 1*: the human person is called to the self-transcendence of a love that is centered on God, which is then concretized as it passes by way of the persons and things of the environment, and the situations of the person's life (cf., in *Vol. 1*, the comment on Gal. 5:13–14, in Sec. 9.3.1). The same matter has been taken up here, p. 433, when the self-transcending of theocentric love, expressed as maturity on the Index of Developmental Maturity and on the second dimension, are taken as basic dispositions correlated with a mature interpersonal orientation, that is, with an interpersonal orientation that favors, in social relationships, a prevalence of theocentric self-transcendence over a self-transcendence that is merely egocentric or sociophilanthropic.

Third, Chapter II of GS avoids stating, or even insinuating, that the *primary mission of the Church* is of a social nature. Rather, this chapter, in the light of biblical revelation and of reason, emphasizes and insists upon the *close links that exist between social living and a sound Christian anthropology*. In other words, as in the whole first part of GS, stress is laid on the need to Christianize the social thinking of the Church, so that this thinking, which has its bases in the theological and ontological call addressed to humanity (cf. preceding paragraph), can permeate all social living. It is this point that we have sought to express, in terms of an existential psychosocial anthropology, in formulating a basic hypothesis, given on pp. 433–434, according to which there is a correlation between maturity as reflected in the person's Index of Developmental Maturity and maturity as reflected in the Index of Interpersonal Orientation. This adds emphasis to the pastoral usefulness of developing, in individual persons, a sound Christian anthropology. In brief, as we read in No. 23 of GS, brotherly dialogue among persons is not realized just by multiplying communications between them, but on a different plane: that of a communion between persons that has its own requirements, going far beyond the mere organization of things. Clarification of the spiritual and moral nature of the human person, by means of a sound christocentric anthropology, has helped to understand what the laws of a well-ordered social life must be. For these reasons, the Church is concerned with the social order above all in terms of the human person, of what the person is, and of his or her divine vocation calling him or her to a self-transcendence centered on God.

Fourth, the three preceding observations are not meant as a defense of any *"individualistic ethic"*; their purpose is precisely the contrary. GS itself has shown concern, right from the first chapter of Chapter I, to state that "God did not create man as a solitary," but that "by his innermost nature man is a social being, and unless he relates himself to others he can neither live nor develop his potential" (No. 12, par. 4). This theme is taken up at length in Chapter II, especially in Nos. 24, 30–32. Number 30 calls attention to an excellent antidote to individualism: institutional commitment as a modern way of fulfilling the duties of justice and of charity. At the end of this article, it is stressed that these suggestions for going beyond an individualistic ethic cannot become reality "unless individual men and their associations cultivate in themselves the moral and social virtues, and promote them in society. Thus, with the needed help of divine grace, men who are truly new and the artisans of a new humanity can be forthcoming." In other words, "Social obligations are pointed out as duties before God, as material in which to embody an attitude to God. That is a task for the community, yet has to be carried out by individuals" (Semmelroth,[38] p. 178). One sees clearly the stress on the need for a theocentric self-transcendence on the part of individuals, which can then express itself on the level of social institutions.

This theme is further developed in the following No. 31, which highlights the fact that a person's participation in social life is based on the sense of responsibility of a strong personality, and on values that can attract persons and dispose them to the service of others.

In the same line, it is worth noting that No. 32 stresses, as does the Council at a number of other points, that God's real partner in the Alliance and in the history of salvation is the People of God, the individual person being a partner only in the measure in that he or she belongs to this people. Human solidarity thus opens toward, and is transformed in, the solidarity between the members of the Church; human community is accomplished in Christ and his unity of life with the Father; the mystical body of Christ is the fulfillment of human solidarity.

Our *Vol. 2*, Sec. 8.1, also calls attention to the same idea of an ethic that is not individualistic, showing, in fact, that maturity in human solidarity (expressed as a mature "interpersonal orientation") is correlated with the individual's maturity in a theocentric and christocentric sense (as indicated by the Index of Developmental Maturity and by the second dimension), and vice versa. Besides, some structures are common to the person's Index of Developmental Maturity and to his or her Index of Interpersonal Orientation, which goes to show how deeply rooted in the human person is the nature and the role of being social. The person's maturity on the Index of Developmental Maturity and on the second dimension takes effect and finds expression as maturity on the Index of Interpersonal Orientation. The findings presented in *Vol. 2*, Sec. 8.1, are matched by the doctrinal-pastoral formulation of No. 24, which draws on various biblical texts centered on the basic statement that all persons are "created in the image of God" and that "all men are called to one and the same goal, namely, God Himself." Noteworthy also is the reminder of "a certain likeness between the union of the divine Persons, and the union of God's sons in truth and charity. This likeness reveals that man . . . cannot fully find himself except through a sincere gift of himself (cf. Lk. 17:33)."

Fifth, the second chapter of GS, discussing in No. 29 the fundamental equality of all persons, men and women, and social justice, emphasizes the principle that *human institutions* must aim at the goal of a self-transcendence centered on God; for they "must labor to minister to the dignity and purpose of man," and "must be accommodated by degrees to the highest of all realities, spiritual ones . . .".

We have attempted to call attention to some important points of convergence between Chapter II of Part I of GS and the ideas and research findings of *Vol. 2*, Sec. 8.1, since these points of convergence are a concrete indication of the possibility of formulating general Christian principles on the basis of a scientific psychosocial anthropology, one which keeps in mind the self-transcending values of Christ. Such convergence shows above all how theology and the human sciences can find many meeting points. Further, such instances of convergence offer the pastoral advantage of making it possible to approach concrete existential problems with a better knowledge of the issues; and this is no small advantage since, in the words of a theological *peritus* of the Council, sometimes "theologians are only too accustomed to prescind from concrete existential situations" (Moeller,[39] p. 112).

Chapter II and Observations on Those Who Are Immature

Thus far, we have considered those persons who are mature on the Index of Developmental Maturity, the second dimension, and the Index of Interpersonal Orientation. Yet the basic hypothesis regarding relationships with creatures, formulated on pp. 433–434, takes account also of immature persons, who are, after all, more numerous than the mature (cf. *Vol. 2*, Secs. 8.1.3–8.1.5, and 8.2.7 at no. 7).

GS takes note of this problem, and deals with defects in relations with others, especially in Nos. 25–28. It will be useful to compare the contribution of the Council with the anthropology presented in *Vol. 1* and *Vol. 2*, with a view to deriving some pastoral applications.

Article No. 25. This article discusses the thesis that the person and society are in a constant and reciprocal interaction resulting from the nature of each. But the article notes that the increased complexity of contemporary social life can have ambivalent effects on the genuine development of the human person: effects that can be positive or negative. In this context, the article makes two anthropological statements that are very important.

The first of these reads, "To be sure the disturbances which so frequently occur in the world order result in part from the natural tensions of economic, political, and social forms. But at a deeper level they flow from man's pride and selfishness, which contaminate even the social sphere." Here we have a clear parallel to other statements of GS: "The truth is that the imbalances under which the modern world labors are linked with that more basic imbalance rooted in the heart of man. For in man himself many elements wrestle with one another," so that "man suffers from internal divisions, and from these flow so many and such great discords in society" (No. 10).

These statements, taken together, tell us above all that in pastoral practice, one must begin with a profound formation of the individual conscience so as to arrive at a social orientation, and not vice versa. The same conclusion was reached by Farahian in a recent doctoral dissertation in biblical theology, "Le 'je' paulinien dans Galates 2:19–21" (in press). Second, these statements of the Council, taken together, recall the conscious dialectics of the first dimension, those that dispose to sin or to virtue. These form part of the Index of Developmental Maturity discussed in Sec. 8.1 of *Vol. 2*, this index being related to the Index of Interpersonal Orientation dealing with relations with others. But there is more to the problem than this.

For the text of No. 25, as already cited, continues with a second statement: "When the structure of affairs is flawed by the *consequence of sin*, man, *already born with a bent towards evil*, finds there new *inducements* to sin, which cannot be overcome without *strenuous efforts* and the assistance of grace" (emphases added). One seems to find here a noteworthy parallel to the dialectics of the first and second dimensions, as described in Gal. 5:16–17 and discussed in *Vol. 1*, Secs. 9.3.2 and 10.3.5; what is involved is the concupiscence that comes from original sin, with its consequences. On the other hand, as research findings have shown, immaturity on the second dimension is an important factor influencing immaturity in relationships with others (see *Vol. 2*, Sec. 8.1).

One might say that the just-cited pages of *Vol. 1* dealing with the second dimension, and also the ideas and data of Sec. 8.1 of *Vol. 2*, serve to make more explicit this part of GS. A further confirmation of this possibility is provided by a point recalled by Haubtmann[40] (p. 269), who was a *peritus* involved in preparing GS: the draft of No. 25 prior to the final text did not speak of "disturbances" but of "evil." A change in terminology was suggested by the fact that social disorders can exist without being sinful. In fact, the dialectics of the second dimension are dispositions to *nonculpable error*, and from such dispositins arise *some* social disturbances. But other social disturbances are culpable.

Article No. 26. The content of this article deals, more or less explicitly, with the ultimate purpose for which the common good is to be promoted. This final purpose is to be found in promoting the development of the person; for ". . . the disposition of affairs is to be subordinate to the personal realm and not contrariwise . . ." And what is this order in which the development of persons is to be promoted? The first and last paragraphs of this article indicate that this order or development of persons should "allow social groups and their individual members relatively thorough and ready access to their own fulfillment" (first par.), and that this fulfillment of persons is the fruit of the "ferment of the Gospel" that "has aroused and continues to arouse in man's heart the irresistible requirements of his dignity" (last par.). The parallel to Galatians 5:13–14, in terms of God calling the human person to freedom for the self-transcendence of theocentric love, seems clear.

It is therefore a theocentric and christocentric self-transcendence that is proclaimed as the ultimate goal of the common good. Yet, experience shows that people who know how to take care of themselves often do so at the expense of the common good. For example, some leaders, even spiritual ones, can, singly or in groups, subordinate the common good for which they are responsible to a "good" of personal advantage. In so doing, they favor the kind of self-centeredness that marks immature persons, and confuse the development of persons with an individualistic quest for self-interest. At the other extreme lies a different form of immaturity that seeks the common good by following the principle that the common interest must prevail over individual interests, in such a way that they desire, more or less consciously, that the individual be absorbed anonymously into the collectivity (Semmelroth,[41] p. 170).

As shown by the research findings of Sec. 8.1 of *Vol. 2*, the immature are those persons in whom an egocentric or merely sociophilanthropic form of self-transcendence prevails over theocentric self-transcendence in their relations with others.

Article No. 27. In this article, the Council passes from principles to practical applications, these being listed as actions to be done or to be avoided. These obligations, considered together, imply certain principles that deserve attention.

First of all, every social duty and relationship should be animated by the Christian commandment of love of God and neighbor. This theocentric and christocentric orientation is clearly emphasized in the middle of the article by reference to Matthew 25:40: "As long as you did it for one of these, the least of my brethren, you did it for me."

Second, in our love of neighbor, we should follow the example of God's love for us. God's love is absolutely free and creative. God creates the partners of his love, and approaches them in love expressed as creation and as grace. And so also should be our own love, going beyond a merely humanistic level, and not waiting for the other person to prove himself deserving of love (Semmelroth, *op. cit.*, pp. 171–173).

Third, we should avoid betraying the dignity of a self-transcendent and theocentric love, for which the human person was created, in favor of an immature motivation that is only sociophilanthropic or egocentric; we must respect the theocentric end for which every single person has been created.

Finally, this article unites the cause of human dignity to that of the honor due to the Creator: the forms of immaturity in the love of persons, listed in the article's final paragraph, "are a supreme dishonor to the Creator."

As can be seen, these four principles emphasize *respect for the human person in his or her totality;* his or her origin and end, which have their foundation in God and in Christ, can be easily forgotten by those who are immature in the sense of Sec. 8.1 of *Vol. 2;* for their strong inclination to confine themselves to a merely egocentric or sociophilanthropic self-transcendence can be a serious obstacle to respecting the *total* person of the other.

The respect due to the person of the other is considered in No. 27 in the perspective of sin and virtue of the first dimension. There is *missing* a vision of relationships with others, and good done to others, in terms of a good that is prevalently apparent rather than genuine and real, such as is possible in the second dimension. Yet our research findings, given in Sec. 8.1 of *Vol. 2,* show the importance that maturity or immaturity on the second dimension can have in leading persons to establish relationships that are not totally Christian.

So the love of others that arises from immaturity can be in part an egocentric love of concupiscence, in which one seeks subconsciously what is gratifying for oneself, rather than the true Christian good of the other. Or else an immature love of others can be a love of benevolence, which seeks the good of the other, but only in terms of natural values, rather than aiming at self-transcendent values, so that the relationship of love does not have its origin in God and does not lead to God, but subconsciously stops at a natural and sociophilanthropic level. Many examples of such *merely apparent good* might be offered; a few will have to suffice.

Friendships that are not really helpful (and at times a real hindrance) toward growth in theocentric love on the part of those involved, and for their development toward an internalization of the self-transcendent values of Christ, are among the most obvious examples: the friendship is limited to a relationship of noninternalizing identification or of compliance (cf. Vol. 1, Sec. 9.4.2B), involving not a *self*-transcending growth in Christ, but only a feeling of gratification and an improved self-image. Such friendships can be pleasant, but they do not help ascetically toward the assimilation of the values of Christ or toward transformation in him.

C. S. Lewis,[42] examining the different kinds of love that underlie all human relationships, and discussing disorder in any kind of human love, stresses that "disordered love" does not mean a love that is insufficiently cautious or that is too great; for it is not possible to love a human being too much; but it *is* possible to love a person too greatly *in proportion* to our love of God. It is insufficient love of God, and not excessive love for a human person, that constitutes the disorder (p. 170). It should not be forgotten that what Lewis says is to be understood in relation to the Christian ideal of human relationships.

The Index of Interpersonal Orientation makes possible an existential and verifiable confirmation of such a proportion between love of God and love of a person; and so it makes possible a discernment of order or disorder in the interpersonal aspect of human action. For this index, as already noted, reflects the person's readiness for an orientation to theocentric self-transcendence, and thus unmasks possible forms of love of God that are false and merely proclaimed (cf. Mt. 7:21–27.) When the Index of Interpersonal Orientation reflects a substantial difficulty with theocentric self-transcendence in love, one has an existential verification, at least on the level of dispositions, of the vulnerability and ambivalence of human relationships; St. Paul makes a similar point in stating (1 Cor. 13:3), "If I give away all that I have, and if I deliver my body to be burned, but have not love, I gain nothing."

A second example has to do with possible ways of governing. One can govern subjects, not as a servant who helps them to draw nearer to Christ and to grow in him, but so as to please them (and, subconsciously, so as to be accepted, praised, and gratified by them); in which case, one lacks the altruism and Christian self-transcendence needed to help the subjects grow toward the theocentric goal for which they were created, even when such a service goes against the spontaneous desires of the subjects themselves. Christianity is not a popularity contest; in this, the example of Christ is very clear; he did not seek to content everyone, but to love everyone so as to lead them *to the Father*, even when this meant paying the personal price of making some enemies. It is clear, on the other hand, that one cannot appeal to "values" as a justification for trampling on the rights of others. When such apparent goods are sought by leaders, they may give them such names as "prudence," "charity," or "realism"; sometimes such names may be quite justified, but at other times, they only mask the leaders' subconscious lack of Christian courage in taking initiative and decisions, in undertaking and resolutely pursuing apostolic activities that are guided by what is important in itself for the kingdom of the Father. Maritain[43] remarks in this regard that Freud's unconscious is a heavy blow to rationalism and to pharisaic pride, to false self-awareness, to the denial of concupiscence and the cult of self-worship. All these are factors that contaminate relations with others and undermine their pursuit of their ultimate goal, that of contributing to the growth of the People of God, of the Mystical Body of Christ.

It is clear that what has just been said about ways of governing can also be applied, *mutatis mutandis*, to ways of carrying on apostolic activities. Here, too, people are not helped toward christocentric growth by a merely social kind of relationship, which is often a mutual self-incensing and gratification, or an *omission* of needful challenges and exhortations to theocentric love, in order to retain the acceptance, approval, and praise of the faithful. Here, too, the subconscious needs of the second dimension, which are oriented only to an egocentric or sociophilanthropic self-transcendence, can lead subconsciously to a loss of respect for the person of the other in its *totality*, created and called to transcend itself in love of Christ and of the Father.

This problem of apostolic effectiveness for the Kingdom of God is anything but marginal or secondary; it is enough to recall the high percentage of immature persons found in our research (cf. *Vol. 2*, Sec. 8.1). To these data, we can add the fact that from 60 to 80 percent of persons are immature on the second dimension (cf. *Vol. 2*, Sec. 5, and the reflections given in *Vol. 1*, Secs. 9.3.2 and 10.3.5).

A fourth problem has to do with community living or with groups within a community. The possibility that people can be led to seek membership in various groups or communities by motivations that are *immature* or prevalently *natural,* rather than by motivations that are prevalently of theocentric self-transcendence, has been heavily documented by a long series of studies and research findings (see the many contributions cited in *Vol. 2*, Sec. 8.3.1). The same possibility is there when a community elects its own superiors.

It was also shown in the research given in *Vol. 2* that a high percentage of those who remain in religious institutions are "nesters," meaning persons who tend to "build themselves a nest" rather than to transcend themselves theocentrically (69 percent of a sample of 267 subjects, and 72 percent of a sample of 103 subjects, were "nesters"; see Sec. 5.6.3). "Nesters" are persons who persevere in vocation while being immature on the second dimension. In such persons, compliance and noninternalizing identification prevail over internalizing identification and internalization (for this distinction, see *Vol. 1*, Sec. 9.4.2B). The influence exercised by the immature interpersonal behavior of these persons upon the life of a community is easy to imagine. The same can happen in the Church in general; there are "nesters" in the Church who call themselves Christians, but are basically led also by non-Christian motivations of the second dimension.

A community that is religious and ecclesial is called to live out its anthropological reality of theocentric self-transcendence in interpersonal relationships and also in apostolic activity. If the community does not want to go on being conditioned by recurrent problems impeding the attainment of its characteristic purpose, including witness and apostolate, it should possess the means of discernment and of growth needed to deal with the roots of these difficulties, such as immaturity in the first, and especially in the second dimension, which, by way of the limitations they impose on individuals, hinder communities and groups in the pursuit of their goals.

Article No. 28. This article bears the title "Reverence and Love for Enemies," "enemies" translating the Latin "adversarii." But the text speaks of "those who think or act differently than we do in social, political, and religious matters." This difference between title and text should not cause surprise; since concupiscence, to which both the first and second dimensions can be dispositions, can easily turn a difference of thought or action into enmity or tension in interpersonal relationships.

It follows that such respect and love for one's *adversarii* is a kind of acid test for those who are immature in relating to others; since their immaturity often tends to transform what is merely a difference of opinion into personal animosity or hostility.

There is also another reason for this. Being able to accept another person's diversity in opinion or action requires that one be able, without ceasing to uphold the truth that one believes in, to treat the other with the respect and love needed for a real dialogue, in which there can be discussion with willingness to receive as well as to give. Receiving is much more difficult for immature persons, who are inclined to cling to what is egocentric or social, rather than integrating both with what is theocentric, that is to say, with values that often require renouncing what is gratifying or defensive, either directly (egocentrically) or indirectly (socially).

Such disinclination to receive as well as to give may be particularly felt in religious matters. Those who are immature on the first or second dimension are persons divided within themselves, also and perhaps especially with regard to the self-transcendent values, moral and religious, for which the human person has been specially created. Hence, immature persons can feel particularly threatened in their own inner division and so in their sense of security. In consequence, they will tend to react to a divergence of views not so as to defend the truth, but in subconscious self-defense, to protect their own self-esteem; and they will tend to do this by making subconscious distortions in their way of listening, judging, and discerning. This subconscious tendency to distortion has been discussed in *Vol. 1,* Sec. 9.4.2C. Here it may be recalled that this tendency can seriously affect growth in the Christian vocation, as well as the relationships of persons in community and the apostolic activity of a group.

Human Activity Throughout the World

Premises

The Second Vatican Council also wishes to recognize the importance of human activity, including the daily tasks of the vocation of humanity as the partner in the dialogue that the Church seeks with the modern world. In this context, Thils[44] reminds us of the danger of a certain devaluation of activity (*praxis*, as opposed to *theoria*), in consequence of the great influence that Greek culture has had upon our world; a danger from which the Christian tradition has not been exempt. The Greeks had devoted themselves to the search for a divine *state* rather than a person.

For the Christian, human activity is to be seen not only in the light of a personalist principle, but also in keeping with the words of Paul: "whether you eat or drink, or whatever you do, do all to the glory of God" (1 Cor. 10:31).[45]

If it is true that the original concern of this part of GS was with external action on the world and on material things, it is also true that such action was immediately related to an overall vision of human activity, and thus placed in the context of humanity's *integral* vocation and specifically of the development of his or her personality, of his or her action on material things, and of his or her relations with others (Articles 33 and 35; cf. the comment of Auer,[46] pp. 185–186 and 189–190).

Chapter III and Observations on Its Articles

Article No. 33: The Problem. Chapter III of GS deals with human activity in the world, under the impulse of two sociocultural phenomena that have had a marked effect on modern persons: technology and socialization, these being considered in the context of humanity's *integral* vocation, and of the specific mission of the Church in the world of today (Auer, *op. cit.*, pp. 186–187).

The limitations of Chapter III have been noted by Smulders,[47] as well as the commentaries already referred to of Thils and Auer. Some of these limitations are due to contingent factors arising from the history of the text, and to lack of time for a full discussion, since the end of the Council was approaching (cf. Smulders, *op. cit*, pp. 394–396). Among others, the following points of basic incompleteness can be noted: (a) the lack of an exploration in depth of the themes of liberty and liberation, which are however mentioned as the supreme fruits of activity in the world; (b) a similar defect in exploring the relationship between such freedom and evangelical liberty; and (c) the fact that the theology of history is not introduced explicitly into this reflection (cf. Smulders, *op. cit.*, p. 419).

The very term "human activity" is not without ambiguity, since it can have many meanings (Smulders, *op. cit.*, p. 398; Flick,[48] p. 581). Perhaps because of such imprecision, and discussions hastened by circumstances, the three basic questions raised in the second paragraph of Article 33 are not given an adequate answer in the text. These three questions are, first, what is the meaning and value of human activity?; second, how should one use the realities involved?; and third, what is the goal of human striving, individual and collective?

Chapter III, therefore, which should in theory have crowned the preceding chapters dealing with the person and the community, seeking to formulate the Christian idea of personal and social activity and then introducing Part II, turns out to be rather incomplete (Smulders, *op. cit.*, p. 394).

Yet it has a value and a historical meaning. The Council has taken serious account of modern humanity and has sought to listen to what concerns and fascinates contemporary people. In contrast to an earlier outlook, not always surpassed, the Council strove to reach a better understanding of the modern mentality so as to offer encouragement and to open new perspectives, rather than to build a dam against it. Chapter III is marked by the simplicity and the single law of the gospel, even though the task of giving form to this law in the complex reality of our existence and society is difficult and endless (Smulders, *op. cit.*, p. 420). Its value and its authority are therefore necessarily limited in comparison with those of the two great Constitutions (on the Church and on Revelation), in spite of its having the same intent as these Constitutions (Smulders, *op. cit.*, p. 397).

In commenting briefly on the articles of Chapter III, we will try to show how the basic concern of *Vol. 1* and *Vol. 2* correspond to some of the problems raised by these articles. This concern was that of defining the terms of an interdisciplinary anthropology (with theological, philosophical, and psychosocial bases) and then providing existential confirmation of some basic elements of this anthropology.

The references to the reflections and to some of the results presented in *Vol. 1* and *Vol. 2* indicate some possible contributions, of limited scope, to grasping the intention of Chapter III of GS. As already mentioned, apart from the success achieved and the limitations observed by commentators, this chapter intends to offer guiding principles for a Christian attitude to the activities and values of the world.

Article No. 34: The Value of Human Activity. This article emphasizes that human creativity, expressed in various forms of activity is a participation in the creative work of God. Such *creativity*—which is not absolute—is a call to *responsibility*.

In the preparatory scheme (1965) of Chapter III, it was desired to extend this participation in creative activity to include explicitly the most ordinary activities of daily life: the mother of a family caring for the well-being of her children, physical, intellectual and moral; the worker performing useful labor and struggling for greater social justice; the researcher trying to uncover the laws of nature; the farmer, the employee, the technician, and all those whose activities are directed to the service of the community.

Divine transcendence is not in itself opposed to the development and maturity that result from human activity; on the contrary, the Christian message calls men to be concerned for the well-being of their fellows and to help to build up the world. These truths are to be understood together with the points made in Nos. 35 and 36.

In the light of these considerations of the Council, human activity has been considered in *Vol. 2*, Sec. 8.3, in relation to certain basic components of the anthropology of the Christian vocation.

Concretely, the Index of Interpersonal Orientation represents in a satisfactory way certain characteristics of human activity in the world that are existential and so can be measured in the research itself. This index provides a measure of the degree in which certain tendencies or dispositions are present or absent in each person: the tendency to accomplish various tasks or projects (attitudes of achievement on the level of the ideal self and of the actual self); to establish bonds of collaboration and loyalty (attitudes of achievement on the level of the ideal self and of the actual self); to establish bonds of collaboration and loyalty (attitudes of affiliation); to help those in need, to sustain, console, protect, comfort, care, and heal (attitudes of nurturance); to explore and understand new fields of human knowledge and action (attitudes of knowledge); to control the human environment by dominating the forces present in the community or in society (attitudes of domination); to organize or arrange the environment with precision (attitudes of order); and also to overcome difficulties, resisting the tendency to evade or retreat from tasks that can be frustrating or embarrassing (attitudes of counteraction.)

These characteristics of human interaction that can reflect in a suitable way (also because they are concrete) the *responsibility* and *creativity* that the Council recognizes as values that respond to the demands of the Christian vocation in the world of today. In the Index of Interpersonal Orientation, these dispositions are related to the greater or lesser disposition to theocentric self-transcendence present in each individual.

Article No. 35: The Regulation of Human Activity. In No. 35, the Council reminds us that while human activity is centered on humanity in the sense that all of creation is related to humanity, it is also true that the person is more precious for what he or she is than for what he or she has. The values of *justice*, of *brotherhood*, and of a *more humane ordering* of social relationships, introduce the importance of a norm that must be related to the Absolute, but which also has a value in itself. The Council here intended to indicate the hierarchy of values in the world, namely their culmination in the human person and the person's orientation to transcendence (Auer,[49] p. 190, citing the *Textus Recognitus et Relationes* of 1965, p. 49). In spite of a certain ambiguity (cf. Auer, who speaks of the failure to distinguish between the ontological and moral values of human activity, and between moral and religious value; *op. cit.*, p. 190), here is reaffirmed the relationship that human activity must have to the *genuine good* of humanity, and to the *total* vocation of the human person (cf. Thils,[50] who refers to Article 36 in connection with this ordering of activity to total happiness).

The "norm of human activity" is that it should serve the *genuine good* of humankind. And, according to the Council, the good of humankind is not a collective development to which the individual person might be sacrificed, but "it should . . . allow men as individuals and as members of society to pursue their total vocation and fulfill it" (par. 3).

In using the word "vocation," the Council means that what is involved is not some blind tendency, but the faithful response to a call and to an invitation to a dialogue. The vocation in which human activity finds its place is, therefore, the manifestation of "the divine plan and will" (par. 3). The norm for judging the value of human activity is religious since it is based on the mission, given to humanity by God, to dominate the world so as to become a more perfect image of God (cf. Flick,[51] p. 608).

In this sense, the reference to theocentrically self-transcendent values in the very structure of the Index of Interpersonal Orientation serves to make explicit and concrete this basic requirement of the Christian meaning of human activity. The reference to theocentrically self-transcendent values in this index is further explained in the reflections that now follow.

Article No. 36: The Rightful Independence of Earthly Affairs. In this article, the Council shows eagerness to uphold the autonomy of human values and does so without ambiguity, distinguishing, however, between an *authentic autonomy* and an autonomy that is false and, for the believer, not acceptable.

Thils,[52] commenting on this paragraph, writes: "the Christian will strive not to live out his tendency towards the Absolute in such a way that the value of earthly realities and their autonomy and dignity are diminished to the point of vanishing. He will also strive not to value these realities to the point where one of them becomes, in a concrete and vital sense, an absolute" (p. 293). The Council, as noted by another commentator (Flick[53]), presents this truth from a twofold point of view. Above all, to value earthly realities without relating them to God is to falsify their true nature, since they gravitate with all their being toward God (Rom. 11: 36). Anyone who fails to hear "His revealing voice in the discourse of creatures" (No. 36, par. 5) has only a partial grasp of the reality of creatures. Further, anyone seeking to value earthly realities while excluding the organic unity that they find only in God, condemns them to a kind of disappearance and makes them opaque (*ibid.*).

The Council seems to intend establishing a *negative* norm: one cannot work for real human progress while *excluding* all reference to God (Flick, *op. cit.*, p. 610).

In this sense, in research seeking an existential verification of the meaning of human interaction, it is crucial to be able to evaluate a person's dispositions to various forms of activity in the world, as considered before (cf. Nos. 34 and 35), in *relation* to those dispositions that are closely linked to *theocentric self-*

transcendence in particular and to the person's entire motivation in general. The Index of Interpersonal Orientation is composed precisely of the totality of those dispositions that can more directly favor or hinder theocentric self-transcendence. A marked immaturity on this index, connected especially with immaturity on the second dimension, can lead to the exclusion of an authentically lived orientation of human activity to the Creator (cf. *Vol. 2*, Sec. 8.1), producing that kind of "independence of temporal affairs [that] is taken to mean that created things do not depend on God, and that man can use them without any reference to their Creator" (par. 5). On this point, one can also consult the Final Relation of the Synod of Bishops on the Second Vatican Council (1985), at II, A, 1, concerning secularism.

Article No. 37: Human Activity as Infected by Sin. In this article, the Council begins to frame the Church's answer to the question of the meaning and value of human activity in the world, *in the perspective of the history of salvation.*

Number 37 approaches this theme from the starting point of the presence of evil in the world and the ambivalence of human activity. It had seemed to some of the Fathers of the Council that the vision presented in earlier drafts at the start of the Council was excessively optimistic (cf. Thils,[54] p. 294, and Auer,[55] p. 194.) As Thils points out (p. 294), the ambiguity intended is not ontological but existential; and one can note that this last term seems to imply a need for considerations of a more dynamic and motivational kind. The comments of Thils and Auer indicate that in the Council there was a confrontation of the basic optimism of Christianity with the reality of evil and of existential disorder in life, but that the equilibrium produced seems to require further clarification. It is not our intention to deal with the complexity of this whole problem; but a comment of Thils is worth recalling: "The permanent renewal which we witness in our knowledge of human mechanisms will lead to a revision of our ideas on the exercise of liberty, on conscience, and on responsibility; but they will not eliminate the fact of sin" (*op. cit.*, p. 295).

Smulders[56] further notes how the Council, before pointing to the dangers implicit in progress, recalls once more that "progress is a *great advantage* to man." But it is this very advantage that brings a temptation with it. One can go further, says Smulders, and add that it is precisely because it is good that progress becomes a stronger temptation. The new *power* of humanity in modern times, the new awareness of self, and the new dominion he or she has over the world, bring with them the danger of humanity overestimating itself (the root of all sin), and the danger of attributing an absolute value to partial goods: comfort, property, knowledge, or power (Smulders, *op. cit.*, p. 408).

At this point, there comes spontaneously to mind the dialectic between the apparent good and the real good that characterizes the second dimension. This dialectic, which is distinct from the conscious dialectic between virtue and sin characterizing the first dimension, can lead to the person's closing himself or herself within natural horizons.

The Index of Interpersonal Orientation, setting dispositions to human activity in relation to dispositions that are more or less favorable to theocentric self-transcendence, takes account of the fact that human action, as a part of human anthropological reality in the wider sense, is involved in a struggle between good and evil. Concretely, it takes account of the fact that human activity and so also interpersonal relations are daily endangered by humanity's pride and disordered self-love (No. 37). Characteristics such as humility or pride, a sense of inferiority, exhibitionism, aggression, sexual desire, affective dependency, the fear of pain and of death, enter as possible dialectics, conscious or subconscious, in the evaluation of the difficulties encountered by persons who are called to a theocentric self-transcendence in interpersonal relationships. In this sense, human action is to be related to a possible disorder having a conscious disposition in the first dimension, but also a subconscious disposition in the second dimension: cf. *Vol. 1*, Sec. 9.3.2. The correlation between the Index of Interpersonal Orientation (on the one hand) and the Index of Developmental Maturity, as well as maturity on the second dimension (on the other hand), is an existential confirmation of an anthropological vision that recognizes this *existential ambivalence* and permits its assessment. The existence of such ambivalence implies the need for a serious discernment of the motivations (including subconscious ones) that underlie different forms of action in the world, as well as discernment of external actions or of conscious intentions.

Article No. 38: Human Activity as Finding Perfection in the Paschal Mystery. Explicit reference to self-transcendent values as the ultimate meaning of human activity is found again in this article. Here it is explicitly stated that it is in the paschal mystery of Christ dead and risen that human activity finds its perfection, through the gift of the Spirit of the risen Christ. The Spirit arouses a desire for the age to come (theocentric self-transcendence) and animates, purifies, and strengthens the longings by which the human family strives to make its life more human and to render the whole earth submissive to this goal.

Smulders[57] stresses the importance of the connection made in the text between the *Christian desire for the age to come* and the effort to *give a more human form* to this world, as had been requested by several Fathers of the Council (cf. Modus 31). These two forces are not in opposition. Since heaven consists essentially in the fulfillment of mankind as a universal community of persons in the love of all for God in Christ, earthly efforts should try to build up the earth, as far as possible, as a community of persons that offers to everyone the means to develop himself or herself in a conscious freedom (p. 413); further, "The desire of heaven and the will to earthly progress can stimulate and reinforce each other; in keeping with this, and with the desire of the Council, this will is the gift of the same Spirit, as long as *it is authentic and not a cover for a latent egoism*" (p. 423, with emphasis added.)

In *Vol. 2*, it emerges in a number of ways that in 60 to 80 percent of the persons studied such latent egoism is present as different forms of immaturity connected above all with the second dimension. For the purpose of discerning such possible latent egoism in the form of apparent goods sought by human activity in the world, the Index of Interpersonal Orientation and the dimensions (especially the second, with which this index is correlated) can make a useful contribution.

Number 38 thus provides an answer to one of the basic questions inspiring the third chapter of GS: What importance has the gospel for man in his earthly activity? The drama of human striving is seen in the context of the history of salvation, with special reference to the paschal mystery as the passage from slavery to freedom. This passage is a liberation that is accomplished in Christ, dead and risen.

This is meant to be a liberation for the human person *as a whole*, not only as tending to God with his ideals, but involving the complex of anthropological factors brought to light by the interdisciplinary approach of *Vol. 1* and *Vol. 2*. The contribution of these volumes to understanding human activity is to be taken in connection with what was said about freedom, with reference to No. 17.

The relation of human activity to freedom for self-transcendent love (cf. Gal. 5:13–14 and *Vol. 1*, Sec. 9.3.1) throws light also on a theme often encountered in vocational life, particularly in apostolic life. This problem was already discussed in a book we published in 1976 (Chapter 10),[58] and in *Vol. 1*, Sec. 10.4.2; it lies in a tendency to live a vocation as an orientation to a role rather than to values. Number 38 reminds us that the gifts of the Spirit are diverse; some are called to give witness to the desire for a heavenly home, and others to dedicate themselves to the earthly service of people and to make ready the material of the celestial realm (see par. 5).

Beyond such differences, present in the external and visible form of the gifts received, the Council recalls that there must be a liberation common to all Christians, effected by the Spirit who "frees all . . . so that by putting aside love of self and bringing all earthly resources into the service of human life they can devote themselves to that future when humanity itself will become an offering accepted by God" (par. 4). Once again, we see an explicit reference to self-transcendent values as the common denominator of the various forms of life and activity in the Church and as *that which gives them value*. This approach, while it *gives value to* every form of life and activity that can be expressed in the variety of roles (including social roles) found in the Church, *relativizes* such roles and activities that, without a reference to self-transcendent values, are deprived of their basic anthropological truth.

Article No. 39: A New Earth and New Heaven. This last article of Chapter III deals with the value of human action in the perspective of eschatology. To what extent does human activity, and the relations with creatures involved in such activity, have only a transitory value, or to what extent do they have an eternal permanence? The perspectives here opened are vast indeed, going well beyond the range of this essay.

The Council recalls that human action, with its progress and its conquests, *is not to be identified with* the growth of Christ's kingdom, but still that these efforts (as explained in the preceding articles) are *part of a plan*, which has a goal to be conceived as the point of arrival of this preparation, not as the arrest or interruption of the process of becoming (Thils,[59] p. 299).

It is worth noting in this context that in pastoral and educational work (always based on some anthropology), it is easy to see, from the pastoral experience of the Church, that *a certain human development* is needed to be able to accept evangelization, and observe the moral law, without expecting grace to work continuous miracles (Flick,[60] p. 627). Physiological factors (handicaps or underdevelopment), crushing misery, or social structures without justice or charity are recognized examples that illustrate possible difficulties in opening oneself to the gospel and the tendency to close in upon oneself in a climate of individual egoism or class struggle: since the Christian commandment of love seems no more than meaningless language, when the words do not correspond to any reality experienced by the hearer.

It is equally worth noting (as pointed out in connection with No. 17, on freedom) that there is less explicit concern with the kind of pastoral work that would deal with those conditionings and limits that do more direct damage to the person in his or her interiority, and that *may* be a hindrance, in human activity, to being oriented to self-transcendent values centered on God and to the love that remains forever (cf. *Vol. 1*, Sec. 9.3.2, and *Vol. 2*, Sec. 9). And yet this was one of the principles placed by the Council as inspiring the whole of GS (cf. No. 10, par. 1, on the "more basic imbalance rooted in the heart of man").

The observations of the present essay, as developed in *Vol. 1* and *Vol. 2*, have shown how difficulties in opening oneself to the gospel can have their roots not only in *external* realities, but also in realities *internal* to the person, and how these difficulties can be identified, on the level of a basic anthropological reality in the person, as forms of immaturity connected with one or more of the three dimensions.

On the other hand, human action can, for those who are mature on the Index of Interpersonal Orientation (which is connected with developmental maturity and with maturity on the second dimension) become a "kind of foreshadowing of the new age." Relations with creatures, if lived with a Christian maturity as described, acquire the value of *permanence*, because they are rooted in love as a value that is self-transcending and centered on God, and acquire also the value of *witness* that is strongly felt by our contemporaries. Here again, the three dimensions (especially the first and second) and the Index of Interpersonal Orientation can contribute, in a modest way, to the discernment of, and growth in, the kind of relations with creatures that produce such Christian witness.

Conclusion

The Second Vatican Council suggests an *interdisciplinary* approach to anthropology, both in the field of doctrine and that of pastoral practice (GS, No. 62, paras. 2 and 3; see above, pp. 405 and 406).

We have tried to follow this suggestion, which was expressed from the very beginning of the Council as one of its principal purposes (cf. John XXIII, *Opening Speech to the Council,* 11 October 1962; AAS, 54 [1962], 792). Such an interdisciplinary approach, as outlined within the limits of the present pages, can make it possible to reach a more concrete vision of the human person, with many apostolic advantages, both doctrinal and pastoral; these advantages can be summarized under the following headings: a vision that is more concrete, more explicit, and so more realistic and more useful for the pastoral care of the human person in his or her existential reality. If these advantages are actually attained, it becomes more possible to reach the goal that was desired by the Synod of Bishops on the Second Vatican Council of 1985: to favor an interior assimilation and an internalization of the Council, which will make its documents alive and a source of life (*Report,* 1, 5 and 6).

Translated from the Italian by Bartholomew Kiely.

Notes

1. John XXIII, *Discorsi, messaggi, colloqui del Santo Padre* (Rome, 1964), V, 274.

2. John Paul II, *L'Osservatore Romano* (7–8 October 1985), 1.

3. O. Semmelroth, "The community of Mankind," in H. Vorgrimler (ed.), *Commentary on the Documents of Vatican II,* Vol. 5 (New York, 1969), 165.

4. J. Mouroux, "Situation et significance du chapitre I: la dignité de la personne humaine," in Y. M.-J. Congar and M. Peuchmaurd (eds.), *L'Eglise dans le monde de ce temps,* Tome II (Paris, 1967), 229.

5. B. Lambert, *ibid.,* pp. 166–167.

6. Y. M.-J. Congar, "In luogo di conclusione," in G. Baraúna (ed.), *La Chiesa del Vaticano II,* (Florence, 1965), 1268.

7. C. Moeller, 'History of the Constitution," in H. Vorgrimler (ed.), *Commentary on the Documents of Vatican II*, Vol. 5 (New York, 1969), 271.

8. G. Alberigo, 'La Costituzione in rapporto al magistero globale del Concilio," in G. Baraúna (ed.), *La Chiesa nel mondo di oggi* (Florence, 1966), 192–195.

9. L. M. Rulla, *Anthropology of the Christian Vocation. Vol. I; Interdisciplinary Bases* (Rome: Gregorian University Press, 1986). L.M. Rulla, J. Ridick, F. Imoda, *Anthropology of the Christian Vocation. Volume 2: Existential Confirmation*, is expected from the Gregorian University Press in 1988. Both volumes are also available from Loyola University Press, Chicago. In the text, both volumes are referred to as *Vol. 1* and *Vol. 2*, respectively.

10. P. Delhaye, "La dignità della persona umana," in G. Baraúna (ed.), *La Chiesa nel mondo di oggi* (Florence, 1966), 268.

11. J. Ratzinger, "The Dignity of the Human Person," in H. Vorgrimler (ed.), *Commentary on the Documents of Vatican II*, Vol. 5 (New York, 1969), 121–122.

12. The transcendent character of the human person is stressed also by GS, although in another context; see Article 76.

13. P. Delhaye, "La dignità della persona umana," 269.

14. J. Ratzinger, "The Dignity of the Human Person," 122–123.

15. Z. Alszeghy, "La dignità della persona umana, I. L'immagine di Dio nella storia della salvezza," in A. Favale (ed.), *La Chiesa nel mondo contemporaneo* (Leuman, Turin, 1966), 427.

16. J. Mouroux, "La dignité de la personne humaine," 235.

17. The Index of Developmental Maturity was assessed by means of in-depth interviews of two hours with each person (cf. *Vol. 2*, Sec. 2.2.1C). These interviews were based on the analysis of much information previously obtained about each person: (a) an earlier interview and a biographical inventory on his past family life, and (b) a study and interpretation of the results of various tests. These tests had been given three times: at the time of entry into vocational life for the religious and seminarians, or into college for the lay students; again two years after entry, and once more four years after entry. On each of the three occasions, the same tests were given, so that each time 162 aspects of each person were examined in terms of 162 scales, each scale representing a combination of several questions or items.

18. J. Ratzinger, "The Dignity of the Human Person," 122–123.

19. P. Delhaye, "La dignità della persona umana," 269.

20. In theology, the technical term "concupiscence" refers to the fact that the person, because of original sin, no longer has perfect control of natural spontaneity and emotions (on emotions, see *Vol. 1*, Secs. 7.2.2 and 8.4.2). For a theological treatment, see K. Rahner,

"The Theological Concept of Concupiscentia," *Theological Investigations*, Vol. 1 (London, 1974), 347–382.

21. P. Delhaye, "La dignità della persona umana," 270, note 13.

22. J. Ratzinger, "The Dignity of the Human Person," 125–126.

23. Z. Alszeghy, "La dignità della persona umana," I, 436.

24. J. Ratzinger, "The Dignity of the Human Person," 124.

25. *Ibid.*, 126.

26. *Ibid.*, 126–127.

27. J. Mouroux, "La dignité de la personne humaine," 238–239.

28. J. Ratzinger, "Zum Personenverständnis in der Dogmatik," in J. Speck (ed.), *Das Personenverständnis in der Pädagokik und ihren Nachbarwissenschaften* (Göttingen, 1966), 157–171.

29. B.J.F. Lonergan, *Method in Theology* (London, 1973²), 35.

30. J. Ratzinger, "The Dignity of the Human Person," 136.

31. B.J.F. Lonergan, *Method in Theology*, 101–124.

32. J. Ratzinger, "The Dignity of the Human Person," 136–139.

33. K. Rahner, *Betrachtungen zum ignatianischen Exercitienbuch* (Munich, 1964).

34. J. Ratzinger, "The Dignity of the Human Person," 121–123.

35. R. Guardini, "Realismo cristiano," *Humanitas*, 30 (1975), 95–101.

36. P. Haubtmann, "La communauté humaine," in Y. M.-J. Congar and M. Peuchmaurd (eds.), *L'Eglise dans le monde de ce temps*, Tome II (Paris, 1967), 255–277.

37. O. Semmelroth, "The community of mankind," in H. Vorgrimler (ed.), *Commentary on the Documents of Vatican II*, Vol. 5 (New York, 1969), 164–181.

38. *Ibid.*, 178.

39. C. Moeller, "History of the Constitution," 112.

40. P. Haubtmann, "La communauté humaine," 269.

41. O. Semmelroth, "The community of mankind," 170.

42. C.S. Lewis, *The Four Loves* (New York, 1960), 170.

43. J. Maritain, "Freudianism and Psychoanalysis: A Thomist View," in B. Nelson (ed.), *Freud and the Twentieth Century* (Cleveland/New York, 1957), 230–257.

44. G. Thils, "L'activité humaine dans l'univers," in Y. M.-J. Congar and M. Peuchmaurd (eds.), *L'Eglise dans le monde de ce temps*, Tome II (Paris, 1967), 280.

45. Thils emphasizes that the dogmas of the creation and incarnation have freed matter from condemnation, but that stoicism has continued to have an influence on moral thinking. Attention to human action has been brought into the foreground by cultural influences such as the philosophy of Kant, which remains however limited by its formalism and by its separation of intention from action. The problem of

action is in any case in the foreground, and the modern person has become ever more aware of the fact that it is he or she who must give meaning to his or her action: it is in the world, and with other persons, that his or her destiny must be worked out. This destiny is not accomplished by intention alone, but by transforming the world (himself or herself, material things, and other persons): humanity must incarnate its responsibility in the different areas of life (cf. GS, No. 36).

46. A. Auer, "Man's Activity Throughout the World," in H. Vorgrimmler (ed.), *Commentary on the Documents of Vatican II*, Vol. 5 (New York, 1969), 185–186 and 189–190.

47. P. Smulders,"L'activité humaine dans le monde," in G. Baraùna (ed.), *L'Eglise dans le monde de ce temps*, II (Bruges, 1968), 394–421.

48. M. Flick, "L'attività umana nell'univeso," in A. Favale (ed.), *La Chiesa nel mondo contemporaneo* (Leuman, Turin, 1966), 427.

49. A. Auer, "Man's Activity Throughout the World," 190.

50. G. Thils, "L'activité humaine dans l'univers," 283.

51. M. Flick, "L'attività umana nell'universo," 608.

52. G. Thils, "L'activité humaine dans l'univers," 293.

53. M. Flick, "L'attività umana nell'universo," 606–610.

54. G. Thils, "L'activité humaine dans l'univers," 294.

55. A. Auer, "Man's Activity Throughout the World," 194.

56. P. Smulders, "L'activité humaine dans le monde," 408.

57. *Ibid.*, p. 413.

58. L.M. Rulla, J. Ridick, and F. Imoda, *Entering and Leaving Vocation: Intrapsychic dynamics* (Rome/Chicago, 1976), Chap. 10.

59. G. Thils, "L'activité humaine dans l'univers," 299.

60. M. Flick, "L'attività umana nell'universo," 627.

CHAPTER 39

The Foundations of Human Rights in Biblical Theology Following the Orientations of *Gaudium et spes*

Édouard Hamel, S.J.

Summary

Many of the approaches used in the attempt to provide a theological basis for human rights in these past twenty years can already be found in *Gaudium et spes*, although maybe in embryo form or as fleeting allusions. Among these various theological approaches, we have chosen the following: (1) the human being as created in the image of God, and as the possessor of inalienable rights; (2) the covenant, or the history of Israel as freed by Yahweh who proclaims and protects the rights of all; (3) the kingdom of God, defined as it now exists for the present, and as hope in its future fulfillment; (4) the Pauline understanding of solidarity (texts on the "body"), which is linked to the new realization of human solidarity.

Gaudium et spes did not reach its full perfection due to a lack of the time needed for a complete maturation process. Even so, the document does have value as foreshadowing future developments, and is very precious for its underlying intuitions, the various pointers it gives, and above all the seeds of growth that it includes and that have borne fruit since its publication.

The two particular points on which there were deficiencies to be made up and lines to be followed further were that of the biblical sources and that of teaching on human rights.

The use of Scripture in the document was not entirely successful. In their wish to provide the document with a universal approach and thus reach all people (although we may wonder whether it did in fact reach any more people because of this), the Fathers thought it best to limit references to revelation. Although we can speak of the biblical sources of the document,[1] the actual use of Scripture is relatively marginal. Various texts are cited, but in isolated fashion, without much exegetical evaluation and without exercising any decisive influence on the central lines of the Constitution.[2] Because of the ascending approach adopted, Christ is seen more as Omega than as Alpha. In short, if *Gaudium et spes* were to be written today, it would probably take a different form.

Nor does teaching on human rights occupy the place it might have. It must be admitted that in the 1960s, development was still the burning issue of the day for the Church, and was therefore the favorite theme of international congresses and publications on social matters.[3] Paul VI would say in 1967 that "the new name for peace is development."[4] The eclipse of the subject of development only started in the 1970s, as the subject of human rights came to take on an ever greater importance. As John Paul II would say in 1979, "After all, peace comes down to respect for man's inviolable rights."[5]

Even if human rights are frequently discussed in *Gaudium et spes*, it can hardly be claimed that the document provides a systematic, fully articulated, and complete presentation of the subject.[6] Still less can we claim that it presents a theology of human rights. It does certainly contain important theological statements, but it would be left above all to John Paul II to fill these out and develop them. And the biblical foundation of human rights hardly appears at all.

In this short study, we should like to show how some of the biblical-theological approaches used in these past twenty years (1965–1985) to provide a biblical and theological foundation for human rights were already found in *Gaudium et spes*, either in an embryonic state or under the form of passing references.

Humanity as Created in the Image of God

How can theological perspectives provide better understanding of the age-old subject of human rights? Since it is a question
of the rights innate to humanity as such, a theological reflection
on humanity as such is indispensable in order to provide an
answer to this question. What does the Constitution have to say
about humanity and its dignity? This question suggests a first
reference point: the person as created in the image of God. And
Gaudium et spes bases the dignity of all people on the biblical and
patristic concept of the "image of God": "For sacred Scripture
teaches us that man was created 'to the image of God,' as able to
know and love his creator, and as set by him over all earthly
creatures that he might rule them, and make use of them, while
glorifying God" (GS 12c).

Recent biblical studies have expanded on this theme abun-
dantly. Created last of all, humanity is God's masterpiece, the
summit and crown of creation. Whereas for the creation of the
other things, the divine command is entrusted to a fulfilling word
(Gen. 1:3), in the case of humanity God says, "Let us make man
in our image" (Gen. 1:26), as if he were in some way giving
himself an order. Only people are said to be created in the image
of their Maker, and only of them is it said that God "breathed
into [their] nostrils the breath of life" (Gen. 2:7). Human life is
thus seen as a mysterious contact between people and God.[7]
Created in the image of their Maker as a living reproduction of
great value, people are connected to God in a special way, and
are set before him as personal subjects whose inner dynamics
orient them toward the one who created them, although this
does not compromise their freedom. As "man's friend," God
looks to a person for a free response. The incomparable dignity of
a person does not come in the first place from the fact that he or
she is called to reign over the cosmos (Gen. 1:28), but from the
fact that he or she is raised to the rank of responsible dialogue
partner with him who created him or her. And this is above all
why a person's fundamental rights are inalienable.

It is normally accepted today that the expression "the image of
God" comes from the royal ideology that was widespread in the
Middle East in ancient times. In Egypt and Mesopotamia, only
the king was the image of the divinity, and his statue was set up
in a given place to signify and recall his sovereignty over that

place. He alone was the mediator between the deity and human beings, and his was the task of acting as viceroy in the place of the absent deity. As a proverb said, "The prince is the shadow of the deity, while the people are the shadow of the prince"—which led to the danger of the divinization of the prince and the use of despotism in the exercise of power.

Previously reserved to the sovereign, when this concept is introduced in Genesis, it is "democratized" and applied to all persons, who are created in the image of God, as the icon of God, and placed on the earth as God's viceroy and the lord of all creation, entrusted with the exercise of sovereignty over the earth and the other creatures on behalf of God, and thus with the continuation of the work of the Creator.[8]

Since there is only one Creator, all persons have been created by the same God, which means that they are brothers and sisters of one another and are all of them equal before him. All people, without any distinction as to sex, race, or social position, can say that Genesis 1:26–27 speaks of them. All people are created equal and are called to share, according to their capacities, in this dominion over the earth. In the perspective of Genesis, this is the deep root of human dignity and the respect that is due to all human beings.

God's Right

God's right is first of all his very excellence, which gives rise to duties on the part of his creatures. Despite their eminent dignity, human beings are not God and only resemble him: they are literally created *in* the image of God, in other words, as dependent on him, with the task of reflecting him, and therefore of being something other than God. They are neither divinized, nor enslaved, but are free and different from God. Sin is contempt for God's right. *Gaudium et spes* speaks implicitly of this "right of God" when it says that "Man was created in God's image and was commanded to conquer the earth with all it contains and to rule the world in justice and holiness: he was to acknowledge God as maker of all things and relate himself and the totality of creation to him" (GS 34a).

However, the expression "God's right" can also have another derived sense, since, thanks to the concept of the image of God, all fundamental human rights are rooted in God, and can only be absolute to the extent that they share in the absoluteness of God. Respect for human rights does not therefore depend on some social convention, but is called for by God himself. In this sense, "God's right" is the protection he grants humanity as created in his image—in other words, his strength placed at the service of humanity's weakness, since a person is nothing but an enthroned beggar before God, a handful of dust (Gen. 2:7) raised up to royal dignity. "All men are endowed with a rational soul and are created in God's image; they have the same nature and origin, and . . . there is here a basic equality between all men and it must be given ever greater recognition" (GS 29a).

In a special way, God's right is the right of the person who is poor in economic or social terms: "He who oppresses a poor man insults his Maker" (Prov. 14:31), since such oppression means depriving him of his right to be under God's protection and at his service. *Gaudium et spes* quotes the following saying of the Fathers: "Feed the man dying of hunger, because if you do not feed him you are killing him" (GS 69a).

Features of the Concept of the Image of God

The concept of the image of God as offered in Genesis has both a relational and a dynamic dimension. "Male and female he created them" (Gen. 1:27). In the bible, a person is also defined through interpersonal relationship, which is indissolubly united to his or her relationship with God. As created by love and for love, a being of communion created for communion, a person can enter into personal relationship with others. "For by his innermost nature man is a social being; and if he does not enter into relations with others he can neither live nor develop his gifts" (GS 12c). And a man's love for a woman in marriage is the fundamental touchstone for human beings as a group, inasmuch as they must all, in the image of the united couple, also live in communion, harmony and peace.[9] Hence, the importance of social rights and community rights: they can never be in conflict, and one set is not possible without the other, so that they must always both be respected.

"And God blessed them, and God said to them, 'Be fruitful and multiply, and fill the earth and subdue it' " (Gen. 1:28). This blessing is also a vocation and a destiny: God, so to speak, launches the man and the woman into history (of which he remains Master and Lord), and confers powers on them that enable them to continue his work together by exercising, in his name, a dominion that is a continual growth and development. For human beings, this dynamic conception of the image of God means initiative and progress, with regard to the exterior world of course, but also—and primarily—in the ever-growing awareness of their own identity, in other words, of everything entailed in their relationship with God and with the other "images of God," and hence their spiritual and moral life. This jibes well with the contemporary approach to human rights as summed up in the phrase "the right to development." "Modern man is in a process of fuller personality development and of a growing discovery and affirmation of his own rights" (GS 41a).

Human Life: Divine Gift and Human Right

What destiny did God assign to human beings from the very beginning? According to the first chapter of Genesis, which is a hymn to life and to God's creative power, and also according to the narration of the fall (Gen. 3:22–24), this destiny was life, bodily life, life in communion with God and people, life on a fraternal earth (the "Canticle of the Creatures"): "The glory of God is living man." And this destiny was not destroyed by the flood, for immediately after it, the scene from the first chapter is renewed, with its blessings (Gen. 9:1). God "who lovest the living" (Wis. 11:26) is the source of life; he protects it and does not want people to destroy it. "Guardian" of creation (Gen. 2:15), a person is also the "guardian" or "keeper" of his or her brother or sister (Gen. 4:10): "Whoever sheds the blood of man, by man shall his blood be shed, for God made man in his own image" (Gen. 9:6). The ultimate basis of human rights is the dignity of human beings as creatures made in the image of God.

In the image of God who governs the world by creating life, not by destroying it, human beings must rule the world "in justice and holiness" (GS 34a). The *Dominamini* is a blessing with corresponding obligations. The actions of dominion that man legitimately performs are linked to ecological duties and the protection of the environment. The exercise of economic rights must neither threaten the present quality of human life, nor compromise the life of future generations. There is a right to the future and also a right *of* the future—that is, the right of those who will follow us. Since material resources are limited, they must not be exploited irresponsibly: "dominating," "subduing," or "having dominion over" does not mean "destroying."[10] Today, there is an ecological crisis of cosmic proportions, which has been brought about by human beings, who are then its first victims. However, this crisis also indicates violence against creation itself. Human beings have the duty of a fundamental respect for creation as reflecting the very beauty of the Creator. God did not only tell people to subdue the earth, but also to admire it; "And the Lord God planted a garden in Eden, in the East; and there he put the man whom he had formed. And out of the ground the Lord God made to grow every tree that is pleasant to the sight . . . " (Gen. 2:8–9). In Genesis, apart from the *Dominamini*, there is also a *Miramini*, to which *Gaudium et spes* makes fleeting and overly timid reference: " . . . the world . . . has been created and is sustained by the love of its maker" (GS 2b).

Contemporary men and women must, therefore, relearn the fact that they must treat the created world with respect, admiring its beauty and wisdom, respecting its laws, and remaining in harmony with it. Otherwise, they are shutting themselves off from an authentic value. They must, of course, organize a world in which people will live better, but they must also admire and respect a creation that, in its beauty, is a gift of God for the good of humanity.

Contemporary men and women have the terrible power to "de-create" the world in which they live. *Gaudium et spes* speaks of the danger of going "from the grave crisis of the present day to that dismal hour, when the only peace it [humanity] will experience will be the dread peace of death" (GS 82d).

In the perspective of a nuclear catastrophe, the fundamental right to life appears in a different context. It is no longer a case only of the individual's right to life, but of the right to life in general. The most personal of human rights has thus also become a social right, in other words, the right to the possibility of life for each person, to existence on this earth as given to all, to the existence of the earth itself.[11]

A Twofold Image of God

Gaudium et spes speaks of an image of God based on right reason (No. 15), freedom (No. 17), and conscience (No. 16), and then of a supernatural image of God that is not only superimposed on the "natural" image of God, but aims at expressing it in its full breadth. Humanity was created in a twofold justice: natural— "Man was created in God's image and was commanded . . . to rule the world in justice and holiness" (GS 34a); and supernatural— "set by God in a state of justice" (GS 13a). The concept of the creation of humanity in the image of God takes on its full meaning and reaches its perfection in Christ, the "perfect man" (GS 22), "the image of the invisible God" (Col. 2:15), who "reflects the glory of God and bears the very stamp of his nature" (Heb. 1:3). Through the incarnation of his Son, God gives everybody the "power to become children of God" (Jn. 1:12) and predestines them to be "conformed to the image of his Son, in order that he might be the first-born among many brethren" (Rom. 8:29).

It is thus the bond between creation and redemption that gives human dignity its final perfection.

> In reality it is only in the mystery of the Word made flesh that the mystery of man truly becomes clear. . . . Christ . . . fully reveals man to himself and brings to light his most high calling . . . [for] by his incarnation he, the son of God, has in a certain way [*quodammodo*] united himself with each man (GS 22a–b).

The statements are there, but the theological development remains minimal. It would be left to John Paul II to expand on them and provide them with greater depth by showing more clearly the meaning of the incarnation for teaching on human rights.

However, we are then faced with the following question: If the supernatural image is complete and all-encompassing, why should we continue to speak of the natural image, which is basically an abstraction drawn from a supernatural reality? The use of the natural image can facilitate dialogue with nonbelieving theists. The expression "the image of God" is undeniably biblical and may be difficult for those who do not share our faith to understand, but a theist philosopher reflecting on the capacity of the human spirit to open itself to the universal could maybe see in this expression a certain affinity between man and God—a participation of human reason in divine reason. There would then be a shift from revelation to philosophy, or, quite simply, a return to human reason, which would be taking up a truth that belongs to it, too, and would thus be giving its own witness, as a sort of confirmation, to a truth known historically through revelation.

Moreover, once the natural image of God is accepted, it would constitute a call and a preparation for the image of Christ, which is pure gift and grace, and which human reason can neither demand nor declare impossible. As Saint Thomas says, man's greatness lies in the fact that he has been made for a destiny that goes beyond his own capacities.[12] In a pluralistic society, this use of the natural image of God also makes it possible to provide the basis for human dignity as absolute. The distinction between the two images of God, obviously as made by faith, is thus legitimized. We can speak of a dialectic tension between the two, with the image of God based on God the Creator only reaching its fullness and perfection under the influence of the image of Christ. Here the "law of upward attraction" applies:

> . . . an order only goes to the full extent of its possibilities under the influence of a higher order, whatever form such influence may take. The highest achievement of the lower order is only possible through the attraction—or whatever we choose to call it—of a higher form as it was sought.[13]

Although the institutions retain their full meaning as such, in the light of the gospel, they take on a significance and fullness that they would not have of themselves. It is only in the light of the gospel that they find their ultimate perfection and their final meaning. This is because the gospel reveals to humanity God's plan for it, and thus provides an overall view of humanity and its vocation, not only in earthly terms but also for eternity. The gospel thus gives a new meaning to natural law that takes up and moves beyond its own meaning.

The light of the gospel, which casts a new clarity over everything, finally enables men and women to find solutions to the problems of their times—solutions that take into account the overall vocation of human beings, without ignoring any human or Christian element, solutions that are in harmony with the full dignity of the human person, solutions that are *fully human* and are therefore valid not only for Christians, but also for all people of good will. The full truth about human beings and the world can only be found in the light of the gospel. The brighter the light of the gospel shines, the more radiant human dignity will be and the more it will be proclaimed and defended. The divine order "does not mean that the autonomy of the creature, of man in particular, is suppressed; on the contrary, it is re-established in its own dignity and strengthened in it" (GS 41b).

The Concept of the Image of God in Lutheran Theology

For Lutherans, a person is not ontologically the image of God, or, in other words, a creature similar to his or her Creator or a sort of reflection of his splendor, because this would mean taking something away from God. Any gift of God that subsisted in a stable manner in a person would be seen as something withdrawn from God. There can be no true correspondence between God and a person, for this would mean denying pure grace (*gratia pura*). A person can only be the image of God to the extent that God deigns to enter into relationship with him or her, without any possible counterpart from a person. "Man is not phosphorus, but simply mirror."[14] The concept of the image of God as applied to a person constitutes a profane foundation that makes it possible to establish a relationship of love that goes from God to a person, without telling us anything ontologically about the human person as such. The underlying Lutheran objection with regard to human dignity and human rights is mainly over the practice of a direct claim to the autonomy of the person with regard to an order given by God. Human dignity can only come from Christ and from his grace (*gratia sola*). The justification from sin that Christ gave to humanity confers on the latter a dignity that it does not deserve, cannot destroy, and of which it cannot dispose. The State must protect this dignity, not only in Christians, but also in all people, since Christ died for all and offers the grace of salvation to all. (Here we can see the influence of K. Barth: everything comes from Christ, and from him alone.)

Human rights are thus not based on direct reference to the concept of humanity as the image of God. They are essentially linked to the secular order, and are principally explained by their basis in political ethics, because they play a constructive role with regard to the State, which must allow the person sufficient space and thus allow its authority to be limited. For Lutherans, the various civil declarations on human rights are *secular analo-*

gies with the basic ideas of the gospel, which represents the blueprint for the life of every Christian.

The Covenant

Another theological approach to human rights is provided by the theme of the covenant, which is the second great pillar of Old-Testament ethics. The perspective is no longer the universalist one of man as created in the image of his Maker, but that of the history of Israel as freed by Yahweh, no longer that of the God of creation, but that of the God of redemption, Yahweh as Liberator of his people. "At the outset of salvation history he [God] chose certain men as members of a given community, not as individuals, and revealed his plan to them, calling them 'his people' (Ex. 3:7–12) and making a covenant on Mount Sinai with them (cf. Ex. 24:1–8)" (GS 32a).

"I am the Lord your God, who brought you . . . out of the house of bondage" (Ex. 20:2). This text expresses the right of ownership that devolves on the person who has ransomed a slave, and therefore proclaims that the people thus freed from slavery belong to God. Israel owes its existence as a people to God's salvific action, so that the main bond between Yahweh and his people is not primarily moral but soteriological.

Yahweh calls himself a just king, who is the defender and protector of the weaker members of his people, and who intervenes on their behalf, demanding that the "strong" members extend the benefits of freedom even to the "weaker" ones and do not deprive the latter of their rights. It is Yahweh himself who has created Israel as a people, and who upholds it and keeps it in unity. It is he who gives the community its rights, who proclaims the right of each and every person, and demands that everybody respect this right. Yahweh's right is in a special way the right of the poor: they are the object of special care in Israel because their situation is in contradiction of the ideal wanted by God, which indicates fundamental equality between all. The right of the poor person is his right to existence, the recognition of his personal needs, his right to be himself, and his dignity as a human person: "The bread of the needy is the life of the poor; whoever deprives them of it is a man of blood. To take away a neighbor's living is to murder him; to deprive an employee of his wages is to shed blood" (Sir. 34:21–22). "Woe to those who decree iniquitous decrees, . . . to turn aside the needy from justice and to rob the poor of my people of their right" (Is. 10:1–2).[15]

The Rights of Liberated Israel

The fact that there was a deliverance as the starting point of the history of Israel marked its social life deeply. The Ten Commandments start by recalling this, and the whole law is simply the charter of those who have known this deliverance, so that the concept of justice and rights is influenced by this.[16]

The Ten Commandments and the code of the covenant proceed from the situation of manumission granted to the people. The Ten Commandments—or ten great freedoms—are the charter of those who have experienced deliverance from Egypt, while the social code is to protect the right of all to live in freedom and peace on the earth given by Yahweh to all the people. Nobody who has himself been freed from slavery can treat another person as an object, disposing of his life, his wife, his children, his honor and his belongings. Precisely because of the covenant, Israel discovers that it does not belong to itself, but to Yahweh, and that, as a result, no member of the community can dispose of his brother.[17] Any violation of the rights of another not only represents a refusal of the agreement to respect others, but is first and foremost an attack on the covenant between God and his people.

The commandments of the second tablet of the Decalogue protect fundamental human rights. They can all of them be summarized in the fifth: "You shall not kill" (Ex. 20:13). They are an affirmation of life, an exhortation to allow life to blossom and develop—bodily life, family life, social life—and a safeguarding of the quality of human life against egoistic, arbitrary, and capricious attacks. They proclaim the minimal conditions for a social life, the minimal moral rules without which a society cannot subsist, and they provide a common denominator on which all men of good will should be able to agree. In this sense, we can say that the second tablet of the Decalogue is a charter of fundamental human rights.[18]

The New Covenant

There is continuity between the actions of God in the old covenant and those performed by Christ under the new, for there is only one plan of salvation. All the biblical covenants are circles of revelation, with Christ the Savior as their common center, although the distance of each one from this center is different.[19] Yahweh's "wonderful works" for Israel are still repeated for us today through his Son who was made man.

In the subsection entitled "The Word Made Flesh, and Human Solidarity," *Gaudium et spes* states: "This communitarian character [of the people of God] is perfected and fulfilled in the work of Jesus Christ, for the Word made flesh willed to share in human fellowship. . . . This solidarity must be constantly increased" (GS 32b and e). The Christian faith tells us that all people without exception have been saved by the blood of Christ who calls especially on Christians to say "Yes" to human beings, and to respect the incomparable dignity that comes to them from the incarnation and redemption. The "rights" of God become the "rights" of Christ: "In his preaching he clearly outlined an obligation on the part of the sons of God to treat each other as brothers" (GS 32c).

In the incarnate Christ, God has sealed a covenant of justice and peace with humanity, accepting human beings completely, and taking them to him in his Son Jesus Christ. Constantly extending the sphere of human rights further, ceaselessly upholding and fostering them, making sure they are ever more firmly rooted, and building up a moral system that provides them with a solid basis and facilitates their promotion, means making human beings always more themselves as such, and taking Christ's incarnation seriously. The inalienable right to be fully human is proclaimed in the gospel. The gospel cannot, of course, be reduced to a human rights declaration, and it does not invent these rights, although the fact that it gives human dignity such a high position means that it does light up these rights from within, and fosters their promotion by giving Christians a special basis for action in this field.

The Kingdom of God and Human Rights

A theology of the kingdom is also of significance for the respect and promotion of human rights. In the subsection entitled "A New Earth and a New Heaven," *Gaudium et spes* has this to say: "Here on earth the kingdom . . . 'of truth and life, a kingdom of holiness and grace, a kingdom of justice, love, and peace' . . . is mysteriously present; when the Lord comes it will enter into its perfection" (GS 39c). However, we must be careful to distinguish between the two cities: " . . . although we must be careful to distinguish earthly progress clearly from the increase of the kingdom of Christ, such progress is of vital concern to the kingdom of God, insofar as it can contribute [conferre potest] to the better ordering of human society" (GS 39b). " . . . the Church has but one sole purpose—that the kingdom of God may come and the salvation of the human race may be accomplished" (GS 45a).

It is in function of the kingdom as already present but still to come that the Christian can place his commitments in the world in their proper perspective, and connect the effort to build a better world to the transcendence of the already accomplished kingdom. The kingdom of God represents the last stage, when at the final consummation, Christ will "deliver the kingdom to God the Father after destroying every rule and every authority and power" (1 Cor. 15:24). Now, if there is unity of origin, dignity, and vocation, there is also unity of destiny: protology is linked to eschatology. Created in the image of God, all human beings are called to share in the kingdom of God, where there will be only one people, one single human family.

The kingdom of Christ expresses an essentially dynamic reality and describes the kingdom of God as already present and working within the world. The concept of kingdom or reigning is closely connected to the person of the king. For Paul, Christ is Lord, and is reigning now: "For he must reign until he has put all his enemies under his feet" (1 Cor. 15:25). According to Psalm 72, Christ exercises his rights and reigns when he acts to correct unjust situations, and when he proclaims the "rights" of the poor, which must be recognized and respected.

The kingdom of Christ, therefore, indicates the power that flows from Christ the King and that, whatever the cost and despite human uncertainty and weakness, fills the world in order to make it bring forth fruits. This certainty gives rise to an immense hope within the Christian and within all men. In this sense, we can speak of a "right to hope,"[20] a hope that is a promise for the future, but also a challenge for the present. According to Isaiah, the kingdom of Christ is a kingdom of justice and peace (Is. 9:6; 11:4). The Christian contributes to the spread of this kingdom on earth, and thus fulfills a part of the gospel message, when he works for the promotion of the rights of others with a view to establishing a more just social order here below, in accordance with the archetype of the eschatological kingdom.

The sole purpose of the Church is the service of the kingdom of Christ, which it announces (GS 45a). It is a sign of this kingdom as it moves forward on its pilgrimage toward its fulfillment. Even if the full message of Christ is not confined simply to the establishment of social justice, it certainly includes the defense and promotion of human rights.

> The Church, . . . being founded in the love of the Redeemer, contributes towards the spread of justice and charity among nations and within the borders of the nations themselves. By preaching the truths of the Gospel and clarifying all sectors of human activity through its teaching and the witness of its members, the Church respects and encourages the political freedom and responsibility of the citizen (GS 76c).

The Lutheran Doctrine of the Two Kingdoms

The Lutheran tradition, with its doctrine of the two kingdoms, has led to a certain skepticism with regard to human rights, so that human rights as asserted at the time of the Enlightenment and by nineteenth-century socialism were for a long time seen as a usurpation of the divine right (and of grace) and were thus opposed.

The earthly kingdom, which is based on the creation, is wanted by God the Creator in order to allow and safeguard the life of society. However, it has no connection with the kingdom of grace. It has no salvific value except through the charity of the person who dedicates himself to it. The separation between the two kingdoms is so marked that the Church seems to remain the only sphere on this earth in which the kingship of Christ is effective and adequate. The two kingdoms remain distinct until Christ's victory is manifested. Thus, the fundamental union between the two kingdoms under the lordship of Christ is no longer evident. It then becomes more difficult to find a theological basis for the need for the Church to provide a witness to the kingship of Christ in the world and over the world. Earthly things are the concern of the secular powers, whereas the Church is addressed only to individuals, whose salvation must be brought about out-side the Church.[21]

Human Solidarity According to Saint Paul

According to the book of Genesis, each person must respect the image of God in his brother, for all people have an equal dignity before God. Today's sharper awareness of the violation of human rights is paralleled by increased attention to that human solidarity of which Saint Paul reveals the whole fullness. He uses the shape of solidarity between the different members of the body in order to explain what should exist within the body of Christ and thus provide us with a Christian understanding of human solidarity in general. "For just as the body is one and has many members, and all the members of the body, though many, are one body, so it is with Christ" (1 Cor. 12:12). " . . . we, though many, are one body in Christ, and individually members one of another" (Rom. 12:5). The basic values proclaimed in the vari-ous declarations of human rights have their place within this "body." Freedom: "For you were called to freedom" (Gal. 5:12). Equality: "There is neither Jew nor Greek, . . . for you are all one in Christ Jesus" (Gal. 3:28). Brotherhood or solidarity: "Bear one another's burdens, and so fulfill the law of Christ" (Gal. 6:2). There were tensions within the community of the Corin-thian church, with the less-gifted Christians feeling that they were discriminated against, while the more gifted despised the others. Paul points out that they must all retain the sense of ecclesial solidarity and have special consideration for "ordinary" Christians:

> For the body does not consist of one member but of many. If the foot should say, "Because I am not a hand, I do not belong to the body," that would not make it any less a part of the body. And if the ear should say, "Because I am not an eye, I do not belong to the body," that would not make it any less a part of the body. If the whole body were an eye, where would be the hearing? If the whole body were an ear, where would be the sense of smell? . . . The eye cannot say to the hand, "I have no need of you," nor again the head to the feet, "I have

no need of you." . . . But God has so adjusted the body, giving the greater honor to the inferior part, that there may be no discord in the body, but that the members may have the same care for one another. If one member suffers, all suffer together; if one member is honored, all rejoice together (1 Cor. 12:14–26).

No Christian can remain untouched when the rights of others are infringed or threatened. The sufferings of the oppressed concern us all.

Gaudium et spes did not refer to this Pauline explanation of human solidarity, although we do find the seeds of the same teaching in the document. In line with the approach of the Apostle, the Constitution declares the fundamental equality of all persons with one another, while taking into account the diversity in their individual qualities and capabilities: "Undoubtedly not all men are alike as regards physical capacity and intellectual and moral powers. But forms of social or cultural discrimination in basic personal rights . . . must be curbed and eradicated as incompatible with God's design" (GS 29b). What is being confirmed is therefore not egalitarianism, but equal dignity, which allows for complementarity and diversity, fosters the maximum development of each person and his or her participation according to individual capacities, and is oriented toward evening out existing inequalities in the spheres of knowledge (information), power (participation), and possessions (a more equal style of life).

Gaudium et spes emphatically stresses the fact that God created human beings not to live in solitude but in solidarity (GS 32a). "God desired that all men should form one family" (GS 24a).

The social nature of man shows that there is an interdependence between personal betterment and the improvement of society. . . . Life in society is not something accessory to man himself: through his dealings with others, through mutual service, and through fraternal dialogue, man develops all his talents and becomes able to rise to his destiny (GS 25a).

" . . . freedom . . . can . . . be strengthened by accepting the inevitable constraints of social life, by undertaking the manifold demands of human fellowship, and by service to the community at large" (GS 31b). It is therefore necessary to move beyond individualistic ethics and open ourselves to the requirements of the common good, which is today taking on an ever more universal dimension, so that "the whole human race is consequently involved with regard to the rights and obligations which result" (GS 26a).

Among the positive values of contemporary culture, the Constitution mentions "a living feeling of unity and of compelling solidarity, of mutual dependence" (GS 4d) and "the sense of international solidarity" that "calls for greater international cooperation" (GS 57e, 85a).

The Constitution *Gaudium et spes* was born during the Council and is full of rich and potentially fruitful insights, although it stands as an unfinished symphony. We therefore felt it was possible to develop its orientations in the specific area of a biblical and theological presentation of human rights. In conclusion, we should recall that even with regard to human rights, *Gaudium et spes* is only one chapter in the conciliar "volume," and in order to gain a fuller picture, we should have studied the other documents as well, especially the Declaration on Religious Freedom, *Dignitatis humanae.*

Translated from the French by Leslie Wearne.

Notes

1. S. Lyonnet, "Les fondements bibliques de la Constitution pastorale *Gaudium et Spes,*" in G. Baraúna (ed.), *L'Eglise dans le monde de ce temps,* 1 (Bruges, 1967), 196–212.

2. G. Alberigo, "La Constitution dans le cadre général du Concile," in *ibid.,* 1, 233.

3. J.H. Pelaez, *Los Derechos Humanos en el Magisterio de Pablo VI* (Rome, 1981), 47.

4. Paul VI, *Populorum progressio,* in *AAS,* 59 (1967), 87; English translation by Catholic Truth Society (London, 1967).

5. John Paul II, *Redemptor hominis,* in *AAS,* 71 (1979), 17; English translation by Libreria Editrice Vaticana (Vatican City, 1979).

6. Those who have written on human rights in the recent magisterium usually tend not to linger over *Gaudium et spes,* but concentrate more on the Encyclical *Pacem in terris* of John XXIII (1963), the document of the Synod of Bishops, *Convenientes ex universo,* on justice

in the world (1971), and above all, the study *The Church and Human Rights*, published by the Justice and Peace Commission in 1975.

7. N. Loss, "La dottrina antropologica di Genesi I-II," in G. de Gennaro (ed.), *L'antropologia biblica* (Naples, 1982), 181; A. Soggin, "Alcuni testi-chiave per l'antropologia dell'Antico Testamento," in *ibid.*, 48.

8. Soggin, "Alcuni testi-Chieave per l'antropologia," 52.

9. A. Fanuli, "L'uomo e il suo Habitat secondo Gen. 1," in de Gennaro (ed.), *L'antropologia biblica*, 91.

10. J. Moltmann, "Théologie et droits de l'homme," *RechScRel*, 52 (1982), 12–13.

11. F. Viola, "Les droits de l'homme: point de rencontre entre la nouvelle chrétienté et l'humanisme contemporain," *Nova et Vetera*, 57 (1982), 12–13.

12. *In Boetium de Trinitate*, q. 6, a. 4, ad 5.

13. J. de Finance, *Citoyen de deux mondes* (Rome, 1980), 104.

14. H. Thielicke, *Theologische Ethik*, 1 (Tubingen, 1951), No. 879.

15. J. Guillet, "De l'Ancien Testament à l'Évangile," *RechScRel*, 63 (1975), 397–406.

16. E. Jacob, "Les bases théologiques de l'éthique de l'Ancien Testament," *SupplVetusTest*, 7 (1968), 43.

17. P. Beauchamp, "Propositions sur l'Alliance de l'Ancien Testament," *RechScRel*, 58 (1970), 174–175.

18. M. Limbeck, "Damit sie das Leben haben und es in Fulle haben," *Bibel und Kirche*, 34 (1979), 74.

19. W. Vischer, *La loi ou les cinq livres de Moise* (Neuchatel, 1940), 141.

20. Paul VI, Message in union with the Fathers of the Synod, *Documentation Catholique*, 71 (1974), 965–966; English translation, *L'Osservatore Romano* (English edition) (7 November 1974), 3.

21. W.A. Visser't Hooft, *La Royauté de Jésus-Christ* (Geneva, 1948), 19 and 23.

CHAPTER 40

A Harmonization
of the Conciliar Statements
On Christian Moral Theology

Josef Fuchs, S.J.

Summary

It can hardly be stated that the Second Vatican Council made a *systematic* pronouncement on basic questions of fundamental moral theology. Nevertheless, there are many occasional statements on such questions scattered through the texts. This article sets itself the task of reflecting on these statements. Two groups of questions are selected here: (1) God's salvation, personal morality, and correct moral behavior; and (2) divine law, objective moral order, ecclesiastical magisterium, and conscience.

———

———

The council gave detailed treatment to certain individual questions of Christian morality—for example, marriage, family, peace and war—above all in the Pastoral Constitution *Gaudium et spes*. It made a reserved statement concerning the Christian character of moral teaching and moral theology in *Optatum totius*.[1] *Gaudium et spes* gives valuable indications for the way to resolve major contemporary human questions.[2] However, at no point does the Council give a systematic account of the basic questions of fundamental moral theology. It is true that the subjects of individual problem areas are to be found here and there; however, the statements concerning these are not systematically justified, nor are they placed in relationship to each other. Other fundamental moral problems are only briefly and occasionally touched on, but are not even given the same solution each time. Not infrequently, these solutions originate from particular ideas that cannot be overall internally reconciled. Already in the preconciliar years, but above all in postconciliar years, moral theology posed itself such questions to an ever greater extent. This could lead us in retrospect to think of attempting to harmonize conciliar statements on certain fundamental moral questions. This is the task we have set ourselves here. This attempt is limited to the following areas: (1) God's salvation, personal morality, and correct moral behavior; and (2) divine law, objective moral order, ecclesiastical magisterium, and conscience—all of these with respect to correct moral behavior in the world of human beings.

God's Salvation, Personal Morality, and Correct Behavior in the World

If we wished to indicate a document of the Council in which we would imagine finding more discussion of questions of Christian morality than in other documents, we would think of the Pastoral Constitution *Gaudium et spes*. Indeed, this Constitution begins by presenting the many problems that confront the Christian in today's world and in the face of which he must decide on responsible action. Yet we soon become aware that behind this there is another, more profound moral problem: that of the interior morality of the human person as such, who, in the last analysis, acting on the basis of his or her personal moral code, intervenes in the world of humanity. For its part, personal morality, according to the Council, presupposes the "healing" and "sanctifying" transformation of the human being who is sinful in himself. It is in calling him to this salvation that God permits him to be "good" in his eyes. The three subjects we have mentioned—salvation, morality, and correct behavior—are not systematically differentiated by the Council, nor are they discussed separately. Nevertheless, we shall not be able to understand the "Christian moral teaching" of the Council if we fail to see that when speaking about humanity, for the Council, the first subject is salvation as given by God, to which personal morality corresponds as a second subject; the human attempt at correct behavior in the world derives from this personal morality and is the third subject.

God's Salvation

How very much humanity's salvation from God and before God is the central anthropological idea of the Council can be grasped even from its concern not to exclude the possibility of salvation as sharing in the earthly and eternal paschal mystery even for the many who, in fidelity to their conscience, innocently live without knowledge of God and Christ (LG 16, GS 22, AG 7, cf. LG 14). The two documents that more than the others emphasize above all the central importance of salvation as granted by God are, on account of their special subjects, the Dogmatic Constitution on Divine Revelation, Dei Verbum, and the Dogmatic Constitution on the Church, Lumen gentium.

According to Dei Verbum, the reason for God's revelation of himself to men and for its transmission is that it is a "summons to salvation" (DV 1). On the basis of this statement, the Council wishes to indicate how the revelation as transmitted to us is to be understood as a whole and in particular, and how its significance is to be assessed. The Council speaks of a history of God's revelation, which we accept in faith, hope, and love (DV 1, 5). The gospel is seen as a transmission and hence as the "source of all saving truth" (DV 7). What the Bible states "for our salvation" is truth (DV 11). The same holds good for the "history of salvation" in the Old Testament (DV 14), and also for what in the New Testament Jesus "really did and taught for our salvation" (DV 19). Only on one occasion is the expression "saving truth" explicitly followed by the other expression "moral discipline," yet here there is no indication of an internal connection; this occurs in the context of the gospel (DV 7).

The Constitution Lumen gentium on the Church understands its mystery on the deepest level as the mystery of salvation. The Church is basically seen as "a sign and instrument . . . of communion with God and of unity among all men" as "full unity in Christ" (LG 1). Since the goal of creation was "to share in . . . divine life," and since, following sin, we have been given "the means of salvation, bestowed in consideration of Christ" (LG 2), the saving action and power of God in the world continue

Christ's mission through the Church, which grows visibly (*LG* 3); and the Spirit who operates within mankind is a power for eternal life (*LG* 4). In the Church, the "kingdom of God" is already present and has become a visible reality (*LG* 5). The teaching of *Lumen gentium* on the Church as the "people of God" points in the same direction: God revealed his "will to save," made his "people holy unto himself," transformed its intimate dimension, its "heart" (following Jer. 31:31–34), and concluded with them a covenant in the blood of Christ and in the Holy Spirit (*LG* 9). Here the following point is already seen in greater clarity: one who is in "salvation" is personally "holy" in personal moral "goodness."

The primacy of the reality of salvation is also, however, to be found in other documents. When the Decree *Optatum totius* speaks of the theological education of future priests, it urges that the first course given should be an introduction "into the mystery of salvation" (*OT* 14), while in general all theological disciplines are to be taught "in contact with the mystery of Christ and the history of salvation." The relationship between salvation and morality is suggested in the admonition that moral theology should teach in the first place not human morality, but God's saving action (*OT* 16). There is an interesting remark in the Decree *Apostolicam actuositatem* concerning the apostolate of the laity, which unambiguously states; "The work of Christ's redemption concerns essentially the salvation of men." However, in the course of the Decree, albeit without any explanation, we find the additional statement to the effect that this work of redemption also takes in "the whole temporal order" (*AA* 5). Elsewhere, we read that anyone who shirks his temporal duties "endangers his eternal salvation" (*GS* 43). Hence, the texts concerning the primacy of divine salvation also indicate—albeit only occasionally— its reference not only to personal morality, but also to right social promotion in the world.

As we have already observed, the Pastoral Constitution *Gaudium et spes,* according to its particular aim, takes as its starting point the problem of the formation of the world of people as creatures of God (*GS* 1), but it also sees in our attempt to continue forming the created world (*GS* 34, 57) a—no doubt moral and religious—perfecting of the human agent itself (*GS* 37–39, 57), and a promotion of the "kingdom of Christ" (*GS*

39). However, the formation of this world takes place as we await a new earth (GS 39).

Personal Morality

"Salvation" is not a "thing," but rather a vocation wrought by God and an interior transformation of the human person, as we have already seen. According to the Council, salvation is found in its free acceptance as offered by God—in faith, hope, and love. The personal decision for the God of salvation, therefore, directly affects not humanity's actions, but each as a person. The person lets himself or herself be transformed and he or she transforms himself or herself in interior freedom, and thus he or she is not a sinner, but one who is redeemed—whether in categorical knowledge of God's saving work (GS 11–13), or without such knowledge (cf. GS 22).

In our reflection on these statements by the Council, it is important to bear in mind that salvation is in direct relationship not with action in the world, but with the human person in his freedom. Morality in the strict sense of the word can be applied only to a free human person, and not to actions as such. Indeed, in all free actions in the world, the person's realization of himself or herself (GS 52, 37–39) and his or her interior convictions (GS 26, 71) are simultaneously the most profound issue. Personal morality signifies the opposite of egoistic closedness of self, and thus the openness of the person as such—for God, for humanity, and for all that is good and right—and in this way, it is "an offering accepted by God" (GS 38). Personal morality is also interior openness and readiness to work for the good of others (GS 39), concern for the right shaping of the world of humanity (GS 39), a tendency toward right action and truth of life (GS 42), readiness to contribute to the temporal world (GS 43), motivation for a right ordering of the world (GS 4). Justice, readiness to sacrifice, generosity, fidelity and chastity, as openness and readiness to correct behavior in different areas of life, as well as open readiness to correct behavior in traffic, industrial life, international interests, and so on, are all elements of personal morality, and constitute moral goodness.

Instead of speaking of personal openness as the antithesis of egoistic closedness, the Council repeatedly refers to love as the basic attitude of personal morality. Love is called "the fundamental law of human perfection" (GS 38); it has the effect of fruitfulness for the life of the world (OT 16), and it is readiness to accord the brethren help and justice (GS 72) and to collaborate in the transformation of the world (GS 38). The commandment of love is described in accordance with Tradition and Scripture as the "new commandment" of love (e.g., GS 38; LG 32). This, of course, does not mean that without Christianity love would not equally be the basic attitude of personal morality. The conciliar Decree on the Apostolate of Lay People, thinking rather of the history of its effect, calls love of our neighbor a commandment that particulary "distinguishes" Christian morality, and that in the overall Christian context receives a new and richer "meaning." Characteristic of the concept of personal morality—goodness—in the texts of the Council is the frequent mention of conscience (the judgment of conscience) instead of laws, commandments, and norms as the point of reference of a moral decision and hence also of personal morality. In a fundamental manner, a sentence in *Gaudium et spes* speaks of "the right to act according to the dictates of conscience" (GS 26). A more correct translation of the original text would be "right dictates"; this addition is no doubt intended to invalidate the "normative force" of a culpably insufficiently formed conscience. The reason for this reference to the conscience in our (always interior) moral decisions is, according to the Council, to be sought in the fact that norms and commandments, and thus also "the will of God," are known and recognized in the conscience and thus become part of our "interiority"; hence, fidelity to the "interiority" of the conscience is the morality of the "interiority" of the person (cf. DH 3). In other words, the interior moral decision can have as its point of reference only interior knowledge concerning correct behavior, that is, the conscience. Hence, the conscience retains its dignity in the field of personal morality even when it innocently considers as correct an erroneous opinion concerning human behavior (GS 16). Atheism and nonmembership of the Church are personally blameworthy and hence exclusive of salvation only if the conscience registers the possibility and necessity of belief in God and of membership of the Church (GS, 14, 16, 19). The Council considers that the Church respects conscience and a free decision based on conscience (GS 41), and demands that the State do likewise, especially as regards freedom of religion (DH 2).

Correct Behavior in the World

Moral goodness and salvation are never experienced purely as such, but always within the parallel realization of our human world in time and space. This realization of the world itself as such is nothing but the formation and development of the world itself. Moral goodness demands that this realization of the world occur not in an arbitrary, but in a "right" manner. Yet the Council understands the formation of the world as a task of creation for the continuation and perfecting of this world (e.g., GS 34, 57), as the transformation of created realities into human culture (GS 53–62). Hence, faith and love and eschatological hope also motivate the Christian to participate in forming the world (GS 43).

The world is understood by the Council as the world of people, as the personal individual in his or her dignity (seen also in religious and moral terms), as the various interpersonal relationships, as the many institutions, as human society, as scientific discoveries and technical possibilities today, and so on. Following their particular slant, it is above all the Constitution on the Church in the Modern World and the Decree on the Apostolate of Lay People that make statements on this question. They find the occasion to speak on this subject above all because of the enormous human questions that are raised because of the immense possibilities of a humanity living according to a "dynamic and . . . evolutionary concept of nature" (GS 5) and that affect human society, its institutions, and its individual members. While it is true that the Council directs its attention primarily to "major human questions," we should not forget that the questions of marriage (cf., e.g., GS 53–62), sexuality, more "private" interpersonal relationships, and general formation of culture (cf., e.g., GS 53–62), and so on, also belong to the formation of the world and to human cultural creative activity; in other words, they are as such not questions of personal morality.

The two documents we have just mentioned take as their point of departure the obvious fact that the reality of the modern world is new to an extent that was not previously even suspected, that its right formation presumes a high degree of technical competence, and that it represents an extremely difficult task. There is no problem whatsoever about the "that" dimension in these two documents. The difficulties start, rather, when we turn to the dimension of "how" to solve this problem. It is interesting to note that in both documents, it is expressly stated that it depends on the "right" or "correct" solutions (GS 21; AA 7). The problem of the rightness of human formation of the world is thus evidently distinguished from the question of personal morality. We should turn our attention to the characteristic statement to the effect that for the problems of modern human society a good "intention" (i.e., personal morality) is not sufficient, for society itself must be changed, and thus the material world must be correctly formed (GS 26). Hence, the phrase "human behavior" refers to the reflection on the criteria of correctness of such behavior in the world of men—in all its spheres.

In this respect, the title of the third chapter of *Guadium et spes,* "Man's Activity in the World," has a twofold meaning: "Human activity *proceeds from man:* it is also *ordered to him*" (GS 35). It is amazing to see how frequently this ordering and thus the human dimension as a practical criterion of the correctness of human behavior in the modern world is emphasized in the conciliar texts: it no doubt occurs more frequently than the indication of stipulated norms. Evidently, even in the human dimension, the norms of correct behavior have their own criterion. Thus, in *Gaudium et spes,* the Council can finally—and only in this way—address itself clearly (GS 2) to all men, including non-Christians.

In today's attempt to master the major questions of mankind, the Council sees a new kind of humanism at work (GS 55). It approves of this humanism insofar as it is not "purely earthbound and even hostile to religion" (GS 56). It means a humanism that tries to "achieve true and full humanity by means of [true] culture, that is, through the cultivation of the goods and values of nature" (GS 53), in order to "develop the whole human person" (GS 56), so that man, constantly changing, may "transcend himself" (GS 35), and correspondinglly work toward forming a "more humane" life (GS 38), a "more human" society (GS 53), and "towards the establishment of a world that is more human" (GS 57). Hence, all formative work in this world must "harmonize with the authentic interests of the human race" (GS 35) with regard to all "that belongs to a life which is human in every respect" (GS 74). In short, in keeping with the kind of humanism proposed by the Council, the "human being" is the criterion for "correct" behavior in the world of humanity; in this sense, it recognizes along with other religions "the voice . . . of God in the language of creatures" (GS 36). This is the properly under-stood doctrine of the natural law according to the Council. It does not exclude, but rather includes, the possibility of the exis-tence of different cultures in which there may be life-styles and "moralities" that are to some extent different, even though in the modern world, life-styles and ethical attitudes are becoming more and more uniform (GS 53, 54, cf. 43).

When dealing with individual questions, the Council also stresses the human aspect of behavior: the family is to be "a school for human enrichment" (GS 52), the marriage act must be human (GS 47), people must carry out conception "in a manner worthy of themselves," and it must be ordered "according to authentic human dignity" (GS 51), and "laws should make hu-mane provision for the case of conscientious objectors (GS 79).

However, it is not always easy to find in practical terms what is humane, and thus a human and correct solution to human prob-lems. The Council confirms this and hence calls for the coopera-tion of all those who are competent in the relevant questions, and since they are "human" (and not specifically "Christian") problems, it also calls for cooperation between believing Chris-tians and nonbelievers (GS 21, 43, 57; AA 7). The Council Fathers also expressly emphasize that in many practical ques-tions, even truly believing, conscientious Christians may "legiti-mately" reach differing or opposing solutions (GS 43) and that the Church as such (GS 33) and its pastors (GS 48) may also not always have a ready solution for practical questions, and that this is not part of their mission (GS 43). This does not mean that the religious message of the "Church" (GS 11, 12), the light of "faith" or of the "gospel" (GS 11, 43), true "holiness" (LG 40), and knowledge of "divine wisdom" (GS 15) and the "divine law," although they may all be incapable of offering a direct solution themselves, may not in fact also represent a great help toward finding humane solutions (the word humanus is employed in each of the references given) or lead to such solutions.

These indications on the part of the Council are linked to the fact that contemporary human questions are not among the ques-tions that, according to Dei Verbum, are revealed "for our salva-tion," nor are they part of what formally constitutes personal morality, although they are human—and remain "human"—questions within a context of redemption. Above all, the conciliar Decree on the Apostolate of Lay People stresses that the work of redemption is also "to improve the whole range of the temporal" (*AA* 5) and that we must speak of a "Christian renewal of the temporal order" (*AA* 31). In a like manner, *Gravissimum Educationis* sees all "natural values assimilated into the full understanding of man redeemed by Christ" (*GE* 2). No doubt this can be seen in connection with the albeit rather vague statement in *Lumen gentium* to the effect that the message of faith must be applied to moral life (*LG* 25). We are, however, prompted to ask what this actually means in practical terms. One of the possible answers may be seen in the remark of *Gaudium et spes* to the effect that "we must seek light for each of these problems from the principles which Christ has given" in order that the Church may reply to individual practical problems (*GS* 46). However, this clarification is only possible by means of a "human" evaluation of the practical circumstances of a person's life. A further reply may be seen in the remark of the same Constitution to the effect that the values that hold sway today "stem from the natural talents given to man by God" and thus "are exceedingly good," although, "owing to corruption of the human heart, they are distorted, so that they need to be set right" (*GS* 11). However, this latter observation means that they must be brought to their true and full humanness. More problematic is the attempt in the Decree on the Apostolate of Lay People (*AA* 16), for here we read that Christians "should, by the light of faith, try to find the higher motives that should govern their behavior" in the world. Yet this demands considerably more than merely a more profound understanding of "humane" norms; it could also refer to setting aright and thus authentically humanizing such principles. It would be more difficult to understand if it meant what this remark appears to mean at a first reading, namely, that we should be concerned with "higher" in the sense of "superhuman" motives.

We must not forget that when the Council speaks of human behavior in the world it is not dealing with morality in the strict sense, but rather with the problem of the correctness of the active shaping of the world of people by people. However, it is aware that a person is obliged by his or her personal morality to assume responsibility for the world of people and thus to set out in search of right or correct action in the world, so as to behave according to the solution he or she has found. This is why, nowadays, it is rightly customary to call the problem of "human

behavior in the world" (whether that of Christians or of nonbelievers) the problem of "*moral* rectitude," which is thus not de-
void of any relation to moral goodness (i.e., morality in the strict
sense of the word), even though it is distinct from it. Hence, in
its remarks on moral goodness, the Council repeatedly recalls
that it is dictated by fidelity to the interior word of the conscience and not by the moral rightness or wrongness of behavior.

Divine Law, Objective Moral Order, Magisterium— and Moral Knowledge in the Conscience

Since the question of moral rightness is presented in the
conciliar documents as distinct from personal morality, but is not
the object of separate reflection, we are forced to ask certain
significant questions. For example, is the Church's competence
in moral questions the same for what is "morally good" and for
what is "morally correct"? On the one hand, the different documents do not always speak in the same way of the "divine law," of
an "objective moral order" and of the ecclesiastical magisterium
as the guideline for correct behavior, while, on the other hand,
they emphasize that, in the human subject, knowledge of moral
rightness takes place in the "conscience." We must now discuss
these questions with respect to "moral rectitude" in the conciliar
texts.

"Divine Law" and Moral Knowledge in the Conscience

Dignatatis humanae declares succinctly: " . . . the highest
norm of human life is the divine law" (*DH* 3). The context
makes it clear that here it is not a question (or not principally so)
of a supernatural law, for when the Council speaks of revelation,
the gospel, faith, Christ, etc., it uses other language (cf. AG 22).
There can be no doubt as to the correctness of the expression
used by *Dignitatis humanae,* although we may ask what was understood by the divine law: Might it have been "given" somewhere,
or can it be discovered? However, this is certainly not what is
meant by this formula. From the context, it is clear that the
divine law is identical with the "eternal law" that had always
been a tenet of Tradition. This eternal law is, however, nothing
other than God himself and, hence, as such is not directly acces-

sible for us, and thus the same would have to be said concerning
the divine law. Doubtless, God knows what is humanly correct
and incorrect behavior, but this knowledge has not been directly
communicated to us as a "revealed truth."

However, we then read that God has enabled us "to participate in this law of his" (*DH* 3), in other words, through our
conscience, he lets us "arrive at a deeper and deeper knowledge"
of it (*DH* 3). Here it is clear, in contrast to other texts, that
"conscience" is understood not as a situational judgment of conscience, but simply as the capacity for moral consciousness.
Thus, this would mean that the divine law, which at first glance
could be imagined as being a divine institution, is basically nothing other than the natural moral law or natural law that is frequently mentioned in the conciliar documents. Divine law and
eternal law are nothing other than an interpretation of natural
moral law (A. Auer). This becomes clearer still when the Council observes that, in common with many religions, we can recognize "the voice . . . of God in the language of creatures" (here,
naturally, principally that of humanity itself) (*GS* 36).

We run into greater difficulties when the Council exhorts
married people to *conform* their conscience to the law of God
(*GS* 50). Since we cannot understand this as the revealed word
of God, this produces a problem inasmuch as in this context, the
conscience itself is seen as the tribunal for recognition of what is
morally right, that is, the divine law. Here clarity is lacking.
Presumably, the intention is to draw attention to a certain objective fund of moral knowledge in the ecclesial community (particularly under the influence of the ecclesiastical magisterium),
which must not be ignored when searching for further moral
knowledge. Indeed, in this context, mention is made of the
importance of the magisterium, which has the task of interpreting the divine law—in the light of the gospel and with the aid of
the Holy Spirit (*GS* 50, 51; *LG* 25). Nonetheless, the magisterium also has no "direct" access to the divine, eternal law,
and is thus dependent on human moral knowledge. Correspondingly, it must be evident that we must arrive at knowledge of the
divine law both with the aid of the magisterium and also of other
teaching as well as by mutual exchange (*DH* 3).

We must now come back once more to the first quotation from
Dignitatis humanae on the divine law, as the latter is more precisely
described there as "eternal, objective and universal" (*DH* 3). This

is a well-known formula for describing the "eternal law." What would the Council Fathers have had in mind when employing this formula? The divine law is called "eternal." Naturally, it is eternal, even if it has never been "given," "known," or "recognized"—in eternity. It is God's eternal knowledge and judgment concerning everything that is "right." It is his eternal presence in everything, however "concretely" or "specifically" it may exist, so that nothing, including each thing's "correctness," is unknown to him. The divine law is called "objective" and not "arbitrary," for in his presence, which extends to the most intimate and ultimate of man's reality, God understands what is the "right" answer for a person who acts both in terms of abstract reflection and also in practical terms, that is, "relative to" total reality (and thus not relativistically!). The divine law is called "universal." Truly, nothing is excepted, not even the smallest detail of human reality. Hence, the following statement is universally valid: "What is identical must be dealt with and realized in an identical fashion, and what is different must be dealt with in a different fashion." It is also true in this connection that there are good reasons for quite diverse solutions to problems of practical moral rightness, and thus for a "legitimate" pluralism (GS 43). It is no rare matter to read— even in the works of moral theologians—a different interpretation of the formula that was selected by the Council. We must presume that this was also the case for quite a number of the Council Fathers. Might they not, without reflecting on it and without saying so, have thought of a God who decides and establishes everything in eternity ("from all eternity"): thus, the opposite of the natural law, which is nothing more than a consideration of God's knowledge and judgment? If so, the eternal law and natural law would not be essential laws, and thus there would be no true natural law.

The "Objective Moral Order" and the "Correct" Formation of the World

In place of the theological-sounding expression "divine law," the conciliar texts often speak of the "objective moral order"— although this sounds rather ethical. These two expressions are equivalent. On first reading, we have the impression that the Council imagines that both the divine law and also an objective moral order somehow "exist objectively." This must, of course, be understood correctly. If not, we would be obliged to posit the use of a formula with its true significance being unknown to the user.

Let us look at this formulation. The Council calls for laws within society that are "moral laws" (GS 36), or, to put it another way, that "conform to the norm of morality." Our formation of the world of people must be achieved in conformity with the objective norm of morality (GS 39). In its demographic policy, the State must not contradict the "moral law" (GS 87). Citizens under the oppression of a public authority that oversteps its competence must defend themselves against the abuses of this authority within the limits of the "natural law" and the law of the gospel (GS 74).

The famous passage of *Gaudium et spes* 16 on the conscience is interesting in this connection. Here the conscience is understood on the one hand as the absolute concrete call to what is good, but on the other hand, it is also conceived of as the tribunal that recognizes the "law" God has written in our hearts, which teaches us about correct behavior and finds its fulfillment in the twofold commandment of love. Here it is a question of an objective moral law, which we must simply "obey." Later, we read that believers and nonbelievers are capable, if they remain faithful to their conscience—which is here no doubt understood as the seat of categorical knowledge of the "law"—of seeking "the right solution to so many moral problems which arise both in the life of individuals and from social relationships." In this way, they will "turn aside from blind choice" and "be guided by the objective standards of moral conduct."

These formulas could lead us to believe that the "objective law of morality" is thought of as limited in extent, if it is true that in seeking correct solutions for the endless number of moral problems, we should see no more than a numerically single use of an individual norm already given in the "objective moral law" (which is no doubt formulated by people). In autonomous ordering of society, in our formation of the world, in our Christian collaboration within society with non-Christians, and in our concrete search whereby we take into account, as is required of us, "the principles of the moral order which spring from human nature itself" (DH 14), we "autonomously" find the solutions, that is to say, concrete norms of moral behavior in the world. In this, the Council does not rule out the possibility that in differ-

ent cultures—which are largely created by people—there may be
different life-styles and norms of behavior (GS 43, 53, 54). No
doubt these are to be considered "objectively" correct solutions.
In this, we are told, we are to be guided by the "objective moral
law." This kind of moral law, even if understood (following
Rom. 2) as "written in the heart" (cf. GS 16), is not a ready-
made and only passively accepted "law," but rather a law that is
discovered actively by us men and women and in human (and
ecclesiastical) society and is found *in this way*. It is clearly objective not because it is recognized in our society (or in the
Church), but because it is not an arbitrary law, and thus because,
in the light of the gospel, it has been rightly decided upon by the
reason given us by God on the basis of knowledge of the reality of
our world. On the one hand, we could understand the objective
moral law that is so strongly emphasized by the Council according to a particular interpretation (among others) of the natural
moral law by Thomas Aquinas as a little *Summa* of the most
general and of generally illuminating first moral principles: in the
light of these, more concrete norms of correct behavior would
have to be sought. On the other hand, the objective moral order,
according to another interpretation, could be conceived of as the
(possible) knowledge of *every* norm of correct moral behavior in
the world, that is, without drawing a fundamental distinction
between an objective law and the concrete solutions, for in this
case, these latter, too, would be objective moral law. In both
cases, the Council would insist that when acting in the world,
one must not abandon oneself to arbitrary behavior, but rather,
through honest reflection on self (in human society), one must
attempt to find correct manners of human behavior. The texts of
the Council do, however, suggest that neither the first nor the
second of these two alternatives determined the conception of
the Council Fathers, but, rather, another view that understands
the objective moral law in practical terms as a certain (and not so
little) *Summa* of already recognized norms of moral behavior that
in the search for manners of human behavior must first of all not
be directly infringed, and second must help the person who is
conducting the concrete search as a guiding light. This might not
be theoretically the best conception, but it is one that is possible
in practice. Nonetheless, it is not then so clear in practice which
norms precisely belong to an "objective moral law" understood in
this way, and which do not.

The Magisterium of the Church:
Basic Principles and Directives

With respect to the "divine law" or the "objective moral law," the Council attributes a God-given competence and a decisive role to the magisterium of the Church. It emphasizes the requirement to follow the pronouncements of the magisterium in moral questions (cf. *LG* 25, and also the explanations of *LG* 69, *GS* 50, *DH* 3, and *IM* 14). The basic task of the bishop (and thus also of the magisterium in general) is the proclamation of "the gospel" (*LG* 27). However, *Dei Verbum* states that the gospel is "the source of all saving truth and *moral discipline*" (*DV* 7), although the latter is distinguished here from the former. Without specifying this relationship of moral teaching with the gospel, *Dignitatis humanae* declares that the Church must "proclaim and teach with authority the truth which is Christ and, at the same time, . . . declare and confirm by her authority the principles of the moral order which spring from human nature itself" (*DH* 14). In a rather vague formulation, *Lumen Gentium* establishes a relationship between these two areas: the bishops "preach the faith to the people assigned to them, the faith which is destined to inform their thinking and direct their conduct" (*LG* 25). The basis for this is the formula adopted from the First Vatican Council, stating that the magisterium is competent "in matters of faith and morals" and is also in certain circumstances infallible in this (*LG* 25).

In response to the question that arises as to whether the competence of the magisterium extends not only to all revealed questions of faith but also to *non*revealed (and thus the vast majority of cases) questions of morals (natural law!), Vatican II appears to have no more to say than Vatican I. Although it is simply observed in the Decree on Missionary Activity that the people who are evangelized must naturally lead a life in accordance "with the standard proposed by divine revelation" (*AG* 22), this is no doubt expressed without a great deal of theological reflection, just like the statement in *Inter mirifica* to the effect that in forming public opinion, "the natural law and Catholic doctrines and directives" must be observed (*IM* 14). In contrast, the distinction between saving truth and moral discipline in *Dei Verbum* 7 is important, for here, in a document dealing specifically with saving truth, moral teaching is seen (at least to a very great extent) as not forming part of revealed truth. This is echoed in the statement of Lumen gentium 25 to the effect that the infallibility of the magisterium (and hence, no doubt, also the magisterium itself) restricts itself to the same limits as those of divine revelation, and thus does not extend to the whole area of what is morally right. The field of what is morally right in behavior in the world requires, especially according to *Gaudium et spes* and *Apostolicam actuositatem,* an immense degree of specialized knowledge, which we can certainly not derive from revelation. What is more, as Bishop Gasser explained in the *Relatio* he delivered at Vatican I, the ethical principles of natural law are not entirely in the sphere of the doctrine of faith, which is the sole object of the magisterium of the Church.[3] It is interesting to note that the Council expresses the competence of bishops in essentially different terms in the Decree on the Pastoral Office of Bishops, where it states that synods advise on the doctrine of the faith and questions of discipline (CD 36)—or has moral teaching been made part of the doctrine of the faith through lack of reflection?

While the conciliar texts normally speak simply of the moral law, in several passages, they speak (restrictively?) of the principles (cf. DH 14 and GS 45) and fundamentals (cf., e.g., IM 14, GS 33, and AA 31) of moral teaching as the object of the magisterium. Does *Gaudium et spes* understand the principles "which Christ has given us" only as the most general insights of faith, when it states that their concrete clarification is the task of the Church (GS 46)? This would represent a way of talking that is different from that employed in *Dignitatis humanae,* according to which a distinction must be drawn between the truth that is Christ himself and the principles that derive from humanity's nature (DH 14). Nonetheless, in both cases, we seem to find a difference expressed between what are more general principles and what are more concrete norms of behavior in the world.

Something similar is true as concerns the case of the word "fundamentals." The Council observes expressly that over and above the fundamentals, the Church also gives "aids" for what are often very difficult (GS 33, 43) solutions to concrete problems (AA 31). Do these fundamentals maybe mean only basic truths of personal morality (e.g., justice, fidelity, mercy, chastity)? The context suggests rather that morally correct behavior is also understood as fundamentals (e.g., in questions of social and sexual ethics). Nevertheless, the question remains somewhat open as to

how we are to distinguish between fundamentals and more concrete norms of moral rightness. Did the ecclesiastical magisterium
intend proposing fundamentals or norms (as distinct from and as
concretizations of fundamentals) in *Personae humanae* (1975) and
Humanae vitae (1968)? As such, fundamentals and norms—
however we may distinguish them—are equally accessible to human knowledge ("in the conscience") and are so in the same way:
norms are not simply deductions from fundamentals.

The texts of the Council do not speak expressly of the
breadth of validity or the breadth of applicability of principles/
fundamentals/norms. Nevertheless, we frequently find an admonition to the effect that pronouncements of the magisterium
with respect to the "divine law" or the "objective moral order"
of correct behavior are to be followed, and this is difficult to
reconcile with the idea of validity and applicability that are
only general rather than universal and without exception. Universality is also suggested by the expression "divine law" (or
"eternal law"). Nowhere do we find the idea that there is a
distinction between *intrinsece malum* (intrinsically evil) (a) as
universale (universal) and thus applied to statements concerning
personal morality in which it is uncontrovertibly a question of
universalia/intrinsece mala, and (b) as applied to the many statements concerning moral rightness that are by no means rarely
formulated only "approximatively."

The Conscience as the Norm of Correct Behavior

We have seen that the Council also referred to the conscience
with regard to the moral rightness of behavior in the world. This
is not so rare a custom in moral theology, even though many
decry this as an improper use of the word "conscience." No
reflection is made in the documents of the Council on the fact
that the word "conscience" is understood in a different fashion
from when it is referred to in the area of the moral goodness of
the acting person. On occasion, the two meanings of conscience
are to be found directly juxtaposed in the same text (cf. GS 16).

Although we have already discussed the reference made by the
Council to the conscience as regards knowledge of the moral
rightness of behavior, it would appear that a more explicit, yet
brief, return to this subject is called for, in view of the ever-
burning issue of "conscience versus objective norm."

On repeated occasions, the Council admonishes that when forming our conscience, that is, when producing a statement (abstract or concrete) expressing the content of the conscience concerning the moral rightness of behavior, we must proceed not arbitrarily but "conscientiously," carefully, and objectively (cf. GS 16, 27, 50, 87; GE 1; AA 5). This admonition implies that a person (or persons) actively obtains this knowledge of moral rightness in the conscience.

Corresponding to this, we find the positive statement that we share in the law "written in our hearts" (GS 16) or in the "divine law" (DH 3) by means of our conscience (DH 3). However, alongside this conception, we find the other, that requires the conscience to conform itself to the divine law when forming its judgments (GS 50). Evidently, here attention has not been paid to the fact that according to the first conception, the conscience shares in the divine law by means of itself. Theoretically, in accordance with this, the admonition really only means that we must seek right knowledge of morally correct behavior honestly and not arbitrarily. In practical terms, this admonition apparently presumes "already known" moral rightness in the Church (especially in the magisterium), but it does not take into consideration the fact that it has also been found by means of human knowledge ("in the conscience").

Postconciliar Moral Teaching

We may regret that the Council did not give a systematic account of the relationships between its statements on salvation, personal morality, and correctness of behavior in the world. A systematic attempt of this kind would also have been significant, for the frequent confusion of the goodness of the person and the correctness of behavior has often led to regrettable consequences both in discussions of moral theology and also in interpretations by the ecclesiastical authorities. However, the state of moral theological discussion could not permit the Council Fathers to undertake such a reflection.

Similar regret may be expressed at the Council's approach to the themes we have presented, namely, "objective moral law," "divine law," "magisterium in moral questions," and "conscience." Here, at the Council, statements were made from case to case without considering their more profound implications or their internal consistency. An attitude was adopted that was largely similar to that assumed in previous, obsolescent days in moral theology. The conciliar theologians were also not in a position to suggest a more profound reflection to the Fathers of the Council.

We can hardly expect the conciliar documents to have stimulated postconciliar moral theology to reflect positively on the questions we have dealt with before—in contrast to the case, for example, of the question of the christological character of moral theology (OT 16). What follows is intended as a very brief overview of the reflection of moral theology itself, independently of the Council, on those truths that were not examined by the Council.

Postconciliar Moral Theology

In the years following the Council, the work of harmonizing the themes of salvation, personal morality, and morally correct behavior, which are present in the Council but not harmonized by it, has slowly been tackled in ever greater depth. Above all, systematic differentiation of personal morality and moral rightness of behavior leads to important consequences. To start with, on the one hand, it has an effect on the still developing discussion concerning a gradation in the competence of the magisterium of the Church in questions of personal morality, and on the other hand, of the rightness of behavior in the world. It then contributes to further clarification of the question as to how, by reasoned argument, we can obtain judgments on the moral rightness of behavior. Here we concentrate, for example, more strongly than in former times on the necessity of a judgment that evaluates "teleologically" morally relevant earthly goods or values that are not yet, however, moral (and, hence, also absolute) in themselves.

Such considerations have demanded, for their part, that a discussion be pursued that had already begun here and there before the Council concerning the breadth of validity and the concrete applicability of norms of moral rightness; this also throws new light on the problem, ignored by the Council, of universal moral values and the *intrinsece malum* ("what is intrinsically evil").

However, by no means all moral theologians see their way to following the development we have just indicated. Hence, we can still find moral theological publications today that ignore, confuse, or else even expressly reject the distinction between "morally good" and "morally correct." What is more, they frequently forget that the teleological manner of justification (which is today often called proportionalism) refers exclusively to questions of moral rightness of behavior and thus not to statements concerning personal morality (such as being merciful, being just, being chaste, following the dictates of one's conscience, etc.), for such questions as these can be justified exclusively "deontologically." Universality and *intrinsece malum* belong to their nature, otherwise than as concerns the statements on moral rightness, even though in the case of the latter, they are also not necessarily excluded. Correspondingly, these moral theologians do not, as they should, undertake a further fundamental precise formulation of the res fidei *et morum* ("matters of faith *and morals*") as the area of competence of the ecclesiastical magisterium. Neither the First nor the Second Vatican Council attempted this precise formulation.[4]

Correspondingly, these theologians also refrain from examining critically or developing the obvious lack of clarity in the Council in the area of the questions of "the objective moral order," "the divine law," "the magisterium," and "the conscience" (as the means communicating insight into moral rightness). The true problem of the all too numerous universal norms and *intrinsece mala* ("things that are intrinsically bad") appears to be insufficiently perceived, and the same is true for the decisive distinction between "morally good" and "morally correct."

This difference between two tendencies in contemporary moral theology is also reflected in the animated discussion surrounding the problem of "ethics of belief" and "ethical autonomy in the Christian context."

The Postconciliar Magisterium and Moral Theology

The postconciliar situation is considerably different from the situation of postconciliar moral theology. The language of the magisterium when dealing with questions of fundamental moral teaching is largely identical with that of the conciliar texts. This may be regretted. And it may also be regretted that certain— even esteemed—members of the college of bishops who have become aware of reflection in the field of moral theology do not always recognize the internal continuity of certain statements in moral theology with positions in the moral theology of the past, so that they react in a somewhat negative fashion, occasionally even polemically and categorically. How often we could show in such cases that these declarations and admonitions are based on a fundamental misunderstanding of the positions in moral theology that they are contesting and on manifest ignorance of the distinctions drawn by the moral theologians as their point of departure! Declarations such as these are, indeed, well suited to impeding the necessary task of harmonizing the statements of the Council.

Translated from the German by Ronald Sway.

Notes

1. Cf. J. Fuchs, "Erneuerung der Moraltheologie. Eine Forderung des Zweiten Vatikanischen Konzils," in *Moral und Moraltheologie nach dem Konzil* (Freiburg im Breisgau, 1967), 9–61.

2. Cf. J. Fuchs, "Berufung und Hoffnung. Konziliäre Weisungen für eine christliche Moral," in F. Groner (ed.), *Die Kirche im Wandel der Zeit (Festgabe Kardinal J. Höffner)* (Cologne, 1971), 271–284.

3. Mansi, 52, 1224A.

4. Cf. in this connection, W. Levada, *Infallible Church Magisterium and the Natural Law,* excerpt from a doctoral dissertation at Pontifical Gregorian University (Rome, 1971); A. Riedl, *Die kirchliche Lehrautorität nach den Aussagen des Ersten Vatikanischen Konzils* (Freiburg im Breisgau, 1975); F.A. Sullivan, *Magisterium. Teaching Authority in the Catholic Church* (Dublin, 1983); J. Schuster, *Ethos und kirchliches Lehramt,* Frankfurter Studien 31 (Frankfurt, 1984).

CHAPTER 41

Reflections on the
Eschatology of Vatican II

Juan Alfaro, S.J.

Summary

This article is a theological reflection on the eschatology of Vatican II, carried on in the light of Christian christology and soteriology, that is, of the unique event of Christ, considered both in its totality and unity, and in the light of its salvific meaning for humankind, for the world and history.

Eschatology and Christology

Christian eschatology, christology, and soteriology comprise an indivisible whole, because the event of Christ is in itself salvific and definitive, unique and ultimate: it is eschatological. By reason of its fundamental character as "already" and "not yet," Christian eschatology derives its originality from the Christ event, as the personal presence of the Son of God in history and as the anticipation of the final coming last of the glorified Christ (Parousia): thus, because of its double and inseparable dimension, christology is both ascending and descending. We have the implicit christology of the pre-Easter Jesus and the explicit christology of the risen Lord. Hence, Christian eschatology can be understood only if it is based on the absolutely unique relationship of Christ to God, to humankind, to the world and to history. First and foremost, a theological reflection on the eschatol-

501

ogy of Vatican II (which is found mostly in *LG, GS, DV,* and
SC)[1] should ask why the Christ event, as a single unit (life,
death, resurrection), is in itself the supreme and therefore ultimate *eschaton;* and then why in this event, the definitive salvation of humankind, the world, and history is achieved.

The incarnation is the act by which the personal word of God
"became man" (Jn. 1:14); it is both God's supreme self-
communication to humanity and the supreme achievement of
humanity that cannot be repeated (Heb. 10:10). What are human
beings? They are not perfect essences closed in on themselves, but
beings called to perfect themselves through their free decisions,
and open to the responsibility and hope of an ultimate future
through death. Historicity makes a radical distinction between
human beings and any other reality of this world: they are called to
create their own history, to realize themselves by means of a temporality marked by the anticipated presence of death. It is precisely
death that structures the existence of every human being into a
whole and renders the free decisions irreversible. Temporal duration limited by death is a duration that will come to an end and
therefore lends an irrevocability to decisions, whereas an indefi-
nite duration of life would deprive free decisions of their irrevocable character: human beings could then continually postpone
their decisions until an endless "afterwards." Because it is limited
by death, time implies a permanent call to the decisions to hope in
a future beyond death.[2]

The incarnation, the fact that the Son of God became *man,*
was not an instantaneous event, therefore, but a permanent one:
the process of becoming man in time until death, with a permanent opening to God as transcendent Future.

We might well say that the event of incarnation was accomplished through the gradual deifying transformation of Christ's
humanity, that is, through the historical evolution of the man
Jesus, whose transcendence (or personal relationship to God)
was absolutely unique. In other words, the divinity of Christ was
actuated, completed, and manifested through what happened in
his humanity, his progressive becoming man until his death. In
short, the incarnation of the Son of God and the divinization of
the man Jesus were inseparably united as the transcendent and
historico-immanent dimensions of one and the same event. The
irreplaceable starting point of christology is found in the history
and life, the action and message of Jesus: this is where the Christ
event was realized and revealed as eschatological.

The coming into the world and history of the Son of God had to be a work of the creative power of God (Lk. 1:35), and by this very fact, an absolutely new event, surpassing all possibilities of nature and history: a qualitatively supreme and unique event, one irrepeatable and definitive: *eschaton*. No other salvific act of God is conceivable that surpasses it: God made himself "God-with-us" (Mt. 1:23), in our world and history. Thus, we understand that in the person, the activity, and the message of Jesus, the kingdom of God is already present (Lk. 11:20): in these acts, the definitive salvific act of God accomplished and revealed itself.[3]

The existence of Christ in history was marked by the fallen state and by the tension of human time. It is a time of ordeal, temptation, inner struggle, and suffering; a time in which the anticipated presence of the end of life lends an irreversibility to free choices, and integrates them into the definitive dimension of death ("once for all": Heb. 9:27). Because of death, each moment of life is given an ultimate meaning (*eschaton*). Human time finally sinks into the "no more time" of death.

But the time lived by Jesus was different from ours: in him there was not this division, this inner contradiction, called *sin*, which alienates us from God. The human existence of Jesus was internally unified by his constant and growing attitude both of self-gift to God on behalf of humanity and of confident abandonment to the Father: *a time of hope in the coming of the Kingdom.* In him, the fallen state of time that is oriented toward death was integrated into and overcome by the ultimate salvation, already anticipated in his option of hoping in the Father and of giving up his life for humanity.

The temporal existence of Jesus in our world and history reached its greatest depth in the mystery of his experience of God the Father: his personal and filial relationship to God, attested by the synoptic gospels and deepened in the fourth gospel, was the reflection of his divine sonship.[4] Jesus enjoyed a unique, absolutely singular experience of God that cannot be repeated (*eschaton*), because it is peculiar to the man who is personally the Son of God. The self-communication of God, which rendered Jesus his Son, was achieved and expressed through his commitment to the Father for our sake, and through his fundamental option in favor of the kingdom.

Therefore, the time of Christ the man was a singularly unique time that, although undermined by death, was definitively saved through his communion of life with God: an existence in the *eschaton*, that is, always lived in supreme union with God for the sake of humanity, an experience oriented toward future plenitude with God, toward his own final salvation and that of others.

Christ's death was by nature eschatological: it not only put an end to his existence in the world, but also consummated his definitive commitment to the Father; Jesus' death was the means by which he embodied in a supreme way his filial relationship to God. Therefore, the death of Jesus did not concern the simple *fact* of undergoing a painful death inflicted with violence, but *the act* of dying, of freely accepting his death by committing his life to the Father for the sake of humanity.[5]

Christ underwent his death with all the enigmatic, annihilating, and heart-rending experience each dying entails: the feeling of being abandoned by the Father. Jesus lived his death as the crisis of his mission, the ordeal that summarized the meaning of his life (Mt. 27:46; Mk. 15:35–37). Abandoned by God, Jesus committed himself to him with confidence. And, thus, he transformed the *eschaton* of his death into the *eschaton* of his life, the ultimate and supreme consummation of his self-giving to the Father: he conquered death and integrated it into the hope of the kingdom (Mt. 26:29; Mk. 14:25; Lk. 22:14–18, 30). He made of his death a victory over dying, a defeat of the fallen temporality of his existence: the definitive moment of becoming man that was peculiar to the Son of God.

By his attitude of definitive self-giving and by abandoning himself to God "who could deliver Him from death" (Heb. 5:7), Jesus allowed his experience of time to reach the supreme degree of tension between death and communion of life with God. And by maintaining this attitude, Jesus received from the creative power of God new and ultimate life, the resurrection: "he lives for God" (Rom. 6:10); he entered into the imperishable plenitude of life with God. The fullness of the divinization of Christ's humanity and the fullness of his incarnation are indistinguishable. The resurrection confers the character of *eschaton* on the whole Christ event, from his coming into the world until his death.

In coming into the world, in existing in history, in dying and finally in being raised to life, Jesus embodied in himself the inner dimension of what is final and definitive, the *eschaton*. His temporality was oriented toward the supratemporal plenitude to come, toward the immediate encounter with God. His future resurrection was anticipated in his hope in the kingdom, in his actual

communion of life with God, in his experience of a filial relationship to the Father, that is, in his incarnation. Through all the
stages of its becoming, the Christ event kept its definitive,
unique "once for all" character (Rom. 6:10; Heb. 9:26–28;
10:10). The incarnation as the anticipation of the resurrection,
and the resurrection as the plenitude of the incarnation, are both
the work of the creative power of God.

The incarnation, death, and resurrection of the Son of God
are then the three fundamental stages of a single event: they can
be understood only in terms of their mutual interrelation within
the total existence of Christ.

Only in the death and resurrection of Christ was the incarnation fully achieved and revealed, since the paschal mystery manifests that "the full content of divine nature lives" in Christ's
humanity (Col. 2:9). On the other hand, Christ's resurrection
cannot be interpreted as appended to his existence in the world;
rather it is the eschatological plenitude of the incarnation, the
"becoming man" of the Son of God. Precisely because of the real
process entailed in the incarnation, Jesus' free acceptance of
death is of decisive importance: by freely committing his life to
the Father for the salvation of humankind, Jesus received the
grace of resurrection.

Eschatology and Soteriology

The early Christian communities expressed their faith and
hope in the risen Jesus with the christological, soteriological, and
eschatological title of the Lord (1 Cor. 16:22; 1,7; 12,3; Rom.
10:9; Phil. 3:20). By proclaiming and invoking him with this
title, they acknowledged his divine rank, his salvific sovereignty
over creation and history (Phil 2:5–11). One, therefore, should
not be amazed at the importance of eschatological hope in the
life of the early Church: the plenitude of history will be achieved
with the glorious coming of the Lord Jesus, the Parousia that is
his final manifestation. This is a major theme of Paul's writings:
the "christofinalization" of humankind, creation and history
that, because of the resurrection of Christ, are called to share his
glory.[6]

One cannot understand the integration of history and creation
into the eschatological glorification of the risen Jesus without

taking into account the work of the Holy Spirit, precisely as the gift of the risen Son (Jn. 7:39). According to Paul, the dynamic presence of the Spirit of Christ transforms human existence even in its corporeal dimension: in the "filial adoption," brought about by the Spirit, man becomes heir to the glory of Christ risen (Rom. 8:12–18). The gift of the Spirit is not only the initial possession (the first fruits) and the anticipated guarantee, but also the vital principle of the resurrection to come: "God who raised Christ from death will also give life to your mortal bodies by the presence of his Spirit in you" (Rom. 8:11). Sharing the resurrection of Christ is a reality that from now on takes place in believers: the whole existence of the human persons, in their interiority and corporeity, is oriented toward a full share in the new life of the risen Christ. The presence of the Spirit within the human person corresponds to two main themes of Pauline theology: it essentially takes place within persons, making them living temples of God; but it also extends to their corporeity that is destined to rise from death.

With these reflections, we have arrived at the chief characteristics of Paul's soteriology and anthropology: (a) Christian salvation entails the complete salvation of human persons, both in their interiority and corporeity; (b) corporeity is not just a part of human beings, it is a unifying dimension of their existence, the dimension by which they are open to the world and to the others; (c) in Christ, corporeity is the basis of his union with the human community, the world, and history; (d) the world was created by God for humanity, in the final instance for a person Christ and for a person conformed to Christ.[7]

The complete transformation of the human person, brought about by the work of the Holy Spirit, is described by Paul as a "new creation" (Gal. 6:15); "the end of time," "the fullness of time" (Eph. 1:10; 3:11): the new and definitive era has come. Eschatological salvation is anticipated in the new existence of the believers under the influence of the Spirit who invites them to hope in the resurrection to come, the "redemption of their bodies" (Rom. 8:23). Paul's theology of the salvific and eschatological meaning of Christ's resurrection, and of the complete salvation of humanity presupposes a unified view of salvation, creation, and history. Nothing escapes the salvation achieved by God in Christ: the identity of God the creator and God the savior. Within the history of salvation, creation is an integral part of the covenant that is definitively accomplished in the person of Christ. In the process of the eschatological glorification of humanity, there is both gradation and subordination: the absolute primacy belongs to the resurrection of Christ; then comes the resurrection of the dead, as participation in the glory of the risen Jesus; and, finally, the whole creation shares the glory of "the children of God" (Rom. 8:17, 21–23).

Vatican II appropriated the eschatological vision of Paul both on the completion of history in the glorified Christ and on the integration of creation into the final salvation still to come: "The promised restoration which we are awaiting has already begun in Christ, is carried forward in the mission of the Holy Spirit, and through Him continues in the Church . . ., with hope of good things to come, the task committed to us in this world by the Father, and work out our salvation." "The final age of the world has already come upon us. The renovation of the world has been irrevocably decreed and in this age is already anticipated in some real way. For even now on this earth the Church is marked with a genuine though imperfect holiness" (LG 48). "God's Word was made flesh . . . so that He might save all men and sum up all things in Himself. The Lord is the goal of human history, the focal point of the longings of history. . . . Enlivened and united in His Spirit, we journey toward the consummation of human history: to re-establish all things in Christ" (GS 45). In the final salvation for which we hope, "charity and its fruits will endure": we shall find again, but in a transfigured state, the values of human dignity, brotherly communion and liberty, and indeed all the goods emerging from our nature and our activity (GS 39).

History of Humankind and History of Salvation

The history of humankind by itself cannot reach a perfect plenitude in the world: the fundamental condition of the historical development consists in the unlimited "hope which hopes," which always aims to go beyond what has been attained in history. Any concrete objective reached by humanity bears the indelible mark of that which remains penultimate, temporary; it is inevitably surpassed by the unlimited tendency that conditions the possibility of every historical growth. The idea of an intrahistorical plenitude of history turns out to be contradictory.

The "hope which hopes" constitutes the human person's ontological dimension, so that he or she is open to a final plenitude
that left to himself or herself he or she cannot reach: this hope is
open to a metahistorical plenitude, as a final and supreme possibility of the human person and as a possibility of absolute grace.
This permanent opening, which no intrahistorical reality can
fulfill, is the insertion point of Christian salvation into human
type. Salvation is the perfectly free gift of the metahistorical
plenitude of history, that is, the salvation of history itself.[8]

Primacy in history falls to human beings, not only because
they are the authors of history, but because by making history,
they become more human. The growth of the person as such is
the fundamental aspect of historical development. That is why
the ultimate salvation of persons does not consist in saving only
their essence but also their reality, which is made more human in
history as they transform the world. The experience of their
action in the world marks forever the personal destiny of human
beings. They make their own history and make themselves by
doing so; creating history entails not just making decisions, but
also carrying them out actively in the world. By rising from
death, human persons will receive the grace of new life, not only
in the realm of their subjectivity, but also in that characterized
by their decisions and actions in the world: every fragment of
history will be integrated into the final salvation still to come.
The mastery of nature won by humanity throughout history will
be assumed and advanced through the new link between the
world and glorified humankind. The "hope which hopes" will
not be deprived of its concrete achievements in the world, as if
they had not been truly human: those realities will be saved, that
is, brought to their metahistorical consummation, which were
practically attained as intrahistorical fulfilled hopes. The radical
capacity of the human person to receive the free gift of ultimate
salvation will surpass its merely transcendental character and will
participate in transcendence itself, the goal of all action in the
world.

When we say that history as such will be saved, we mean that
it will be freed of its fallen state and temporality: it will be
integrated into the metaphorical duration of humankind that has
been raised and glorified with Christ, and thus will share God's
"eternal life."

In accordance with Christ's grace, the gift of the Holy Spirit to humanity not only opens to the possibility of receiving the gift of the metahistorical plenitude: indeed, in the risen Christ, history is also already participating in its metahistorical completion. History does not contain in itself this orientation toward its definitive plenitude: it receives it from Christ's grace. Consequently, the truth that history is heading toward the metahistorical plenitude still to come is not discovered by human reason, but is revealed as a mystery of Christian faith: the very mystery of Christ, Son of God, made flesh, crucified, and risen.

One must avoid all ambiguity when speaking of the "unity" between the history of humankind and the history of salvation. Between the two there is a unity not of "identity" but of "existential inseparability." These two histories are not parallel or placed side by side: the history of salvation unfolds within the history of humankind. But the history of salvation is not the mere result of human effort to transform the world: it is the absolute grace of God inserted into the historical destiny of humankind: "the Christian existential" (Christ's grace) is inserted into the "human element" (into human history) and sets it on the road toward the metahistorical plenitude to come. The unity between the divine element and human element in Christ, which the Chalcedonian council has qualified by using the expressions "without confusion, division or separation,"[9] is a definitive paradigm that we cannot leave aside if we want to maintain a correct notion of the unity between Christian grace and the human effort, between the history of salvation and the history of humankind.

Eschatology and the Christian Code of Ethics

Eschatology, as presented by Vatican II, accurately reflects the fundamental features of Christian salvation as described in the core texts of the New Testament: human salvation, bestowed by God through Christ, begins in time and on earth, and reaches its plenitude in the resurrection of the dead. This is the integral salvation of humanity, which includes relationship to God, to the others, to the world and to history.

Christian salvation is, therefore, not only transcendent and metahistorical, but indivisibly immanent and transcendent, that is, both intrahistorical and metahistorical: it takes place on this side of death, as anticipation of the ultimate future beyond death. It is not a merely future reality, but one begun here and now through the conversion of humanity to God and to love and justice toward his neighbor. Christian eschatology thus bases its code of ethics on fraternity and hope. Christ, by calling all people to salvation through participation here and now in communion of life with him, has created a new bond of solidarity among them. The whole of humanity is called to form one single people of God, which as a communion of brotherly love and of shared hope is heading toward its promised homeland.[10] Christian hope cannot remain hidden within the person: it has to manifest and express itself through the structures of society. The only way for Christians to contribute to setting up the kingdom of Christ is to foster a world of love and justice, and thus to arouse true hope among people.[11]

Christian life in this world, therefore, is not only the time for individuals to determine their ultimate salvation still to come, but also the time for the whole Church to establish the kingdom of God in the world, which is marked by fraternity and justice, and in which the goods of the earth created by God for all people will be shared and transformed into means to serve the whole human family. Hence, commitment to establish a more just and human world is required by Christian hope. Such a commitment is at the very center of the present human decisions concerning future salvation.

By proclaiming that all humanity is destined to take part, as a community, in a future salvation that has already begun on earth, Christianity insists that this participation in the new future must actualize itself in this world and in all dimensions of human existence. The salvation to come could not really begin otherwise. Humanity cannot be saved by the mere promise of a happy beyond: persons need the tangible reality of a fraternity dedicated to justice so as to have a hint of a better future life.

In no other way will the Church be able to make hope in "eternal life" credibile as participation of the human community in the glory of Christ. To proclaim Christian hope without practicing the works of Christian love is to bring about its discredit, to provide a contradictory testimony, and to deny in actions what is attested in words.

Paul VI has spoken of the necessity for the Church to *free itself from the historical structures that are now perceived to be deformations of its evangelic character and apostolic mission; and to undertake a critical, historical, and ethical examination so as to give back to the Church its authentic form, in which the present generation wishes to recognize Christ's face.* [12] It is indeed undeniable that in the past, the Church has relied on the political and socioeconomic powers of the world, and on the authority of its own institutions. And even nowadays, to various degrees and more or less conspicuously, the Church pays for the protection it obtains from the powers of the world, sometimes with the connivance of silence, sometimes with a covert collaboration.

Vatican II has declared many times that the present situation of the Church calls for a radical reform and renewal. [13] To accomplish its mission as God's avant-garde in the world and to fix its gaze on Christ's promise, the Church must first have enough courage to reflect on itself. With determination, it must undertake the changes called for if it is to be faithful to the essence of Christianity: to free itself from the merely human elements it appropriated in the course of history and eventually considered as indispensable for its very survival; to cleanse itself of the dross gradually accumulated by many concrete forms of its institutions and considered as so many guarantees of its security, whereas in fact it slowed down the dynamism of the Spirit. The Church needs the audacity that comes from hope in Christ and from confidence in Christ who is "the power of God" (1 Cor. 1:24).

We all form the people of God; we all are the Church. Conscious of the urgency of Church reform, we must first of all confess our personal and corporate condition as sinners. Conscious of our incapacity to overcome sin, we must do what Paul did so convincingly: place our confidence in nothing human, in nothing that comes from us, that is, in nothing in the Church that is merely human (positions of prestige or power), but trust solely the grace of Christ. Our reaction in the face of the present situation of the Church should essentially be undertaking a new exodus of hope in Christ.

Once renewed in Christian hope, the Church will become a sign of hope for a world marred by enormous injustices at both the national and the international levels: its technical and industrial progress keeps widening the economic gap between the rich nations and the poor ones, so that a minority amasses wealth while poverty keeps great majorities from the resources necessary not only to lead a worthy human life, but also to survive. Yet, at the same time, the world has become aware of universal fraternity and of urgent need to reform economic and political structures so as to eliminate inequalities and establish sharing among human beings.

Since humankind exists in such a situation, the contemporary Church must carry out its mission of testifying, through word and action, to the Good News of salvation and hope for all: a hope articulated in terms of the concrete longings of humankind for improved social structures.

On account of its mission to testify to Christian hope before the world, the Church must radically commit itself to justice, and proclaim that the Christian message finds its fulfillment in freeing the oppressed.

Because Vatican II declared, "the world, more than ever, needs the Church to denounce injustice,"[14] we must not forget that the Church will lack the moral authority required for its mission, as long as it cooperates with the economic and social structures oppressing the needy classes. The Church will have to win its own true freedom and liberation, by committing itself to the freedom of the oppressed.

Nowadays, Christian hope demands from the entire Church and from each of its members a task that is both difficult and urgent: opting for the poor and the second-class citizens of society. In the words of Vatican II, Christian hope today demands "universal changes in ideas and attitudes."[15]

If we do not sense the necessity of such a "conversion," we do not understand the simple and radical truth of the gospel messages and do not know from experience the real situation of the oppressed. To become aware of our ignorance, we have only to read, with a heart open to the word of Jesus, the parables of the Good Samaritan and the Last Judgment (Lk. 10:30–37; Mt. 25:31–46). The priest and the Levite walked away from the suffering man lying on the edge of the road who had been stripped and rendered helpless; they did not come near the neighbor who needed help, but left him half dead. Yet, Jesus viewed this violated and abandoned "neighbor" as his "brother" par excellence. If, on the road of life, we walk by these "brothers" of Christ—and today there are millions of them—we have not yet found the true Christ, and if we still consider ourselves to be his disciples, we deceive ourselves miserably.

And if these poor still believe and hope in Christ and in the justice of his kingdom, and if they still remain open to the message of a liberating God, how shall we preach the Good News to them without committing ourselves to preserve their dignity as children of God and brothers of Christ? We can fully liberate them, only if we increase their participation in all levels of human life—social, economic, political, and cultural.

Every structure that fosters oppressive disparity is contrary to Christian eschatology and hope. For this hope of the final salvation is such that, by anticipating the kingdom at every moment of history, it renders all human achievements penultimate. Christian hope realizes and manifests itself only when it overcomes egoism through practical commitment to fraternity and justice in the world: the truth of the gospel finds its fulfillment in the love of one's neighbor (Eph. 4:15).

Translated from the Spanish by Louis-Bertrand Raymond.

Notes

1. In this article, I merely present a few reflections inspired by the eschatology of Vatican II. For an exhaustive analysis of this theme, cf. A. Dos Sangos Marto, *Esperanza cristiana, futuro do homen. Doctrina escatológica del Concilio Vaticano II* (Rome: Gregorian University, 1978).

2. Vatican II, GS 10, 12, 17, 18, 21, 38, 39.

3. DV 4.17.

4. Cf. W. Marchel, *Abba, Père. La prière du Christ et des chrétiens* (Rome, 1965), 162–165; J. Jeremias, *Vaterunser im Lichte der neueren Forschung* (Stuttgart, 1966), 152–171.

5. Mk. 10:45; 14:32–36; Jn. 10:15–18; Heb. 2:9; 5:7–9; 10:5–8.

6. 1 Cor. 15:20–28; 35–37; 1 Thess. 4:13–18; Rom. 8:17–25; Col. 1:15–20; Eph. 1:3–11; 20:23; 3:11.

7. Cf. J. Alfaro, *Esperanza cristiana y liberación del hombre* (Barcelona, 1972), 143–151; id., *Cristología y antropología* (Madrid, 1973), 105–114.

8. GS 20, 21.

9. DS 302.

10. GS 1, 13, 18, 24–45.

11. LG 35, 36, 48; GS 39, 93.

12. *Insegnamenti di Paolo VI* (1970), VIII, 672–676.

13. LG 8, 15; GS 21, 42, 76, 88; UR 6.

14. *Message of the Council*, 20 October 1962.

15. GS 63.

Bibliography

This bibliography contains the books and articles published on the Second Vatican Council by the contributors to Volume Two.

Juan Alfaro, S.J.
"Unitas institutionis theologicae iuxta Vaticanum II," *Seminarium*, 23 (1971), 219–239.
"Cristología y Eclesiología en el Concilio Vaticano II," in *Cristologia y antropologia* (Madrid, 1973), 121–140.
"Compito della teologia cattolica dopo il Vaticano II," *La Civiltà Cattolica*, 127/2 (1976), 530–540.
"La Mariología del Vaticano II," in *María la bienaventurada porque ha creido* (Rome, 1983), 7–27.

Gerardo J. Békés, O.S.B.
"Eucharisztia és az egyház egysége," *Teologia*, 20 (1968), 10–16.
"Dimensioni riscoperte della teologia eucaristica. Riflessioni provenienti dal dialogo ecumenico," in *Eucaristica sfida alle Chiese divise* (Padua, 1984), 197–221.
Eucaristia e Chiesa. Ricerca dell'unità nel dialogo ecumenico, Collana Liturgica: Fonte e Culmine (Casale Monferrato, 1985).
"La successione nella tradizione apostolica. Il problema del rapporto fra la successione del ministero e la paradosis apostolica," in *Il ministero ordinato nel dialogo ecumenico*, Studia Anselmiana 92 (Rome, 1985), 143–164.
"Le dimensioni della dottrina eucaristica nel documento di Lima," *Salesianum*, 47 (1985), 167–179.

Josef Fuchs, S.J.
"Theologia moralis perficienda: Votum Concilii Vaticani II," *Periodica*, 55 (1966), 499–548.

"Erneuerung der Moraltheologie. Eine Forderung des zweiten Vatikanischen Konzils," in *Moral und Moraltheologie nach dem Konzil* (Freiburg im Breisgau, 1967), 9–61.

"Berufung und Hoffnung. Konziliäre Weisungen für eine christliche Moral", in F. Groner (ed.), *Kirche im Wandel der Zeit Festagabe . . . Josef Kard. Höffner* (Cologne, 1971), 271–284.

"Vocazione e speranza. Indicazioni conciliari per una morale cristiana," *Seminarium*, 23 (1971), 491–510.

Gianfranco Ghirlanda, S.J.

"De caritate ut elemento iuridico fundamentali constitutivo iuris ecclesialis," *Periodica*, 66 (1977), 621–655.

"La carità, principio giuridico costitutivo del diritto ecclesiale," *La Civiltà Cattolica*, 128/2 (1977), 454–471.

"De hierarchica communione ut elemento constitutivo officii episcopalis iuxta 'Lumen Gentium,' " *Periodica*, 69 (1980), 31–57.

"Hierarchica communio. Significato della formula nella 'Lumen Gentium,' " Analecta Gregoriana 216 (Rome, 1980).

'De notione communionis hierarchicae iuxta Vaticanum secundum," *Periodica*, 70 (1981), 41–68.

"La notion de communion hiérarchique dans le Concile Vatican II," *L'Année Canonique*, 25 (1981), 231–254.

"Episcopato e Presbiterato nella 'Lumen Gentium,' " *Communio*, 59 (1981), 53–70.

"Il mistero della Chiesa una sola complessa realtà," *Ecclesia Mater*, 20 (1982), 2–9.

"De variis ordinibus et condicionibus iuridicis in Ecclesia," *Periodica*, 71 (1982), 379–296.

"De definitione Ecclesiae universalis particularis, localis iuxta Concilium Vaticanum secundum," *Periodica*, 71 (1982), 605–636.

"De Christifidelibus," in P. A. Bonnet and G. Ghirlanda, *De Christifidelibus De eorum iuribus, de laicis, de consociationibus* (Adnotationes in Codicem) (Rome, 1983), 3–18.

"De obligationibus et iuribus christifidelium laicorum," *ibid.*, 53–70.

De Ecclesiae munere sanctificandi. De Ordine (Adnotationes in Codicem) (Rome, 1983).

"De laicis iuxta novum Codicem," *Periodica*, 73 (1983), 53–70.

"Ecclesialità della vita consacrata," in *La vita consacrata*, Coll. Il Codice del Vaticano II (Bologna, 1983), 13–52.

"Elementi ecclesiologici per una lettura del nuovo Codice di Diritto Canonico," *Communio*, 69 (1983), 93–109; Netherlands ed., 8 (1983), 136–148; in AA.VV., *Chi è il Vescovo?* (1984), 165–181.

"Elementos eclesiológicos de nuovo Código de dereito canónico," *Broteria*, 117 (1983), 363–374.

"I laici nella Chiesa secondo il nuovo Codice di diritto canonico," *La Civiltà Cattolica*, 134/2 (1983), 531–543; *Aggiornamenti sociali*, 34 (1983), 484–496.

"Vangelo, legge e diritto: senso evangelico del nuovo Codice," *Seminarium*, 33 (1983), 479–495.

"De obligationibus et iuribus Christifidelium in communioni ecclesiali deque eorum adimpletione et exercitio," *Periodica*, 73 (1984), 329–378.

"La vita consacrata nella vita della Chiesa," *Informationes SCRIS*, 10 (1984), 79–96.

"De natura, origine et exercitio potestatis regiminis iuxta novum Codicem," *Periodica*, 74 (1985), 109–164.

"La tipologia degli istituti di vita consacrata dal Concilio al nuovo Codice," *Vita Consacrata*, 21 (1985), 210–227.

Édouard Hamel, S. J.

"Justitia in Constitutione Pastorali 'Gaudium et Spes,' " *Periodica*, 65 (1966), 315–353.

"Aequalitas fundamentalis omnium christifidelium in Ecclesia secundum Concilium Vaticanum II," *Periodica*, 56 (1967), 247–266.

"Lumen rationis et lux Evangelii," *Periodica*, 59 (1970), 215–249.

"Lux Evangelii in Const. 'Gaudium et Spes,' " *Periodica*, 60 (1971), 103–120.

"L'Écriture, âme de la théologie," *Gregorianum*, 52 (1971), 511–535.

Pedro Romano Rocha, S. J.

Almeida, C. F. de [pseud.], "Traduções litúrgicas," *Brotéria*, 86 (1968), 90–97.

Almeida, C.F. de [pseud.], "Os novos textos da Oração Eucarística," *Brotéria*, 87 (1968), 198–202.

Almeida, C.F. de [pseud.], "Novos rituais do Baptismo," *Brotéria*, 87 (1968), 536–542.

Almeida, C.F. de [pseud.], "Liturgia 1968," *Brotéria*, 88 (1969), 39–44.

Almeida, C.F. de [pseud.], "O novo calendário litúrgico," *Brotéria*, 89 (1969), 145–153.

"O novo breviário," *Lumen*, 33 (1969), 99–107.

"A renovação litúrgica e o Vaticano II," *Lumen*, 33 (1969), 514–518.

"A Missa na perspectiva do novo missal," *Lumen*, 33 (1969), 530–536.

"Celebrar o Mistério Pascal," *Lumen*, 34 (1970), 134–142.

"O novo ritual das ordenações e a teologia do sacramento da Ordem," *Lumen*, 34 (1970), 458–466.

"A solenidade de Cristo-Rei," *Lumen*, 34 (1970), 600–604.

"O novo calendário litfgico," *Ora et labora*, 17 (1971), 45–54.

Almeida, C.F. de [pseud.], "Os sacramentos dos doentes," Brotéria, 96 (1973), 313–323.

Almeida, C.F. de [pseud.], "Reflexõs sobre um documento (Immensae caritatis), Brotéria, 96 (1973), 563–572.

"Dez anos de liturgia. No 10° aniversário da Constituição litúrgica," Brotéria, 98 (1974), 172–183.

"A 'Instrução geral do missal romano,' " Boletim de Pastoral Litúrgica, 9 (1978), 17–21; 10 (1978), 3–9.

"No 20° aniversário da Constituição litúrgica," Brotéria, 118 (1984), 508–522.

"Sentire con la Chiesa in un'época di disenso," in "Sentire con la Chiesa." Sfida, storia, pedagogia (Rome, 1980), 81–95.

"Sentir con la Iglesia en una época de disenso," in Sentire cum Ecclesia. Historia, pedagogia, disafío actual (Rome, 1983), 81–95.

"Penser avec l'Eglise à une époque marquée par les dissentiments," in Sentire cum Ecclesia. Histoire, Pédagogie, Défi pour aujourd'hui (Rome, 1983), 83–97.

"Thinking with the Church in an Age of Dissent," in Sentire cum Ecclesia. History, Pedagogy, Challenge Today (Rome, 1983), 82–97.

"Deus e a Praxis," Perspectiva Teológica, 17 (1985), 179–200.

"O Deus dos Pobres," Brotéria, 121 (1985), 389–401.

Félix-Alejandro Pastor, S.J.

"Concilio pastoral, positivo y ecuménico, " SIC, 26/252 (1963), 79-82.

"Teología del ministerio eclesial," Estudios Eclesiástico, 45 (1970), 53–90.

"Sacerdozio ministeriale: teologia del ministero eclesiale," Rassegna di Teologia, Supp. No. 2 (1971), 30–43.

"Carisma e Missão. Considerações teológicas sobre o problema da renovação da vida consagrada," Síntese 3/6 (1975), 35–56.

"Consecratae vitae renovatio ecclesiologice perspecta," Periodica, 66 (1977), 47–72.

"Romani episcopi ordinatio et primatialis potestas," Periodica, 69 (1980), 321–350.

"A Igreja como problema. A questão de "sentir com a Igreja" em uma época de contestação e pluralismo," Convergencia, 13/129 (1980), 21–32.

Francis A. Sullivan, S.J.

"On the Infallibility of the Episcopal College in the Ordinary Exercise of its Teaching Office," in Acta Congressus Internationalis de Theologia Concilii Vaticani II (Vatican City, 1968), 189–195.

Magisterium. Teaching Authority in the Catholic Church (Ramsey/Dublin, 1983).

Il Magistero nella Chiesa cattolica (Assisi, 1986).

Robert Taft, S.J.

"The Neo-Orthodox View on Ecumenical Councils," *Sciences Ecclésiastiques*, 13 (1961), 437–444; *Diakonia*, 2 (1967), 266–277.

"The Nature of the Church. An Eastern Orthodox View," *Irish Ecclesiastical Record*, 100 (1963), 150–164.

"Il concilio ecumenico secondo e i neo-ortodossi," *Russia Cristiana*, 9/96 (1968), 7–13.

"The Continuity of Tradition in a world of Liturgical Change: the Eastern Liturgical Experience," *Seminarium*, 27 (1975), 445–459.

"De Geest van de Oosterse Liturgie," *Het Christelijk Oosten*, 28 (1976), 229–245.

"The Spirit of Eastern Christian Worship," *Diakonia*, 12 (1977), 103–120.

" 'Thanksgiving for the Light.' Toward a Theology of Vespers," *Diakonia, 13 (1978), 27–50.*

"Der Geist des christlichen Gottesdienstes im Osten," *Der Christliche Osten*, 34 (1979), 147–156.

"Concelebration," in P.K. Meagher, T.C. O'Brien, and C.M. Ahearne (eds.), *Encyclopedic Dictionary of Religion I* (Washington, DC, 1979), 858–859.

"Ex Oriente lux? Some Reflections on Eucharistic Concelebration," *Worship*, 54 (1980), 308–325; in K. Seasolz (ed.), *Living Bread, Saving Cup. Readings on the Eucharist* (Collegeville, MN, 1982), 242–259.

'Ex Oriente Lux? Zur eucharistischen Konzelebration," *Theologie der Gegenwart*, 25 (1982), 266–277.

"Chronicle: Interritual Concelebration," *Worship*, 55 (1981), 441–444.

"The Frequency of the Eucharist throughout History," *Concilium*, 152 (1982), 13–24; "La fréquence de l'eucharistie à travers l'histoire," *Concilium*, 172 (1982), 27–44; "La frequenza dell'eucaristia nella storia," *Concilium*, 172 (1982), 35–53; "Die Häufigkeit der Eucharistie im Laufe der Geschichte," *Concilium*, 172 (1982), 86–95; "De frequentie de eucharistie in de loop der geschiedenis," *Concilium*, 172 (1982), 19–31; "La frecuencia de la eucaristia a traves la historia," *Concilium*, 172 (1982), 169–188.

"Iqāmat al-iwhāristiyyaā 'abr al-tārīh, *Al-Fikr a-Masīhī*, 18/177 (Mosul, Iraq, 1982), 321–328.

"Das Dankgebet für das Licht. Zu einer Theologie der Vesper," *Der Christliche Osten*, 37 (1982), 127–133, 151–161.

"On the Question of Infant Communion in the Byzantine Catholic Churches of the U.S.A.," *Diakonia*, 17 (1982), 201–214.

"Sunday in the Eastern Tradition," in M. Searle (ed.), *Sunday Morning: A Time for Worship*, (Collegeville, MN, 1982), 49–74.

"Receiving Communion—a Forgotten Symbol?" *Worship*, 57 (1983), 412–418.

Beyond East and West. Problems in Liturgical Understanding (Washington, DC, 1984).

The Liturgy of the Hours in East and West. The Origins of the Divine Office and its Meaning for Today (Collegeville, MN, 1986).

Ivan Žužek, S.J.

"Oriental Canon Law: Survey of Recent Developments," *Concilium*, 8/1 (1965), 67–78.

"Animadversiones quaedam in Decretum de Ecclesiis Orientalibus Catholicis Concilii Vaticani II," *Periodica*, 55 (1966), 266–288.

"Opinions on the Future Structure of Oriental Canon Law," *Concilium*, 8/3 (1967), 65–75.

"Some Aspects of the Sacramental Canon Law of the Christian East," *Concilium* 8/4 (1968), 75–82.

"La giuridizione dei vescovi ortodossi dopo il Concilio Vaticano II," *La Civiltà Cattolica*, 122/3 (1971), 550–562.

"Hat die Katholische Kirche die Jurisdiction der orthodoxen Bischöfe nach dem Zweiten Vatikanischen Konzil anerkannt oder nicht?" *Österreichisches Archiv für Kirchenrecht*, 22 (1971), 109–128.

"Dopo il Vaticano II la Chiesa Cattolica ha riconosciuto la giurisdizione dei vescovi ortodossi?" *Unitas*, 26 (1971), 255–270.

"Che cosa è una Chiesa, un rito orientale," *Seminarium*, 37 (1975), 263–275.

"Les textes non publiés du Code de Droit Canon Oriental," *Nuntia*, 1 (1975), 23–31.

"Canon concerning the Authority of Patriarchs over the Faithful of Their Own Rite Who Live outside the Limits of Patriarchal Territory," *Nuntia*, 6 (1978), 3–33.

"L'économie dans les travaux de la Commission Pontificale pour la révision du Code de Droit Canonique Oriental," *Kanon*, 6 (1983), 66–83.

Contents
of All Three Volumes

521

Volume Two

PART IV

Liturgy and Sacraments

PART VI

The View of Humanity

Volume Three

PART VII

The Consecrated Life

PART VIII

Religion and Religions

PART IX

Questions of Theological Formation

PART X

New Prospects